CONTENTS

4 TOKYO NEIGHBORHOODS & SUGGESTED ITINERARIES 63

5 WHERE TO STAY 81

6 WHERE TO DINE 122

7 WHAT TO SEE & DO IN TOKYO 171

Frommer's®

Tokyo

11th Edition

by Beth Reiber

WILEY

Wiley Publishing, Inc.

Published by:

WILEY PUBLISHING, INC.

111 River St.
Hoboken, NJ 07030-5774

ISBN 978-0-470-53764-0

Editor: Stephen Bassman
Production Editor: Michael Brumitt
Cartographer: Guy Ruggiero
Photo Editor: Richard Fox
Production by Wiley Indianapolis Composition Services

Front cover photo: A comic book shop in the Shibuya district. ©Jochen Tack/imagebroker.net/PhotoLibrary
Back cover photo: The Sensoji Temple and Five-Story Pagoda in the Asakusa neighborhood. ©Seiji Tajima/amanaimages/Corbis

For information on our other products and services or to obtain technical support, please contact our Customer Care Department within the U.S. at 877/762-2974, outside the U.S. at 317/572-3993 or fax 317/572-4002.

Wiley also publishes its books in a variety of electronic formats. Some content that appears in print may not be available in electronic formats.

Manufactured in the United States of America

5 4 3 2 1

8 TOKYO STROLLS

204

9 SHOPPING

224

10 TOKYO AFTER DARK

246

11 SIDE TRIPS FROM TOKYO

267

12 FAST FACTS

306

13 A GLOSSARY OF USEFUL JAPANESE TERMS

316

14 A JAPANESE-CHARACTER INDEX

324

INDEX

327

TOKYO

CONTENTS

LIST OF MAPS

DEDICATION

To Debbie Howard, for being my best friend since we were 4 years old and for giving me my own futon at Ebisu Palace whenever I'm in Tokyo; to my sons Matthias and Johannes, for being such great traveling companions and providing a teenager's perspective on Tokyo; and to Jack, for everything.

ACKNOWLEDGMENTS

I would like to thank some fine and very special people who were instrumental in the completion of this book: Nori Akashi and Naoko Marutani of the Japan National Tourist Organization; and Tokyoite Junko Matsuda, for keeping me up to date on Tokyo and her friendship since student days in Kansas.

HOW TO CONTACT US

In researching this book, we discovered many wonderful places—hotels, restaurants, shops, and more. We're sure you'll find others. Please tell us about them, so we can share the information with your fellow travelers in upcoming editions. If you were disappointed with a recommendation, we'd love to know that, too. Please write to:

Frommer's Tokyo, 11th Edition
Wiley Publishing, Inc. • 111 River St. • Hoboken, NJ 07030-5774

AN ADDITIONAL NOTE

Please be advised that travel information is subject to change at any time—and this is especially true of prices. We therefore suggest that you write or call ahead for confirmation when making your travel plans. The authors, editors, and publisher cannot be held responsible for the experiences of readers while traveling. Your safety is important to us, however, so we encourage you to stay alert and be aware of your surroundings. Keep a close eye on cameras, purses, and wallets, all favorite targets of thieves and pickpockets.

ABOUT THE AUTHOR

Long before she could read, **Beth Reiber** spent hours pouring over her grandparents' latest *National Geographic* magazines. After living several years in Germany, first as a university student and then as a freelance travel writer writing for major U.S. newspapers, and in Tokyo as editor of *Far East Traveler,* she authored several Frommer's guides, including *Frommer's Japan* and *Frommer's Hong Kong.* She also contributes to *Frommer's USA* and *Frommer's China.* Online, she writes a blog for www.japantravelinfo.com. In 2009 she was appointed a YOKOSO! Japan Ambassador by Japan's Ministry of Land, Infrastructure, Transport and Tourism for her many years writing about Japan, the only recipient residing in the United States to receive the honorary award. When not on the road, she resides in an 1890 Victorian home in Lawrence, Kansas, with her two sons, a dog, and a cat.

FROMMER'S STAR RATINGS, ICONS & ABBREVIATIONS

Every hotel, restaurant, and attraction listing in this guide has been ranked for quality, value, service, amenities, and special features using a **star-rating system.** In country, state, and regional guides, we also rate towns and regions to help you narrow down your choices and budget your time accordingly. Hotels and restaurants are rated on a scale of zero (recommended) to three stars (exceptional). Attractions, shopping, nightlife, towns, and regions are rated according to the following scale: zero stars (recommended), one star (highly recommended), two stars (very highly recommended), and three stars (must-see).

In addition to the star-rating system, we also use **seven feature icons** that point you to the great deals, in-the-know advice, and unique experiences that separate travelers from tourists. Throughout the book, look for:

(Finds)	Special finds—those places only insiders know about
(Fun Facts)	Fun facts—details that make travelers more informed and their trips more fun
(Kids)	Best bets for kids and advice for the whole family
(Moments)	Special moments—those experiences that memories are made of
(Overrated)	Places or experiences not worth your time or money
(Tips)	Insider tips—great ways to save time and money
(Value)	Great values—where to get the best deals

The following **abbreviations** are used for credit cards:

AE	American Express	**DISC**	Discover	**V**	Visa
DC	Diners Club	**MC**	MasterCard		

TRAVEL RESOURCES AT FROMMERS.COM

Frommer's travel resources don't end with this guide. Frommer's website, **www.frommers. com**, has travel information on more than 4,000 destinations. We update features regularly, giving you access to the most current trip-planning information and the best airfare, lodging, and car-rental bargains. You can also listen to podcasts, connect with other Frommers.com members through our active-reader forums, share your travel photos, read blogs from guidebook editors and fellow travelers, and much more.

The Best of Tokyo

Describing Tokyo to someone who has never been there is a formidable task. After all, how do you describe a city that—as one of my friends visiting Tokyo for the first time put it—seems like part of another planet?

To be sure, Tokyo is very different from Western capitals, but what really sets it apart is its people. Approximately 12.5 million people reside within Tokyo's 2,100 sq. km (811 sq. miles), and almost one-fourth of Japan's total population lives within commuting distance of the city. This translates into a crush of humanity that packs the subways, crowds the sidewalks, and fills the department stores beyond belief. In some parts of the city, the streets are as crowded at 3am as they are at 3pm. With its high-energy, visual overload, Tokyo makes even New York seem like a sleepy, laid-back town.

And yet, despite its limited space for harmonious living and some of the crime inherent in every major city, Tokyo remains one of the safest cities in the world. No matter how lost I may become, I know that people will go out of their way to help me. Hardworking, honest, and helpful to strangers, the Japanese are their country's greatest asset.

With Tokyo so densely packed, it comes as no shock to learn that land here is more valuable than gold. Buildings are built practically on top of each other, shaped like pieces in a jigsaw puzzle to fit the existing plots of real estate. More than perhaps any other city in the world, Japan's capital is a concrete jungle, stretching on and on as far as the eye can see, with a few parks but not many trees to break the monotony. Fires, earthquakes, wars, the zeal for modernization, and the price of land have taken their tolls on the city, eradicating almost all evidence of previous centuries. It's as though Tokyo was born only this morning, with all the messy aftermath of a city conceived without plan and interested only in the future.

Thus, first-time visitors to Tokyo are almost invariably disappointed. They come expecting an exotic Asian city but instead find a megalopolis, Westernized to the point of drabness. Used to the grand edifices and monuments of Western cities, visitors look in vain for Tokyo's own monuments to its past—ancient temples, exquisite gardens, Imperial palaces, or whatever else they've imagined. Instead they find what may be, quite arguably, one of the ugliest cities in the world.

So, while Tokyo is one of my favorite cities, my appreciation came only with time. When I first moved here, I was tormented by the unsettling feeling that I was somehow missing out on the "real" Tokyo. Even though I was living and working here, Tokyo seemed beyond my grasp: elusive, vague, and undefined. I felt that the meaning of the city was out there, if only I knew where to look.

With time, I learned that I needn't look farther than my own front window. Tokyo has no center, but rather is made up of a series of small towns and neighborhoods clustered together, each with its own history, flavor, and atmosphere. There are narrow residential streets, ma-and-pa shops, fruit stands, and stores. There's the neighborhood tofu factory, the lunchbox stand, the grocery shop, and the tiny police station, where the cops know the residents by name and patrol the area by bicycle. There are carefully pruned bonsai trees gracing sidewalks, and wooden homes on impossibly narrow streets. Walk in the old downtown neighborhoods of Asakusa or Yanaka and you're worlds apart from the trendy quarters of Harajuku or the high-rises of Shinjuku. Neighborhoods like these make Tokyo lovable and livable.

What's more, once visitors get to know Tokyo better, they learn that you can't judge Tokyo by what it looks like on the outside, for this is a city of interiors. Even those concrete monsters may house interiors that are fascinating in design and innovation. In the basement of that drab building could well be a restaurant with wooden beams, mud walls, and thatched ceiling, imported intact from a farmhouse in the Japan Alps; on its roof could be a small Shinto shrine, while the top floor could house a high-tech bar or a tony French restaurant with dreamy views over the city.

And beneath Tokyo's concrete shell is a thriving cultural life left very much intact. In fact, if you're interested in Japan's performing arts as well as such diverse activities as the tea ceremony or sumo, Tokyo is your best bet for offering the most at any one time. It is rich in museums and claims the largest repository of Japanese art in the world. It also gets my vote as the pop-art capital of the world, so if you're into kitsch or *anime* (Japanese animation), you'll be in high heaven. And if you're into style, you'll find Tokyo a mecca for cutting-edge fashion and innovative design.

While Tokyo isn't representative of all of Japan, just as New York isn't representative of the entire United States, it's a fairly good barometer of where the country is heading, if not the world. I can't imagine being bored here for even a minute.

1 THE MOST UNFORGETTABLE TRAVEL EXPERIENCES

- **Taking Part in a Festival.** Tokyo and its surrounding cities offer a myriad of annual festivals, ranging from processions of portable shrines to ladder-top acrobatics. Be ready to battle good-natured crowds, as festivals can be unbelievably packed. See "Tokyo Calendar of Events," in chapter 3.

- **Strolling a Japanese Landscaped Garden.** There's no better escape from Tokyo's urban jungle than a stroll through one of its landscaped gardens, especially in spring when irises, wisteria, peonies, azaleas, and other flowers are in bloom. Top picks are Rikugien Garden, Shinjuku Gyoen, and—in nearby Yokohama—Sankeien Garden. See "Parks & Gardens," in chapter 7, and "Yokohama," in chapter 11.

- **Soaking Away Your Cares.** Tokyo now has its own hot-spring spas, thanks to drilling that released therapeutic waters from deep below the surface. Top on my list is Oedo-Onsen Monogatari, a theme-based spa that emulates bathing houses of yore, with its feudal-era replica architecture, shops, restaurants, indoor and outdoor baths, and more. See "Five Unforgettable Ways to Immerse Yourself in Japanese Culture," in chapter 7.

- **Hunting for Bargains at Flea Markets.** You never know what treasure you might find at one of Tokyo's weekend outdoor flea markets, where vendors sell everything from used kimono to antiques and curios. Go early, and be sure to bargain. See "Shopping A to Z," in chapter 9.

- **Experiencing the Serenity of the Tea Ceremony.** Developed in the 16th century as a means to achieve inner harmony with nature, the tea ceremony is a highly ritualized process that takes years to learn. You can experience a shortened version at several Tokyo hotels. See "Five Unforgettable Ways to

Immerse Yourself in Japanese Culture," in chapter 7.

- **Getting the Royal Treatment at Department Stores.** Tokyo's department stores are huge, spotless, and filled with merchandise you never knew existed; many also have first-rate art galleries. Shibuya, Shinjuku, and Ginza boast the greatest concentration of department stores. Service in a Japanese department store is an unparalleled experience: Be there when it opens, and you'll see employees lined up at the front door, bowing to incoming customers. See "Shopping A to Z," in chapter 9.

- **Attending a Kabuki Play.** Kabuki has served as the most popular form of entertainment for the masses since the Edo Period. Watch the audience as they yell their approval; watch the stage for its gorgeous costumes, stunning settings, and easy-to-understand dramas of love, duty, and revenge. See "The Performing Arts," in chapter 10.

2 THE BEST SPLURGE HOTELS

- **Four Seasons Hotel Tokyo at Chinzan-So** (2–10–8 Sekiguchi, Bunkyo-ku; ℂ **800/819-5053** in the U.S. and Canada, or 03/3943-2222): Set amid luscious grounds, this top-notch property has virtually everything going for it (with the exception of a rather obscure location in northeast Tokyo). Enjoy European comfort blended with Asian decor, one of Tokyo's best and most attractive spas, and rooms with peaceful garden views. See p. 97.

- **Mandarin Oriental, Tokyo** (2–1–1 Nihombashi Marumachi, Chuo-ku; ℂ **866/526-6566** in the U.S. and Canada, or 03/3270-8950): Located across from the famous Mitsukoshi department store, this luxurious property boasts outstanding views, massive guest rooms with sophisticated entertainment centers, a spa, high-end restaurants, and fabrics and textiles made especially for the hotel by artisans throughout Japan. See p. 91.

- **Park Hyatt Tokyo** (3–7–1–2 Nishi-Shinjuku, Shinjuku-ku; ℂ **800/233-1234** in the U.S. and Canada, or 03/5322-1234): This was one of my favorite hotels long before it became a *Lost in Translation* celebrity. Quite simply, it's among the most gorgeous and sophisticated hotels in Japan, with rooms to die for, stunning views, and one of Tokyo's best restaurants. It also wins kudos for free entry for hotel guests to its dramatic, sunlit, 20m (66-ft.) indoor pool, on the 47th floor, with great views over Tokyo. See p. 91.

- **The Peninsula Tokyo** (1–8–1 Yurakucho, Chiyoda-ku; ℂ **866/382-8388** in the U.S. and Canada, or 03/6270-2888): Low-key compared to sister property Hong Kong's The Peninsula, this hotel places its emphasis on luxurious rooms, complete with gorgeous bathrooms equipped with mood lighting (and tubs big enough for two), dryers just for nails, and bedside controls that light up with the slightest touch. Its location near the Ginza, Marunouchi, and Hibiya also make it hotel central for both business and leisure traveler; a Rolls Royce delivers guests in style within a 1km (1.2-mile) radius, free of charge. See p. 90.

- **The Ritz-Carlton, Tokyo** (9–7–1 Akasaka, Minato-ku; ℂ **800/241-3333** in the U.S. and Canada, or 03/3423-8000): Occupying the lofty reaches of Tokyo's tallest building, this luxury property in Tokyo Midtown ranks as one of Japan's best hotels, with Tokyo's largest rooms, complete with two large closets and huge bathrooms with two separate sinks and counters, making it a best bet for couples. It cocoons guests from the mad whirl of central Tokyo with the best that money can buy, including service above and beyond the call of duty. See p. 97.

3 THE BEST MODERATELY PRICED HOTELS

- **Hilltop Hotel** (1–1 Surugadai, in Kanda; ☎ 03/3293-2311): Established in 1937, this unassuming hotel is the closest that Tokyo has to a historic hotel. With an Art Deco facade, it boasts such endearing touches as fringed lampshades, doilies, cherry-wood furniture, velvet curtains, and old-fashioned heaters. With only 74 rooms, it also boasts a surprising number of restaurants and bars. See p. 113.
- **Hotel Century Southern Tower** (2–2–1 Yoyogi, Shibuya-ku; ☎ 03/5354-0111): Occupying the top floors of a Shinjuku skyscraper just a couple minutes' walk from Shinjuku Station, this bright and modern property offers great views, a convenient location, and comfortable rooms. See p. 110.
- **Hotel Gracery** (7–10–1 Ginza, Chuo-ku; ☎ 03/6686-1000): Although rooms are tiny, they're smartly decorated, and there's even a floor just for ladies. Even better is this hotel's location, smack dab in the Ginza. See p. 107.
- **Park Hotel Tokyo** (1–7–1 Higashi Shimbashi, Minato-ku; ☎ 03/6252-1111): An attractive 10-story light-filled lobby, restaurants offering organic dishes, rooms with views of Tokyo Bay or Tokyo Tower, and walking distance from the Ginza make this a low-cost alternative to similarly designed but pricier hotels. See p. 108.
- **Tokyu Stay Aoyama Premier** (2–27–18 Minami-Aoyama, Minato-ku; ☎ 03/3497-0109): Road-weary travelers can park here, taking advantage of this chain's lower rates for longer stays and rooms complete with kitchenettes and in-room laundry facilities. Bonuses are its central location and high floors offering expansive views. See p. 110.

4 THE MOST UNFORGETTABLE DINING EXPERIENCES

- **Feasting on a Kaiseki Meal:** Although expensive, a *kaiseki* feast, consisting of dish after dish of artfully displayed delectables, may well be the most beautiful and memorable meal you'll ever have. Splurge at least once on the most expensive kaiseki meal you can afford, and you'll feel like royalty. See "Eating & Drinking in Tokyo," in chapter 2.
- **Dining with a View:** There's no way you can forget you're in Tokyo when you're dining with views of the city as far as you can see. This category has many options, not all of them expensive, like the **Mado Lounge** on the 52nd floor of Mori Tower, Roppongi Hills, 6–10–1 Roppongi (☎ 03/3470-0052). However, the very top splurge has long been the **New York Grill**, located on the 52nd floor of the Park Hyatt Tokyo hotel (☎ 03/5322-1234). Surrounded by glass, it offers great American cuisine, live jazz, and breathtaking views of the endless city. On

clear days, you can see Mount Fuji, making this the closest you can get to dining on a cloud. See p. 143.

- **Eating Sushi and Sashimi:** Sushi restaurants have spread to the four corners of the earth, but they're rarely as good—or authentic—as those in Japan. Not only do Japanese sushi chefs train for years, but also the variety of fresh fish is astounding. For an especially unique experience, eat at Tsukiji Fish Market. See p. 178.
- **Rubbing Elbows in a Yakitori-ya:** There's no better place to observe Tokyo's army of office workers at play than at a *yakitori-ya*, a drinking man's pub that also sells skewered grilled chicken and bar snacks. It's fun, noisy, and boisterous. See "Eating & Drinking in Tokyo, in chapter 2.

5 THE BEST THINGS TO DO FOR FREE (OR ALMOST)

- **Catching the Action at Tsukiji Fish Market.** Get up early your first morning in Japan (you'll probably be wide awake with jet lag anyway) and head straight for the country's largest fish market, where you can browse through stalls of seafood and sample the freshest sushi you'll ever have. See p. 178.
- **Sitting Pretty in Shinjuku.** On the 45th floor of the Tokyo Metropolitan Government Office (TMG), designed by well-known architect Kenzo Tange, an observatory offers a bird's-eye view of Shinjuku's cluster of skyscrapers, the never-ending metropolis, and, on fine winter days, Mount Fuji. Best of all, it's free. See p. 199.
- **Walking the Imperial Moat.** It's an easy, 4.8km (3-mile) walk around the Imperial Palace moat, especially beautiful in spring when the many cherry blossoms are aflame. Don't miss the attached (and free) East Garden. See p. 182.
- **Appreciating the Beauty of Ikebana.** After seeing how flowers, branches, and vases can be combined into works of art, you'll never be able to simply throw flowers into a vase again. You can learn the basics of *ikebana,* Japanese flower arranging, at several schools in Tokyo. Exhibitions of ikebana are held regularly at Yasukuni Shrine and department stores. Shows are often free. See "Five Unforgettable Ways to Immerse Yourself in Japanese Culture," in chapter 7.
- **Visiting Company Showrooms.** Several of Tokyo's biggest companies have showrooms, including Toyota, Panasonic, and Sony, where you can ogle their latest products for free. Panasonic even has a cool house of the future (reservations required). See "Specialty Museums & Showrooms," in chapter 7.

6 THE BEST OFFBEAT EXPERIENCES

- **Viewing Cherry Blossoms at Ueno Park.** Ueno Park is famous throughout Japan for its 1,000 cherry trees, attracting multitudes of company employees and organizations. It's not, however, the communing with nature you might think, as everyone drinks and eats, seemingly oblivious to the shimmering blossoms above. Observing Tokyoites at play here is a cultural experience you won't forget. See "Parks & Gardens," in chapter 7, and "Walking Tour: Ueno," in chapter 8.

- **Watching the Big Guys Wrestle.** Nothing beats watching huge, almost-nude sumo wrestlers, most weighing well over 300 pounds, throw each other around. Matches are held in Tokyo in January, May, and September; catch one on TV if you can't make it in person. Great fun and not to be missed. See "Spectator Sports," in chapter 7.
- **Browsing the Electronics and Anime Shops of Akihabara.** Even if you don't buy anything, it's great fun—and very educational—to see the latest in electronic gadgetry in Japan's largest electronics district, which offers many products unknown in Western markets. In recent years, shops specializing in *manga* (Japanese comic books) and anime have also opened, along with so-called "maid cafes." See "Shopping A to Z," in chapter 9.
- **Getting a Massage.** After a hard day of work or sightseeing, nothing beats a relaxing massage. *Shiatsu,* or pressure-point massage, is available in the privacy of your room at virtually all first-class and most midrange Tokyo hotels, as well as at a number of clinics in the city, many of which offer acupuncture as well. See "Five Unforgettable Ways to Immerse Yourself in Japanese Culture," in chapter 7.
- **Browsing the Food Floors of a Department Store.** Often occupying two basement floors, these food emporiums are updated versions of the local food market, with hawkers yelling out specials, and rows upon rows of glass cases offering everything from fresh seafood to fantastic chocolate creations. It's an education to simply walk through and see what's available in this food-obsessed nation. See "Department Stores," in chapter 9.

7 THE BEST NEIGHBORHOODS FOR GETTING LOST

- **Strolling Through Asakusa.** No place better conveys the atmosphere of old Tokyo than Asakusa. Sensoji Temple is the city's oldest and most popular temple, and Nakamise Dori, the pedestrian lane leading to the temple, is lined with shops selling souvenirs and traditional Japanese goods. As in days of yore, arrive by boat via the Sumida River. See "Walking Tour: Asakusa," in chapter 8.
- **Hanging Out in Harajuku.** Nothing beats Sunday in Harajuku, where you can begin the day leisurely with brunch, stroll the promenade of Omotesando Dori, shop the area's many boutiques, take in a museum and perhaps a flea market, visit Meiji Shrine, and then relax over drinks at a sidewalk cafe watching the hordes of teeny-boppers parading past.

Also on Sundays, youths dressed in costumes gather in front of the entrance to Meiji Shrine and in Yoyogi Park, happy to pose for pictures. See "Walking Tour: Harajuku & Aoyama," in chapter 8.
- **Escaping Big-City Life in the Temple Town of Yanaka.** With its many temples, offbeat attractions, sloping hills, and peaceful narrow streets, Yanaka makes for a wonderful half-day escape from the crowds of Tokyo. See "Walking Tour: Yanaka," in chapter 8.
- **Taking a Spin Through Kabuki-cho.** Shinjuku's Kabuki-cho has the craziest nightlife in all of Tokyo, with countless strip joints, porn shops, restaurants, bars, and the greatest concentration of neon (and drunks) you're likely to see anywhere. It's a fascinating place for an evening stroll. See "The Club & Music Scene," in chapter 10.

- **Tokyo National Museum** (Ueno Park, Taito-ku; ✆ **03/3822-1111**): Even professed museum-phobes should make a point of visiting the largest museum of Japanese art in the world, where you can see everything from samurai armor and lacquerware to kimono and woodblock prints. If you visit only one museum in Tokyo, this should be it. See p. 177.

- **Edo-Tokyo Museum** (1–4–1 Yokoami, Sumida-ku; ✆ **03/3626-9974**): Housed in a high-tech modern building, this ambitious museum chronicles the fascinating and somewhat tumultuous history of Tokyo (known as Edo during the Feudal Period), with models, replicas, artifacts, and dioramas. Guided tours in English are available for free. See p. 173.

- **Mori Art Museum** (6–10–1 Roppongi, Minato-ku; ✆ **03/5777-8600**): Tokyo's highest museum, on the 53rd floor of Mori Tower in Roppongi Hills, offers fantastic views of Tokyo along with innovative shows of emerging and established artists from around the world. And it's open late most nights, too, making it my top pick for a romantic cultural experience. See p. 188.

- **Open-Air Folk House Museum** (7–1–1 Masugata, Tama-ku, Kawasaki; ✆ **044/922-2181**): It's in the neighboring town of Kawasaki, but the 30-minute train ride to this "village" of 34 traditional houses and historic buildings in a beautiful wooded setting makes for a lovely, educational outing. And the photographs you'll get of thatched farmhouses and other architectural gems will make you feel you've left Tokyo—not to mention the 21st century—far behind. See p. 196.

Tokyo in Depth

No matter how many times I visit the observatory on the 45th floor of the Tokyo Metropolitan Government Office, I'm always struck anew by the city's surreal vastness, stretching in all directions as far as the eye can see. Yet despite its seemingly forbidding size, Tokyo is actually easy to navigate and explore. Everything runs like clockwork, Tokyoites will go out of their way to help strangers, and the entire city is strikingly clean and orderly. Although skyscrapers are definitely on the rise, there are many diverse neighborhoods with small-town atmospheres. And while the nation's capital takes a no-nonsense approach when it comes to conducting business, it's also one of the quirkiest cities you'll find anywhere (coffee in a so-called "maid cafe," anyone?). Like most destinations around the world, Tokyo is a product of its geography, history, and people. This chapter highlights how Tokyo came to be the way it is today, providing, I hope, some insight into what I consider to be one of the most interesting—not to mention fun!—cities in the world.

---

1 TOKYO TODAY

With a population of about 12.5 million, Tokyo is one of the largest cities in the world—and one of the most intriguing and invigorating. As the nation's capital and financial nerve center, Tokyo has long been a major player in Asia. In a nation of overachievers, Tokyo has more than its fair share of intelligentsia, academics, politicians, businesspeople, artists, and writers, and it's the country's showcase for technology, fashion, art, architecture, music, and advertising. People rush around here with such purpose and determination, it's hard not to feel that you're in the midst of something important, that you're witnessing history in the making.

As for innovation, Tokyo has long been recognized as a leader. Indeed, Japan, once dismissed as merely an imitator with no imagination of its own, has long been at the forefront of all things technological, from robots and cars to audiovisual equipment and kitchen and office gadgetry. Walking through the stores of Akihabara, Tokyo's electronics center, provokes an uneasiness few visitors can shake, for it's here that the latest goods are sold long before they reach Western markets. Tokyo also stands at the center of Japan's cool pop culture—*anime* (Japanese animation), Hello Kitty, Pokémon—one of the fastest-growing subcultures in the world. In other words, this trend-setting Asian capital is in.

Yet despite outward appearances, all is not rosy in the land of the rising sun. Its unparalleled economic growth of the 1980s, generating both admiration and envy worldwide, has never quite recovered from the burst of its economic bubble in 1992. While the economy seemed to be on the mend by mid-2000, the 2008 international financial meltdown brought Japan's economy to a screeching halt, as demand for Japanese cars, electronics, and other exports dropped dramatically around the world.

Meanwhile, homelessness is so common in Tokyo that it no longer draws stares, even in the swank Ginza district. Crime, once almost unheard of, has been a

Moments A Face in the Crowd

My first morning in Japan took place more than 25 years ago, but I remember it vividly because of an unexpected act of kindness. Shouldering my backpack, I was making my way from my Tokyo hotel to Shinagawa Station, a sea of people streaming past me on their way to work. A soft, wet snow was falling from the gray sky.

Suddenly, a woman appeared at my side and fell in sync with my stride, holding her umbrella aloft to shelter me from the cold snow. We walked like that all the way to the station, where, to my surprise, she whipped a towel from her bag and proceeded to dry my wet hair. Back then, my Japanese was limited to phrases like "Where's the bathroom?" so all I could manage was a polite *arigatoo.* But my guardian angel's job wasn't over yet. She helped me find the Yamanote Line bound for Tokyo Station and, finally satisfied, sent me on my way.

Over the years I have been the recipient of so many acts of kindness that I have to wonder whether it's because people in Japan are so nice or whether it's because I'm so inept (I suppose if I didn't get lost so often, I wouldn't need so much help). Strangers have gone out of their way to deliver me to my destination, made telephone calls on my behalf, helped me choose meals from indecipherable menus, and showered me with small gifts.

But no one stands out in my memory as much as that woman who took me under her wing that very first day. I was excited to be in a new foreign country, nervous about finding my way, tired from the long flight, and feeling just a tad lonely in the sea of unfamiliar faces. Of course, she didn't know any of these things when she stepped up to help. I was just a face in the crowd, but when she left me, I no longer felt quite the stranger in a very strange land.

major topic of concern for more than a decade. My former Tokyo landlady fears burglary so much that she no longer opens her door to strangers.

Another pressing long-term concern is a declining birth rate coupled with an aging population, with Japan's over-65 generation, which now accounts for more than 22% of its population, expected to double by 2055. Meanwhile, Japan's ratio of children ages 14 and younger is believed to be the lowest in the world, accounting for only 13.5% of the population. The government has predicted that Japan's total population could plunge by nearly one-third by 2055, causing tax-revenue shortfalls and a shortage of labor.

Discontent with the status quo played a major role in Japan's national elections held in August 2009, when the left-of-center Democratic Party of Japan (DPJ) defeated the conservative Liberal Democratic Party, which had ruled for all but 10 months since its founding in 1955. Whether the DPJ, which also cruised to victory in a Tokyo Metropolitan Assembly election, can truly effect change remains to be seen. Its first real test, critics say, will be in drafting the annual budget from April 2010.

Meanwhile, almost every Japanese company you can think of, from Sony to Toyota, has suffered devastating losses the past year, as exports to other countries plunged.

Impressions

The Japanese are in general intelligent and provident, free and unconstrained, obedient and courteous, curious and inquisitive, industrious and ingenious, frugal and sober, cleanly, good-natured and friendly, upright and just, trusty and honest, mistrustful, superstitious, proud, and haughty, unforgiving, brave, and invincible.
—Charles Peter Thunberg, *Travels in Europe, Africa, and Asia* (1795)

All my friends living in Tokyo, both Japanese and foreign, have had to tighten their belts, whether it's because their annual bonuses have been drastically cut or because income from clients—who are also having financial difficulties—has dried up. In other words, the economic crisis isn't much different in Japan than elsewhere; it's just been going on much longer.

Yet oddly, more museums and other highly visible buildings are undergoing major renovations in Tokyo right now than almost any year I can think of, including the Kabuki-za and the Central Post Office (I find it encouraging that a proposed demolition of the post office building, built in 1931, caused such a furor that as much as 30% of the old building will be preserved). Although some of my favorite restaurants and hotels have closed as victims of the economy, new ones have sprung up to take their place. In other words, it's business as usual in Tokyo, though bargains abound in these troubled times, whether it's for goods, hotel rooms, or a meal. One of the most favorable results of the recession is Japan's growing desire to attract foreign visitors, with more English-language brochures, websites, and user-friendly services than ever before. Tobu, which operates train service to Nikko, introduced a train pass strictly for foreigners. There's also a new dedicated tourist bus that makes a circular route to Tokyo's major sightseeing districts, such as Ueno and Asakusa, making it easier to move around the metropolis.

One of the most fascinating changes in Tokyo over the past few years, in my opinion, is the explosion of personal expression, making it a mecca for seekers of cool, edgy design. Long gone are the same drab office clothes and nonquestioning conformity. Tokyo today is a kaleidoscope of various fashions, from hip street clothing to a wide range of personal styles that reflect a wide spectrum of international influences. The *otaku* (geek) culture has come out of the closet and into the mainstream, bringing with it such a newfound interest in anime (Japanese animation) and *manga* (Japanese graphic novels) that Akihabara is no longer a mecca just for buyers of electronics but also for those in search of pop culture. Tokyo's Design Festa, held twice a year, is one of the most exuberant art events you'll find anywhere, drawing more than 8,500 artists from more than 30 countries.

In many ways, Tokyo is more interesting and diverse now than it ever was. With the DPJ at the helm, and its promise to shift the country's emphasis from a business-oriented society to one that is more people-oriented, it will be very interesting to see what's coming down the road.

For the short-term visitor to Tokyo, however, problems that loom in the public psyche—economic uncertainty, a revolving door of prime ministers, political scandal, and rising crime—are not readily apparent (unless you go to Ueno or Yoyogi parks, where the number of homeless is nothing short of astounding). Crime, though undeniably on the increase over the past years, is still negligible when compared to levels in the United States, and Tokyo remains one of the safest cities in the world. (According to an article published September 11, 2007, in the *Yomiuri Shimbun,* the number of thefts and burglaries in the Tokyo metropolitan area decreased 30% to 50% after the arrest in 2006 of 16 Chinese suspected of operating two burglary rings.)

Although it's true that I am more careful than I was 20 years ago—I guard my purse in crowded subways and I avoid parks after dark—for Americans, such precautions seem merely self-evident. But while I'm cautious about theft and purse-snatching, I never worry about personal safety when I'm walking the streets of Tokyo. In fact, it never even crosses my mind. Violent crime—especially against

strangers—remains virtually unheard of in Japan.

Moreover, while Tokyo remains one of the most expensive cities in the world, it now offers something that would have been unthinkable during the spend-happy 1980s, when only designer goods would do and expense accounts seemed unlimited: bargains. Tony French restaurants serve value-conscious fixed-price lunches, there are buffets virtually everywhere, secondhand clothing stores sell last year's designer wear, 100-Yen discount shops do a brisk business, and many hotels offer bargain rates on their websites.

Despite what the future may bring, I'm convinced Tokyo at street level will remain as it's always been—humming with energy, crowded beyond belief, and filled with acts of human kindness.

2 LOOKING BACK AT TOKYO

EARLY HISTORY

Archaeological finds show that the region was inhabited as early as 30,000 B.C., but it wasn't until the 6th century that Japan began spreading its cultural wings. Taking its cues from China, its great neighbor to the west, Japan adopted Buddhism, the character system of writing, and Chinese art forms and architecture, and molded them into a style of its own.

In A.D. 794, the Japanese Imperial family established a new capital in Heiankyo (present-day Kyoto), where it remained for more than 1,000 years. The arts flourished, and extravagant temples and pavilions were erected. Noh drama, the tea ceremony, flower arranging, and landscape gardening developed. But even though Kyoto served as the cultural heart of the nation, it was often the nation's capital in

DATELINE

- **794** Kyoto becomes Japan's capital.
- **1192** Minamoto Yoritomo becomes shogun and establishes his shogunate government in Kamakura.
- **1333** The Kamakura shogunate falls and the Imperial system is restored.
- **1603** Tokugawa Ieyasu becomes shogun and establishes his shogunate in Edo

(present-day Tokyo), marking the beginning of a 264-year rule by the Tokugawa clan.
- **1612** Silver mint opens in the Ginza.
- **1633** Japan closes its doors to foreign trade and subsequently forbids all foreigners from landing in Japan and all Japanese from leaving.
- **1787** The population of Tokyo reaches 1.3 million.

- **1853** Commodore Matthew C. Perry of the U.S. Navy persuades the Japanese to sign a trade agreement with the United States.
- **1867** The Tokugawa regime is overthrown, bringing Japan's feudal era to a close.
- **1868** Emperor Meiji assumes power, moves his Imperial capital from Kyoto to Tokyo, and begins the industrialization of Japan.

continues

name only. Preoccupied by their own luxurious lifestyle, the nobles and royal court of Kyoto were no match for rebellious military clans in the provinces.

THE FEUDAL PERIOD

The first successful clan uprising took place at the end of the 12th century, when a young warrior named Minamoto Yoritomo won a bloody civil war that brought him supremacy over the land. Wishing to set up his rule far away from the Imperial family in Kyoto, he made his capital in a remote and easily defended fishing village called Kamakura, not far from today's Tokyo. He created a military government, a shogunate, ushering in a new era in Japan's history in which the power of the country passed from the aristocratic court into the hands of the warrior class. In becoming the nation's first shogun, or military dictator, Yoritomo laid the groundwork for the military governments that lasted for another 700 years in Japan—until the Imperial court was restored in 1868.

The Kamakura Period, from 1192 to 1333, is perhaps best known for the unrivaled ascendancy of the warrior caste, called samurai. Ruled by a rigid code of honor, the samurai were bound in loyalty to their feudal lord and would defend him to the death. If they failed in their duties, they could redeem their honor by

committing ritualistic suicide, or *seppuku*. Spurning the soft life led by the noble court in Kyoto, the samurai embraced a harsher and simpler set of ideals and a spartan lifestyle, embodied in the tenets of Zen Buddhism's mental and physical disciplines.

The Kamakura Period was followed by 200 years of vicious civil wars and confusion as *daimyo* (feudal lords) staked out their fiefdoms throughout the land and strove for supremacy. Not unlike a baron in medieval Europe, a daimyo had absolute rule over the people who lived in his fiefdom and was aided in battles by his samurai retainers.

THE RISE OF TOKUGAWA

In the second half of the 16th century, several brilliant military strategists rose to power, but none proved as shrewd as Tokugawa Ieyasu, a statesman so skillful in eliminating his enemies that his heirs would continue to rule Japan for the next 250 years. It was with him that Tokyo's history began.

For centuries, present-day Tokyo was nothing more than a rather obscure village called Edo, which means simply "mouth of the estuary." Then, in 1590, Tokugawa acquired eight provinces surrounding Edo, much of it marsh and wilderness, with little fresh water available. Undaunted, Tokugawa chose Edo as his base and

- 1873 Ueno Park opens to the public as Tokyo's first city park.
- 1878 Establishment of the Tokyo Stock Exchange.
- 1922 The Imperial Hotel, designed by Frank Lloyd Wright, opens in Hibiya, opposite the Imperial Palace.
- 1923 Tokyo and Yokohama are devastated by a major earthquake in which more than 100,000 people lose their lives.

- 1937 Japan goes to war with China and conquers Nanking.
- 1940 Japan forms a military alliance with Germany and Italy.
- 1941 The Pacific War begins as Japan bombs Pearl Harbor.
- 1945 Hiroshima and Nagasaki suffer atomic bomb attacks; Japan agrees to surrender.

- 1946 The emperor renounces his claim to divinity; Japan adopts a new, democratic constitution; women gain the right to vote.
- 1952 The Allied occupation of Japan ends; Japan regains its independence.
- 1956 Japan is admitted to the United Nations.
- 1964 The XVIII Summer Olympic Games are held in Tokyo.

immediately set to work correcting the area's shortcomings by reclaiming land, building a conduit for fresh water, and constructing a castle surrounded by moats.

By 1603, Tokugawa had succeeded in defeating every one of his rivals in a series of brilliant battles, becoming shogun over all of Japan. He declared the sleepy village of Edo the seat of his shogunate government, leaving the emperor intact but virtually powerless in Kyoto. He then set about expanding Edo Castle to make it the most impressive castle in the land, surrounding it with an ingenious system of moats that radiated from the castle in a great swirl, giving him access to the sea and thwarting enemy attack.

THE EDO PERIOD

Edo grew quickly as the shogunate capital. For greater protection, and to ensure that no daimyo in the distant provinces could grow strong enough to usurp the shogun's power, the Tokugawa government ordered every daimyo to reside in Edo for a prescribed number of months every other year, thus keeping the feudal lords under the watchful eye of the shogunate. Furthermore, all daimyo were required to leave their families in Edo as permanent residents, to serve as virtual hostages. There were as many as 270 daimyo in Japan in the 17th century, with each maintaining several mansions in Edo for family members and retainers, complete with elaborate compounds and expansive landscaped gardens. Together with their samurai, who made up almost half of Edo's population in the 17th century, the daimyo and their entourage must have created quite a colorful sight on the dusty streets of old Edo. By expending so much time and money traveling back and forth and maintaining residences in both the provinces and Edo, a daimyo would have been hard put to wage war against the shogun.

To cater to the needs of the shogun, daimyo, and their samurai retainers, merchants and craftsmen from throughout Japan swarmed to Edo. To accommodate them, hills were leveled and marshes filled in, creating what is now the Ginza, Shimbashi, and Nihombashi. By 1787, the population had swelled to 1.3 million, making Edo one of the largest cities in the world. It was a city few outsiders were ever permitted to see, however. Fearing the spread of Western influence and Christianity in Japan, not to mention daimyo growing rich through international trade, the Tokugawa shogunate adopted a policy of complete isolation in 1633, slamming Japan's doors to the outside world for more than 200 years. The shogunate forbade foreigners to enter Japan and forbade the Japanese to leave. Those who defied the strict decrees paid with their lives. The

- **1989** Emperor Hirohito dies after a 63-year reign.
- **1990** Hirohito's son, Akihito, formally ascends the throne and proclaims the new "Era of Peace" (Heisei).
- **1991** Tokyo's new city hall, the Tokyo Metropolitan Government Office, designed by Kenzo Tange, opens in Shinjuku.
- **1992** The worst recession since World War II hits Japan. The Diet (Japanese parliament) approves use of military forces for United Nations peacekeeping efforts.
- **1993** Liberal Democratic party loses election for the first time since 1955. Akebono, a Hawaiian, becomes first non-Japanese to reach sumo's highest rank of *yokozuna*.
- **1995** Japan's sense of security is shaken by the Great Hanshin Earthquake (and the subsequent mishandling of rescue aid), which flattens the city of Kobe, and by the sarin-gas attack upon Tokyo's crowded commuter trains.
- **1998** The XVIII Winter Olympic Games are held in Nagano.
- **1999** A nuclear plant 113km (70 miles) northeast of Tokyo suffers Japan's worst nuclear accident, exposing dozens to radiation.

continues

only exception to this policy of isolation was a colony of tightly controlled Chinese merchants in Nagasaki, and a handful of Dutch confined to a small trading post on a tiny island in Nagasaki.

The Edo Period (1603–1867) was a time of political stability, with all policy dictated by the shogunate government. Japanese society was divided into four distinct classes: samurai, farmers, craftsmen, and merchants. After daimyo and nobles, samurai occupied the most exalted social position and were the only ones allowed to carry two swords. At the bottom of the social ladder were the merchants. They occupied squalid tenements, which were typically long row houses constructed of wood and facing narrow meter-wide alleys, with open sewers running down the middle. Family homes were unimaginably small, consisting of a tiny entryway that also doubled as the kitchen and a single room about 9.2 sq. m (99 sq. ft.) in size. Because most of Edo was built of wood, it goes without saying that fires were a constant threat. In fact, rare indeed was the person who didn't lose his house at least several times during his lifetime. Between 1603 and 1868, almost 100 major fires swept through Edo, along with countless smaller fires. One of the most tragic fires occurred in 1657, after a severe drought had plagued the city for almost 3 months. Buffeted by strong winds, the

flames ignited wooden homes and thatched roofs like tinder, raging for 3 days and reducing three-fourths of the city to smoldering ruins. More than 100,000 people lost their lives.

Despite such setbacks, the merchants of Tokyo grew in number and became so wealthy that new forms of luxury and entertainment arose to occupy their time. Kabuki drama and woodblock prints became the rage, while stone and porcelain ware, silk brocade for elaborate and gorgeous kimono, and lacquerware were elevated to wondrous works of art. Japan's most famous pleasure district was an area in northeast Edo called Yoshiwara, the "floating world of pleasure," where rich merchants spent fortunes to cavort with beautiful courtesans.

THE OPENING OF JAPAN

By the mid-19th century, it was clear that the feudal system was outdated. With economic power in the hands of the merchants, money rather than rice became the primary means of exchange. Many samurai families found themselves on the brink of poverty, and discontent with the shogunate grew widespread.

In 1854, Commodore Matthew C. Perry of the U.S. Navy succeeded in forcing the shogun to sign an agreement granting America trading rights, thus ending 2 centuries of isolation. In 1868, the

- **2001** A man storms into an elementary school in Osaka Prefecture and fatally stabs eight children. Public spirits rise with the birth of a baby girl to the crown prince and princess.
- **2002** North Korea admits that it kidnapped 11 young Japanese in the 1970s and 1980s to teach Japanese language and customs to North Korean spies.

- **2003** Tokyo's Shinagawa Station becomes a stop on the Tokaido-Sanyo Line with connections to Kyoto, Hiroshima, and other points west.
- **2005** Anti-Japanese protests are held throughout China in response to new school textbooks in Japan that gloss over Japan's World War II atrocities.

- **2007** A full-page ad appearing June 14 in the *Washington Post*, endorsed by 44 Japanese lawmakers, disputes that women in Asia were forced into prostitution by the Japanese army during World War II.
- **2009** Sony reports its first annual net loss in 14 years. The Democratic Party of Japan defeats the long-running Liberal Democratic Party in national elections.

Tokugawas were overthrown, and Emperor Meiji was restored as ruler. The feudal era drew to an end.

THE MEIJI RESTORATION

Rather than remain in Kyoto, Emperor Meiji decided to take Edo for his own and moved his Imperial capital to its new home in 1868. Renaming Edo Tokyo, or "Eastern Capital" (to distinguish it from the "western" capital of Kyoto), the emperor was quick to welcome ideas and technology from the West. The ensuing years, known as the Meiji Period (1868–1911), were nothing short of amazing, as Japan progressed rapidly from a feudal agricultural society of samurai and peasants to an industrial nation. The samurai were stripped of their power and were no longer permitted to carry swords; a prime minister and cabinet were appointed; a constitution was drafted; and a parliament, called the Diet, was elected. The railway, postal system, and even specialists and advisers were imported from the West. Between 1881 and 1898, 6,177 British, 2,764 Americans, 913 Germans, and 619 French were retained by the Japanese government to help transform Japan into a modern society.

As the nation's capital, Tokyo was hardest hit by this craze for modernization. Ideas for fashion, architecture, food, and department stores were imported from the West—West was best, and things Japanese were forgotten or pushed aside. It didn't help that Tokyo was almost totally destroyed *twice* in the first half of the 20th century: In 1923, a huge earthquake, measuring 7.9 on the Richter scale and known as the Great Kanto Earthquake, struck the city, followed by tsunami (tidal waves). More than 100,000 people died and a third of Tokyo was in ruins. Disaster struck again during World War II, when incendiary bombs laid more than half the city to waste and killed another 100,000 people.

WORLD WAR II & ITS AFTERMATH

Japan's expansionist policies in Asia during the 1930s and early 1940s spread the flag of the rising sun over Hong Kong, China, Singapore, Burma, Malaysia, the Philippines, the Dutch East Indies, and Guam. World War II, however, halted Japan's advance. Shortly after the United States dropped the world's first atomic bombs—over Hiroshima on August 6, 1945, and over Nagasaki 3 days later—surrender came, on August 14, 1945.

The end of the war brought American occupation forces to Japan, where they remained until 1952. It was the first time in Japan's history that the island nation had suffered defeat and occupation by a foreign power. The experience had a profound effect on the Japanese people. Emerging from their defeat, they began the long effort to rebuild their cities and economy. In 1946, under the guidance of the Allied military authority, headed by U.S. Gen. Douglas MacArthur, they adopted a new, democratic constitution that renounced war and divested the emperor of his claim to divinity. A parliamentary system of government was set up and in 1947 the first general elections were held. The following year, the militarists and generals who had carried out the Pacific War were tried, and many of them were convicted. To the younger generation of Japanese, the occupation was less a painful burden that had to be suffered than an opportunity to remake their country, with American encouragement, into a modern, peace-loving, and democratic state.

A special relationship developed between the Japanese and their American occupiers. In the early 1950s, as the Cold War between the United States and the communist world erupted into hostilities in Korea, that relationship grew into a firm alliance, strengthened by a security treaty between Tokyo and Washington. In 1952, the occupation ended and in 1956 Japan joined the United Nations as an independent country.

POSTWAR TOKYO

Perhaps unsurprising in a city trained in natural calamities, Tokyo was so adept at rebuilding that a decade later not a trace of wartime destruction remained. Avoiding involvement in foreign conflicts, the Japanese concentrated on economic recovery. Through a series of policies that favored domestic industries and shielded Japan from foreign competition, the country achieved rapid economic growth. By the mid-1960s—only a century after Japan had opened its doors to the rest of the world and embraced modernization—the Japanese had transformed their nation into a major industrial power, with Tokyo riding the crest of the economic wave. In 1964, in recognition of Japan's increasing importance, the Summer Olympic Games were held in Tokyo, thrusting the city into the international limelight.

As their economy continued to expand, the Japanese sought new markets abroad; by the early 1970s, they had attained a trade surplus, as Japanese products—cars and electronic goods—attracted more and more foreign buyers. By the 1980s, "Japan, Inc." seemed on the economic brink of ruling the world, as Japanese companies bought prime real estate around the globe, books flooded the Western market expounding Japanese business principles, and Japan enjoyed unprecedented financial growth. With the exception of a top tier of the very wealthy, virtually everyone in Japan considered him- or herself a member of the middle class.

In 1992, recession hit Japan, bursting the economic bubble and plunging the country into its worst recession since World War II. Bankruptcies reached an all-time high, Tokyo real-estate prices plummeted 70% from what they were in 1991, the Nikkei (Japan's version of the

American Dow) fell a gut-churning 63% from its 1989 peak, and the country was rocked by one political scandal after another. Public confidence was further eroded in 1995, first by a major earthquake in Kobe that killed more than 6,000 people and proved that Japan's cities were not as safe as the government had maintained, and then by an attack by an obscure religious sect that released the deadly nerve gas sarin on Tokyo's subway system during rush hour, killing 12 people and sickening thousands. The nation had another scare in 1999 when an accident at a nuclear power plant only 113km (70 miles) from Tokyo exposed dozens to radiation; two workers subsequently died from the radiation. But the worst blow of all was in 2001, when a knife-wielding man stormed into an elementary school in Osaka Prefecture, fatally stabbing eight children and wounding 15 others. For many Japanese, it seemed that the very core of their society had begun to crumble.

Since 1999, Tokyo has been led by outspoken governor Ishihara Shintaro, a nationalist writer who, together with former Sony chairman Morita Akio, penned the 1989 best-selling *The Japan That Can Say No.* His election was regarded as a clear rejection of the status quo and a belief that change in Japan must come from within, with Tokyo clearly at the forefront. In 2001, that desire for change ushered in long-haired, 59-year-old Koizumi Junichiro as the new prime minister, long considered a maverick for his battles against the established power brokers and his cries for reform.

While Koizumi instigated policies that helped decrease the number of bad loans at major banks—once considered a financial time bomb—to half what they were in 2002, public opinion polls eventually turned sour over his achievements. In addition, relations with Japan's closest neighbors, China and North and South Korea, hit rock bottom, with disputes that included island territorial claims; North Korea's admission to abducting young Japanese decades earlier to teach its spies Japanese language and customs; Japan's lack of accountability in school textbooks of atrocities it committed during World War II; and Japan's denial of sex slavery in neighboring countries during the war. Koizumi further outraged his neighbors with repeated visits to Tokyo's Yasukuni Shrine, vilified by critics for honoring Japanese war dead, including those executed for wartime atrocities in Asia.

After more than a decade of recession, the economy seemed to be on the mend by mid-2000. Tokyo property prices rose for the first time in 2004, spurring investors to return. In fact, after years of no new attractions, few new hotels, deflated prices, and only a handful of new developments, Tokyo experienced something of a development boom in the latter half of the last decade, led by auctions of massive land tracts once owned by Japan Railways near train stations, especially Tokyo Station. Several major urban developments mushroomed, most notably the Marunouchi district east of Tokyo Station, with its spanking-new skyscrapers and tree-lined shopping street; Omotesando Hills, a posh residential and shopping center designed by renowned architect Tadao Ando; Roppongi's Tokyo Midtown, which boasts Tokyo's tallest building along with shops, restaurants, an art museum, apartments, and offices; and leader of the pack Roppongi Hills, which stretches over 12 hectares (30 acres) and contains 230 shops and restaurants, offices, luxury apartments,

and an art museum (my favorite part of the Roppongi Hills story: It took developer Mori Minoru 18 years of negotiation with 500 property owners to secure the land for development).

In or near these new developments was a blitz of foreign-owned luxury hotels, including the Mandarin Oriental, Tokyo; Grand Hyatt Tokyo; Ritz-Carlton, Tokyo; and The Peninsula Tokyo. In 2007, Tokyo witnessed the development of new major museums in more than a decade: The National Art Center, Tokyo, and Suntory Museum of Art, which, together with Roppongi Hills' Mori Art Museum, formed the new Art Triangle Roppongi.

But then came the 2008 international financial meltdown, and Japan, whose foremost trading partner had shifted from the United States to China, was left reeling from a downward spiral in foreign trade. Furthermore, after Koizumi's rare 5-year term ended in 2006, Japan once again suffered a revolving door of prime ministers, with three coming and going over the next 3 years.

In August 2009, widespread dissatisfaction with the status quo brought a landslide victory for the opposition Democratic Party of Japan and defeat for the business-friendly Liberal Democratic party, which had ruled for more than a half-century. Under the helm of the new prime minister, Hatoyama Yukio, the DPJ has pledged to cut government waste; provide support for farmers, fishermen, and small and medium-size businesses; and boost disposable household income in an attempt to bolster Japan's middle class.

3 SHRINES & TEMPLES: RELIGION IN JAPAN

The main religions in Japan are Shintoism and Buddhism, and many Japanese consider themselves believers in both. Most Japanese, for example, will marry in a

Shinto ceremony, but when they die, they'll have a Buddhist funeral.

A native religion of Japan, **Shintoism** is the worship of ancestors and national heroes, as well as of all natural things, both animate and inanimate. These natural things are thought to embody gods and can be anyone or anything—mountains, trees, the moon, stars, rivers, seas, fires, animals, rocks, even vegetables. Shintoism also embraces much of Confucianism, which entered Japan in the 5th century and stressed the importance of family and loyalty. There are no scriptures in Shintoism, nor any ordained code of morals or ethics.

The place of worship in Shintoism is called a *jinja,* or shrine. The most obvious sign of a shrine is its *torii,* an entrance gate, usually of wood, consisting of two tall poles topped with either one or two crossbeams. Another feature common to shrines is a water trough with communal cups, where the Japanese will wash their hands and sometimes rinse out their mouths. Purification and cleanliness are important in Shintoism because they show respect to the gods. At the shrine, worshippers will throw a few coins into a money box, clap their hands twice to get the gods' attention, and then bow their heads and pray for whatever they wish—good health, protection, the safe delivery of a child, or a prosperous year. The most famous shrine in Tokyo is **Meiji Shrine.**

Founded in India in the 5th century, **Buddhism** came to Japan in the 6th century via China and Korea, bringing with it the concept of eternal life, and, by the end of the 6th century, it had gained such popularity that it was declared the state religion. Of the various Buddhist sects in Japan today, Zen Buddhism is probably the most well known in the West. Considered the most Japanese form of Buddhism, Zen is the practice of meditation and a strictly disciplined lifestyle to rid yourself of desire so that you can achieve enlightenment. There are no rites in Zen Buddhism, no dogmas, no theological conceptions of divinity. You do not analyze rationally, but rather know things intuitively. The strict and simple lifestyle of Zen appealed greatly to Japan's samurai warrior class, and many of Japan's arts, including the tea ceremony, arose from the practice of Zen.

Whereas Shintoists have shrines, Buddhists have temples, called *otera.* Instead of torii, temples will often have an entrance gate with a raised doorsill and heavy doors. Temples may also have a cemetery on their grounds (which Shinto shrines never have) as well as a pagoda. Tokyo's most famous temple is **Sensoji Temple** in Asakusa.

---

4 TOKYO IN POPULAR CULTURE: BOOKS & FILM

BOOKS

Kodansha International (www.kodansha-intl.com), a Japanese publisher, has probably published more books on Japan in English—including Japanese-language textbooks—than any other company. Available at major bookstores in Japan, they can also be ordered online at www.amazon.com.

HISTORY The definitive work of Japan's history through the ages is *Japan: The Story of a Nation* (Alfred A. Knopf, 1991), by Edwin O. Reischauer, a former U.S. ambassador to Japan. For more recent coverage, there's *A Modern History of Japan: From Tokugawa Times to the Present,* by Andrew Gordon (Oxford University Press, 2003).

For an overview of Tokyo's history, refer to Edward G. Seidensticker's *Low City, High City* (Harvard University Press, 1991), which covers the period from 1867 to 1923, when the city rapidly grew from an isolated and ancient shogun's capital into a great modern city. Its sequel, *Tokyo Rising* (Harvard University Press, 1991), describes the metropolis after the Great Earthquake of 1923 and follows its remarkable development through the postwar years until the end of the 1980s. Describing the daily lives of samurai, farmers, craftsmen, merchants, courtiers, and outcasts, with a special section devoted to life in Edo, is Charles J. Dunn's fascinating *Everyday Life in Traditional Japan* (Tuttle, 2000).

SOCIETY Reischauer's *The Japanese Today* (Tuttle, 1993) offers a unique perspective on Japanese society, including the historical events that have shaped and influenced Japanese behavior and the role of the individual in Japanese society; an updated version is Reischauer's *Japanese Today: Change and Continuity* (Belknap Press, 1995). A classic description of the Japanese and their culture is found in Ruth Benedict's brilliant *The Chrysanthemum and the Sword: Patterns of Japanese Culture* (New American Library, 1967), first published in the 1940s but reprinted many times since. For a more contemporary approach, read Robert C. Christopher's insightful *The Japanese Mind: The Goliath Explained* (Linden Press/Simon & Schuster, 1983).

For a look into life in the capital—education, employment, home life, and more—check your school or public library for *Life in Tokyo: The Way People Live* (Lucent Books, 2001), by Stuart A. Kallen. More entertaining is *Tabloid Tokyo: 101 Tales of Sex, Crime, and the Bizarre from Japan's Wild Weeklies* (Kodansha, 2005), by Mark Schreiber, and its sequel, *Tabloid Tokyo 2* (Kodansha, 2007).

CULTURE & THE ARTS *Introduction to Japanese Culture,* edited by Daniel Sosnoski (Tuttle, 1996), gives a great overview and covers major festivals, the tea ceremony, flower arranging, Kabuki, sumo, Buddha, kanji, and much more. For a historical perspective on Tokyo's cultural development through the centuries, including literature, architecture, Kabuki, and the arts, see *Tokyo: A Cultural History* by Stephen Mansfield (Oxford University Press, 2009).

The Japan Travel Bureau puts out nifty pocket-size illustrated booklets on things Japanese, including *Eating in Japan, Living Japanese Style, Martial Arts & Sports in Japan,* and *Japanese Family & Culture.* My favorite is *Salaryman in Japan* (JTB, 1986), which describes the private and working lives of Japan's army of white-collar workers who receive set salaries.

FICTION Tokyo bookstores have entire sections dedicated to English translations of Japan's best-known modern and contemporary authors, including Mishima Yukio, Soseki Natsume, Abe Kobo, Tanizaki Junichiro, and Nobel prize winners Kawabata Yasunari and Oe Kenzaburo. An overview of Japanese classical literature is provided in *Anthology of Japanese Literature* (Grove Press, 1955), edited by Donald Keene. *Modern Japanese Stories: An Anthology* (Tuttle, 1962), edited by Ivan Morris, introduces short stories by some of Japan's top modern writers, including Mori Ogai, Tanizaki Junichiro, Kawabata Yasunari, and Mishima Yukio.

Soseki Natsume, one of Japan's most respected novelists of the Meiji Era, writes of Tokyo and its tumultuous time of change in *And Then* (Putnam, 1982), translated by Norma Moore Field, and in *Kokoro* (Regnery Publishing, 1985), translated by Edwin McClellan. Although not well known in the West, Enchi Fumiko writes an absorbing novel about women trapped by social constraints in 19th-century Tokyo in *The Waiting Years* (Kodansha, 2002), first published in 1957.

Favorite writers of Japan's baby-boom generation include Murakami Ryu, who captured the undercurrent of decadent urban life in his best-selling *Coin Locker Babies* (Kodansha, 1995) and wrote a shocking expose of Tokyo's sex industry in

In the Miso Soup (Kodansha, 2003), though its murder descriptions might be too graphic for some; and Murakami Haruki, whose writings include *Dance Dance Dance* (Kodansha, 1994), about a 30-something protagonist living in a glittering high-rise but searching for more meaning in life, and *South of the Border, West of the Sun* (Knopf, 1999), another story of a bewildered man in contemporary Tokyo.

FILMS

Probably the most internationally well-known film shot in Tokyo in recent years is Sophia Coppola's *Lost in Translation* (2003), in which two lost characters played by Bill Murray and Scarlett Johansson find solace in each other's company as they drift through an incomprehensible—and at times hilarious—Tokyo.

Love and Pop (1998), by director Anno Hideaki, best known for anime films, is a low-budget film based on a novel by Murakami Ryu about "compensated dating," in which teenage girls are paid to go out with older businessmen. Another film dealing with this phenomenon rarely covered in the Western press is Harada Masato's *Bounce Ko Gals* (1998), which presents a shocking but heart-felt story of sexual exploitation and loss of innocence.

Adrift in Tokyo (2007), directed by Satoshi Miki, gives an up-close and personal view of Tokyo's back streets and neighborhoods as two men—a debt collector and a university student who owes money—walk across the city on a journey that seems aimless but provides a turning point in the lives of both men.

Other movies partly or wholly filmed in Tokyo include German writer-director Doris Dorrie's *Cherry Blossoms* (2008), about a middle-aged Bavarian, who, mourning the death of his wife, takes a trip to Tokyo and meets a young Butoh dancer also grieving over the death of a loved one; and *Tokyo Sonata* (2008), directed Kurosawa Kiyoshi, about an ordinary family in contemporary Tokyo in which the father loses his job but is too ashamed to tell his family and thus pretends he's going to work every day. Spanish director Isabel Coixet's *Map of the Sounds of Tokyo* (2009) centers on two star-crossed lovers in Tokyo, with rich imagery of the city's neon streets, love hotels, noodle shops, fish market, and other true-to-life scenes.

5 EATING & DRINKING IN TOKYO

Tokyo is a foodie's paradise. In fact, I'd have to say that Tokyoites are obsessed with food, fanatics ever on the prowl for the best of the best, whether it's for the city's best sushi or its best burger. If you see a long queue outside a restaurant, chances are it's been written up in some magazine, inducing food-crazed hordes to endure long waits for the privilege of dining at the newest hot spot.

But I have to admit, whenever I leave Japan, it's the food I miss the most. Sure, there are sushi bars and other Japanese specialty restaurants in major cities elsewhere, but they don't offer nearly the variety available in Japan (and they often aren't nearly as good). Just as America has more to offer than hamburgers and steaks, Japan has more than sushi and *teppanyaki*. For both the gourmet and the uninitiated, Tokyo is a treasure-trove of culinary surprises.

JAPANESE CUISINE

There are more than a dozen different and distinct types of Japanese cuisine, plus countless regional specialties. A good deal of what you eat may be completely new to you, as well as completely unidentifiable.

There is a saying that the Chinese eat with their stomachs and the Japanese with their eyes.

—Bernard Leach, *A Potter In Japan* (1960)

No need to worry—even the Japanese themselves don't always know what they're eating, so varied and so wide is the range of available edibles. The rule is simply to enjoy, and enjoyment begins even before you raise your chopsticks to your mouth.

To the Japanese, presentation of food is as important as the food itself, and dishes are designed to appeal to the eye as well as to the palate. In contrast to the Western way of piling as much food as possible onto a single plate, the Japanese often use many small plates, each arranged artfully with bite-size morsels of food. After you see what can be done with maple leaves, flowers, bits of bamboo, and even pebbles to enhance the appearance of food, your relationship with what you eat may change forever.

Below are explanations of some of the most common types of Japanese cuisine. Generally, only one type of cuisine is served in a given restaurant—for example, only raw seafood is served in a sushi bar, while tempura is served at a tempura counter. There are some exceptions to this, especially in regard to raw fish and vegetables, which are served as appetizers and side dishes in many restaurants. In addition, some of Japan's drinking establishments (called *izakaya* or *nomiya*) offer a wide range of foods, from soups to sushi to skewered pieces of chicken known as *yakitori*. Japanese restaurants in hotels may also offer great variety in order to appeal to as large a customer base as possible.

For a quick rundown of individual dishes, refer to the food terms in appendix B.

FUGU   Known as blowfish, puffer fish, or globefish in English, fugu is one of the most exotic and adventurous foods in Japan—if it's not prepared properly, it means almost certain death for the consumer! In the past decade or so, some 50 people in Japan have died from fugu poisoning, usually because they tried preparing it at home. The ovaries and intestines of the fugu are deadly and must be entirely removed without being punctured. So why eat fugu if it can kill you? Well, for one thing, it's delicious, and for another, fugu chefs are strictly licensed by the government and greatly skilled in preparing fugu dishes. You can order fugu raw (*fugu-sashi*), sliced paper-thin and dipped into soy sauce with bitter orange and chives; in a stew (*fugu-chiri*) cooked with vegetables at your table; or in a rice porridge (*fugu-zosui*). There's even fugu-laced sake. The season for fresh fugu is October or November through March, but some restaurants serve it year-round.

KAISEKI   The king of Japanese cuisine, kaiseki is the epitome of delicately and exquisitely arranged food, the ultimate in aesthetic appeal. It's also among the most expensive meals you'll ever find. A kaiseki dinner can cost ¥25,000 or more per person; some restaurants, however, do offer more affordable mini-kaiseki courses. In addition, the better *ryokan* (Japanese inns) serve kaiseki, one reason for a ryokan's high cost. Kaiseki, which is not a specific dish but rather a complete meal, is expensive because much time and skill are involved in preparing each of the many dishes, with the ingredients cooked to preserve natural flavors. Even the plates are chosen with great care to enhance the color, texture, and shape of each piece of food.

Kaiseki cuisine, both in selection of food and presentation, is based on the four seasons. In spring, for example, cherries and cherry blossoms are often incorporated into dishes. The kaiseki gourmet can tell what time of year it is just by looking at a meal.

A kaiseki meal is usually a lengthy affair, with various dishes appearing in set order. First come the appetizer, clear broth, and one uncooked dish. These are followed by boiled, broiled, fried, steamed, heated, and vinegared dishes, which are finally followed by another soup, rice, pickled vegetables, and fruit. Although meals vary greatly depending on what's fresh, common dishes include some type of sashimi, tempura, cooked seasonal fish, and an array of bite-size pieces of vegetables. Because kaiseki is always a set meal, there's no problem in ordering; let your budget be your guide.

KUSHIAGE Kushiage foods (also called kushikatsu) are breaded and deep-fried on skewers and include chicken, beef, seafood, and lots of seasonal vegetables (snow peas, green peppers, gingko nuts, lotus roots, and the like). They're served with a slice of lemon and usually a specialty sauce. The result is delicious, and I highly recommend trying it. Ordering the set meal is easiest; what you receive may be determined by the chef and the season. A restaurant serving kushiage, called a *kushiage-ya,* is often open only for dinner.

OKONOMIYAKI *Okonomiyaki,* which originated in Osaka after World War II and literally means "as you like it," is often referred to as Japanese pizza. To me, it's more like a pancake to which meat or fish, shredded cabbage, and vegetables are added, topped with a thick Worcestershire sauce. Because it's a popular offering of street vendors, restaurants specializing in this type of cuisine are very reasonably priced. At some places the cook makes it for you, but at other places it's do-it-yourself at your table, which can be

quite fun if you're with a group. Yakisoba (fried Chinese noodles and cabbage) are also usually on offer at okonomiyaki restaurants.

RICE As in other Asian countries, rice has been a Japanese staple for about 2,000 years. In fact, rice is so important to the Japanese diet that *gohan* means both "rice" and "meal." In the old days, not everyone could afford the expensive white kind of rice, which was grown primarily to pay taxes or rent to the feudal lord; the peasants had to be satisfied with a mixture of brown rice, millet, and greens. Today, some Japanese still eat rice three times a day, although they're now just as apt to have bread and coffee for breakfast. In any case, Japanese rice is sticky, making it easier to pick up with chopsticks. It's eaten plain—no salt, no butter, no soy sauce (it's considered rather uncouth to dump a lot of sauces in your rice)—though trendy restaurants nowadays may sprinkle rice bowls with black sesame seeds, plum powder, or other seasoning. Most restaurants serve polished white rice, while health-conscious restaurants may also offer unpolished brown rice (*genmai*).

ROBATAYAKI *Robatayaki* refers to restaurants in which seafood, meats, and vegetables are cooked over an open charcoal grill. In the old days, an open fireplace *(robata)* in the middle of an old Japanese house was the center of activity for cooking, eating, socializing, and simply keeping warm. Today's robatayaki restaurants are like nostalgia trips into Japan's past and are often decorated in rustic farmhouse style, with staff dressed in traditional clothing. Robatayaki restaurants, usually open only in the evening, are popular among office workers for both eating and drinking.

There's no special menu in a robatayaki restaurant—rather, it includes just about everything eaten in Japan. The difference is that most of the food will be grilled. Favorites of mine include gingko nuts *(ginnan)*, asparagus wrapped in bacon (asparagus bacon), green peppers *(piman)*, mushrooms (various kinds), potatoes *(jagabataa)*, and just about any kind of fish. You can also usually get skewers of beef or chicken as well as a stew of meat and potatoes *(nikujaga)*—delicious during cold winter months. Some restaurants offer set meals. If ordering is only a la carte, you'll just have to look and point (some restaurants display all their foods available for grilling).

SASHIMI & SUSHI   It's estimated that the average Japanese eats 38 kilograms (84 lb.) of seafood a year—that's six times the average American consumption. Although this seafood may be served in any number of ways, from grilled to boiled, a great deal of it is eaten raw.

Sashimi is raw seafood, usually served as an appetizer and eaten alone (that is, without rice). If you've never tried it, a good choice to start with is *maguro*, or lean tuna, which doesn't taste fishy at all and is so delicate in texture that it almost melts in your mouth. The way to eat sashimi is to first put wasabi (pungent green horseradish) into a small dish of soy sauce, and then dip the raw fish in the sauce using chopsticks.

Sushi, which is raw fish with vinegared rice, comes in many varieties. The best known in Tokyo is *nigiri-zushi*: raw fish or seafood placed on top of vinegared rice with just a touch of wasabi. It's also dipped in soy sauce. Use chopsticks or your fingers to eat sushi; remember, you're supposed to eat each piece in one bite—quite a mouthful, but about the only way to keep it from falling apart. Another trick is to turn it upside down when you dip it in the sauce, to keep the rice from crumbling.

Also popular is *maki-zushi*, which consists of seafood, vegetables, or pickles rolled with rice inside a sheet of nori seaweed. *Inari-zushi* is vinegared rice and chopped vegetables inside a pouch of fried tofu bean curd.

Typical sushi includes tuna (maguro), flounder *(hirame)*, sea bream *(tai)*, squid *(ika)*, octopus *(tako)*, shrimp *(ebi)*, sea eel *(anago)*, and omelet *(tamago)*. Ordering is easy because you usually sit at a counter, where you can see all the food in a refrigerated glass case in front of you. You also get to see the sushi chefs at work. The typical meal begins with sashimi and is followed by sushi, but if you don't want to order separately, there are always various set courses *(seto)*. Pickled ginger is part of any sushi meal.

By the way, the least expensive way to enjoy sushi is **chiraishi,** which is a selection of fish, seafood, and usually tamago on a large flat bowl of rice. Because you get more rice, those of you with bigger appetites may want to order chiraishi. Another way to enjoy sushi without spending a fortune is to eat at a **kaiten sushi** shop, in which plates of sushi circulate on a conveyor belt on the counter—customers reach for the dishes they want and pay for the number they take.

SHABU-SHABU & SUKIYAKI   Until about 120 years ago, the Japanese could think of nothing so disgusting as eating the flesh of animals (though fish was okay). Considered unclean by Buddhists, meat consumption was banned by the emperor in the 7th century. It wasn't until late in the 19th century, when Emperor Meiji himself announced his intention to eat meat, that the Japanese accepted the idea. Today, the Japanese have become skilled in preparing a number of beef dishes.

Sukiyaki is among Japan's best-known beef dishes and is preferred by many Westerners. Sukiyaki is thinly sliced beef cooked at the table in a broth of soy sauce, stock, and sake, with scallions, spinach, mushrooms, tofu, bamboo shoots, and other vegetables. All diners serve themselves from the simmering pot and then dip their morsels into their own bowl of raw egg. You can skip the raw egg if you want (most Westerners do), but it adds to the taste and cools the food down enough so that it doesn't burn your tongue.

Shabu-shabu is also prepared at your table and consists of thinly sliced beef cooked in a broth with vegetables, in a kind of Japanese fondue. (It's named for the swishing sound the beef supposedly makes when cooking.) The main difference between the two dishes is the broth: Whereas in sukiyaki it consists of stock flavored with soy sauce and sake and is slightly sweet, in shabu-shabu it's relatively clear and has little taste of its own. The pots used are also different.

Using their chopsticks, shabu-shabu diners hold pieces of meat in the watery broth until they're cooked. This usually takes only a few seconds. Vegetables are left in longer, to swim around until fished out. For dipping, there's either sesame sauce with diced green onions or a more bitter fish-stock sauce. Restaurants serving sukiyaki usually serve shabu-shabu as well.

SOBA & UDON NOODLES The Japanese love eating noodles, and I suspect at least part of the joy comes from the way they eat them—they slurp, sucking in the noodles with gravity-defying speed. What's more, slurping noodles is considered proper etiquette. Fearing that it would stick with me forever, however, I've neglected to learn the technique. Places serving noodles range from stand-up eateries—often found at train and subway stations and the ultimate in fast food—to more refined noodle restaurants with tatami seating. Regardless of where you eat them, noodles are among the least expensive dishes in Japan.

There are many different kinds of noodles—some are eaten plain, some are eaten in combination with other foods such as shrimp tempura; some are served hot, others cold. **Soba,** made from buckwheat flour, is eaten hot (*kake-soba*) or cold (*zaru-soba* or *mori-soba*). **Udon** is a thick, white wheat noodle originally from Osaka; it's usually served hot. **Somen** is a fine, white noodle eaten cold in the summer and dunked in a cold sauce.

TEMPURA Today a well-known Japanese food, tempura was actually introduced by the Portuguese in the 16th century. Tempura is fish and vegetables delicately coated in a batter of egg, water, and wheat flour and then deep-fried; it's served piping hot. To eat tempura, you usually dip it in a sauce of soy, fish stock, radish (*daikon*), and grated ginger; in some restaurants, only some salt, powdered green tea, and perhaps a lemon wedge are provided as accompaniments. Tempura specialties include eggplant (*nasu*), mushroom (*shiitake*), sweet potato (*satsumaimo*), small green pepper (*shishito*), sliced lotus root (*renkon*), shrimp (*ebi*), squid (*ika*), lemon-mint leaf (*shiso*), and many kinds of fish. Again, the easiest thing to do is to order the set meal, the teishoku.

TEPPANYAKI A teppanyaki restaurant is a Japanese steakhouse. As in the well-known Benihana restaurants in many U.S. cities, the chef slices, dices, and cooks your meal of tenderloin or sirloin steak and vegetables on a smooth hot grill right in front of you—though with much less fanfare than in the U.S. Because beef is relatively new in Japanese cooking, some people categorize teppanyaki restaurants as "Western." However, I consider this style of cooking and presentation unique, and in this book I refer to such restaurants as Japanese. Teppanyaki restaurants tend to be expensive, simply because of the price of beef in Japan, with Kobe beef among the most prized.

TONKATSU *Tonkatsu* is the Japanese word for "pork cutlet," made by dredging pork in wheat flour, moistening it with egg and water, dipping it in bread crumbs, and deep-frying it in vegetable oil. Because restaurants serving tonkatsu are generally inexpensive, they're popular with office workers and families. The easiest order is the teishoku, which usually features either lean pork filet *(hirekatsu)* or pork loin with some fat on it *(rosukatsu)*. In any case, your tonkatsu is served on a bed of shredded cabbage, and one or two sauces will be at your table—a Worcestershire sauce and perhaps a specialty sauce. If you order the teishoku, it will come with rice, miso soup, and shredded cabbage.

UNAGI   I'll bet that if you eat *unagi* without knowing what it is, you'll find it very tasty—and you'll probably be very surprised to learn you've just eaten eel. Popular as a health food because of its high vitamin A content, eel is supposed to help fight fatigue during hot summer months but is eaten year-round. Broiled eel *(kabayaki)* is prepared by grilling filet strips over a charcoal fire; the eel is repeatedly dipped in a sweetened barbecue soy sauce while cooking. A favorite way to eat broiled eel is on top of rice, in which case it's called *unaju* or *unagi donburi.* Do yourself a favor and try it.

YAKITORI   Yakitori is chunks of chicken meat or chicken parts basted in a sweet soy sauce and grilled over a charcoal fire on thin skewers. Places that specialize in yakitori *(yakitori-ya,* often identifiable by a red paper lantern outside the front door) are technically not restaurants but drinking establishments; they usually don't open until 5 or 6pm. Most yakitori-ya are popular with workers as inexpensive places to drink, eat, and be merry.

The cheapest way to dine on yakitori is to order a set course, which will often include various parts of the chicken, including the skin, heart, and liver. If this is not to your taste, you may wish to order a la carte, which is more expensive but gets you exactly what you want. In addition to chicken, other skewered, charcoaled delicacies are usually offered (called *kushiyaki*). If you're ordering by the stick, you might want to try chicken breast *(sasami),*

chicken meatballs *(tsukune),* green peppers *(piman),* chicken and leeks *(negima),* mushrooms (shiitake), or gingko nuts (ginnan).

OTHER CUISINES   During your dining expeditions you might also run into these types of Japanese cuisine: **Kamameshi** is a rice casserole, served in individual-size cast-iron pots, with different kinds of toppings that might include seafood, meat, or vegetables. **Donburi** is also a rice dish, topped with tempura, eggs, and meat such as chicken or pork. **Nabe,** a stew cooked in an earthenware pot at your table and popular mostly in winter, consists of chicken, beef, pork, or seafood; noodles; and vegetables. **Oden** is a broth with fish cakes, tofu, eggs, and vegetables, served with hot mustard. If a restaurant advertises that it specializes in **Kyodo-Ryori,** it serves local specialties for which the region is famous and is often very rustic in decor. **Shojin Ryori** is a vegetarian meal, created centuries ago to serve the needs of Zen Buddhist priests and pilgrims. A more recent trend is **crossover fusion cuisine**— creative dishes inspired by ingredients from both sides of the Pacific Rim. A precursor to fusion cuisine is **Yoshoku,** dishes created in Japan after it opened its doors to the outside world and which are considered Western but are unique to Japan, including omelet with fried rice.

Although technically Chinese fast-food restaurants, **ramen shops** are a big part of inexpensive dining in Japan. Serving what I consider to be generic Chinese noodles, soups, and other dishes, ramen shops can be found everywhere; they're easily recognizable by red signs, flashing lights, and quite often pictures of dishes displayed beside the front door. Many are stand-up affairs—just a high counter to rest your bowl on. In addition to ramen (noodle and vegetable soup), you can also get such items as **yakisoba** (fried noodles) or—my favorite—**gyoza** (fried pork dumplings). What these places lack in atmosphere is made up for by cost: Most dishes average about ¥650 to ¥800, making them one of the cheapest places in Japan for a quick meal.

Note that some Japanese restaurants, but more commonly Japanese-style pubs, levy a per-person **table charge,** or snack charge *(otsumami),* which usually includes a snack.

JAPANESE DRINKS

All Japanese restaurants serve complimentary Japanese **green tea** with meals. If that's a little too weak for your taste, you may want to try **sake** (pronounced *sah-kay*), also called *Nihon-shu,* an alcoholic beverage made from rice and served either hot or cold. It goes well with most forms of Japanese cuisine. Produced since about the 3rd century, sake varies by region, production method, alcoholic content, color, aroma, and taste. Altogether, there are more than 1,800 sake brewers in Japan producing about 10,000 varieties of sake. Miyabi is a prized classic sake; other popular brands are Gekkeikan, Koshinokanbai, Hakutsuru (meaning "white crane"), and Ozeki.

Japanese **beer** is also very popular. The biggest sellers are Kirin, Sapporo, Asahi, and Suntory, each with its own bewildering variety of brews. There are also many microbreweries. Businessmen are fond of **whiskey,** usually mixed with ice and water. Popular in recent years is **shochu,** an alcoholic beverage produced mainly in southern Japan and generally made from rice but sometimes from wheat, sweet potatoes, or sugar cane. It used to be considered a drink of the lower classes, but sales have increased so much that it's threatening the sake and whiskey businesses. A clear liquid, comparable, perhaps, to vodka, it can be consumed straight but is often combined with soda water in a drink called *chu-hai.* My own favorite mixture is *ume-shu,* a plum-flavored shochu. But watch out—the stuff can be deadly. **Wine,** usually available only at restaurants serving Western food, has gained in popularity in recent years, with both domestic and imported brands available. Although **cocktails** are available in discos, hotel lounges, and fancier bars at rather inflated prices, most Japanese stick with beer, sake, or whiskey.

DINING PROCEDURE & ETIQUETTE

UPON ARRIVAL Although rare in Tokyo, you may be asked to remove your shoes at the entryway and place them in a wooden locker near the door. Then, as soon as you're seated in a Japanese restaurant (that is, a restaurant serving Japanese food), you'll be given a wet towel, which will be steaming hot in winter or pleasantly cool in summer. Called an *oshibori,* it's for wiping your hands. In all but the fanciest restaurants, men can get away with wiping their faces as well, but women are not supposed to (I ignore this if it's hot and humid outside). The oshibori is a great custom, one you'll wish would be adopted back home. Sadly, some cheaper Japanese restaurants now resort to a paper towel wrapped in plastic, which isn't nearly the same. Oshibori are generally not provided in Western restaurants.

CHOPSTICKS The next thing you'll probably be confronted with is chopsticks (though knives and forks are used in restaurants serving Western food). The proper way to use a pair is to place the first chopstick between the base of the thumb and the top of the ring finger (this chopstick remains stationary), and the second one between the top of the thumb and the middle and index fingers (this second chopstick is the one you move to pick up food). The best way to learn to use chopsticks is to let a Japanese person show you. How proficiently foreigners handle chopsticks is a matter of great curiosity for the Japanese, and they're surprised if you know how to use them; even if you were to live in Japan for 20 years, you would never stop receiving compliments on how talented you are with chopsticks. And it's perfectly okay to pick up a bowl of rice or small dish while eating.

As for etiquette involving chopsticks, if you're taking something from a communal bowl or tray, turn your chopsticks upside down and use the part that hasn't been in your mouth to transfer the food to your plate. Then you turn the chopsticks back to their proper position. The exceptions are shabu-shabu and sukiyaki. Never point your chopsticks at anyone. Also, never stick your chopsticks down vertically into your bowl of rice and leave them there, and never pass anything from your chopsticks to another person's chopsticks—both actions have origins relating to funerary rites but are now mostly considered bad manners.

EATING SOUP If you're eating soup, you won't use a spoon. Rather, you'll pick up the bowl and drink from it. Use your chopsticks to fish out larger morsels of food. It's considered in good taste to slurp with gusto, especially if you're eating noodles. Noodle shops in Japan are always well orchestrated with slurps and smacks.

DRINKING If you're drinking in Japan, the main thing to remember is that you never pour your own glass. Bottles of beer are so large that people often share one. The rule is that, in turn, one person pours for everyone else in the group, so be sure to hold up your glass when someone is pouring for you. Only as the night progresses do the Japanese get sloppy about this rule. It

took me a while to figure this out, but if no one notices your empty glass, the best thing to do is to pour everyone else a drink so that someone will pour yours. If someone wants to pour you a drink and your glass is full, the proper thing to do is to take a few gulps so that he or she can fill your glass; or, if you truly don't want to drink any more, leave your glass full and politely refuse any more offers. At any rate, because each person is continually filling everyone else's glass, you never know exactly how much you've had to drink, which (depending on how you look at it) is either very good or very bad.

PAYING THE BILL If you go out with a group of friends (not as a visiting guest of honor and not with business associates), it's customary to split the dinner bill equally, even if you all ordered different things. This makes it difficult if you're trying to spend wisely, especially if others had a lot more to eat and drink. But even foreigners living in Japan adopt the practice of splitting the bill; it certainly makes figuring everyone's share easier, especially since there's no tipping in Japan.

OTHER ETIQUETTE TIPS It's considered bad manners to walk down the street in Japan eating or drinking (except at a festival). You'll notice that if a Japanese buys a drink from a vending machine, he'll stand there, gulp it down, and throw away the container before moving on. To the chagrin of the elders, young Japanese sometimes ignore this rule.

6 SOCIAL SKILLS 101

Because of its physical isolation and the fact that it was never successfully invaded before World War II, Japan is one of the most homogeneous nations in the world. Almost 99% of Japan's population is Japanese, with hardly any influx of other genes into the country since the 8th century. The Japanese feel they belong to one huge

tribe different from any other people on earth. A Japanese person will often preface a statement or opinion with the words "We Japanese," implying that all Japanese think alike and that all people in the world can be divided into two groups, Japanese and non-Japanese.

While in the West, the recipe for a full and rewarding life seems to be that elusive attainment of "happiness," in Japan, it's the satisfactory performance of duty and obligation. Individuality in Japan is equated with selfishness and a complete disregard for the feelings and consideration of others. The Japanese are instilled with a sense of duty toward the group— whether it be family, friends, co-workers, or Japanese society as a whole. In a nation as crowded as Japan, such consideration of others is essential, especially in Tokyo, where space is particularly scarce.

MINDING YOUR P'S & Q'S

When European merchants and missionaries began arriving in Japan almost 400 years ago, the Japanese took one look at them and immediately labeled them barbarians. After all, these hairy and boisterous outsiders rarely bathed and didn't know the first thing about proper etiquette and behavior.

The Japanese, on the other hand, had a strict social hierarchy that dictated exactly how a person should speak, sit, bow, eat, walk, dress, and live. Failure to comply with the rules could bring swift punishment and sometimes even death. More than one Japanese literally lost his head for committing a social blunder.

Of course, things have changed since then, and the Japanese have even adopted some of the Western barbarians' customs. However, what hasn't changed is that the Japanese still attach much importance to proper behavior and etiquette, which developed to allow relationships to be as frictionless as possible—important in a country as crowded as Japan. The Japanese don't like confrontations, and although I'm told they do occur, I've never seen a fight in Japan.

One aspect of Japanese behavior that sometimes causes difficulty for foreigners is that the Japanese find it very hard to say no. They're much more apt to say that your request is very difficult to fulfill, or else they'll beat around the bush without giving a definite answer. At this point you're expected to let the subject drop. Showing impatience, anger, or aggressiveness rarely gets you anywhere in Japan. Apologizing sometimes does. And if someone does give in to your request, you can't thank the person enough.

BOWING The main form of greeting in Japan is the bow rather than the handshake. Although at first glance it may seem simple enough, the bow—together with its implications—is actually quite complicated. The depth of the bow and the number of seconds devoted to performing it, as well as the total number of bows, depend on who you are and to whom you are bowing. In addition to bowing in greeting, the Japanese also bow upon departing and to express gratitude. The proper form for a bow is to bend from the waist with a straight back and to keep your arms at your sides, but as a foreigner you'll probably feel foolish and look pretty stupid if you try to imitate what the Japanese have spent years learning. A simple bob of the head is enough. Knowing that foreigners shake hands, a Japanese person may extend a hand but probably won't be able to stop from giving a little bow as well. I've even seen Japanese bow when speaking to an invisible someone on the telephone.

VISITING CARDS You're a nonentity in Japan if you don't have a business or visiting card, called a *meishi*. Everyone from housewives to plumbers to secretaries to bank presidents carries meishi to give out upon introduction. If you're trying to conduct business in Japan, you'll be regarded suspiciously if you don't have business cards. As a tourist, you don't have to have business cards, but it certainly doesn't hurt, and the Japanese will be greatly impressed by your preparedness. The card should have your address and occupation on it. As a nice souvenir, you might consider having your meishi made in Japan with the Japanese syllabic script (*katakana*) written on the reverse side.

The proper way to present a meishi depends on the status of the two people involved. If you are of equal status, you exchange meishi simultaneously; otherwise, the lower person on the totem pole presents the meishi first and delivers it underneath the card being received, to show deference. Turn it so that the other person can read it (that is, upside down to you) and present it with both hands and a slight bow. Afterward, don't simply put the meishi away. Rather, it's customary for both of you to study the meishi for a moment and, if possible, to comment on it (such as "You're from Kyoto? My brother lived in Kyoto!" or "Sony! What a famous company!").

SHOES Nothing is so distasteful to the Japanese as the bottoms of shoes, andthere-fore shoes are taken off before entering a home, a Japanese-style inn, a temple, and even some museums and restaurants. Usually, there will be plastic slippers at the entryway for you to slip on, but whenever you encounter tatami floors you should remove even these slippers—only bare feet or socks are allowed to tread upon tatami.

Restrooms present another whole set of slippers. If you're in a home or Japanese inn, you'll notice a second pair of slippers—again plastic or rubber—sitting just inside the restroom door. Step out of the hallway plastic shoes and into the toilet-room slippers and wear these the whole time you're in the restroom. When you're finished, change back into the hallway slippers. If you forget this last changeover, you'll regret it—nothing is as embarrassing as walking into a room wearing toilet slippers and not realizing what you've done until you see the mixed looks of horror and mirth on the faces of the Japanese.

GUEST ETIQUETTE If you are invited to a Japanese home, you should know it is both a rarity and an honor. Most Japanese consider their homes too small and humble

for entertaining guests, which is why there are so many restaurants, coffee shops, and bars. If you are lucky enough to get an invitation, don't show up empty-handed. Bring a small gift, such as candy, fruit, flowers, or a souvenir of your hometown. Alcohol is also appreciated.

Instead of being invited to a private home, you may be invited out for dinner and drinks, especially if you're in Japan on business, in which case your hosts may have an expense account. In any event, it's nice to reciprocate by taking them out later to your own territory, say, to a French or other Western-style restaurant, where you'll feel comfortable playing host.

If you're with friends, the general practice is to divide the check equally among everyone, no matter how much or how little each person consumed.

In any case, no matter what favor a Japanese has done for you—whether it was giving you a small gift, buying you a drink, or making a telephone call for you—be sure to give your thanks profusely the next time you meet. The Japanese think it odd and rude not to be remembered and thanked upon your next meeting, even if a year has elapsed.

OTHER CUSTOMS Don't blow your nose in public if you can help it, and never at the dinner table. It's considered disgusting. On the other hand, even though the Japanese are very hygienic, they are not averse to spitting on the sidewalk. And even more peculiar, men often urinate when and where they want, usually against a tree or a wall and most often after a night of carousing in the bars.

THE JAPANESE BATH

On my very first trip to Japan, I was certain that I would never get into a public Japanese bath (*sento*). I was under the misconception that men and women bathed together, and I couldn't imagine getting into a tub with a group of smiling and bowing Japanese men. I needn't have worried. In almost all circumstances, bathing is gender-segregated. There are some exceptions, primarily at outdoor hot-spring spas in the countryside, but the women who go to these are usually grandmothers who couldn't care less. Young Japanese women wouldn't dream of jumping into a tub with a group of male strangers.

Japanese baths are delightful—and I, for one, am addicted to them. You'll find them at Japanese-style inns, at hot-spring spas, and at neighborhood baths (not everyone has his or her own bath in Japan). Sometimes they're elaborate affairs with many tubs both indoor and outdoor, and sometimes they're nothing more than a tiny tub. Public baths have long been regarded as social centers for the Japanese—friends and co-workers visit hot-spring resorts together; neighbors exchange gossip at the neighborhood bath. Sadly, however, the neighborhood bath has been in great decline over the past decades, as more and more Japanese acquire private baths. In 1968, Tokyo alone had 2,687 neighborhood baths; today that number has dropped to about 1,000. On a positive note, several hot-spring spas *(onsen)* have opened in Tokyo and its vicinity in recent years, complete with open-air baths *(rotenburo)*.

In any case, whether large or small, the procedure at all Japanese baths is the same. After you remove your shoes at the entryway, completely disrobe in the changing room, and put your clothes in either a locker or a basket, you hold a washcloth—provided free or available for sale—in front of your vital parts and walk into the bath area. There you'll find plastic basins and stools (sometimes they're still made of wood), and faucets along the wall. Sit on a stool in front of a faucet and repeatedly fill

your basin with water or use the adjacent showerhead, rinsing your whole body. If there's no hot water from the faucet, it's acceptable to dip your basin into the hot bath. Most Japanese will soap down before entering the bath (though increasingly many simply rinse off), but all traces of soap should be rinsed off before entering the bath. Like in a Jacuzzi, everyone uses the same bathwater. For that reason, you should never wash yourself in the tub, never put your washcloth into the bath (place it on your head or lay it beside the bath), and never pull the plug when you're done. After your bath is when you scrub your body and wash your hair. I have never seen a group of people wash themselves so thoroughly as the Japanese, from their ears to their toes. All sento provide shampoo and body soap, along with interesting products provided free by companies hoping to rope in new customers, but in small public baths you might have to provide your own.

Your first attempt at a Japanese bath may be painful—simply too scalding for comfort. It helps if you ease in gently and then sit perfectly still. You'll notice all tension and muscle stiffness ebbing away, a decidedly relaxing way to end the day. The Japanese are so fond of baths that many take them nightly, especially in winter, when a hot bath keeps you toasty warm for hours afterward. With time, you'll probably become addicted, too. ***Note:*** Because tattoos in Japan have long been associated with *yakuza* (Japanese mafia), many sento and onsen do not admit people with tattoos. If your tattoo is discreet, however, and you're at, say, a small Japanese inn, you probably won't have any problems.

Without a doubt, the hardest part of being in Tokyo is the language barrier. Suddenly you find yourself transported to a crowded city of 12.5 million people, where you can neither speak nor read the language. To make matters worse, many Japanese cannot speak English, and signs, menus, and shop names are often in Japanese only.

Realizing the difficulties foreigners have with the language, the **Japan National Tourism Organization (JNTO)** puts out a nifty booklet called *The Tourist's Language Handbook,* with sentences in English and their Japanese equivalents for almost every activity, from asking directions, to shopping, to ordering in a restaurant, to staying in a Japanese inn. In addition, a glossary of common phrases and words appears in appendix B of this book. For more in-depth coverage, there are many guide books geared toward travelers, including *Japanese for Travelers,* by Scott Rutherford (Tuttle, 2009), with useful phrases and travel tips.

If you need to ask directions in Tokyo, your best bet is to **ask younger people.** They have all studied English in school and are most likely to be able to help you. Japanese businessmen also often know some English. And as strange as it sounds, if you're having problems communicating with someone, try writing your question instead of speaking it. The emphasis in schools is on written rather than oral English (even many English-language teachers can't speak English very well), so Japanese who can't understand a word you say may know all the subtleties of syntax and English grammar. If you still have problems communicating, you can call the **Tourist Information Center** (© 03/3201-3331). And if you're heading for a particular restaurant or shop, have your destination written out in Japanese by someone at your hotel to show to taxi drivers or passersby. If you get lost along the way, look for one of the police boxes, called *koban,* found in virtually every neighborhood. They have maps of their district and can pinpoint exactly where you want to go if you have the address with you.

THE WRITTEN LANGUAGE   No one knows the exact origins of the Japanese language, but we do know that it existed only in spoken form until the 6th century. It was then that the Japanese borrowed Chinese characters, called **kanji,** and used them to develop their own form of written language. Later, two phonetic alphabet systems, **hiragana** (used for Japanese words that aren't written in kanji) and **katakana** (used for all foreign words), were added to kanji to form the existing Japanese writing system. Thus, Chinese and Japanese use some of the same pictographs, but otherwise there's no similarity between the languages; while they may be able to recognize some of each other's written language, the Chinese and Japanese cannot communicate verbally.

The Japanese written language—a combination of kanji, hiragana, and katakana—is probably one of the most difficult systems of written communication in the modern world. As for the spoken language, there are many levels of speech and forms of expression relating to a person's social status, age, and sex. Even nonverbal communication is vital to understanding Japanese, since what isn't said is often more important than what is. It's little wonder that Saint Francis Xavier, a Jesuit missionary who came to Japan in the 16th century, wrote that Japanese was an invention of the devil designed to thwart the spread of Christianity. And yet, astoundingly, adult literacy in Japan is estimated to be 99%.

A note on establishment names: Many hotels, restaurants, and sightseeing attractions in Tokyo now have signs in *romaji*

(Roman, or English-language, characters); many others do not. For places mentioned in this book that have only Japanese signs, I've included an appendix of the Japanese character names so that you'll be able to recognize them. When you see a number in an oval preceding the name of a restaurant, Japanese-style inn, or other establishment, turn to "Chapter 14: A Japanese-Character Index" and look for the corresponding number to find the Japanese character name of that establishment.

PRONUNCIATION If you're having difficulty communicating with a Japanese-speaker, it may help to pronounce an English word in a Japanese way. Foreign words, especially English, have penetrated the Japanese language to such an extent that they're now estimated to make up 20% of everyday vocabulary. The problem is that these words change in Japanese pronunciation, because words always end in either a vowel or an *n,* and because two consonants in a single syllable are usually separated by a vowel. Would you recognize *terebi* as "television," *koohi* as "coffee," or *rajio* as "radio"?

OTHER HELPFUL TIPS It's worth noting that Japanese nouns do not have plural forms; thus, for example, *ryokan,* a Japanese-style inn, can be both singular and plural. Plural sense is indicated by context. In addition, the Japanese custom is to list the family name first, followed by the given name. That is the format followed in this book, but note that many things published in English—business cards, city brochures, and so on—may follow the Western custom of listing family name last.

And finally, you may find yourself confused because of suffixes attached to Japanese place names. For example, *dori* can mean street, avenue, or road, and sometimes it's attached to the proper noun with a hyphen while at other times it stands alone. Thus, you may see Chuo-dori, Chuo Dori, or even Chuo-dori Avenue on English-language maps and street signs, but they are all one and the same street. Likewise, *dera* means "temple" and is often included at the end of the name, as in Kiyomizudera; *ji* means shrine.

WRITTEN ENGLISH IN JAPAN You'll see English on shop signs, billboards, posters, shopping bags, and T-shirts. The words are often wonderfully misspelled, however, or used in such unusual contexts that you can only guess at the original intent. My days have been brightened innumerable times by the discovery of zany or unfathomable English. What, for example, could possibly be the meaning behind "Today birds, tomorrow men," which appeared under a picture of birds on a shopping bag? I have treasured ashtrays that read "The young boy grasped her heart firmly" and "Let's Trip in Hokkaido." In Matsue a "Beauty Saloon" conjures up images of beauties chugging mugs of beer, while in Gifu you can only surmise at the pleasures to be had at the Hotel Joybox. I appreciated the honesty of a Hokkaido Tourist Association employee whose business card identified him as working for the "Propaganda Section." But imagine my consternation upon stepping on a bathroom scale that called itself the "Beauty-Checker."

The best sign I saw was at Narita Airport many years ago. At all check-in counters was a sign telling passengers they would be required to pay a departure tax at "the time of check in for your fright." I explained the cause of my amusement to the person behind the counter, and when I came back 2 weeks later, I was almost disappointed to find that all signs had been corrected. That's Japanese efficiency.

Planning Your Trip to Tokyo

Much of the anxiety associated with travel comes from a fear of the unknown—not knowing what to expect can give even seasoned travelers butterflies. This chapter will help you prepare for your trip to Tokyo—but don't stop here. Reading through the other chapters before leaving will also help you in your planning. Just learning that Tokyo's hotels provide a *yukata* (cotton robe), for example, may prompt you to leave your pajamas behind. In any case, Japan doesn't require the advance preparations that some other Asian destinations require, such as visas for most nationalities or inoculations, but if you use prescription drugs, you'll want to bring enough to last the trip. However, keep in mind that information given here may change during the lifetime of this book.

For additional help in planning your trip and for more on-the-ground resources in Tokyo, please turn to "Fast Facts," on p. 306.

1 WHEN TO GO

Although Tokyo's busiest foreign-tourist season is summer, the city lends itself to visiting year-round. In fact, when the rest of Japan is besieged with vacationing Japanese during Golden Week (Apr 29–May 5) and summer vacation (mid-July through Aug), Tokyo can be blissfully empty, as Tokyoites pour out of the city to the countryside. Keep in mind, however, that in mid-February, hotel rooms may be in short supply as high-school students from around the nation converge on Tokyo to compete in entrance exams for the city's prestigious universities. In addition, popular tourist destinations outside Tokyo, such as Nikko, Kamakura, and Hakone, will be jam-packed on major holidays. And from December 31 through the first 2 to 4 days of January, it seems as though the entire nation shuts down, including most restaurants and museums.

CLIMATE

The Japanese are very proud of the fact that Japan has four distinct seasons; they place much more emphasis on the seasons than people do in the West. Kimono, dishes and bowls used for *kaiseki* (elaborate feasts utilizing seasonal food), and Noh plays all change with the seasons, and most festivals are tied to seasonal rites. Even Tokyoites note the seasons: Almost as though on cue, businesspeople will change virtually overnight from their winter to summer business attire. And when the cherry blossoms burst forth, it seems like the entire metropolis comes out to greet them.

Summer, which begins in June, is heralded by the rainy season, which lasts from about mid-June to mid-July in Tokyo. July, on the average, has 10 to 12 rainy days, but even though it doesn't rain every day, umbrellas are imperative. When the rain stops, it gets unbearably hot and humid through August—you might want to head for Hakone for a bit of fresh air. Otherwise, you'll be most comfortable in light cottons, and you'd be wise to pack sunscreen and a hat (Japanese women are also fond of sun parasols), but be sure to pack a lightweight jacket for unexpected cool evenings and overly air-conditioned rooms. The period from the end of August through September is typhoon season, though most storms stay out at sea and vent their fury on land as thunderstorms.

Autumn, which lasts September through November, is one of the best times to visit Tokyo. The days are pleasant and slightly cool, the skies are a brilliant blue, and the maple trees turn scarlet. Bring a warm jacket.

Winter lasts from about December to March in Tokyo, with days that are generally clear and cold with extremely low humidity. Tokyo doesn't get much snow, but it can, so be prepared. I remember one winter when snow fell in a slushy mush through March and into the cherry-blossom season. In any case, the temperature is usually above freezing.

Spring is ushered in by a magnificent fanfare of plum and cherry blossoms in March and April, an exquisite time of year when all of Japan is set ablaze in whites and pinks. The blossoms last only a few days, symbolizing to the Japanese the fragile nature of beauty and of life itself. Tokyo may still have cool, rainy weather until May, so be sure to bring a light raincoat or jacket.

Tokyo's Average Daytime Temperatures & Rainfall

	Jan	Feb	Mar	Apr	May	June	July	Aug	Sept	Oct	Nov	Dec
Temp. (°F)	42	45	50	61	69	71	78	81	76	68	57	48
Temp. (°C)	5	7	10	16	21	22	26	27	24	20	14	9
Days of Rain	4.3	6.1	8.9	10	9.6	12.1	10	8.2	10.9	8.9	6.4	3.8

HOLIDAYS

National holidays are January 1 (New Year's Day), second Monday in January (Coming-of-Age Day), February 11 (National Foundation Day), March 20 (Vernal Equinox Day), April 29 (Showa Day, after the late Emperor Showa), May 3 (Constitution Memorial Day), May 4 (Greenery Day), May 5 (Children's Day), third Monday in July (Maritime Day), third Monday in September (Respect-for-the-Aged Day), September 23 (Autumn Equinox Day), second Monday in October (Health Sports Day), November 3 (Culture Day), November 23 (Labor Thanksgiving Day), and December 23 (Emperor's Birthday). For more information on holidays, see the "Tokyo Calendar of Events," below.

When a national holiday falls on a Sunday, the next day, Monday, becomes a holiday. The most important holidays for the Japanese are **New Year's, Golden Week** (Apr 29–May 5), and the **O-Bon Festival** (about a week in mid-Aug). Avoid traveling on these dates at all costs, since long-distance trains and most accommodations are booked solid (and are often more expensive), including most of those listed in chapter 11, "Side Trips from Tokyo." The weekends before and after these holidays are also likely to be very crowded. Luckily, Tokyo is an exception—since the major exodus is back to hometowns or the countryside, holidays such as Golden Week can be almost blissful in the metropolis. Another busy travel time is during summer-school holidays, around July 19 through August, when the Japanese take vacations en masse.

Although government offices and many businesses are closed on public holidays, restaurants and most stores remain open. The exception is during the New Year's celebration, the end of December through January 3 or 4, when almost all restaurants, public and private offices, and stores close up shop; during that time, you'll have to dine in hotels.

All **museums** close for New Year's for 1 to 4 days, but most major museums remain open for the other holidays. If a public holiday falls on a Monday (when most museums are closed), many museums will remain open but will close instead the following day, on Tuesday. Note that privately owned museums, however, such as art museums or special-interest museums, generally close on public holidays. To avoid disappointment, be sure to phone ahead if you plan to visit a museum on or the day following a holiday.

TOKYO CALENDAR OF EVENTS

Because Japan has two major religions, Shintoism and Buddhism, it celebrates festivals throughout the year. Every major shrine and temple observes at least one annual festival with events that might include traditional dances, colorful processions, and booths selling souvenirs and food. For an exhaustive list of events beyond those listed here, check http://events.frommers.com, where you'll find a searchable, up-to-the-minute roster of what's happening in cities all over the world.

JANUARY

New Year's Day, nationwide. The most important national holiday in Japan, this is a time of family reunions and gatherings with friends to drink sake and eat special New Year's dishes. Because the Japanese spend this day with families, and because almost all businesses, restaurants, shops, and museums are closed, it's not a particularly rewarding time of the year for foreign visitors. The best bets are shrines and temples such as Meiji Jingu and Sensoji Temple, where Japanese come dressed in their best (many wear traditional kimono) to pray for good health and happiness in the coming year. January 1.

Dezomeshiki (New Year's Parade of Firemen), Tokyo Big Sight, Odaiba, Tokyo. This annual event features agile firemen in traditional costumes who prove their worth with acrobatic stunts atop tall bamboo ladders. January 6.

Coming-of-Age Day, a national holiday. This day honors young people who have reached the age of 20, when they are allowed to vote, drink alcohol, and assume other responsibilities. They visit shrines to pray for their future; in Tokyo, the most popular shrine is Meiji Shrine. Many women wear traditional kimono. Second Monday in January.

Sumo Tournament, Kokugikan (sumo stadium), Tokyo (www.sumo.or.jp; take the JR or Oedo Line to Ryogoku Station). One of three Grand Tournaments held in Tokyo, held for 15 consecutive days in mid-January.

FEBRUARY

Setsubun (Bean-Throwing Festival), at leading temples throughout Japan. This festival celebrates the last day of winter according to the lunar calendar. People throng to temples to participate in the traditional ceremony of throwing soybeans to drive away imaginary devils and welcome spring. In Tokyo, popular sites include Kanda Myojin Shrine, Hie Shrine, and Sensoji Temple. February 3 or 4.

National Foundation Day (Kigensetsu), a national holiday. It celebrates the founding of Japan by Emperor Jimmy in 660 B.C. February 11.

Hinamatsuri (Doll Festival), observed throughout Japan. This festival is held in honor of young girls to wish them a future of happiness. In homes where there are girls, dolls dressed in ancient costumes representing the emperor, empress, and dignitaries are set up on a tier of shelves, along with miniature household articles. Many hotels also showcase doll displays in their lobbies. March 3.

Daruma Ichi Doll Festival, Jindaiji Temple (take the Keio Line to Tsutsujigaoka Station). A *daruma* is a legless, pear-shaped doll modeled after Bodhidharma, who founded the Zen sect in the 6th century and is said to have lost the use of his limbs from sitting 9 years in the lotus position on the way to enlightenment. Stalls here sell daruma with blank spots for eyes—according to custom, you're supposed to paint in one eye while making a wish; when your wish is fulfilled, you paint in the other eye. March 3 and 4.

Vernal Equinox Day, a national holiday. Throughout the week, Buddhist temples hold ceremonies to pray for the souls of the departed. March 20.

Sakura Matsuri (Cherry-Blossom Season). The bursting forth of cherry blossoms represents the birth of spring for Tokyoites, who gather en masse under the trees to drink sake, eat, and be merry. Popular cherry-viewing spots in Tokyo include Ueno Park, Yasukuni Shrine, Shinjuku Gyoen, Aoyama Bochi Cemetery, Sumida Koen Park in Asakusa, and the moat encircling the Imperial Palace, especially Chidorigafuchi Park. Late March to early April.

Tokyo International Anime Fair, Tokyo Big Sight, Odaiba (www.tokyo anime.jp). One of the world's largest Japanese animation events draws more than 100 production companies, TV and film agencies, toy and game software companies, publishers, and other *anime*-related companies. Usually last weekend in March.

APRIL

Kanamara Matsuri, Kanayama Shrine, Kawasaki (just outside Tokyo). This festival extols the joys of sex and fertility (and, more recently, raised awareness about AIDS), featuring a parade of giant phalluses, some carried by transvestites. Needless to say, it's not your average festival, and you can get some unusual photographs here. First Sunday in April.

Buddha's Birthday (also called Hana Matsuri, or Floral Festival), nationwide. Ceremonies are held at every Buddhist temple, where a small image of Buddha is displayed and doused with a sweet tea called *amacha* in an act of devotion. April 8.

Asakusa Yabusama (Horseback Archery), Sumida Koen Park, Asakusa. Marksmen in traditional costume show their prowess in archery while galloping on horses. A Saturday in mid-April.

Kamakura Matsuri, Tsurugaoka Hachimangu Shrine in Kamakura. The festival honors heroes from the past, including Yoritomo Minamoto, who made Kamakura his shogunate capital back in 1192. Highlights include horseback archery (truly spectacular to watch), a parade of portable shrines, and sacred dances. Second to third Sunday in April.

Yayoi Matsuri, Futarasan Shrine in Nikko. Featured is a parade of gaily decorated floats. April 16 and 17.

Showa Day, a national holiday. Named after Emperor Showa and celebrated on his birthday. April 29.

Golden Week, a major holiday period nationwide. It's a crowded time to travel, so making reservations is a must.

Because so many factories and businesses close during the week, this is said to be the best time of year for a clear view of the city and beyond from atop Tokyo's tallest buildings. April 29 to May 5.

MAY

Constitution Memorial Day, a national holiday. The Japanese Constitution went into effect on this day in 1947. May 3.

Greenery Day, a national holiday. A new holiday, established in 2007, to promote and appreciate nature. May 4.

Children's Day, a national holiday. This festival is for all children but especially honors young boys. Throughout Japan, colorful streamers of carp are flown from poles to symbolize perseverance and strength, considered desirable attributes for young boys. May 5.

Sumo Tournament, Kokugikan (sumo stadium), Tokyo (www.sumo.or.jp; take the JR or Oedo Line to Ryogoku Station). One of three Grand Tournaments held in Tokyo, held for 15 consecutive days in mid-May.

Kanda Myojin Festival, Kanda Myojin Shrine, Ochanomizu, Suehirocho or Akihabara station (www.kandamyoujin.or.jp/English/top.html). This festival, which commemorates Tokugawa Ieyasu's famous victory at Sekigahara in 1600, began during the Feudal Period as the only time townspeople could enter the shogun's castle and parade before him. Today, this major Tokyo festival features a parade of dozens of portable shrines carried through the district, plus geisha dances and a tea ceremony. Held in odd-numbered years (with a smaller festival held in even-numbered years) on the Saturday and Sunday closest to May 15.

Grand Spring Festival of Toshogu Shrine, in Nikko. Commemorating the day in 1617 when Tokugawa Ieyasu's remains were brought to his mausoleum in Nikko, this festival re-creates that drama, with more than 1,000 armor-clad men escorting three palanquins through the streets. May 17 and 18.

Design Festa, Tokyo Big Sight. Tokyo's biggest (and quirkiest) international art exhibition (www.designfesta.com) takes place biannually (2010, 2012, 2014, and so on), in May and October or November, with more than 8,500 artists from more than 30 countries working in mediums ranging from art and fashion to design, film, and music. Impromptu street performances, stalls with working artists, theaters and indoor and outdoor stages provide lots of entertainment. Mid-May.

Sanja Matsuri, Asakusa Shrine. This is one of Tokyo's best-known and most colorful festivals, featuring a parade of 100 portable shrines carried through the streets of Asakusa on the shoulders of men and women dressed in traditional garb. Third Sunday and preceding Friday and Saturday of May.

JUNE

Sanno Matsuri, Hie Shrine, Akasaka (Tameike-sanno Station). One of Tokyo's largest, this first began in the Edo Period as a festival in which the shogun permitted participants to enter the grounds of Edo Castle. It features the usual portable shrines transported through the busy streets of the Akasaka district and more than 300 people dressed in ancient costumes. June 10 to 16.

JULY

Tanabata (Star Festival), celebrated throughout Japan. According to myth, the two stars Vega and Altair, representing a weaver and a shepherd, are allowed to meet only once a year, on this day. If the skies are cloudy, however, the celestial pair cannot meet and must wait another year. July 7.

Hozuki Ichi (Ground Cherry Pod Fair), on the grounds of Asakusa's Sen-soji Temple. Hundreds of street stalls sell Hozuki (Lantern Plants), colorful wind bells, and festival snacks. July 9 and 10.

O-Bon Festival, nationwide. This festival is held in memory of dead ancestors who, according to Buddhist belief, revisit the world during this period. O-Bon Odori folk dances are held in neighborhoods everywhere. Many Japanese return to their hometowns for the event, especially if a member of the family has died recently. As one Japanese, whose grandmother had died a few months earlier, told me, "I have to go back to my hometown—it's my grandmother's first O-Bon." Mid-July or mid-August.

Antique Jamboree, Tokyo Big Sight, Odaiba. One of Japan's largest antique shows features 500 Japanese, European, and American dealers. Weekend in mid-July.

Maritime Day, a national holiday. The holiday commemorates the vital role of the sea in Japan's livelihood and honors those involved in the marine industry. Third Monday in July.

Hanabi Taikai (Fireworks Display). Tokyo's largest summer celebration features spectacular fireworks displays over the Sumida River in Asakusa. Get there early and spread a blanket on the bank of the river or in Sumida Koen Park (near Kototoibashi and Komagatabashi bridges). There are also fireworks displays over Tokyo Bay in August. Last Saturday of July.

AUGUST

Waraku Odori, in Nikko. This is one of the most popular events for folk dances, with thousands of people dancing to music. August 5 and 6.

SEPTEMBER

Sumo Tournament, Kokugikan (sumo stadium), Tokyo (www.sumo.or.jp; take the JR or Oedo Line to Ryogoku Station). One of three Grand Tournaments held in Tokyo, held for 15 consecutive days in mid-September.

Respect-for-the-Aged Day, a national holiday. Third Monday in September.

Yabusame (Horseback Archery), Tsu-rugaoka Hachimangu Shrine in Kamakura. The archery performances by riders on horseback recall the days of the samurai. September 16.

Autumnal Equinox Day, a national holiday. September 23.

OCTOBER

Health Sports Day, a national holiday, established in commemoration of the Tokyo Olympic Games. Second Monday in October.

Oeshiki Festival, Ikegami-Honmonji Temple, Ikegami (Ikegami or Nishi-magome station; www.honmonji.jp/English.html). This is the largest of Tokyo's commemorative services held for Nichiren (1222–82), who founded the Buddhist Nichiren Sect and died at this temple. A nighttime procession features lanterns and huge paper decorations joined by the sound of flutes and drums. October 12 and 13.

Autumn Festival of Toshogu Shrine, Toshogu Shrine in Nikko. A parade of warriors in early-17th-century dress are accompanied by spear-carriers, gun-carriers, flag-bearers, Shinto priests, pages, court musicians, and dancers as they escort a sacred portable shrine. October 17.

NOVEMBER

Culture Day, a national holiday. November 3.

Daimyo Gyoretsu, Yumoto Onsen, in Hakone. On this day the old Tokaido

The Masterless Samurai

Every Japanese schoolchild knows the story of the 47 ronin (masterless samurai), a story also immortalized in a popular Kabuki play. In 1701, a feudal lord (daimyo) named Kira was ordered by the Tokugawa shogun to instruct another daimyo, Asano, in the etiquette of court ritual in preparation for a visit from an Imperial entourage from Kyoto. The two quarreled, and the quick-tempered Asano, angered at the insults hurled by the older daimyo, drew his sword. Because the drawing of a sword in Edo Castle was strictly forbidden, Asano was ordered to commit ritual suicide, his family was disinherited and turned out of their home, his estate and castle were confiscated by the shogun, and his retainers (samurai) became masterless. Kira, on the other hand, was found innocent and went unpunished.

In those days, masterless samurai were men without a future. Their loyalty in question, they were unlikely to find daimyo willing to retain them, so many turned to a life of crime, hiring themselves out as mercenaries or becoming highway robbers. The 47 ronin, however, decided to avenge their master's death by killing Kira. Knowing that Kira was on the lookout for revenge, they bided their time until one snowy December night in 1702, when they attacked Kira's mansion, cut off his head, and paraded it through the streets of Edo on the way to their master's grave at Sengakuji Temple. Although the public was sympathetic toward the ronin for the steadfast loyalty they had shown their dead master, the shogun ordered all of them to commit ritual suicide through disembowelment.

In Tokyo today, all that remains of Kira's mansion, located near the Kokugikan sumo stadium at 3-13-9 Ryogoku, is a white-and-black wall crowned by a weeping willow and a small inner courtyard. The 47 ronin and their master, on the other hand, are memorialized by tombs at **Sengakuji Temple,** 2-11-1 Takanawa (✆ **03/3441-5560;** subway: Sengakuji, exit A2, a 2-min. walk), and by a small museum (daily 9am–4pm; closed Mar 31 and Sept 30) containing some clothing, armor, and personal items belonging to the ronin but is most interesting for its three short videos about the ronin and their era (usually shown in Japanese, you can request to see them in English if there are no other visitors; otherwise you can skip the museum). Across from the museum, up a flight of stairs, are carved wooden statues of the ronin (included in the museum admission), while their tombstones are located past the museum on the hill. Admission to the temple and tombs is free; admission to the museum is ¥500 for adults, ¥400 for students, and ¥250 for children. Every December 14, 47 men dressed as ronin walk 3 hours from Kira's mansion to deliver a replica of Kira's head to Sengakuji Temple.

Highway that used to link Kyoto and Tokyo comes alive again with a faithful reproduction of a feudal lord's procession in the old days, as he traveled between Edo (present-day Tokyo) and his domain accompanied by his retainers. November 3.

Shichi-go-san (Children's Shrine-Visiting Day), held throughout Japan. *Shichi-go-san* literally means "seven-five-three"; it refers to children of these ages who are dressed in their best kimono and taken to shrines by their elders to express thanks and to pray for their future. In Tokyo, the most popular sites are the Meiji, Yasukuni, Kanda Myojin, Asakusa, and Hie shrines. November 15.

Tori-no-Ichi (Rake Fair), Otori Shrine in Asakusa. This fair features stalls selling rakes lavishly decorated with paper and cloth, which are thought to bring good luck and fortune. The date, based on the lunar calendar, changes each year. Mid-November.

Labor Thanksgiving Day, a national holiday. November 23.

DECEMBER

Gishi-sai, Sengakuji Station. This memorial service honors 47 masterless samurai *(ronin),* who avenged their master's death by killing his rival and parading his head; for their act, all were ordered to commit suicide. Forty-seven men dressed as the ronin travel to Sengakuji Temple (site of their master's burial) with the enemy's head to place on their master's grave (see "The Masterless Samurai" box, below). December 14.

Hagoita-Ichi (Battledore Fair), Sensoji Temple. Popular since Japan's feudal days, this fair features decorated paddles of all types and sizes, as well as shuttlecocks and kites. Most have designs of Kabuki actors—images made by pasting together silk and brocade—and make great souvenirs and gifts. December 17 to 19.

Emperor's Birthday, a national holiday. The birthday of Akihito, Japan's 125th emperor, became a national holiday in 1989. December 23.

New Year's Eve, celebrated nationwide. At midnight, many temples ring huge bells 108 times to signal the end of the old year and the beginning of the new (each peal represents a sin). Many families visit temples and shrines to pray for good luck and prosperity and to usher in the coming year. In Tokyo, Meiji Shrine is the place to be for this popular family celebration; many coffee shops and restaurants in nearby Harajuku stay open all night to serve the revelers. Other popular sites are Kanda Myojin Shrine, Sensoji Temple, and Sanno Hie Shrine.

2 ENTRY REQUIREMENTS

Note: As of 2007, all foreigners entering Japan are fingerprinted and photographed in a measure to prevent terrorism, despite the fact that terrorism in Japan has been mostly homegrown. Exceptions include children younger than 16, diplomats, and some permanent residents of Japan.

PASSPORTS

For most tourists, including those from the United States, Canada, Australia, New Zealand, and the United Kingdom, the only document necessary to enter Japan is a passport. For information on how to get a passport, go to "Passports," in chapter 12.

VISAS

Foreign visitors from many countries can enter Japan without a visa for purposes of tourism. **Americans, Australians,** and **New Zealanders** traveling to Japan as tourists for a stay of 90 days or less need only a valid passport to gain entry into the country. **Canadians** don't need a visa for

---

Tips Passport Savvy

Safeguard your passport in an inconspicuous, inaccessible place, such as a money belt, and keep a photocopy of your passport's information page in your luggage. If you lose your passport, visit your nearest consulate as soon as possible for a replacement (see "Embassies and Consulates," on p. 307). *Note:* All foreigners must present their passports for photocopying when checking into lodging facilities. In addition, foreigners are required to carry with them at all times either their passports or, for those who have been granted longer stays, their alien registration cards. Police generally do not stop foreigners, but if you're caught without an ID, you'll be taken to local police headquarters. It happened to me once, and believe me, I can think of better ways to spend an hour and a half than explaining in detail who I am, what I am doing in Japan, where I live, and what I plan to do for the rest of my life. I even had to write a statement explaining why I rushed out that day without my passport, apologizing and promising never to do such a thoughtless thing again. The policemen were polite and were simply doing their duty.

---

stays of up to 3 months, and **United Kingdom** and **Irish citizens** can stay up to 6 months without a visa.

If your nationality requires a visa for Japan, please visit "Fast Facts," on p. 306, for more information.

CUSTOMS

If you're 20 or older, you can bring duty-free into Japan up to 400 non-Japanese cigarettes or 500 grams of tobacco or 100 cigars; three bottles (760cc each) of alcohol; and 2 ounces of perfume. You can also bring in goods for personal use that were purchased abroad whose total market value is less than ¥200,000.

What You Can Take Home from Tokyo

For information on what you're allowed to bring home, contact one of the following agencies:

U.S. Citizens: U.S. Customs & Border Protection (CBP), 1300 Pennsylvania Ave., NW, Washington, DC 20229 (© 877/287-8667; www.cbp.gov).

Canadian Citizens: Canada Border Services Agency (© 800/461-9999 in Canada, or 204/983-3500; www.cbsa-asfc.gc.ca).

U.K. Citizens: HM Customs & Excise at © 0845/010-9000 (from outside the U.K., 020/8929-0152), or consult the website at www.hmce.gov.uk.

Australian Citizens: Australian Customs Service at © 1300/363-263, or log on to www.customs.gov.au.

New Zealand Citizens: New Zealand Customs, The Customhouse, 17–21 Whitmore St., Box 2218, Wellington (© 04/473-6099 or 0800/428-786; www.customs.govt.nz).

MEDICAL REQUIREMENTS

Unless you're arriving from an area known to be suffering from an epidemic (particularly cholera or yellow fever), inoculations or vaccinations are not required for entry into Japan. Note, however, that at press time, all passengers arriving at Narita Airport are requested to fill out a questionnaire in-flight regarding symptoms of the

H1N1 influenza, such as fever or coughing. In addition, the temperature of all arriving passengers is taken upon entering the customs area; if you have a fever, you may be quarantined as a protection against H1N1 or avian flu.

3 GETTING THERE & GETTING AROUND

GETTING TO TOKYO

Tokyo has two airports, both of which will soon be international. As we go to print, all international flights land at Narita International Airport (NRT) in Narita about 66km (41 miles) outside Tokyo. If you're arriving in Tokyo from elsewhere in Japan, your flight will probably land at Haneda Airport (HND), used primarily for domestic flights, though note that Haneda is opening an international terminal, complete with the world's first airport aquarium, in October 2010.

With dozens of airlines serving Tokyo from around the world, it's certainly not difficult to get here. Below are some pointers to get you headed in the right direction.

By Plane

Because the flight to Tokyo is such a long one (about 12 hr. from Los Angeles or London and 13½ hr. from Chicago or New York), you may wish to splurge for a roomier seat and upgraded service, including special counters for check-in, private lounges at the airport, and better meals, though these come with a price. You should also consider a mileage program, because you'll earn lots of miles on this round-trip.

Japan's major carriers, flagship Japan Airlines and All Nippon Airways, offer more international flights to Tokyo than any other carriers. Other airlines flying between North America and Tokyo include American Airlines, Asiana Airlines, Continental Airlines, Delta Air Lines, Korean Air, Northwest Airlines, Singapore Airlines, Thai Airways International, and United Airlines.

From the United Kingdom, British Airways and Virgin Atlantic Airways also offer daily nonstop service from London to Tokyo. Air New Zealand, Jetstar, and Qantas fly from Australia to Tokyo.

For contact information and websites for these airlines, as well as other airlines that fly into Tokyo, see "Airline Websites," p. 314.

Long-haul Flights: How to Stay Comfortable

- Your choice of airline and airplane will definitely affect your legroom. Find more details about U.S. airlines at **www.seatguru.com**. For international airlines, research firm Skytrax has a list of average seat pitches at www.airlinequality.com.

- Emergency-exit seats and bulkhead seats typically have the most legroom. Emergency-exit seats are usually left unassigned until the day of a flight (to ensure that someone able-bodied fills the seats); it's worth getting to the ticket counter early to snag one of these spots for a long flight. Many passengers find that bulkhead seating (the row facing the wall at the front of the cabin) offers more legroom, but keep in mind that bulkhead seats have no storage space on the floor in front of you.

- To have two seats for yourself in a three-seat row, try for an aisle seat in a center section toward the back of coach. If you're traveling with a companion, book an aisle and a window seat. Middle seats are usually booked last, so chances are good that you'll end up with three seats to yourselves. And in the event that a third passenger is assigned the middle seat, he or she will probably be more than happy to trade for a window or an aisle.

- Ask about entertainment options. Many airlines offer seatback video systems where you get to choose your movies or play video games—but only on some of their planes (Boeing 777s are your best bet).
- To sleep, avoid the last row of any section or a row in front of an emergency exit, as these seats are the least likely to recline. Avoid seats near highly trafficked toilet areas. Avoid seats at the backs of many jets—these can be narrower than those in the rest of coach class. Or reserve a window seat so that you can rest your head and avoid being bumped in the aisle.
- Get up, walk around, and stretch every 60 to 90 minutes to keep your blood flowing. This helps avoid **deep-vein thrombosis,** or "economy-class syndrome," a potentially deadly condition that can be caused by sitting in cramped conditions for too long.
- If you're flying with kids, don't forget to carry on toys, books, pacifiers, and snacks and chewing gum to help them relieve ear-pressure buildup during ascent and descent.

Arriving at Narita Airport

Narita International Airport (✆ **0476/ 34-8000;** www.narita-airport.jp) consists of two terminals (1 and 2). Arrival lobbies in both terminals have ATMs and counters for money exchange, open daily 6:30am to 11pm (change enough money here to last several days, since the exchange rate is the same as in town, the process is speedy, and facilities in town are somewhat limited). Both are connected to all ground transportation into Tokyo.

A **Tourist Information Center (TIC),** managed by the Japan National Tourism Organization, is located in the arrival lobbies of both Terminal 1 (✆ **0476/30- 3383**) and Terminal 2 (✆ **0476/34-5877**).

The TIC offers free maps and pamphlets and can direct you to your hotel or inn. Both TICs are open daily 8am to 8pm; if you don't yet have a hotel room and want one at a modest price, you can make reservations here for free until 7:30pm.

Other facilities and services at both terminals include post offices, medical clinics, cellular phone rentals, luggage storage and lockers, shower rooms, day rooms for napping, children's playrooms, observation decks, and coin-operated computers with Internet connection (¥100 for 10 min.).

Getting into Town from Narita Airport

Everyone grumbles about Narita Airport because it's so far away from Tokyo. In fact, Narita is a different town altogether, with miles of paddies, bamboo groves, pine forests, and urban sprawl between it and Tokyo.

BY TRAIN *Note:* As we go to print, the new **Keisei Skyliner** (✆ **03/3831-0131;** www.keisei.co.jp) is set to become the fastest way to get from Narita Airport to Nippori Station downtown; you'll get there in just 36 minutes. See their website (and click on "English") for further details. Thus, the quickest way to reach Tokyo is by train. Trains depart directly from the airport's two underground stations, called Narita Airport Station (in Terminal 1) and Airport Terminal 2 Station. The JR **Narita Express (N'EX;** ✆ **050/2016-1603;** www.jreast.co.jp) was the fastest way to reach Tokyo Station, Shinagawa, Shibuya, and Shinjuku, with departures approximately once an hour, or twice an hour during peak hours. The hour-long trip to Tokyo Station costs ¥2,940 one-way. At Tokyo Station, the train splits, with the front cars going to Shibuya, Shinjuku, and Ikebukuro, and rear cars going to Shinagawa (cost to these stations: ¥3,110). *Note:* Because seats are sometimes sold out in advance, especially during peak travel times, you might consider purchasing

(Tips) Saving on Airport Transportation

If you're going to be traveling around Tokyo by public transportation (and who doesn't?), you can save money by purchasing a N'EX and Suica card for ¥3,500, which includes the Narita Express into Tokyo plus ¥2,000 worth of travel in Tokyo. The discount ticket, available only at Narita Airport to foreign visitors, can be purchased at JR East Travel Service Centers in the basement of both terminals. Likewise, there's an Airport Limousine & Metro Pass combination ticket that includes one Airport Limousine trip to or from the airport plus 1 day of unlimited rides on Metro subways (it doesn't have to be the same day of arrival) for ¥3,100. This ticket is available at Airport Limousine counters at the airport, TCAT, Shinjuku Station West Exit, and Tokyo Metro Pass offices around town. A round-trip from and to the airport plus 2 days traveling on Metro subways costs ¥6,000; it's available only at Narita Airport. Finally, there are also 1- and 2-day Metro passes available only in the arrival lobbies of both terminals at Narita for ¥600 and ¥980, respectively (these do not include transportation from the airport). For more information on the Suica and 1-day Metro cards, see "Getting Around," below.

your return ticket to Narita Airport here at the airport, at major JR stations in Tokyo, or at a travel agency or online; time your arrival to the airport at least 2 hours before your plane's departure.

If the N'EX is sold out, take the slower JR Airport Liner rapid train, which will get you to Tokyo Station in 80 minutes and costs ¥1,280.

The privately owned **Keisei Skyliner** train departs directly from both Narita Airport Station (Terminal 1) and Airport Terminal 2 and travels to Ueno Station in Tokyo in about an hour, with a stop at Nippori Station on the way. (See above; the latest Skyliner will put the Narita Express to shame at 36 minutes, though these hour-long trains will still be available at these lesser fares.) You'll find Keisei Skyliner counters in the arrival lobbies of both terminals. Trains depart Narita approximately every 40 minutes between 7:52am and 10pm. The fare from Narita Airport to Ueno Station in Tokyo is ¥1,920 one-way. Travelers on a budget can take one of Keisei's slower limited express trains to Ueno Station; fares start at ¥1,000 for the 71-minute trip.

BY TAXI Obviously, jumping into a taxi is the easiest way to get to Tokyo, but it's also prohibitively expensive—and may not even be the quickest method during rush hours. Fares are fixed but average around ¥19,000 to ¥21,000 for a 1½- to 2-hour taxi ride from Narita to central Tokyo.

BY AIRPORT BUS The most popular and stress-free way to get from Narita to Tokyo is via the **Airport Limousine Bus** (© **03/3665-7220;** www.limousinebus. co.jp), which picks up passengers and luggage from just outside the arrival lobbies of terminals 1 and 2 and delivers them to downtown hotels. This is the best mode of transportation if you have heavy baggage or are staying at one of the 40 or so major hotels served by the bus. Buses depart for the various hotels generally once an hour, and it can take almost 2 hours to reach a hotel in Shinjuku. Buses also travel to both Tokyo and Shinjuku Station and the Tokyo City Air Terminal (TCAT) in downtown Tokyo, with more frequent departures (up to four times an hour).

If your hotel is not served by Airport Limousine Bus, take it to the hotel or station nearest your destination. TCAT,

Shinjuku Station, and Tokyo Station are served by public transportation as well as taxis. TCAT is connected to the Hanzomon subway line via moving walkways and escalators; Shinjuku and Tokyo stations are hubs for subway lines and commuter trains, but if it's your first trip to Japan, you might want to avoid these big, crowded stations.

Check with the staff at the Airport Limousine Bus counter in the arrival lobbies to inquire which bus stops nearest your hotel and the time of departure. The fare to most destinations is ¥3,000. Children 6 to 12 are charged half-fare; those under 6 ride free.

Getting from Haneda Airport to Central Tokyo

If you're arriving at **Haneda Airport,** also called Tokyo International Airport (✆ **03/ 5757-8111;** www.tokyo-airport-bldg. co.jp), located near the center of Tokyo and used mainly for domestic flights, you can take the **Airport Limousine Bus** to Shinjuku Station, Tokyo Station, the Tokyo City Air Terminal (TCAT) in downtown Tokyo, and hotels in Shinjuku, Ikebukuro, Shibuya, and Akasaka. Fares run ¥900 to ¥1,200. Locals, however, are more likely to take the **monorail** from Haneda Airport 15 minutes to Hamamatsucho Station (fare: ¥470), or the **Keikyu Line** 19 minutes to Shinagawa (fare: ¥400). Both Hamamatsucho and Shinagawa connect to the very useful Yamanote Line, which travels to major stations, including Tokyo and Shinjuku stations. Be sure to stop by the **Tokyo Tourist Information Center** (✆ **03/5757-9345**) in Haneda Airport, open daily 9am to 10pm.

By Train

If you're arriving from elsewhere in Japan, you'll most likely arrive via Shinkansen bullet train at Tokyo, Ueno, or Shinagawa station. All are well served by trains (including the useful JR Yamanote Line), subways, and taxis.

By Boat

There are no international ferry services to Tokyo, but domestic long-distance ferries arrive at Ariake Ferry Terminal, located on an artificial island adjacent to Odaiba in Tokyo Bay; the nearest station is Kokusai-Tenjijo-Seimon. Cruise lines usually dock at Harumi Terminal.

GETTING AROUND

Your most frustrating moments in Tokyo will probably occur when you find you're totally lost. Maybe it will be in a subway or train station, where all you see are signs in Japanese, or on a street somewhere as you search for a museum, restaurant, or bar. At any rate, accept here and now that you will get lost if you are at all adventurous and eager to strike out on your own. It's inevitable. But take comfort in the fact that Japanese get lost, too—even taxi drivers!

Another rule of getting around Tokyo: It will always take longer than you think. For short-term visitors, calculating travel times in Tokyo is tricky business. Taking a taxi is expensive and involves the probability of getting stuck interminably in traffic, with the meter ticking away. Taking the subway is usually more efficient, even though it's more complicated and harder on your feet: Choosing which route to take isn't always clear, and transfers between lines are sometimes quite a hike in themselves. If I'm going from one end of Tokyo to the other by subway, I usually allow myself anywhere from 30 to 60 minutes, depending on the number of transfers and the walking distance to my final destination. The journey from Roppongi or Shibuya to Ueno, for example, takes approximately a half-hour because it's a straight shot on the subway, but a trip requiring transfers can take much longer. Traveling times to destinations along each line are posted on platform pillars, along with diagrams showing which train compartments are best for making quick transfers between lines.

Your best bet for getting around Tokyo is to take the subway or Japan Railways (JR) commuter train to the station nearest your destination. From there you can either walk, using a map and asking directions along the way, or take a taxi.

For all hotels, *ryokan,* restaurants, sights, shops, and nightlife venues listed in this book, I've included both the nearest station and, in parentheses, the number of minutes' walk required to get from the station to the destination.

BY TAXI

Taxis are shamefully expensive in Tokyo. Fares start at ¥710 for the first 2km (1¼ miles) and increase ¥90 for each additional 288m (950 ft.) or 40 seconds of waiting time. There are also smaller, more compact taxis for a maximum of four persons that charge slightly less, but they are fewer in number. Fares are posted on the back of the front passenger seat. If you're like me, you probably won't shop around—you'll gratefully jump into the first taxi that stops. Note that from 10pm to 5am, an extra 30% is added to your fare. Perhaps as an admission of how expensive taxis are, fares can also be paid by all major credit cards (though some companies require a minimum fare of ¥5,000).

With the exception of some major thoroughfares in the downtown area, you can hail a taxi from any street or go to a taxi stand or a major hotel. A red light above the dashboard shows if a taxi is free to pick up a passenger; a yellow light indicates that the taxi is occupied. Be sure to stand clear of the back left door—it swings open automatically. Likewise, it shuts automatically once you're in. Taxi drivers are quite perturbed if you try to maneuver the door yourself. The law requires that back-seat passengers wear seat belts.

Unless you're going to a well-known landmark or hotel, it's best to have your destination written out in Japanese, since most taxi drivers don't speak English. But even that may not help. Tokyo is so complicated that taxi drivers may not know a certain area, although many now have navigation systems. If a driver doesn't understand where you're going, he may refuse to take you.

There are so many taxis cruising Tokyo that you can hail one easily on most thoroughfares—except when you need it most: when it's raining, or just after 1am on weekends, after all subways and trains have stopped. To call a major taxi company for a pickup, try **Nihon Kotsu** (© **03/5755-2336**) for an English-speaking operator, or **Kokusai** (© **03/3505-6001;** Japanese only). Note, however, that you'll be required to pay extra (usually not more than ¥400) for an immediate pickup. I have rarely telephoned for a taxi—as in the movies, one usually cruises by just when I raise my hand.

BY PUBLIC TRANSPORTATION

Each mode of transportation in Tokyo—subway (with two different companies), JR train (like the Yamanote Line), and bus—has its own fare system and therefore requires a new ticket each time you transfer from one mode of transport to another. If you're going to be in Tokyo for a few days, it's much more convenient to purchase a **Suica,** a contactless prepaid card issued by JR East that automatically deducts fares and can be used on virtually all modes of transportation, including JR trains, private railways (such as the Rinkai Line to Odaiba or Minato Mirai Line to Yokohama), subways, and buses in the greater Tokyo area (including trips to Kamakura). It can even be used for purchases at designated vending machines, convenience stores, and fast-food outlets that display the Suica sign. First-time buyers must purchase the Suica from vending machines for ¥2,000, which includes a ¥500 deposit. The Suica is rechargeable, at amounts ranging from ¥1,000 to ¥10,000. Note, however, that when you return your

Suica to get your deposit back, be sure that the card is depleted, or you'll be charged a ¥210 handling fee for any remaining stored balance on the card. A similar card to the Suica is the **Pasmo,** which can also be used on various modes of transportation throughout Tokyo. Although there are other options available, including 1-day cards and Metro-only cards, the Suica is by far my favorite. If you're going to be in Tokyo at least 3 days, it will save you a lot of time that you'll otherwise spend trying to figure out your fare.

That being said, if you think you're going to be traveling a lot by public transportation on any given day, consider purchasing a **Tokyo Free Kippu** (Tokyo Round Tour Ticket), which, despite its name, costs ¥1,580, but does allow unlimited travel for 1 day on all Metro subways, JR trains, and Toei buses within Tokyo's 23 wards. It's available at all JR stations with a Midori-no-madoguchi (Reservation Ticket Office) or View Plaza (Travel Service Center), and most Metro subway stations.

Tips on Traveling by Train or Subway

Avoid taking the subway or JR train during the weekday morning **rush hour,** from 8 to 9am—the stories you've heard about commuters packed into trains like sardines are all true. There are even "platform pushers," men who push people into compartments so that the doors can close. If you want to witness Tokyo at its craziest, go to Shinjuku Station at 8:30am—but go by taxi unless you want to experience the crowding firsthand. Most lines provide women-only compartments weekdays until 9:30am.

Another thing you'll want to keep in mind are **station exits,** which are always numbered. Upon alighting from the subway onto the platform, look for the yellow signboards designating which exit to take for major buildings, museums, and addresses. If you're confused about which exit to take, ask someone at the window near the ticket gate. Taking the right exit can make a world of difference, especially in Shinjuku, where there are more than 60 station exits.

Please note that all cellphones should be switched to silent mode (called *manner mode* in Japanese) on public conveyances. There's a four-color **Tokyo Metro map,** with subway and train lines, on the inside back cover of this book.

BY SUBWAY

To get around Tokyo on your own, it's imperative that you learn how to ride its subways. Fortunately, the Tokyo **Metro** system (which uses a symbol "M" vaguely reminiscent of McDonald's famous arches) is efficient, modern, clean, and easy to use; in fact, I think it's one of the most user-friendly systems on the planet. All station names are written in English. Many cars also display the next station in English on digital signs above their doors and announce stops in English. Altogether, there are 13 underground subway lines crisscrossing the city, operated by two companies: Tokyo Metro (the bigger of the two) and Toei (which operates four lines, including the Oedo Line). Each line is color-coded. The Ginza Line, for example, is orange, which means that all its trains and signs are orange. If you're transferring to the Ginza Line from another line, follow the orange signs and circles to the Ginza Line platform. Each line is also assigned a letter (usually its initial), so that the Ginza has the letter "G" and Hibiya the letter "H." Additionally, each station along each line is assigned a number in chronological order beginning with the first station (Asakusa Station, for example, is G19, the 19th stop from Shibuya on the Ginza Line), so you always know how many stops to your destination. Before boarding, however, make sure the train is going in the right direction—signs on the platform of each station show both the previous and the next stop, so you can double-check you're heading in the right direction. Tokyo's newest line, Toei's Oedo Line, makes a zigzag loop around the city and is useful for traveling between Roppongi and Shinjuku; be aware, however, that it's buried deep underground and that platforms take a while to reach, despite escalators.

Whereas it used to be a matter of skill to know exactly which train compartment to board if making transfers down the line, diagrams at each station (usually on a pillar at the entrance to each platform) show which end of the train and compartment is most useful for connections. There are also signs that show exactly how many minutes it takes to reach every destination on that line. See the inside back cover for a map of Tokyo subways and other trains.

TICKETS   **Vending machines** at all subway stations sell tickets, which begin at ¥160 for the shortest distance and increase according to the distance you travel. Children 6 to 11 pay half-fare; children 5 and under ride free. Vending machines give change, even for a ¥10,000 note. To purchase your ticket, insert money into the vending machine until the fare buttons light up, and then push the amount for the ticket you want. Your ticket and change will be deposited at the bottom of the machine.

Before purchasing your ticket, you first have to figure out your fare. Fares are posted on a large subway map above the vending machines, but they're often in Japanese; most stations also post a smaller map or table listing fares in English, but you may have to search for it. An alternative is to look at the subway map contained in the "Tourist Map of Tokyo," issued by the Tourist Information Center—it lists stations in both Japanese and English. Once you know what the Japanese characters look like, you may be able to locate your station and its corresponding fare. If

you still don't know the fare, ask a station attendant, or buy the cheapest ticket for ¥160. When you reach your destination, look for the **fare adjustment machine** just before the exit wicket; insert your ticket to find out how much more you owe, or go to the exit, where a subway employee will tell you how much you owe. In any case, be sure to hang on to your ticket, since you must give it up at the exit wicket at the end of your journey.

Because buying individual tickets is a hassle (and vending machines are unfortunately not as user-friendly as the subway system is), I suggest buying either a Suica or Pasmo card (see above). There are also **One-Day Open Tickets** for unlimited 1-day rides on subways. The ¥710 1-day ticket (¥600 if you buy it at Narita Airport) is for use on Tokyo Metro lines (including the Ginza, Hibiya, Marunouchi, and Chiyoda lines), while the ¥1,000 1-day ticket can be used on all subway lines of both the Metro and Toei companies. These are sold at vending machines and are inserted into the ticket gate at the entrance to the platform, just like a regular ticket, except this time you'll retrieve it when you reach your destination.

HOURS   Most subways run from about 5am to midnight, although the times of the first and last trains depend on the line, the station, and whether it's a weekday or weekend. Schedules are posted in the stations, but most days, trains arrive every 3 to 5 minutes.

For more information on tickets, passes, and lines for the subway, as well as a detailed subway map and brochure, stop by **Metro Information desks** located at Ginza, Shinjuku, Omotesando, and other major stations in Tokyo. Or check the website **www.tokyometro.jp/global.en**. Staff at the Metro's Customer Relations Center, (€ **03/3941-2004,** speak Japanese only. Information on **Toei Subway** is available at **www.kotsu.metro.tokyo.jp**.

Transfers on the Subway & Train

You can transfer between most subway lines without buying another ticket, and you can transfer between JR train lines on one ticket. However, your ticket or prepaid card does not allow a transfer between Tokyo's two subway companies (Metro and Toei), JR train lines, and private train lines connecting Tokyo with outlying destinations such as Nikko. You usually don't have to worry about this, though, because if you exit through a wicket and have to give up your ticket, you'll know you have to buy another one.

There are a few instances, however, when you pass through a ticket wicket to transfer between subway lines, in which case your ticket will be returned to you if your destination is farther along. The general rule is that if your final destination and fare are posted above the ticket vending machines, you can travel all the way to your destination with only one ticket. But don't worry about this too much—the ticket collector will set you straight if you've miscalculated. Note, however, that if you pay too much for your ticket, the portion of the fare that's left unused is not refundable—so, again, the easiest thing to do if in doubt is to buy the cheapest fare. Even better, buy a Suica.

BY JR TRAIN

As an alternative to subways, electric commuter trains operated by the East Japan Railway Company (JR) run aboveground. These trains are also color-coded, with fares beginning at ¥130. Buy your ticket from vending machines the same as you would for the subway, but more convenient is the Suica.

The **Yamanote Line** (green-colored coaches) is the best-known and most convenient JR line. It makes an oblong loop around the city, stopping at 29 stations along the way, all of them announced in English and with digital signboards in each compartment. In fact, you may want to take the Yamanote Line and stay on it for a roundup view of Tokyo; the entire trip takes about an hour, passing stations such as Shinjuku, Tokyo, Harajuku, Akihabara, and Ueno on the way.

Another convenient JR line is the orange-colored **Chuo Line;** it cuts across Tokyo between Shinjuku and Tokyo stations, with both express (which doesn't make as many stops) and local trains available. The yellow-colored **Sobu Line** runs between Shinjuku and Akihabara and beyond to Chiba. Other JR lines serve outlying districts for the metropolis's commuting public, including Yokohama and Kamakura. Because the Yamanote, Chuo, and Sobu lines are rarely identified by their specific names at major stations, look for signs that say JR LINES.

If you think you'll be traveling by JR lines on any given day, consider purchasing a **1-Day Tokunai Pass,** which allows unlimited travel for ¥730.

For more information on JR lines and tickets, stop by one of JR's **Information Centers** at Tokyo Station, Ueno, Shinjuku, Shibuya, or Shinagawa or call the English-language **JR East Infoline** at ✆ **050/2016-1603,** daily from 10am to 6pm. You can also check its website at www.jreast.co.jp/e.

BY BUS

Buses are not as easy to use as trains or subways unless you know their routes, since only the end destination is written on the bus and routes listed at bus stops are usually not in English. In addition, many bus drivers don't speak English. Buses are sometimes convenient for short distances, however. If you're feeling adventurous, board the bus at the front and drop the exact fare (usually ¥200) into the box. If you don't have the exact amount, fare boxes accept coins or bills; your change minus the fare will come out below. Suica and Pasmo cards are also accepted. A signboard at the front of the bus displays the next stop, usually in English. When you wish to get off, press one of the buttons on the railing near the door or the seats. You can pick up an excellent Toei bus map showing all major routes at one of the Tokyo Tourist Information Centers operated by the Tokyo Metropolitan Government (see "Visitor Information," p. 313). Or check the Toei website at www.kotsu. metro.tokyo.jp.

An exception to the city buses above is Toei's **Tokyo Shitamachi Bus,** a user-friendly sightseeing bus that follows a fixed route to seven major sightseeing spots. Departing from the Marunouchi north exit of Tokyo Station, buses stop at Nihombashi's Mitsukoshi Department Store; Akihabara, with its many anime and electronic stores; Ueno Park; Kappabash-dougugai Dori, with its many kitchen stores; and Asakusa before terminating at Ryogoku Station with the Edo-Tokyo Museum. Buses travel in both directions at 30-minute intervals daily between 9am and 6:30pm. The fare is ¥200 each time you board (you can use a Suica card); or purchase a one-day Toei bus pass for ¥500. For information about the Tokyo Shitamachi Bus, including a schedule and map, stop by the Tokyo Tourist Information Center in Shinjuku or Ueno (p. 313).

BY BOAT
Although all tourist destinations are accessible by land transportation, some sights in Tokyo Bay or on the Sumida River are served by sightseeing boat, an enjoyable way to travel and see the Tokyo skyline. Boats depart from **Hinode Pier** near Hamamatsucho and Hinode stations and travel to **Asakusa** via the Sumida River; the trip takes approximately 40 minutes and costs ¥760. You can also reach Asakusa by boat from Hama Rikyu Garden, while another route travels between Asakusa and Odaiba. Pick up a brochure at the TIC or call the **Tokyo Cruise Ship Co.** at ⓒ **03/5733-4812.** A timetable is posted on its website at www.suijobus.co.jp.

4 MONEY & COSTS

The Value of Yen vs. Other Popular Currencies

Yen	US$	Can$	UK£	Euro (€)	Aus$	NZ$
100	$1.10	C$1.13	68p	€.76	A$1.19	NZ$1.49

Frommer's lists prices in the local currency. The currency conversions quoted above were correct at press time. However, rates fluctuate, so before departing consult a currency exchange website such as **www. oanda.com/convert/classic** to check up-to-the-minute rates.

There's no getting around it: Tokyo is among the most expensive cities in the world (according to Economist.com, it was *the* world's most expensive city in February 2009). Hopefully, this guide will help reduce some potential costs by showing you how to take advantage of deals on public transportation, dine more cheaply,

What Things Cost in Tokyo	Japanese Yen
Narita Express from airport to Tokyo Station	2,940
Metro subway ride from Ginza to Asakusa	1.90
Local telephone call (per 1 min.)	.10
Double room at The Peninsula Tokyo (deluxe)	60,000
Double room at Courtyard by Marriott Tokyo Ginza (moderate)	30,000
Double room at Asia Center of Japan (inexpensive)	12,390
Lunch for one at Ginza Daimasu (moderate)	2,100
Lunch for one at Limapuluh (inexpensive)	1,050
Dinner for one, without drinks, at New York Grill (deluxe)	11,000
Dinner for one, without drinks, at Waentei-Kikko (moderate)	6,825
Dinner for one, without drinks, at Gonpachi	3,500
Glass of beer	600
Coca-Cola	300
Cup of coffee	400
Admission to the Tokyo National Museum	600

and see some of Tokyo's sights with reduced admission.

In any case, you'll probably want to arrive in Tokyo with cash, credit cards, and maybe even traveler's checks. Luckily, it's much easier to obtain yen than it used to be even just a decade ago.

CURRENCY

The currency in Japan is called the *yen,* denoted by ¥. Coins come in denominations of ¥1, ¥5, ¥10, ¥50, ¥100, and ¥500. Bills come in denominations of ¥1,000, ¥2,000, ¥5,000, and ¥10,000, though ¥2,000 notes are rarely seen. All coins get used (though you may find it hard to get rid of ¥1 coins).

Some people like to arrive in a foreign country with that country's currency already in hand, but I do not find it necessary for Tokyo. **Narita Airport** has several exchange counters for all incoming international flights that offer better exchange rates than what you'd get abroad, as well as ATMs. Change enough money to last several days, since exchanging money is

not as convenient in Japan as it is in many other countries. And remember, Tokyo is one of the most expensive cities in the world; see the chart above and refer to the listings in this book to get an idea of how much money you should have on hand each day.

Personal checks are not used in Japan. Most Japanese pay with credit cards or cash—the country's overall crime rate is so low, you can feel safe walking around with money (but always exercise caution). The only exception is on a crowded subway during rush hour or in heavily touristed areas such as Tsukiji or Asakusa. Although the bulk of your expenses—hotels, major purchases, meals in classier restaurants—can be paid for with credit cards, bring traveler's checks for those times when you might not have convenient access to an ATM for cash withdrawals, especially outside Tokyo in more rural areas.

ATMs

The best way to get cash away from home is from an ATM (automated teller machine). Because most ATMs in Japan accept only cards issued by Japanese banks, your best bet for obtaining cash is a **7-Eleven** convenience store, most of which are open 24 hours and have ATMs that accept foreign bank cards operating on the **Cirrus** (www.mastercard.com) and **PLUS** (www.visa.com) systems, as well as American Express. Another good bet is a post office, though ATM machines located at every post office in Japan may be operable only during limited hours (depending on the post office, that may be until 6 or 7pm weekdays and until 5pm on weekends).

Other places with ATMs that might accept foreign-issued cards include most Citibanks (which usually accept cards on the PLUS and Cirrus systems, as well as Visa and MasterCard and sometimes American Express, but note that not all foreign cards may be accepted), large department stores, and Narita Airport. Note that there is no public American Express office in Japan.

Be sure you know your four-digit personal identification number (PIN) and your daily withdrawal limit before leaving home. *Note:* Many banks impose a fee every time you use a card at another bank's ATM, and that fee can be higher for international transactions than for domestic ones. In addition, the bank from which you withdraw cash may charge its own fee. Because Tokyo is expensive and because there is a limit to how much money you can withdraw with each transaction, you'll find these bank fees especially annoying here. For international withdrawal fees, ask your bank.

CREDIT CARDS

Credit cards are a safe way to carry money, provide a convenient record of all your expenses, and generally offer relatively good exchange rates. You can withdraw cash advances from your credit cards at banks or ATMs, provided you know your 4-digit PIN. Keep in mind that you'll pay

interest from the moment of your withdrawal, even if you pay your monthly bills on time. Also, note that many banks now assess a 1% to 3% "transaction fee" on *all* charges you incur abroad (whether you're using the local currency or your native currency).

The most readily accepted cards in Japan are **American Express, Diners Club, MasterCard** (also called Eurocard), **Visa,** and the Japanese credit card **JCB** (Japan Credit Bank). Shops and restaurants accepting credit and charge cards will usually post which cards they accept at the door or near the cash register (you can even use credit cards to pay for taxis). However, smaller establishments may be reluctant to accept cards for minor purchases and inexpensive meals, so inquire beforehand. In addition, note that the vast majority of Tokyo's least expensive businesses, including noodle shops, fast-food joints, ma-and-pa establishments, and the cheapest accommodations, often do not accept credit cards.

TRAVELER'S CHECKS

Although traveler's checks are something of an anachronism now that ATMs have come onto the scene, traveler's checks are still useful in Japan. Traveler's checks generally fetch a better exchange rate than cash and also offer protection in case of theft; *you'll need your passport to exchange traveler's checks.* Note, however, that in some very remote areas, even banks won't cash them. Before taking off for small towns, be sure you have enough cash.

You can get traveler's checks at most banks. They are offered in denominations of $20, $50, $100, $500, and sometimes $1,000. Generally, you'll pay a service charge ranging from 1% to 4%.

Be sure to keep a record of the traveler's checks' serial numbers separate from your checks in the event that they are stolen or lost. You'll get a refund faster if you know the numbers.

In Tokyo, all banks displaying an AUTHORIZED FOREIGN EXCHANGE sign can exchange currency and traveler's checks, with exchange rates usually displayed at the appropriate foreign-exchange counter. **Banks** are generally open Monday through Friday from 9am to 3pm, though business hours for exchanging foreign currency usually don't begin until 10:30 or 11am (be prepared for a long wait; you'll be asked to sit down as your order is processed).

More convenient—and quicker—are **Travelex** foreign-exchange kiosks, with several locations across town, including one in Hibiya at 1–5–2 Yurakucho (✆ **03/5157-8311**; station: Hibiya or Yurakucho), open Monday to Friday from 10am to 6pm; Tokyo Station (✆ **03/5220-5021**), open daily from 9am to 8pm; 3rd floor of Tokyo Midtown Tower, 9–7–1 Akasaka (✆ **03/3408-2280;** station: Roppongi), open from Monday to Friday from 11am to 7pm and Saturday from 10am to 5pm. Other locations are in Shinjuku, Shibuya, Shimbashi, Akasaka, and Odaiba. See www.travelex.com for more information.

If you need to exchange money outside of the hours above, inquire at your **hotel.** Likewise, large **department stores** also offer exchange services and are often open until 8pm. Note, however, that hotels and department stores may charge a handling fee and offer a slightly less favorable exchange rate.

5 HEALTH

STAYING HEALTHY

It's safe to drink tap water and eat to your heart's content everywhere in Japan (pregnant women, however, are advised to avoid eating raw fish and to avoid taking hot baths). Although Japan had nine cases of mad cow disease after its first confirmed case in 2001, all slaughtered cows must now be checked for the disease before the meat is authorized for consumption. To prevent the spread of avian and H1N1 flu, all incoming passengers are monitored upon arrival at Narita Airport for fever; those with a higher than normal temperature may be quarantined. To be on the safe side, therefore, you may opt for an influenza vaccine before departing from home.

Otherwise, you don't need any inoculations to enter Japan. **Prescriptions** can be filled at Japanese pharmacies *only if they're issued by a Japanese doctor.* To avoid hassle, bring more prescription medications than you think you'll need, clearly labeled in their original containers, and be sure to pack them in your carry-on luggage. But to be safe, bring copies of your prescriptions with you, including generic names of medicines in case a local pharmacist is unfamiliar with the brand name. Over-the-counter items are easy to obtain, though name brands are likely to be different from those back home, some ingredients allowed elsewhere may be forbidden in Japan, and prices are likely to be higher.

WHAT TO DO IF YOU GET SICK AWAY FROM HOME

Tokyo has some Western-trained physicians and many more who speak some English. If you get sick, you may want to contact the concierge at your hotel—some upper-range hotels have in-house doctors or clinics (see the individual hotel listings in chapter 5). Otherwise, your embassy in Tokyo can provide a list of area doctors who speak English (see p. 307 for embassy contact information), as can the local tourist office. You can also contact the **International Association for Medical Assistance to Travellers** (✆ **716/754-4883,** or 416/652-0137 in Canada; www.iamat.org), an organization that lists many

> **Healthy Travels to You**
>
> The following government websites offer up-to-date health-related travel advice:
> **Australia:** www.smartraveller.gov.au/tips/travelwell.html
> **Canada:** www.hc-sc.gc.ca/index-eng.php
> **U.K.:** www.nhs.uk/Healthcareabroad/Pages/Healthcareabroad.aspx
> **U.S.:** www.cdc.gov/travel

local English-speaking doctors and also posts the latest developments in global outbreaks. Otherwise, if you can't find a doctor who can help you right away, try the local hospital. Many have walk-in clinics for cases that are not life-threatening.

Doctors and hospitals generally do not accept credit cards and require immediate cash payment for health services. See "Fast Facts: Tokyo," in chapter 12 for Tokyo hospitals, medical clinics, and emergency numbers (p. 306).

6 SAFETY

Tokyo is one of the safest cities in the world. In all the years I've lived and worked in Tokyo, I've never had even one fearful encounter, and I never hesitate to walk anywhere any time of the night or day. If you lose something, say on a subway or in a park, chances are good that you'll get it back.

That being said, however, crime—especially pickpocketing—is on the increase,

and there are precautions you should always take when traveling: Stay alert and be aware of your immediate surroundings. Be especially careful with cameras, purses, and wallets, particularly in crowded subways, department stores, or tourist attractions (such as the retail district around Tsukiji Market). Some Japanese caution women against walking through parks alone at night.

7 SPECIALIZED TRAVEL RESOURCES

In addition to the destination-specific resources listed below, please visit Frommers.com for additional specialized travel resources.

GAY & LESBIAN TRAVELERS

While there are many gay and lesbian establishments in Tokyo (concentrated mostly in Shinjuku's Ni-chome district), the gay community in Japan is not a vocal one, and in any case, information in English is hard to come by. A useful website for gay club listings is www.utopia-asia.

com/tokyobars.htm. Otherwise, the best bet for getting up to speed on the current Tokyo gay and lesbian scene is to head to Ni-chome and stop by one of the establishments listed in chapter 10 (p. 264).

TRAVELERS WITH DISABILITIES

Tokyo can be a nightmare for travelers with disabilities. City sidewalks can be so jam-packed that getting around on crutches or in a wheelchair is exceedingly difficult.

Although most train and subway stations have elevators, they are often difficult to locate. A few stations are accessible only by stairs or escalators, but in recent years some have been equipped with powered seat lifts. While some buses are now no-step conveyances for easy access, subway and train compartments are difficult for solo wheelchair travelers to navigate on their own due to a gap or slight height difference between the coaches and platforms. In theory, you can ask a station attendant to help you board, though you might have to wait if he's busy; you can also request that someone at your destination help you disembark. Finally, although trains and buses have seating for passengers with disabilities, subways can be so crowded that there's barely room to move. Moreover, these seats are almost always occupied by commuters—so unless it's obvious that you have a physical disability, no one is likely to offer you a seat.

As for accommodations, most expensive hotels have at least one or two barrier-free rooms (sometimes called a "universal" room in Japan), though lower-priced hotels and Japanese inns generally do not. Lower-priced accommodations may also lack elevators. In a positive move, the Tokyo Metropolitan Government provides subsidies to hotels wishing to upgrade their facilities to make them more accessible for people with physical disabilities; for a list of accommodations that have received the subsides and to see the work they've accomplished, go to www.tourism. metro.tokyo/jp/English/administration/ barrier_free/barrierlist.html.

Restaurants can also be difficult to navigate, with raised doorsills, crowded dining areas, and tiny bathrooms that cannot accommodate wheelchairs. Best bets for ramps and easily accessible restrooms include restaurants in department stores and upper-end hotels. Even Japanese homes are not very accessible, since the main floor is traditionally raised about a foot above the entrance-hall floor.

For information on traveling in Japan with a wheelchair, see Accessible Japan at www.tesco-premium.co.jp/aj/index.htm. It gives limited information on a handful of sights and hotels that offer facilities for people with disabilities.

When it comes to **facilities for the blind,** Japan has a very advanced system. At subway stations and on many major sidewalks in Tokyo, raised dots and lines on the ground guide blind people through intersections and subway platforms. In some cities, streetlights chime a theme when the signal turns green east–west, and chime another for north–south. Even Japanese yen notes are identified by a slightly raised area in their top corners—the ¥1,000 note has one circle in a corner, while the ¥10,000 note has two. And finally, many elevators have floors indicated in Braille, and some hotels identify rooms in Braille.

FAMILY TRAVEL

The Japanese are very fond of children, which makes traveling in Japan with kids a delight. All social reserve seems to be waived for children. Taking along some small and easy-to-carry gifts (such as colorful stickers) for your kids to give to other children is a great icebreaker.

Safety also makes Japan a good destination for families. Still, plan your itinerary with care. To avoid crowds, visit tourist sights on weekdays. Never travel on city transportation during rush hour or on trains during popular public holidays. And remember that with all the stairways and crowded sidewalks, strollers are less practical than baby backpacks. Many of Tokyo's major hotels provide babysitting services, although they are prohibitively expensive. Expect to fork over a minimum of ¥5,000 for 2 hours of babysitting.

Children 6 to 11 years old are generally charged half-price for everything from temple admission to train tickets, while children 5 and under are often admitted free. Tourist spots in Japan almost always have a table or counter with a stamp and inkpad so that visitors can commemorate their trip; you might wish to give your children a small notebook so that they can collect imprints of every attraction they visit.

If your child under 6 sleeps in the same bed with you, you generally won't have to pay for him or her in most *ryokan* (a Japanese-style inn), and some hotels don't charge extra for children. However, it's always advisable to ask in advance.

As for dining, most family-style restaurants, especially those in department stores, offer a special children's meal that often includes a small toy or souvenir. For those real emergencies, Western fast-food places, such as McDonald's and KFC, are everywhere in Tokyo.

To locate those accommodations, restaurants, and attractions that are particularly kid-friendly, refer to the "Kids" icon throughout this guide. For lists of kid-friendly hotels and restaurants, see p. 96 and 141, respectively. "Especially for Kids," on p. 199, describes attractions and activities geared toward children.

SENIOR TRAVEL

A few museums in Tokyo offer **free admission** to seniors over 65 or 70 (be sure to have your passport handy), including the **Tokyo National Museum;** others in Tokyo and elsewhere may offer discounts. However, discounts may not be posted, so be sure to ask. In addition, visitors to Japan should be aware that there are many stairs to navigate in metropolitan areas, particularly in subway and train stations and on pedestrian overpasses. Remember that it is very hot and humid in summer.

STUDENT TRAVEL

Students sometimes receive discounts at museums, though occasionally discounts are available only to students enrolled in Japanese schools. Furthermore, discounted prices are often not displayed in English. Your best bet is to bring along an **International Student Identity Card (ISIC)** with your university student ID and show them both at museum ticket windows. For information on the card and where and how to obtain one, check the website www.isic.org.

8 SUSTAINABLE TOURISM

Tokyo may be crowded and land may be scarce, but it's certainly clean and cared for. Littering is rare in Japan, and Japanese are taught practically at birth about separating trash for recycling. You can do your part by depositing all your trash—newspapers, plastic water bottles, cans—into the appropriate recycle bins found in parks, subway stations, and other public places.

Other actions you can take include refusing extra packaging at department stores (which may otherwise wrap your purchase and then place it in a shopping bag), carrying your own chopsticks (in cheap restaurants they are likely to be disposable), reusing your towels and sheets in hotels, and opting for public transportation over taxis.

Luckily for a megalopolis this size, public transportation is efficient and most people I know in Tokyo don't own a car. Japan is no newcomer to the idea of

General Resources for Green Travel

In addition to the resource for Tokyo listed above, the following websites provide valuable wide-ranging information on sustainable travel. For a list of even more sustainable resources, as well as tips and explanations on how to travel greener, visit www.frommers.com/planning.

- **Responsible Travel** (www.responsibletravel.com) is a great source of sustainable travel ideas; the site is run by a spokesperson for ethical tourism in the travel industry. **Sustainable Travel International** (www.sustainable travelinternational.org) promotes ethical tourism practices and manages an extensive directory of sustainable properties and tour operators around the world.

- In the U.K., **Tourism Concern** (www.tourismconcern.org.uk) works to reduce social and environmental problems connected to tourism. The **Association of Independent Tour Operators** (AITO; www.aito.co.uk) is a group of specialist operators leading the field in making holidays sustainable.

- In Canada, **www.greenlivingonline.com** offers extensive content on how to travel sustainably, including a travel and transport section and profiles of the best green shops and services in Toronto, Vancouver, and Calgary.

- In Australia, the national body that sets guidelines and standards for ecotourism is **Ecotourism Australia** (www.ecotourism.org.au). **The Green Directory** (www.thegreendirectory.com.au), **Green Pages** (www.thegreen pages.com.au), and **Eco Directory** (www.ecodirectory.com.au) offer sustainable travel tips and directories of green businesses.

- **Carbonfund** (www.carbonfund.org), **TerraPass** (www.terrapass.org), and **Carbon Neutral** (www.carbonneutral.org) provide info on "carbon offsetting," or offsetting the greenhouse gas emitted during flights.

- **Greenhotels** (www.greenhotels.com) recommends green-rated member hotels around the world that fulfill the company's stringent environmental requirements; although there are no member hotels in Japan, the website describes what it means to be a green hotel. **Environmentally Friendly Hotels** (www.environmentallyfriendlyhotels.com) offers more green accommodations ratings, including three in Tokyo.

- **Volunteer International** (www.volunteerinternational.org) has a list of questions to help you determine the intentions and the nature of a volunteer program. For general info on volunteer travel, including opportunities in Japan, see www.volunteerabroad.com/Japan.cfm.

hybrids, however, with Toyota introducing the Prius many years back and Honda's Insight now the best-selling car in Japan.

For a look at sustainability in Japan and grass-root organizations, or to get involved, go to www.greenz.jp.

9 SPECIAL-INTEREST TRIPS & ESCORTED GENERAL-INTEREST TOURS

LANGUAGE CLASSES & CULTURAL EXPERIENCES

You won't become fluent in Japanese in a week or two, but for longer stays there are language schools throughout Tokyo that cater to both the beginner and the intermediate. Check the classified sections of city magazines such as *Metropolis* for lists of language schools.

Two Hong Kong import luxury hotels offer a variety of cultural classes for its guests—all at a price, of course. The Peninsula Tokyo (p. 90) offers a flower-arranging class and a sushi-making class, among others, while the Mandarin Oriental, Tokyo (p. 91), offers private lessons in the tea ceremony, ikebana flower arranging, and calligraphy lasting from 60 to 90 minutes.

Several hotels have tea ceremony rooms and demonstrations open to the public, including the New Otani, Okura, and Imperial. See p. 180 in chapter 7 for more information.

For extra pampering, many upper-range hotels also offer spas (see individual hotel listings in chapter 5), but for the traditional Japanese spa experience, you'll want to visit a hot-spring bath. Tokyo has two hot-spring baths, the Ooedo-Onsen Monogatari and Spa LaQua (p. 182), but for a real hot-spring experience, consider a trip to Hakone or Izu (p. 289 and 299, respectively).

For more information on cultural experiences in Japan, including flower-arranging schools and acupuncture, see "Five Ways to Immerse Yourself in Japanese Culture" in chapter 7.

ESCORTED GENERAL-INTEREST TOURS

Escorted tours are structured group tours, with a group leader. The price usually includes everything from airfare to hotels, meals, tours, admission costs, and local transportation.

Despite the fact that escorted tours require big deposits and predetermine hotels, restaurants, and itineraries, many people derive security and peace of mind from the structure they offer. Escorted tours—whether they're navigated by bus, motor coach, train, or boat—let travelers sit back and enjoy the trip without having to drive or worry about details. They take you to the maximum number of sights in the minimum amount of time with the least amount of hassle. They're particularly convenient for people with limited mobility, and they can be a great way to make new friends.

On the downside, you'll have little opportunity for serendipitous interactions with locals. The tours can be jam-packed with activities, leaving little room for individual sightseeing, whim, or adventure—plus they often focus on the heavily touristed sites, so you miss out on many a lesser-known gem.

That said, lots of tour companies offer group trips that include a stop in Tokyo, including **General Tours** (© 800/221-2216; www.generaltours.com), which offers tours to major tourist destinations in Japan. **JTB USA** (© 800/235-3523; www.jtbusa.com) offers tours that may highlight anything from Japanese cuisine to art. **Esprit Travel & Tours** (© 800/377-7481; www.esprittravel.com) specializes in small-group walking, hiking, and cultural tours that cover such interests as textile arts, Japanese gardens, and the old Tokaido Road. If you want someone else to take care of logistics but don't like group tours, **Artisans of Leisure** (© 800/214-8144; www.artisansofleisure.com) provides luxury tours with private guides that are tailored to your interests. For more information on escorted tours departing from North America, go to www.japantravelinfo.com; for tours departing from England, go to www.seejapan.co.uk.

For more information on escorted general-interest tours, including questions to ask before booking your trip, see www.frommers.com/planning.

10 STAYING CONNECTED

TELEPHONES

To call Tokyo from outside Japan: First, dial the international access code: **011** from the U.S.; **00** from the U.K., Ireland, or New Zealand; or **0011** from Australia. Next, dial the country code for Japan, **81.** Finally, dial the city code for Tokyo, **3,** and then the number.

Domestic calls: If you're calling Tokyo from outside Tokyo but within Japan, the **area code** for Tokyo is **03.**

Despite the proliferation of cellphones, you can still find public telephones in telephone booths on the sidewalk, in or near train stations, in hotel lobbies, and in restaurants and coffee shops. A local call costs ¥10 for each minute; a warning chime will ring to tell you to insert more coins or you'll be disconnected. I usually insert two or three coins at the start so that I won't have to worry about being disconnected; ¥10 coins that aren't used are returned at the end of the call. Most public phones accept both ¥10 and ¥100 coins. The latter is convenient for long-distance calls, but no change is given for unused minutes. All gray ISDN telephones are equipped for international calls and have dataports for Internet access.

If you think you'll be making a lot of domestic calls from public telephones and don't want to deal with coins, purchase a magnetic **prepaid telephone card.** These are available in a value of ¥1,000 and are sold at vending machines (sometimes located right beside telephones), station kiosks, and convenience stores. Green and gray telephones accept telephone cards. In fact, many nowadays accept telephone cards exclusively. Insert the card into the slot. On the gray ISDN telephones, there's a second slot for a second telephone card, which is convenient if the first one is almost used up or if you think you'll be talking a long time. Domestic long-distance calls are cheaper at night, on weekends, and on national holidays for calls of distances more than 60km (37 miles).

Toll-free numbers: Numbers beginning with **0120** or **0088** are toll-free. Calling a 1-800 number in the U.S. from Japan is not toll-free and costs the same as an international call.

To make international calls: For a collect call or to place an operator-assisted call through KDDI, dial the international telephone operator at © **0051.** From a public telephone, look for a specially marked INTERNATIONAL AND DOMESTIC CARD/COIN TELEPHONE. Although many of the specially marked green or gray telephones, the most common public telephones, accept both coins and magnetic telephone cards for domestic calls, most in Tokyo do not accept magnetic cards for direct overseas calls (due to illegal usage of telephone cards), except for those in a few key facilities like the airport and some hotels. You'll therefore either have to use coins or purchase a special prepaid international telephone card that works like telephone cards issued by U.S. telephone companies. That is, an access number must first be dialed, followed by a secret telephone number, and then the number you wish to dial. Such cards are often sold from vending machines next to telephone booths in hotels or in convenience stores such as Sunkus, Circle K, Family Mart, or Lawson. There are numerous such cards (with instructions in English), including the rechargeable **Brastel Smart Phonecard** (ⓒ **0120/659-543**; www.brastel. com), which charges ¥49 to ¥54 per minute from a payphone to a landline in the U.S. or United Kingdom; or the **KDDI Super World Card** (ⓒ **0057**; www.kddi. com), which gives approximately 21 minutes of weekday talk time to the U.S. on its ¥1,000 card. Some hotels have special phones equipped to accept credit cards.

International rates vary according to when you call, which telephone company you use, and what type of service you use. Direct-dial service is cheaper than operator-assisted calls. The cheapest time to call is between 11pm and 8am Japan time, while the most expensive time is weekdays from 8am to 7pm.

If you're not using a prepaid card (which has its own set of instructions and access numbers), to make a direct-dial international call, you must first dial one of the international access codes offered by the various telephone companies— **001** (KDDI), **0033** (NTT Communications), or **0061** (Softbank Telecom)— followed by **010,** and then the country code. The country code for the United States and Canada is **1;** for the United Kingdom, it's **44;** for Australia, it's **61;** and for New Zealand, it's **64.** Next you dial the area code and number. For example, if you wanted to call the British Embassy in Washington, D.C., using KDDI you would dial **001-010-1-202-588-6500.** If you're dialing from your hotel room, you must first dial for an outside line, usually **0.**

If you wish to be connected with an operator in your home country, you can do so from green international telephones by dialing ⓒ **0039** followed by the country code. (For the United States, dial ⓒ **0039-111.**) These calls can be used for collect calls or credit card calls. Some hotels and other public places are equipped with special phones that will link you to your home operator with the push of a button, and there are instructions in English.

If you have a U.S. calling card, ask your phone company for the direct access number from Japan that will link you directly to the United States. If you have AT&T, for example, dial ⓒ **00539-111** to place calls using KDDI or ⓒ **00665-5111** to use Softbank Telecom.

CELLPHONES

The three letters that define much of the world's wireless capabilities are GSM (Global System for Mobiles). Unfortunately, Japan uses a system that is incompatible with GSM. You can, however, use your **own mobile phone number** in Japan by bringing your own SIM card from home and inserting it into a handset rented from **Softbank Global Rental** or **NTT DoCoMo.** It only works, however, if your home service provider has a roaming agreement with Softbank or NTT. For more information, contact your mobile phone company, NTT DoCoMo (http://roaming.nttdocomo.co.jp), or Softbank Global Rental (www.softbank-rental.jp), where you can also find out about rental costs and rental locations and make online reservations. Another option is to bring your own mobile phone and rent a SIM card from Softbank.

Otherwise, if you want to have a telephone number before arriving in Japan, consider renting a phone before leaving home. North Americans can rent one before leaving home from **InTouch USA** (ⓒ **800/872-7626**; www.intouchglobal. com) or **Roadpost** (ⓒ **888/290-1606**; www.roadpost.com).

You can also rent a phone in Japan (unfortunately, foreign visitors are not allowed to buy cellphones in Japan). If you're in Japan for only a few days and are staying in an upper-class hotel, most convenient but most expensive is to rent a mobile phone from your hotel. A check of several hotels in Tokyo turned up rental fees ranging from ¥600 to ¥1,200 per day (the more expensive the hotel, the more expensive the rental). I suggest, therefore, that you rent a phone at Narita Airport. Lots of companies maintain counters at both terminals, including NTT DoCoMo and Softbank Global Rental (see above), as well as **G-Call** (www.g-call.com/e), **Telecom Square** (www.telecomsquare.co.jp), and **PuPuRu** (www.pupuru.com), which have the extra convenience of easy pickup and drop-off and offer online reservations. Most rentals start at ¥525 per day, though bargains are often offered online or on-site. Charges for domestic and international calls vary, but incoming calls are usually free.

For travelers staying in Japan a week or longer, **Go Mobile** (www.gomobile.co.jp) offers 1-week, 2-week, and 30-day rentals, including a limited number of free local calls. A 1-week rental costs ¥2,995 and includes 15 minutes of free local calls. Phones are shipped to an address in Japan (such as your hotel) and returned via a prepaid, pre-addressed envelope.

VOICE-OVER INTERNET PROTOCOL (VOIP)

If you have Web access while traveling, you might consider a broadband-based telephone service (in technical terms, **Voice over Internet protocol,** or **VoIP**) such as Skype (www.skype.com).

INTERNET & E-MAIL

Without your own computer: Cybercafes are growing in number. In any case, avoid **hotel business centers** unless you're willing to pay exorbitant rates, though some accommodations provide a computer in the lobby that guests can use for free.

The best place to set up a temporary office in Tokyo is at the sophisticated **Gran Cyber Café Bagus,** on the 12th floor of the Roi Building, 5–5–1 Roppongi (② 03/5786-2280; station: Roppongi). Open 24 hours, it offers individual cubicles with prices that depend on the chair you select: ¥500 the first hour for a straight-back chair, ¥530 for a recliner, and ¥600 for a massage chair. Unsurprisingly, given Tokyo's high taxi prices, it also offers a "night pack" in a reclining chair, available for a maximum of 6 hours between 11pm and 8am for ¥1,450, as well as—brace yourself—booths for couples. A "Ladies Only" section is also available. Another 24-hour Gran Cyber Café Bagus is located in Shibuya, on the seventh floor of the HMV music store at 24–1 Udagawacho (② 03/5456-8922).

For free access, try **Marunouchi Café,** located on the tree-lined Marunouchi Naka Dori avenue in the Shin Tokyo Building, 3–3–1 Marunouchi (② 03/3212-5025; stations: Marunouchi or Tokyo), with six computers available Monday to Friday 8am to 9pm and Saturday and Sunday 11am to 8pm (you'll need to show a photo ID, such as a passport). Or try the **Apple Store,** Ginza, 3–5–12 Ginza (② 03/5159-8200; station: Ginza), with approximately five Macs on the 4th floor available daily from 10am to 9pm. Note that waits can be long.

Although expensive, **Kinko's** has more than 30 locations throughout Tokyo, including one at Tokyo Station at the Yaesu north exit (② 03/3213-1811). Most are open 24 hours and charge ¥210 per 10 minutes of computer time.

With your own computer: With the exception of some budget hotels, virtually all hotels in Tokyo provide Internet access in guest rooms (see individual hotel listings in chapter 5). While most provide high-speed dataports, more and more are going **Wi-Fi** (wireless fidelity). I'm also happy to report that more and more are also offering Internet connections for free. Otherwise, expect to pay anywhere from ¥500 to ¥1,050.

Wherever you go, bring a phone cord and a spare Ethernet network cable—or find out whether your hotel supplies them to guests (many do, for free). For Japan's electricity requirements, see "Fast Facts," on p. 306.

4

Tokyo Neighborhoods & Suggested Itineraries

If your time in Tokyo is limited, the suggested itineraries below will make the most of it by guiding you to the best the city has to offer, coordinating sightseeing with dining and evening plans. Keep in mind that some attractions are closed 1 day of the week, so plan your days accordingly.

1 GETTING TO KNOW TOKYO

CITY LAYOUT

Tokyo is located on the mideastern part of **Honshu,** Japan's largest and most historically important island, and sprawls westward onto the **Kanto Plain** (the largest plain in all Japan). It is bounded on the southeast by **Tokyo Bay,** which in turn opens into the Pacific Ocean.

If you look at a map, you'll see that Tokyo retains some of its Edo Period features, most notably a large green oasis in the middle of the city, site of the former Edo Castle and today home of the Imperial Palace and its grounds. Surrounding it is the castle moat; a bit farther out are remnants of another circular moat built by the Tokugawa shogun. The **JR Yamanote Line** forms another loop around the inner city; most of Tokyo's major hotels, nightlife districts, and attractions are near or inside this oblong loop.

For administrative purposes, Tokyo is divided into 23 wards, known as ku. Its business districts of Marunouchi and Hibiya, for example, are in Chiyoda-ku, while Ginza is part of Chuo-ku (Central Ward). These two ku are the historic hearts of Tokyo, for it was here that the city had its humble beginnings. Greater Tokyo is also a prefecture (similar to a state or province) and includes 26 cities, five towns, and eight villages in addition to its 23 wards, as well as Pacific islands. For most purposes, however, references to Tokyo in this guide pertain mostly to central Tokyo's 23 wards.

MAIN STREETS & ARTERIES

One difficulty in finding your way around Tokyo is that hardly any streets are named. Think about what that means—some 12 million people living in a huge metropolis of nameless streets. Granted, major thoroughfares and some well-known streets in areas such as Ginza and Shinjuku received names after World War II at the insistence of American occupation forces, and a few more have been labeled or given nicknames only the locals know. But for the most part, Tokyo's address system is based on a complicated number scheme that must make the postal workers' jobs here a nightmare. To make matters worse, most streets in Tokyo zigzag—an arrangement apparently left over from the past to confuse potential attacking enemies. Today they confuse Tokyoites and visitors alike.

Among Tokyo's most important named streets are **Meiji Dori,** which follows the loop of the Yamanote Line and runs from Minato-ku ward in the south through Ebisu,

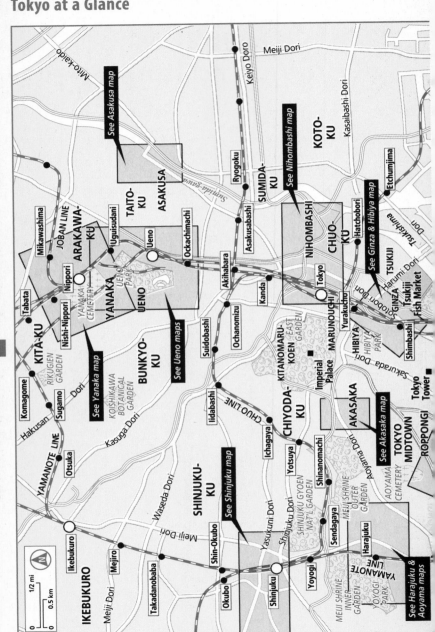

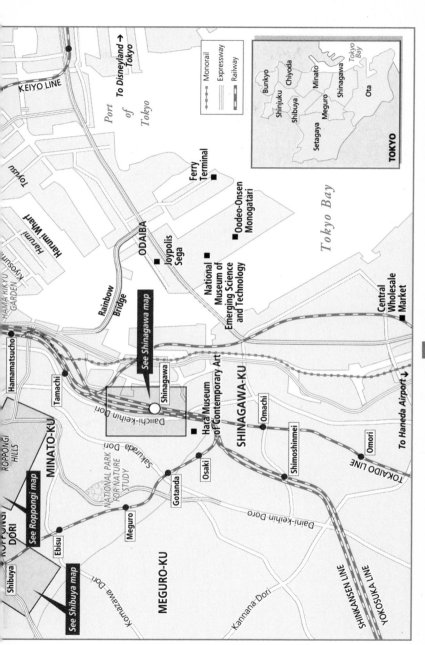

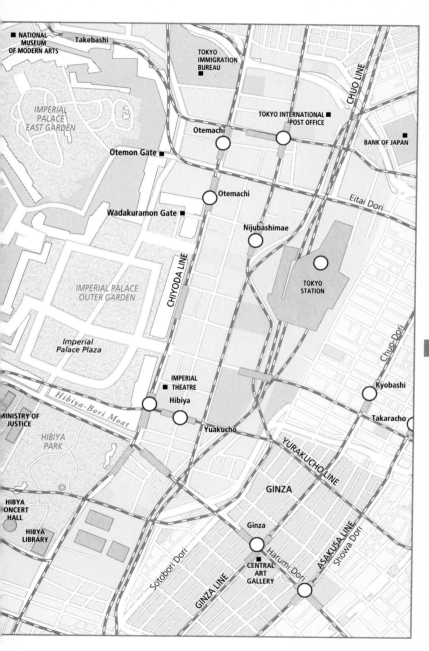

Shibuya, Harajuku, Shinjuku, and Ikebukuro in the north; **Yasukuni Dori** and **Shinjuku Dori,** which cut across the heart of the city east and west from Shinjuku to Chiyoda-ku; and **Sotobori Dori, Chuo Dori, Harumi Dori,** and **Showa Dori,** which pass through Ginza. Other major thoroughfares are named after the districts they're in, such as **Roppongi Dori** in Roppongi and **Aoyama Dori** in Aoyama (dori means "avenue" or "street," as does michi).

An intersection in Tokyo is called a crossing; it seems every district has a famous crossing. Ginza 4–chome Crossing is the intersection of Chuo Dori and Harumi Dori. Roppongi Crossing is the intersection of Roppongi Dori and Gaien-Higashi Dori.

FINDING AN ADDRESS

Because streets did not have names when Japan's postal system was established, the country has a unique address system. A typical Tokyo address might read 6–4–21 Ginza, Chuo-ku, which is the address of the Ginza Nikko Hotel. Chuo-ku is the name of the ward. Wards are further divided into named districts, in this case, Ginza. Ginza itself is broken down into *chome* (numbered subsections), the first number in the series, here 6–chome. The second number (4 in the example) refers to a smaller area within the chome—usually an entire block, sometimes larger. Thus, houses on one side of the street will usually have a different middle number from houses on the other side. The last number, in this case 21, refers to the actual building. Although it seems reasonable to assume that next to a no. 21 building will be a no. 22, that's not always the case; buildings were assigned numbers as they were constructed, not according to location.

Addresses are usually, but not always, posted on buildings beside doors, on telephone poles, and at major intersection traffic lights, but sometimes they are written in kanji only. One frustrating trend is that new, modern buildings omit posting any address whatsoever on their facades, perhaps in the belief that no one understands the address system anyway.

FINDING YOUR WAY AROUND

If you're traveling by subway or JR train, the first thing you should do upon exiting your compartment is look for yellow signs posted on every platform that tell which exit to take for particular buildings, attractions, and chome. At Roppongi Station, for example, you'll find yellow signboards that tell you which exit to take for Roppongi Hills, which will at least get you pointed in the right direction once you emerge from the station. Stations also have detailed maps of the area complete with addresses, either inside the station or at the exit; these are your best plans of attack when you're trying to find a particular address.

As you walk around Tokyo, you will notice maps posted beside sidewalks, giving a breakdown of the postal number system for the area (look for a white circle with an "i" in the middle). The first time I tried to use one, I stopped one Japanese, then another, and asked each to point to the location of a particular address on the map. Each person studied the map and pointed out the direction. Both turned out to be wrong. Not very encouraging, but if you learn how to read these maps, they're invaluable. Nowadays, many of them include landmarks translated in English.

Other invaluable sources of information are the numerous police boxes, called *koban,* located in every neighborhood throughout the city. Police officers have area maps, and helping lost souls seems to be their main occupation. You should also never hesitate to ask a Japanese person for directions, but be sure to ask more than one. You'll be amazed at the conflicting advice you'll receive. Apparently, the Japanese would rather hazard a guess than impolitely shrug their shoulders and leave you standing there. The best thing to do is ask several Japanese and then follow the majority opinion. Or you can duck into a shop and ask someone where a nearby address is, although in my experience, employees do not know the address of their own store. They may, however, have an area map.

MAPS

The maps in this guide are accurate and up-to-date and will help you find the businesses listed in this guide—but you'll need to arm yourself with a few more maps to properly navigate Tokyo. Maps are so much a part of life in Tokyo that they're often included in shop or restaurant advertisements, on business cards, and even on party invitations. Although I've spent years in Tokyo, I rarely venture forth without a map. The Tourist Information Center issues a "Tourist Map of Tokyo," which includes a subway map. Better, in my opinion, are the free maps from the Tokyo Metropolitan Government, which range from a city map to detailed maps of Tokyo's many districts. Armed with these maps, you should be able to locate at least the general vicinity of every place mentioned in this book. Hotels sometimes distribute their own maps. In short, never pass up a free map.

For more detailed maps, head for Tower Books, Kinokuniya, or one of the other bookstores with an English-language section, where you'll find several variations of city maps. My favorite is Shobunsha's Bilingual Map of Tokyo, listing chome and chome subsections for major areas; the compact folded map can be carried in a purse or backpack. If you plan to write a guidebook, consider the Bilingual Atlas of Tokyo, by Tokyo Chizu Publishing Company, or Kodansha International's Tokyo City Atlas, both of which cover all 23 of Tokyo's wards with specific postal maps, provide both Japanese and English-language place names, rail and subway maps, and an index to important buildings, museums, and other places of interest.

NEIGHBORHOODS IN BRIEF

Taken as a whole, Tokyo seems formidable. Instead, think of Tokyo as a variety of neighborhoods scrunched together, much like the pieces of a jigsaw puzzle. Holding the pieces together, so to speak, is the **Yamanote Line,** a commuter train loop around central Tokyo, passing through such important stations as Yurakucho, Tokyo, Akihabara, Ueno, Ikebukuro, Shinjuku, Harajuku, Shibuya, and Shinagawa.

Hibiya (map on p. 92) This is not only the business heart of Tokyo, but its spiritual heart as well. Hibiya is where the Tokugawa shogun built his magnificent castle and was thus the center of old Edo. Today, Hibiya, in Chiyoda-ku, is no less important as the home of the **Imperial Palace,** built on the ruins of Edo Castle and today the residence of Japan's 125th emperor. Bordering the palace is the wonderful **East Garden** and **Hibiya Park,** both open free to the public.

Marunouchi (map on p. 174) Bounded by the Imperial Palace to the west and Tokyo Station to the east, Marunouchi is one of Tokyo's oldest business districts, with wide avenues and office buildings. Since the turn of this century, it has undergone a massive revival, beginning with the replacement of the historic 1923 Marunouchi Building, with a 36-story complex of restaurants, shops, and offices, followed by construction of the Shin-Marunouchi Building, the Oazo Building, and the Peninsula Tokyo. Currently, the historic west side of Tokyo Station and the Central Post Office are undergoing renovations. At Marunouchi's center is the fashionable, tree-lined **Marunouchi Naka Dori,** home to international designer boutiques from Armani and Burberry to Tiffany & Co., as well as a growing number of restaurants and bars. Traveling in a long oblong around the perimeter of Marunouchi is the free Marunouchi Shuttle, operating daily from 10am to 8pm at 15- to 20-minute intervals.

Nihombashi (map on p. 99) Back when Edo became Tokugawa's shogunate capital, Nihombashi (also spelled Nihonbashi) was where merchants set up shop, making it the commercial center of the city and therefore of all Japan. Nihombashi, which stretches east of Tokyo Station, still serves as Tokyo's financial center, home of the computerized **Tokyo Stock Exchange** and headquarters for major banks and companies. Two of Tokyo's oldest department stores, **Mitsukoshi** and **Takashimaya,** are also here. The area takes its name from an actual **bridge,** Nihombashi, which means "Bridge of Japan," that served as the starting point for all main highways leading out of the city to the provinces during the Edo Period; distances to other destinations were also measured from here. Today the bridge is overshadowed by super highways rising above it.

Ginza (map on p. 92) Ginza is the swankiest and most expensive shopping area in all Japan. When the country opened to foreign trade in the 1860s, following 2 centuries of self-imposed seclusion, it was here that Western imports and adapted Western architecture were first displayed. Today, Ginza is where you'll find a multitude of department stores, international brand-name boutiques, exclusive restaurants,

hotels, art galleries, hostess clubs, and drinking establishments. Although Tokyo's younger generation favors less staid districts such as Harajuku, Shibuya, and Shinjuku, the Ginza is still a good place to window-shop and dine, especially on Sunday, when its major thoroughfare, Chuo-Dori, is closed to vehicular traffic, giving it a festive atmosphere. On the edge of Ginza is **Kabuki-za,** the nation's main venue for Kabuki productions but closed for renovations until 2013.

Tsukiji (map on p. 174) Located only two subway stops from Ginza, Tsukiji was born from reclaimed land during the Tokugawa shogunate; its name, in fact, means "reclaimed land." During the Meiji Period, it housed a large foreign settlement. Today it's famous for the **Tsukiji Fish Market,** one of the largest wholesale fish markets in the world.

Shiodome (map on p. 174) This new urban development project south of the Ginza has the usual skyscrapers with offices and hotels, as well as the Caretta Shiodome shopping mall. Most famous here is **Hama Rikyu Garden,** one of Tokyo's most famous gardens. From Hama Rikyu Garden, sightseeing boats depart for Asakusa in the north.

Akihabara (map on p. 174) Two stops north of Tokyo Station on the Yamanote Line, Akihabara has long been Japan's foremost shopping destination for electronic and electrical appliances, with hundreds of shops offering a look at the latest in gadgets and gizmos, including Yodobashi Camera, Japan's largest appliance store. In recent years, Akihabara has also become a mecca for *otaku* (geek) culture, home of *anime* and *manga* stores and the **Tokyo Anime Center.** This is a fascinating area for a stroll, even if you aren't interested in buying anything. About a 12-minute walk to the west is

Kanda, with many stores specializing in new and used books.

Asakusa (map on p. 109) Located in the northeastern part of central Tokyo, Asakusa and areas to its north served as the pleasure quarters for old Edo. Even older, however, is the famous **Sensoji Temple,** one of Tokyo's top and oldest attractions. Asakusa also has a wealth of tiny shops selling traditional Japanese crafts, most clustered along a pedestrian street called **Nakamise Dori** that leads straight to Sensoji Temple; the street's atmosphere alone makes it one of the most enjoyable places to shop for Japanese souvenirs. About a 15-minute walk west is **Kappabashi-dougugai Dori,** lined with shops dealing in kitchen appliances, plastic food, pots and pans, and everything else needed to run a restaurant. When Tokyoites talk about *shitamachi* (old downtown), they are referring to the traditional homes and tiny narrow streets of the Asakusa and Ueno areas.

Ueno (map on p. 117) Located just west of Asakusa, on the northern edge of the JR Yamanote Line loop, Ueno retains some of the city's old shitamachi atmosphere, especially at its spirited **Ameya Yokocho** street market, which began life as a black market after World War II and is spread underneath the Yamanote train tracks. Ueno is most famous, however, for **Ueno Park,** a huge green space comprising a zoo, a concert hall, a temple, a shrine, and several acclaimed museums, including the **Tokyo National Museum,** which houses the largest collection of Japanese art and antiquities in the world. North of Ueno is **Yanaka,** a delightful residential area of traditional old homes, neighborhood shops, and temples; several of Tokyo's most affordable Japanese-style inns are located here.

Shinjuku (map on p. 94) Originating as a post town in 1698 to serve the needs of feudal lords and their retainers traveling between Edo and the provinces, Shinjuku was hardly touched by the 1923 Great Kanto Earthquake, making it an attractive alternative for businesses wishing to relocate following the widespread destruction. In 1971, Japan's first skyscraper was erected here with the opening of the Keio Plaza Hotel in western Shinjuku, setting a dramatic precedent for things to come. Today more than a dozen skyscrapers, including several hotels, dot the Shinjuku skyline; and with the opening of the **Tokyo Metropolitan Government Office (TMG)** in 1991 (with a tourist office and a great free observation floor), Shinjuku's transformation into the capital's upstart business district was complete. Separating eastern and western Shinjuku is **Shinjuku Station,** the nation's busiest commuter station, located on the western end of the Yamanote Line loop. Surrounding the station is a bustling shopping district, particularly the huge **Takashimaya Shinjuku** complex and the many discount electronics stores. Shinjuku is also known for its nightlife, especially in **Kabuki-cho,** one of Japan's most famous—and naughtiest—amusement centers; and in **Shinjuku Ni–chome,** Tokyo's premier gay nightlife district. An oasis in the middle of Shinjuku madness is **Shinjuku Gyoen Park,** a beautiful garden for strolling and with a tranquil Japanese garden at its center.

Ikebukuro Located north of Shinjuku on the Yamanote Line loop, Ikebukuro is the working person's Tokyo, less refined and a bit rougher around the edges. Ikebukuro is where you'll find **Seibu** and **Tobu,** two of the country's largest department stores, as well as the **Japan Traditional Craft Center,** with its beautifully crafted traditional items. The **Sunshine City Building,** one of Japan's tallest skyscrapers, is home to a huge indoor shopping center and aquarium, while **Jiyugakuen Myonichikan** is a former girls' school–turned-museum that draws visitors because of its architect, Frank Lloyd Wright.

Harajuku (map on p. 149) The mecca of Tokyo's younger generation, Harajuku swarms throughout the week with teenagers in search of fashion and fun. **Takeshita Dori** is a narrow pedestrian lane packed elbow to elbow with young people looking for the latest in inexpensive clothing; at its center is Harajuku Daiso, a ¥100 discount shop. Harajuku is also home to one of Japan's major attractions, the **Meiji Jingu Shrine,** built in 1920 to deify Emperor and Empress Meiji; and to the small but delightful **Ukiyo-e Ota Memorial Museum of Art,** with its woodblock prints. Another draw is the **Oriental Bazaar,** Tokyo's best shop for products and souvenirs of Japan. Two Sundays a month, nearby **Togo Shrine** holds an antiques flea market. Linking Harajuku with Aoyama (see below) is **Omotesando Dori,** a fashionable tree-lined avenue flanked by trendy shops, restaurants, and sidewalk cafes, making it a premier promenade for people-watching.

Aoyama (map on p. 149) While Harajuku is for Tokyo's teeny-boppers, nearby chic Aoyama is its playground for trend-setting yuppies, boasting sophisticated restaurants, pricey boutiques, and more cutting-edge designer-fashion outlets than anywhere else in the city. It's located on the eastern end of **Omotesando Dori** (and an easy walk from Harajuku), centered on Aoyama Dori. The upscale **Omotesando Hills** shopping center on Omotesando

Dori stretches from Harajuku to Aoyama.

Shibuya (map on p. 155) Located on the southwestern edge of the Yamanote Line loop, Shibuya serves as an important commuter nucleus. More subdued than Shinjuku, more down-to-earth than Harajuku, and less cosmopolitan than Roppongi, it caters to bustling throngs of students and young office workers with its many shops and thriving nightlife, including more than a dozen department stores specializing in everything from designer clothing to housewares. Don't miss the light change at Shibuya Crossing near the Hachiko statue, reportedly Japan's busiest intersection, with its hordes of pedestrians, neon, and five video billboards that have earned it the nickname "the Times Square of Tokyo" (and a spot in the movie *Lost in Translation*).

Ebisu (map on p. 174) One station south of Shibuya on the JR Yamanote Line, Ebisu was a minor player in Tokyo's shopping and nightlife league until the 1995 debut of **Yebisu Garden Place,** a smart-looking planned community of apartments, concert halls, two museums (one highlighting Sapporo Beer, the other Japanese photography), restaurants, a department store, and a first-class hotel, all connected to Ebisu Station via moving walkway. The vicinity east of Ebisu Station, once a sleepy residential and low-key shopping district, has blossomed into a small but thriving nightlife mecca, popular with expats who find Roppongi too crass or commercial.

Roppongi (map on p. 159) Tokyo's best-known nightlife district for young Japanese and foreigners, Roppongi has more bars and nightclubs than any other district outside Shinjuku, as well as a multitude of restaurants serving international cuisine. The action continues until dawn. Nearby **Nishi Azabu,** once a residential neighborhood (many foreigners live here), offers a quieter and saner dining alternative to frenetic Roppongi. Between Roppongi and Nishi Azabu is the eye-popping, 11-hectare (27-acre) **Roppongi Hills,** Tokyo's largest urban development with 230 shops and restaurants, a first-class hotel, a garden, apartments, offices, a cinema complex, a playground, and Tokyo's highest art museum, on the 53rd floor of Mori Tower. Astonishingly, Roppongi Hills was upstaged in 2007 by the 10-hectare (25-acre) **Tokyo Midtown,** which boasts Tokyo's tallest building, a Ritz-Carlton, a medical center, 130 fashion boutiques and restaurants, apartments, offices, a garden, and the Suntory Museum of Art. Nearby is **The National Art Center, Tokyo,** focusing on changing exhibitions of modern and contemporary art.

Akasaka (map on p. 103) Close to Japan's seat of government and home to several large hotels and a small nightlife district, Akasaka caters mostly to businessmen and bureaucrats, making it of little interest to tourists. It does, however, boast some good restaurants; in recent years, so many Koreans have opened restaurants and other establishments here that it has been dubbed "Little Korea."

Shinagawa (map on p. 105) Once an important post station on the old Tokaido Highway, Shinagawa remains an important crossroads in large part because of **Shinagawa Station,** a stop on the Shinkansen bullet train and on the southern end of the Yamanote Line loop. Home to several hotels, it has also witnessed a major blossoming of office construction in recent years, making it a serious rival of Shinjuku's business

district. Other than the **Hara Museum of Contemporary Art** and **Sengakuji Temple,** however, there's little here to attract sightseers.

Ryogoku (map on p. 174) Located outside the Yamanote Line loop east of the Sumida River, Ryogoku has served as Tokyo's sumo town since the 17th century. Today it's home not only to Tokyo's large **sumo stadium and museum,** but also to about a dozen sumo stables, where wrestlers live and train. You can often see the giants as they stroll the district in their characteristic *yukata* robes. In 1993, Ryogoku became a tourist destination with the opening of the **Edo-Tokyo Museum,** which outlines the history of this fascinating city.

Odaiba (map on p. 174) This is Tokyo's newest district, quite literally—it was constructed from reclaimed land in Tokyo Bay. Connected to the mainland by **Rainbow Bridge** (famous for its chameleon colors after nightfall), the Yurikamome Line monorail, the Rinkai Line, and a vehicular harbor tunnel, Odaiba is home to hotels, Japan's largest convention space, several shopping complexes (including the very fancy Venus Fort), futuristic buildings (including the Kenzo Tange–designed Fuji TV building), several museums (such as the Museum of Maritime Science and the National Museum of Emerging Science and Innovation), a hot-spring public bath that harkens back to the Edo era, a monolithic Ferris wheel, the Panasonic Center showcasing its products, and Megaweb (a huge multimedia car amusement and exhibition center sponsored by Toyota). For young Japanese, Odaiba is one of Tokyo's hottest dating spots.

Seeing the top sights of Tokyo in a single day requires a very early start, discipline, and a bit of stamina. This "greatest hits" tour begins with an early morning spin through Japan's largest fish market and a sushi breakfast, and includes a garden tour, a cruise, a museum stop, swanky shopping, and a great meal. *Start: Subway to Tsukijijio or Tsukiji.*

❶ Tsukiji Fish Market ★★★

You'll need a very early start here, but if you've just flown in from the other side of the globe, you'll be suffering from jet lag anyway, so you should be wide awake by 5am. Head to Japan's largest wholesale fish market for an action-packed morning. After boats unload their catches from around the world in the wee hours of the morning, seafood auctions are held for wholesalers (only a small area of the tuna auctions is open to the public, 5–6:15am). Wholesalers then set up stalls, hawking about 450 different kinds of seafood; it's a great education simply walking through the aisles. The market is closed Sundays, holidays, and some Wednesdays. See p. 178.

> **❷ SUSHI DAI ★**
> For the freshest sushi breakfast you'll ever have, head to this tiny sushi bar (**© 03/3547-6797**) on the market grounds. See p. 138.

Take a taxi from Tsukiji Fish Market to Hama Rikyu Garden, or walk for 12 minutes.

❸ Hama Rikyu Garden

There are better, more famous gardens elsewhere in Japan, but Hama Rikyu Garden is convenient for a quick tour. Created more than 300 years ago, today it features a traditional Japanese garden complete with moon-viewing pavilions, teahouses, and other vestiges of its Edo-era origins, as well as a bird refuge. The garden opens at 9am daily. See p. 184.

❹ Sumida River Boat Cruise ★★

Inside Hama Rikyu Garden is a pier, where you can board a sightseeing boat for a 40-minute cruise up the Sumida River to Asakusa. In the days of old Edo (present-day Tokyo), taking a boat was the most popular way to reach Asakusa and its famous temple, and though the scenery has changed, it's still the most relaxing and interesting way to reach this destination. Boats depart Hama Rikyu at 10:35 and 11:15am, with subsequent departures every half-hour or hour. See p. 172.

❺ Nakamise Dori

Asakusa is one of Tokyo's oldest neighborhoods, filled with narrow lanes, traditional Japanese homes, and shops selling handmade crafts and souvenirs. At the heart of Asakusa is Nakamise Dori, a narrow pedestrian lane lined on both sides with booths selling a wide variety of Japanese souvenirs—a good place to stock up on inexpensive gifts for the folks back home. On side streets radiating from Nakamise Dori are also shops offering traditional crafts. See p. 240.

❻ Sensoji Temple ★★★

Nakamise Dori leads straight to Tokyo's oldest and most popular temple, founded in A.D. 628 to house the Buddhist goddess of mercy and happiness. Destroyed during World War II and lovingly rebuilt with donations from the Japanese people, it attracts 20 million worshippers a year, giving it a festive atmosphere virtually every day. See p. 177.

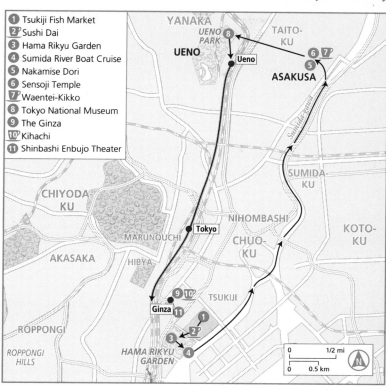

1. Tsukiji Fish Market
2. Sushi Dai
3. Hama Rikyu Garden
4. Sumida River Boat Cruise
5. Nakamise Dori
6. Sensoji Temple
7. Waentei-Kikko
8. Tokyo National Museum
9. The Ginza
10. Kihachi
11. Shinbashi Enbujo Theater

7 WAENTEI-KIKKO ★★★

This traditional house offers reasonably priced *obento* box lunches. Try to time your visit to coincide with a free performance of the *shamisen* or other Japanese musical instrument, given daily at 12:15 and 1:30pm. Located at 2-2-13 Asakusa (📞 **03/5828-8833**). See p. 140.

Take the Tokyo Shitamachi bus from Kaminarimon Dori (in front of Nakamise Dori) two stops to Ueno; or take the Ginza subway line three stops to Ueno.

8 Tokyo National Museum ★★★

This is the most important museum to see in Tokyo, if not all of Japan. It houses the country's largest collection of historic treasures, including swords, samurai gear, lacquerware, ceramics, Buddhist sculptures, calligraphy, woodblock prints, and much, much more. Its most priceless treasures are Buddhist statues, masks, and other religious works of art from Horyuji Temple in Nara, founded in 607. Closed Monday. See p. 177.

Take the Ginza Line from Ueno Station to Ginza Station.

9 The Ginza

The Ginza is Japan's most fashionable—and expensive—shopping address, home to international designer boutiques, art galleries, and huge department stores. My favorite department store is **Matsuya** on

Chuo Dori, with everything from Japanese folk crafts to designer togs for sale, plus an art gallery, restaurants, and a huge food emporium in its basement. See p. 231.

10 KIHACHI ★★

There are many different kinds of restaurants in the Ginza in all price ranges, but for a contemporary take on fusion Japanese-French cuisine you can't go wrong here. Located at 2–2–6 Ginza. (*C* 03/3567-6281). See p. 130.

11 Shinbashi Enbujo Theater ★★★

If you've managed to stay awake this long, about a 10-minute walk from the Ginza is the Shinbashi Enbujo Theater, where you can see performances of Kabuki with its gorgeous costumes; plots that revolve around love, loyalty, revenge, and other easy-to-understand themes; and great stage presentations. (Keep in mind that performances end by 9pm.) See p. 248.

3 THE BEST OF TOKYO IN 2 DAYS

You'll be packing in the activities for Day 2 as well, starting out at the Edo-Tokyo Museum, and then strolling through the electronic-goods haven, Akihabara, also home to anime and manga shops. Next, it's on to Harajuku, one of Tokyo's most vibrant neighborhoods; Tokyo's most venerable Shinto shrine; a museum devoted to woodblock prints; and Oriental Bazaar, a great shop for souvenirs. Finish the day with a trip to Shinjuku, where you'll have a bird's-eye view of the sprawling metropolis from an observation deck (it's free!). After dinner, take a stroll through Shinjuku's Kabuki-cho happening nightlife district, ablaze with neon. *Start: Subway or JR Sobu Line to Ryogoku.*

1 Edo-Tokyo Museum ★★★

This wonderful museum chronicles what life was like for the people who lived here, beginning with Edo's founding in 1590 and continuing to 1964 (when Tokyo hosted the Olympics). The museum presents vivid accounts of the lives of shoguns, merchants, craftsmen, and townspeople. Be sure to take advantage of free museum tours. Closed Monday. See p. 173.

Take the JR Sobu Line from Ryogoku Station two stops to Akihabara Station.

2 Akihabara

For a mind-numbing spin through the latest in Japanese electronic wizardry, check out a few of the 600-some shops and stalls vying for your attention in the nation's largest electronics district.

In recent years, a growing number of shops specialize in manga and anime (Japanese animation). See p. 225 and 226, respectively.

Take the JR Yamanote Line, which loops around central Tokyo, directly to Harajuku Station (via Tokyo Station). Quicker is the Sobu Line which cuts across Tokyo, but you have to transfer to the Yamanote at Yoyogi Station.

3 Harajuku

Harajuku is teeny-bopper heaven, with throngs of young Japanese combing shops for the latest fashions. It's one of Tokyo's most energetic neighborhoods, full of sidewalk cafes, boutiques, accessory stalls, and street vendors. Don't miss Takeshita Dori, the quintessential Harajuku street. See p. 237.

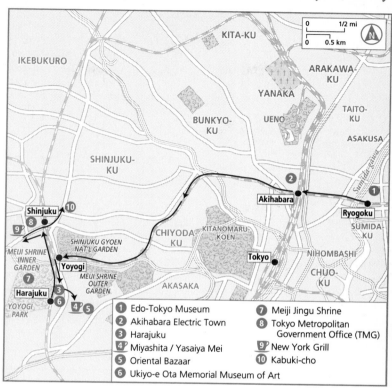

① Edo-Tokyo Museum
② Akihabara Electric Town
③ Harajuku
④ Miyashita / Yasaiya Mei
⑤ Oriental Bazaar
⑥ Ukiyo-e Ota Memorial Museum of Art
⑦ Meiji Jingu Shrine
⑧ Tokyo Metropolitan Government Office (TMG)
⑨ New York Grill
⑩ Kabuki-cho

④ **MIYASHITA OR YASAIYA MEI** ★
Omotesando Hills, 4–12–10 Jingumae, a swank shopping complex, offers a sophisticated respite from the teenage crowds. On its third floor are several restaurants, including Miyashita (© **03/5785-0707**), serving its own take on French and Japanese fusion dishes, and Yasaiya Mei (© **03/5785-0606**), which specializes in seasonal vegetables along with choices for carnivores. See p. 148 and 160, respectively.

⑤ **Oriental Bazaar**
With a facade that resembles a Shinto shrine, this is Tokyo's best bet for one-stop souvenir shopping: four floors packed with tableware, *yukata* (light cotton robes), new and used kimono, antique furniture, and more. Closed Thursday. See p. 243.

⑥ **Ukiyo-e Ota Memorial Museum of Art** ★
This diminutive museum packs a wallop with its themed exhibits of *ukiyo-e* (woodblock prints). I've seen everything from Edo-era beauties to varied views of Mount Fuji. Closed Monday and from the 27th to the end of every month for exhibit changes. See p. 191.

⑦ **Meiji Jingu Shrine** ★★
It's not old—it dates from only 1920—but it was built in honor of Emperor and Empress Meiji, whose role in opening

Japan to the rest of the world cannot be overstated. After walking through a lush forest, once the private grounds of a feudal lord, and passing under two *torii* (traditional entry gates of a Shinto shrine), you'll come to the shrine, designed with an austere, dignified simplicity. On weekends, the entrance to the shrine serves as a stage for teenagers dressed in bizarre costumes. See p. 176.

Take the JR Yamanote Line from Harajuku one stop north to Yoyogi Station, and then transfer to the Oedo Line to Tochomae Station.

⑧ Tokyo Metropolitan Government Office (TMG) ★★★

Nothing conveys Tokyo's vastness better than this building's observatory 45 stories above ground. From here you have unparalleled views of Shinjuku's skyscrapers and even Mount Fuji on clear days. Best of all? It's free. Hours are daily 9:30am to 10:30pm. See p. 199.

☕ NEW YORK GRILL ★★★

You may recognize this gorgeous hotel as the premier setting for *Lost in Translation*. For the same expansive views featured in the film, head to this top-notch venue on the 52nd floor of the Park Hyatt Hotel. You'll pay for the memorable experience to dine here on superb American cuisine—but only if you make a reservation in advance. Located at 3-7-1-2 Nishi-Shinjuku (*☎* **03/5322-1234**). See p. 143.

Take the free shuttle bus from the Park Hyatt to Shinjuku Station (last departure: 9:20pm), or take a taxi to Kabuki-cho.

⑩ Kabuki-cho

Kabuki-cho ranks as one of Japan's most famous—and notorious—nightlife districts. Neon galore heralds restaurants, bars, dance clubs, strip joints, peep shows, and hostess bars. Once the domain of Japanese businessmen carousing with fellow office workers, Kabuki-cho's narrow streets now attract a college crowd as well, until the wee hours. It's fun to take a spin through, if only to see what all the hubbub is about. See p. 251.

---

4 THE BEST OF TOKYO IN 3 DAYS

While you could spend a third day—and even a fourth and a fifth—visiting more attractions and soaking up the atmosphere of Tokyo's diverse neighborhoods (see suggested walking tours in chapter 8), visitors with limited time in Japan and confined to the Tokyo area should consider a day trip to the nearby town of Kamakura, located an hour south of Tokyo by train. One of Japan's most important historical sites, Kamakura served as Japan's first feudal capital when the ruling shogun set up military headquarters here in 1192. Many noteworthy temples and shrines of the Kamakura Shogunate (1192–1333) remain, including one of Japan's most celebrated bronze Buddhas. *Start: JR Yokosuka Line from Shinagawa or Tokyo Station to Kamakura Station.*

---

❶ Komachi Dori

After exiting Kamakura Station, walk catty-corner to the left across the square to Kamakura's main shopping street, a narrow pedestrian lane lined with shops selling clothing, accessories, and other goods. It's always bustling with shoppers, giving it a fun, lively atmosphere. At the end of the street, to the right, is the entrance to Tsurugaoka Hachimangu Shrine.

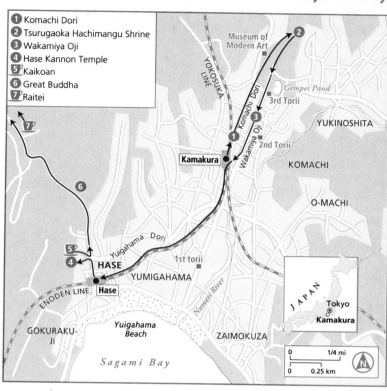

1 Komachi Dori
2 Tsurugaoka Hachimangu Shrine
3 Wakamiya Oji
4 Hase Kannon Temple
5 Kaikoan
6 Great Buddha
7 Raitei

Museum of Modern Art
YOKOSUKA LINE
Komachi Dori
Gempei Pond
3rd Torii
YUKINOSHITA
2nd Torii
Wakamiya Oji
Kamakura
KOMACHI
O-MACHI
Yuigahama Dori
1st torii
HASE
YUMIGAHAMA
Hase
Nameri River
ENODEN LINE
GOKURAKU-JI
Yuigahama Beach
ZAIMOKUZA
JAPAN
Tokyo
Kamakura
Sagami Bay
0   1/4 mi
0   0.25 km

2 Tsurugaoka Hachimangu Shrine ★★★

It's just a 10-minute walk from Kamakura Station, but this vermilion-colored shrine, built by Japan's first shogun, Yoritomo Minamoto, is a millennium away from Kamakura's modern center in age. The shrine itself, providing a sweeping view of a grand processional leading straight to the sea, contains a small collection of ancient swords, suits of armor, and other items relating to Yoritomo's rule. A counter sells individual fortunes, as well as good-luck charms that ensure good health, a long life, success in business, and other endeavors. See p. 268.

3 Wakamiya Oji

The wide processional that runs from Tsurugaoka Hachimangu Shrine 1.8km (about 1 mile) to Yuigahama Beach is called Wakamiya Oji. Marked by three massive torii gates, it was once more than three times wider at its far end near the sea, an optical illusion that reportedly made the lane appear longer than it actually was. In the middle of the lane is an elevated median with a footpath flanked by cherry trees and azaleas. Lining the street are restaurants, cafes, and souvenir stores offering *Kamakura-bori* (a locally made lacquerware), pottery, and other crafts, making it good for a stroll back to Kamakura Station.

Take the old-fashioned JR Enoden Line from Kamakura Station to Hase Station.

④ Hase Kannon Temple ★★★

The founding of this Buddhist temple, on a hill with views of the sea, is shrouded in myth. In A.D. 721, a priest supposedly carved two statues of the 11-headed goddess of mercy from a single camphor trunk. One of the statues was enshrined in a temple near Nara (another ancient capital), while the other was thrown into the sea. It turned up in Hase 16 years later, prompting the construction of this temple. More than 9m (30 ft.) high, the gilded statue is the tallest wooden image in Japan. On the stairway to the temple are hundreds of likenesses of Jizo, the guardian deity of children, donated by those grieving over miscarried, stillborn, or aborted children. See p. 272.

> **5 HASE KANNON TEMPLE**
> Sit with a drink and enjoy the sweeping views toward the sea on the small open-air pavilion. Next to the pavilion is a restaurant, **Kaikoan,** serving noodles, other simple fare, and drinks. Located at 3–11–2 Hase (℃ **0467/22-6300**). See p. 273.

⑥ Great Buddha ★★★

This is Kamakura's top attraction, and with good reason. Measuring 11m (36 ft.) high and weighing 93 tons, it was cast in 1252 and was once enclosed in a huge hall washed away by a tidal wave. Set against a dramatic background of rising wooded hills, it ranks second in size after Japan's tallest bronze Buddha in Nara, but this one with its outdoor setting is much more impressive. See p. 272.

> **7 RAITEI ★★★**
> There's no finer conclusion to a trip to Kamakura than a meal at this traditional restaurant, situated among rolling hills on the outskirts of the city. You can dine on inexpensive noodles and obento lunchboxes or splurge on *kaiseki*. In any case, be sure to wander the verdant grounds of the restaurant after your meal. Located at Takasago (℃ **0467/32-5656**). See p. 274.

Where to Stay

Tokyo has no old, grand hotels in the tradition of the Peninsula in Hong Kong or the Raffles in Singapore; it has hardly any old hotels, period. But what the city's hotels may lack in quaintness or old grandeur is more than made up for by excellent service—for which the Japanese are legendary—as well as cleanliness and efficiency. Be prepared, however, for small rooms. Space is at a premium in Tokyo, so with the exception of some rooms in very expensive hotels, rooms seem to come in three sizes: minuscule, small, and barely adequate.

Unfortunately, neither does Tokyo have many first-class *ryokan,* or Japanese-style inns. I suggest, therefore, that you wait for your travels outside Tokyo (see chapter 11, "Side Trips from Tokyo," for recommended excursions) to experience a first-rate ryokan. Alternatively, most of Tokyo's upper-bracket hotels offer at least a few Japanese-style rooms, with tatami mats, Japanese bathtubs (deeper and narrower than the Western version), and futons. Although these rooms tend to be expensive, they're usually large enough for four people. There are also inexpensive Japanese-style inns in Tokyo. In fact, if you're on a tight budget, a simple Japanese-style inn is often the cheapest way to go.

On the other hand, if you're looking for luxury, Tokyo certainly doesn't disappoint. First-class Japanese hotels have always prided themselves in providing the utmost in care and service, and the recent infusion of foreign-owned luxury hotels, including The Peninsula Tokyo, Mandarin Oriental, and the Ritz-Carlton, has only upped the ante.

Other trends in the hotel industry include a boom in business-oriented hotels; among my favorites is the Tokyu Stay chain, offering rooms complete with kitchens and laundry machines and reduced rates for guests staying longer than a week. Thankfully, a growing number of hotels are also switching from paid in-room Internet connections to free service, though Wi-Fi is not as ubiquitous as in the U.S. Nonsmoking floors are common in virtually all hotels except for some of the inexpensive ones, particularly Japanese-style inns. All hotels also have air-conditioning (a must in Tokyo) and all but the cheapest also have private bathrooms (most with tub/shower combinations).

Finally, the recent economic downturn has also affected Japan's hotels, which translates into bargain rates once unheard of. Whereas in the not-too-distant past hotels adhered to their published rack rates, today they are just as likely to offer deals, especially on their websites.

1 BEST BETS FOR ACCOMMODATIONS

- **Best Historic Japanese-Style Inn: Homeikan,** 5–10–5 Hongo (© **03/3811-1181**), consists of three historic buildings, one with a Japanese garden and very nice tatami rooms. A great choice for those who don't mind roughing it a bit (there are no private bathrooms), this is traditional Japanese living at inexpensive rates. See p. 116.
- **Best for Business Travelers:** Although not as centrally located as other hotels, the **Royal Park Hotel,** 2–1–1 Nihombashi-Kakigara-cho (© **800/457-4000** in the U.S.,

or 03/3667-1111), wins my vote as the best for business travelers, with its easy and frequent access to Narita airport, excellent service (including a Woman's Traveler Desk), nine restaurants and bars, 24-hour room service, a 24-hour business center, and comfortable rooms complete with a computerized TV system that allows guests to access the Internet and send e-mail for free. See p. 100.

- **Best for a Romantic Getaway:** Nothing beats a weekend getaway to the historic **Fujiya Hotel,** in Hakone (© **0460/82-2211**). Established in 1878, it is one of Japan's finest, most majestic hotels, boasting great views, Japanese- and Western-style architecture, a wonderful 1930s dining hall, and a large landscaped garden perfect for moonlit walks. See p. 295.

- **Best Budget Accommodations:** Although the building is rather nondescript, **Ryokan Sawanoya,** 2–3–11 Yanaka, in Ueno (© **03/3822-2251**), is nestled in a delightful neighborhood of traditional shops and old wooden houses; the English-speaking owner goes out of his way to introduce the neighborhood and make guests feel at home with such extras as complimentary tea and instant coffee, and free laundry detergent. An added bonus is the free lion dances performed by his son. See p. 118.

- **Best for Long Stays:** For stays of a week or longer, a comfy home-away-from-home is **Tokyu Stay Aoyama Premier,** 2–27–18 Minami-Aoyama (© **03/3497-0109**), which offers rooms complete with kitchenettes, combination washer/dryers, lots of storage space, and such extras as complimentary breakfast and Internet connections. See p. 110.

- **Best Views:** If it's winter, when Mount Fuji is most likely to be visible, the **Park Hyatt Tokyo,** 3–7–1–2 Nishi-Shinjuku (© **800/233-1234** in the U.S. and Canada, or 03/5322-1234), affords great views of Japan's tallest mountain. For city views, nothing can beat panoramas from Tokyo's highest hotel, the **Ritz-Carlton, Tokyo,** 9–7–1 Akasaka (© **800/241-3333** in the U.S. and Canada, or 03/3423-8000). See p. 91 and 97, respectively.

- **Best Hotel Garden: Hotel New Otani,** 4–1 Kioi-cho, in Akasaka (© **800/421-8795** in the U.S. and Canada, or 03/3265-1111), has a beautiful 400-year-old Japanese garden that once belonged to a feudal lord. Its sprawling 4 hectares (10 acres) contain ponds, waterfalls, bridges, bamboo groves, and manicured bushes. See p. 101.

- **Best Health Club & Spa:** For complete pampering, the spa at **Four Seasons Hotel Tokyo at Chinzan-So,** 2–10–8 Sekiguchi (© **800/819-5053** in the U.S. and Canada, or 03/3943-222), offers 10 treatment rooms, including two rooms for couples and a suite with its own private open-air bath. Other facilities include traditional Japanese cedar indoor baths, a heated outdoor pool with a retractable roof, and a fully equipped gym. Finish off with a relaxing stroll through the adjacent 100-year-old Chinzan-so garden. See p. 97.

- **Best Hotel for Pretending You're Not in Tokyo:** Located on the man-made island of Odaiba, **Hotel Nikko Tokyo,** 1–9–1 Daiba (© **800/645-5687** in the U.S. and Canada, or 03/5500-5500), has a resortlike atmosphere, is surrounded by parks and gardens, and is just a short walk away from a sandy swimming beach, museums, and shopping malls. A glance outside your hotel room, however, serves as a reminder—the city skyline crowds the edge of Tokyo Bay. See p. 104.

2 JAPANESE & WESTERN-STYLE ACCOMMODATIONS

JAPANESE-STYLE ACCOMMODATIONS
Ryokan

Although it can be very expensive, spending the night in a traditional Japanese inn (ryokan) is worth the splurge at least once during your trip. Unfortunately, you won't find many first-class ryokan in Tokyo itself. Unable to compete with the more profitable high-rise hotels, most closed long ago, so you'll need to travel to a resort or hot-spring spa, such as Hakone (chapter 11), for the true experience. If you don't have time for a side trip from Tokyo, however, you can still find some decent ryokan in the city, though they won't provide the full experience. Alternatively, most of Tokyo's upper-class hotels offer some Japanese-*style* rooms.

The full ryokan experience is unforgettable. Nothing conveys the simplicity and beauty—indeed, the very atmosphere—of old Japan like these inns, with their gleaming polished wood, tatami floors, rice-paper sliding doors, and meticulously pruned gardens. Exquisitely prepared *kaiseki* meals and personalized service by kimono-clad hostesses are the trademarks of such inns, and staying in one is like taking a trip back in time.

Traditionally, ryokan are small—only one or two stories high and containing about 10 to 30 rooms—and are made of wood with a tile roof. Most guests arrive at their ryokan around 3 or 4pm. The entrance is often through a gate and small garden, where you're met by a bowing woman in a kimono. Remove your shoes, slide on the proffered plastic slippers, and follow the hostess down long wooden corridors until you reach the sliding door of your room. After taking off the slippers, step into your tatami room, almost void of furniture except for a low table in the middle of the room, floor cushions, an antique scroll hanging in an alcove, and a simple flower arrangement. Best of all is the view past rice-paper sliding screens of a Japanese landscaped garden with bonsai, stone lanterns, and a meandering pond filled with carp. Notice that the room has no bed.

Almost immediately, your hostess welcomes you with hot tea and a sweet, served at your low table so that you can sit there for a while and appreciate the view, the peace, and the solitude. Next comes a hot bath, either in your own room (if it has one), or in the communal bath. (Be sure to follow the procedure outlined in "Social Skills 101," in chapter 2—soap and rinse yourself *before* you get into the tub.) After bathing and soaking away travel fatigue, aches, and pains, change into your *yukata,* a cotton kimono provided by the ryokan.

When you return to your room, you'll find the maid ready to serve your kaiseki dinner, an elaborate spread that is the highlight of a ryokan stay. It generally consists of locally grown vegetables, sashimi (raw fish), grilled or baked fish or another meat dish, and various regional specialties, served on many tiny plates; the menu is determined by the chef. Admire how each dish is in itself a delicate piece of artwork; it all looks too wonderful to eat, but finally hunger takes over. If you want, you can order sake or beer to accompany your meal (you'll pay extra for drinks).

After you've finished eating, the maid returns to clear away the dishes and to lay out your bed. The bed is really a futon, a kind of mattress with quilts, and is laid out on the tatami floor. The next morning the maid will wake you, put away the futon, and serve a breakfast of fish, pickled vegetables, soup, and other dishes. Feeling rested, well fed, and

Love Hotels

In addition to Japanese-style inns, Japan has another unique form of accommodations—so-called love hotels. Usually found close to entertainment districts, such as Shinjuku and Shibuya, such hotels do not, as their name might suggest, provide sexual services; rather, they offer rooms for rent by the hour to lovers. Even married couples use love hotels, particularly if they share small quarters with in-laws.

There are an estimated 35,000 such love hotels in Japan, often gaudy affairs shaped like ocean liners or castles and offering such extras as rotating beds, mirrored walls, video cameras, and fantasy-provoking decor. Love hotels are usually clustered together. You'll know you've wandered into a love-hotel district when you notice discreet entryways and—a dead giveaway—hourly rates posted near the front door. Many have reasonable overnight rates as well. I have friends who, finding themselves out too late and too far from home, have checked into love hotels, solo.

pampered, you're then ready to pack your bags and pay your bill. Your hostess sees you to the front gate, smiling and bowing as you set off for the rest of your travels.

Such is life at a good ryokan. Sadly, however, the number of upper-class ryokan diminishes each year. And, although ideally a ryokan is an old wooden structure that once served traveling feudal lords or was perhaps the home of a wealthy merchant, today most are actually modern concrete affairs with as many as 100 or more rooms, with meals served in dining rooms. What they lack in intimacy and personal service, however, they make up for with slightly cheaper prices and such amenities as modern bathing facilities and perhaps a bar and outdoor recreational facilities. Most guest rooms are fitted with a TV, telephone, safe for locking up valuables, and yukata, as well as amenities such as soap, shampoo, razor, toothbrush, and toothpaste.

Rates in a ryokan are always based on a per-person charge rather than a straight room charge and include breakfast, dinner, and often service and tax. Thus, while ryokan rates may seem high, they're actually competitive compared to what you'd pay for a hotel room and comparable meals in a restaurant. Although rates can vary from ¥9,000 to an astonishing ¥150,000 per person, the average cost is generally ¥12,000 to ¥20,000. Even within a single ryokan the rates can vary greatly, depending on the room you choose, the dinner courses you select, and the number of people in your room. If you're paying the highest rate, you can be certain you're getting the best room, the best view of the garden, or perhaps your own private garden, as well as a much more elaborate meal than that given to lower-paying guests. All the rates for ryokan in this book are based on double occupancy; if there are more than two of you in one room, you can generally count on a slightly lower per-person rate.

Although I heartily recommend spending at least 1 night in a ryokan, there are a number of **disadvantages** to these accommodations. The most obvious is that you may find it uncomfortable sitting on the floor. And because the futon is put away during the day, there's no place to lie down for an afternoon nap or rest, except on the hard, tatami-covered floor. In addition, some of the older ryokan, though quaint, can be bitterly cold in the winter and may have only Japanese-style toilets (see "Fast Facts: Tokyo," in chapter 12). As for breakfast, you might find it difficult to swallow fish, rice, and seaweed in the morning (I've even been served grilled grasshopper—quite crunchy). Sometimes you can get a Western-style breakfast if you order it the night before, but more often than not the fried or scrambled eggs arrive cold, leading you to suspect that they were cooked right after you ordered them.

A ryokan is also quite rigid in its **schedule.** You're expected to arrive sometime between 3 and 5pm, take your bath, and then eat at around 6 or 7pm. Breakfast is served early, usually by 8am, and checkout is by 10am. That means you can't sleep in, and because the maid is continually coming in and out, you have a lot less privacy than you would in a hotel.

You should always make a **reservation** if you want to stay in a first-class or medium-priced ryokan, since the chef has to shop for and prepare your meals. You can make reservations through any travel agency in Japan or by contacting a ryokan directly. You may be required to pay a deposit. Another good source is the **Japan Ryokan Association** (© 03/3231-5310; www.ryokan.or.jp), which lists some 1,400 ryokan as members.

Japanese Inn Group

If you want the experience of staying in a Japanese-style room but cannot afford the extravagance of a ryokan, consider staying in one of the participating members of the Japanese Inn Group—a special organization of more than 80 Japanese-style inns and hotels throughout Japan offering inexpensive lodging and catering largely to foreigners. Although you may balk at the idea of staying at a place filled mainly with foreigners, keep in mind that some inexpensive Japanese-style inns are not accustomed to guests from abroad and may be quite reluctant to take you in if you don't speak Japanese. I have covered several Japanese Inn Group members in this book over the years and have found the owners, for the most part, to be an exceptional group of friendly people eager to offer foreigners the chance to experience life on tatami and futons. In many cases, these are good places in which to exchange information with other world travelers, and they are popular with young people and families alike.

Although many of the group members call themselves ryokan, they are not ryokan in the true sense of the word, because they do not offer the trademark personalized service or the beautiful setting common to ryokan. However, they do offer simple tatami rooms that generally come with TVs and air-conditioners; most have towels and cotton yukata. Some offer Western-style rooms as well, and/or rooms with private bathrooms. Facilities generally include a coin-operated washer and dryer and a public bath. The average cost of a 1-night stay is about ¥5,000 to ¥6,000 per person, without meals. Breakfast is usually available if you pay extra; dinner is also sometimes available.

You can view member inns at **www.jpinn.com.** Or, upon your arrival in Tokyo, head to the Tourist Information Center for the free pamphlet called *Japanese Inn Group*. Make reservations directly with the inn (most have home pages and e-mail). In some cases, you'll be asked to pay a deposit (most accept American Express, MasterCard, and Visa). Many member inns belong to the Welcome Inn Group as well, which means you can make reservations through one of the methods described above in this chapter.

Minshuku

Technically, a *minshuku* is inexpensive Japanese-style lodging in a private home—the Japanese version of a bed-and-breakfast—usually located in resort areas or smaller towns. Because minshuku are family-run affairs, there's no personal service, which means that you're expected to lay out your own futon at night, stow it away in the morning, and tidy up your room. Most also do not supply towels or yukata, nor do they have units with private bathrooms. Meals are served in a communal dining room.

Officially, what differentiates a ryokan from a minshuku is that the ryokan is more expensive and provides more services, but the difference is sometimes very slight. I've stayed in cheap ryokan providing almost no service and in minshuku too large and modern to be considered private homes. The average per-person cost for a night in a minshuku is ¥7,000 to ¥9,000, including two meals.

WESTERN-STYLE ACCOMMODATIONS

Western-style lodgings range from exclusive first-class hotels to inexpensive ones catering primarily to Japanese businessmen.

When you book a hotel room, contact the hotel directly to inquire about rates, even if a toll-free 800 number is provided; sometimes there are special packages, such as weekend or honeymoon packages, that central reservations desks do not know about. Special, cheaper rates are also often offered on the hotel's website. In addition, always ask what kinds of rooms are available. Many hotels, especially those in the upper and medium range, offer a variety of rooms at various prices, with room size the overwhelming factor in pricing. Other aspects that often have a bearing on rates include bed size, floor height (higher floors are more expensive), and in-room amenities. Views are generally not a factor in Tokyo (though some hotels near Tokyo Bay charge more for harbor views; Mt. Fuji in the far distance is generally visible only in the winter or on rare, clear days). In Japan, a **twin room** refers to a room with two twin beds, while a **double room** refers to a room with one double bed (for convenience, the "double" rates for hotels listed below refer to two people in one room and include both twin and double beds). Most hotels charge more for a twin room, but sometimes the opposite is the case. When making your reservation, therefore, inquire about the differences in rates and what they entail.

Once you decide on the type of room you want, ask for the best in that category. For example, if you want a standard room, and deluxe rooms start on the 14th floor, ask for a standard on the 13th floor. In addition, be specific about the kind of room you want, whether it's a nonsmoking room, a room with a view of Mount Fuji, a room with Internet connection, or a room away from traffic noise. If possible, give the hotel your approximate time of arrival, especially if you'll be arriving after 6pm, when unclaimed rooms are sometimes given away.

3 SELECTING ACCOMMODATIONS

PRICE CATEGORIES

The hotel recommendations below are arranged first according to price, then by geographical location. Because Tokyo's attractions, restaurants, and nightlife are widely scattered, and because the public transportation system is fast and efficient (I've provided the nearest subway or train stations for each listing), there's no one location in Tokyo that's more convenient than another—and because this is one of the most expensive hotel cities in the world, the overriding factor in selecting accommodations will likely be cost. I've divided Tokyo's hotels into price categories based upon two people per night, including tax and service charge: **Very Expensive** hotels charge ¥50,000 and above, **Expensive** hotels range from ¥32,000 to ¥50,000, **Moderate** hotels offer rooms from ¥16,000 to

¥32,000, and **Inexpensive** accommodations offer rooms for less than ¥16,000. Unless otherwise indicated, units have private bathrooms.

TAXES & SERVICE CHARGES   Most hotel rates provided in the listings below include a 5% government **tax.** In addition, an additional local hotel tax will be added to bills that cost more than ¥10,000 per person per night: ¥100 is levied per person per night for rates between ¥10,000 and ¥14,999; rates of ¥15,000 and up are taxed at ¥200. Furthermore, upper-class hotels and most midrange hotels add a **service charge** of 10% to 15% (cheaper establishments do not add a service charge, because no service is provided). *Unless otherwise stated, the prices given in this chapter include all taxes and service charges.*

VERY EXPENSIVE & EXPENSIVE   Tokyo's top hotels can rival upper-range hotels anywhere in the world. Although many of the city's best hotels may not show much character from the outside, inside they're oases of subdued simplicity where hospitality reigns supreme. In addition to fine Japanese- and Western-style restaurants, they may also offer travel agencies, business centers, guest relations officers to help with any problems or requests you may have (from making a restaurant reservation to finding an address), shopping arcades, cocktail lounges with live music, spas, and health clubs with swimming pools. Unfortunately, health clubs and swimming pools usually cost extra—anywhere from ¥2,000 to an outrageous ¥5,000 per single use; I've noted below where extra fees are imposed (if no fee is given, entrance is free). Some hotel chains have membership clubs, allowing you to use pools for free. Best of all, membership is free. Note, too, that outdoor pools are generally open only in July and August.

Rooms in upper-range hotels come with such standard features as minibars, cable TVs with international broadcasts such as CNN and on-demand pay movies, high-speed Internet or wireless connections (the more expensive the hotel, the more likely you'll have to pay extra for it), clocks, radios, yukata, duvet-covered beds, hot-water pots and tea (and sometimes coffee, but you usually pay extra for it), hair dryers, and private bathrooms with tub/showers (very expensive hotels usually have separate tub and shower areas, as well as small TVs you can watch from the tub). All also have washlet toilets, a combination toilet and spray bidet. Because they're accustomed to foreigners, all upper-range hotels employ English-speaking staff and offer nonsmoking floors. Services provided include 24-hour room service, same-day laundry and dry-cleaning service, and complimentary English-language newspapers, such as the *Japan Times,* delivered to your room. Many hotels also offer executive floors, which are generally on the highest floors and offer such perks as private lounges with separate check-in, more in-room amenities, free continental breakfasts and cocktails, extended check-out times, and privileges that can include free use of the health club. At just a few thousand yen more than regular rates, these can be quite economical.

MODERATE   Moderately priced accommodations vary from tourist hotels to business hotels, with business hotels making up the majority. Catering primarily to traveling Japanese businessmen, a business hotel is a no-frills establishment with tiny, sparsely furnished rooms, most of them singles along with a few twins (double rooms are in the minority), with barely enough space to unpack your bags. If you're a large person, you may have trouble sleeping in a place like this. Primarily just a place to crash for the night, these rooms usually have everything you need—minuscule private bathroom, TV, telephone, radio, clock, yukata, Internet connections (either charged or free), hair dryer, hot-water pot with tea, and usually a minibar or an empty fridge you can stock yourself. There's usually no room service, and sometimes not even a lobby or coffee shop, although there may be vending machines that dispense beer and soda. There may be same-day laundry service as well, if you give up your laundry by 10am (no laundry service is available Sun or holidays). Some business hotels may not offer nonsmoking rooms, though this is increasingly rare, especially in Tokyo. On the plus side, they're usually situated in convenient locations near train or subway stations. If you're interested simply in a clean and functional place to sleep rather than in roomy comfort, a nondescript business hotel may be the way to go.

INEXPENSIVE   It's difficult to find inexpensive lodgings in Tokyo; the price of land is simply prohibitive. You can, however, find rooms—tiny though they may be—for less than ¥15,000 a night for two people, which is pretty good considering that you're in one of the most expensive cities in the world. Inexpensive accommodations include a bed or futon and (usually) phone, TV, heating, air-conditioning, and usually Internet connections (either in-room or via lobby computers, usually at no charge). Unless otherwise indicated, units also have private bathrooms and are generally spotless. Inexpensive Japanese-style rooms account for about half in this category; they're described in more detail above in "Japanese & Western-Style Accommodations."

Many foreigners find Japan so expensive that they end up becoming **youth hostel** regulars, even though they may never consider staying in one in other countries. There's no age limit at hostels in Japan (except children younger than 4 may not be accepted), and although most require a youth-hostel membership card, they often let foreigners stay without one for about ¥600 extra per night. However, there are usually quite a few restrictions, such as a 9 or 10pm curfew, a lights-out policy shortly thereafter, an early breakfast time, and closed times through the day, generally from about 10am to 3pm. In addition, rooms usually hold many bunk beds or futons, affording little privacy. On the other hand, these are certainly the cheapest accommodations in Tokyo.

TIPS ON ACCOMMODATIONS

Although Tokyo doesn't suffer from a lack of hotel rooms during peak holidays (when most Japanese head for the hills and beaches), rooms may be in short supply because of **conventions** and other events. If possible, avoid coming to Tokyo in **mid-February** unless you book well in advance—that's when university entrance exams bring multitudes of aspiring high-school students and their parents to the capital for a shot at entering one of the most prestigious universities in the country. In **summer,** when many foreign tourists are in Japan, the cheaper accommodations are often the first to fill up. It's always best, therefore, to **make your hotel reservations in advance,** especially if you're arriving in Tokyo after a long transoceanic flight and don't want the hassle of searching for a hotel room.

WELCOME INN RESERVATION CENTER   If you're looking for help in booking moderately priced and budget accommodations, at the top of my list is the Welcome Inn Reservation Center, operated in cooperation with the Japan National Tourism Organization (JNTO). Some 50 modestly priced accommodations in Tokyo, including business hotels and Japanese-style inns, are members of Welcome Inn, with rates of ¥8,000 for a single and ¥13,000 or less for a double. There's no fee for the service, but you are asked to guarantee your reservation with a credit card. This is a good option also if you decide to travel outside Tokyo for a night or more and wish to secure reservations beforehand.

In addition to booking rooms via the Internet at **www.itcj.jp**, you can book a room by appearing in person at one of the three TIC offices in Tokyo—at Narita Airport (in the arrivals lobbies of terminals 1 and 2), or near Yurakucho Station in the heart of the

Ⓥalue Tips for Saving on Your Hotel Room

Although Japanese hotels have traditionally remained pretty loyal to their published **rack rates,** which are always available at the front desk, the recession has opened possibilities for bargains.

- **Check the Internet.** If the hotel has a website, check to see whether discounts or special promotions are offered. Some hotels offer discounts exclusively through the Internet. In addition, check hotel booking sites such as Expedia and Rakuten Travel (see "Surfing for Hotels," above).
- **Always ask politely whether a room less expensive than the first one mentioned is available.** Because there are usually many categories, ask what the difference is, say, between a standard twin and a superior twin. If there are two of you, ask whether a double or a twin room is cheaper. Ask whether there are corporate discounts. Find out the hotel's policy on children—do children stay free in the room or is there a special rate?
- **Contact the hotel directly.** In addition to calling a hotel's toll-free number, call the hotel directly to see where you can get the best deal.
- **Ask about promotions and special plans.** Hotels frequently offer special "plans," including "Spring Plans," "Ladies' Plans," and even "Shopping Plans," which provide cheaper rates and services.
- **Remember the law of supply and demand.** Resort hotels are more crowded and therefore more expensive on weekends and during peak travel periods such as Golden Week. Discounts, therefore, are often available for midweek and off-season stays.
- **Ask about hotel membership plans.** Some chain business hotels offer hotel memberships with discounts on meals and free stays after a certain number of nights. Others, such as the New Otani, Okura, and the Imperial in Tokyo, allow free use of the hotel swimming pool simply if you become a member at no extra charge. Ask the concierge or front desk for a membership application.

city, on the 10th floor of the **Kotsu Kaikan Building** (2–10–1 Yurakucho; ℂ **03/3201-3331**). Reservations are accepted at the Narita TIC daily from 8am to 7:30pm; and at the Tokyo TIC daily from 9 to 11:30am and 1 to 4:30pm.

SURFING FOR HOTELS   In addition to the online travel booking sites **Travelocity, Expedia, Orbitz,** and **Priceline,** other good sites to check include **Hotels.com, Asia travel.com,** and **Asia-hotels.com.** In any case, be sure to compare rates at several booking sites, as well as with individual hotel websites to make sure you're getting a good deal.

For Japan-specific websites, government-approved moderate and higher-priced hotels that are members of the Japan Hotel Association are listed at **www.j-hotel.or.jp.** Likewise, high-priced, government-registered members of the Japan Ryokan Association can be found at **www.ryokan.or.jp.** Budget-priced Japanese inns—which do not offer the service or the class of high-priced inns, but do offer the experience of sleeping Japanese-style—who are members of the Japanese Inn Group (see above for details)—are listed at

www.jpinn.com. Japan's largest online hotel reservations company for budget and moderately priced accommodations is Rakuten Travel, at **http://travel.rakuten.co.jp/en/index.html**.

In any case, it's always a good idea to **get a confirmation number** and **make a print-out** of any online booking transaction.

4 VERY EXPENSIVE

Hotels in this section charge ¥50,000 and up. In addition to the recommendations here, **The Shangri-La Hotel, Tokyo,** 1–8–3 Marunouchi (© **866/565-5058** in the U.S., or 03/6739-7888; www.shangri-la.com), opened in 2009 adjacent to Tokyo Station as Tokyo's newest luxury property, with 202 rooms, two restaurants, a health club, pool, and spa, with rates beginning at ¥60,000 for a single or double.

NEAR THE GINZA
The Peninsula Tokyo ★★★ Travelers who love the ornate lobby of Hong Kong's the Peninsula may experience culture shock here. While the lobby layouts are the same—dominated by a restaurant popular for people-watching and afternoon tea served to live music—here the decor is stunningly austere and Zen-like. I doubt it will ever reach the tourism status of its Hong Kong counterpart, but that's hardly the point. The emphasis here is on the rooms, and in this the Peninsula excels. Beginning at 51 sq. m. (544 sq. ft.), with the most expensive facing the Imperial Palace and Hibiya Park, rooms include amenities you'd be hard pressed to find anywhere else in town, including bedside controls that light up with the slightest touch, the Peninsula's signature valet box for shoe polishing and newspaper delivery, gorgeous bathrooms with mood and "spa" lighting (and tubs big enough for two), dryers just for nails, humidifiers, and mobile phones for use throughout the hotel. Add a fantastic location between the Imperial Palace and the Ginza, gratis transportation via Rolls Royce within a 2-km (1.2-mile) radius, free iPod tours of the surrounding area, and the Peninsula Academy offering tours of Tsukiji Fish Market or classes for cooking and flower arranging, and it's clear this hotel is in a class all its own.

1–8–1 Yurakucho, Chiyoda-ku, Tokyo 100-0006. © **866/382 8388** in the U.S., or 03/6270-2888. Fax 03/6270-2000. www.peninsula.com. 314 units. ¥60,000–¥80,000 single or double; from ¥100,000 suite. Rates exclude all taxes and service charge. AE, DC, MC, V. Station: Yurakucho (3 min.); Hibiya (1 min.). **Amenities:** 5 restaurants, including Peter (p. 131); lounge; babysitting; concierge; health club and spa; indoor pool w/outdoor terrace; room service. *In room:* A/C, TV/DVD and DVD library, CD player, fax/printer, hair dryer, minibar, Free Wi-Fi.

NIHOMBASHI & AROUND TOKYO STATION
Four Seasons Hotel Tokyo at Marunouchi ★★★ (Kids) With only 57 rooms, this property, next to Tokyo Station and within walking distance of the Ginza, offers the ultimate in service, privacy, and exclusivity, with a well-trained staff that goes out of its way to make guests feel welcome (including special amenities and services for children). For first-timers leery of traveling between Narita Airport and Tokyo Station, the hotel offers a unique "greeting" service at the airport to assure a seamless transition all the way to the hotel (cost: ¥6,300). Guests are then escorted to rooms by guest-relations officers, and with good reason, as rooms are so high-tech it's almost impossible to figure out even such mundane tasks as double-locking the doors or engaging the bathtub stopper. At 44

Once you've chosen accommodations that appeal to you, you can locate many of them using the following neighborhood maps:

- **Akasaka,** p. 103.
- **Asakusa,** p. 109.
- **Ginza** and **Hibiya,** p. 92.
- **Harajuku,** p. 149.
- **Ueno,** p. 117.

- **Nihombashi,** p. 99
- **Roppongi,** p. 159.
- **Shinagawa,** p. 105.
- **Shinjuku,** p. 94.

sq. m (474 sq. ft.) and larger, the attractive rooms offer such standouts as wall-mounted TVs with Internet connections, leather-covered desks, and floor-to-ceiling windows. Unfortunately, the hotel's location on the lower levels of an office high-rise affords views only of Tokyo Station and its Shinkansen bullet trains or surrounding buildings. Still, this is a great place to stay—if you can get someone else to pay for it.

Pacific Century Place, 1-11-1 Marunouchi, Chiyoda-ku, Tokyo 100-6277. ℂ **800/819-5053** in the U.S. and Canada, or 03/5222-7222. Fax 03/5222-1255. www.fourseasons.com/marunouchi. 57 units. ¥65,100–¥75,600 single or double; from ¥115,500 suite. Rates exclude service charge and hotel tax. AE, DC, MC, V. Station: Tokyo (2 min.). **Amenities:** Restaurant; bar; lounge; babysitting; free use of bikes; concierge; exercise room; public bath w/imported hot springs mineral water and steam room; room service, spa. *In room:* A/C, TV/DVD, CD player, hair dryer, minibar, MP3 docking station, Wi-Fi (fee: ¥1,995 for 24 hr.).

Mandarin Oriental, Tokyo ★★★   Located in the historic Nihombashi district just steps away from the venerable Mitsukoshi department store, this sophisticated hotel occupies the top floors of the soaring Nihombashi Mitsui Tower, affording outstanding city views from its 38th-floor lobby, its restaurants, and guest rooms. Modern in design, the hotel boasts fabrics and textiles made expressly for the hotel by artisans across Japan, who used techniques handed down for generations to create everything from the wall coverings in public spaces to guest room bedcovers and upholstery. Starting at 50 sq. m (538 sq. ft.) and affording views of the Sumida River or—for a higher price—Tokyo Bay, the Imperial Palace garden, or Mount Fuji on clear days, rooms feature such unique touches as a lacquered box for the robe and slippers; yoga mat; a safe with an electrical outlet for recharging a phone or laptop; and a special delivery box at the entrance to allow your cleaned shoes or laundry to be returned without disturbing you. Bathrooms, separated from the room by a wall of glass, have separate showers and deep sunken tubs. Be sure to check with the concierge for cultural excursions offered by the hotel, ranging from Tsukiji tours to lessons in the tea ceremony or flower arranging.

2-1-1 Nihombashi Marumachi, Chuo-ku, Tokyo 103-8328. ℂ **866/526-6566** in the U.S. and Canada, or 03/3270-8950. Fax 03/3270-8886. www.mandarinoriental.com/tokyo. 179 units. ¥73,500–¥85,050 single or double; from ¥141,750 suite. Rates exclude service charge and hotel tax. AE, DC, MC, V. Station: Mitsukoshimae (2 min.). **Amenities:** 4 restaurants; 2 bars; lounge; tea lounge; babysitting; concierge; state-of-the-art exercise room w/views; room service; spa. *In room:* A/C, TV/DVD, CD player, hair dryer, minibar, MP3 docking station, Wi-Fi (fee: ¥1,800 for 1 day).

SHINJUKU

Park Hyatt Tokyo ★★★   Located in West Shinjuku on the 39th to 52nd floors of Kenzo Tange's granite-and-glass Shinjuku Park Tower, the Park Hyatt has spurred lots of

WHERE TO STAY

5

VERY EXPENSIVE

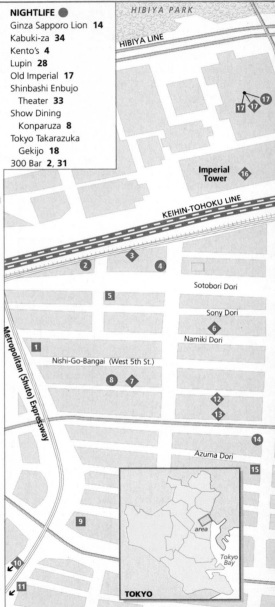

ACCOMMODATIONS ■
Hotel Com's Ginza (formerly Mitsui Urban Hotel Ginza) **1**
Courtyard by Marriott Tokyo Ginza Hotel **23**
Four Seasons Hotel Tokyo at Marunouchi **40**
Ginza Nikko Hotel **5**
Hotel Gracery (formerly Ginza Washington Hotel) **15**
Hotel Monterey La soeur **44**
Imperial Hotel **17**
Mitsui Garden Hotel Premier **9**
Park Hotel Tokyo **11**
The Peninsula Tokyo **35**
Hotel Villa Fontaine Shiodome **11**

DINING ◆
Any Shin's Hinomoto **37**
Aux Bacchanales **24**
Botejyu San **10**
Donto **36**
Fukusuke **26**
Ginza Daimasu **22**
Gonpachi **43**
The Imperial Viking Sal **17**
Inakaya **7**
Itamae Sushi **3**
Kamon **17**
Kihachi **41**
La Boheme **25, 43**
L'Osier **6**
Manpuku **38**
Meal Muji **39**
Monsoon **43**
Ohmatsuya **29**
Ohmatsuya Kura **21**
Peter **35**
Rangetsu **42**
Ristorante Sabatini di Firenze **27**
Shabusen **30**
Sushiko **19**
Tarafuku **12**
Tatsutano **13**
Ten-ichi **16, 20**
Tsukiji Sushi Sen **32**
Zest Cantina **43**
Zipangu **10**

NIGHTLIFE ●
Ginza Sapporo Lion **14**
Kabuki-za **34**
Kento's **4**
Lupin **28**
Old Imperial **17**
Shinbashi Enbujo Theater **33**
Show Dining Konparuza **8**
Tokyo Takarazuka Gekijo **18**
300 Bar **2, 31**

WHERE TO STAY

5

VERY EXPENSIVE

HIBIYA PARK

HIBIYA LINE

Imperial Tower **16**

KEIHIN-TOHOKU LINE

Sotobori Dori

Sony Dori

Namiki Dori

Metropolitan (Shuto) Expressway

Nishi-Go-Bangai (West 5th St.)

Azuma Dori

area

Tokyo Bay

TOKYO

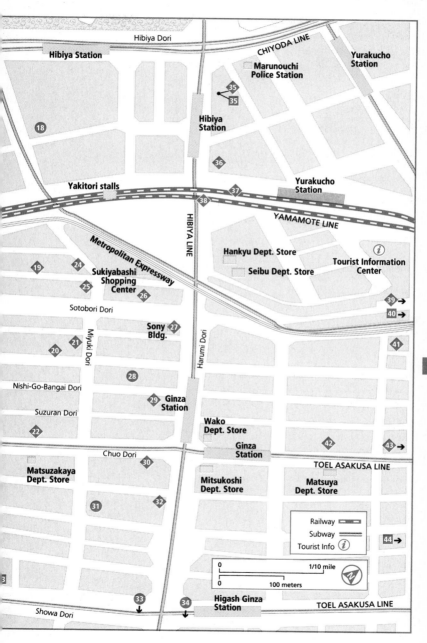

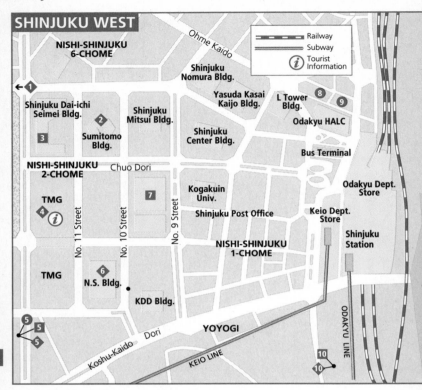

SHINJUKU WEST

Ohme Kaido

Railway
Subway
ⓘ Tourist Information

NISHI-SHINJUKU 6-CHOME

Shinjuku Nomura Bldg.

Yasuda Kasai Kaijo Bldg.

L Tower Bldg.

Shinjuku Dai-ichi Seimei Bldg.

Shinjuku Mitsui Bldg.

Odakyu HALC

Sumitomo Bldg.

Shinjuku Center Bldg.

Bus Terminal

NISHI-SHINJUKU 2-CHOME

Chuo Dori

Odakyu Dept. Store

TMG

Kogakuin Univ.

Keio Dept. Store

Shinjuku Post Office

Shinjuku Station

No. 11 Street
No. 10 Street
No. 9 Street

NISHI-SHINJUKU 1-CHOME

TMG

N.S. Bldg.

KDD Bldg.

ODAKYU LINE

Dori

YOYOGI

Koshu-Kaido

KEIO LINE

imitators since its 1994 opening, yet it remains among the most gorgeous and sophisticated hotels in Japan, a perfect reflection of high-tech, avant-garde Tokyo in the 21st century. If you can afford it, stay here. Check-in, on the 41st floor, is comfortably accomplished at one of three sit-down desks. Though it doesn't attract as much off-the-street foot traffic as Shinjuku's other hotels, the Park Hyatt's debut in *Lost in Translation* assures a steady stream of curious fans to its lounges and restaurants. Be sure to book early, therefore, for the 52nd-floor New York Grill, one of Tokyo's best restaurants (p. 143), offering a spectacular setting. All rooms average at least 45 sq. m (484 sq. ft.) and have original artwork, stunning and expansive views (including Mt. Fuji on clear days), bathrooms to die for, with deep tubs (plus separate showers), walk-in closets, and even Japanese/English dictionaries. Although no longer the only high-in-the-sky luxury hotel, this property remains high on my short list of great places to stay.

3–7–1–2 Nishi-Shinjuku, Shinjuku-ku, Tokyo 163-1055. ⓒ **800/233-1234** in the U.S. and Canada, or 03/5322-1234. Fax 03/5322-1288. www.tokyo.park.hyatt.com. 178 units. ¥69,300–¥87,780 single or double; from ¥167,475 suite. Rates exclude hotel tax. AE, DC, MC, V. Station: Shinjuku (a 13-min. walk or 5-min. free shuttle ride); Hatsudai, on the Keio Line (7 min.); or Tochomae (8 min.). **Amenities:** 3 restaurants, including New York Grill (p. 143); 2 bars; lounge; babysitting; concierge; health club and spa;

WHERE TO STAY

5

VERY EXPENSIVE

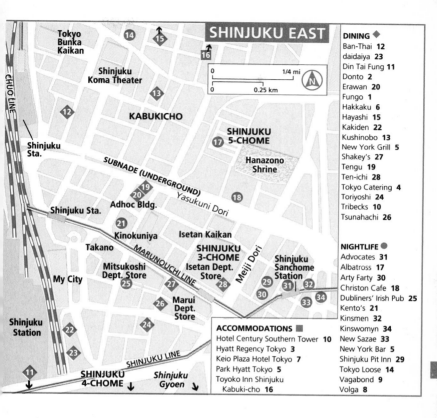

SHINJUKU EAST

DINING ◆
Ban-Thai **12**
daidaiya **23**
Din Tai Fung **11**
Donto **2**
Erawan **20**
Fungo **1**
Hakkaku **6**
Hayashi **15**
Kakiden **22**
Kushinobo **13**
New York Grill **5**
Shakey's **27**
Tengu **19**
Ten-ichi **28**
Tokyo Catering **4**
Toriyoshi **24**
Tribecks **10**
Tsunahachi **26**

NIGHTLIFE ●
Advocates **31**
Albatross **17**
Arty Farty **30**
Christon Cafe **18**
Dubliners' Irish Pub **25**
Kento's **21**
Kinsmen **32**
Kinswomyn **34**
New Sazae **33**
New York Bar **5**
Shinjuku Pit Inn **29**
Tokyo Loose **14**
Vagabond **9**
Volga **8**

ACCOMMODATIONS ■
Hotel Century Southern Tower **10**
Hyatt Regency Tokyo **3**
Keio Plaza Hotel Tokyo **7**
Park Hyatt Tokyo **5**
Toyoko Inn Shinjuku
  Kabuki-cho **16**

Map labels: Tokyo Bunka Kaikan; Shinjuku Koma Theater; KABUKICHO; CHUO LINE; Shinjuku Sta.; SUBNADE (UNDERGROUND); Adhoc Bldg.; Shinjuku Sta.; Kinokuniya; Takano; Mitsukoshi Dept. Store; My City; Shinjuku Station; MARUNOUCHI LINE; SHINJUKU LINE; SHINJUKU 4-CHOME; Shinjuku Gyoen; SHINJUKU 5-CHOME; Hanazono Shrine; Yasukuni Dori; Isetan Kaikan; SHINJUKU 3-CHOME; Isetan Dept. Store; Meiji Dori; Shinjuku Sanchome Station; Marui Dept. Store; SHINJUKU EAST; 0 1/4 mi; 0 0.25 km

dramatic 20m indoor pool w/great views; room service; free shuttle service to Shinjuku Station up to 3 times an hr. *In room:* A/C, TV/DVD, CD player and CD library, hair dryer, minibar, free Wi-Fi.

EBISU

The Westin Tokyo ★★★ A black marble floor, neoclassical columns and statuary, huge floral bouquets, and palm trees set this smart-looking hotel apart from other Tokyo hotels—it would be a perfect fit in Hong Kong. Set in the attractive Yebisu Garden Place (Tokyo's first planned community), it's still a hike from Ebisu Station, even with the aid of the elevated moving walkways. It's also far from Tokyo's business center. But the largely Japanese clientele (though North Americans account for 25% of the guests) favors it for its European ambience, relaxed atmosphere, Westin name, and Yebisu Garden Place with its restaurants and shopping. The spacious, high-ceilinged rooms blend luxurious 19th-century Biedermeier styles with contemporary furnishings and Westin's trademark Heavenly Beds that are either king-size (in double rooms) or two double beds (in twins) and oversize desks. Rooms on higher floors cost more, with the best views considered those facing Tokyo Tower, though on clear days those facing west treat you to views of Mount Fuji. Executive Club rooms include Guest Office rooms (with printer/fax machines and

WHERE TO STAY

5

VERY EXPENSIVE

Kids Family-Friendly Hotels

Four Seasons Hotel Tokyo at Marunouchi (p. 90)   If money is no object (though children 18 and under can stay in their parents' room at no extra charge), little princes and princesses receive the royal treatment here, including a welcome amenity, child-size robes, children's menus, complimentary toiletries, and bedtime cookies and milk. And for those hard-to-please teenagers, there's even free use of TV video games. The Four Seasons Hotel Tokyo at Chinzan-So has a similar offer.

Hotel New Otani (p. 101)   This huge hotel has an outdoor pool (which you can use free of charge by becoming a Hotel Club member), but best for parents is the babysitting room for children ages 1 month to 5 years. For a small fortune, you can even leave the darlings overnight.

Imperial Hotel (p. 98)   This famous hotel makes it easier to bring the family along, with its day-care center for children ages 2 weeks to 6 years, its babysitting service, and an indoor pool, which you can use free of charge by becoming a member of the Imperial Club.

Keio Plaza Hotel Tokyo (p. 101)   A children's day-care center for children 2 months and older, and free admission to an outdoor pool with children's pool are family pleasers, but if that's not enough, maybe the kids will find it cool to stay in one of Tokyo's tallest hotels.

Shinagawa Prince Hotel (p. 112)   Japan's largest hotel boasts a children's day-care center, cinema complex, amusement arcade, indoor and outdoor pools, aquarium, bowling alley, sports center, and much more.

office supplies), Workout Rooms (with exercise equipment), and a Ladies Floor with heightened security along with a yoga DVD and mat, jewelry box, vanity, humidifiers, female toiletries, and free espresso.

1–4–1 Mita, Meguro-ku, Tokyo 153-8580. ℂ **800/WESTIN-1** (937-8461) in the U.S. and Canada, or 03/5423-7000. Fax 03/5423-7600. www.westin-tokyo.co.jp. 438 units. ¥65,100–¥68,250 single or double; from ¥73,500 Executive Club; from ¥157,500 suite. Rates exclude service charge and hotel tax. AE, DC, MC, V. Station: Ebisu (7 min. via Yebisu Sky Walk). **Amenities:** 5 restaurants; 2 bars; lounge; babysitting; concierge; executive-level rooms; exercise room (fee: ¥1,000; free for Starwood Preferred Guest and Executive Club members); access to nearby health club w/heated indoor pool and gym (fee: ¥4,000; ¥2,500 for Executive Club and Preferred Guest members); room service; spa. In room: A/C, TV/DVD, hair dryer, high-speed Internet (fee: ¥1,800 for 24 hr.), minibar, iron.

ROPPONGI & AKASAKA

Grand Hyatt Tokyo ★★★   Depending on the surrounding Roppongi Hills development with its 200-some shops and restaurants to act as a major draw, this ambitious hotel wows with a wide range of recreational and dining facilities, as well as technically advanced rooms that older hotels can only dream about. In contrast to sister Park Hyatt's subdued, sophisticated atmosphere that attracts bigwigs hoping to escape the limelight, the Grand Hyatt strives for a livelier clientele who relish being in the center of it all. Still, key cards inserted into elevators block public access to guest floors, and those seeking pampering can opt for the Grand Club floor. Rooms, starting at 42 sq. m (452 sq. ft.), feature Italian furnishings, large mahogany desks, blackout blinds, safes designed for laptops with plug-ins for recharging, and duvet-covered beds with focused reading lights. One-quarter of each unit's space is taken up by a huge bathroom equipped with separate shower and tub areas and a small TV that swivels from the tub to the sink.

6–10–3 Roppongi, Minato-ku, Tokyo 106-0032. ⓒ **800/233-1234** in the U.S. and Canada, or 03/4333-1234. Fax 03/4333-8123. www.tokyo.grand.hyatt.com. 389 units. ¥60,060–¥68,145 single; ¥65,835–¥73,920 double; from ¥77,385 Grand Club double; from ¥112,035 suite. Rates exclude hotel tax. AE, DC, MC, V. Station: Roppongi (exit 1, 3 min.) or Azabu-Juban (exit A3, 5 min.). **Amenities:** 7 restaurants; 3 bars; babysitting; concierge (plus technology concierge to address your computer woes); executive-level rooms; health club w/20m indoor pool and spa (fee: ¥4,200); room service. *In room:* A/C, TV/DVD and DVD library, hair dryer, high-speed Internet, minibar.

The Ritz-Carlton, Tokyo ★★★   Of the several luxury hotels that have come online over the past few years, the Ritz-Carlton literally tops them all: It occupies the lofty upper reaches of Tokyo's tallest building, making it the highest hotel in a city that prides itself on skyscraper hotels. The crowning glory of Roppongi's Midtown urban renewal project, it boasts superlatives in almost every category you can think of, including Tokyo's largest rooms (starting at 52 sq. m/560 sq. ft.), its most expensive suite (¥2,100,000, in case you're considering it), and the city's highest ratio of nonsmoking rooms (80%). Reception, on the 45th floor, is markedly contemporary, yet oddly, views of the surrounding city are restricted to only a few select tables in the lobby lounge. That's remedied when guests are escorted to their rooms for individual check-in, where rooms from the 47th to 53rd floors provide eye-popping views of Tokyo in all its glory. Everything you'd expect from a top-rated hotel is here, including king-size (the majority) or two double beds, wireless telephones you can take with you anywhere in the hotel, a safe with plug-ins to recharge laptops, a good working desk, and—great for couples—two large closets. Bathrooms, which account for a third of the room's space, are among the best I've seen in Japan. It's hard to imagine a new hotel coming onto the scene with larger and higher rooms, but this being Tokyo, one undoubtedly will.

Tokyo Midtown, 9–7–1 Akasaka, Minato-ku, Tokyo 107-6245. ⓒ **800/241-3333** in the U.S. and Canada, or 03/3423-8000. Fax 03/3423-8001. www.ritzcarlton.com. 248 units. ¥68,250–¥71,400 single; ¥73,500–¥76,650 double; Grand Floor from ¥84,000 single, ¥94,500 double; from ¥115,500 suite. Rates exclude service charge and hotel tax. AE, DC, MC, V. Station: Roppongi or Nogizaka (3 min.). **Amenities:** 3 restaurants, including Hinokizaka (p. 158); bar; lounge; babysitting; concierge; executive-level rooms; health club w/20m indoor lap pool and spa (free entrance to health club; spa entrance fee: ¥5,250); room service. *In room:* A/C, TV/DVD, CD player, hair dryer, minibar, free Wi-Fi.

OTHER NEIGHBORHOODS

Four Seasons Hotel Tokyo at Chinzan-So ★★★ ⓕ**Finds**   Although inconveniently located in northwest Tokyo (about a 15-min. taxi ride from Ikebukuro), the Four Seasons Tokyo is a superb hotel set in the luscious 6.8-hectare (17-acre), 100-year-old Chinzan-So Garden, making it extremely inviting after a bustling day in Tokyo. It also has what may be Tokyo's best spa, including a gorgeous glass-enclosed indoor pool surrounded by greenery with a glass ceiling that opens in summer and a Japanese hot-spring bath (the water is shipped in from Izu Peninsula). In contrast to the starkly modern Four Seasons at Marunouchi, the luxurious interiors here make this one of the most beautiful European-style hotels in Japan. Because the hotel embraces the park, most rooms have peaceful garden views from their V-shaped bay windows (those that don't are cheaper, but the garden views are worth the splurge). Don't miss a stroll through the garden, which contains several charming, traditional Japanese restaurants; a pagoda; and stone monuments.

2–10–8 Sekiguchi, Bunkyo-ku, Tokyo 112-8667. ℂ **800/819-5053** in the U.S. and Canada, or 03/3943-2222. Fax 03/3943-2300. www.fourseasons.com/tokyo. 259 units. ¥52,500–¥57,750 single; ¥57,750–¥70,350 double; from ¥84,000 suite. Rates exclude service charge and hotel tax. AE, DC, MC, V. Station: Edogawabashi (exit 1a, a 10-min. walk along a cherry-tree-lined canal or a 2-min. ride). **Amenities:** 3 restaurants (plus 3 tenant restaurants in the garden); 2 lounges; babysitting; concierge; executive-level rooms; health club w/indoor pool and spa (fee: ¥4,200); room service. In room: A/C, TV/DVD and DVD library, CD player, hair dryer, high-speed Internet, minibar, MP3 docking station.

---

5 EXPENSIVE

Prices for hotels in this section range from ¥32,000 to ¥50,000.

GINZA & HIBIYA

Imperial Hotel ★★★ **Kids**   Located across from Hibiya Park, within walking distance of the Ginza and Imperial Palace, this is one of Tokyo's best-known and most popular hotels. The Imperial's trademark is impeccable service: Guests are treated like royalty. The Imperial's history goes back to 1890, when it opened at the request of the Imperial family to house the many foreigners coming to Japan; it was rebuilt in 1922 by Frank Lloyd Wright, but the present hotel dates from 1970, with a 31-story tower added in 1983. Wright's legacy lives on in the hotel's Art Deco Old Imperial Bar (p. 257) and Wright-inspired designs and furniture in public spaces. (Part of Wright's original structure survives at Meiji-Mura, an architectural museum outside Nagoya.) A full range of facilities includes one of the few hotels with a children's day-care center. Rooms in the main building are quite large for Tokyo, while Tower rooms, slightly smaller, are higher up, have floor-to-ceiling bay windows, and offer fantastic views of either Imperial Palace grounds or, my preference, the Ginza. All come with first-class amenities you'd expect from one of Tokyo's top hotels, as well as such appreciated extras as a hands-free phone, safes with plug-ins for laptops, and one-touch bedside controls for lights, drapes, and music. *Tip:* Become a member of the Imperial Club (membership is free), and you can use the small pool and gym free of charge.

1–1–1 Uchisaiwaicho, Chiyoda-ku, Tokyo 100-8558. ℂ **800/223-6800** in the U.S. and Canada, or 03/3504-1111. Fax 03/3581-9146. www.imperialhotel.co.jp/e/tokyo. 1,019 units. ¥33,600—¥57,750 single; ¥38,850–¥63,000 double; from ¥63,000 suite. Imperial Floor ¥45,150–¥63,000 single; ¥50,400–¥68,250 double. Rates exclude service charge and hotel tax. AE, DC, MC, V. Station: Hibiya (1 min.). **Amenities:** 13 restaurants, including Kamon, Ten-ichi, and the Imperial Viking Sal (p. 129, 131 and 132); 2 bars; 2 lounges; babysitting; children's day-care center, for ages 2 weeks to 6 years (fee: ¥5,250 for 2 hr.); concierge; executive-level rooms; exercise room (fee: ¥1,050; free for Imperial Club members); 20th-floor indoor pool (fee: ¥1,050; free for Imperial Club members); room service; sauna; in-house doctor; tea-ceremony room; post office. In room: A/C, TV, hair dryer, high-speed Internet, minibar.

NIHOMBASHI & AROUND TOKYO STATION

Marunouchi Hotel ★   Opened in 2004 as a modern replacement of a 1924 hotel, this low-key accommodation is well situated in the heart of Tokyo's business district; its location, just north of Tokyo Station's Marunouchi exit, makes it also convenient to both train and plane travel. Occupying the top 11 floors of the Marunouchi Oazo glass high-rise, it exudes an almost Zen-like solemnity, with bare wooden floors and shoji-like walls

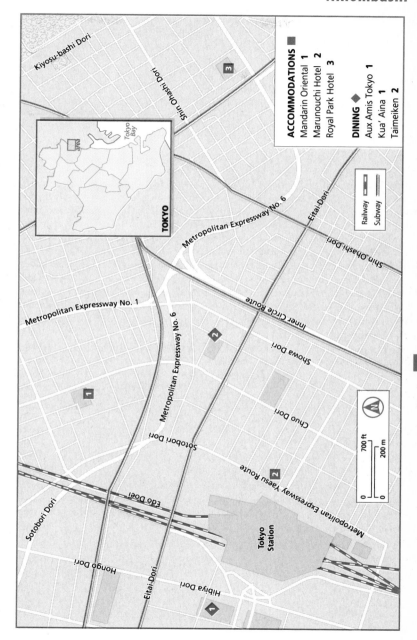

ACCOMMODATIONS ■
Mandarin Oriental **1**
Marunouchi Hotel **2**
Royal Park Hotel **3**

DINING ◆
Aux Amis Tokyo **1**
Kua' Aina **1**
Taimeiken **2**

Railway
Subway

TOKYO

Tokyo Bay

area

Kiyosu-bashi Dori

Shin Ohashi Dori

Metropolitan Expressway No. 6

Eitai-Dori

Shin Ohashi Dori

Metropolitan Expressway No. 1

Inner Circle Route

Metropolitan Expressway No. 6

Showa Dori

Chuo Dori

Sotobori Dori

Edo Dori

Metropolitan Expressway Yaesu Route

Sotobori Dori

Hongo Dori

Eitai-Dori

Hibiya Dori

Tokyo Station

700 ft
200 m

N

in a lobby that overlooks a rooftop garden that seems almost surreal. Key cards are required to access elevators to guest rooms, which are of standard size and decorated in warm browns. Small bathrooms have deep Japanese-style tubs with pillows for relaxing (the first I've seen in Japan). Roomy deluxe twins have "Japanese corners," a tatami area with a low table (and a "leg well" under the table for those errant limbs), but for the best view ask for a room facing Tokyo Station, where triple-pane glass allows you to watch bullet trains silently glide by. Though quite classy (and pricey), the Marunouchi is lacking in facilities and services, placing it more squarely in the business-hotel category.

1–6–3 Marunouchi, Chiyoda-ku, Tokyo 100-0005. ℂ **03/3217-1111.** Fax 03/3217-1115. www.marunouchi-hotel.co.jp. 205 units. ¥23,300–¥29,075 single; ¥31,385–¥52,375 double; ¥115,900 suite. AE, DC, MC, V. Station: Tokyo (1 min. via underground passageway) or Otemachi (2 min.). **Amenities:** 3 restaurants; bar; concierge; room service. *In room:* A/C, TV, fridge, high-speed Internet, trouser presser.

Royal Park Hotel ★★★   The Royal Park is located east of Tokyo Station (about a 10-min. ride by taxi), not far from the Tokyo Stock Exchange and Suitengu Shrine (popular with expectant mothers hoping for safe deliveries). One of its greatest assets, aside from the friendly and superbly efficient staff and its interesting environs, is that it's connected via enclosed walkway to the Tokyo City Air Terminal, the main terminus of the Airport Limousine Bus (which shuttles passengers to and from Narita Airport frequently), making this a convenient place for visitors with only a night or two to spend in Tokyo. It's also the first hotel I've seen with a Woman's Traveler Desk, offering check-in and other special services. But what makes it particularly attractive to business travelers, including many Americans, is its up-to-date guest rooms with a sophisticated computerized TV system that allows guests to access 80 channels and the Internet, send e-mail, and check airline schedules for free, plus, for a fee, watch videos on demand, play computer games, and more. Its views are uninspiring, however, even the so-called "city views," considered the hotel's best.

2–1–1 Nihombashi-Kakigara-cho, Chuo-ku, Tokyo 103-8520. ℂ **800/457-4000** in the U.S., or 03/3667-1111. Fax 03/3667-1115. www.rph.co.jp. 406 units. ¥27,300–¥45,150 single; ¥35,700–¥49,350 double. Executive floor from ¥34,650 single; ¥44,100 double. Rates exclude service charge and hotel tax. AE, DC, MC, V. Station: Suitengu-mae (underneath the hotel). **Amenities:** 6 restaurants; bar; 2 lounges; babysitting; concierge; executive-level rooms; health club w/20m indoor pool (fee: ¥1,575 for either alone); room service. *In room:* A/C, TV/DVD w/free high-speed Internet access, hair dryer, high-speed Internet (fee: ¥1,200 for 24 hr.), minibar.

SHINJUKU

In addition to the recommendations below, there's the nearby **Hilton Tokyo,** 6–6–2 Nishi-Shinjuku (ℂ **800/HILTONS** [445-8667] in the U.S., or 03/334-5111; www.hilton.com), with 815 rooms, 5 restaurants, a health club with an indoor pool, and free shuttle service to Shinjuku Station. Look online or call for room prices, as Hilton maintains "floating" rates that ebb with the law of demand. *Tip:* Join Hilton HHonors for free, and you also gain free entrance to its health club.

Hyatt Regency Tokyo ★   Located on Shinjuku's west side next to Shinjuku Chuo (Central) Park (popular with joggers), this least expensive and oldest of the Hyatt's three Tokyo properties celebrated its 25th anniversary in 2005 with renovated restaurants and rooms. Remaining is the hotel's impressive seven-story atrium lobby with three of the most massive chandeliers you're likely to see anywhere. Many foreigners (mostly American) pass through the hotel's doors, ably assisted by the excellent staff, which meets the Hyatt's usual high standards. However, because this hotel is popular with both business and leisure groups, those seeking a quieter, more personalized experience will want to book elsewhere. Rates are based on size; even the cheapest units are adequate, but they do face another building and don't receive much sunshine. If you can afford it, spring for a more expensive room on a high floor with bay windows overlooking the park (in winter, you might also have a view of Mt. Fuji).

2–7–2 Nishi-Shinjuku, Shinjuku-ku, Tokyo 160-0023. Ⓒ **800/233-1234** in the U.S. and Canada, or 03/3348-1234. Fax 03/3344-5575. http://tokyo.regency.hyatt.com. 744 units. ¥32,270 single; ¥42,735–¥47,355 double. Regency Club from ¥49,665 single; ¥53,130 double. Rates exclude hotel tax. AE, DC, MC, V. Station: Tochomae (1 min.), Nishi-Shinjuku (3 min.), or Shinjuku (a 10-min. walk, or a free 3-min. shuttle ride). **Amenities:** 6 restaurants; bar; concierge; executive-level rooms; health club w/indoor pool (fee: ¥2,000) and spa; room service; free shuttle service to Shinjuku Station every 20 min. *In room:* A/C, TV, hair dryer, high-speed Internet, minibar.

Keio Plaza Hotel Tokyo ★ ⟨**Kids**⟩ The closest hotel to Shinjuku Station's west side, the Keio Plaza is also West Shinjuku's oldest and biggest hotel, built in 1971. It has the distinction of being not only Japan's first skyscraper, but also, at 47 stories high, still one of Tokyo's tallest and largest hotels. It's popular with both Japanese and foreign travelers, including group tours, and the lobby bustles with activity—sometimes too much, making it difficult to get personalized service. But the hotel boasts a number of first-class facilities and services, including several that appeal to families, such as day care for children 2 months and older, and free access to an outdoor pool and children's pool. With almost 20 restaurants and bars, choices seem limitless. Rooms are small but comfortably furnished, with views of the surrounding Shinjuku area. Most expensive are the Plaza Premier rooms on the 35th to 37th floors, with MD/CD players, air purifiers, and safes with electric outlets so that laptops can recharge while being stowed. *Tip:* Become a member of the Executive International Club (it's free), and you qualify for discounted room rates, complimentary buffet breakfast, and use of a club lounge.

2–2–1 Nishi-Shinjuku, Shinjuku-ku, Tokyo 160-8330. Ⓒ **800/222-KEIO** (5346) in the U.S., or 03/3344-0111. Fax 03/3345-8269. www.keioplaza.com. 1,438 units. ¥31,500–¥45,150 single; ¥34,650–¥48,300 double; from ¥97,650 suite. Rates exclude service charge and hotel tax. AE, DC, MC, V. Station: Tochomae (1 min.) or Shinjuku (5 min.). **Amenities:** 12 restaurants; 3 bars; 1 lounge; children's day-care center (daily 10am–6pm; evenings by reservation only: fee: ¥3,150 for 1 hr.); concierge; executive-level rooms; fitness room; outdoor pool w/wading pool; room service; in-house doctor and dentist. *In room:* A/C, TV, hair dryer, high-speed Internet, minibar.

AKASAKA & ROPPONGI

Hotel New Otani ★★ ⟨**Kids**⟩ If you like small, quiet hotels, this monolith is not for you. Like a city unto itself, the New Otani is so big that two information desks are needed to assist lost souls searching for a particular restaurant or one of the shops in the meandering arcade. The hotel's most splendid feature is its garden, the best of any Tokyo hotel—a 400-year-old Japanese garden that once belonged to a feudal lord, with 4 hectares (10 acres) of ponds, waterfalls, bridges, bamboo groves, and manicured bushes. The large outdoor pool, flanked by greenery, is also nice. A variety of rooms, in a main building built for the 1964 Olympics and a newer tower, are available. Those in the main building are comfortable, with full-length windows to take advantage of city and garden views. Tower rooms, including "*fusui* healing" rooms with such extras as in-room humidifier and foot bath, offer the best views—of the garden, the skyscrapers of Shinjuku, and, on clear days, Mount Fuji. Because rates are the same no matter which way you face, be sure to request a room overlooking the garden. Parents appreciate the 24-hour Baby Room and the fact that the outdoor pool is free for those who become Hotel Club members (membership is free).

4–1 Kioi-cho, Chiyoda-ku, Tokyo 102-8578. ✆ **800/421-8795** in the U.S. and Canada, or 03/3265-1111. Fax 03/3221-2619. www.newotani.co.jp. 1,533 units. ¥31,500–¥34,650 single; ¥37,800–¥73,500 double; from ¥50,400 Executive House Zen; from ¥89,250 suite. Rates exclude service charge and hotel tax. AE, DC, MC, V. Station: Akasaka-mitsuke or Nagatacho (3 min.). **Amenities:** 38 restaurants and cafes, including La Tour d'Argent, Sekishin-tei, and the Sky (p. 165, 166 and 168); 6 bars and lounges; children's day-care center, for ages 1 month to 5 years old (fee: ¥6,300 for 2 hr.); concierge; executive-level rooms; small exercise room; health club w/indoor pool and spa (fee: ¥5,250); outdoor pool (fee: ¥2,000; free for Hotel Club members); room service; lighted outdoor tennis courts; medical and dental clinics; art museum (free for hotel guests); post office; tea-ceremony room. *In room:* A/C, TV, hair dryer, high-speed Internet (fee: ¥1,260 for 24 hr.), minibar.

Hotel Okura ★★★ Located across from the U.S. embassy and long considered one of Tokyo's most venerable hotels, the Okura is struggling to keep up with pricier—and newer—top-rated hotels in the city. Still, it remains a favorite home-away-from-home of visiting U.S. dignitaries, and the service is gracious and impeccable. Rich decor elegantly combines *ikebana* and shoji screens with an old-fashioned Western spaciousness. The atmosphere is low-key, almost Zen-like, with none of the flashiness inherent in some younger hotels. All rooms are comfortable, with opaque windows designed to resemble shoji and gold colors offset by fuchsia or other bright-colored armchairs and pillows. My favorite rooms are in the main building facing the garden; some on the fifth floor here have balconies overlooking the garden and pool. Other rooms have views of a rooftop garden or Tokyo Tower, while "Grand Comfort rooms" on the 9th and 10th floors offer free entrance to the spa. *Tip:* Fees are charged for use of the health club and pools, but become a member of Okura Club International (membership is free) and you can use them for free; fill out an application at the guest relations desk.

2–10–4 Toranomon, Minato-ku, Tokyo 105-0001. ✆ **800/526-2281** in the U.S. and Canada, or 03/3582-0111. Fax 03/3582-3707. www.okura.com/tokyo. 833 units. ¥36,750–¥44,100 single; ¥42,000–¥49,350 double; from ¥78,750 suite. Grand Comfort rooms ¥52,500 single; ¥66,150 double. Rates exclude service charge and hotel tax. AE, DC, MC, V. Station: Toranomon or Kamiyacho (5 min.). **Amenities:** 10 restaurants; 3 bars; children's day-care center (fee: ¥6,300 for 2 hr.); concierge; health club w/indoor 20m pool (fee: ¥5,775) and spa; nicely landscaped outdoor pool (fee: ¥2,100/$17); room service; free shuttle service to the nearest subways (Sat–Sun only); tea-ceremony room; in-house dentist; private museum showcasing Japanese art (free for hotel guests); pharmacy; packing and shipping service; post office. *In room:* A/C, TV, hair dryer, high-speed Internet (fee: ¥1,500 for 1 day), minibar.

The Prince Park Tower Tokyo ★★ Rising high above the pastoral surroundings of a parkland and Zozoji Temple, this 33-story monolith is the Prince chain's most luxurious Tokyo property. After a sit-down check-in, you'll cross a bridge over water and through the triangular-shaped building's hollow core before reaching the elevators. Designed by Tange Associates (the firm created by architect Kenzo Tange), the hotel certainly gets your attention. Rooms, from the 3rd to 31st floors, are what you'd expect from a hotel of this caliber (including whirlpool tubs and separate showers), so it's the views that stand out, with about half the rooms possessing balconies. You'll pay more for higher floors (from the 19th floor and higher), accessed only by special key and including a floor just for ladies (with humidifiers and air purifiers, scales, massage chairs, and curling irons). The hotel is within spitting distance of Tokyo Tower and a sobering walk from Roppongi's nightlife district.

4–8–1 Shiba-koen, Minato-ku, Tokyo 105-8563. ✆ **800/542-8686** in the U.S. and Canada, or 03/5400-1111. Fax 03/5400-1110. www.princehotels.com/en/parktower. 673 units. ¥34,000–¥45,000 single or double; from ¥52,000 executive floor; from ¥65,000 suite. Rates exclude hotel tax. AE, DC, MC, V. Station: Akabane-bashi (2 min.), Shiba-koen (3 min.), Daimon (9 min.), or Hamamatsucho (12 min.). **Amenities:** 8 restaurants; lounge; concierge; executive-level rooms; health club w/25m indoor pool, fitness room, and

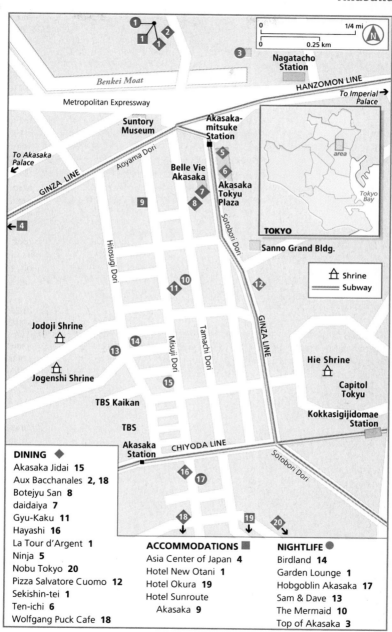

Benkei Moat

Metropolitan Expressway

Nagatacho Station

HANZOMON LINE

To Imperial → Palace

Suntory Museum

Akasaka-mitsuke Station

To Akasaka Palace ↙

Aoyama Dori

GINZA LINE

Belle Vie Akasaka

Akasaka Tokyu Plaza

Sotobori Dori

Sanno Grand Bldg.

TOKYO

area

Tokyo Bay

Hitosugi Dori

⌂ Shrine
═══ Subway

Jodoji Shrine ⌂

Jogenshi Shrine ⌂

Misuji Dori

Tamachi Dori

GINZA LINE

Hie Shrine ⌂

Capitol Tokyu

Kokkasigijidomae Station

TBS Kaikan

TBS

Akasaka Station

CHIYODA LINE

Sotobori Dori

DINING ◆
Akasaka Jidai **15**
Aux Bacchanales **2, 18**
Botejyu San **8**
daidaiya **7**
Gyu-Kaku **11**
Hayashi **16**
La Tour d'Argent **1**
Ninja **5**
Nobu Tokyo **20**
Pizza Salvatore Cuomo **12**
Sekishin-tei **1**
Ten-ichi **6**
Wolfgang Puck Cafe **18**

ACCOMMODATIONS ■
Asia Center of Japan **4**
Hotel New Otani **1**
Hotel Okura **19**
Hotel Sunroute
  Akasaka **9**

NIGHTLIFE ●
Birdland **14**
Garden Lounge **1**
Hobgoblin Akasaka **17**
Sam & Dave **13**
The Mermaid **10**
Top of Akasaka **3**

hot-spring bath (fee: ¥4,200; available for guests older than 24); room service; free shuttle service to Hamamatsucho Station 30 min; bowling alley w/darts and billiards. *In room:* A/C, TV, hair dryer, high-speed Internet, minibar.

SHINAGAWA

Sheraton Miyako Hotel Tokyo ★★ (Value)

This hotel is one of my favorites in Tokyo, for its calm peacefulness as well as its small-luxury-hotel service. Because it's a bit off the beaten path, it has a quieter, more relaxed atmosphere than those found at more centrally located hotels, evident the moment you step into its lobby lounge with its gas-flame fireplace (winter only) on one end and the lush greenery of a garden on its other. It offers average-size rooms, with good bedside reading lamps and beds so comfortable you'd sneak them into your luggage if you could. The best rooms are on higher floors, with huge floor-to-ceiling windows overlooking the hotel's own lush garden, a famed garden next door, or Tokyo Tower. This is a fine choice of hotel, despite its out-of-the-way location (mitigated by frequent complimentary shuttle service to Meguro Station).

1–1–50 Shirokanedai, Minato-ku, Tokyo 108-8640. (©) **800/325-3535** in the U.S. and Canada, or 03/3447-3111. Fax 03/3447-3133. www.miyakohotels.ne.jp/tokyo. 495 units. ¥28,350–¥44,100 single; ¥31,500–¥47,250 double; from ¥74,550 suite. Rates exclude service charge and hotel tax. AE, DC, MC, V. Station: Shirokanedai (4 min.), Shirokane-Takanawa (5 min.), or free shuttle from Meguro Station. **Amenities:** 3 restaurants; bar; lounge; concierge; health club w/25m indoor heated pool and spa (fee: ¥735); room service; free shuttle service to Meguro Station every 15 min. and Shinagawa Station (mornings only); dental/medical clinics. *In room:* A/C, TV, hair dryer, high-speed Internet, minibar.

The Strings by InterContinental Tokyo ★★★

The Strings has many things working in its favor, including its affiliations with InterContinental and ANA (All Nippon Airways) and its location just a short walk from Shinagawa Station, surrounded by a sea of office buildings. Guests—corporate CEOs during the week and well-heeled tourists on weekends—take express elevators to the 26th floor of an office high-rise, where the lobby soars seven stories in a light-filled atrium featuring slatted wood and a reflecting pond. In fact, natural sunlight, stone, wood, and water are dominant themes throughout public areas, in almost defiant rejection of the marble so favored by hotels in the past. Brown is the color of choice for contemporary, high-ceilinged rooms occupying the top six floors, with sofas and walnut furnishings that are low-slung so as not to obstruct city views; but the beds are higher than normal, so guests can see outside while resting.

Shinagawa East One Tower, 2–16–1 Konan, Minato-ku, Tokyo 108-8282. (©) **800/424-6835** in the U.S. and Canada, or 03/5783-1111. Fax 03/5783-1112. www.intercontinental-strings.jp. 206 units. ¥31,000–¥38,000 single or double; from ¥96,000 suite. Club Room ¥43,000–¥50,000 single or double. Rates exclude taxes and service charge. Children 11 and under stay free in parent's room. AE, DC, MC, V. Station: Shinagawa (Konan exit, 2 min.). **Amenities:** 2 restaurants; bar; lounge; babysitting; concierge; executive-level rooms; exercise room w/steam room; room service. *In room:* A/C, TV/DVD, CD player, hair dryer, high-speed Internet, minibar.

ODAIBA

Hotel Nikko Tokyo ★★

This is by far the most un-Tokyo-like hotel in the city. Located on Odaiba in Tokyo Bay with its convention center, shopping malls, and sightseeing attractions, this grand, elegant lodging is surrounded by parks and sea, which give it a relaxed, resort-evoking atmosphere. Billing itself as an "urban resort," it's especially popular with young well-to-do Japanese in search of an exotic weekend getaway. A curved facade assures waterfront views from most rooms, which have the added benefit of private balconies with two chairs. The most expensive rooms offer commanding views

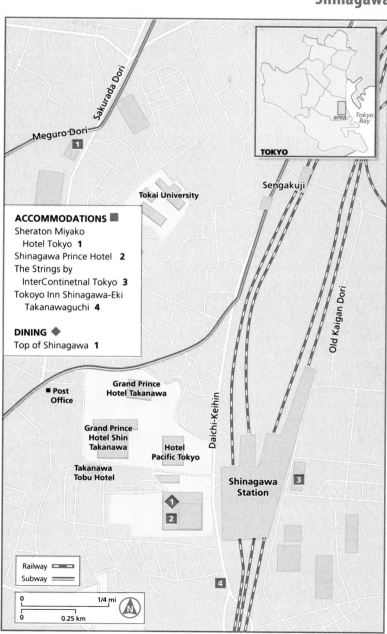

ACCOMMODATIONS ■

Sheraton Miyako
   Hotel Tokyo **1**
Shinagawa Prince Hotel **2**
The Strings by
   InterContinetnal Tokyo **3**
Tokoyo Inn Shinagawa-Eki
   Takanawaguchi **4**

DINING ◆

Top of Shinagawa **1**

Sakurada Dori

Meguro-Dori

TOKYO

area

Tokyo
Bay

Tokai University

Sengakuji

Old Kaigan Dori

■ Post
Office

Grand Prince
Hotel Takanawa

Grand Prince
Hotel Shin
Takanawa

Daichi-Keihin

Hotel
Pacific Tokyo

Takanawa
Tobu Hotel

Shinagawa
Station

Railway
Subway

0   1/4 mi
0   0.25 km

WHERE TO STAY

5

EXPENSIVE

of Tokyo Bay, Rainbow Bridge, and the city skyline (impressive at night); the least expensive rooms, smaller in size, face another hotel or the Maritime Museum and Haneda Airport across the bay. This is a great choice if you want to get away from the bustle of Tokyo, but the location can be a disadvantage; it's served only by the expensive monorail Yurikamome Line, the JR Saikyo Line to Shibuya, and the inconvenient Rinkai Line, all of which can be quite crowded on weekends, as can bus and taxi travel via the Rainbow Bridge or harbor tunnel.

1–9–1 Daiba, Minato-ku, Tokyo 135-8625. ℂ **800/645-5687** in the U.S. and Canada, or 03/5500-5500. Fax 03/5500-2525. www.hnt.co.jp. 453 units. ¥42,000–¥68,000 single or double; from ¥150,000 suite. Rates exclude hotel tax. AE, DC, MC, V. Station: Daiba (1 min.) or Tokyo Teleport Station (10 min., or free shuttle bus to hotel). **Amenities:** 8 restaurants; bar; lounge; babysitting; concierge; room service; spa w/indoor pool linked to outdoor heated tub, Jacuzzi, and sun terrace overlooking Rainbow Bridge (fee: ¥3,150 the 1st day; thereafter ¥1,000); free shuttle service from Tokyo Teleport Station every 15 min. *In room:* A/C, TV, hair dryer, high-speed Internet (fee: ¥2,600 per stay), minibar.

6 MODERATE

Prices of hotels in this section range from ¥16,000 to ¥32,000.

GINZA & SHIODOME

Courtyard by Marriott Tokyo Ginza Hotel ★   This small, classy, and personable hotel, located on Showa Dori, behind the Ginza Matsuzakaya department store and within easy walking distance of shopping and nightlife, attracts a foreign clientele as high as 60%, thanks mainly to its association with Marriott. Primarily a business hotel, it has limited facilities—you are clearly paying for location here. Rooms are contemporary but small, including small windows (there's nothing to see anyway) and small bathrooms. Be sure to pick up the hotel's sightseeing leaflets at the concierge's desk, which give information on the city's top attractions, opening hours, and how to reach them from the hotel.

6–14–10 Ginza, Chuo-ku, Tokyo 104-0061. ℂ **888/321-2211** in the U.S. and Canada, or 03/3546-0111. Fax 03/3546-8990. www.marriott.com/TYOCY. 206 units. ¥25,500 single; ¥30,000 double. AE, DC, MC, V. Station: Ginza (5 min.) or Higashi-Ginza (1 min.). **Amenities:** 2 restaurants; bar; lounge; concierge; executive-level rooms; exercise room; room service. *In room:* A/C, TV, hair dryer, high-speed Internet (fee: ¥1,000 for 24 hr.), minibar, iron.

Ginza Nikko Hotel Ⓞⓥⓔⓡⓡⓐⓣⓔⓓ   I'm glad this hotel underwent a much-needed renovation, but I'm shocked at its raised rack rates (even the desk clerk seemed embarrassed by them). It doesn't offer any of the facilities you'd expect at this price, but if you can snag a better price off the Internet, its Ginza location alone may make it worth it (that, essentially, is what you're paying for). Rates are based on room size, with the cheapest rooms very tiny indeed; even the largest tend to be cramped and dark because of surrounding taller buildings, but all have duvet-covered beds, the windows can be opened, and the tubs are deep.

Sotobori Dori, 8–4–21 Ginza, Chuo-ku, Tokyo 104-0061. ℂ **800/645-5687** in the U.S. and Canada, or 03/3571-4911. Fax 03/3571-8379. www.ginza-nikko-hotel.com. 112 units. ¥21,000–¥24,000 single; ¥32,000–¥42,000 double. AE, DC, MC, V. Station: Shimbashi, Ginza, or Hibiya (5 min.). **Amenities:** Restaurant. *In room:* A/C, TV, hair dryer, high-speed Internet, minibar.

Hotel Com's Ginza (formerly Mitsui Urban Hotel Ginza)   Because of its great location, convenient to the Ginza, Shimbashi, and Hibiya shopping and business centers, this attractive hotel caters mostly to business travelers, but tourists like it, too. The lobby,

| (Tips) **A Double or a Twin?**

For the sake of convenience, the price for two people in a room is listed as a "double" in this chapter. Japanese hotels, however, differentiate between rooms with a double bed or two twin beds, usually with different prices. Most hotels charge more for a twin room, but sometimes the opposite is true; if you're looking for a bargain, therefore, be sure to inquire prices for both. Note, too, that hotels usually have more twin rooms than doubles, for the simple reason that Japanese couples, used to their own futon, traditionally prefer twin beds.

on the second floor, has a friendly staff and an exceptionally long front desk, which hopefully translates into quicker service. Rooms, from the 3rd to 11th floors, are tiny but pleasant, with the more expensive rooms sporting comfortable leather chairs, good-size desks, espresso machines, a TV with headphones, and duvet-covered beds (but no closets). Note that the cheapest rooms (also without closets) don't have desks or space to unpack, a good example of what ¥25,000 buys in Tokyo. I suggest asking for a room away from the highway overpass beside the hotel.

8–6–15 Ginza, Chuo-ku, Tokyo 104-0061. (✆ **03/3572-4131.** Fax 03/3572-4254. www.granvista.co.jp. 267 units. ¥14,500–¥21,500 single; ¥25,000–¥34,800 double. AE, DC, MC, V. Station: Shimbashi (2 min.). **Amenities:** 3 restaurants; bar; lounge. In room: A/C, TV, hair dryer, high-speed Internet.

Hotel Gracery (formerly Ginza Washington Hotel) ★★ (**Value**) You can't beat the rates and prime Ginza location of this budget hotel, just off Chuo Dori behind Ginza Sapporo Lion. Part of a business hotel chain targeting downtown metropolises, it offers tiny rooms smartly decorated in beige and red, with duvet-covered beds, unit bathrooms, and clothes racks filling in for closets. Female travelers may opt for the Lady's Floor, which features wooden floors (in the belief that walking barefoot makes one feel more relaxed) and amenities geared toward women, while those looking for an upgrade can try the Executive Floor, with TVs that double as computers.

7–10–1 Ginza, Chuo-ku, Tokyo 104-0061. (✆ **03/6686-1000.** Fax 03/6858-1020. www.gracery-ginza.com. 270 units. ¥15,600–¥22,200 single; ¥22,200–¥24,200 double. AE, DC, MC, V. Station: Ginza (3 min.) or Shimbashi (7 min.). **Amenities:** Restaurant. In room: A/C, TV, fridge, hair dryer, high-speed Internet.

Hotel Monterey La Soeur ★ The Monterey chain targets female travelers with its feminine decor, and this hotel, designed by a woman, is no exception. A small, boutique-like property with a slight European ambience (note the display of Art Deco perfume bottles in the tiny lobby), it rises above the ordinary business hotel with small but comfortable rooms that demonstrate a woman's touch without being fussy. If rooms here are full, try the nearby sister **Hotel Monterey Ginza** (✆ **03/3544-7111**), with the same boutique-hotel concept and similar prices.

1–10–18 Ginza, Chuo-ku, Tokyo 104-0061. (✆ **03/3562-7111.** Fax 03/3562-6328. www.hotelmonterey.co.jp. 141 units. ¥18,000–¥21,000 single; ¥24,000–¥48,000 double. AE, DC, MC, V. Station: Ginza Itchome (2 min.) or Ginza (4 min.). **Amenities:** Restaurant. In room: A/C, TV, hair dryer, high-speed Internet, minibar.

Mitsui Garden Hotel Ginza Premier ★★ (**Finds**) This chic hotel is a notch above older Ginza properties and a good choice for business travelers looking for stylish rooms with good views. Located at the edge of Ginza close to Shimbashi, it occupies the upper floors of an office building (reception is on the 16th floor), with guest rooms providing

WHERE TO STAY

5

MODERATE

panoramic views of either Tokyo Bay or the Ginza with its glittering night views. As with most business hotels, rooms are mostly singles, with desks and love seats both placed strategically at windows to take advantage of the hotel's best feature. Even bathrooms take advantage of the views, with those in single rooms boasting windows that look out past the bedroom toward the views beyond (thankfully, the glass can be switched from transparent to opaque with the flip of a switch), while those in the most expensive double and twin rooms have windows that let you gaze upon Tokyo right from the tub.

8–13–1 Ginza, Chuo-ku, Tokyo 104-0061. ℂ **03/3543-1131.** Fax 03/3543-5531. www.gardenhotels.co.jp/ eng/ginza.html. 361units. ¥18,900–¥21,000 single; ¥25,200–¥34,650 double. Rates exclude hotel tax. AE, DC, MC, V. Station: Shimbasi (5 min.) or Ginza (7 min). **Amenities:** Restaurant; bar. *In room:* A/C, TV, fridge, hair dryer, high-speed Internet.

Park Hotel Tokyo ★★ (Finds) Occupying the top 10 floors of the building it shares with international media organizations, this hotel, well located downtown just a few minutes' walk from the Ginza, emulates the high-priced Strings by InterContinental Tokyo, but on a less grand, less expensive scale. Its lobby, on the 25th floor and decorated with large trees and dark woods in a theme of "nature and health," is bathed in the natural sunlight afforded by its 10-story atrium topped with an opaque ceiling. Complying with the hotel theme, restaurants follow a natural-foods concept, using organic ingredients. The front desk is one of the most dramatic I've seen, backed by nothing but great views of Tokyo Tower and the city. Rooms are simply decorated, with original art; they also provide views, the best of which can be found on the 30th floor and above facing Hama Rikyu Garden and Tokyo Bay or facing Tokyo Tower (and Mt. Fuji on clear winter days). The hotel even has a trained "pillow fitter," who can take your measurements and provide one made to fit, at no extra cost.

Shiodome Media Tower, 1–7–1 Higashi Shimbashi, Minato-ku, Tokyo 105-7227. ℂ **03/6252-1111.** Fax 03/6252-1001. www.parkhoteltokyo.com. 273 units. ¥21,000 single; ¥26,250–¥37,800 double. Rates exclude service charge and hotel tax. AE, DC, MC, V. Station: Shiodome (1 min.) or Shimbashi (8 min.). **Amenities:** 3 restaurants; bar; lounge; room service. *In room:* A/C, TV, hair dryer, high-speed Internet, minibar.

ASAKUSA

Asakusa View Hotel This upper-bracket, modern hotel in the Asakusa area looks out of place rising 28 stories above this famous district's older buildings. Still, it's a good place to stay if you want to be in Tokyo's old downtown but don't want to sacrifice any creature comforts. The midsize guest rooms are pleasant, with contemporary furnishings and bay windows that let in plenty of sunshine (and smaller windows that can be opened, a rarity in Tokyo). Rooms facing the front (east) have views over the famous Sensoji Temple, but those on the top floor facing west have views of Mount Fuji on clear days (mostly in winter).

Kokusai Dori, 3–17–1 Nishi-Asakusa, Taito-ku, Tokyo 111-8765. ℂ **03/3847-1111.** Fax 03/3842-2117. www.viewhotels.co.jp/asakusa. 337 units. ¥15,750–¥18,900 single; ¥31,500–¥34,650 double. Executive floor from ¥33,600 double. Rates exclude service charge and hotel tax. AE, DC, MC, V. Station: Tawaramachi (8 min.) or Tsukuba Express Asakusa (1 min.). **Amenities:** 4 restaurants; 2 bars; lounge; executive-level rooms; 20m indoor pool w/retractable roof (fee: ¥3,150); room service. *In room:* A/C, TV, hair dryer, high-speed Internet, minibar.

Hotel Sunroute Asakusa Located on Kokusai Dori, this modern, pleasant business hotel is a good choice for leisure travelers as well. Not only does it boast a good location near the sightseeing attractions of Asakusa, but it is also classier than most business hotels, with Miró reprints in the lobby and modern artwork in each guest room. Though

ACCOMMODATIONS ■
Asakusa View Hotel 4
Hotel Asakusa & Capsule 12
Hotel Sunroute Asakusa 11
Ryokan Asakusa Shigetsu 6
Ryokan Kamogawa 7
Sadachiyo Sukeroku-no-yado 3
Sakura Ryokan 1

NIGHTLIFE ●
Daimasu 8
Ichimon 2
Sky Room 18

DINING ◆
Chinya 9
Kamiya Bar 17
Komagata Dojo 13
La Ranarita Azumabashi 18
Mugitoro 14
Namiki Yabusoba 15
Sansado 16
Sometaro 10
Waentei-Kikko 5

WHERE TO STAY

5

MODERATE

small, the (mostly single) rooms come with all the comforts, with slightly larger beds and bathrooms than those found at most business hotels. Double rooms, however, are very small for two people, so you might want to spring for a more expensive twin-bedded room. The hotel's one coffee shop, a chain called Jonathan's serving both Japanese and Western food, is open daily 24 hours, a huge plus if you're suffering from jet lag.

1–8–5 Kaminarimon, Taito-ku, Tokyo 111-0034. © 03/3847-1511. Fax 03/3847-1509. www.sunroute-asakusa.co.jp. 120 units. ¥10,498–¥11,550 single; ¥16,275–¥21,000 double. Rates exclude hotel tax. AE, DC, MC, V. Station: Tawaramachi (1 min.) or Asakusa (8 min.). **Amenities:** Restaurant, free use of lobby computers. *In room:* A/C, TV, fridge, hair dryer, high-speed Internet.

Sadachiyo Sukeroku-no-yado ★★ Located in the heart of Asakusa's traditional neighborhood, this 65-year-old ryokan entices with its whitewashed walls, stone and paper lanterns, bamboo screens, traditionally clad staff, and rickshaw beside its front door. Inside, antiques line hallways that lead to tatami guest rooms. Even the public areas and cypress-and-granite public baths are Japanese-style, and Japanese dinners typical of old Tokyo are available, beginning at ¥7,000 (make dinner reservations when you reserve your room), making this inn a great choice for those wishing to experience a bit of old Edo in the modern metropolis.

2–20–1 Asakusa, Taito-ku, Tokyo 111-0032. © 03/3842-6431. Fax 03/3842-6433. www.sadachiyo.co.jp. 20 units. ¥14,000 single; ¥19,000 double. ¥1,000 extra Fri, Sat, and night before holidays. AE, MC, V. Station: Tawaramachi (8 min.) or Asakusa (15 min.) or Tsukuba Express Asakusa (3 min). **Amenities:** Restaurant. *In room:* A/C, TV, fridge.

SHINJUKU

Hotel Century Southern Tower ★★★ (Finds) This chic, modern hotel is located just southwest of Shinjuku Station and just a footbridge away from the huge Takashimaya Shinjuku shopping complex. Because it occupies the top floors of a sleek white building, it seems far removed from the hustle and bustle of Shinjuku below. Its 20th-floor lobby (with free wireless access), is simple and uncluttered and boasts almost surreal views of Tokyo stretching in the distance. Ask for a room on a higher floor. Rooms facing east or south are considered best (and are therefore pricier), especially at night when neon is in full regalia. Rooms facing west have views of Shinjuku's skyscrapers and, on clear days (mostly in winter), of Mount Fuji. A playful touch: Maps in each room outline the important buildings visible from your room.

2–2–1 Yoyogi, Shibuya-ku, Tokyo 151-8583. © 03/5354-0111. Fax 03/5354-0100. www.southerntower. co.jp. 375 units. ¥18,480–¥20,790 single; ¥27,720–¥34,650 double. Rates exclude hotel tax. AE, DC, MC, V. Station: Shinjuku (south exit, 3 min.). **Amenities:** 3 restaurants, including Tribecks (p. 145); lounge; executive-level rooms; exercise room. *In room:* A/C, TV, fridge, hair dryer, high-speed Internet.

AOYAMA

Tokyu Stay Aoyama Premier ★★ (Finds) Finally, a Tokyo hotel chain that provides discounts for guests staying longer than a week, plus in-room extras road-weary travelers can appreciate. All Tokyu Stay hotels offer rooms with kitchenettes (complete with cooking and dining utensils) in all but the cheapest singles (which come instead with microwaves but no hot plates), as well as combination washer/dryers and plenty of storage space, but this Aoyama property is the cream of the crop, with a central location convenient to both Aoyama and Roppongi and high floors affording expansive city views. Of course, these advantages also come with a price (note that only singles and twins are available; that is, no rooms with double beds). Cheaper alternatives include **Tokyu Stay Shibuya Shin-Minamiguchi**, 3–26–21 Shibuya (© **03/5466-0109**; station: Shibuya), and **Tokyu Stay Higashi-Ginza,** with a colorful location near the Tsukiji Fish Market at 4–11–5 Tsukiji (📞 **03/5551-0109;** station: Tsukiji or Tsukijijo).

2-27-18 Minami-Aoyama, Minato-ku, Tokyo 107-0062. 📞 **03/3497-0109.** Fax 03/3497-1091. www. tokyustay.co.jp. 170 units. ¥14,000–¥16,500 single; ¥24,500–¥26,500 double. Rates exclude hotel tax. Rates include breakfast. Discounts for stays longer than 6 nights. AE, DC, MC, V. Station: Gaienmae (exit 1a, 2 min.). **Amenities:** Restaurant. *In room:* A/C, TV/DVD, hair dryer, high-speed Internet, kitchenette (most rooms), trouser press.

SHIBUYA

In addition to the recommendation below, the **Tokyu Stay Shibuya Shin-Minamiguchi,** 3–26–21 Shibuya (📞 **03/5466-0109;** station: Shibuya) offers single rooms starting at ¥9,500 and twins and doubles at ¥17,900, most with small balconies; see above for a review of this hotel chain.

Shibuya Excel Hotel Tokyu ★★ Across from bustling Shibuya Station and connected by a footbridge and underground passage, this busy, modern hotel has an excellent location above Mark City shopping mall (reception is on the fifth floor). The hotel tries hard to appeal to everyone: For business travelers, "Excel" rooms offer use of a hallway computer free of charge (there are also coin-operated computers off the lobby for ¥100 for 10 min.); for female travelers, there are two women-only floors accessed by a special key and with special in-room amenities such as face cream and jewelry boxes. Rooms are available for visitors with disabilities, and 50% of all rooms are for nonsmokers. Ask for an upper-floor room facing Shinjuku (rooms run from the 7th to 24th floors); the night view is great.

1-12-2 Dogenzaka, Shibuya-ku, Tokyo 150-0043. 📞 **800/428-6598** in the U.S., or 03/5457-0109. Fax 03/5457-0309. www.tokyuhotelsjapan.com. 408 units. ¥21,945–¥23,100 single; ¥28,875–¥34,650 double. Rates exclude hotel tax. AE, DC, MC, V. Station: Shibuya (1 min. by footbridge). **Amenities:** 3 restaurants, including Abientot (p. 154), plus many more in Mark City mall; room service. *In room:* A/C, TV, hair dryer, high-speed Internet, minibar.

ROPPONGI & AKASAKA

the b roppongi ★★ (Finds) This boutique business hotel, within walking distance of both Roppongi and Akasaka, has more style than most business-oriented hotels, making it attractive to business and leisure travelers alike. Although it doesn't offer much in the way of facilities, rooms are functional and pleasant, with comfortable beds, good bedside reading lamps, and shades that can be drawn for added darkness. If you're claustrophobic, you might want to spring for a deluxe room (the most expensive of which has a kitchenette), as standard and superior choices are quite small. Free coffee in the lobby is a plus, not to mention that it's only a short walk from Roppongi's nighttime madness. Less convenient but also less expensive is **the b akasaka,** 7–6–13 Akasaka (📞 **03/3586-0811;** station: Akasaka).

3-9-8 Roppongi, Minato-ku, Tokyo 106-0032. 📞 **03/5412-0451.** Fax 03/5412-9353. www.ishinhotels. com. 65 units. ¥18,000–¥23,000 single; ¥22,000–¥43,000 double. Rates exclude hotel tax. AC, MC, V. Station: Roppongi (1 min.). **Amenities:** Restaurant, free use of lobby computer. *In room:* A/C, TV, fridge, hair dryer, high-speed Internet.

Hotel Ibis (Value) Once the only hotel in Roppongi, this is still as close as you can get to the night action of Roppongi, just a minute's walk away from Roppongi Crossing. It caters to businessmen and couples alike, who come to Roppongi's discos and don't make (or don't want to make) the last subway home. The lobby, with public computers available for accessing the Internet (¥500 for 25 min.), is on the fifth floor, with the guest rooms above. Tiny but comfortable, the rooms feature modern furniture and windows that you can open—though with a freeway nearby, I'm not sure you'd want to. The cheapest doubles come with semi-double-size beds, just slightly wider than a single. On the 13th floor is a reasonably priced Italian restaurant, Sabatini (p. 147), with views of the city.

7–14–4 Roppongi, Minato-ku, Tokyo 106-0032. ✆ **03/3403-4411.** Fax 03/3479-0609. www.ibis-hotel. com. 182 units. ¥13,382–¥16,023 single; ¥16,285–¥26,765 double. AE, DC, MC, V. Station: Roppongi (1 min.). **Amenities:** 2 restaurants, including Sabatini Roppongi (p. 162); room service. *In room:* A/C, TV, hair dryer, high-speed Internet, minibar.

Hotel Sunroute Akasaka   Smack dab in the middle of Akasaka's nightlife, this chain business hotel offers mostly tiny single rooms, with duvet-covered double-size beds taking up most of the space. There are also eight twins, but no doubles, though if two people want to squeeze into a single, they can do so for ¥16,500. What I like best are the large desks, complete with TVs that double as computers with keyboards guests can use free of charge (except for the computer games). There's no view, but rooms on the top floors facing the front have a bit more breathing space, overlooking rooftops of surrounding buildings.

Misuji Dori, 3–21–7 Akasaka, Minato-ku, Tokyo 107-0052. ✆ **03/3589-3610.** Fax 03/3589-3619. www. sunroute.jp. 91 units. ¥14,400 single; ¥19,500–¥22,500 double. Rates exclude hotel tax. AE, DC, MC, V. Station: Akasaka-mitsuke (1 min.), Nagatacho (5 min.), or Akasaka (10 min.). **Amenities:** Coffee shop. *In room:* A/C, TV w/keyboard, fridge, hair dryer, high-speed Internet.

Shiba Park Hotel ★ Finds   This small, older hotel in an out-of-the-way location offers enthusiastic, personalized service, a boon to those who don't like getting lost in the shuffle of larger hotels. Popular with budget-conscious overseas business travelers, it's a bit far from Roppongi nightlife but close to Shiba Park, Tokyo Tower, and Zozoji Temple. Rooms, in a main building and an annex across the street, are mostly small singles with just the basics. Those in the main building lack Internet connections, and single rooms also lack refrigerators. Higher-priced rooms, in the annex, are slightly larger and offer free high-speed Internet access, refrigerators, and huge bathrooms; here, too, are the Business Class Rooms (singles only), which add large desks, an ergonomic chair, and a fax/copy machine.

1–5–10 Shiba-koen, Minato-ku, Tokyo 105-0011. ✆ **03/3433-4141.** Fax 03/3433-4142. www.shibapark hotel.com. 382 units. ¥14,175–¥19,950 single; ¥21,525–¥32,025 double. Rates exclude service charge and hotel tax. AE, DC, MC, V. Station: Onarimon (2 min.), Daimon (4 min.), or Hamamatsucho (8 min.). **Amenities:** 5 restaurants; bar; room service; coin-op laundry room w/iron and ironing board; lobby computer (¥100 for 5 min.). *In room:* A/C, TV, fridge (some rooms), hair dryer, high-speed Internet (some rooms).

SHINAGAWA

Shinagawa Prince Hotel Kids   With four gleaming white buildings added at various stages (each with its own check-in), the Shinagawa Prince Hotel is the largest sleep factory in Japan. It's a virtual city within a city, with more than a dozen food and beverage outlets, a 10-screen cinema complex, a small aquarium with dolphin shows, a large sports center with nine indoor tennis courts, an 80-lane bowling center, an indoor golf practice center, a SEGA amusement/arcade-game center, indoor and outdoor pools, and a fitness center. It caters to Japanese businessmen on weekdays and to students and family vacationers on weekends and holidays. Rooms vary widely depending on which building you select: The 17-story East Tower has only very small singles, at the cheapest rates; the 17-story North Tower has singles, twins, and doubles in a medium price range; the

39-story Main Tower features renovated rooms (mostly twins) with the ubiquitous brown color scheme, Internet access in most rooms, and duvet-covered beds (those on the highest floors have views of Tokyo Bay); the upscale Annex, with only doubles, has smart-looking rooms, Internet connections, and correspondingly high prices. Assuming you can find it, be sure to have a drink or meal at the 39th-floor Top of Shinagawa (p. 264); its views of Tokyo Bay and the city are among the best in town. With its many diversions, this hotel is like a resort getaway, but is too big and busy for my taste.

4–10–30 Takanawa, Minato-ku, Tokyo 108-8611. ⊘ **800/542-8686** in the U.S. or Canada, or 03/3440-1111. Fax 03/3441-7092. www.princehotelsjapan.com. 3,679 units. ¥9,300–¥20,500 single; ¥16,300–¥36,000 double. Rates exclude hotel tax. AE, DC, MC, V. Station: Shinagawa (2 min.). **Amenities:** 13 restaurants, including a 24-hr. Internet cafe; bar; sports center (various fees charged: ¥1,050 for indoor pool, ¥1,100 for outdoor pool); children's day-care center; (fee: ¥2,000–¥2,500 for 1 hr.); cinema complex; aquarium. *In room:* A/C, TV, fridge, hair dryer, high-speed Internet (some rooms; fee: ¥1,050 for 24 hr.).

OTHER NEIGHBORHOODS
Hilltop Hotel (Yama-no-Ue Hotel) ★★ (Finds)
This is a delightfully old-fashioned, unpretentious (some might say dowdy) hotel with character. Built in 1937 and boasting an Art Deco facade, it was once the favorite haunt of writers, including novelist Mishima Yukio. Avoid the cheaper, more boring rooms in the 1954 annex, unless you spring for the higher-priced Art Septo rooms with their flower boxes outside the windows, black leather furnishings, LCD TV with CD player, and fancier bathrooms. Otherwise, rooms in the main building have such endearing, homey touches as fringed lampshades, doilies, cherrywood furniture (and mahogany desks), velvet curtains, vanity tables, and old-fashioned heaters with intricate grillwork. Some twins even combine a tatami area and shoji with beds; the most expensive twin overlooks its own Japanese garden. Don't be surprised if the reception desk remembers you by name. Although the Hilltop is not as centrally located or up-to-date as other hotels, nearby Meiji University brings lots of young people and liveliness to the area.

1–1 Surugadai, Kanda, Chiyoda-ku, Tokyo 101-0062. ⊘ **03/3293-2311.** Fax 03/3233-4567. www.yamanoue-hotel.co.jp. 74 units. ¥12,600–¥21,000 single; ¥23,100–¥33,600 double. Rates exclude service charge and hotel tax. AE, DC, MC, V. Station: Ochanomizu or Shin-Ochanomizu (8 min.) or Jimbocho (5 min.). **Amenities:** 7 restaurants; 3 bars; room service. *In room:* A/C, TV, hair dryer, high-speed Internet, minibar.

7 INEXPENSIVE

Hotels in this section charge less than ¥16,000. In addition to the recommendations here, **Tokyu Stay Higashi-Ginza,** which, despite its name, is actually near the Tsukiji Fish Market at 4–11–5 Tsukiji (⊘ **03/5551-0109;** station: Tsukijijo), offers single rooms starting at ¥9,400 and twins at ¥14,700, all with TVs with DVD/video players, microwaves, combination washers/dryers, and free Internet; all but the cheapest rooms also have kitchenettes. See p. 110 for a review of this hotel chain.

SHIODOME
Hotel Villa Fontaine Shiodome (Value)
If you're looking for a business hotel in a good location with comfortable rooms but absolutely no facilities or services (except a business center with computers you can use free of charge), this is a good choice. Situated in Shiodome, with direct access to the station and about a 5-minute walk from the Ginza, it is located in a marbled office building, its lobby separated from the ground-floor

A Note on Japanese Symbols

Many hotels, restaurants, and other establishments in Japan do not have signs giving their names in Roman (English-language) letters. Those that don't have the corresponding Japanese symbols listed within the review. So if you see Japanese *kanji*, or alphabet, within a review you'll know that business does *not* have an English sign, and you'll need to work a bit harder to find it.

entranceway and office elevators only by glass panels and a sliding door. Standard rooms, with twin, full, or double-size beds, are long and narrow and tend to be dark, while larger, more expensive Business Rooms have king-size beds and large working desks complete with computers. There are also Ladies Rooms, which come with bubble bath and other female-oriented toiletries, as well as Healing Rooms with foot massagers and humidifiers. Rooms face Hama Rikyu Garden or Tokyo Tower, but none are high enough for outstanding views. At these prices for this location, it's a good choice for travelers who only need a room.

1–9–2 Higashi-Shimbashi, Minato-ku, Tokyo 105-0021. ℂ **03/3569-2220** or 03/5339-1200 for reservations. Fax 03/3569-2111. www.hvf.jp. 497 units. ¥11,000–¥16,000 single; ¥14,000–¥18,000 double. Rates include buffet breakfast. AE, DC, MC, V. Station: Shiodome (2 min.). *In room:* A/C, TV, fridge, hair dryer, high-speed Internet.

ASAKUSA

Ryokan Asakusa Shigetsu ★ Ⓕⁱⁿᵈˢ   Whenever a foreigner living in Tokyo, soon to host first-time visitors to Japan, asks me to recommend a moderately priced ryokan in Tokyo, this is the one I most often suggest. It has a great location in Asakusa just off Nakamise Dori, a colorful, shop-lined pedestrian street leading to the famous Sensoji Temple—an area that gives you a feel for the older Japan. A member of the Japanese Inn Group, it represents the best of modern yet traditional Japanese design—simple yet elegant, with shoji, unadorned wood, and artwork throughout. Two public Japanese baths have views of the nearby five-story pagoda. There are eight Western-style rooms, but I prefer the 15 slightly more expensive Japanese-style tatami rooms, which include Japanese-style mirrors and comfortable chairs for those who don't like relaxing on the floor. This ryokan costs no more than a regular business hotel but has much more class. What a pity that the front-desk staff can be brusque.

1–31–11 Asakusa, Taito-ku, Tokyo 111-0032. ℂ **03/3843-2345.** Fax 03/3843-2348. www.shigetsu.com. 23 units. ¥7,700–¥9,450 single; ¥14,700–¥16,800 double. Japanese or Western breakfast ¥1,300 extra. AE, DC, MC, V. Station: Asakusa (4 min.). **Amenities:** Restaurant; lobby computer w/free high-speed Internet access. *In room:* A/C, TV, hair dryer, high-speed Internet, minibar.

Ryokan Kamogawa ★ Ⓚⁱᵈˢ   If Ryokan Asakusa Shigetsu (see above) is full, this is a very good alternative. Established in 1948 by the present owner's parents and located just off Nakamise Dori, it's small and personable, with a coffee shop (and computer you can use for free) and tatami rooms with shoji screens. Four room sizes are available, with and without private bathrooms. The largest sleep four to six persons, making them a good choice for families, as is the family bath you can use privately (reserve in advance). Note that the inn is usually fully booked in April and December, so if you hope to stay here then, book far ahead.

(Fun Facts) Capsule Hotels

There's another inexpensive lodging option in Tokyo, but it's not for the claustrophobic. So-called capsule hotels, which became popular in the early 1980s, are used primarily by Japanese businessmen who have spent an evening out drinking with fellow workers and missed the last train—a capsule hotel can be cheaper than a taxi ride home. They're located mostly near nightlife districts or major train stations. Sleeping units are small (no larger than a coffin) yet contain a bed and often a private TV, alarm clock, and radio; the units are usually stacked two deep in rows down a corridor, and the only thing separating you from your probably inebriated neighbor is a curtain. A cotton kimono and locker are provided, and facilities usually include public baths, sauna, and vending machines selling everything from beer to instant noodles to toothbrushes.

Most capsule hotels do not accept women. Two that do, with separate facilities for the sexes, are ①**Hotel Asakusa & Capsule,** 4–14–9 Kotobuki, Taito-ku (☎ **03/3847-4477,** but no English is spoken and no reservations are accepted; station: Tawaramachi, 3 min.), which is located about a 6-minute walk south of Asakusa's Sensoji Temple; and **Ace Inn,** 5–2 Katamachi, Shinjuku-ku (☎ **03/3350-6655;** www.ace-inn.jp; station: Akebonobashi, 1 min.), which caters mostly to backpacking foreigners with bare-bone capsules (no TV or radio here), plus a commons room, free Wi-Fi on most floors, a computer you can use for free for 30 minutes, and coin-operated showers and laundry facilities; note that the front doors are locked from 2 to 4:30am. Hotel Asakusa & Capsule starts at ¥2,400, while Ace Inn starts at ¥3,150. Otherwise, prices for most capsule inns average about ¥4,000 per night; credit cards are usually not accepted. Check-in is generally 4 or 5pm, and check-out is about 9:30 or 10am. Because everyone has to pack up and vacate cubicles during the day (coin lockers are generally available but may not be large enough for a big suitcase), curious foreigners may wish to experience a capsule hotel only as a 1-night stand. An even cheaper alternative if you're suddenly in need of a place to spend the night: springing for a night package on a private cubicle in an Internet/*manga* cafe.

1–30–10 Asakusa, Tokyo 111-0032. ☎ **03/3843-2681.** Fax 03/3843-2683. www.f-kamogawa.jp. 13 units (8 with bathroom). ¥6,400 single without bathroom, ¥6,800–¥8,200 single with bathroom; ¥12,600–¥13,000 double without bathroom, ¥12,800–¥14,600 double with bathroom; ¥19,200 triple without bathroom, ¥21,300 triple with bathroom. Rates include coffee and toast. Japanese breakfast ¥1,000 extra. Japanese dinner ¥4,000 extra (reservations required). AE, DC, MC, V. Station: Asakusa (3 min.). **Amenities:** Coffee shop. *In room:* A/C, TV, fridge, hair dryer (in rooms w/bathroom).

Sakura Ryokan (**Kids**   A member of the Japanese Inn and Welcome Inn groups, this family-run establishment, in a nondescript concrete building, is a combination business-tourist hotel and caters to both Japanese and foreign guests. It's located in Asakusa just northwest of the Kappabashi Dori and Kototoi Dori intersection, about a 12-minute walk from Sensoji Temple. The reception area, along with a computer you can use for free, is on the second floor, and the friendly owner speaks some English. Each spotless room comes with a sink and an alarm clock. Both Western- and Japanese-style units are available with or without private bathroom. The single rooms are quite spacious compared to those in business hotels. Two Japanese-style rooms with a bathroom connect, making them good for a family of up to six people.

2–6–2 Iriya, Taito-ku, Tokyo 110-0013. ℂ **03/3876-8118.** Fax 03/3873-9456. www.sakura-ryokan.com. 18 units (8 with bathroom). ¥5,500 single without bathroom, ¥6,600 single with bathroom; ¥9,600–¥10,000 double without bathroom, ¥10,500–¥11,000 double with bathroom; ¥13,200 triple without bathroom, ¥13,800 triple with bathroom. Japanese or Western breakfast ¥840 extra, Japanese dinner ¥1,680 extra (reservations required). AE, MC, V. Station: Iriya (exit 1 or 2, 6 min.). *In room:* A/C, TV.

UENO

Annex Katsutaro ★★ (Finds) This thoroughly modern concrete ryokan is a standout for its simple yet chic designs, spotless Japanese-style rooms (all with bathroom), and location—right in the heart of Yanaka with its old-fashioned neighborhood and about a 20-minute walk northwest of Ueno Park (the Keisei Skyliner from Narita Airport stops at nearby Nippori Station). The English-speaking proprietress, Arakawa-san, distributes a free map of the area showing the best way to get around and offers free coffee in the lobby. If the ryokan is full, don't let management talk you into taking a room in its much older main Ryokan Katsutaro; it's not nearly as nice as the annex.

3–8–4 Yanaka, Taito-ku, Tokyo 110-0001. ℂ **03/3828-2500.** Fax 03/3821-5400. www.katsutaro.com. 17 units. ¥6,300 single; ¥10,500–¥12,600 double; ¥14,700–¥16,800 triple. Continental breakfast ¥840 extra. MC, V. Station: Sendagi (2 min.) or Nippori (7 min.). **Amenities:** Lobby computers w/free high-speed Internet. *In room:* A/C, TV, fridge, hair dryer, high-speed Internet.

Homeikan ★★★ (Finds) Although a bit of a hike from Ueno Park (about 30 min.) and not as conveniently located as the other ryokan, this lovely place is my number-one choice if you want to experience an authentic, traditional ryokan in a traditional neighborhood. It consists of three separate buildings acquired over the last century by the present owner's grandfather. Homeikan, the main building (Honkan), was purchased almost 100 years ago; today it is listed as a "Tangible Cultural Property" and is used mainly by groups of students and seniors. Across the street is Daimachi Bekkan, built after World War II to serve as the family home. A beautiful, 31-room property, it boasts a private Japanese garden with a pond, public baths (including one open 24 hr.), and wood-inlaid and pebbled hallways leading to nicely detailed tatami rooms adorned with such features as gnarled wood trim and sitting alcoves, as well as simpler tatami rooms for budget travelers. This is where most foreigners stay. If you opt for meals, they will be served in your room in true ryokan fashion. The third building, Morikawa Bekkan, about a 5-minute walk away, was built as an inn about 45 years ago and, with 35 rooms, is the largest. Owner Koike-san, who speaks excellent English, points out that travelers who need the latest in creature comforts (including private bathrooms) should go elsewhere; those seeking a traditional ryokan experience, however, will not be disappointed.

5–10–5 Hongo, Bunkyo-ku, Tokyo 113-0033. ℂ **03/3811-1181** or 03/3811-1187. Fax 03/3811-1764. www.homeikan.com. 89 units (none with private bathroom). ¥6,825–¥7,350 single; ¥11,550–¥12,600 double; ¥14,175–¥15,750 triple. ¥525 more per person in peak season; ¥525 less per person in off season. Western- or Japanese-style breakfast ¥1,050; Japanese dinner ¥3,150 (not available 1st night of stay). AE, DC, MC, V. Station: Hongo Sanchome (8 min.) or Kasuga (5 min.). *In room:* A/C, TV, minibar.

Hotel Park Side Located across from the south end of Shinobazu Pond, this hotel has a good location near Ueno Park's many attractions and views of the park. Otherwise, it's rather ordinary, with clean, modern, and very small rooms with 19-inch LCD TVs plus keyboards so that they double as computers (the first 30 min. are free; thereafter it costs ¥1,000 until 11am the next day). Ask for a room on an upper floor facing the park,

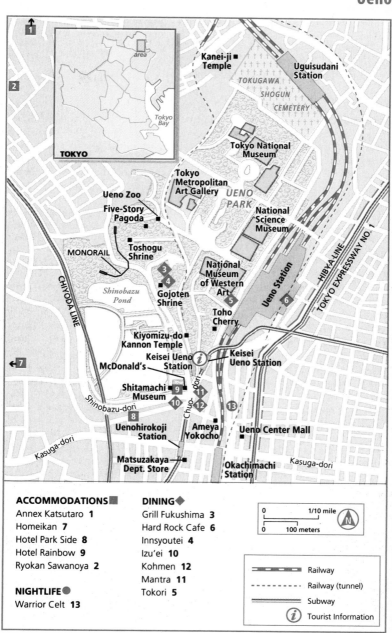

TOKYO

ACCOMMODATIONS■
Annex Katsutaro **1**
Homeikan **7**
Hotel Park Side **8**
Hotel Rainbow **9**
Ryokan Sawanoya **2**

NIGHTLIFE●
Warrior Celt **13**

DINING◆
Grill Fukushima **3**
Hard Rock Cafe **6**
Innsyoutei **4**
Izu'ei **10**
Kohmen **12**
Mantra **11**
Tokori **5**

0		1/10 mile
0	100 meters	

▬▬▬ ▬▬ Railway
– – – – – Railway (tunnel)
═══════ Subway
ⓘ Tourist Information

WHERE TO STAY

5

INEXPENSIVE

as that view is this hotel's best feature. I also like the sky lounge on the top (10th) floor for its panoramic views, inexpensive lunches, and evening cocktails with live piano music. Rooms with semi-double-size beds are available for ¥14,000 for couples on a budget, as well as Japanese-style tatami rooms, including one with its own open-air bath for ¥39,600 for two people.

2–11–18 Ueno, Taito-ku, Tokyo 110-0005. ℂ **03/3836-5711.** Fax 03/3831-6641. www.parkside.co.jp. 128 units. ¥9,200–¥10,800 single; ¥15,500–¥18,000 double. AE, MC, V. Station: Yushima (1 min.), Ueno Okachi-machi or Ueno Hirokoji (4 min.), or Ueno (6 min.). **Amenities:** 3 restaurants; lounge. *In room:* A/C, WebTV, fridge, hair dryer, high-speed Internet.

Hotel Rainbow ⟨**Value**⟩ Just minutes from Ueno Park's southern end, the Ameya Yokocho market, and Keisei Station with service to Narita Airport, this older, spotless hotel is tucked away inside a nondescript building next to McDonald's; you'll find the lobby on the third floor. In addition to single and twin rooms (all with double-size beds), it also offers a variety of double rooms at various prices, the best of which are corner rooms with views of Shinobazu Pond. It's a good choice for budget travelers in a colorful part of town.

2–13–1 Ueno, Taito-ku, Tokyo 110-0005. ℂ **03/3833-7716.** Fax 03/3833-7857. www.hotel-rainbow.jp. 48 units. ¥8,930 single; ¥10,500–¥14,700 double. AE, MC, V. Station: Ueno (5 min.). *In room:* A/C, TV, fridge, high-speed Internet.

Ryokan Sawanoya ★★ Although this family-run, smoke-free ryokan, open since 1949, looks relatively unexciting, it's delightfully located in a wonderful residential area of old Tokyo, northwest of Ueno Park and within walking distance of the park's attractions and Nezu Shrine. Upon your arrival, the owner, English-speaking Sawa-san, gives a short tour of the establishment before taking you to your tatami room; throughout the ryokan are written explanations to help the novice. The owner also gives you a map outlining places of interest in the vicinity. Several times a month, Sawa-san's son provides guests with a special treat—a traditional Japanese lion dance, free of charge. His daughter-in-law sometimes gives demonstrations of the tea ceremony. The nice public baths (which you can lock for privacy) have a view of a small garden, and there's free coffee and a computer in the lobby. This is a great place to stay thanks to Sawa-san's enthusiastic devotion to his neighborhood, which he readily imparts to his guests (he's even written a book about his years as an innkeeper). Highly recommended.

2–3–11 Yanaka, Taito-ku, Tokyo 110-0001. ℂ **03/3822-2251.** Fax 03/3822-2252. www.sawanoya.com. 12 units (2 with bathroom). ¥5,040–¥5,355 single without bathroom; ¥9,450 double without bathroom; ¥10,080 double with bathroom; ¥12,915 triple without bathroom, ¥14,490 triple with bathroom. Breakfast of toast and fried eggs ¥315 extra; Japanese breakfast ¥945 extra. AE, MC, V. Closed Dec 29–Jan 3. Station: Nezu (exit 1, 7 min.). **Amenities:** 2 rental bikes (¥200 for 1 day); lobby computer w/free high-speed Internet; ironing board, iron, and trouser press (on 3rd floor). *In room:* A/C, TV, hair dryer, high-speed Internet.

SHINJUKU

In addition to the recommendation here, there's the **Toyoko Inn Shinjuku Kabuki-cho,** 2–20–15 Kabuki-cho (ℂ **03/5155-1045;** station: Shinjuku), offering singles starting at ¥6,510 and twins and doubles at ¥9,240, along with such extras as free Japanese breakfast, free in-room Internet connections, and free use of lobby computers.

Tokyo International Hostel ⟨**Value**⟩ This spotless hostel, operated by the Tokyo Metropolitan Government and situated in a high-rise, is definitely the best place to stay in its price range—it offers fantastic Tokyo views. Even the public baths boast good views (especially at night). All beds are dormitory style, with two, four, or five bunk beds to a room. Rooms are very pleasant, with big windows, and each bed has its own curtain for privacy. If there are vacancies, you can stay longer than the normal 6-day maximum. In summer, it's a good idea to reserve about 2 months in advance (reservations can be made up to 3 months in advance). The hostel is closed from 10am to 3pm and locked at 11pm (lights out also at 11pm).

1–1 Kagura-kashi, Shinjuku-ku, Tokyo 162-0823. ☎ **03/3235-1107.** Fax 03/3264-4000. www.tokyo-ih.jp. 158 beds. ¥3,860 adult, ¥2,000 child. Breakfast ¥450; dinner ¥900. No youth-hostel card required; no age limit. AE, MC, V. Closed Dec 29–Jan 3. Station: Iidabashi (take the west exit from the JR station or the B2b subway exit, 2 min.). Reception is on the 18th floor of the Central Plaza Building. **Amenities:** Coin-op computer w/Internet access; communal kitchen. *In room:* A/C, no phone.

AKASAKA & ROPPONGI

Arca Torre (Value)

This smart-looking, 10-story property looks expensive from the outside but is actually a business hotel. It has a great location on Roppongi Dori, between Roppongi Crossing and Roppongi Hills, making it popular with both business types and tourists on a budget. Its (mostly single) rooms are small but cheerful, with flatscreen TVs and complimentary bottled water in the otherwise empty fridge. Rooms facing the back are quiet but face another building with glazed windows and are rather dark. If you opt for a room facing the front, spring for the more expensive rooms on higher floors above the freeway; otherwise, from the cheaper rooms on lower floors your view will be of cars and, at certain times of the day, traffic jams.

6-1-23 Roppongi, Minato-ku, Tokyo 106-0032. ☎ **03/3404-5111.** Fax 03/3404-5115. www.arktower. co.jp/arcatorre. 77 units. ¥11,550–¥13,650 single; ¥14,700–¥22,050 double. AE, DC, MC, V. Station: Roppongi (1 min.). **Amenities:** Restaurant. *In room:* A/C, TV, fridge, hair dryer, high-speed Internet.

Asia Center of Japan (Asia Kaikan) ★ (Value)

Great rates make this a top choice if you're looking for inexpensive Western-style accommodations in the center of town (it's wise to reserve months in advance). Everyone—from businessmen to students to travelers to foreigners teaching English—stays here; I know one teacher who lived here for years. Resembling a college dormitory, the Asia Center is popular with area office workers for its inexpensive cafeteria with outdoor seating. Accommodations are basic, with few frills, and in the singles you can almost reach out and touch all four walls. The cheapest doubles are actually single rooms with small, semi-double-size beds (not quite full size but larger than single/twin size). Avoid rooms on the ground floor—windows can open, and in Japan there are no screens. Tucked on a side street off Gaien-Higashi Dori not far from Aoyama Dori, the center is a 15-minute walk to the nightlife of Roppongi or Akasaka, one station away by subway.

8-10-32 Akasaka, Minato-ku, Tokyo 107-0052. ☎ **03/3402-6111.** Fax 03/3402-0738. www.asiacenter. or.jp. 173 units. ¥8,610–¥10,290 single; ¥12,390–¥18,690 double. AE, MC, V. Station: Aoyama-Itchome (exit 4, 5 min.) or Nogizaka (exit 3, 5 min.). **Amenities:** Restaurant; coin-op computer w/Internet access. *In room:* A/C, TV, fridge, hair dryer, Internet.

SHINAGAWA

Toyoko Inn Shinagawa-Eki Takanawaguchi ★ (Value)

I like this hotel chain for its clean functional rooms, complimentary breakfast of coffee and pastries served in the lobby, free in-room Internet connections and free wireless access in the lobby (and for those who don't have their own laptops, free use of computers in the lobby), and complimentary movies (only occasionally in English). Rooms are all very small singles and doubles. Other convenient Tokyo locations of this popular chain include **Toyoko Inn**

Shinjuku Kabuki-cho, 2–20–15 Kabuki-cho (✆ **03/5155-1045**; station: Shinjuku), and **Toyoko Inn Ikebukuro Kita-guchi No. 1,** 2–50–5 Ikebukuro (✆ **03/5960-1045**; station: Ikebukuro), both with single, double, and twin rooms at similar costs and the same freebies.

4-23-2 Takanawa, Minato-ku, Tokyo 108-0074. ✆ **03/3280-1045.** Fax 03/3280-1046. www.toyoko-inn. com. 180 units. ¥7,140 single; ¥9,240 double. Rates include continental breakfast. AE, DC, MC, V. Station: Shinagawa (3 min.). From JR station's Takanawa (west) exit, turn left. *In room:* A/C, TV, fridge, hair dryer, high-speed Internet.

IKEBUKURO

In addition to the recommendation below, the **Toyoko Inn Ikebukuro Kita-guchi No. 1,** 2–50–5 Ikebukuro (✆ **03/5960-1045**; station: Ikebukuro), offers singles for ¥7,140 and twins and doubles for ¥9,240, along with such extras as free Japanese breakfast, free in-room Internet connections, and free use of lobby computers.

Kimi Ryokan ★ Finds This has long been a Tokyo favorite for inexpensive Japanese-style lodging. Spotlessly clean and with such Japanese touches as sliding screens, a cypress public bath, flower arrangements in public spaces, and traditional Japanese music playing softly in the hallways, it caters almost exclusively to foreigners (mostly 20-somethings) and is so popular there's sometimes a waiting list. A bulletin board and newsletter list rental apartments and job opportunities (primarily teaching English); a lounge with cable TV is a favorite hangout and a good place to network with other travelers. Rooms are Japanese style, with single and the cheapest double the size of four and one-half tatami mats, and the larger double the size of six tatami mats (a single tatami measures 1m×1.8m/3¼ ft.×6 ft.). Note that there's a 1am curfew.

2-36-8 Ikebukuro, Toshima-ku, Tokyo 171-0014. ✆ **03/3971-3766.** Fax 03/3987-1326. www.kimi-ryokan. jp. 38 units (none with private bathroom). ¥4,500 single; ¥6,500–¥7,500 double; ¥10,000–¥12,000 triple. Prices exclude tax. No credit cards. Station: Ikebukuro (west exit; 7 min.). The police station (take the west exit from Ikebukuro Station and turn right) has maps that will guide you to Kimi; there's also an area map outside the station. *In room:* A/C, free Wi-Fi (some rooms).

OTHER NEIGHBORHOODS

Andon Ryokan Finds Located two subway stops north of Ueno on the Hibiya Line, this contemporary ryokan opened in 2003 and received an award by the Architectural Institute of Japan 2 years later. Its facade is a sheet of milky glass (particularly stunning at night, when light pouring out of individual guest rooms gives it a lanternlike glow), while its interior sports black walls and mesh. Antiques from the owner's own collection, however, fill nooks and crannies, and rooms (all nonsmoking) are traditional tatami style. The staff speaks English, there's a small inviting lounge on the ground floor offering free tea and coffee and use of a computer, a tea ceremony is held three times a month (fee: ¥500), and the top-floor Jacuzzi can be reserved for free. There's a lift for luggage, but you'll have to take the stairs in this four-story ryokan.

2-34-10 Nihonzutsumi, Taito-ku, Tokyo 111-0021. ✆ **03/3873-8611.** Fax 03/3873-8612. www.andon. co.jp. 24 units (none with private bathroom). ¥8,190 single or double. MC, V. Station: Minowa (exit 3, 5 min.). Turn left, then cross and turn left at Meiji Dori; look for the Andon sign, where you'll take a right and then a left. **Amenities:** Jacuzzi, lounge computer w/free high-speed Internet; communal kitchen. *In room:* A/C, TV/DVD player and DVD library, high-speed Internet.

The Hotel Bellegrande ★ This hotel is outside the Yamanote loop line, east of the Sumida River, but it's just minutes from central Tokyo via the JR Sobu line and the Oedo subway line. Sumo fans will appreciate its location right next to the sumo stadium (reserve far in advance if you're here for one of Tokyo's three annual tournaments), and with many sumo training stables nearby, you're more likely to catch sight of the giant athletes here than anywhere else in town. Here, too, is the Edo-Tokyo Museum. Otherwise, the hotel's best features are its large balconies, which help mitigate the small size of its rather basic rooms. For the best views, ask for a room facing the front on a high floor.

2–19–1 Ryogoku, Sumida-ku, Tokyo 130-0026. ℃ **03/3631-8111.** Fax 03/3631-8112. www.hotel-bellgrande. co.jp. 150 units. ¥9,450 single; ¥14,700–¥42,000 double. AE, DC, MC, V. Station: Ryogoku (1 min.). **Amenities:** 3 restaurants; bar. *In room:* A/C, TV, hair dryer, fridge, high-speed Internet.

Sakura Hotel Value   Popular with backpackers, this inexpensive property in central Tokyo offers dormitory beds and sparsely furnished tiny singles, doubles (with semi-double-size beds), and twins with bunk beds. Although rooms are all designated non-smoking, not everyone follows the rules, so you might want to inspect before signing on. The Sakura is best if you just need a place to crash for the night; for longer stays of a month or more, contact Sakura House (℃ **03/5330-5250;** www.sakura-house.com) for inexpensive apartments and guesthouses all over Tokyo.

2–21–4 Kanda-Jimbocho, Chiyoda-ku, Tokyo 101-0051. ℃ **03/3261-3939.** Fax 03/3264-2777. www. sakura-hotel.co.jp. 43 units (none with private bathroom). ¥6,090–¥7,140 single; ¥8,200–¥8,400 double; ¥3,150–¥3,780 dormitory. AE, DC, MC, V. Station: Jimbocho (exit A6, 2 min.). Turn right and take the 2nd right. **Amenities:** 24-hr. Internet cafe. *In room:* A/C, TV, high-speed Internet (free Wi-Fi available on lower floors).

Where to Dine

From stand-up noodle shops and pizzerias to sushi bars and exclusive *kaiseki* restaurants serving elaborate multicourse meals, restaurants in Tokyo number at least 80,000—which gives you some idea of how fond the Japanese are of eating out. In a city where apartments are so small and cramped that entertaining at home is almost unheard of, restaurants serve as places for socializing, meeting friends, and wooing business associates—as well as great excuses for drinking a lot of beer, sake, wine, and whiskey.

1 BEST BETS FOR DINING

- **Best Spot for a Romantic Dinner:** Great Pacific Rim fusion cuisine, attentive yet unobtrusive service, dim lighting in a comfortable setting, a year-round open deck for after-dinner drinks, and a row of massage chairs make **Casita,** 5–51–8 Jingumae (© **03/5485-7353**), a perfect rendezvous for a romantic evening. See p. 147.
- **Best Spot for a Business Lunch:** Join the other movers and shakers at **Nobu Tokyo,** 4–1–28 Toronomon (© **03/5733-0070**), located near the U.S. embassy and offering something for everyone with its Pacific Rim fusion cuisine. See p. 167.
- **Best Spot for a Celebration:** Peter, 1–8–1 Yurakucho (© **03/6270-2763**), has all the makings of a joyous occasion: great food, a theatrical setting, excellent service, and views of surrounding Hibiya. See p. 131.
- **Best View:** Located 52 stories above the city, **Mado Lounge,** 6–10–1 Roppongi (© **03/3470-0052**), boasts stunning views of an endless Tokyo. Because it's located in the Mori Art Museum, you have to pay the museum's admission to dine here, but the Italian/French cuisine is reasonably priced and the museum's cutting-edge exhibitions and great views are a bonus. See p. 165.
- **Best Late-Night Dining:** Gonpachi, with several convenient locations around Tokyo, has made a name for itself by offering inexpensive Japanese fare daily until 3:30 or 5am, depending on the location. Ditto for **La Boheme** serving Italian food; **Zest Cantina,** which serves Mexican food; and **Monsoon,** offering Asian dishes, all under the same ownership and with the same hours. See p. 162, 134, 157, and 135.
- **Best Theatrics:** There's never a dull moment at **Inakaya,** 4–10–11 Roppongi (© **03/5775-1012**), with waiters shouting out orders, U-shaped counter seating, mountains of food, and kneeling cooks laboring over charcoal grills. See p. 158.
- **Best Weekend Brunch:** The weekend brunch at **New York Grill,** 3–7–1–2 Shinjuku (© **03/5322-1234**), where you'll be treated to breathtaking views, is so popular there's practically a waiting list. See p. 143.
- **Best Buffets: The Imperial Viking Sal,** on the 17th floor of the Imperial Hotel, 1–1–1 Uchisaiwai-cho (© **03/3504-1111**), with views of the Ginza and Hibiya, was a pioneer of all-you-can-eat buffets in Japan. After 40-some years, it still offers great lunch and dinner buffets with international selections. See p. 132.

Notes on Dining

The restaurants listed below are organized first by neighborhood, then by price category.

- Note that the **5% consumption tax** is included in menu prices. However, many first-class restaurants, as well as hotel restaurants, will add a **10% to 15% service charge** to the bill. Unless otherwise stated, the prices given below include the tax but not the service charge.
- Restaurants that have no signs in English letters are preceded by a **numbered icon,** which is keyed to a list of *kanji* **(Japanese writing symbols)** in Chapter 14.
- Finally, keep in mind that the **last order** is taken at least 30 minutes before the restaurant's actual closing time, sometimes even an hour before closing at the more exclusive restaurants.

- **Best Vegetarian:** Everything I've had at **Yasaiya Mei,** 4–12–10 Jingumae (✆ **03/5785-0606**), which specializes in fresh, seasonal vegetables, has been delicious, but the wild plant tempura is my absolute favorite. See p. 148.
- **Best Traditional Decor:** With its beautifully landscaped Japanese garden and 200-year-old farmhouse imported from the Japanese Alps, **Tokyo Shiba Toufuya Ukai,** 4–4–13 Shibakoen (✆ **03/3436-1028**), specializing in classic tofu cuisine, seems like it's in the countryside rather than the middle of Tokyo. See p. 160.
- **Best Traditional Music:** Located in the traditional Asakusa neighborhood in a Japanese-style wooden house, **Waentei-Kikko,** 2–2–13 Asakusa (✆ **03/5828-8833**), offers *obento* lunchboxes and kaiseki meals, along with *shamisen* and other traditional music performances. See p. 140.

2 RESTAURANT ESSENTIALS

ORDERING

The biggest problem facing the hungry foreigner in Tokyo is ordering a meal in a restaurant without an English-language menu. I've tried to alleviate this problem somewhat by giving sample dishes and prices for recommended restaurants. I've also noted which restaurants have English-language menus.

One aid to simplified ordering is the common use of **plastic-food models** in glass display cases either outside or just inside the front door of many restaurants. Sushi, tempura, daily specials, spaghetti—they're all there in mouthwatering plastic replicas, along with the corresponding prices. Decide what you want and point it out to your waiter.

Unfortunately, not all restaurants in Japan have plastic display cases, especially the more exclusive or traditional ones. In fact, you'll miss a lot of Tokyo's best cuisine if you restrict yourself to eating only at those with displays. If there's no display from which to choose, look at the menu to see whether there are pictures of the available dishes, or look at what people around you are eating and order what looks best. An alternative is to order the *teishoku*, or daily special meal (also called "set course" or simply "course," especially in restaurants serving Western food); these are fixed-price meals that consist of a main dish and several side dishes, often including soup, rice, and Japanese pickles. Although most restaurants have special set courses for dinner as well, lunch is the usual time for the teishoku, generally from 11 or 11:30am to about 2pm.

Once you've decided what you want to eat, flag down a waiter or waitress; waitstaff will not hover around your table waiting for you to order, but come only when you summon them. In any case, in many restaurants there are no assigned servers to certain tables; rather, servers are multitaskers, so don't be shy about stopping anyone who passes by.

HOURS

Most Japanese restaurants (that is, restaurants serving Japanese food) hang a rod of *noren* (split curtains) outside their front door to signal they are open for business. Otherwise, restaurants in Tokyo are usually open from about 11am to 10 or 11pm. Of course, some establishments close earlier, while others stay open past midnight; many close for a few hours in the afternoon. Try to avoid the lunchtime rush from noon to 1pm.

Keep in mind that the closing time posted for most restaurants is exactly that—everyone is expected to pay his or her bill and leave. A general rule of thumb is that the last order is taken at least a half-hour before closing time, sometimes an hour or more for kaiseki restaurants. To be on the safe side, therefore, try to arrive at least an hour before closing time so that you have time to relax and enjoy your meal.

HOW TO DINE IN TOKYO WITHOUT SPENDING A FORTUNE

Tokyo is one of the most expensive cities in the world. During your first few days here, money will seem to flow out of your pockets like water. (Many people become convinced they must have lost it somehow.) Here are some invaluable dining tips on getting the most for your money.

SET LUNCHES I know people in Tokyo who claim they haven't cooked in years—and they're not millionaires. They simply take advantage of one of the best deals in Tokyo—the fixed-price lunch, usually available from 11am to 2pm. Called a *teishoku* in a Japanese restaurant, a fixed-price meal is likely to include soup, perhaps an appetizer like sashimi, a main dish such as tempura or whatever the restaurant specializes in, pickled vegetables, rice, and tea. In restaurants serving Western food, the fixed-price lunch is variously referred to as a set lunch, *seto coursu*, or simply *coursu*, and usually includes an appetizer, a main course with one or two side dishes, coffee or tea, and sometimes dessert. Even restaurants listed under **Very Expensive** (where you'd otherwise spend at least ¥13,000 or more per person for dinner, excluding drinks) and **Expensive** (where you can expect to pay ¥9,000–¥13,000) usually offer set-lunch menus, allowing you to dine in style at very reasonable prices. To keep costs down, therefore, try having your biggest meal at lunch, avoiding, if possible, the noon-to-1pm weekday crush when Tokyo's army of office workers floods area restaurants. Because the Japanese tend to order fixed-price meals rather than a la carte, set dinners are also usually available (though they're not as cheap as set lunches). All-you-can-eat buffets (called *viking* in Japanese, probably because Japan's first buffet was in a restaurant called Viking in the Imperial Hotel), offered by many hotel restaurants, are also bargains for big appetites.

So many of Tokyo's good restaurants fall into the **Moderate** category that it's tempting simply to eat your way through the city—and the range of cuisines is so great you could eat something different at each meal. Dinner in this category will average ¥4,000 to ¥9,000, lunch likely half as much.

Many of Tokyo's most colorful, noisy, and popular restaurants fall into the **Inexpensive** category, where meals usually go for less than ¥4,000; many offer meals for less than ¥2,000 and lunches for ¥1,000 or less. The city's huge working population heads to these places to catch a quick lunch or to socialize with friends after hours. Because I can cover only a limited number of cheap restaurants in each neighborhood, ask your concierge or hotel manager for recommendations; a great, little place may be just around the corner.

COFFEE & BREAKFAST Because prices are markedly different here (steeper), a bit of readjustment in thinking and habits is necessary. Coffee, for example, is something of a luxury, and some Japanese are astonished at the thought of drinking four or five cups a day. Traditional coffee shops (as opposed to imports such as Starbucks) offer what's called "morning service" until 10 or 11am; it generally consists of a cup of coffee, a small salad, a boiled egg, and the thickest slice of toast you've ever seen for about ¥650. That's a real bargain when you consider that just one cup of coffee can cost ¥250 to ¥500, depending on where you order it. (With the exception of hotel buffets, it's rare to find a bottomless cup in Japan.) For a coffee break later in the day, look for an inexpensive chain such as Doutour, Excelsior, or Pronto. Starbucks has also conquered Japan, with more than 700 branches throughout the country (and probably a good deal more by the time you read this).

If you like starting the day with a big meal, hotel buffet breakfasts are a good way to go, with the best offering an array of Western and Japanese selections. The cheapest ones, however, aren't very tasty, consisting almost invariably of scrambled eggs, processed ham, lettuce, miso soup, rice, and pickled vegetables. If you're on a strict budget, therefore, you're best off buying fruit, snacks, and juice at the grocery store.

CHEAP EATS Inexpensive restaurants can be found in department stores (often an entire floor will be devoted to restaurants, most with plastic-food displays), in underground shopping arcades, in nightlife districts, and in and around train and subway stations. Look for **yakitori-ya** (evening drinking establishments that sell skewered meats and vegetables), **noodle** and **ramen shops, coffee shops** (which often offer inexpensive pastries and sandwiches), and **conveyor-belt sushi bars,** where you reach out and take the plates that interest you. Tokyo also has American fast-food chains, such as McDonald's (where Big Macs cost about ¥320), Wendy's, and KFC, as well as Japanese chains— Freshness Burger and First Kitchen among them—that sell hamburgers.

There are also many excellent yet inexpensive **French bistros, Italian trattorie,** and **ethnic restaurants,** particularly those serving Indian, Chinese, Thai, and other Asian cuisines. **Hotel restaurants** are good bargains for inexpensive set lunches and buffets. Finally, remember to check the nightlife section in chapter 10 for suggestions on **inexpensive drinking places** that serve food.

PREPARED FOODS You can save even more money by avoiding restaurants altogether. There are all kinds of prepared foods you can buy; some are complete meals, perfect for picnics in the park or right in your hotel room.

Perhaps the best known is the *obento,* or box lunch, commonly sold in major train stations, in food sections of department stores, and at counter windows of tiny shops throughout Tokyo. Costing usually between ¥800 and ¥1,500, the basic obento contains a piece of meat (generally fish or chicken), various side dishes, rice, and pickled vegetables. Sushi box lunches are also readily available.

My favorite places to shop for prepared foods are **department stores.** Located in basements, these enormous food and produce sections hearken back to Japanese markets of yore, with vendors yelling out their wares and crowds of housewives deciding on the evening's dinner. Different counters specialize in different items—tempura, yakitori, eel, Japanese pickles, cooked fish, sushi, salads, vegetables, and desserts. Almost the entire spectrum of Japanese cuisine is available, and numerous samples are available (some travelers have been known to "dine" in department-store basements for free). What I love about buying my dinner in a department store is that I can compose my own meal exactly as I wish—perhaps some sushi, some mountain vegetables, boiled soybeans, maybe even Chinese food—in combinations never available in most restaurants. Obento box meals are also available, and some department stores (such as Isetan in Shinjuku) have sit-down counters for meals of tempura and other fare on the perimeter of their food floor. In any case, you can eat for less than ¥1,200, and there's nothing like milling with Japanese housewives to make you feel like one of the locals. Though not as colorful, 24-hour convenience stores also sell packaged foods, including sandwiches and obento, as do local grocery stores such as Peacock and the budget-friendly Lawson 100.

Street-side stalls, called *yatai,* are also good sources of inexpensive meals. These restaurants-on-wheels sell a variety of foods, including *oden* (fish cakes), *yakitori* (skewered barbecued chicken), and *yakisoba* (fried noodles), as well as sake and beer. A popular sight at festivals, they otherwise appear mostly at night, illuminated by a single lantern or a string of lights, and many have a counter with stools as well, protected in winter by a tarp wall. These can be great places for rubbing elbows with the locals. Sadly, traditional pushcarts are slowly being replaced by motorized vans, which are not nearly as romantic and don't offer seating.

3 RESTAURANTS BY CUISINE

American
Good Honest Grub (Shibuya, $, p. 156)
Hard Rock Cafe (Roppongi, Ueno, $, p. 163)
Kua' Aina ★ (Around Tokyo Station, Aoyama, Shibuya, Odaiba, $, p. 151)
New York Grill ★★★ (Shinjuku, $$$$, p. 143)
Roti Roppongi ★ (Roppongi, $, p. 165)
Wolfgang Puck Cafe (Roppongi, Akasaka, $$, p. 168)
Wolfgang Puck Express (Harajuku, $, p. 153)
Zip Zap (Harajuku, $, p. 153)

Chinese
Daini's Table ★★ (Aoyama, $$, p. 147)
Din Tai Fung (Shinjuku, $, p. 145)

Continental
Tribecks (Shinjuku, $$, p. 145)

Desserts
Tatsutano ★ (Ginza, $, p. 136)

Dojo
Komagata Dojo ★ (Asakusa, $$, p. 139)

Donburi/Kamameshi (Rice Casseroles)
Hayashi ★★★ (Akasaka, $, p. 144)
Tatsutano ★ (Ginza, $, p. 136)
Torigin (Roppongi, $, p. 165)

Key to Abbreviations: $$$$ = Very Expensive $$$ = Expensive $$ = Moderate $ = Inexpensive

Eel

Izu'ei (Ueno, $$, p. 142)
Kandagawa ★ (Kanda, $$, p. 169)

French

Abientot ★ (Shibuya, $$, p. 154)
Aux Amis Tokyo ★ (Around Tokyo
 Station, $$, p. 136)
Aux Bacchanales (Akasaka, Ginza, $$,
 p. 167)
Grill Fukushima ★ (Ueno, $$$,
 p. 142)
La Table de Joël Robuchon ★★
 (Ebisu, $$$, p. 156)
La Tour d'Argent ★★ (Akasaka,
 $$$$, p. 165)
L'Osier ★★★ (Ginza, $$$$, p. 130)
Mado Lounge ★ (Roppongi, $,
 p. 165)

Fugu (Blowfish)

Tarafuku (Ginza, $$, p. 133)
Tentake (Tsukiji, $$, p. 137)

Fusion

Casita ★★★ (Aoyama, $$$, p. 147)
Kihachi ★★ (Ginza, $$$, p. 130)
Legato ★★ (Shibuya, $$, p. 154)
Limapuluh ★★ (Aoyama, $, p. 151)
Miyashita (Harajuku, $$, p. 148)
Nobu Tokyo ★★★ (Akasaka, $$$,
 p. 167)
Selan (Aoyama, $$, p. 148)
Wolfgang Puck Cafe (Roppongi, Aka-
 saka, $$, p. 168)

Gyoza

Harajuku Gyoza Lou ★ (Harajuku, $,
 p. 150)
Ippudo ★ (Ebisu, $, p. 157)

Indian

Mantra (Ueno, $, p. 143)

International

Fungo ★ (Shinjuku, $, p. 146)
The Imperial Viking Sal ★ (Hibiya,
 $$, p. 132)
Kitchen Five ★ (Roppongi, $, p. 164)

Meal Muji (Ginza, $, p. 133)
Peter ★★★ (Hibiya, $$$, p. 131)
The Sky (Akasaka, $$, p. 168)
Taimeiken (Nihombashi, $, p. 137)
Toriyoshi (Harajuku, Aoyama, Rop-
 pongi, Shinjuku, $, p. 152)

Italian

Fungo ★ (Shinjuku, $, p. 146)
La Boheme (Aoyama, Ginza, Hara-
 juku, Roppongi, Nishi Azabu,
 Odaiba, Shibuya, $, p. 134)
La Ranarita Azumabashi ★ (Asakusa,
 $$, p. 139)
Legato ★★ (Shibuya, $$, p. 154)
Mado Lounge ★ (Roppongi, $,
 p. 165)
Pizzeria Sabatini (Aoyama, $, p. 152)
Ristorante Il Bianco (Roppongi, $$,
 p. 161)
Ristorante Sabatini di Firenze ★★
 (Ginza, $$$, p. 131)
Sabatini ★ (Aoyama, $$$, p. 147)
Sabatini Roppongi ★ (Roppongi, $$,
 p. 162)
Selan (Aoyama, $$, p. 148)
Taimeiken (Nihombashi, $, p. 137)
Venire Venire (Harajuku, $, p. 152)
ViVi La Verde (Ebisu, $$, p. 157)

Japanese (Varied)

Akasaka Jidaiya (Akasaka, $$, p. 167)
Andy's Shin-Hinomoto (Hibiya, $,
 p. 134)
daidaiya ★ (Akasaka, Shinjuku, $$,
 p. 168)
Donto ★★ (Hibiya, Shimbashi, Shin-
 juku, $$, p. 131)
Gonpachi ★★ (Ginza, Nishi Azabu,
 Shibuya, Odaiba, $, p. 162)
Hakkaku ★ (Shinjuku, $, p. 146)
Hinokizaka ★★★ (Roppongi, $$$$,
 p. 158)
Hiroba (Aoyama, $, p. 151)
Honoji ★ (Roppongi, $, p. 163)
Kamiya Bar (Asakusa, $, p. 140)
Ninja ★ (Akasaka, $$$, p. 166)
The Sky (Akasaka, $$, p. 168)

Tengu (Shibuya, Shinjuku, $, p. 156)
Tokyo Catering (Shinjuku, $, p. 146)
Toriyoshi (Harajuku, Aoyama, Shinjuku, $, p. 152)
Yasaiya Mei★ (Aoyama, $$, p. 148)

Kaiseki/Obento

Ginza Daimasu (Ginza, $$, p. 132)
Hinokizaka★★★ (Roppongi, $$$$, p. 158)
Innsyoutei★ (Ueno, $$, p. 142)
Kakiden★★ (Shinjuku, $$$, p. 144)
Mikura (Shibuya, $$, p. 153)
Mugitoro (Asakusa, $$, p. 139)
Rangetsu (Ginza, $$, p. 132)
Tamura★ (Tsukiji, $$$, p. 137)
Waentei-Kikko★★★ (Asakusa, $$, p. 140)

Korean Barbecue

Gyu-Kaku (Akasaka, Roppongi, $, p. 169)
Tokori (Ueno, $$, p. 142)

Kushikatsu

Kushinobo (Roppongi, Shinjuku, $$, p. 161)

Mexican

Fonda de la Madrugada (Harajuku, $, p. 150)
La Colina★ (Roppongi, $$, p. 161)
La Fiesta (Roppongi, $, p. 164)
Zest Cantina (Ebisu, Ginza, Odaiba, Shibuya, $, p. 157)

Noodles (Japanese)

Kanda Yabusoba★ (Kanda, $, p. 170)
Namiki Yabusoba★ (Asakusa, $, p. 140)

Nouvelle Japanese

daidaiya★ (Akasaka, Shinjuku, $$, p. 168)
Ichioku★ (Roppongi, $, p. 163)
Mominoki House★ (Harajuku, $, p. 152)
Nobu Tokyo★★★ (Akasaka, $$$, p. 167)
Zipangu (Shimbashi, $$, p. 133)

Okonomiyaki

Botejyu (Shibuya, $, p. 154)
Sometaro★ (Asakusa, Akasaka, Shimbashi, $, p. 141)
Yai Yai (Harajuku, $, p. 153)

Pizza

Pizza Salvatore Cuomo (Akasaka, $, p. 169)
Pizzeria Sabatini (Aoyama, $, p. 152)
Shakey's (Harajuku, Shinjuku, Ikebukuro, $, p. 146)

Ramen

Ippudo★ (Ebisu, $, p. 157)
Kohmen (Roppongi, Ueno, Harajuku, Ebisu, $, p. 164)

Robatayaki (Japanese Grill)

Hakkaku★ (Shinjuku, $, p. 146)
Hayashi★★★ (Akasaka, $$$, p. 166)
Hayashi★★ (Shinjuku, $$, p. 144)
Inakaya★★ (Roppongi, Ginza, $$$$, p. 158)
Ohmatsuya★★ (Ginza, $$, p. 132)

Shabu-Shabu

Chinya★ (Asakusa, $$, p. 138)
Rangetsu (Ginza, $$, p. 132)
Shabusen★ (Ginza, $, p. 135)

Southeast Asian

Monsoon (Ginza, Aoyama, Shibuya, Ebisu, Nishi Azabu, Odaiba, $, p. 135)

Sukiyaki

Chinya★ (Asakusa, $$, p. 138)
Rangetsu (Ginza, $$, p. 132)

Sushi

Edogin (Tsukiji, $, p. 138)
Fukusuke (Ginza, $, p. 134)
Fukuzushi★★ (Roppongi, $$$, p. 160)
Ginzo (Akihabara, $, p. 170)
Heirokuzushi (Harajuku, $, p. 150)
Itamae Sushi (Ginza, $, p. 134)
Sushi Dai★ (Tsukiji, $, p. 138)

Sushiko ★★★ (around Tokyo Station, Ginza, $$$$, p. 130)
Tsukiji Sushi Sen (Ginza, $, p. 136)

Tempura

Sansado (Asakusa, $, p. 140)
Ten-ichi ★ (Akasaka, Ginza, Hibiya, Shinjuku, $$$, p. 131)
Tsunahachi (Shinjuku, $$, p. 145)

Teppanyaki

Kamon ★★★ (Hibiya, $$$$, p. 129)
Sekishin-tei ★★ (Akasaka, $$$$, p. 166)

Thai

Ban-Thai (Shinjuku, $$, p. 144)
Erawan ★ (Roppongi, Shinjuku, $$, p. 161)

Tofu

Tokyo Shiba Toufuya Ukai ★★★ (Shibakoen, $$$, p. 160)

Tonkatsu (Pork Cutlet)

Maisen ★ (Harajuku, $, p. 151)

Vegetarian

Good Honest Grub (Shibuya, $, p. 156)
Hiroba (Aoyama, $, p. 151)
Mominoki House ★ (Harajuku, $, p. 152)
Yasaiya Mei ★ (Harajuku, Roppongi, $$, p. 160)

Yakitori

Ganchan ★ (Roppongi, $, p. 162)
Gonpachi ★★ (Ginza, Nishi Azabu, Shibuya, Odaiba, $, p. 162)
Kamakura (Roppongi, $, p. 164)
Manpuku (Hibiya, $, p. 135)
Tengu (Shibuya, Shinjuku, $, p. 156)
Torigin (Roppongi, $, p. 165)

Yam

Mugitoro (Asakusa, $$, p. 139)

Yoshoku (Japanese Version of Western Food)

Kamiya Bar (Asakusa, $, p. 140)
Taimeiken (Nihombashi, $, p. 137)
Miyashita (Harajuku, $$, p. 148)

WHERE TO DINE

6

GINZA, HIBIYA & SHIMBASHI

---

4   GINZA, HIBIYA & SHIMBASHI

Note: To locate these restaurants, see the map on p. 92.

VERY EXPENSIVE

In addition to the recommendations here, there's also a branch of **Inakaya,** 8–7–4 Ginza (✆ **03/3569-1708**), a robatayaki restaurant, open daily 5 to 11pm, for grilled foods (see p. 156 for a review).

Kamon ★★★ TEPPANYAKI   Kamon, which means "Gate of Celebration," has an interior that could be a statement on Tokyo itself—traditionally Japanese yet ever so high-tech. Located on the 17th floor of the Imperial Hotel, the restaurant offers seating at one of several large counters (some with views over Hibiya) centered around grills where expert chefs prepare excellent teppanyaki before your eyes according to your wishes. Japanese sirloin steaks or filets, cooked to succulent perfection, are available, as well as seafood ranging from fresh prawns and scallops to crabmeat and fish, and seasonal vegetables, served with traditional Japanese accompaniments. The service is, of course, imperial.

On the 17th floor of the Imperial Hotel, 1-1-1 Uchisaiwai-cho. ✆ **03/3539-8116.** www.imperialhotel. co.jp. Reservations recommended for dinner. Set dinners ¥13,650–¥31,500; set lunches ¥3,675–¥7,875. AE, DC, MC, V. Daily 11:30am–2:30pm and 5:30–9:30pm. Station: Hibiya (1 min.).

Tips A Note on Establishments with Japanese Signs

Many restaurants, hotels, and other establishments in Japan do not have signs giving their names in Roman (English-language) letters. Those that don't are indicated in this guide by an oval with a number that corresponds to a number in chapter 14 showing the Japanese equivalent. Thus, to find the Japanese kanji, or alphabet, for, say, **Sushiko,** refer to no. 2 on p. 324.

L'Osier ★★★ FRENCH   Chef Bruno Menard reigns at this elegant, modern restaurant decorated with an understated Art Deco motif. Serving only 40 lucky diners, Mr. Menard and his staff of 40 are able to coddle, pamper, amaze, and seduce with excellent service and superb cuisine that combines classic French cooking with modern ingredients and methods of preparation. Set meals start with *amuse-bouche* (literally "mouth amusers") and end with *les petit fours* and *café* (small cakes and coffee); in between may be such dishes as the French classic *foie gras de canard* (duck's liver), lobster, French sea bass with braised fennel, or roast suckling lamb. An ample wine selection, a large variety of cheeses, and a dessert trolley overflowing with some 30 temptations round out the meal. To join the politicians and other movers and shakers who flock here, reserve well in advance.
Shiseido Building, 7-5-5 Ginza. ✆ 03/3571-6050. www.shiseido.co.jp/losier. Reservations required. Jacket required. Main dishes ¥7,200–¥12,000; set dinners ¥19,000–¥25,000; set lunches ¥6,800–¥11,000. AE, DC, MC, V. Mon–Sat noon–2pm and 6–9pm. Closed holidays. Subway: Ginza (2 min.). On Namiki Dori.

②**Sushiko ★★★** SUSHI   If you're in pursuit of top-quality sushi, your search will eventually bring you here, considered by some to be one of the best sushi bars in town. There's no written menu, and the counter seats 11 customers only. Owned by a fourth-generation restaurateur, this establishment doesn't display its fish, as most sushi bars do, but keeps it freshly refrigerated until the moment it meets the swift blade of the expert chefs. Unless you know your sushi, you're best off telling the chef how much you want to spend and letting him take it from there.
There's a less expensive branch on the 35th floor of the Marunouchi Building, 2–4–1 Marunouchi (✆ 03/3240-1908; station: Tokyo), offering views along with an English menu and set lunches, starting at ¥3,990, and set dinners that start at ¥7,350.
6-3-8 Ginza. ✆ 03/3571-1968. Reservations required. Meals ¥15,000–¥20,000. AE, MC, V. Daily 11:30am–10:30pm. Station: Ginza or Hibiya (4 min.). A block east of the elevated tracks of the JR Yamanote Line, on the Ginza side, on Sukiyabashi Dori.

EXPENSIVE

Kihachi ★★ FUSION   With a cool, crisp interior accented with Art Nouveau trimmings, this second-floor restaurant offers an interesting French-influenced menu that combines flavors of the West with Japanese and Asian ingredients, creations of its French-trained chef. Past choices on the English-language menu have included starters such as pan-fried foie gras or half-baked egg wrapped in smoked salmon and topped with carrot and crab; mains have included grilled sea bream with cumin and roasted vegetables, or Japanese-flavored duck breast. The hardest part of dining here? Limiting yourself to one meal—you just might have to come back. To spare your wallet, consider dining in the first-floor cafe, which offers set lunches, beginning at ¥2,000, and dinner entrees ranging from a fish of the day to grilled duck with yuza pepper and lemon.

2-2-6 Ginza. ✆ **03/3567-6281.** Main dishes ¥2,000–¥3,000; set dinners ¥8,400–¥13,650; set lunches ¥3,675–¥6,300. AE, DC, MC, V. Daily 11:30am–2:30pm and 6–9:30pm (last order). Station: Yurakucho (5 min.). Near the Tourist Information Center and Printemps department store.

Peter ★★★ (**Value**) INTERNATIONAL Perched on the 24th floor of the Peninsula Tokyo and offering inspiring views of Hibiya Park and the Imperial Palace's gardens from three walls of windows, this restaurant wows with its internationally inspired cuisine and theatrical setting that puts guests "on stage" as they walk via a raised platform and catwalk to their table. With an emphasis on fresh ingredients, simple preparation, and healthy meals, the menu may include such main dishes as roasted cod with asparagus, potatoes confit and fricassee of mushrooms and bacon, chicken jus or grilled quail with black trumpets, parsley polenta, and poached Japanese eggplant with a citrus jus. This is a great choice for a romantic or celebratory meal (note that children younger than 12 are not allowed).

On the 24th floor of the Peninsula Tokyo, 1-8-1 Yurakucho. ✆ **03/6270-2763.** www.peninsula.com. Reservations recommended. Main dishes ¥2,700–¥5,200; set dinners ¥8,500–¥12,000; set lunches ¥4,800–¥8,500. AE, DC, MC, V. Daily 11:30am–2:30pm and 5:30–10pm. Station: Hibiya (1 min.).

Ristorante Sabatini di Firenze ★★ ITALIAN Open since 1980, on the seventh floor of the Sony Building, this top-act Italian restaurant boasts good views over the Ginza from its elegant drawing-room-style dining room. Sister restaurant of a well-known Florence mainstay, it is famous for its handmade pasta, cooked to al dente perfection, along with traditional and contemporary renditions of seafood and meat dishes, including a classic Milanese-style veal cutlet and Japanese beef filet with foie gras and black truffle sauce. To complement the food are more than 500 Italian wines.

On the 7th floor of the Sony Building, 5-3-1 Ginza. ✆ **03/3573-0013.** Reservations recommended for dinner. Main dishes ¥4,000–¥9,000; set dinners ¥12,000–¥16,000; set lunches ¥3,600–¥7,000. AE, DC, MC, V. Daily 11:30am–2:30pm and 5:30–9:30pm (last order). Station: Ginza (exit B9, 1 min.).

Ten-ichi ★ TEMPURA In this restaurant, located on Namiki Dori, in the heart of Ginza's nightlife, you can sit at a counter and watch the chef prepare your meal. This is the main outlet of an 80-year-old restaurant chain that helped the tempura style of cooking gain worldwide recognition by serving important foreign customers. Today Ten-ichi still has one of the best reputations in town for serving the most delicately fried foods, along with its special sauce (or, if you prefer, you can dip the morsels in lemon juice with a pinch of salt).

Other Ten-ichi restaurants in Tokyo are in the Imperial Hotel's Tower basement (✆ **03/3503-1001;** station: Hibiya); Akasaka Tokyu Plaza (✆ **03/3581-2166;** station: Akasaka-mitsuke); and Isetan department store, 3–14–1 Shinjuku (✆ **03/5379-3039;** station: Shinjuku Sanchome).

6-6-5 Ginza. ✆ **03/3571-1949.** Reservations recommended for lunch, required for dinner. Set dinners ¥10,500–¥18,900; set lunches ¥8,400–¥12,600. AE, DC, MC, V. Daily 11:30am–9:30pm. Station: Ginza (3 min.). On Namiki Dori.

MODERATE

③ **Donto** ★★ (**Finds**) VARIED JAPANESE Located in Hibiya, on Harumi Dori, in the basement of an unlikely looking office building, this is a great place for lunch. Popular with the local working crowd (and therefore best avoided noon–1pm), it's pleasantly decorated in a rustic style with shoji screens, wooden floors, and an open kitchen. Take off your shoes at the entryway and put them into one of the wooden lockers. Choose what you want from the plastic-food display case by the front door, which shows various teishoku and set meals. Everything from noodles, sashimi, tempura, and obento to kaiseki is available. Unfortunately, the best deals are daily specials that are written in Japanese only; ask about them or look around at what others are eating.

There are other Donto restaurants at 2–6–1 Shimbashi (✆ **03/3501-0123;** station: Shimbashi) and on the 49th floor of the Sumitomo Building in Shinjuku (✆ **03/3344-6269;** station: Tochomae).

Yurakucho Denki Building basement, 1-7-1 Yurakucho. ✆ **03/3201-3021.** Set dinners ¥3,500–¥4,500; set lunches ¥800–¥950. AE, DC, MC, V. Mon–Sat 11am–2pm and 5–11pm. Closed holidays. Station: Hibiya (1 min.). On Harumi Dori.

④ **Ginza Daimasu** KAISEKI/OBENTO   This 90-year-old restaurant has a simple, modern decor with Japanese touches. Experienced, kimono-clad waitresses serve artfully arranged set meals from the English-language menu. The *Fukiyose-zen obento*—many delicate dishes served in three courses—includes beautiful tempura delicacies for ¥3,675. A plastic-food display in the front window will help you recognize the restaurant. Set lunches are served until 4pm.

6-9-6 Ginza. ✆ **03/3571-3584.** Reservations required for kaiseki meals costing more than ¥9,450. Kaiseki ¥5,250–¥12,600; obento ¥2,415–¥3,675; set lunches ¥2,100–¥2,940. AE, DC, MC, V. Daily 11:30am–8:30pm (last order). Station: Ginza (2 min.). Across from Matsuzakaya department store on Chuo Dori.

The Imperial Viking Sal ★ INTERNATIONAL   No, this has nothing to do with Scandinavian invaders; rather, *viking* is the Japanese word for "all-you-can-eat buffet." Although lots of Tokyo hotels now offer such spreads, this 17th-floor restaurant was the first and has been serving buffets for more than 50 years. It offers more than 40 mostly European and some international dishes, which vary according to seasonal food promotions spotlighting a country's cuisine, from Indonesian to Swiss. Views are of the Ginza and Hibiya Park, and there's live jazz in the evenings. This restaurant has enjoyed great popularity for decades, making reservations a must.

Imperial Hotel, 17th floor, 1–1–1 Uchisaiwai-cho. ✆ **03/3504-1111.** www.imperialhotel.co.jp. Reservations strongly recommended. Buffet dinner ¥7,875; buffet lunch ¥5,250. AE, DC, MC, V. Daily 11:30am–2:30pm and 5:30–9:30pm. Station: Hibiya (1 min.).

⑤ **Ohmatsuya** ★★ (**Finds** ROBATAYAKI   Enter this restaurant of a nondescript building and you're instantly back in time: After you're greeted by waitresses clad in traditional country clothing, you'll find yourself enveloped in an old farmhouse atmosphere. (Part of the decor is from a 17th-century samurai house in northern Japan.) Even the style of cooking is traditional, as customers grill their own food over a hibachi. Sake, served in a length of bamboo, is drunk from bamboo cups. Dinner menus (in English) include such delicacies as grilled fish, skewered meat, and vegetables. This is a true find—and easy to find at that—just off Harumi Dori on West Fifth Street. If this place is full, there's a nearby sister restaurant, **Ohmatsuya Kura,** 6–6–19 Ginza (✆ **03/3574-4200**), with the same atmosphere and two set meals starting at ¥5,250; it's open Monday to Friday from 5 to 10pm.

5-6-13 Ginza, 7th floor. ✆ **03/3571-7053.** Reservations required. Set dinners ¥5,040–¥9,450, plus a ¥500 table charge. AE, DC, MC, V. Mon–Fri 5–10pm; Sat 5–9pm (last order). Closed holidays. Station: Ginza (3 min.). On West Fifth St.

⑥ **Rangetsu** SUKIYAKI/SHABU-SHABU/KAISEKI/OBENTO   This well-known Ginza restaurant has been dishing out sukiyaki, shabu-shabu, obento (traditional box meals), and steaks since 1947. It uses only Matsuzaka beef (bought whole and carved up by the chefs), which ranges from costlier fine-marbled beef to cheaper cuts with thick marbling. There are also crab dishes (including a crab sukiyaki), kaiseki, sirloin steaks, and eel dishes. Especially good deals are the obento box meals (available day and night and offering a variety of small dishes) and the set lunches served until 2:30pm. In the basement is a sake bar with more than 80 different kinds of sake from all over Japan, which you can also order with your meal.

3–5–8 Ginza. 𝓒 **03/3567-1021.** Reservations recommended. Beef sukiyaki or shabu-shabu set meals from ¥8,000 for dinner, ¥2,500 for lunch; obento meals and mini-kaiseki ¥2,400–¥5,800. AE, DC, MC, V. Daily 11:30am–10pm. Station: Ginza (3 min.). On Chuo Dori, across from the Matsuya department store.

⑦ **Tarafuku** FUGU   Located 1 block west of Chuo Dori, this simple restaurant specializes in *fugu,* or blowfish (not available in summer). There's no English-language menu, but a lit signboard outside the front door shows various set-meal options that include fugu cooked in various ways, including fugu kaiseki meals. In addition to the regular menu, less expensive seasonal meals are also available. For something different, try the *fugu hirezake,* consisting of fugu fin immersed in sake and set ablaze. All I can say is that charred fugu must be an acquired taste. In addition to this location, there are two nearby branches within a block, so if you make a reservation, make sure you have the right one. Before you eat here, be sure you read about fugu, in "Japanese Cuisine," in chapter 2 (p. 21).

Suzuran Dori, 7–8–18 Ginza. 𝓒 **03/3573-0129.** Reservations recommended. Set dinners ¥6,090–¥13,650; set lunches ¥2,500–¥4,980. AE, DC, MC, V. Mon–Fri 11:30am–2pm and 4:30–11pm; Sat 11:30am–2pm and 4–10pm; Sun and holidays 11:30am–10pm. Station: Ginza (3 min.).

Zipangu NOUVELLE JAPANESE   Just outside the Ginza and located high in the sky—on the 47th floor of the Caretta Shiodome Building, with shimmering views over Tokyo Bay—this contemporary Japanese restaurant offers set meals for lunch that are difficult to describe—the constantly changing presentations border on nouvelle Japanese cuisine, with international influences (luckily, there's an English-language menu). In the evenings, the stone-and-wood venue is more of a drinking bar, with an a la carte menu offering chargrilled steak or salmon, yakitori, sashimi, and dishes that go well with wine. In any case, this is a great choice if you're visiting nearby Hama Rikyu Garden.

Caretta Shiodome, 1–8–1 Higashi-Shimbashi. 𝓒 **03/6215-8111.** Reservations required. Main dishes ¥1,460–¥4,536; set lunches ¥2,940–¥6,300. AE, DC, MC, V. Daily 11:30am–2:30pm and 5–10pm (last order). Station: Shiodome (2 min.) or Shimbashi (5 min.).

INEXPENSIVE

In addition to the restaurants here, check out **Meal Muji,** 3–8–3 Marunouchi (𝓒 **03/5208-8241**), a cafeteria on the second floor of the popular minimalist Muji clothing and housewares store, where you can load up on salads and mostly vegetarian choices daily from 11am to 8:30pm. There are also a number of restaurants on the eighth floor of **Matsuya Ginza department store** serving everything from French and Chinese food to sushi, tempura, noodles, and more. **Aux Bacchanales,** a brasserie offering sandwiches, salads, and daily specials, has a branch at 6–3–2 Ginza (𝓒 **03/3569-0202**) and is open daily from 9am to 11pm (p. 167). **Botejyu San,** an okonomiyaki restaurant originally from Osaka, has a branch in the basement of Caretta Shiodome, 1–8–2 Higashi Shimbashi (𝓒 **03/5537-7808;** p. 154), and is open daily from 11am to 3pm and 5 to 11pm (to 10pm Sat–Sun). **Gonpachi,** at the G-Zone, 1–2–3 Ginza (𝓒 **03/5524-3641**), serves a variety of Japanese food from 11:30am to 3:30am.

For atmospheric dining, head to an arch underneath the elevated Yamanote railway tracks, about halfway between Harumi Dori and the Imperial Hotel Tower. It has a hand-

WHERE TO DINE

6

GINZA, HIBIYA & SHIMBASHI

ful of **tiny yakitori stands,** each with a few tables and chairs, which cater to a rather boisterous working-class clientele, mainly men. The atmosphere, unsophisticated and dingy, hearkens back to prewar Japan, somewhat of an anomaly in the otherwise chic Ginza. Stalls are open from about 5pm to midnight Monday to Saturday.

Andy's Shin-Hinomoto (Value VARIED JAPANESE Occupying its own arch underneath the Yamanote tracks, this Japanese-style pub is owned by Andy, a Brit, who buys all his seafood and vegetables fresh daily at Tsukiji Market. The upstairs is the place to be, with its arched ceiling and mixed foreign and Japanese crowd. If you don't have reservations, you'll be shunted into the less ambient downstairs, where you'll feel like a refugee in a fallout shelter as you sit elbow-to-elbow with local office workers at long tables under fluorescent lighting. Sashimi, grilled fish, tempura, sautéed vegetables, deep-fried chicken, tofu, salad, and much more are offered on the English-language menu.

2–4–4 Yurakucho. ⦿ **03/3214-8021.** Reservations strongly recommended. Main dishes ¥500–¥1,600. No credit cards. Mon–Sat 5pm–midnight. Station: Yurakucho or Ginza (1 min.). Underneath the Yamanote elevated tracks, across from the Yurakucho Denki Building.

⑧**Fukusuke** SUSHI In this basement full of cheap restaurants, called Ginza Palmy (look for the outdoor sign saying "Mosaic"), walk all the way to the back (away from Harumi Dori). There are two branches here; the one to the right offers cheaper lunches, starting at ¥945, that include soup, sushi, Japanese pickles and tea, while the one at the right has lunches beginning at ¥1,365. Both are popular with area office workers, so try to avoid the noontime rush. Otherwise, their all-day set meals are the same.

Ginza Toshiba Building B2, 5–2–1 Ginza. ⦿ **03/3573-0471.** Sushi a la carte ¥126–¥630; set dinners ¥1,575–¥4,725; set lunches ¥945–¥3,675. AE, DC, MC, V. Daily 11:30am–9:30pm (last order). Station: Ginza or Hibiya (4 min.). In the 2nd basement on Sotobori Dori, at Sukiyabashi Crossing.

Itamae Sushi SUSHI This user-friendly sushi restaurant is a natural for both novices and more experienced fans of raw fish. Order a la carte for your favorites, or stick to one of the set meals if you don't know much about sushi. A signboard outside shows pictures and prices for individual sushi, while plastic models show various sets available. Two counters give everyone a ringside seat.

8–2–13 Ginza. ⦿ **03/3571-9970.** Sushi a la carte ¥98–¥398; set meals ¥1,050–¥2,980. AE, DC, MC, V. Daily 11:30am–2:30pm; Mon–Fri 5pm–4am; Sat–Sun 5–11pm. Closed some holidays. Station: Shimbashi (1 min.) or Hibiya (5 min.). Across from the elevated hwy.

La Boheme ITALIAN The food is passable, but what sets La Boheme apart is that it's open every day until 5am, making it a good bet for a late-night meal. I also like its huge, open kitchen in the middle of the room, surrounded by a U-shaped counter that provides a ringside view of the action. The pasta ranges from spaghetti with eggplant and tomato sauce to spaghetti Bolognese, along with Japanese-style versions such as steamed breast of chicken with Japanese baby leek, spinach, and sesame oil.

You'll find other La Boheme restaurants at many popular spots around Tokyo, including the Ginza at 1–2–3 Ginza (⦿ **03/5524-3616;** station: Ginza); in Aoyama at 7–11–4 Minami Aoyama (⦿ **03/3499-3377;** station: Omotesando), 6–2–2 Minami Aoyama (⦿ **03/6418-4242;** station: Omotesando), and 3–6–25 Kita-Aoyama (⦿ **03/5766-1666;** station: Gaienmae); in Harajuku at 5–8–5 Jingumae (⦿ **03/5467-5666l;** station: Meiji-Jingumae); in Roppongi at 4–11–13 Roppongi (⦿ **03/3478-0222;** station: Roppongi); in Nishi Azabu at 2–25–18 Nishi Azabu (⦿ **03/3407-1363;** station: Roppongi); in Shibuya at 1–6–8 Jinnan (⦿ **03/3477-0481;** station: Shibuya); and on the fourth floor of Mediage on Odaiba (☎ **03/3599-4801;** station: Odaiba). All are open daily from 11:30am to 3:30am or later.

6–4–1 Ginza. ☎ **03/3572-5005.** www.boheme.jp. Pizza and pasta ¥550–¥1,480; set lunches ¥900–¥1,300. AE, DC, MC, V. Daily 11:30am–5am. Station: Hibiya (5 min.) or Ginza (10 min.). Behind Mosaic, on a corner.

Manpuku (Value) YAKITORI   This yakitori restaurant differs from the others under the Yamanote tracks in that it offers tables along a covered passageway where you can watch office workers bustling by. Decorated with old posters inside and out, it has a slight post–World War II retro feel; its sign even boasts RETRO DINING. Manpuku offers an English-language menu of yakitori, braised tofu with meat, noodles, and other pub grub. The food isn't the greatest, but prices are cheap and it's often packed.

2–4–1 Yurakucho. ☎ **03/3211-6001.** Main dishes ¥504–¥1,134; set lunches ¥810–¥1,449. No credit cards. 24 hr., except 1st and 3rd Sun when it's closed 1am–6am. Station: Yurakucho or Hibiya (1 min.). On Harumi Dori, underneath the elevated Yamanote tracks btw. the Sony and Yurakucho Denki buildings.

Monsoon SOUTHEAST ASIAN   With ethnic music and a mock Southeast Asian decor, this restaurant offers dishes from China, Vietnam, Singapore, Thailand, Malaysia, Indonesia, and Japan, including satays, Thai hot-and-sour soup, steamed dumplings, noodles and rice dishes (such as Nasi Goreng and pad Thai), curries (you choose the curry—red, green, or yellow—plus the meat and rice), and much more. While the food is mediocre, the decor is interesting, the staff is friendly, and it's open late. This restaurant is actually one of four restaurants ensconced under a freeway in a nifty dining complex called **G-Zone.** Each of the restaurants, part of the Global Dining group, offers English-language menus, inexpensive food, friendly and polished staff, and late opening hours (see also **Zest Cantina,** p. 157; **La Boheme,** p. 134; and **Gonpachi,** p. 162).

You'll find other Monsoons at 7–3–1 Minami Aoyama (☎ **03/3400-7200;** station: Omotesando); in Shibuya at 1–6–8 Jinnan (☎ **03/5489-1611;** station: Shibuya); in Ebisu at 4–4–6 Ebisu (☎ **03/5789-3811;** station: Ebisu); in Nishi Azabu at 2–10–1 Nishi Azabu (☎ **03/5467-5221;** station: Roppongi); and on the fourth floor of Mediage on Odaiba (☎ **03/3599-4805;** station: Odaiba), all open 11:30am to 3:30am or later.

1–2–3 Ginza. ☎ **03/5524-3631.** www.monsoon-cafe.jp. Main dishes ¥900–¥1,380; set lunches ¥850–¥1,580. AE, DC, MC, V. Daily 11:30am–3:30am. Station: Kyobashi (exit 3, 2 min.) or Ginza-Itchome (exit 7, 1 min.). On Chuo Dori, at the northern edge of Ginza.

(9) **Shabusen** ★ (Value) SHABU-SHABU   With an improbable location on the second floor of a fashion department store just a stone's throw from Ginza 4–chome Crossing (the Harumi Dori–Chuo Dori intersection), this is a fun restaurant where you can cook your own sukiyaki or shabu-shabu in a boiling pot as you sit at a round counter or at your private table. It's also one of the few restaurants that caters to individual diners (shabu-shabu is usually shared by a group). Orders are shouted back and forth among the staff, service is rapid, and the place is lively. There's an English-language menu, complete with cooking instructions, so it's user-friendly. The special shabu-shabu dinner for ¥4,147, with appetizer, tomato ("super dressing") salad, beef, vegetables, noodles or rice porridge, and dessert, is enough for most voracious appetites. You'll find a branch of Shabusen in the basement of the same building (☎ **03/3572-3806**).

Core Building 2F, 5–8–20 Ginza. ☎ **03/3571-1717.** Set dinners ¥2,310–¥5,880; set lunches ¥1,155–¥3,150. AE, DC, MC, V. Daily 11am–10pm. Station: Ginza (1 min.). On Chuo Dori, next to the Nissan Building.

⑩**Tatsutano** ★ DESSERTS/KAMAMESHI   If you'd like to try a traditional Japanese dessert, head to this 100-year-old shop, famous for its sweets. Most popular is *anmitsu*, a dessert made from beans, molasses, sweet-bean paste, and gelatin. Other traditional desserts are *oshiruko*, a hot sweet-bean porridge; and sweet-bean ice cream. If you crave something more substantial, you might wish to order a reasonably priced *kamameshi* (rice casserole) or *zosui* (rice porridge) from the English-language menu.

7-8-7 Ginza. ✆ **03/3571-1850.** Desserts ¥651–¥1,150; kamameshi ¥1,100–¥1,650; kamameshi set meals ¥1,250–¥2,250. No credit cards. Daily 11am–8pm. Station: Ginza (3 min.). On Chuo Dori, across from H&M.

⑪**Tsukiji Sushi Sen** SUSHI   Too brightly lit and possessing as much charm as an interrogation room, this second-floor Ginza branch nevertheless offers fresh sushi at bargain prices, served at a counter or at tables overlooking busy Harumi Dori. Other dishes are also available on the English-language menu, including salads, tofu, grilled seafood, tempura, and sushi rolls. If you find yourself hungry in the Ginza in the dead of night, this all-nighter is a good choice.

5-9-1 Ginza. ✆ **03/5537-2878.** Sushi a la carte ¥52–¥514; set lunches ¥892–¥945; set dinners ¥1,260–¥3,150. AE, MC, V. Daily 24 hrs. Station: Higashi Ginza or Ginza (2 min.). On the south side of Harumi Dori, btw. Chuo Dori and Showa Dori.

5 TOKYO STATION—MARUNOUCHI & NIHOMBASHI

Note: To locate these restaurants, see the map on p. 99.

MODERATE

Sushiko, on the 35th floor of the Marunouchi Building (✆ **03/3240-1908**), offers set sushi meals for lunch and dinner daily from 11am to 2:30pm and 5:30 to 10pm (p. 130).

Aux Amis Tokyo ★ FRENCH   This small, tony restaurant specializing in creative French cuisine is one of several on the top two floors of the Marunouchi Building (called *Maru Biru* by locals), located on the marunouchi (west) side of Tokyo Station. Sweeping views make it a dining hot spot (reserve one of the few coveted window seats), as do an extensive wine list and a changing French/Japanese menu that might include such entrees as roast lamb with shiitake mushrooms, pork filet in a red-wine sauce, and a fish of the day. It's also a great spot for lunch, but note that the rather bare dining room fails to absorb the constant chatter of this popular venue. Other restaurants on the two floors serve shabu-shabu, sushi, tempura, and kaiseki, as well as Italian, Thai, French, and Chinese cuisines. There are many more inexpensive eateries in the basement.

Marunouchi Building, 35th floor, 2-4-1 Marunouchi. ✆ **03/5220-4011.** Main dishes ¥2,940–¥5,114; set dinners ¥6,300–¥12,600; set lunches ¥2,940–¥7,140, plus a weekday lunch for ¥1,800. AE, DC, MC, V. Daily 11am–2:30pm and 5:30–11:30pm (last order). Station: Tokyo (Marunouchi exit, 2 min.).

INEXPENSIVE

There's a **Kua' Aina** outlet selling burgers in the Marunouchi Building on the fifth floor, across from Tokyo Station at 2-4-1 Marunouchi (✆ **03/5220-2400**), open daily from 11am to 10:30pm (p. 151).

12 **Taimeiken** WESTERN (JAPANESE VERSION)/INTERNATIONAL This old-fashioned, Western-style restaurant, located in the same building as the **Kite Museum** (p. 195), has been in business since 1931. It's simple, inexpensive, and often crowded with mainly middle-age and older Japanese; it was also one of the first nonsmoking restaurants I saw in Japan. Its English-language menu lists such dishes as crab croquette, beef filet steak with garlic sauce, crab and macaroni gratin, omelets with rice, spaghetti, curry rice, and ramen. To Western eyes, the food looks Japanese; to Japanese, it's Western fare. In other words, this restaurant serves the classic Japanese version of Western food (*yoshoku*) and, in that respect, has probably changed little since it opened. Diners are usually given both chopsticks and silverware, as though even the management isn't sure what it serves. However you classify it, it's an interesting place for a quick, cheap meal.

1–12–10 Nihombashi. ☎ **03/3271-2463.** Main dishes ¥980–¥2,880; set lunch (Mon–Fri only) ¥860. No credit cards. Daily 11am–8:30pm (last order). Station: Nihombashi (3 min.). Off Eitai Dori, btw. Chuo Dori and Showa Dori and behind Coredo shopping center.

6 TSUKIJI

Because Tsukiji is home to the nation's largest wholesale fish market, it's not surprising that this area abounds in sushi and seafood restaurants. In addition to the recommendations here, don't neglect the many stalls in and around the market, where you can eat everything from noodles to fresh sashimi.

EXPENSIVE

13 **Tamura** ★ KAISEKI This modern kaiseki restaurant has a friendly staff of smiling and bowing kimono-clad waitresses and hostesses who make you feel as though they've been waiting all this time just for you. The menu is in Japanese only, so they can help you decide what to order, but because the meals are set ones, your budget will probably decide for you. Lunch is by far the most economical meal; many Japanese housewives come for the obento lunchbox, served in a pleasant dining room with tables and chairs. If you order a kaiseki meal for more than ¥20,000, you are ushered to a tatami room upstairs; frankly, I can't even imagine what the ¥52,500 meal looks like.

2–12–11 Tsukiji. ☎ **03/3541-2591.** Reservations required for dinner, recommended for lunch. Set kaiseki dinners ¥8,400–¥52,500; lunch obento ¥3,500. AE, DC, MC, V. Thurs–Tues 11:30am–3pm (last order 2pm) and 5:30–10pm. Station: Tsukiji (Honganji exit, 1 min.). Off Shinohashi Dori, catty-corner from Honganji Temple, down the street running btw. Doutour Coffee Shop and a schoolyard.

MODERATE

14 **Tentake** FUGU People who really know their fugu, or blowfish, will tell you that the proper time to eat it is October through March, when it's fresh. You can eat fugu year-round, however, and a good place to try this Japanese delicacy is Tentake, popular with the Tsukiji working crowd. An English-language menu lists dishes such as tempura fugu, along with complete fugu dinners with all the trimmings. Otherwise, if you want suggestions, try the fugu-chiri for ¥280, a do-it-yourself blowfish-and-vegetable stew in which you cook raw blowfish, cabbage, dandelion leaves, and tofu in a pot of boiling water in front of you—this was more than I could eat, but you can make a complete meal of it by ordering the Tsukiji course for ¥6,500, which adds tempura, salad, and other dishes. You can wash it all down with fugu sake. If someone in your party doesn't like fugu, I recommend the crab set menu for ¥4,090. And yes, that's fugu swimming in the fish tank. (Before you eat here, be sure you read about fugu, in "Japanese Cuisine," in chapter 2.)

6-16-6 Tsukiji. © **03/3541-3881.** Fugu dishes ¥520–¥4,090; fugu set dinners ¥4,800–¥13,500; set lunches ¥840–¥1,570. AE, MC, V. Daily 11:30am–9:30pm (last order). Station: Tsukiji (7 min.). From the Harumi Dori/Shinohashi intersection, walk on Harumi Dori in the opposite direction of Ginza; the restaurant is on the left in a modern building just before the Kachidoki-bashi Bridge.

INEXPENSIVE

⑮ **Edogin** SUSHI   There are two Edogin sushi restaurants in Tsukiji, within walking distance of one another. Because they're close to the famous fish market, you can be sure that the fish will be fresh. There's nothing aesthetic about the main Edogin, first established about 80 years ago—the lights are bright, it's packed with the locals, and it's noisy and busy. It's particularly crowded during lunch and dinnertime because the food is dependably good and plentiful. The menu is in Japanese only, but an illustrated menu outside displays some of the set meals, with most prices ¥3,700 or less. There are also sushi platters for ¥1,600 to ¥4,200. As an alternative, look at what the people around you are eating or, if it's lunchtime, order the teishoku (served until 2pm). The nigiri-zushi teishoku for ¥1,050 offers a variety of sushi, along with soup and pickled vegetables; if you're really hungry, a more plentiful nigiri-zushi teishoku is available for ¥1,470.

4-5-1 Tsukiji. © **03/3543-4401.** Set meals ¥1,800–¥5,500; lunch teishoku ¥1,050–¥1,470. AE, DC, MC, V. Mon–Sat 11:30am–9:30pm; Sun and holidays 11:30am–9pm. Station: Tsukiji or Tsukijijo (3 min.). Located near the Harumi and Shinohashi Dori intersection behind McDonald's; anyone in the neighborhood can point you in the right direction.

⑯ **Sushi Dai** ★ SUSHI   Located right in the Tsukiji Fish Market, this sushi bar boasts some of the freshest fish in town (and often a long line of people queuing for one of the dozen seats; waits can be up to an hour). The easiest thing to do is order the *seto,* a set sushi course that usually comes with tuna, eel, shrimp, and other morsels, plus six rolls of tuna and rice in seaweed *(onigiri).* You won't get plates here—food is served directly on the raised counter in front of you.

Tsukiji Fish Market. © **03/3547-6797.** Sushi a la carte ¥315–¥1,000; sushi seto ¥2,500–¥3,900. No credit cards. Mon–Sat 5am–2pm. Closed Wed if the market is closed, and on holidays. Station: Tsukijijo (2 min.) or Tsukiji (10 min.). Located in a row of barracks housing other restaurants and shops beside the covered market, in Building no. 6 in the 3rd alley (just past the mailbox); it's the 3rd shop on the right.

7 ASAKUSA

Note: To locate these restaurants, see the map on p. 103.

MODERATE

⑰ **Chinya** ★ (**Value** SHABU-SHABU/SUKIYAKI   Established in 1880, Chinya is an old sukiyaki restaurant with a new home in a seven-story building to the left of Kaminarimon Gate, adjacent to its own butcher shop. The entrance to this place is open-fronted; all you'll see is a man waiting to take your shoes and a hostess in a kimono ready to lead you to one of the tatami-floored dining areas above. Chinya offers very good shabu-shabu and sukiyaki set lunches for ¥4,300, available until 3pm and including an appetizer, miso soup, rice or noodles, and side dishes. Otherwise, dinner set meals of shabu-shabu or sukiyaki, including sashimi, rice, and soup, begin at ¥5,500 (reservations required). The English-language menu and an English pamphlet include instructions, making this a good bet for the sukiyaki/shabu-shabu novice.

1–3–4 Asakusa. ©̶ **03/3841-0010.** www.chinya.co.jp. Reservations required for set dinners. Sukiyaki or shabu-shabu ¥3,200–¥8,100; set dinners ¥5,500–¥12,000; set lunch ¥4,300. AE, DC, MC, V. Mon–Sat noon–9pm; Sun and holidays 11:30am–9pm (last order 7pm). Station: Asakusa (1 min.). On Kaminarimon Dori; located to the left of the Kaminarimon Gate, if you stand facing Asakusa Kannon Temple (look for the sukiyaki sign).

⑱ **Komagata Dojo** ★ (Finds) DOJO   This is a restaurant very much out of the Edo Period. Following a tradition spanning 200 years and now in its sixth generation of own-ers, this old-style dining hall specializes in *dojo*, a tiny, sardinelike river fish that translates as "loach." It's served in a variety of styles listed on an English-language menu, from grilled to stewed. Easiest is to order one of the set meals (described in Japanese only), which includes a popular *dojo nabe*, cooked on a charcoal burner in front of you (dojo nabe ordered a la carte costs ¥1,700). Otherwise, look around and order what someone else is eating. The dining area is a single large room of tatami mats, with ground-level boards serving as tables, and waitresses in traditional dress moving quietly about.

1–7–12 Komagata, Taito-ku. ©̶ **03/3842-4001.** Reservations recommended for dinner. Dojo dishes ¥850–¥1,700; set dinners ¥2,450–¥7,300; set lunches ¥2,400–¥2,550. AE, DC, MC, V. Daily 11am–9pm. Station: Asakusa (3 min.). Walk south on Asakusa Dori (away from Kaminarimon Gate/Sensoji Temple); the restaurant—a large, old-fashioned wood house on a corner, with blue curtains at its door—is on the right side of the street, about a 5-min. walk from Kaminarimon Gate, past the MUFJ Bank.

La Ranarita Azumabashi ★ ITALIAN   The Asahi Beer Tower may not mean any-thing to you, but if I mention the building with the golden hops poised on top, you'll certainly know it when you see it (the building was designed by Philippe Starck). The Asahi Beer Tower is the high-rise next to the golden hops, looking like : . . a foaming beer mug? On the top floor (in the foam), this Italian restaurant has soaring walls and great views of Asakusa. It's a perfect perch from which to watch barges on the river or the sun set over Asakusa as you dine on everything from pasta and grilled lamb with rosemary to fresh fish of the day prepared baked, grilled, or meunière. The set lunches include an antipasto, salad, a main dish, and coffee. If you want a ringside seat, make a reservation at least 3 days in advance, avoid weekends and holidays, or arrive just when they open.

Asahi Beer Tower (on the opposite side of the Sumida River from Sensoji Temple), 22nd floor, 1–23–1 Azumabashi. ©̶ **03/5608-5277.** Reservations recommended on weekends. Pizza and pasta ¥1,300–¥1,800; main dishes ¥2,200–¥5,000; set lunches ¥1,800–¥4,800. AE, DC, MC, V. Mon–Sat 11:30am–2pm and 5–9pm; Sun and holidays 11:30am–3pm and 5–9pm (last order). Station: Asakusa (4 min.).

⑲ **Mugitoro** YAM/KAISEKI   Founded about 65 years ago but now housed in a new building, this restaurant specializes in *tororo-imo* (yam) kaiseki and has a wide fol-lowing among middle-age Japanese women. Popular as a health food, the yams used here are imported from the mountains of Akita Prefecture and are featured in almost all the dishes. If you're on a budget or want a quick meal, come for the weekday lunch buffet offered until 1pm; it includes a main dish such as fish or beef, yam in some form, vege-table, soup, and rice—just deposit ¥1,000 into the pot on the table and help yourself.

2–2–4 Kaminarimon. ©̶ **03/3842-1066.** Reservations recommended. Set dinners ¥5,250–¥10,500; set lunches Sat–Sun and holidays ¥2,625–¥3,675. AE, DC, MC, V. Mon–Fri 11:30am–9pm; Sat–Sun and holi-days 11am–9pm (last order). Station: Asakusa (2 min.). From Sensoji Temple, walk south (with your back to Kaminarimon Gate) until you reach the 1st big intersection with the stoplight. Komagata-bashi Bridge will be to your left; Mugitoro is beside the bridge on Edo Dori, next to a tiny temple.

20 **Waentei-Kikko** ★★★ Finds KAISEKI Just southeast of Sensoji Temple, Waentei-Kikko is actually a tiny, traditional house tucked behind a tiny garden. Inside, it's like a farmhouse in the countryside with its flagstone entry, wooden rafters, and tatami seating. A warm and friendly husband-and-wife team manage it, but what makes this establishment especially compelling are the shamisen performances by the husband, Fukui Kodai, playing with the fervor of a rock star, or by other staff members, as well as performances of other traditional Japanese music (performances are at 12:15, 1:30, 6:30, and 8pm). Of course, the food shines, too, with obento lunchboxes and kaiseki dinners that change with the seasons. Fugu kaiseki dinners, beginning at ¥9,975, are also available with advance reservations. This place is a true find.

2-2-13 Asakusa. ✆ **03/5828-8833.** www.waentei-kikko.com. Reservations recommended. Obento lunches ¥2,500 and ¥3,500; kaiseki dinners ¥6,825–¥14,175. AE, DC, MC, V. Thurs-Tues 11:30am–1:30pm and 5–8:30pm (last order). Station: Asakusa (5 min.). Walk on Nakamise Dori toward Sensoji Temple, turning right after the last shop; go past the 2 stone Buddhas, and then turn right again at the tiny Benten-do Temple with the large bell. The restaurant is on the right side of the street across from the playground.

INEXPENSIVE

Kamiya Bar VARIED JAPANESE/WESTERN This inexpensive restaurant, established in 1880 as the first Western bar in Japan, serves both Japanese and Western fare on its three floors. The first floor is the bar, popular with older, tobacco-smoking Japanese men and famous for its Denki Bran (a concoction of brandy, gin, wine, vermouth, Curacao, and herbs). The second floor offers Western food of a sort (that is, the Japanese version of Western food), including fried chicken, smoked salmon, spaghetti, fried shrimp, and hamburger steak. The third floor serves Japanese food ranging from udon noodles and yakitori to tempura and sashimi. I personally prefer the third floor for both its food and its atmosphere. Although the menus are in Japanese only, extensive plastic-food display cases show set meals of Japanese food costing ¥1,500 to ¥3,500. This is a very casual restaurant, very much a place for older locals, and it can be quite noisy and crowded.

1-1-1 Asakusa. ✆ **03/3841-5400.** Main dishes ¥700–¥1,500. AE, DC, MC, V (2nd/3rd floors only). Wed-Mon 11:30am–9:30pm (last order). Station: Asakusa (1 min.). Located on Kaminarimon Dori in a plain, brown-tiled building btw. Kaminarimon Gate and the Sumida River.

21 **Namiki Yabusoba** ★ NOODLES Asakusa's best-known noodle shop, founded in 1913, offers plain buckwheat noodles in cold or hot broth as well as more substantial tempura with noodles, all listed on an English-language menu. Seating is at tables or on tatami mats., It's a small place, so there's often a queue outside the front door, and you won't be able to linger if people are waiting.

2-11-9 Kaminarimon. ✆ **03/3841-1340.** Dishes ¥700–¥1,700. No credit cards. Fri-Wed 11:30am–7:30pm. Station: Asakusa (2 min.). From Kaminarimon Gate, walk south (away from Sensoji Temple) 1 min.; Namiki is on the right side of the street, a brown building with bamboo trees, a small maple, and a stone lantern by the front door.

22 **Sansado** TEMPURA Located right beside Kaminarimon Gate, next to the Kurodaya paper shop, this simple tempura restaurant specializes in Edo-style tempura, fried in a light oil. On the first floor, seating is either at tables or on tatami, while the upstairs is more traditional with tatami seating; one room overlooks the temple gate. Sansado is run by an army of very able grandmotherly types, and because the menu is in Japanese only, they're more than happy to go outside with you to help you make a selection from the plastic-food display case.

> (Kids) **Family-Friendly Restaurants**
>
> ---
>
> **Hard Rock Cafe** (p. 163)   This internationally known establishment, with two locations in Tokyo, should pacify grumbling teenagers. They can munch on hamburgers, gaze at famous guitars and other rock 'n' roll memorabilia, and, most importantly, buy that Hard Rock T-shirt.
>
> **Kua' Aina** (p. 151)   When your kids start asking for "real food," take them here for some of the best burgers in town.
>
> **Shakey's** (p. 146)   When nothing but pizza will satisfy the kids, head for one of these chain pizza parlors for an all-you-can-eat bargain lunch.
>
> **Sometaro** (p. 141)   This traditional restaurant specializes in Japanese-style pancakes filled with meat and vegetables, and fried noodles that you cook yourself at your table, which might delight more adventuresome little eaters, especially because they get to pick their own ingredients.
>
> **Tokyo Catering** (p. 146)   This inexpensive cafeteria won't break the bank and, with everything from sushi to noodles, offers enough to satisfy most diners. Your kids will be impressed, too, with the views from its location on the 32nd floor, but to really wow the little ones, take them also to the free observatory on the 45th floor.

1-2-2 Asakusa. (C) **03/3841-3400.** Set meals ¥1,385–¥3,235. AE, DC, MC, V. Daily 11:30am–9pm (last order). Station: Asakusa (1 min.). East of Kaminarimon Gate, with entrances beside Kurodaya paper shop and on Kaminarimon Dori.

(23) **Sometaro** ★ (Kids) OKONOMIYAKI   This very atmospheric neighborhood restaurant specializes in okonomiyaki, a working-class meal that is basically a Japanese pancake filled with beef, pork, and vegetables, and prepared by the diners themselves as they sit on tatami at low tables inset with griddles. Realizing that some foreigners may be intimidated by having to cook an unfamiliar meal, this restaurant makes the process easier with an English-language menu complete with instructions. The busy but friendly staff can also help you get started. In addition to okonomiyaki, *yakisoba* (fried noodles) with meat or vegetables and other do-it-yourself dishes are available. This is a fun, convivial way to enjoy a meal, especially for kids who might like to try their own hand in cooking their meal (and selecting their own ingredients). Before entering the restaurant, be sure to deposit your shoes in the proffered plastic sacks by the door.

2-2-2 Nishi-Asakusa. (C) **03/3844-9502.** Main dishes ¥588–¥880; set meals ¥1,575. No credit cards. Daily noon–10pm (last order). Station: Tawaramachi (2 min.) or Asakusa (5 min.). Just off Kokusai Dori, on the side street that runs btw. the Drum Museum and the police station, in the 2nd block on the right.

---

8 UENO

Note: To locate these restaurants, see the map on p. 117.

Grill Fukushima ★ CLASSIC FRENCH   Parent company Seiyoken opened one of Japan's first restaurants serving Western food in 1876. Its restaurant here, ensconced in a nondescript building dating from the 1950s, is nonetheless the classiest place to eat in Ueno Park, serving pricey but quite good French cuisine, with a relaxing view of greenery outside its large windows and classical music playing softly in the background. The a la carte menu, in French and Japanese, includes seafood such as lobster in an orange sauce and meat dishes ranging from filet mignon in red-wine sauce to roast lamb, but most people order one of the many fixed-price meals. There's a varied selection of French wines as well as wines from Germany, California, and Australia. The Grill is located to the right as you enter the building and is not to be confused with the much cheaper utilitarian restaurant to the left.

In Ueno Park. ✆ **03/3821-2181.** Main dishes ¥4,200–¥7,875; set dinners ¥10,500–¥18,900; set lunches ¥4,800–¥10,500. AE, DC, MC, V. Daily 11am–8pm (last order). Station: JR Ueno (6 min.). Btw. Kiyomizu Temple and Toshogu Shrine.

MODERATE

㉔ **Innsyoutei** ★ KAISEKI/OBENTO   This traditional Japanese restaurant in Ueno Park has been a Tokyo landmark since 1875. Downstairs is a simple tearoom, but for a meal you'll be ushered upstairs to a dining room with tables overlooking trees or a private tatami room. For lunch, it offers a variety of set meals (including a vegetarian meal), obento, and kaiseki meals from an English-language menu, while dinner features kaiseki and chicken sukiyaki. If you've never had kaiseki, this is a good choice, but it's also a convenient lunch spot after visiting Ueno Park's many museums.

In Ueno Park. ✆ **03/3821-8126.** Reservations recommended. Set dinners ¥5,300–¥10,500; set lunches ¥1,680–¥6,300. No credit cards. Daily 11am–4pm and 5–11pm (to 10pm Sun). Station: JR Ueno (6 min.). Btw. Grill Fukushima (see above) and the row of orange torii leading downhill.

㉕ **Izu'ei** EEL   Put aside all your prejudices about eels and head for this modern yet traditionally decorated multistoried restaurant with a 260-year history dating back to the Edo Period, and with views of Shinobazu Pond. Because eels are grilled over charcoal, the Japanese place a lot of stock in the quality of the charcoal used, and this place boasts its own furnace in the mountains of Wakayama Prefecture, which is said to produce the best charcoal in Japan. *Unagi donburi* (rice topped with strips of eel), tempura, and sushi are available, as well as set meals. There's no English-language menu, but there is a display case outside, and the menu has some pictures.

2-12-22 Ueno. ✆ **03/3831-0954.** Reservations recommended. Main dishes ¥1,595–¥5,250; set meals ¥2,100–¥10,500. AE, DC, MC, V. Daily 11am–9:30pm (last order). Station: JR Ueno (3 min.). On Shinobazu Dori, across the street from Shinobazu Pond and the Shitamachi Museum, next to KFC.

Tokori KOREAN BARBECUE   One of three restaurants in a modern concrete building called Bamboo Garden (the other two restaurants serve Chinese and Japanese food), this friendly establishment offers Korean-style barbecued meats, which you grill yourself at your table, as well as salads, kimchi (spicy Korean cabbage), Korean-style pancakes, rice porridge, noodles, and soups from an English-language menu with photographs. Set lunches feature one-pot meals or grilled beef, along with side dishes of soup, salad, and *kimchi.*

1-52 Ueno Park. ✆ **03/5807-2255.** Main dishes ¥840–¥1,880; set lunches ¥1,000–¥2,200. AE, DC, MC, V. Daily 11am–11:30pm. Station: JR Ueno (2 min.). On a steep hillside across the street from JR Ueno Station's west side, in Ueno Park next to the Ueno Royal Museum.

The **Hard Rock Cafe Ueno,** 7–1–1 Ueno (© **03/5826-5821**), located in JR Ueno Station, is open daily 7am to 11pm (p. 163), while **Kohmen,** 4–8–8 Ueno (© **03/5807-4535**), offers tasty ramen and gyoza daily from 11am to 5am (p. 164).

Mantra INDIAN   Decorated in pink, with etched mirrors and lots of brass, this tiny, spotless restaurant offers curries, tandoori, and Halal food at inexpensive prices. A good way for lone diners to try a variety of dishes is the all-you-can-eat lunch buffet served from 11am to 4pm, or one of the meat or vegetarian set meals *(thali)*. Another good choice for budget travelers: a set dinner for ¥2,395 that's all you can eat within 90 minutes; add ¥1,050 for all you can drink.

Nagafuji Building Annex, 3rd floor, 4–9–6 Ueno. © **03/3835-0818.** Main dishes ¥890–¥1,680; set meals ¥1,980–¥3,300; lunch buffet ¥998 Mon–Fri, ¥1,300 Sat–Sun and holidays. AE, DC, MC, V. Daily 11am–9:30pm (last order). Station: JR Ueno (2 min.). From the south end of Ueno Park, look for the modern Nagafuji Building on Chuo Dori; the annex is in the back, facing the north end of Ameyokocho shopping street.

---

9   SHINJUKU

In addition to the suggestions below, be sure to check out the restaurant floors of several skyscrapers in Shinjuku, where you can find eateries in all price categories serving a variety of Japanese and international cuisines; some even have the bonus of great city views. These include the 29th and 30th floors of the **N. S. Building** where, in addition to Hakkaku (p. 146), other restaurants serve tempura, tonkatsu, teppanyaki, and Italian fare; the top four floors of the **Sumitomo Building** where, in addition to Donto (p. 131), you'll find more than 20 outlets offering everything from tempura to Chinese cuisine; and the 12th, 13th, and 14th floors of **Takashimaya Shinjuku** where, in addition to Din Tai Fung (p. 145), restaurants serve sushi, eel, tonkatsu, noodles, tempura, hamburgers, and more.

Note: To locate these restaurants, see the map on p. 94.

VERY EXPENSIVE

New York Grill ★★★ AMERICAN   On the 52nd floor of one of Tokyo's most exclusive hotels, the New York Grill has remained *the* place to dine ever since its 1994 opening; some swear it's the most romantic restaurant in all of Japan. Surrounded on four sides by glass, it features stunning views (especially at night), live jazz in the evenings, and a 1,600-bottle wine cellar (with an emphasis on California wines). The restaurant backs up its dramatic setting with generous portions of steaks, seafood, and other fare, ranging from delectable roast duck to Australian veal chop, all prepared in an open kitchen with counter seating for close-up views of the action. Both the set lunch and the weekend and holiday brunches are among the city's best and most sumptuous (reservations required)—and are great options for those who don't want to pawn their belongings to eat dinner here. I wouldn't miss it.

Park Hyatt Tokyo, 3–7–1–2 Nishi-Shinjuku. © **03/5322-1234.** www.parkhyatttokyo.com. Reservations required. Main dishes ¥4,800–¥11,000; set lunches ¥5,200; set dinners ¥11,000–¥21,000; Sat–Sun and holiday brunch ¥6,600. AE, DC, MC, V. Daily 11:30am–2:30pm and 5:30–10:30pm. Station: Shinjuku (west exit, 13-min. walk or 5-min. free shuttle ride), Hatsudai on the Keio Line (7 min.), or Tochomae on the Oedo Line (8 min.).

There's a branch of the famous tempura restaurant **Ten-ichi** on the seventh floor of Isetan department store, 3–14–1 Shinjuku (☎ **03/5379-3039**; p. 131), open daily from 11am to 8pm.

㉖ **Kakiden** ★★ KAISEKI   Although it's located on the eighth floor of a rather uninspiring building, Kakiden has a relaxing teahouse atmosphere, with low chairs, shoji screens, bamboo trees, and soothing traditional Japanese music playing softly in the background. Sibling restaurant to one in Kyoto founded more than 260 years ago as a catering service for the elite, this kaiseki restaurant serves set meals that change with the seasons, according to what's fresh and available. An English-language menu lists the set meals, but it's probably best to simply pick a meal to fit your budget. The set lunch is available until 3pm. Set dinners include box kaiseki starting at ¥5,250, mini-kaiseki for ¥8,400, and kaiseki courses ranging from ¥8,400 to ¥15,750. Some of the more common dishes here include fish, seasonal vegetables, eggs, sashimi, shrimp, and mushrooms, but don't worry if you can't identify everything—I've found that even the Japanese don't always know what they're eating.

3–37–11 Shinjuku, 8th floor. ☎ **03/3352-5121.** Reservations recommended for lunch. Set dinners ¥5,250–¥21,000; set lunches ¥4,200–¥6,300. AE, DC, MC, V. Daily 11am–9pm (last order). Station: Shinjuku (east exit, 1 min.). Next to Shinjuku Station's east side.

MODERATE

In addition to the suggestions here, an excellent choice for nouvelle Japanese cuisine is **daidaiya,** located next to the east exit of Shinjuku station on the third floor of the Nowa Building, 3–37–12 Shinjuku (☎ **03/5362-7173**). It's open daily 5pm to midnight (p. 168). I also like **Kushinobo,** a kushikatsu restaurant at 1–10–5 Kabuki-cho (☎ **03/3232-9744**), offering two set dinners: The ¥2,940 course features 10 skewered morsels, including crab, mushrooms, and asparagus, while the Omakase course is the chef's choice and continues until you say you've had enough (16 skewers costs ¥4,500). It's open Monday to Saturday from 5 to 11pm (p. 161). Thai restaurant **Erawan,** on the 8th floor of the Adhoc Shinjuku Building, 3–15–11 Shinjuku (☎ **03/3341-5127**), is open Monday to Friday from 11:30am to 3pm, Saturday and Sunday from 11:30am to 4pm, and daily 5 to 11:30pm (p. 161).

㉗ **Ban-Thai** THAI   One of Tokyo's longest-running Thai restaurants and credited with introducing authentic Thai food to the Japanese, Ban-Thai prepares excellent Thai fare, with 90 mouthwatering items on the menu. My favorites are the cold and spicy meat salad, the chicken soup with coconut and lemongrass, and the pad Thai. Note that set dinners are available only for parties of two or more; also, portions are not large, so if you order several portions and add beer, your tab can really climb. Finally, the service is indifferent. Yet this place is packed every time I come here.

1–23–14 Kabuki-cho, 3rd floor. ☎ **03/3207-0068.** Reservations recommended. Main dishes ¥1,200–¥1,800; set dinners ¥2,500–¥6,000; set lunches ¥630–¥1,365. AE, DC, MC, V. Mon–Fri 11:30am–3pm and 5–11pm; Sat–Sun and holidays 11:30am–11pm (last order). Station: Shinjuku (east exit, 7 min.). In East Shinjuku, in the seediest part of Kabuki-cho (don't worry, the interior is nicer than the exterior), on the west side of a neon-lit pedestrian street running from Yasukuni Dori (look for the red neon archway and 7-Eleven) to Koma Stadium, a Kabuki-cho landmark.

㉘ **Hayashi** ★★ Finds ROBATAYAKI   This restaurant specializes in Japanese set meals cooked over your own hibachi grill. It's small and cozy, with only five grills and a woman in a kimono overseeing the cooking operations, taking over if customers seem the least bit hesitant. The rustic interior was imported intact from the mountain region of Takayama. Four set meals are offered (vegetarian meals are available on request). My ¥5,250 meal came with sashimi, yakitori, tofu steak, scallops cooked in their shells, shrimp, and vegetables, all grilled one after the other. Watch your alcohol intake—drinks can really add to your bill.

Jojoen Daini Shinjuku Building, 2–22–5 Kabuki-cho. © **03/3209-5672.** Reservations recommended. Set dinners ¥4,200–¥7,350. AE, DC, MC, V. Mon–Sat 5–11:30pm. Closed holidays. Station: Shinjuku (east exit, 10 min.). On the northern edge of Kabuki-cho; you'll know you're getting close when you see Godzilla hanging from a building; the restaurant is just a bit farther to the north, on a corner.

Tribecks CONTINENTAL   On the 20th floor of the sleek Hotel Century Southern Tower, this upbeat, contemporary restaurant with an open kitchen offers great city views of Shinjuku Park and central Tokyo along with Continental fare. Although the dishes, ranging from French-inspired cuisine to original creations, don't always live up to expectations, the service is great and the views are sublime, making it popular with shoppers from nearby Takashimaya Shinjuku (make reservations or avoid peak hours). Dinner selections may include roast lamb with garlic and estragon sauce or grilled Iberico pork with orange and basil sauce, while the very popular set lunches offer a choice of main dish such as tuna, sautéed scallops with prawns, or grilled chicken, along with a salad bar, dessert, and coffee.

Hotel Century Southern Tower, 20th floor, 2–2–1 Yoyogi. © **03/5354-2177.** www.southerntower.co.jp. Reservations recommended, especially for lunch. Main dishes ¥2,310–¥5,775; set dinners ¥6,930–¥9,240; set lunches ¥2,100–¥2,940. AE, DC, MC, V. Mon–Fri 11:30am–3pm; Sat–Sun and holidays 11:30am–4pm; daily 5:30–10pm (last order). Station: Shinjuku (south exit, 3 min.).

(29) **Tsunahachi** TEMPURA   Inside a small, old-fashioned brown building in the heart of fashionable East Shinjuku is the main branch of a restaurant that has been serving tempura since 1923. Now there are several dozen outlets in Japan, including one on the 13th floor of Takashimaya Shinjuku (© **03/5361-1860**). The Shinjuku location is the largest outlet, with an open kitchen and counter plus table seating. Though it has an English menu, the easiest option is to order one of three set meals, the least expensive of which includes six pieces of tempura, including deep-fried shrimp, conger eel, seasonal fish, shrimp balls, and vegetables, along with miso soup, Japanese pickles, and rice.

3–31–8 Shinjuku. © **03/3352-1012.** Reservations recommended. Tempura a la carte ¥470–¥1,200; tempura set meals ¥1,995–¥3,990. AE, DC, V. Daily 11am–10pm. Station: Shinjuku Sanchome (2 min.) or Shinjuku (east exit, 5 min.). Off Shinjuku Dori on the side street that runs along the east side of Mitsukoshi department store.

INEXPENSIVE

Donto, on the 49th floor of the Sumitomo Building (© **03/3344-6269**), offers a Japanese lunch buffet and set meals for dinner and is open Monday to Saturday from 11am to 2pm and 5 to 11pm (p. 131). Also, **Tengu,** on Yasukuni Dori at 3–20–5 Shinjuku (© **03/3354-3046**; p. 156), and **Toriyoshi,** 3–34–16 Shinjuku (© **03/3225-1922**; p. 152), are popular Japanese-style pubs with inexpensive meals, both open from 5pm.

Din Tai Fung CHINESE   The Tokyo branch of Taiwan's most popular dim sum (dumpling) restaurant is so popular, you'll probably have to join the long line of people waiting to get in. Luckily, the line moves fast and soon you'll find yourself either dining inside the noisy restaurant or outside on the spacious terrace (unfortunately, there are no views). The English-language menu lists various dim sum, including the signature steamed pork dumplings, served in piping hot bamboo steamers, along with various soups and other dishes such as mashed black sesame seeds and fried pork spareribs.

Takashimaya Shinjuku, 12th floor, 5–24–2 Sendagaya. ✆ **03/5361-1381.** Main dishes ¥600–¥1,365; set meals ¥1,470–¥1,659. AE, DC, MC, V. Daily 11am–11pm. Station: Shinjuku (New South Exit, 1 min.).

Fungo ★ (Value) ITALIAN/INTERNATIONAL   "Going to Be Fun" is the motto (and explanation for its name) of this small, funky place with a hip, young staff. Tables too close together translate into a convivial place for dinner rather than a romantic tête-à-tête, but the English-language menu, though limited, is varied enough to please most palates. Meat dishes might include the likes of grilled Japanese beef with fond-de-veau and balsamic sauce or roasted sea bass with ginger in a cream sauce; there's always a seafood catch of the day, and pasta is available in three different sizes. The cheapest lunch offers a choice of about eight different entrees (such as spaghetti or green Thai chicken curry), plus an appetizer buffet, bread, and a drink, all for only ¥1,000, making this a very popular place indeed.

6–16–7 Nishi-Shinjuku. ✆ **03/5339-7123.** Reservations recommended. Main dishes ¥1,400–¥2,800; set lunches ¥1,000–¥2,000. AE, DC, MC, V. Daily 11am–2:30pm and 5–11pm. Station: Tochomae (8 min.) or Nishi-Shinjuku 5-Chome (3 min.). On Kita Dori, a 3-min. walk west of the Hilton, north of Shinjuku Chuo Park.

(30) **Hakkaku** ★ (Finds) VARIED JAPANESE/ROBATAYAKI   This lively, crowded establishment has a lot going for it: a corner location in a skyscraper with expansive views over Yoyogi Park, inexpensive dishes and meals on an English-language menu, and Kirin beer on tap. Its decor and food resemble those of a bar. During lunch, only set meals are available; choose grilled fish, fried chicken, tempura, or from the display case. Dinner offers a wider range of possibilities, including sashimi, grilled fish, fried noodles, and salads. Yakitori, beginning at ¥399 per two skewers, includes asparagus wrapped in bacon and *tsukune* (chicken meatballs), two of my favorites. There's also a robatayaki counter, where you can point at various dishes, watch them be prepared on the open grill, and then receive them from a wooden paddle passed in your direction.

N. S. Building, 29th floor (be sure to take the dedicated SKY RESTAURANT elevator at the northeast corner of the building), 2–4–1 Nishi-Shinjuku. ✆ **03/3345-1848.** Main dishes ¥700–¥1,869; set lunches ¥780–¥850. AE, DC, MC, V. Daily 11am–2:30pm and 5–9:30pm (last order). Station: Tochomae (3 min.) or Shinjuku (west exit, 8 min.).

Shakey's (Kids) PIZZA   If you want to gorge yourself on pizza, the best deal is at one of several Shakey's around town, offering all-you-can-eat pizza, spaghetti, and fried potatoes for lunch (served at this location every day until 5pm). Although kids may be horrified by the thought of pizza with octopus, they're sure to find other slices more to their liking. There are other Shakey's, including one in Harajuku on Omotesando Dori at 6–1–10 Jingumae (✆ **03/3409-2404;** station: Meiji-Jingumae), and one in Ikebukuro at 1–11–4 East Ikebukuro (✆ **03/3983-4818;** station: Ikebukuro). Both are open for buffet lunches daily from 11am to 4pm.

3–30–11 Shinjuku. ✆ **03/3341-0322.** All-you-can-eat pizza lunch ¥850 Mon–Sat, ¥1,180 Sun and holidays. Individual-size pizzas ¥490–¥1,000. No credit cards. Daily 11am–11pm. Station: Shinjuku Sanchome (1 min.). In E. Shinjuku on Shinjuku Dori, in the basement of a building just east of Mitsukoshi.

Tokyo Catering (Value) VARIED JAPANESE   This is probably the cheapest place in town for a meal with a view. Located on the 32nd floor in the north tower of the Tokyo Metropolitan Government Office (TMG), which offers a free observation room on its 45th floor, this cafeteria is for public employees but is open to everyone. Choose your meal—which can include the likes of pork cutlet, fried fish, sushi, curry rice, or noodles—from the display case, where every item is identified by a number. You then purchase your selections from a vending machine and take your tickets to the cafeteria **147** window. The cafeteria lacks charm, but if you can get a table by the window, you'll have a good view of Tokyo. On the same floor is also a cafe, open Monday to Friday from 10am to 5pm for drinks and dessert.

TMG, 32nd floor of North Tower (take the office elevator, not the elevator to the observatory), 2-8-1 Nishi-Shinjukuku. ☎ **03/5320-7510.** Set meals ¥580–¥660. No credit cards. Mon–Fri 11:15am–2pm and 5–7pm. Station: Tochomae (1 min.), Shinjuku (10 min.), or Nishi-Shinjuku (5 min.).

10 HARAJUKU & AOYAMA

Note: To locate these restaurants, see the map on p. 149.

EXPENSIVE

Casita ★★★ (Finds) FUSION   One of the reasons I'm a great fan of Casita is that I feel truly pampered here. Who wouldn't, with a staff that proffers flashlights to the aged among us who have difficulty reading menus in dim lighting, stands ready to carry out every whim, and, on chilly nights, tucks us under electric blankets so that we can enjoy after-dinner drinks on the deck before we head over to the massage chairs? Casita aims to please, carving its own niche in Tokyo's fiercely competitive market by creating a tropical, resortlike atmosphere, bolstered by great service and a year-round outdoor deck that's heated in winter and covered when it rains. Of course, none of that matters if the food falls short, but Casita turns out dishes that border on awesome, whether it's the Caesar salad with serious shavings of Parmesan, the caramelized foie gras with balsamic sauce, the wrapped langoustines with garam masala–flavored Bearnaise sauce, or the grilled Japanese beef sirloin with seasonal vegetables in a wasabi-flavored red wine sauce. Who wouldn't be a fan?

La Porte Aoyama, 5th floor, 5-51-8 Jingumae. ☎ **03/5485-7353.** www.casita.jp. Reservations required. Main dishes ¥3,200–¥5,500; set dinners ¥8,400–¥12,600. AE, DC, MC, V. Daily 5–11pm (last order). Station: Omotesando (3 min.). Head toward Shibuya on Omotesando Dori; it will be on your right, buried in an unlikely looking building past Kinokuniya and the stoplight.

Sabatini ★ ITALIAN   This restaurant, with its Italian furniture and tableware and strolling musicians, seems as if it has been moved intact from the Old World. In fact, the only thing to remind you that you're in Tokyo is your Japanese waiter. The Italian family that opened Sabatini (no relation to the Sabatini restaurant in the Ginza) has had a restaurant in Rome for more than 50 years, and many of the ingredients—olive oil, ham, salami, tomato sauce, and Parmesan—are flown in fresh from Italy. The menu includes seafood, veal, steak, and lamb, from the traditional saltimbocca to grilled scampi. Naturally, there's a wide selection of Italian wines.

Suncrest Building, 2-13-5 Kita-Aoyama. ☎ **03/3402-3812.** Reservations recommended for dinner. Main dishes ¥3,990–¥7,770; set dinners ¥10,500–¥14,700; set lunches ¥2,310–¥6,090 (from ¥2,730 Sat–Sun and holidays). AE, DC, MC, V. Daily 11:30am–2:30pm and 5:30–10:30pm (last order). Station: Gaienmae (2 min.). On Aoyama Dori, near Gaien-Nishi Dori.

MODERATE

Daini's Table ★★ CHINESE   This elegant Chinese restaurant, located next to the Blue Note jazz club off Kotto Dori, serves intriguing dishes that are nicely presented one dish at a time rather than all at once as in most Chinese restaurants. Its English-language menu offers both traditional dishes (roast Peking duck, boiled prawns with red chili

WHERE TO DINE

6

HARAJUKU & AOYAMA

sauce, and hot-and-sour Peking-style soup) and more unusual combinations that change with the seasons. Everything I've had here has been delicious, though note that set dinners (described in Japanese only) require a two-person minimum; dishes are also for two people. Lone diners, therefore, should come for lunch, but note that the menu for set lunches is also in Japanese only.

6-3-14 Minami Aoyama. 📞 **03/3407-0363.** Reservations recommended. Main dishes ¥2,500–¥3,900; set dinners ¥5,500–¥16,000; set lunches ¥1,100–¥3,000. AE, DC, MC, V. Mon–Fri 11:30am–2pm; daily 5:30–10pm (last order). Station: Omotesando (6 min.).

Miyashita YOSHOKU/FUSION   It could be argued that fusion cuisine has been a staple in Japan ever since its first Western restaurant opened more than 100 years ago, serving Japanese interpretations of popular Western dishes (called *yoshoku* in Japanese). This restaurant in the swank Omotesando Hills shopping complex revels in yoshoku cuisine by offering its own take on French and Japanese fusion dishes, prepared in a bustling open kitchen. The English-language menu changes with the seasons, but you might wish to start with a fresh ginger or onion gratin soup, followed by such classics as seafood gratin (macaroni au gratin with shrimp, scallops, and seasonal seafood), Japanese beef cheeks in a demi-glacé sauce, omelet rice (fried rice wrapped in omelet), and hashed beef and rice served with Japanese steak and foie gras. You won't find dishes like these in Western restaurants back home, making for an only-in-Japan dining experience.

Omotesando Hills, 3rd floor, 4–12–10 Jingumae. 📞 **03/5785-0707.** Main dishes ¥2,500–¥6,500; set dinners ¥3,800–¥6,300; set lunches ¥2,500–¥3,800. AE, DC, MC, V. Mon–Sat 11am–10:30pm; Sun 11am–9pm (last order). Station: Meiji-Jingumae or Omotesando (4 min). On Omotesando Dori.

Selan ITALIAN/FUSION   This restaurant has one of the most envied spots in Tokyo—on a gingko-lined street that serves as the entrance to Meiji-Jingu-gaien Park. The food, Italian with Japanese and French influences, is hit-or-miss, with past offerings on the English-language menu including chicken stewed with Italian red wine, plus a limited assortment of pizzas (available for dinner only) and pastas—but on a warm summer's day, there's nothing more sublime than sitting on the outdoor terrace and reveling in all that greenery. The hours below are for the upstairs restaurant with large picture windows; the ground-floor cafe, which offers the same menu, boasts an outdoor terrace open throughout the day—make that throughout the year, thanks to outdoor heaters.

2-1-19 Kita-Aoyama. 📞 **03/3478-2200.** Pasta and pizza ¥1,470–¥1,680; main dishes ¥2,415–¥3,360; set dinners ¥5,250–¥7,350; set lunches ¥1,890–¥4,725. AE, DC, MC, V. Mon–Sat 11:30am–2:30pm and 6–9:30pm; Sun 11:30am–2:30pm and 6–8:30pm (last order). Station: Gaienmae or Aoyama-Itchome (5 min.). Off Aoyama Dori, at the entrance to Meiji-Jingu-gaien Park.

㉛ **Yasaiya Mei** ★ VARIED JAPANESE/VEGETARIAN   If you like veggies, this restaurant specializing in fresh, seasonal vegetables is a must. For starters you might choose the green papaya kimchi or the Mei Special bagna cauda, which comes with a variety of veggies—such as eggplant, radish and asparagus—plus a dipping sauce. Not to be missed is the wild plant tempura, which changes with the seasons; spring might feature young bamboo shoots, while autumn may include eggplant and water chestnuts. Although the emphasis here is clearly on things that grow in the ground, a few meat dishes are also available, such as grilled pork with mash potatoes. Set lunches feature a vegetable curry or fish, along with an obento served in a charming box with drawers. Seating is either at the U-shaped open kitchen or a table (try to snag one beside the large windows overlooking the trees of Omotesando Dori). There's a branch in Roppongi Hills, on the fifth floor of Mori Tower, in an area called West Walk (📞 **03/5775-2960;** station: Roppongi).

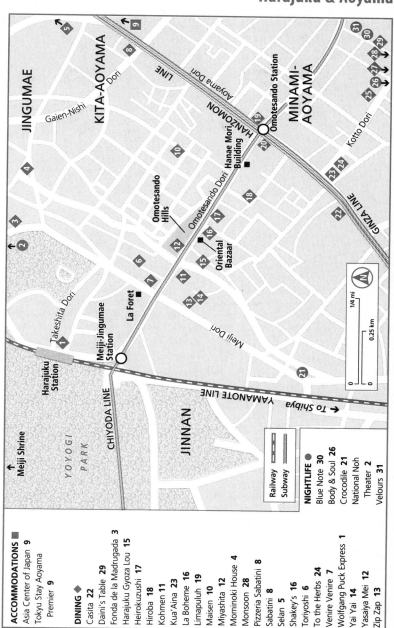

Harajuku & Aoyama

WHERE TO DINE

6

HARAJUKU & AOYAMA

ACCOMMODATIONS ■
Asia Center of Japan **9**
Tokyu Stay Aoyama
Premier **9**

DINING ◆
Casita **22**
Daini's Table **29**
Fonda de la Madrugada **3**
Harajuku Gyoza Lou **15**
Heirokuzushi **17**
Hiroba **18**
Kohmen **11**
Kua'Aina **23**
La Boheme **16**
Limapuluh **19**
Maisen **10**
Miyashita **12**
Mominoki House **4**
Monsoon **28**
Pizzeria Sabatini **8**
Sabatini **8**
Selan **5**
Shakey's **16**
Toriyoshi **6**
To the Herbs **24**
Venire Venire **7**
Wolfgang Puck Express **1**
Yai Yai **14**
Yasaiya Mei **12**
Zip Zap **13**

NIGHTLIFE ●
Blue Note **30**
Body & Soul **26**
Crocodile **21**
National Noh
Theater **2**
Velours **31**

Railway
Subway

Omotesando Hills, 3rd floor, 4-12-10 Jingumae. © **03/5785-0606.** Reservations required. Main dishes ¥900–¥2,100; set dinners ¥5,800; set lunches ¥1,400–¥3,800. AE, DC, MC, V. Mon–Sat 11am–11pm; Sun 11am–10pm (last order). Station: Station: Meiji-Jingumae or Omotesando (4 min). On Omotesando Dori.

INEXPENSIVE

In addition to the choices below, consider **La Boheme,** with locations at 7–11–4 Minami Aoyama (© **03/3499-3377**), 6–2–2 Minami Aoyama (© **03/6418-4242**), 3–6–25 Kita-Aoyama (© **03/5766-1666**), and on Omotesando Dori at 5–8–5 Jingumae (© **03/5467-5666**); all serve pizza and pasta and are open daily from 11:30am to 3:30am or later (p. 134). **Monsoon,** serving Asian dishes from several countries, is at 7–3–1 Minami Aoyama (© **03/3400-7200**) and is open daily from 11am to 3:30am (p. 135). **Shakey's,** on Omotesando Dori near Oriental Bazaar at 6–1–10 Jingumae (© **03/3409-2404;** p. 146), offers an all-you-can eat pizza buffet daily from 11am to 4pm (p. 146). **Kohmen,** 6–2–8 Jingumae (© **03/5468-6344**), is a ramen restaurant open daily from 11am to 4am (p. 164).

Fonda de la Madrugada MEXICAN Serving what is probably Tokyo's most authentic Mexican food, this dark basement restaurant has a cavernous main dining room, several small and cozy offshoots, and a strolling mariachi band, making it seem like you're dining in a Mexican villa. Shrimp marinated in tequila, chicken mole, and soft-tortilla tacos served with chicken, fish, beef, or pork are just some of the items on the trilingual (Japanese/Spanish/English-language) menu, along with the requisite Mexican beers, tequila shots and shooters, margaritas, rum and vodka cocktails, and wine from Mexico, Chile, and Argentina.

2-33-12 Jingumae. © **03/5410-6288.** Reservations required. Main dishes ¥1,050–¥3,045. AE, DC, MC, V. Sun–Thurs 5:30pm–2am; Fri–Sat 5pm–5am. Station: Meiji-Jingumae (10 min.). From the Meiji Dori/Omotesando intersection, walk north on Meiji Dori (toward Shinjuku); it will be on your right after the pedestrian overpass.

(32) **Harajuku Gyoza Lou** ★ GYOZA If you like *gyoza* (pork dumplings), you owe yourself a meal here. Unlike most greasy spoons that specialize in fast-food Chinese (and tend to be on the dingy side), this restaurant in the heart of Harajuku is hip yet unpretentious and draws a young crowd with its straightforward menu posted on the wall (an English-language menu is also available). Only four types of gyoza are offered: steamed (*sui-gyoza*) or fried (*yaki-gyoza*), and with or without garlic (*ninniku*). A few side dishes, such as cucumber, boiled cabbage with vinegar, sprouts with a spicy meat sauce, and rice, are available, as are beer and sake. A U-shaped counter encloses the open kitchen, which diners can watch as they chow down on the very good gyoza.

6-2-4 Jingumae. © **03/3406-4743.** Gyoza ¥290 for a plate of 6. No credit cards. Mon–Sat 11:30am–4:30am; Sun and holidays 11:30am–10:30pm (last order). Station: Meiji-Jingumae (3 min.) or Harajuku (5 min.). From the Meiji/Omotesando Dori intersection, walk on Omotesando Dori toward Aoyama and take the 3rd right (just before Kiddy Land); it's at the end of this alley, on the right.

(33) **Heirokuzushi** SUSHI Bright (a bit too bright), clean, and modern, this is one of those fast-food sushi bars where plates of food are conducted along a conveyor belt on the counter. Customers help themselves to whatever strikes their fancy. To figure your bill, the cashier counts the number of plates you took from the conveyor belt: Green plates cost ¥136, blue ones ¥168, red ones ¥231, gold ones ¥398, and brown ones ¥504. You can order takeout; you might want to eat in nearby Yoyogi Park.

5-8-5 Jingumae. © **03/3498-3968.** Plates of sushi ¥136–¥504. No credit cards. Daily 11am–9pm. Station: Meiji-Jingumae (2 min.) or Omotesando (5 min.). On Omotesando Dori close to the Oriental Bazaar.

Hiroba VARIED JAPANESE/VEGETARIAN Located in the basement of the Crayon House, which specializes in Japanese children's books, this natural-food restaurant offers a buffet lunch of organic veggies, fish, brown rice, and other health foods. For dinner, an English-language menu offers varied fare, including seasonal fish grilled with herbs, tandoori chicken, and stir-fried pork with soy sauce and ginger. The dining hall is very simple (its atmosphere reminds me of a potluck supper in a church basement), and because of the upstairs bookstore, there are likely to be families here.

Crayon House, 3-8-15 Kita-Aoyama. ℂ 03/3406-6409. Lunch buffet ¥1,260; main dishes ¥840–¥1,890. No credit cards. Daily 11am–2pm and 5:30–10pm. Station: Omotesando (2 min.). Off Omotesando Dori on the side street to the right of the Hanae Mori Building.

Kua' Aina ★ (Kids) AMERICAN How far will you go for a burger? Quite simply, one of the best burger chains in town makes this Hawaiian import a smashing success. In fact, if you come at mealtime, you'll probably have to wait for a table in one of the tiny upstairs dining rooms. Burgers come as third- and (whopping) half-pounders. There are also sandwiches ranging from BLTs with avocado to roast beef to tuna. A good carnivore fix.

Branches can be found at 1–10–4 Shibuya (ℂ 03/3409-3200; station: Shibuya), in the Marunouchi Building across from Tokyo Station at 2–4–1 Marunouchi (ℂ 03/5220-2400; station: Tokyo), and in Aqua City on Odaiba (ℂ 03/3599-2800; station: Daiba).

5-10-21 Minami Aoyama. ℂ 03/3407-8001. Burgers and sandwiches ¥750–¥1,330. No credit cards. Mon–Sat 11am–11pm; Sun 11am–10pm. Station: Omotesando (2 min.). On Aoyama Dori (heading toward Shibuya), at its busy intersection with Kotto Dori.

Limapuluh ★★ (Finds) FUSION Not far from the Omotesando Dori-Aoyama Dori intersection, this breezy restaurant with an outdoor terrace wins kudos both for its laid-back atmosphere and its fusion French-Asian cuisine at very reasonable prices. Set lunches offer a meat dish, fish, or pasta of the day, along with a salad, dessert, and drink (such as lychee juice). Offerings for dinner change often and are written in Japanese only on a blackboard but always include the day's pasta, pizza, and heartier fare. Join local hipsters for happy hour, available Monday to Friday from 5 to 7pm, with drinks starting at ¥500. In short, it's hard to imagine going wrong here. What you save on a meal can be spent at Issey Miyake's Pleats Please shop, just a few steps away.

La Place, 3-13-21 Minami Aoyama. ℂ 03/3401-1193. Main dishes ¥1,200–¥2,100; set lunches ¥1,050–¥1,800. AE, DC, MC, V. Daily 11am–11:30pm. Station: Omotesando (1 min.). Off Aoyama Dori in the direction of Gaienmae, almost immediately to the right and hidden in a small shopping complex centered on a plaza.

(34) **Maisen** ★ (Finds) TONKATSU Extremely popular with the locals, this restaurant has been dishing out *tonkatsu* (deep-fried breaded pork cutlet) for more than 25 years and is especially known for its black pork, originally from China and prized for its sweet, intense flavor. But what makes this restaurant a real standout is that it occupies a former pre–World War II public bathhouse; its main dining hall was once the changing room and it sports a high ceiling and original architectural details. There's an English-language menu, but lunch specials (available until 4pm) are listed in Japanese only, though there are photos. It's easiest to order a set meal.

4-8-5 Jingumae. ℂ 03/3470-0071. Set meals ¥1,420–¥2,995; set lunches ¥840–¥1,420. AE, DC, MC, V. Daily 11am–10pm (last order). Station: Omotesando (4 min.). Take the A2 exit and turn right on the side street btw. Ito Hospital and McDonald's (the one with HARAJUKU above it); take the 1st left, and then an immediate right. It will be in the next block on the left.

Mominoki House ★ (Finds) NOUVELLE JAPANESE/VEGETARIAN Mominoki House dishes could be described as French, except they're the creations of a very busy chef (who is also the owner), who uses lots of soy sauce, ginger, Japanese vegetables, and macrobiotic foods (there's even organic wine, beer, and sake). This alternative natural food restaurant, open since 1976 and in a category by itself, has split-level dining, which allows for more privacy than you would think possible in such a tiny place. Its recorded jazz collection is extensive. Dinner features approximately 50 a la carte dishes and may include tofu steak, free-range grilled chicken with ginger sauce, Hokkaido deer steak, brown rice pilaf, tempeh steak, and macrobiotic vegetable gratin with soy cheese and bean sauce. Especially good deals are the lunch specials featuring brown rice, miso soup, seasonal vegetables, and fish or another main dish (including vegetarian selections). There's an English-language menu, but daily specials are written on the blackboard in Japanese only. The chef, Mr. Yamada, speaks English, so if in doubt, ask him what he recommends.

2–18–5 Jingumae. ☎ **03/3405-9144**. www2.odn.ne.jp/mominoki_house. Main dishes ¥1,300–¥4,800; set dinners ¥3,200–¥7,300; set lunches ¥1,150–¥6,000. AE, DC, MC, V. Daily noon–4pm and 5–10pm (last order). Station: Meiji-Jingumae (10 min.) or Harajuku (15 min.). From the Meiji Dori/Omotesando intersection, walk north on Meiji Dori and turn right at the pedestrian overpass; it will be on the left at the 2nd street on the corner.

Pizzeria Sabatini ITALIAN/PIZZA This basement restaurant, opened in 1984 by the same brothers from Rome who also opened Sabatini, an expensive Italian restaurant in the same building (p. 147), is no longer the only game in town, but it still turns out great pizza. Many ingredients are flown in from Italy, including olive oil and huge slabs of Parmesan and other cheeses, as well as the restaurant's large wine selection. In addition to pizza, there's spaghetti, lasagna, fettuccine, and meat and seafood dishes. All you need order, however, is pizza.

Suncrest Building, 2–13–5 Kita-Aoyama. ☎ **03/3402-2027**. Pasta and pizza ¥1,365–¥1,995; main dishes ¥2,500–¥3,150; set lunches ¥1,575–¥3,360. AE, DC, MC, V. Daily 11:30am–2:30pm and 5:30–10:30pm (last order). Station: Gaienmae (1 min.). At the intersection of Aoyama Dori and Gaien-Nishi Dori.

(35) **Toriyoshi** VARIED JAPANESE/INTERNATIONAL This upscale jazz bar is a popular dining spot as well, especially for its chicken specialties such as fried chicken wings and half a fried chicken. The English-language menu lists a variety of Japanese and Asian pub fare as well, including salads, yakitori, tofu (I love the black sesame tofu, called *kuroi gomadofu*), kimchi, and more. A good place for a convivial evening. There are more than a dozen branches in Tokyo, including 3–18–16 Minami Aoyama (☎ **03/3403-7720;** station: Omotesando) and 3–34–16 Shinjuku (☎ **03/3225-1922;** station: Shinjuku).

4–28–21 Jingumae. ☎ **03/3470-3901**. Main dishes ¥620–¥1,400. AE, DC, MC, V. Mon–Fri 5–11pm; Sat–Sun 4–11pm (last order). Station: Meiji-Jingumae (3 min.). From the Meiji Dori/Omotesando intersection, walk on Omotesando toward Aoyama and take the 1st left (there's a Wendy's here); Toriyoshi is down this street, on the right side, beside a willow tree. Look for its VOICE signboard, a reference to the jazz vocals often aired here.

Venire Venire ITALIAN You'll have to see for yourself how inexpensive doesn't necessarily mean drab. This tall-ceilinged trattoria, on the fifth floor of the Y.M. Square Building in Harajaku, is light and airy, with a large outdoor terrace affording sweeping views over the surrounding rooftops (open from Golden Week to Oct). It offers mostly pizzas and pastas, such as fettuccini with scampi or pizza topped with prosciutto ham and mozzarella cheese, as well as a handful of main dishes, including grilled chicken or pork with rosemary. Lunch gives a choice of pizza, pasta, or a main dish, such as fish, along with a trip through the appetizer and salad bar. There's a large selection of Italian wines.

Y.M. Square, 4–31–10 Jingumae. ✆ **03/5775-5333.** Pizza and pasta ¥1,300–¥2,200; main dishes ¥1,400–¥3,000; set lunch ¥1,680. AE, DC, MC, V. Mon–Fri 11:30am–3pm and 5–11pm; Sat 11:30am–4pm and 5–11pm; Sun and holidays 11:30am–4pm and 5–10:30pm. Station: Harajuku (1 min.). On Meiji Dori, just north of Gap and across from La Foret.

Wolfgang Puck Express AMERICAN This is the most casual and least expensive of Puck's invasion of eateries in Japan. It concentrates on burgers, pizza, pasta, roast chicken, salads, and other fast foods. What I like about this location is that it's right at the top of Takeshita Dori (Harajuku's most popular shopping street) across from the station, and it's more stylish than other fast-food competitors that shall remain nameless. Fast service, pop music, and beer—what more could you ask for?

1–17–1 Jingumae. ✆ **03/5786-4690.** Main dishes ¥980–¥1,480; set lunches ¥650–¥1,780. AE, DC, MC, V. Daily 11am–11pm. Station: Harajuku (1 min.). Across the street from Harajuku Station's north exit, at the top of Takeshita Dori.

㊱ **Yai Yai** OKONOMIYAKI Instead of having to cook your own okonomiyaki, all you have to do here is order, whereupon the young staff sets to work cooking your meal on a griddle in front of you. You choose your toppings—such as pork or scallops, together with vegetables such as green onions or kimchi—which are then added to the pancakelike base, cabbage, and egg. Fried noodles and udon, also cooked with a choice of toppings, are also available.

6–8–7 Jingumae. ✆ **03/3406-8181.** Okonomiyaki or fried noodles ¥980–¥1,490. AE, DC, MC, V. Mon–Fri 5pm–3am; Sat noon–3am; Sun and holidays noon–11pm. Station: Meiji-Jingumae (3 min.) or Harajuku (7 min.). From the Meiji Dori/Omotesando intersection, walk on Omotesando toward Aoyama and take the 2nd right; it will be on the left.

Zip Zap AMERICAN I have no idea what its name means, but this trendy Harajuku sidewalk eatery is known for its burgers, which some swear are the best in town. Using 100% *wagyu* beef, considered one of Japan's best, it serves burgers so large you'd need a mouth operation just to fit it all in (I resorted to a knife and fork), but it also serves a club sandwich, tuna melt, BLT, Cajun chicken, salads, and other options, including desserts made on-site. There's a nice terrace on the sidewalk, popular with people who—I am not making this up—like to dine with their pooches.

6–9–11 Jingumae. ✆ **03/3499-1150.** www.zip-zap.jp. Main dishes ¥1,200–¥1,600; set lunches (Mon–Fri only) ¥800–¥900. AE, DC, MC, V. Daily 11:30am–10pm (last order). Station: Meiji-Jingumae (3 min.) or Harajuku (7 min.). From the Meiji Dori/Omotesando intersection, walk on Omotesando toward Aoyama and take the 1st right; it will be on the left.

11 SHIBUYA

Serving as a major commuter nucleus, Shibuya caters primarily to students and young office workers with its many fashion department stores and lively nightlife scene. In addition to the suggestions below, consider the fourth floor of **Mark City,** 1–12–5 Dogenzaka, across from Shibuya Station (and next to the Shibuya Excel Hotel Tokyu), where you'll find a dozen or so restaurants specializing in Japanese, Italian, and Chinese food. Try ㊲ **Mikura** (✆ **03/5459-4011**), simply but elegantly decorated in gold, for its Kyoto-style obento and kaiseki; set lunches cost ¥2,100 to ¥5,460, while dinners (reservations required) start at ¥3,990. It's open daily 11am to 1:30pm and 5 to 9pm (last order).

Note: To locate these restaurants, see the map on p. 155.

MODERATE

Abientot ★ (Value) FRENCH   Even I could come up with a better interior design for this drab hotel restaurant, but luckily its perch on the 25th floor and very good cuisine at reasonable prices more than make up for the lack of imagination. You might start with salmon confit with white asparagus from the English-language menu, followed by stew of lamb shank and navy beans or sautéed guinea fowl thigh with mustard sauce. Reserve a table beside the window with views toward Shinjuku (the night views are especially stunning). And, by the way, as you walk across the footbridge from the station to the hotel, look outside to the right; that busy intersection, with people crossing from all directions when the lights turn red, was featured in the movie *Lost in Translation*.

Shibuya Excel Hotel Tokyu, 25th floor, 1–12–2 Dogenzaka. ⓒ **03/5457-0132.** Main dishes ¥2,310– ¥4,620; set dinners ¥4,620–¥7,507; set lunches ¥2,079–¥5,775. AE, DC, MC, V. Daily 11:30am–2pm and 5:30–10:30pm (last order). Station: Shibuya (1 min. by footbridge).

Legato ★★ (Finds) ITALIAN/FUSION   Walk past the tear-shaped bar with its view over Shibuya (or stop for an aperitif), and then head downstairs to the theatrical setting of this elegant yet low-key restaurant. Dim lighting, an open kitchen, knowledgeable service, and reasonable prices make this a great choice for a splurge without spending a fortune. The menu blends ingredients from Italy and Asia, with starters that range from sautéed foie gras with vanilla-flavored dark cherry sauce to stewed spare ribs with Cantonese-style barbecue sauce. Main dishes offer pasta, fish, and meat choices, such as sautéed sea bass and bamboo shoots with broad beans and Parmigiano risotto, and Japanese sirloin steak with lemongrass-flavored mustard sauce.

E-Space Tower, 15th floor, 3–6 Maruyama-cho. ⓒ **03/5784-2121.** www.legato-tokyo.jp. Main dishes ¥2,100–¥4,200; set dinners ¥3,600–¥8,500; set lunches ¥2,000–¥2,600. AE, DC, MC, V. Mon–Fri 11:30am– 2pm; daily 5:30pm–midnight. Station: Shibuya (Hachiko, 8 min.). From the station, walk straight up Dogenzaka; it will be on the right, just past the koban police box.

INEXPENSIVE

In addition to the choices here, there's **Gonpachi,** on the 14th floor of E-Space Tower, 3–6 Maruyama-cho (ⓒ **03/5784-2011**), offering a wide selection of Japanese fare, from yakitori and noodles to tempura and sushi. It's open daily 11:30am to 3:30am (p. 162). You'll also find branches of the pizza/pasta restaurant **La Boheme** (ⓒ **03/3477-0481;** p. 134); **Monsoon** (ⓒ **03/5489-1611;** p. 135), serving Southeast Asian fare; and Tex-Mex eatery **Zest Cantina** (ⓒ **03/5489-3332;** p. 157), all at 1–6–8 Jinnan and open daily 11:30am to 5am. For burgers, there's **Kua' Aina,** at 1–10–4 Shibuya (ⓒ **03/3409-3200**), open daily 11am to 10pm (p. 151).

(38) **Botejyu** OKONOMIYAKI   Although okonomiyaki is considered plebeian fare (see "Japanese Cuisine," in chapter 2, for a description), this Tokyo branch of an Osaka restaurant, founded in 1946, is classier than most, with dark-wood paneling, an open kitchen, and recorded music that is likely to be jazz. In addition, instead of cooking your food yourself as in most okonomiyaki restaurants, food here is prepared for you, making it much easier to experience this very tasty meal. The English-language dinner menu lists various choices for okonomiyaki and yakisoba (fried noodles), including those made with pork, squid, or shrimp, as well as teppanyaki. The lunch menu, however, is in Japanese only, so you'll have to ask for guidance. There are other branches, in the basement of

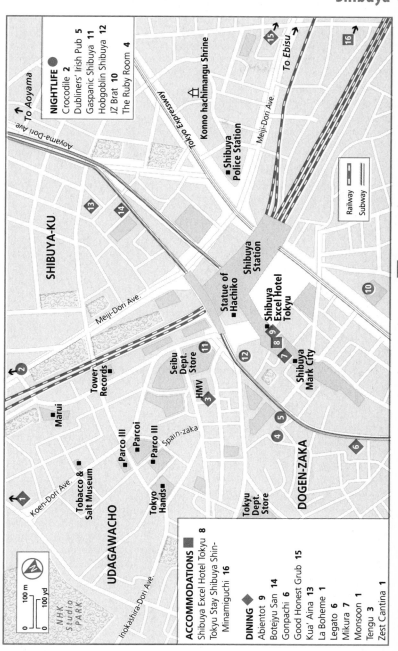

NIGHTLIFE ●
Crocodile **2**
Dubliners' Irish Pub **5**
Gaspanic Shibuya **11**
Hobgoblin Shibuya **12**
JZ Brat **10**
The Ruby Room **4**

To Aoyama

Aoyama-Dori Ave.

SHIBUYA-KU

13
14

Konno hachimangu Shrine

Tokyo Expressway

Shibuya
Police Station

To Ebisu

15

Meiji-Dori Ave.

16

Meiji-Dori Ave.

Railway
Subway

Shibuya
Station

Statue of
Hachiko

Shibuya
Excel Hotel
Tokyu

8 9

1

Shibuya
Mark City

10

12

7

5

4

6

DOGEN-ZAKA

Seibu
Dept.
Store

HMV

3

11

Tower
Records

Marui

2

Parco II
Parcoi
Parco III

Spain-zaka

Tokyo
Hands

Tobacco &
Salt Museum

Koen-Dori Ave.

UDAGAWACHO

1

Tokyu
Dept.
Store

Inokashira-Dori Ave.

NHK
Studio
PARK

0   100 m
0   100 yd

ACCOMMODATIONS ■
Shibuya Excel Hotel Tokyu **8**
Tokyu Stay Shibuya Shin-
Minamiguchi **16**

DINING ◆
Abientot **9**
Boteju San **14**
Gonpachi **6**
Good Honest Grub **15**
Kua' Aina **13**
La Boheme **1**
Legato **6**
Mikura **7**
Monsoon **1**
Tengu **3**
Zest Cantina **1**

Caretta Shiodome, 1–8–2 Higashi Shimbashi (🕾 **03/5537-7808;** station: Shiodome), and on the second floor of the Taisuikan Building, 3–10–1 Akasaka (🕾 **03/3505-2930;** station: Akasaka-mitsuke).

1-12-9 Shibuya. 🕾 **03/3407-8636.** Main dishes ¥950–¥1,530; set lunches ¥1,000–¥1,250. AE, DC, MC, V. Mon–Sat 11:30am–3pm; Mon–Thurs 5–11pm; Fri–Sat 5pm–2am; Sun and holidays 11:30am–11pm. Station: Shibuya (east exit, 3 min.). From the north end of the station's east exit, head up Miyamasuzaka away from the station; it's just past Shibuya's post office on the left, up a short flight of stairs.

Good Honest Grub (Finds) AMERICAN/VEGETARIAN   The owner is Canadian and the food is a compilation of homegrown favorites expatriates—including the health conscious—are likely to crave: eggs Benedict and French toast for the weekend brunch (with bottomless coffee refills), and sandwiches, wraps, chicken quesadillas, vegetarian lasagna and daily specials for lunch. Located in a cute Lilliputian house, with seating upstairs in a sunny, cozy room with hanging plants, it would be right at home at any North American college campus.

2-20-8 Higashi. 🕾 **03/3797-9877.** Main dishes ¥1,000–¥1,700. No credit cards. Mon–Fri 11:30am–3pm; Sat–Sun and holidays 10:30am–4:30pm. Station: Shibuya or Ebisu (10 min.). Just off Meiji Dori midway btw. Ebisu and Shibuya stations, on a side street beside the Lawson 100 store.

Tengu VARIED JAPANESE/YAKITORI   Founded in 1969, this popular chain is a great place for an inexpensive meal. Although it's a drinking establishment and located smack-dab in the middle of Shibuya's Center Gai nightlife district, it is more brightly lit than most Japanese pubs and is popular with young Japanese professionals. An English-language menu with photos makes ordering easy and includes all the typical bar food and snacks you'd expect: yakitori, sashimi, sushi, tofu, salad, gyoza, fried noodles, and more. And there's plenty of beer, *shochu*, sake, wine, and cocktails to wash it all down (you'll be charged an extra ¥294 snack charge if ordering alcoholic drinks). There's another Tengu in East Shinjuku, on Yasukuni Dori, at 3–20–5 Shinjuku (🕾 **03/3354-3046;** station: Shinjuku).

15-3 Udagawacho. 🕾 **03/3496-7397.** Main dishes ¥380–¥700. AE, DC, MC, V. Daily 5–11:30pm. Station: Shibuya (Hachiko exit, 4 min.). Off Center Gai just past HMV on the right; look for the Tengu logo—a red face with a long nose and a sign that reads TENG.

---

12 EBISU

EXPENSIVE

La Table de Joël Robuchon ★★ FRENCH   Housed in a reproduction 18th-century French château planted in the midst of swanky Yebisu Garden Place, this ground-floor restaurant offers nouveau French cuisine at a fraction of what meals cost at its more expensive, more romantic, and much more formal sister **Joël Robuchon Restaurant** (🕾 **03/5424-1347**) upstairs (where lunch courses will set you back ¥8,200 and dinner courses start at ¥20,000). La Table allows you to compose your own set meals from a generous list of soups, appetizers, and main dishes, some of which are Robuchon's original dishes while others are innovations that add Spanish and Italian influences. The wine list is extensive, with more than 300 vintages from throughout France, and at reasonable prices to boot. While La Table, decorated in purple and black and with an outdoor garden in fine weather, is fancy enough for most tastes, serious foodies will likely want to splurge on the gourmet feast upstairs.

Yebisu Garden Place, 1–13–1 Mita. (C) **03/5424-1338.** www.joel-robuchon.com. Reservations recommended. La Table set dinners ¥7,800–¥13,800; set lunches ¥2,950–¥5,250. AE, DC, MC, V. Daily 11:30am–2:30pm and 6–10pm (last order). Station: Ebisu (6 min.).

MODERATE

ViVi La Verde ★ ITALIAN   There are a dozen or so restaurants that comprise the Top of Yebisu on the 38th and 39th floors of this high-rise in Yebisu Garden Place, but few can boast the views of this restaurant. Sleekly decorated with black furniture and an open kitchen, it occupies a corner of the building, with views toward Roppongi, Shinagawa, Odaiba, Haneda, and even Yokohama on clear days, with many tables windowside. For dinner, main dishes range from roasted swordfish with marinated tomato to sautéed pork with a salad of white kidney beans, and, of course, there are plenty of Italian wines to wash it all down. Set dinners allow you to choose your main dish from the a la carte menu, with more expensive meals adding more side dishes. Set lunches are described in Japanese only, with the cheapest set lunch offering a pasta, salad, and coffee.

Yebisu Garden Place Tower, 39th floor, 4–20–3 Ebisu. (C) **03/3444-3225.** Main dishes ¥2,000–¥2,500; set dinners ¥4,800–¥8,000; set lunches ¥1,000–¥3,500. Mon–Fri, ¥2,000–¥3,000 Sat–Sun and holidays. AE, DC, V. Mon–Fri 11:30am–2:30pm and 5:30–10pm; Sat–Sun and holidays 11:30am–3pm and 5:30–10pm. Station: Ebisu (6 min.).

INEXPENSIVE

In addition to the choices here, there's **Monsoon,** 4–4–6 Ebisu ((C) **03/5789-3811**), serving Southeast Asian food daily from 11am to 3:30am (p. 135), and **Kohmen,** 1–9–5 Ebisu ((C) **03/5475-0185**), offering ramen and gyoza daily from 11am to 5am (p. 164).

(39)**Ippudo** ★ GYOZA/RAMEN   An English-language menu, energetic young staff, and background jazz music make this a good choice for a meal, but it's the food that makes it great. I can't resist the gyoza here, tender and juicy, though the ramen, available in three different sizes, is what made the restaurant famous (there's even a branch in New York). Sit down at one of the long wooden tables wherever you find an empty space (you'll probably have to share), help yourself to the extra garlic available at every table, and watch the action in the bustling open kitchen.

1–3–13 Hiroo. (C) **03/5420-2225.** Ramen ¥850–¥1,150; set lunches ¥850–¥1,250. No credit cards. Daily 11am–4am. Station: Ebisu (5 min.). From the West exit, turn right on Komozawa Dori and cross Meiji Dori via the pedestrian bridge. It's on Meiji Dori (in the direction of Hiroo), on the left side; look for its red lit signboard and glass windows.

Zest Cantina MEXICAN   You can probably find better Mexican restaurants at home, but this will do for a quick fix, especially once the margaritas kick in. A huge, multilevel restaurant decorated cantina-style with corrugated sheet metal on the outside and wood and brick on the inside, Zest offers chicken and cheese burritos, enchiladas, tacos, fajitas, and other Tex-Mex fare, as well as steaks, buffalo wings, hamburgers, and very good salads from its English-language menu. Service can be slow. If you're wearing stiletto heels, beware: I saw several lasses snared by the wide-planked flooring, which made for an interesting sideshow.

You'll find other Zest Cantinas in the Ginza at 1–2–3 Ginza ((C) **03/5524-3621**), in Shibuya at 1–6–8 Jinnan ((C) **03/5489-3332**), and on the fourth floor of Mediage on Odaiba ((C) **03/3599-4803**).

1–22–19 Ebisu. (C) **03/5475-6291.** www.zest-cantina.jp. Main dishes ¥750–¥2,600; set lunches ¥850–¥2,200 (not available Sun). AE, DC, MC, V. Daily 11:30am–5am. Station: Ebisu (east exit, 8 min.). Follow the signs for 1-chome Ebisu, and then take the street that runs btw. Kinko's and Mizuho bank; it will be on the left.

13 ROPPONGI & NISHI AZABU

Because Roppongi is such a popular nighttime hangout for young Tokyoites and foreigners, it boasts a large number of both Japanese and Western restaurants. To find the location of any of the Roppongi addresses below, stop by the tiny police station on **Roppongi Crossing** (Roppongi's main intersection of Roppongi Dori and Gaien-Higashi Dori), where you'll find a map of the area. If you still don't know where to go, ask one of the policemen.

Catty-corner to the police station is the number-one meeting spot in Roppongi, in front of Almond coffee shop. Unfortunately, this landmark is under reconstruction until the end of 2010, so gone are the gaudy but instantly recognizable pink and white awnings. However, if you are asked to meet someone in Roppongi, this will likely be the spot.

About a 10-minute walk west of Roppongi (via Roppongi Dori in the direction of Shibuya) is **Nishi Azabu.** Once primarily a residential neighborhood, Nishi Azabu has slowly changed over the years as it began absorbing the overflow of Roppongi. It has restaurants and a few bars, yet remains mellower and much less crowded than Roppongi. Between Roppongi Crossing and Nishi Azabu is **Roppongi Hills,** a sprawling urban development with many choices in dining. **Tokyo Midtown,** Tokyo's newest urban development and attracting huge crowds, also offers dining, but good luck in securing a seat.

Note: To locate these restaurants, see the map on p. 159.

VERY EXPENSIVE

Hinokizaka ★★★ KAISEKI/VARIED JAPANESE   With that inimitable Japanese aesthetics that make even traditional shoji and latticed woodwork seem up-to-the-minute hip, Hinokizaka pairs refined elegance with knock-out views of Tokyo. Along with a main dining area and private tatami rooms (including an imported 200-year-old teahouse), it also has separate counters ensconced in smaller rooms (none with views) for sushi, tempura, and teppanyaki. Needless to say, the prices for its beautifully presented kaiseki dinners are as high as its location, but a celebratory meal here is one you won't soon forget. For a less expensive splurge, come for a lunch obento or one of the set lunches for sushi, tempura, teppanyaki, or kaiseki.

Ritz-Carlton, 45th floor, Tokyo Midtown, 9-7-1 Akasaka. ℂ **03/3423-8000.** www.ritzcarlton.com. Set dinners ¥12,000–¥28,000; set lunches ¥4,200–¥8,500. AE, DC, MC, V. Daily 11:30am–2:30pm and 5:30–10pm. Station: Roppongi or Nogizaka (3 min.).

㊵ **Inakaya** ★★ ROBATAYAKI   Whenever I host first-time foreign visitors in Tokyo, I take them to this festive restaurant, and they've never been disappointed. Although tourist-oriented and overpriced, it's still great fun; the drama of the place alone is worth it. Customers sit at a long, U-shaped counter, on the other side of which are mountains of fresh vegetables, beef, and seafood. And in the middle of all that food, seated in front of a grill, are male chefs—ready to cook whatever you point to in the style of robatayaki. Orders are yelled out by your waiter and are repeated in unison by all the other waiters, resulting in ongoing, excited yelling. Sounds strange, I know, but actually it's a lot of fun. Food offerings may include yellowtail, red snapper, sole, scallops, king crab legs, giant shrimp, steak, meatballs, gingko nuts, potatoes, eggplant, and asparagus, all piled high in wicker baskets and ready for the grill. Although prices for individual dishes may not seem high, they quickly add up. Most meals here average around ¥15,000, including a ¥800 per person table charge.

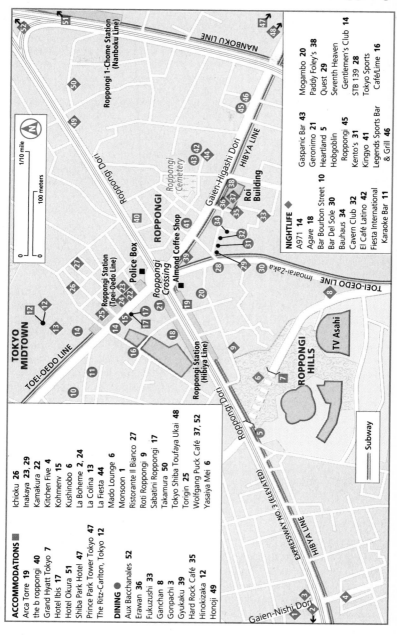

Other branches are at 5–3–4 Roppongi (✆ **03/3408-5040**), open daily 5pm to 5am, and at 8–7–4 Ginza (✆ **03/3569-1708**), open daily 5 to 11pm, but only the one detailed here has an English-language menu.

4-10-11 Roppongi. ✆ **03/5775-1012.** www.roppongiinakaya.jp. Grilled vegetables ¥650–¥900; grilled seafood and meats ¥1,050–¥5,100. AE, DC, MC, V. Daily 5–10:30pm (last order). Station: Roppongi (2 min.). Off Gaien-Higashi Dori on a side street opposite Ibis Hotel; from Roppongi Crossing, walk on Gaien-Higashi Dori in the direction of Midtown and take the 2nd right.

EXPENSIVE

42 **Fukuzushi** ★★ SUSHI   This is one of Tokyo's classiest sushi bars, attracting a cosmopolitan crowd. Although it has a traditional entrance through a small courtyard with lighted lanterns and the sound of trickling water, the interior is slick and modern with bold colors of black and red. Some people swear it has the best sushi in Tokyo, although with 7,000 sushi bars in the city, I'd be hard-pressed to say which one is tops. Certainly, you can't go wrong here. Three different set lunches are available, featuring sushi, *chirashi-zushi* (assorted sashimi with rice), or eel as the main course. Dinners are more extensive, with the ¥8,400 set course consisting of salad, sashimi, steamed egg custard, grilled fish, sushi, miso soup, dessert, and coffee (set dinners require orders by a minimum of two people).

5-7-8 Roppongi. ✆ **03/3402-4116.** www.roppongifukuzushi.com. Reservations recommended, especially for dinner. Set dinners ¥6,300–¥8,400; set lunches ¥2,625–¥4,725. AE, DC, MC, V. Mon–Sat 11:30am–1:30pm and 5:30–10pm (last order); holidays 5:30–9pm. Closed 1 week in mid-Aug. Station: Roppongi (4 min.). From Roppongi Crossing, walk toward Tokyo Tower on Gaien-Higashi Dori, turning right after McDonald's, left in front of Hard Rock Cafe, and then right.

Tokyo Shiba Toufuya Ukai ★★★ Finds TOFU   It's hard to imagine you're in Tokyo when you enter the lush grounds of this exquisite restaurant. Indeed, though it's located at the foot of Tokyo Tower (about a 15-min. walk from Roppongi), it's a world apart from the bustling city, with a landscaped garden complete with ponds (and three fulltime gardeners) and traditional Japanese structures that includes a main building constructed with heavy beams and foot-thick lacquered pillars imported from a 200-year-old Takayama farmhouse. Yet despite its aristocratic atmosphere, this restaurant specializes in classic tofu cuisine, with set meals that change with the seasons and are described on an English-language menu. The least expensive set lunch, for example, may start with an egg custard, deep-fried tofu with sweet miso sauce, and assorted sashimi, followed by deep-fried simmered tofu, sushi topped with cooked eel along with deep-fried burdock root, tofu seasoned in soy milk, rice, and sweet red-bean soup with rice cake. By the way, this restaurant is a branch of the famous Ukai Toriyama in the outskirts of Tokyo near Mount Takao, which specializes in charbroiled chicken (p. 183).

4-4-13 Shibakoen. ✆ **03/3436-1028.** Reservations required. Set dinners ¥8,400–¥12,600; set lunches ¥5,500–¥6,500. AE, DC, MC, V. Daily 11am–10pm (last order 8pm). Station: Akabanebashi (5 min.). Behind Tokyo Tower, to the left.

MODERATE

In addition to the choices here, there's a **Wolfgang Puck Cafe** in the Roi Building, 5–5–1 Roppongi (✆ **03/5775-5401**), open daily 11am to 11pm (p. 168); and **Yasaiya Mei,** specializing in fresh vegetables, in Roppongi Hills, on the fifth floor of Mori Tower in an area called West Walk (✆ **03/5775-2960**), open Monday to Thursday from 11am to 11pm and Friday and Saturday from 11am to 2am (p. 148).

Erawan ★ THAI   Perched 13 floors above the Roppongi madness and offering cool, aloof views on three sides (ask to be seated on the Tokyo Tower side), this restaurant is massive but well divided into intimate dining areas that create a pleasant Thai aura with dark gleaming woods, woodcarvings, plants, bamboo screens, and a smiling Thai staff. Although it has an a la carte menu, most economical is to opt for the dinner buffet (available until 9pm), which includes an appetizer, salad, and dessert bar, plus two main dishes such as stir-fried minced pork with basil wrapped in lettuce of steamed deep-fried chicken wrapped in pandanus leaves. There's a branch in Shinjuku, on the eighth floor of the Adhoc Shinjuku Building, 3–15–11 Shinjuku (© **03/3341-5127**; station: Shinjuku).

Roi Building, 13th floor, 5–5–1 Roppongi. © **03/3404-5741.** Main dishes ¥1,300–¥1,800; set dinner buffet ¥5,300. AE, DC, MC, V. Mon–Fri 5:30–11:30pm; Sat–Sun and holidays 4–10pm. Station: Roppongi (3 min.). From Roppongi Crossing, Erawan is on the right side of Gaien-Higashi Dori (the road leading to Tokyo Tower), just past McDonald's.

Kushinobo KUSHIKATSU   First opened in Osaka in 1950, this small and cozy restaurant specializing in *kushikatsu* (deep-fried skewers of food) is ensconced in Roppongi Hills. Every day it prepares more than 40 different kinds of meat, seafood, and vegetable kushikatsu, drawn from more than 100 in-house recipes. A progression of skewers is served one at a time until you say stop (if you like one especially well, you can ask for it again), along with the restaurant's own special tartar sauce, miso sauce, sweet-and-sour sauce, and other sauces for dipping. Most people average about 16 skewers, which cost about ¥4,500, including a side dish and dessert. By the way, this is the first restaurant I've seen that charges a 10% "night charge," levied to those entering after 10pm or departing after 11pm. Still, I really like kushikatsu and wish there were more restaurants serving it in Tokyo. There's a Kushinobo branch in Shinjuku, at 1–10–5 Kabuki-cho (© **03/3232-9744**; station: Shinjuku).

Roppongi Hills, 5th floor of West Walk, 6–10–1 Roppongi. © **03/5771-0094.** Set dinners ¥3,990–¥4,500; set lunches ¥1,575–¥4,500. AE, DC, MC, V. Mon–Fri 11am–11pm; Sat 11am–4am; Sun and holidays 11am–10pm (last order). Closed holidays. Station: Roppongi (Roppongi Hills exit, 2 min.).

La Colina ★ MEXICAN   Since Tokyo Midtown's 2007 opening, it's been abuzz with curious sightseers, most of whom seem more than willing to brave long queues for the privilege of dining in one of its posh restaurants. A marked contrast to its sister restaurant Fonda de la Madrugada in Harajuku (p. 150), this stylish restaurant, with its modern decor, strolling musicians, and outdoor terrace, offers more hope than most for securing a seat if you haven't made a reservation, simply because Mexican food remains unknown to many Japanese. In any case, the food is more creative and refined (and pricier) than at its sister restaurant, offering the likes of chicken crepe on poblano chili and pistachio sauce, or lamb shank marinated in chili, garlic, and herbs. To be honest, I don't understand the fuss about Midtown; I like Roppongi Hills better, both for its architecture and its facilities.

Tokyo Midtown, Garden Terrace (shop D-0118), 1st floor, 9–7–4 Roppongi. © **03/5413-0092.** Reservations strongly recommended. Main dishes ¥2,200–¥3,050; set dinners ¥6,830–¥8,930; set lunches ¥2,300–¥4,500. AE, DC, MC, V. Daily 11am–11pm (last order). Station: Roppongi (Oedo exit, 2 min.). From Roppongi Crossing, walk on Gaien-Higashi Dori to Midtown, and then head to Garden Terrace.

Ristorante Il Bianco (**Value** ITALIAN   My friends and I don't know how they do it, but this very tiny Italian restaurant offers inexpensive wines (mostly from Chile) beginning at ¥1,575 a bottle. Main courses change often but always include choices of veal, chicken, and fish of the day, and the ¥200 dinner table charge includes bread. The only problem is finding the place—stop at the police station at Roppongi Crossing to look at the map or ask for directions. And once you get there, be sure to take the stairs on the right side of the building to the second-floor restaurant unless you want a cheap thrill—the elevator deposits you directly into the kitchen.

4–5–2 Roppongi. © **03/3470-5678.** Reservations a must for dinner. Main dishes ¥2,500–¥3,000; set dinners ¥4,000–¥5,500; pasta set lunches ¥1,050. AE, DC, MC, V. Mon–Fri 11:30am–2pm and 5:30–10pm; Sat 5:30–10pm (last order). Closed holidays. Station: Roppongi (3 min.). From Roppongi Crossing, head away from Tokyo Tower on Gaien-Higashi Dori and take the last right just before Midtown and then the 2nd right; it will be on the right, up a flight of stairs.

Sabatini Roppongi ★ ITALIAN   There are so many Sabatini restaurants in Tokyo (some with no relationship to each other) that they're hard to keep apart. This one, on the 13th floor of the Ibis Hotel, is the least expensive of them all, with good food and thoughtful service. Offering panoramic views over Roppongi and dominated by a huge floral arrangement in the center of the restaurant, it offers various pasta dishes along with Roman favorites, including rolled swordfish, chicken cacciatore, and *saltimbocca* (veal with sage and ham).

Ibis Hotel, 13th floor, 7–14–4 Roppongi. © **03/5411-2975.** Pasta ¥1,575–¥2,520; main dishes ¥1,995–¥5,250; set dinners ¥5,000–¥8,925; set lunches ¥1,350–¥2,600. AE, DC, MC, V. Daily 11:30am–2:30pm and 5:30–11pm. Station: Roppongi (1 min.). From Roppongi Crossing, walk away from Tokyo Tower on Gaien-Higashi Dori; Hotel Ibis is on your left.

INEXPENSIVE

In addition to the recommendations below, **La Boheme** (p. 134), at 4–11–13 Roppongi (© **03/3478-0222;** Mon–Sat 11am–5am; Sun 5pm–3:30am) and 2–25–18 Nishi Azabu (© **03/3407-1363;** daily 11am–5pm), serves pizza and pasta, while **Monsoon,** 2–10–1 Nishi Azabu (© **03/5467-5221**), offers a wide variety of Asian standards daily from 11am to 5am (p. 135). **Gyu-Kaku,** 5–1–2 Roppongi (© **03/5414-5129**), is a Korean barbecue restaurant, open Monday to Saturday from 5pm to 5am and Sunday and holidays from 5pm to midnight (p. 169).

(43) **Ganchan** ★ YAKITORI   This is one of my favorite yakitori-ya. Small and intimate, it's owned by a friendly and entertaining man who can't speak English worth a darn but keeps trying with the help of a worn-out Japanese–English dictionary he keeps behind the counter. His staff is young and fun-loving. There's an eclectic cassette collection—I never know whether to expect Japanese pop tunes or American oldies. Seating is along a single counter with room for only a dozen or so people. Though there's an English-language menu, it's easiest to order the yakitori seto, a set course that comes with salad and soup and eight skewers of such items as chicken, beef, meatballs, green peppers, and asparagus rolled with bacon. There's a table charge of ¥600 per person, but it includes an appetizer.

6–8–23 Roppongi. © **03/3478-0092.** Yakitori skewers ¥315–¥735; yakitori set course ¥2,625. AE, MC, V. Daily 5:30pm–1:30am. Station: Roppongi (7 min.). From Roppongi Crossing, take the small street going downhill to the left of the Almond coffee shop; Ganchan is at the bottom of the hill on the right.

Gonpachi ★★ (Value) VARIED JAPANESE/YAKITORI   Housed in a re-created *kura* (traditional Japanese warehouse) with a high ceiling, three-tiered seating, and a central, open kitchen, this is one of Tokyo's most imaginative inexpensive Japanese restaurants (it's said to have served as the inspiration for the restaurant scene in the movie *Kill Bill*). It offers a wide variety of dishes, including yakitori (such as duck breast with wasabi), fish (such as miso-glazed black cod), sushi (on the third floor), noodles, tempura, and more.

From the outside, you'd expect this place to be much more exclusive than it is—and you probably will be excluded if you fail to make reservations for dinner.

There are branches of Gonpachi at the G-Zone, 1–2–3 Ginza (© **03/5524-3641;** station: Kyobashi or Ginza-Itchome); in Shibuya on the 14th floor of E-Space Tower, 3–6 Maruyama-cho (© **03/5784-2011;** station: Shibuya); and at Mediage on Odaiba (© **03/3599-4807;** station: Daiba), all open from 11:30am to 3:30am or later. However, they don't match the Nishi Azabu location's atmosphere.

1-13-11 Nishi Azabu. © **03/5771-0170.** www.gonpachi.jp. Reservations recommended for dinner. Yakitori ¥300–¥1,500; main dishes ¥1,000–¥2,800; set meals ¥3,500–¥6,000; set lunches ¥950–¥1,100. AE, DC, MC, V. Daily 11:30am–5am. Station: Roppongi (10 min.). From Roppongi Crossing, walk toward Shibuya on Roppongi Dori. It will be on your right, at Gaien-Nishi Dori.

Hard Rock Cafe (Kids) AMERICAN   Founded by two American expatriates in London in 1971, Hard Rock Cafe has more than half a dozen locations in Japan; this was the first. If you have disgruntled teenagers in tow, bring them to this world-famous hamburger joint dedicated to rock 'n' roll to ogle the memorabilia on the walls, chow down on burgers, and check out the T-shirts for sale. In addition to hamburgers, the menu includes salads, sandwiches, steak, barbecued ribs, barbecued chicken, fish of the day, fajitas, and a few Asian dishes. Be prepared: The music is loud.

A branch is located in JR Ueno Station at 7–1–1 Ueno (© **03/5826-5821**).

5-4-20 Roppongi. © **03/3408-7018.** www.hardrockjapan.com. Main dishes ¥1,480–¥3,980. AE, DC, MC, V. Sun–Thurs 11:30am–2am; Fri–Sat 11:30am–4am. Station: Roppongi (3 min.). From Roppongi Crossing, walk on Gaien-Higashi Dori toward Tokyo Tower and take a right at McDonald's.

(44) **Honoji** ★ (Finds) VARIED JAPANESE   A plain wooden facade and a stark interior of concrete walls with wire-mesh screens set the mood for good, home-style Japanese cooking. Although it looks small at first glance (an open kitchen takes up half the space), quiet back-room nooks give diners a sense of privacy as they enjoy grilled fish, sashimi, yakitori, fried chicken, grilled eggplant with miso, stir-fried dishes such as cabbage with oyster sauce, seasoned pork with potatoes, and a variety of vegetables. Honoji serves the kinds of food offered by neighborhood *nomiya* (drinking establishments) all over Japan, which isn't exactly the kind of fare you'd expect in trendy Roppongi. Still, the crowds that wait at the door, especially on weekend nights, attest to its success. There's no English-language menu, so you might look around at what others are eating or go with one of the above dishes. *Note:* There's a dinner table charge of ¥380, though I was told it will be waived if foreigners don't like the snack that comes with it. The lunch teishoku, available for ¥900 and the only item offered for lunch, draws Japanese from all walks of life.

3-4-33 Roppongi. © **03/3588-1065.** Main dishes ¥500–¥1,000. AE, DC, MC, V. Mon–Fri 11:30am–1:30pm; Mon–Sat 5:30–10pm (last order). Closed holidays. Station: Roppongi (3 min.). On the right side of Roppongi Dori, as you walk from Roppongi Crossing in the direction of Akasaka, at the bottom of the hill just past 7-Eleven.

(45) **Ichioku** ★ NOUVELLE JAPANESE   This is one of my favorite restaurants in Roppongi for casual dining. It's a tiny, cozy place with only eight tables, and you fill out your order yourself using the English-language menu—complete with pictures—which is glued underneath the clear glass tabletop. The food, featuring organically grown vegetables, can best be called nouvelle Japanese, with original creations offered at very reasonable prices. About 25 dishes are available, including tuna and ginger sauté, mushroom sauté, shrimp spring rolls, Thai curry, asparagus salad, fried potatoes, sautéed eggplant, and a dish of grated radish and tiny fish. I personally like the tofu steak (fried tofu and

flakes of dried fish) and the cheese gyoza (fried pork dumpling topped with melted cheese).

4–4–5 Roppongi. ℂ **03/3405-9891.** Main dishes ¥800–¥2,450. AE, DC, MC, V. Mon–Fri 11:30am–2pm and 6pm–12:30am; Sat 6pm–1am; holidays 5–11pm (last order). Station: Roppongi (4 min.). On a side street in the neighborhood behind the police station.

Kamakura YAKITORI   Much more refined than most yakitori-ya, this basement establishment is decorated with paper lanterns and sprigs of fake but cheerful spring blossoms, with traditional koto music playing softly in the background. The English-language menu lists yakitori set courses; a la carte sticks are skewered with shrimp, meatballs, gingko, squid, eggplant, or mushrooms.

4–10–11 Roppongi. ℂ **03/3405-4377.** Yakitori skewers ¥240–¥550; set dinners ¥2,300–¥4,300. AE, DC, MC, V. Mon–Sat 5–11pm. Station: Roppongi (2 min.). From Roppongi Crossing, walk on the right side of Gaien-Higashi Dori in the direction of Tokyo Midtown and take the 2nd right.

Kitchen Five ★ **Finds** INTERNATIONAL   If it's true that love is the best spice for cooking, then perhaps that's why Yuko Kobayashi's 25-year-old, 18-seat restaurant is so popular. She goes to market every morning to fetch ingredients for a dozen main dishes, which may include stuffed eggplant, lasagna, moussaka, and other casseroles and curries that are spread on a counter along with their prices. Every year Kobayashi goes off to search for recipes in Sicily, South America, northern Africa, and other countries that feature garlic, tomatoes, and olive oil in their cuisine. The love for what she does shines in her eyes as she cooks, serves, and walks you through the menu of daily dishes displayed. *Warning:* The food is so delicious, it's tempting to over-order. Highly recommended.

4–2–15 Nishi Azabu. ℂ **03/3409-8835.** Dishes ¥1,300–¥1,900. No credit cards. Tues–Sat 6–9:30pm (last order). Closed holidays, Jan, Golden Week, and late July to early Sept. Station: Hiroo (7 min.) or Roppongi (15 min.). Opposite Gaien-Nishi Dori from the gas station, down a side street.

46 Kohmen **Value** RAMEN   Famished in the wee hours of the morning but spent most of your cash carousing? Head to this quirky ramen restaurant, where black-clad staff move around the dark interior like ninjas, fish swim in a birdcage, and personal-sized TVs at counters and tables broadcast Kohmen commercials, concerts, and movie previews. An English-language menu gives a good choice of various ramen noodles, from thick or thin to crispy, along with various broths and extra toppings ranging from grilled pork to fried leek. I'm crazy about the *kogashi-tantanmen,* a creamy sesame soup with hot chili and chargrilled marinated pork. There are branches across the city, including those at 6–2–8 Jingumae in Harajuku (ℂ **03/5468-6344;** station: Harajuku); 1–9–5 Ebisu (ℂ **03/5475-0185;** station: Ebisu); and 4–8–8 Ueno (ℂ **03/5807-4535;** station: Ueno).

7–14–3 Roppongi. ℂ **03/6406-4565.** Ramen ¥730–¥1,080. No credit cards. Daily 11am–6am. Station: Roppongi (1 min.). From Roppongi Crossing, head away from Tokyo Tower on Gaien-Higashi Dori; it will be on the left, next to the Ibis Hotel.

La Fiesta MEXICAN   Although there is an ever-growing number of Mexican restaurants in Tokyo, the majority serve only passable food. This one is better than most, and even though its renditions may not be what you're used to, they're usually very tasty in their own right and are good for a spicy fix. Colorfully decorated with south-of-the-border memorabilia and set to the pace of lively Mexican music, La Fiesta offers quesadillas, enchiladas, tacos, chimichangas, fajitas, and very good burritos. And, of course, everything goes down better with a margarita. Mexican beers and a good selection of tequilas are also available.

3–15–23 Roppongi. ℂ **03/3475-4412.** www.lafiesta-tokyo.com. Main dishes ¥880–¥3,280. AE, DC, MC, V. Daily 5pm–12:30am. Station: Roppongi (4 min.). From Roppongi Crossing, walk down the left side of Gaien-Higashi Dori in the direction of Tokyo Tower, turning left after passing McDonald's on your right.

Mado Lounge ★ ITALIAN/FRENCH   You have to pay the admission fee to the Mori Art Museum (p. 186) to dine here, but at 52 floors above the city, it's worth it for the views alone (the cutting-edge exhibitions are great, too). For lunch, you'll choose one of the sets, which may include the likes of grilled chicken with tomato sauce or Japanese pork ragu served with penne rigatte, while dinner allows you to nibble on a range of tapas (such as ratatouille with white beans), salads, pastas, pizzas, and main dishes ranging from Norwegian salmon to Japanese beef stewed in red wine. From 2:30 to 6:30pm, there's a curry set for ¥1,200 along with various cakes. Note that on Friday and Saturday nights (usually from 8pm) there's live music or a guest DJ, with a cover charge averaging ¥3,500.

Mori Tower, Roppongi Hills, 6–10–1 Roppongi. ℂ **03/3470-0052.** Main dishes ¥1,300–¥2,300; set lunches ¥1,200–¥2,400. AE, DC, MC, V. Wed–Mon 11am–midnight (last order). Station: Roppongi (Roppongi Hills exit, 2 min.).

Roti Roppongi ★ AMERICAN   A casual brasserie with both indoor (nonsmoking) and outdoor seating, Roti counts many expats among its loyal customers, due in part to its quiet, tucked-away location just a minute's walk from Roppongi Hills and also to its bilingual staff and modern American fare, which includes free-range rotisserie chicken, grilled steaks, burgers, serious Caesar salads, and many other delectable dishes too numerous to mention. More than 90 bottles of New World, Australian, and New Zealand wines, as well as American ales and Belgian microbrews, are on offer.

6–6–9 Roppongi. ℂ **03/5785-3671.** www.roti.jpco.com. Main dishes ¥1,600–¥3,300; set lunches (Mon–Fri only) ¥1,500–¥2,000. AE, DC, MC, V. Mon–Fri 11:30am–2:30pm; Sat–Sun 11:30am–5pm; daily 6–11pm. Station: Roppongi (A1 exit, 1 min.). On a side street that parallels Roppongi Dori, a stone's throw from Roppongi Hills.

㊼ **Torigin** YAKITORI   Part of a chain of yakitori establishments, this no-frills old-timer is typical of the smaller Japanese restaurants all over the country patronized by the country's salarymen, who stop off for a drink and a bite to eat before boarding the commuter trains for home. An English-language menu includes skewers of grilled chicken, gingko nuts, green peppers, quail eggs, and asparagus with rolled bacon, as well as various *kamameshi* (rice casseroles cooked and served in little pots and topped with chicken, bamboo shoots, mushrooms, crab, salmon, or shrimp).

4–12–6 Roppongi. ℂ **03/3403-5829.** Yakitori skewers ¥150–¥260; kamameshi ¥840–¥1,260; set meals ¥2,630. No credit cards. Daily 11:30am–2:30pm and 5–10:30pm. Station: Roppongi (2 min.). From Roppongi Crossing, walk on the right side of Gaien-Higashi Dori in the direction of Midtown and take the 3rd right.

14 AKASAKA

Note: To locate these restaurants, see the map on p. 103.

VERY EXPENSIVE
La Tour d'Argent ★★ CLASSIC FRENCH   Here's the place to dine if you're celebrating a very special occasion, are on a hefty expense account, or fancy yourself a jetsetter. Opened in 1984, La Tour d'Argent is the authentic sister to the one in Paris, which

opened back in 1582 and was visited twice by Japan's former emperor, Hirohito. Entrance to the Tokyo restaurant is through an impressive hallway with a plush interior and displays of tableware used in the Paris establishment throughout the centuries. The dining hall looks like an elegant Parisian drawing room. The service is superb, and the food is excellent. The specialty here is roast duckling—it meets its untimely end at the age of 3 weeks and is flown to Japan from Brittany. Other dishes on the menu, which changes seasonally, may include lobster or Kobe beef sirloin.

Hotel New Otani, 4–1 Kioi-cho, Chiyoda-ku. ☏ **03/3239-3111**. www.newotani.co.jp/en. Reservations required. Jacket and tie required. Main dishes ¥7,600–¥12,500; set dinners ¥21,000–¥29,000. AE, DC, MC, V. Tues–Sun 5:30–10:30pm (last reservation accepted for 8:30pm). Station: Akasaka-mitsuke or Nagata-cho (3 min.).

Sekishin-tei ★★ TEPPANYAKI Nestled in the New Otani's 400-year-old garden (which is the reason this is the hotel's most popular restaurant), this glass-enclosed teppanyaki pavilion has an English-language menu for Kobe beef, fish, lobster, and vegetables, cooked on a grill right in front of you. If you order a salad, try the soy sauce dressing; it's delicious. You'll eat surrounded by peaceful views, making this place a good lunchtime choice.

Hotel New Otani, 4–1 Kioi-cho, Chiyoda-ku. ☏ **03/3238-0024**. www.newotani.co.jp/en. Reservations required. Set dinners ¥15,750–¥29,400; set lunches ¥5,250–¥8,400. AE, DC, MC, V. Mon–Fri 11:30am–2pm; Sat–Sun and holidays 11:30am–3pm; daily 6–9pm. Station: Nagatacho or Akasaka-mitsuke (3 min.).

EXPENSIVE

In addition to the recommendations here, there's a branch of **Ten-ichi**, specializing in tempura, in Akasaka Tokyu Plaza, 2–14–3 Nagata-cho (☏ **03/3581-2166**), open daily 11am to 9:30pm (p. 131).

48 Hayashi ★★★ (Finds) ROBATAYAKI One of the most delightful old-time restaurants I've been to in Tokyo, this cozy, rustic-looking place serves home-style country cooking and specializes in grilled food that you prepare over your own square hibachi. There are only a handful of grills in this small restaurant, some of them surrounded by tatami mats and some by wooden stools or chairs. As the evening wears on, the one-room main dining area can get quite smoky, but that adds to the ambience. Other nice touches are the big gourds and memorabilia hanging about and the waiters in traditional baggy pants. Hayashi serves three set menus, which change with the seasons. The ¥6,300 meal—which will probably end up being closer to ¥8,000 by the time you add drinks and service charge—may include such items as sashimi and vegetables, chicken, scallops, and gingko nuts, which you grill yourself. At lunch, only *oyakodonburi* is served—literally, "parent and child," a simple rice dish topped with egg and chicken.

Sanno Kaikan Building, 4th floor, 2–14–1 Akasaka. ☏ **03/3582-4078**. Reservations required for dinner. Set dinners ¥6,300, ¥8,400, and ¥10,500; set lunches ¥900. AE, DC, MC, V. Mon–Fri 11:30am–2pm; Mon–Sat 5:30–11pm (last order 10pm). Closed holidays. Station: Akasaka (exit 2, 1 min.). Just south of Misuji Dori on the 4th floor of a nondescript, improbable-looking building.

Ninja ★ VARIED JAPANESE At this themed restaurant, diners enter the secret world of the ninja as soon as they step inside the darkened entrance, where costumed waiters appear out of nowhere to lead the hungry through a labyrinth of twisting passageways to private dining nooks. A scroll unrolls to reveal an English-language menu listing various set dinner menus that may include shabu-shabu, as well as a la carte items such as sweet-and-sour pork with asparagus, sole baked with herbs in saffron sauce, and grilled tenderloin beef and foie gras wrapped in *yuba* (soymilk skin). A fun place for a meal, but book early to reserve a seat.

Akasaka Tokyu Plaza, 1st floor, 2–14–3 Nagata-cho. *C* **03/5157-3936.** Reservations required. Main dishes ¥2,000–¥3,800; set dinners ¥7,777–¥20,000. AE, DC, MC, V. Mon–Sat 5pm–2am; Sun and holidays 5–11pm. Station: Akasaka-mitsuke (1 min.). In the candy cane–striped building, below the Akasaka Excel Tokyu Hotel.

Nobu Tokyo ★★★ NOUVELLE JAPANESE/FUSION Sister restaurant to New York's Nobu (and now with 20 locations worldwide), this classy, modern establishment is the place to see and be seen—and you can count on being seen, since the efficient, black-clad staff yells *"Irashaimase!"* ("Welcome!") the moment anyone is ushered into the large dining room. The food, beautifully presented and served one dish at a time, is a unique blend of Pacific Rim ingredients (not quite Japanese) with decidedly American/Latin influences. Sushi and sashimi are served, as well as sushi rolls such as California rolls (with avocado) and soft-shell-crab rolls. Other dishes include the roast fish of the day with jalapeño dressing, sake roasted cod with sansho salsa, baby squid with ginger salsa, wagyu steak with a choice of sauce, and sautéed scallops with wasabi pepper sauce. If ordering is too much of a chore, you can leave your meal to the discretion of Chef Matsuhisa by ordering the *omakase,* a complete chef's-choice dinner starting at ¥12,000. Nobu has an unlikely location in an obscure office building, but the Hotel Okura across the street and the nearby U.S. embassy assure it a steady stream of moneyed customers.

Toronomon Towers Office, 4–1–28 Toronomon. www.nobutokyo.com. **03/5733-0070.** Reservations recommended. Sushi and sashimi (per piece) ¥600–¥1,200; set dinners ¥12,000–¥25,000; set lunches ¥2,300–¥12,000. AE, DC, MC, V. Mon–Fri 11:30am–2pm; Mon–Sat 6–10pm; Sun and holidays 6–9:30pm (last order). Closed for lunch holidays. Station: Kamiyacho (6 min.) or Tameike Sanno (8 min.). Behind Hotel Okura.

MODERATE

(49) **Akasaka Jidaiya** VARIED JAPANESE Although the outside of this building isn't eye-catching, bend down to enter through the small Edo-style front door and you're instantly imported to old Japan. Decorated with antiques and with leg wells under tables for more comfortable floor seating, this Japanese pub has an English-language menu offering kaiseki, tempura, sukiyaki, and shabu-shabu set courses (with a two-person minimum order), as well as main dishes that range from grilled beef and tempura to nabe.

3–14–3 Akasaka. **03/3588-0489.** Reservations recommended. Main dishes ¥2,500–¥3,500; set meals ¥4,000–¥10,000. AE, DC, MC, V. Daily 11:30am–2pm; Mon–Fri 5pm–4am; Sat–Sun and holidays 5–11pm. Station: Akasaka (2 min.) or Akasaka-mitsuke (5 min.). On Misuji Dori.

Aux Bacchanales FRENCH This brasserie made a name for itself as the best people-watching sidewalk cafe in Harajuku, but then it abandoned teenybopper paradise for this grown-up location, where it does a booming trade with area business types. It still has the requisite sidewalk seating of sorts, on a back terrace of the Ark Hills complex, but the parade is not nearly as interesting. Inside it's a faithful brasserie replica, with booths, a tiled floor, and a long bar, making it equally popular for a drink after work. Lunch features specials written on a blackboard, along with such mainstays as croque-monsieur, quiche Lorraine, and hot dog Parisien (though it's hard to imagine there is such a thing), while dinner offers more substantial fare such as grilled scallops in a garlic butter sauce and stewed beef in red wine.

There's another location in Akasaka, in front of the Hotel New Otani, at 4–1 Kioicho (✆ **03/5276-3422;** station: Akasaka-mitsuke or Nagatacho), as well as in the Ginza, at 6–3–2 Ginza (✆ **03/3569-0202;** station: Ginza or Hibiya).

Ark Hills, 1st floor, 1-12-33 Akasaka. ✆ **03/3582-2225.** www.auxbacchanales. Main dishes ¥1,980–¥3,700; set dinner ¥5,000; set lunches ¥950–¥1,900 (¥2,900 Sat–Sun). AE, DC, MC, V. Mon–Sat 10am–11pm; Sun and holidays 11am–10pm. Closed 1 day a month (usually 2nd Sun). Station: Tameiko Sanno (3 min.) or Roppongi Itchome (2 min.). At the back of the Ark Mori Building, off Roppongi Dori.

daidaiya ★★ (Finds) VARIED JAPANESE/NOUVELLE JAPANESE   Upon exiting the elevator, you'll be forgiven for confusedly thinking you've landed in a nightclub rather than a restaurant—daidaiya's dark, theatrical entrance is the first clue that this is not your ordinary Japanese restaurant. The dining room, a juxtaposition of modern and traditional with a slate stone floor, shoji screens, warm woods, and black furniture, is rather like the cuisine—a curious mix of traditional Japanese food and original nouvelle creations, all mouthwateringly good. Pop music or jazz plays in the background, and for dinner, gauzy sheets of fabric are hung from the ceiling to create tiny, tête-à-tête dining cubicles for couples. Tatami seating is also available, with views over Akasaka. An English-language seasonal menu lists such intriguing entrees as Japanese beef filet with foie gras and whole chicken leg deep-fried and then topped with a sweet sauce and served with risotto. Lunch sets, including obento, are equally satisfying. I love this place.

There's a branch located on the third floor of the Nowa Building, 3–37–12 Shinjuku (✆ **03/5362-7173;** station: Shinjuku).

Bellevie Akasaka Building, 9th floor, 3-1-6 Akasaka. ✆ **03/3588-5087.** www.chanto.com. Reservations recommended for dinner. Main dishes ¥1,500–¥3,500; set dinners ¥6,300–¥8,400; set lunches ¥1,300–¥3,500. AE, DC, MC, V. Mon–Sat 11:30am–2pm and 5pm–midnight; Sun 11:30am–3pm and 5–10pm (last order). Station: Akasaka-mitsuke (1 min., underneath the Bellevie Akasaka Building). Take the elevator from inside the BelleVie Shopping Center.

The Sky VARIED JAPANESE/INTERNATIONAL   Located on the 17th floor of the New Otani's main building, with great views of the city, this revolving restaurant provides panoramic views and all-you-can-eat buffets, with mostly Japanese fare as well as a mix of Asian and Western dishes. Appetizers, salads, dim sum, desserts, and other choices are spread at various tables, while tempura, teppanyaki, sushi, and other made-to-order dishes are prepared by chefs according to your specifications (top-grade beef extra). My only complaint is that while the windowside tables revolve (70 min. for a complete cycle), the food stations remain stationary, making for some possible long strolls and confusion trying to find your table again. Also, beverages cost extra. If revolving restaurants aren't your thing, another buffet-style restaurant called **Top of the Tower,** on the 40th floor of the New Otani's tower, also has spectacular views of the city and offers Continental buffet lunches for ¥5,040 and dinners for ¥7,875, with the same open hours.

Hotel New Otani, 4-1 Kioi-cho, Chiyoda-ku. ✆ **03/3238-0028.** www.newotani.co.jp/en. Dinner buffet ¥8,400; lunch buffet ¥5,250. AE, DC, MC, V. Daily 11:30am–2pm and 5:30–9pm. Station: Akasaka-mitsuke or Nagatacho (3 min.).

Wolfgang Puck Cafe AMERICAN/FUSION   This casual, well-managed restaurant, with a colorful, cheerful interior and an outdoor sidewalk terrace, offers pasta, pizza, salads, and burgers for lunch (served to a late 5pm), and adds entrees such as pan-fried catfish, sautéed swordfish, and roasted chicken with garlic potato purée and rosemary jus to its dinner menu. You can depend on a tasty—though uneventful—meal at this chain. There's a branch in the Roi Building, 5–5–1 Roppongi (✆ **03/5775-5401;** station: Roppongi).

Ark Mori Building, 1–12–33 Akasaka. ☎ 03/5575-2100. Pizza and pasta ¥1,080–¥1,700; main dishes ¥1,780–¥2,780; set lunches ¥1,300–¥2,000. AE, DC, MC, V. Daily 11am–11pm. Station: Roppongi Itchome (1 min.) or Tameike Sanno (3 min.). On Roppongi Dori.

INEXPENSIVE

Don't forget **Hayashi,** on the fourth floor of the Sanno Kaikan Building, 2–14–1 Akasaka, described above as an expensive restaurant (p. 166). Although dinner is costly, you can enjoy the same, cozy atmosphere for much, much less at lunch, when only one dish, *oyako donburi* (rice topped with chunks of chicken and egg), is served, with pickled vegetables, clear soup, and tea, for ¥900, with a slightly larger portion available for ¥1,000. Open for lunch Monday through Friday from 11:30am to 2pm. In addition, okonomiyaki restaurant **Botejyu San** is on the second floor of the Taisuikan Building, 3–10–1 Akasaka (☎ 03/3505-2930). It's open Monday to Friday from 11:30am to 3pm and daily from 5:30 to 11pm (p. 154).

Gyu-Kaku KOREAN BARBECUE   Akasaka is known for its Korean restaurants, but this one is easier than most with an English-language menu that describes each dish in almost encyclopedic detail. There are various kinds of meats—beef, pork, chicken—which you grill yourself on charcoal briquettes at your table, along with side dishes ranging from salad and *kimchi* (spicy cabbage) to roasted garlic wrapped in foil. There are also platters for two diners beginning at ¥1,974, and on weeknights there's an all-you-can-eat buffet for ¥2,750; note that the whole table must order it and there's a time limit of 90 minutes. This is a fun, boisterous place, popular with groups of office workers and couples unwinding and letting loose. There's a branch in Roppongi, at 5–1–2 Roppongi (☎ 03/5414-5129; station: Roppongi).

3–10–10 Akasaka. ☎ 03/5572-6129. Meat dishes ¥514–¥1,029. AE, DC, MC, V. Daily 5pm–midnight. Station: Akasaka-mitsuke (2 min.). On Misuji Dori, on the 2nd floor above a pachinko parlor.

Pizza Salvatore Cuomo PIZZA   Nestled between two glass office buildings on a small square and with outdoor seating, this stylish pizzeria with a young staff and contemporary music turns out traditional Neapolitan pizza baked in a wood-fired oven. Pasta, a fish of the day, and a few other dishes are also available, though the emphasis is on the pizza, with two sizes available. The small size is big enough for two to share if ordering a salad as well.

Prudential Plaza, 2–13–10 Nagata-cho. ☎ 03/3500-5700. Small pizza ¥1,300–¥1,900; set lunches (Mon–Fri only) ¥980–¥1,400. AE, DC, MC, V. Daily 11am–2:30pm and 5–11pm (last order). Station: Akasaka-mitsuke (2 min.). On the east side of Sotobori Dori, to the back of a small square btw. two glass office buildings that contain Citibank and Prudential Financial.

15   AKIHABARA/KANDA

MODERATE

(50) **Kandagawa** ★ (Finds) EEL   Dining in this beautiful, old-fashioned, traditional Japanese restaurant, famous for its eel dishes since the Edo Period, is unforgettable. A Japanese-style wooden house, hidden behind a wooden gate, it offers seven private tatami rooms, as well as a larger tatami dining room. The menu, in Japanese only, offers side dishes of soup, rice, and Japanese pickles, and such main dishes as *kabayaki* (broiled and basted eel), *unaju* (broiled eel on rice with a sweet sauce), *shiroyaki* ("white" eel, broiled without soy sauce or oil), and *umaki* (eel wrapped in an omelet). If you've never eaten

eel, I can think of no finer place to first try it. Expect to spend a minimum of ¥7,500 per person, including drinks, appetizers, and service. No one here speaks English, so it's best to have a Japanese-speaking person make your reservation, at which time you must order the dishes you'd like to be served.

2–5–11 Soto-Kanda. ✆ **03/3251-5031.** Reservations required. Main dishes ¥2,600–¥4,100. MC, V. Mon–Sat 11:30am–2pm and 5–8pm. Closed holidays and 2nd Sat of the month Sept–May. Station: Akihabara (5 min.). On Shohei Bashi Dori (Hwy. 17).

INEXPENSIVE

Ginzo (Value) SUSHI   With a long counter from which to watch the sushi chefs in action and with the rumbling of trains overhead, this neighborhood restaurant offers reasonably priced meals from an English-language menu. The ¥980 set meal, for example, comes with six maki-zushi, nine sushi, soup, and *chawamushi* (egg custard). Because this is a very popular restaurant with local workers, avoid the weekday lunchtime rush.

1–8–6 Kanda-Hanaoka-cho. ✆ **03/5298-5161.** Sushi ¥137 per piece; set meals ¥780–¥1,500. No credit cards. Mon–Thurs 11:30am–11pm; Fri–Sun and holidays 11:30am–10pm. Station: Akihabara (1 min.). Underneath the train tracks btw. Chuo and Showa Dori; look for the fake bamboo and a banner showing the various set meals outside its front door.

(51) **Kanda Yabusoba** ★ (Finds) NOODLES   This is one of Tokyo's most famous *soba* (noodle) shops, established in 1880 and rebuilt after the 1923 Great Kanto Earthquake. The house, which is surrounded by a wooden gate with an entryway through a small grove of bamboo, features shoji screens and a dining area with tatami mats and tables. It's often filled with middle-age businessmen and housewives, so you'll probably have to wait on the bench at the entrance if you come during lunchtime. There's an English-language menu. The specialties are hot and cold wheat noodles, which you can order with grated yam, grilled eel, duck, or crispy shrimp tempura. Listen to the woman sitting at a small counter by the kitchen—she sings out orders to the chef, as well as hellos and goodbyes to customers.

2–10 Awajicho, Kanda. ✆ **03/3251-0287.** Main dishes ¥630–¥1,785. No credit cards. Daily 11:30am–7:30pm (last order). Closed 1 week in mid-Aug. Station: Awajicho or Ogawamachi (exit A3, 3 min.) or Akihabara (10 min.). Northeast of the Sotobori Dori and Yasukuni Dori intersection; from Sotobori Dori, take the side street that runs btw. the Tokyo Green Hotel and the Hotel Mystays and look toward the left.

What to See & Do in Tokyo

Some Westerners have a highly romanticized view of Japan, picturing it as a woodblock print—exquisite, mysterious, and ancient.

What a shock, then, to come to Tokyo. In a country known around the world for its appreciation of the aesthetic, Tokyo is disappointingly unimpressive. Some foreigners, unable to reconcile unrealistic expectations with the cold facts of reality, summarily dismiss Tokyo as a monstrosity of the 21st century and go off in search of the "real" Japan. What they don't realize is that beneath Tokyo's concrete shell is a cultural life left very much intact. In fact, Tokyo is the best place in the world to experience Japanese performing arts, such as Kabuki, as well as participate in such diverse activities as the tea ceremony and flower arranging. It's also the nation's foremost repository of Japanese arts and crafts and boasts a wide range of both first-class and unique museums.

SEEING THE CITY BY GUIDED TOUR With the help of this book and a good map, you should be able to visit Tokyo's major attractions easily on your own. Should you be pressed for time, however, you might consider taking one of several group tours of Tokyo and its environs offered by the **Japan Travel Bureau (JTB; ⓒ 03/5796-5454;** www.jtb-sunrise tours.jp) or **Japan Gray Line (ⓒ 03/3595-5939;** www.jgl.co.jp/inbound/index.htm). Day tours may include Tokyo Tower, the Imperial Palace and Ginza districts, Asakusa Sensoji Temple, Meiji Jingu Shrine, and a harbor or river cruise. There are also specialized tours that take in local festivals, the Ghibli Museum, Kabuki,

Tsukiji Fish Market, Akihabara, sumo wrestling, or Tokyo's nightlife, as well as cultural-themed tours that allow participants to experience such activities as the tea ceremony, making sushi, or dressing up in a kimono. Be warned, however, that tours are very tourist-oriented, do not allow much time for exploration, and are more expensive than touring Tokyo on your own. Prices range from about ¥4,500 for a half-day tour to about ¥12,000 for a full-day tour including lunch. You can easily book tours through most tourist hotels and travel agencies.

Although they cover less ground, 10 tours offered by the **Tokyo Metropolitan Government** concentrate on specific areas or themes, such as Japanese gardens, Asakusa, or Harajuku. Lasting 2 to 3 hours, they are conducted mostly on foot or utilize public transportation and vary in price from free (a walking tour of Shinjuku and the food floor of Isetan department store) to ¥3,540 (the Ginza, Tsukiji Outer Market, Hama Rikyu Garden, and Odaiba), plus admission costs of the volunteer guides. Tours depart from the Tokyo Tourist Information Center in the TMG building in Shinjuku at 1pm Monday to Friday (excluding public holidays; some tours depart also at 10am). Preregistration 3 days in advance of the tour is required, and a minimum of one participant must be at least 20 years old. For more information, go to www.tourism.metro.tokyo.jp/english/tourists/guideservice/guideservice/index.html or contact the tourist office (see p. 306 in "Fast Facts").

Volunteer guides are also on hand at the Ueno Green Salon in Ueno Park every

Did You Know?

- Tokyo has been the capital of Japan only since 1868; before that, Kyoto served as capital for more than 1,000 years.
- Ten percent of Japan's total population lives in Tokyo—more than 12 million residents. Almost a quarter of Japan's total population lives within commuting distance.
- Tokyo's workers commute to work an average of 90 minutes one-way. Shinjuku Station handles the most train and subway passengers in all of Japan—more than three million people a day, giving it an entry in the Guinness Book of World Records as the busiest rail station in the world. More than 60 exits lead out of the station.
- Tokyo suffered widespread destruction twice in the last century—in the 1923 Great Kanto Earthquake and from World War II firebombs. In both instances, more than 100,000 people lost their lives.
- During the Edo Period (1603–1867), Edo (former Tokyo) witnessed almost 100 major fires, not to mention countless smaller fires.
- Tokyo sprawls over 1,288 sq. km (497 sq. miles), yet most streets are not named.
- Rickshaws originated in Tokyo in 1869; 4 years later, there were 34,000 of the people-propelled vehicles in the capital city.
- Park space in Tokyo is woefully inadequate—just 4.52 sq. m (5^1/$_2$ sq. yd.) per capita, compared to 45.7 sq. m (55 sq. yd.) in Washington, D.C.
- According to government 2008 estimates, approximately 3,400 homeless were living in Tokyo, mainly in city parks and along riverbanks. There are 15,750 homeless nationwide, a big decline from the peak of 25,296 in 2003, the first year records were kept.

Wednesday, Friday, and Sunday for free 90-minute walking tours departing at 10:30am and 1:30pm; and at the Asakusa Information Center every Sunday for 1-hour tours departing at 11am and 2pm (for locations of these meeting places, refer to my walking tours of Ueno and Asakusa in chapter 8). No registration is required. For more information, call © **03/3842-5566.**

Free guided tours are also offered through www.tokyofreeguide.com, staffed by volunteers. You're expected to pay for the guide's entrance to museums, meals, and transportation fees if applicable, but you get to choose what you'd like to see;

because many of these volunteers work, weekends are the best days to book a tour.

A 1-hour tour of the Marunouchi and Ginza districts is offered by the **Tokyo Sky Bus** (© **03/3215-0008;** www.skybus.jp), with departures from the Mitsubishi Building (across from the Marunouchi South exit of Tokyo Station) every hour on the hour from 10am to 6pm. The open-top, double-decker buses roll past the Imperial Palace, National Theater, Supreme Court, Diet Building, and other downtown sights, and the tours cost ¥1,500.

Otherwise, one tour I especially like is a **boat trip on the Sumida River** ★★ between Hama Rikyu Garden and

Asakusa. Commentary on the 40-minute trip is in both Japanese and English (be sure to pick up the English-language leaflet, too). You'll get descriptions of the 12 bridges you pass along the way and views of Tokyo you'd otherwise miss. Boats depart Hama Rikyu Garden hourly or more frequently between 10:35am and 4:15pm, with the fare to Asakusa costing ¥720 one-way. There are also other cruise routes, including those between Hinode Pier (closest station: Hinode, about a 1-min. walk) and Asakusa (fare: ¥760), Asakusa and Odaiba (fare: ¥1,520), and Hinode Pier and Odaiba (fare: ¥460). For more information, contact the **Tokyo Cruise Ship Co.** (© **0120-977311;** www.suijobus.co.jp).

Another boat company, offering transportation along the Sumida and Arakawa rivers, in the Odaiba area, and to Kasai Rinkai Park, is the **Tokyo Mizube Cruising Line** (© **03/5608-8869;** www.tokyo-park.or.jp/English/business/route.html).

Finally, for personalized, one-on-one tours of Tokyo, contact **Jun's Tokyo Discovery Tours,** managed by Tokyoite Junko Matsuda, which offers tailored sightseeing trips to Tsukiji, Asakusa, Yanaka, Harajuku, Aoyama, Shibuya, Shinjuku, and Kamakura, as well as shopping trips and special trips designed to fit your interests. Tours utilize public transportation and are especially useful if you wish to communicate with shopkeepers and the locals, want to learn more about what you're seeing, or are timid about finding your way on public transportation (if you wish, you'll be met at your hotel). The cost is ¥25,000 for 1 day (7 hr.) for up to four adults or a family. Reserve tours at least 3 days in advance (1 week preferred) by fax (© **03/5477-6022**) or e-mail (me2@gb3.so-net.ne.jp), stating the desired tour date and what you'd like to see; messages can also be left at © **090/7734-0079** (if you're calling from abroad, drop the initial 0).

1 THE TOP ATTRACTIONS

Edo-Tokyo Museum (Edo-Tokyo Hakubutsukan) ★★★ (Kids) The building housing this impressive museum is said to resemble a rice granary when viewed from afar, but to me it looks like a modern *torii,* the entrance gate to a shrine. This is the metropolitan government's ambitious attempt to present the history, art, disasters, science, culture, and architecture of Tokyo from its humble beginnings in 1590—when the first shogun, Tokugawa Ieyasu, made Edo (old Tokyo) the seat of his domain—to 1964, when Tokyo hosted the Olympics. All in all, the museum's great visual displays create a vivid portrayal of Tokyo through the centuries. I wouldn't miss it. Plan on spending 2 hours here.

After purchasing your ticket and taking a series of escalators to the sixth floor, you'll enter the museum by walking over a replica of Nihombashi Bridge, the starting point for all roads leading out of old Edo. Exhibits covering the Edo Period portray the lives of the shoguns, merchants, craftsmen, and townspeople. The explanations are mostly in Japanese only, but there's plenty to look at, including a replica of an old Kabuki theater, a model of a *daimyo's* (feudal lord) mansion, portable floats used during festivals, maps and photographs of old Edo, and—perhaps most interesting—a row-house tenement where Edo commoners lived in cramped quarters measuring only 10 sq. m (108 sq. ft.). Other displays cover the Meiji Restoration, the Great Kanto Earthquake of 1923, and the bombing raids of World War II (Japan's own role as aggressor is disappointingly glossed over), with plenty of old-style conveyances—from a palanquin to a rickshaw—for kids to climb in and have parents take their picture.

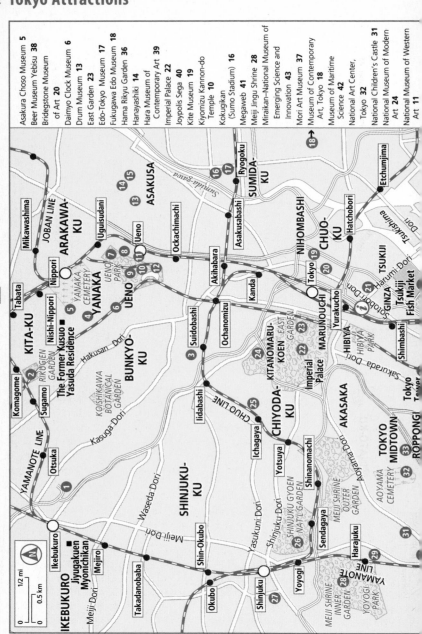

Asakura Choso Museum **5**
Beer Museum Yebisu **38**
Bridgestone Museum of Art **20**
Daimyo Clock Museum **6**
Drum Museum **13**
East Garden **23**
Edo-Tokyo Museum **17**
Fukugawa Edo Museum **18**
Hama Rikyu Garden **36**
Hanayashiki **14**
Hara Museum of Contemporary Art **39**
Imperial Palace **22**
Joypolis Sega **40**
Kite Museum **19**
Kiyomizu Kannon-do Temple **10**
Kokugikan (Sumo Stadium) **16**
Megaweb **41**
Meiji Jingu Shrine **28**
Miraikan–National Museum of Emerging Science and Innovation **43**
Mori Art Museum **37**
Museum of Contemporary Art, Tokyo **18**
Museum of Maritime Science **42**
National Art Center, Tokyo **32**
National Children's Castle **31**
National Museum of Modern Art **24**
National Museum of Western Art **11**

National Museum of Nature
and Science **8**
Nezu Shrine **4**
Ooedo-Onsen Monogatari **44**
Panasonic Center **45**
Rikugien Garden **2**
Sensoji Temple **15**
Shinjuku Gyoen **26**
Shitamachi Museum **12**
Sony Building **21**
Spa LaQua **3**
Sunshine International
Aquarium **1**
Suntory Museum of Art **33**
Tokyo City View **37**
Tokyo Dome City **3**
Tokyo Metropolitan
Children's Hall **30**
Tokyo Metropolitan
Government (TMG)
Observation Platform **27**
Tokyo Metropolitan Museum
of Photography **38**
Tokyo National Museum **7**
Tokyo Tower **34**
Toshogu Shrine **10**
Toyota Auto Salon Amlux
Tokyo **1**
Tsukiji Fish Market **35**
Ueno Zoo **9**
Ukiyo-e Ota Memorial
Museum of Art **29**
Yasukuni Shrine **25**

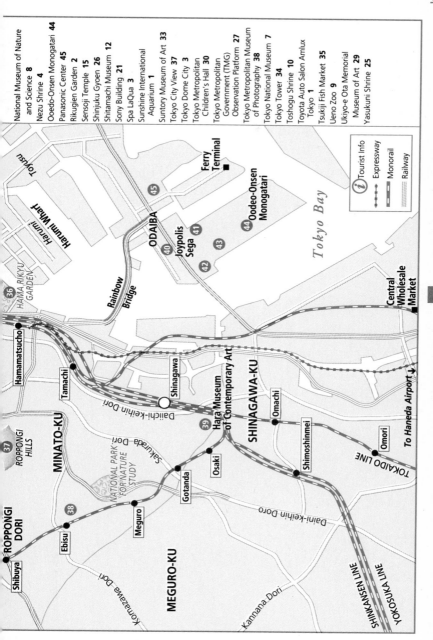

If you wish, take advantage of a free museum tour offered by volunteers daily 10am to 3pm (last tour). Most tours last 1 to 2 hours, depending on the level of visitor interest, and are insightful for their explanations of the Japanese-only displays. However, tours are necessarily rushed and focus on particular displays; you may wish to tour the museum afterward on your own.

1–4–1 Yokoami, Sumida-ku. (C) **03/3626-9974.** www.edo-tokyo-museum.or.jp. Admission ¥600 adults, ¥480 college students, ¥300 seniors and junior-high/high-school students, free for younger children. Tues–Sun 9:30am–5:30pm (to 7:30pm Sat). Station: Ryogoku on the JR Sobu Line (west exit, 3 min.) and Oedo Line (exit A4, 1 min.). Tokyo Shitamachi Bus: Ryogoku Station.

The Imperial Palace (Kyokyo) ★ The Imperial Palace, home of the Imperial family, is the heart and soul of Tokyo. Built on the very spot where Edo Castle used to stand during the days of the Tokugawa shogunate, it became the Imperial home upon its completion in 1888 and is now the residence of Emperor Akihito, 125th emperor of Japan. Destroyed during air raids in 1945, the palace was rebuilt in 1968 using the principles of traditional Japanese architecture. But don't expect to get a good look at it; most of the palace grounds' 114 hectares (282 acres) are off-limits to the public, with the exception of 2 days a year when the royal family makes an appearance before the throngs: January 2 and December 23 (the emperor's birthday). Or, you can visit Imperial grounds on free **guided tours** Monday through Friday at 10am and 1:30pm (1:30pm tour not available July 21–Aug 31), but you must register at least 1 day in advance (reservations are accepted up to 1 month in advance) by calling (C) **03/3213-1111** and then stopping by the Imperial Household Agency (located at the Sakashita-mon Gate, on the east side of the palace grounds) to show your passport number and provide nationality, name, age, gender, and home address. Easier is to book through the Internet at http://sankan.kunaicho.go.jp/English/index.html at least 4 days before the tour. Tours, conducted in Japanese only but with English-language audioguides available, last about 75 minutes and lead past official buildings, the inner moat and historic fortifications, and Nijubashi Bridge. I recommend this tour only if you have time to spare and have already seen Tokyo's other top attractions.

Otherwise, you'll have to console yourself with a camera shot of the palace from the southeast side of **Nijubashi Bridge,** where the moat and the palace turrets show above the trees. Most Japanese tourists make brief stops here to pay their respects. The wide moat, lined with cherry trees, is especially beautiful in the spring. You might even want to spend an hour strolling the 4.8km (3 miles) around the palace and moat. But the most important thing to do in the palace's vicinity is visit its **Higashi Gyoen (East Garden),** where you'll find what's left of the central keep of old Edo Castle, the stone foundation; see "Parks & Gardens," later in this chapter.

Hibiya Dori Ave. Station: Nijubashi-mae (1 min.) or Hibiya (5 min.).

Meiji Jingu Shrine ★★ This is Tokyo's most venerable Shinto shrine, opened in 1920 in honor of Emperor and Empress Meiji, who were instrumental in opening Japan to the outside world more than 120 years ago. Japan's two largest *torii* (the traditional entry gate of a shrine), built of cypress more than 1,700 years old, give dramatic entrance to the grounds, once the estate of a daimyo. The shaded pathway is lined with trees, shrubs, and dense woods. In late May/June, the **Iris Garden** is in spectacular bloom (admission fee charged). About a 10-minute walk from the first *torii*, the shrine is a fine example of dignified and refined Shinto architecture. It's made of plain Japanese cypress

and topped with green-copper roofs. Meiji Jingu Shrine is the place to be on New Year's
Eve, when more than two million people crowd onto the grounds to usher in the New
Year.

Meiji Shrine Inner Garden, 1–1 Kamizono-cho, Yoyogi, Shibuya-ku. © **03/3379-5511.** www.meijijingu.
or.jp. Free admission. Daily sunrise to sunset (about 4:30pm in winter). Station: Harajuku (2 min.).

Sensoji Temple ★★★   Also popularly known as Asakusa Kannon, this is Tokyo's
oldest and most popular temple, with a history dating back to A.D. 628. That was when,
according to popular lore, two brothers fishing in the nearby Sumida River netted the
catch of their lives—a tiny golden statue of Kannon, the Buddhist goddess of mercy and
happiness who is empowered with the ability to release humans from all suffering. Sensoji Temple was erected in her honor, and although the statue is housed here, it's never
shown to the public. Still, through the centuries, worshippers have flocked here seeking
favors of Kannon; and when Sensoji Temple burned down during a 1945 bombing raid,
the present structure was rebuilt with donations by the Japanese people (*Note:* Due to
renovation, Sensoji Temple is under wraps until Dec 2010, but it remains open to the
public).

Colorful **Nakamise Dori,** a pedestrian lane leading to the shrine, is lined with traditional shops and souvenir stands. In fact, the whole Asakusa area is one of my favorite
neighborhoods, and you can easily spend half a day here; see the walking tour in chapter
8 for more on this fascinating part of old Tokyo.

2-3-1 Asakusa, Taito-ku. © **03/3842-0181.** Free admission. Daily 6:30am–5pm. Station: Asakusa (2
min.). Tokyo Shitamachi Bus: Asakusa Kaminarimon.

Tokyo National Museum (Tokyo Kokuritsu Hakubutsukan) ★★★   The
National Museum is not only the largest and oldest museum in Japan, but it also boasts
the largest collection of Japanese art in the world. This is where you go to see antiques
from Japan's past—old kimono, samurai armor, priceless swords, lacquerware, metalwork, pottery, scrolls, screens, *ukiyo-e* (woodblock prints), calligraphy, ceramics, archaeological finds, and more. Items are shown on a rotating basis with about 3,000 on display
at any one time—so no matter how many times you visit the museum, you'll always see
something new. There are also frequent special exhibitions. Schedule at least 2 hours to
do the museum justice.

The museum comprises five buildings. The **Japanese Gallery (Honkan),** straight
ahead as you enter the main gate, is the most important one, devoted to Japanese art.
Here you'll view Japanese ceramics; Buddhist sculptures dating from about A.D. 538 to
1192; samurai armor, helmets, and decorative sword mountings; swords, which throughout Japanese history were considered to embody spirits all their own; textiles and
kimono; lacquerware; ceramics; and paintings, calligraphy, ukiyo-e, and scrolls. Be sure
to check out the museum shop in the basement; it sells reproductions from the museum's
collections as well as traditional crafts by contemporary artists.

The **Asian Gallery (Toyokan)** houses art and archaeological artifacts from everywhere
in Asia outside Japan. There are Buddhas from China and Gandhara, stone reliefs from
Cambodia, embroidered wall hangings and cloth from India, Iranian and Turkish car-
pets, Thai and Vietnamese ceramics, and more. Chinese art—including jade, paintings,
calligraphy, and ceramics—makes up the largest part of the collection, illustrating China's tremendous influence on Japanese art, architecture, and religion. You'll also find
Egyptian relics, including a mummy dating from around 751 to 656 B.C. and wooden

WHAT TO SEE & DO IN TOKYO

178 objects from around 2000 B.C. *Note:* The Toyokan is closed for renovation until 2012. Until its reopening, selections from the collection are on display at the **Hyokeikan,** built on the museum grounds in 1909 to commemorate the marriage of Emperor Taisho.

The **Heiseikan Gallery** is where you'll find archaeological relics of ancient Japan, including pottery and Haniwa clay burial figurines of the Jomon Period (10,000 B.C.– 1000 B.C.) and ornamental, keyhole-shaped tombs from the Yayoi Period (400 B.C.–A.D. 200). The **Gallery of Horyuji Treasures (Horyuji Homotsukan)** displays priceless Buddhist treasures from the Horyuji Temple in Nara, founded by Prince Shotoku in A.D. 607. Although the building's stark modernity (designed by Taniguchi Yoshio, who also designed the expansion of the New York Museum of Modern Art) seems odd for an exhibition of antiquities, the gallery's low lighting and simple architecture lend dramatic effect to the museum's priceless collection of bronze Buddhist statues, ceremonial Gigaku masks used in ritual dances, lacquerware, and paintings.

Ueno Park, Taito-ku. ✆ **03/3822-1111.** www.tnm.jp. Admission ¥600 adults, ¥400 college students, free for seniors and for children. Special exhibits cost more. Tues–Sun 9:30am–5pm (enter by 4:30pm; Apr– Dec till 8pm Fri during special exhibitions; Apr–Sept till 6pm Sat–Sun and holidays). Closed Dec 28–Jan 1. Station: Ueno (10 min.). Tokyo Shitamachi Bus: Ueno Koen Yamashita/Ueno Station.

Tsukiji Fish Market ★★★ This huge wholesale fish market—the largest in Japan and one of the largest in the world—is a must for anyone who has never seen such a market in action. The action here starts early: At about 3am, boats begin arriving from the seas around Japan, from Africa, and even from America, with enough fish to satisfy the demands of a nation where seafood reigns supreme. To give you some idea of its enormity, this market handles almost all the seafood—about 450 kinds of seafood—consumed in Tokyo. The king is tuna, huge and frozen, unloaded from the docks, laid out on the ground, and numbered. Wholesalers walk up and down the rows, jotting down the numbers of the best-looking tuna, and by 5:30am, the tuna auctions are well underway. The entire auction of sea products takes place from about 4:40 to 6:30am, with auctions of vegetables at a corner of the market starting at 6:30am. The wholesalers then transfer what they've bought to their own stalls in the market, subsequently selling fish and produce to their regular customers, usually retail stores and restaurants.

Although I used to be able to arrive before dawn and visit the entire market freely, an increasing number of tourists over the years has prompted authorities to close tuna auctions to visitors, except for a small viewing area open 5–6:15am (get there before 5am and expect to wait in line). Otherwise, I think it's just as fun to the visit the wholesale market area, held in a cavernous, hangarlike building, which means you can visit it even on a dismal rainy morning. There's a lot going on—men in black rubber boots rushing wheelbarrows and forklifts through the aisles, hawkers shouting, knives chopping and slicing. Wander the aisles and you'll see things you never dreamed were edible. This is a good place to bring your camera, but note that no flash photography of auctions or the market is allowed. Also, the floors are wet, so leave your fancy shoes at the hotel. Finally, be mindful of the many forklifts and carts, and please don't touch the fish.

Tsukiji is also a good place to come if you want sushi for breakfast. Alongside the covered market are rows of barracklike buildings divided into sushi restaurants and shops related to the fish trade. In addition, in between the market and Tsukiji Station is the Outer Market *(Jogai),* a delightful district of tiny retail shops and stalls where you can buy the freshest seafood in town, plus dried fish and fish products, seaweed, vegetables, knives, and other cooking utensils. *Warning:* While walking through the Outer Market, my Japanese friend and I were warned several times by local shopkeepers to watch our purses, advice we didn't take lightly. Apparently, pickpockets have been at work here on **179** unsuspecting tourists.

5-2-1 Tsukiji, Chuo-ku. (℃) **03/3542-1111.** www.tsukiji-market.or.jp. Free admission. Mon–Sat 5–11am (best time 5–9am). Closed some Wed, holidays, several days around New Year's, and 3 days in mid-Aug. Station: Tsukijishijo (exit A2, 2 min.) or Tsukiji (Honganji Temple exit, 10 min.).

2 FIVE UNFORGETTABLE WAYS TO IMMERSE YOURSELF IN JAPANESE CULTURE

Just walking down the street could be considered a cultural experience in Japan. But there are a few more concrete ways to learn about this country's cultural life: The best of them involve participating in some of the country's time-honored rituals and traditions.

In addition to the recommendations below, several tour companies offer cultural activities, which you might consider if time is short or you wish to experience an activity not covered in this chapter. Of course, you'll also pay more for the convenience of a tour. JTB's **Sunrise Tours** ((℃) **03/5796-5454;** www.jtb-sunrisetours.jp) offers a wide range of cultural activities, from trying your hand at making sushi or writing calligraphy to learning about bonsai, visiting a sumo stable, participating in a tea ceremony, to trying on a kimono or samurai and ninja outfits. Prices range from ¥5,000 for the bonsai tour to ¥19,000 for a tour that includes an *ikebana* (flower arranging) lesson, a tea ceremony, and the experience of wearing a kimono.

Similarly, **H.I.S. Experience Japan** (http://hisexperience.jp) offers a wide range of hands-on activities, including a ninja training session; a samurai sword class featuring a sword fight demonstration by instructors and a lesson covering the basic movements; a visit to a sumo stable, followed by a typical sumo meal; a taiko drumming or shamisen course; the tea ceremony; a kimono workshop; a survival Japanese-language class; and cooking classes that cover sushi, soba, and traditional Japanese food. Activities are held irregularly, so check the website for dates. Prices range from ¥5,500 for the Japanese-language class to ¥30,000 for the 4-hour Japanese Traditional Cooking class, including lunch.

IKEBANA Japanese flower arranging, or *ikebana,* was first popularized among aristocrats during the Heian Period (A.D. 794–1192). In its simplest form, traditional ikebana is supposed to represent heaven, man, and earth, but there are various forms of the art and several schools of thought. It's considered a truly Japanese art without outside influences; as important as the arrangement itself is the vase chosen to display it.

Today, most young Japanese girls have at least some training in the art. Instruction is available at several schools in Tokyo, a few of which offer English-language classes on a regular basis. Note that you must register in advance to enroll. **Sogetsu Ikebana School,** 7-2-21 Akasaka ((℃) **03/3408-1209** or 03/3408-1151; www.sogetsu.or.jp; station: Aoyama-Itchome, exit 4, 5 min.), offers instruction in English on Monday from 10am to noon (closed in Aug). The cost of one lesson for first-time participants is ¥3,800, including flowers, and reservations should be made by noon on the previous Thursday. Additionally, classes in Japanese, with assistance in English for those who require it, are held the first three Tuesdays and Thursdays of the month from 10am to noon, 2 to 4pm, and 6 to 8pm. The cost of these is ¥3,150, and reservations should be made at least 3 days in advance.

Pachinko Parlors

Brightly lit and garish, pachinko parlors are packed with upright pinball-like machines and—increasingly—slot machines, at which row upon row of Japanese businessmen, housewives, and students sit intently immobile. Originating in Nagoya in the 1920s, *pachinko* is a game in which ball bearings are flung into a kind of vertical pinball machine, one after the other. Humans control the strength with which the ball is released, but otherwise there's very little to do. Some players even wedge a matchstick under the control and just watch the machine with folded arms. Points are amassed according to which holes the ball bearings fall into. If you're good at it, you win ball bearings back, which you can subsequently trade in for food, watches, calculators, gadgets, and the like.

It's illegal to win money in Japan, but outside many pachinko parlors along back alleyways, there are slots where you can trade in the watches, calculators, and other prizes for cash. The slots are so small that the person handing over the goods never sees the person who hands back money. Police, meanwhile, look the other way.

Pachinko parlors compete in an ever-escalating war of themes, lights, and noise. Step inside, and you'll wonder how anyone could possibly think; the noise level of thousands of ball bearings clanking is awesome. Perhaps that's the answer to its popularity: You can't think, making it a getaway pastime. Some people seem to be addicted to the mesmerizing game, newspaper articles talk of errant husbands who are hardly ever home, and psychologists analyze its popularity (an estimated 13% of Japan's population plays the game). At any rate, every hamlet seems to have a pachinko parlor, and major cities, such as Tokyo, are inundated with them. You'll find them in nightlife districts and clustered around train stations, but with their unmistakable clanging and clanking, you'll hear them long before you notice their brightly lit, gaudy facades.

The **Ohara School of Ikebana,** 5–7–17 Minami Aoyama (© **03/5774-5097;** www. ohararyu.or.jp; station: Omotesando, exit B1, 3 min.), offers 2-hour instruction in English at 10am on Wednesday and 10am and 1:30pm on Thursday for ¥4,000. Reservations should be made at least one day in advance (no classes July 15–Sept 3). If you wish to observe the class but not participate, you can do so for ¥800 (no reservations required).

If you wish to see ikebana, ask at the **Tourist Information Office** whether there are any special exhibitions. Department stores sometimes hold special ikebana exhibitions in their galleries. Another place to look is **Yasukuni Shrine,** located on Yasukuni Dori northwest of the Imperial Palace (closest station: Ichigaya or Kudanshita). Dedicated to Japanese war dead, the shrine is also famous for ongoing ikebana exhibitions on its grounds.

TEA CEREMONY Brought to Japan from China more than 1,000 years ago, tea first became popular among Buddhist priests as a means of staying awake during long hours of meditation. Gradually, its use filtered down among the upper classes, and in the 16th century, the tea ceremony, *cha-no-yu,* was perfected by a merchant named Sen-no-Rikyu. Using the principles of Zen and the spiritual discipline of the samurai, the tea ceremony became a highly stylized ritual, with detailed rules on how tea should be prepared, served, and drunk. The simplicity of movement and tranquillity of setting are meant to free the mind from the banality of everyday life and to allow the spirit to enjoy peace and harmony.

Teahouses are traditionally quite small, with a small tatami room, a small brazier for the teapot, and views of a garden. One of my favorite places to enjoy the tea ceremony is at a traditional Japanese garden (see "Parks & Gardens," below). Otherwise, several first-class hotels hold tea-ceremony demonstrations in special tea-ceremony rooms. Reservations are usually required, and because the ceremonies are often booked by groups, you'll want to call in advance to see whether you can participate. **Seisei-an,** on the seventh floor of the Hotel New Otani, 4–1 Kioi-cho, Chiyoda-ku (© **03/3265-1111,** ext. 2443; station: Nagatacho or Akasaka-mitsuke, a 3-min. walk from both), holds 20-minute demonstrations Thursday through Saturday from 11am to 4pm. The cost is ¥1,050, including tea and sweets. **Chosho-an,** on the seventh floor of the Hotel Okura, 2–10–4 Toranomon, Minato-ku (© **03/3582-0111;** station: Toranomon or Kamiyacho, a 10-min. walk from both), gives 40-minute demonstrations anytime between 11am and noon and between 1 and 4pm Monday, Tuesday, and Thursday through Saturday except holidays. Appointments are required; the cost is ¥1,050 for tea and sweets. At **Toko-an,** on the fourth floor of the Imperial Hotel, 1–1–1 Uchisaiwaicho, Chiyoda-ku (© **03/ 3504-1111;** station: Hibiya, 1 min.), demonstrations are given from 10am to 4pm Monday through Saturday except holidays. Reservations are required. The fee is ¥1,500 for tea and sweets.

ACUPUNCTURE & SHIATSU   Although most Westerners have heard of acupuncture, they may not be familiar with *shiatsu* (Japanese pressure-point massage) or *moxibustion* (using moxa, or mugwort, to warm acupuncture points and thereby stimulate circulation and facilitate healing). Most hotels in Japan offer shiatsu in the privacy of your room (look for a bedside placard offering the service or look in the hotel services booklet in your room). There are acupuncture clinics everywhere in Tokyo, and the staff of your hotel may be able to tell you one nearby. As it's not likely the clinic's staff will speak English, it might be a good idea to have the guest relations officer at your hotel not only make the reservation, but also specify the treatment you want.

Otherwise, English is spoken at **Yamate Acupuncture Clinic,** second floor of the ULS Nakameguro Building, 1–3–3 Higashiyama, Meguro-ku (© **03-3792-8989;** station: Nakameguro, 6 min.), open Monday to Friday 9am to 8pm and Saturday 9am to 2pm. Specializing in athletic injuries, it charges ¥3,000 for a specific treatment or ¥5,000 for the whole body, plus a ¥1,000 initial fee. English is also spoken at **Tani Clinic,** third floor of the Taishoseimei Hibiya Building, 1–9–1 Yurakucho, Chiyoda-ku (© **03/3201-5675;** station: Hibiya, 1 min.), open Monday, Tuesday, Wednesday, and Friday 9am to noon and 2 to 5pm, and Saturday 8:30am to noon and 2 to 4:30pm, and charging ¥10,500 for the first visit, ¥6,300 for each subsequent visit. The **Shirokane Oriental Therapy Center,** 1–26–4 Shirokane, Minato-ku (© **03/5789-8222;** www.shirogane-s.com; station: Shirokane-Takanawa, 1 min.), offers 60-minute shiatsu for ¥7,350 and 90-minute massage and acupuncture treatments for ¥10,500.

PUBLIC BATHS   Tokyo has approximately 1,000 *sento* (public baths)—which may sound like a lot but is nothing compared to the 2,687 it used to have in the 1970s. Easily recognizable by a tall chimney and shoe lockers just inside the door, a sento sells just about anything you might need at the bathhouse—soap, shampoo, towels, even underwear. Keep in mind, however, that people bearing tattoos are sometimes prohibited from entering public and hot-spring baths, as tattoos are associated with the Japanese mafia. If your tattoo is discreet, however, or you're using a public bath in, say, a hotel, you probably won't experience any problems.

For a unique bathing experience, nothing beats a 3- or 4-hour respite at the **Ooedo-Onsen Monogatari,** 2–57 Aomi on Odaiba (✆ **03/5500-1126;** www.ooedoonsen.jp; station: Telecom Center Station, 2 min.), which tapped mineral-rich hot-spring waters 1,380m (4,528 ft.) below ground to supply this re-created Edo-era bathhouse village. After changing into a *yukata* (cotton kimono) and depositing your belongings in a locker (your key is bar-coded, so there's no need to carry any money), you'll stroll past souvenir shops and restaurants on your way to massage rooms, sand baths (extra fee charged), and *onsen* (hot-spring baths) complete with outdoor baths, Jacuzzi, steam baths, foot baths, and saunas. Because as many as 6,500 bathers pour into this facility on weekends, try to come on a weekday. Also, signs in English are virtually nonexistent, so observe gender before entering bathing areas (a hint: women's baths usually have pink or red curtains, men's have blue). Open daily 11am to 9am the next day. Admission is ¥2,900 for adults and ¥1,600 for children 4 to 11, with reduced prices after 6pm.

Not quite as colorful is the upscale **Spa LaQua,** 1–1–1 Kasuga (✆ **03/3817-4173;** www.laqua.jp; station: Kasuga, 2 min.), located in the heart of Tokyo at Korakuen's Tokyo Dome City complex. It, too, has hot-spring indoor/outdoor baths, saunas, and massage options, but an adjoining amusement park with roller coasters (and screaming passengers) makes this a less relaxing alternative. It's open daily 11am to 9am the next day, with admission priced at ¥2,565, with higher fees weekends, holidays, and after midnight. Note that this is considered an adult facility; children under 6 are not allowed, and no minors under 18 are allowed after 6pm.

ZAZEN　A few temples in the Tokyo vicinity occasionally offer sitting meditation with instruction in English. You should call in advance to make a reservation and arrive 30 minutes early for instructions. The **Toshoji International Zen Center,** 4–5–18 Yutaka-machi, Shinagawa-ku (✆ **03/3781-4235;** station: Togoshikoen, 5 min.), offers free zazen at 5am every morning (except Sun and holidays), as well as Zen training meetings Saturday from 6 to 8pm, including zazen, a lecture, and tea. Accommodations are also available to those who wish to stay for longer periods to practice Zen. **Sounin Temple,** 4–1–12 Higashi-Ueno, Taito-ku (✆ **03/3844-3711;** station: Ueno, 5 min.), holds zazen the second Sunday and Monday (and preceding Sat) from 7 to 8pm, followed by a talk and tea.

3　PARKS & GARDENS

Although Japan's most famous gardens are not in Tokyo, most of the places listed below use principles of Japanese landscaping and give visitors at least an idea of the scope and style of these gardens. More information on parks and gardens is available at www.tokyo-park.or.jp.

East Garden (Higashi Gyoen) ★★　The 21 hectares (52 acres) of the formal Higashi Gyoen—once the main grounds of Edo Castle and located next to the Imperial Palace—are a wonderful respite in the middle of the city. Yet surprisingly, this garden is hardly ever crowded (except when cherry trees, azaleas, and other blossoms are in

(Finds) A Hiking Getaway

If Tokyo's concrete jungle is getting you down and a stroll through Tokyo's parks and gardens just won't cut it, head west to Mount Takao, a 600-m. (1,969-ft.) wooded hill popular for its seven hiking trails. In addition to scenic lookouts, there's also Takaosan Yakuoin Yuuki-ji Temple, founded in 744 in honor of Yakushi Nyorai, a Buddha believed to cure illness. Today it's a popular destination for mountain worshippers.

To reach Mount Takao, take the Keio Line's semi-express from Shinjuku Station almost an hour to Takaosan-guchi, the last stop (train fare: ¥370). From there, you can take either a cable car or a chairlift (my favorite) halfway to the top (fare for either: ¥470, or ¥900 round-trip). Alternatively, you can hike to the top in about 1¹/₂ hours. If you don't want to purchase individual tickets, there's a combination ticket you can buy at the Keio Line's ticket counter in Shinjuku Station that covers round-trip travel on both the train and cable car or chairlift for ¥1,320 on weekdays or ¥1,480 on weekends. For more information on Mount Takao, see www.takaotozan.co.jp/takaotozan_eng1/index.htm.

For dining, there's **Beer Mount** (© **042/665-9943**) at the top of the chairlift, a beer garden open July through September from 4 to 9:30pm (from 2:30pm weekends and holidays). It offers outstanding views of Tokyo in the distance and all-you-can-eat-and-drink buffets for ¥3,300 for men and ¥3,000 for women. Better in my opinion, however, is either **Ukai Toriyama** (© **042/661-0739**) or **Ukai Chikutei** (© **042/661-8419**), both accessible from Takaosan-guchi Station via free shuttle buses that depart every 20 minutes. Toriyama, opened in 1964, specializes in Japanese-style chargrilled chicken, with set meals ranging from ¥4,730 to ¥8,930, while Chikutei offers beautifully prepared set meals starting at ¥4,200 for lunch and ¥7,140 for dinner. Both boast beautiful settings, with dining in individual thatched huts and traditional houses picturesquely situated in natural surroundings complete with streams and ponds. Dining at either will be an experience you won't soon forget. Both restaurants are open daily from 11 or 11:30am to 8 or 9:30pm, depending on the day of the week. Reservations are required.

full bloom, or at lunchtime when *obento*-eating office workers fill the benches). **Ninomaru** ★★★, my favorite part, is laid out in Japanese style with a pond, stepping-stones, and winding paths; it's particularly beautiful when the wisteria, azaleas, irises, and other flowers are at their peak. Near Ninomaru is the **Sannomaru Shozokan,** with free changing exhibitions of art treasures belonging to the Imperial family. There's also a bamboo grove, a rose garden, a plum grove, and an iris garden with plants introduced from the famous iris garden in Meiji Jingu (see "The Top Attractions," earlier).

On the highest spot of Higashi Gyoen is the **Honmaru** (inner citadel), where Tokugawa's main castle once stood. Built in the first half of the 1600s, the castle was massive, surrounded by a series of whirling moats and guarded by 23 watchtowers and 99 gates around its 16km (10-mile) perimeter. At its center was Japan's tallest building at the time, the five-story castle keep, soaring 50m (164 ft.) above its foundations and offering an

Cherry-Blossom Viewing in Ueno Park

If you happen to come to Ueno Park during that brief single week in late March or early April when the cherry blossoms burst forth in glorious pink, consider yourself lucky. Cherry blossoms have always been dear to the Japanese heart as a symbol of beauty, fragility, and the transitory nature of life.

Ueno Park, with its 1,000 cherry trees, has been popular as a viewing spot since the Edo Period. Today, Tokyoites throng here en masse to celebrate the birth of the new season. It's not, however, the spiritual communion with nature you might think. In the daytime on a weekday, Ueno Park may be peaceful and sane enough, but on the weekends and in the evenings during cherry-blossom season, havoc prevails as office workers break out of their winter shells.

Sending underlings to stake out territory early in the day, whole companies of workers later converge on Ueno Park to sit under the cherry trees on plastic or cardboard, their shoes neatly lined up along the perimeter. They eat obento box lunches and drink sake and beer; many get drunk and can be quite rowdy. Still, visiting Ueno Park during cherry-blossom season is a cultural experience no one should miss.

Other good bets for viewing cherry blossoms (Japan boasts more than 300 different varieties of cherry trees) include Shinjuku Gyoen, Chidorigafuchi (the outer moat of the Imperial Palace), Sumida Park in the Asakusa district, and both Aoyama and Yanaka cemeteries. More than likely, you'll be invited to join one of the large groups—and by all means do so. You'll all sit there drinking and making merry, seemingly oblivious to the fragile pink blossoms shimmering above.

expansive view over Edo. This is where Tokugawa Ieyasu would have taken refuge, had his empire ever been seriously threatened. Although most of the castle was a glimmering white, the keep was black with a gold roof, which must have been quite a sight in old Edo as it towered above the rest of the city. All that remains today of the shogun's castle are a few towers, gates, stone walls, moats, and the stone foundations of the keep.

Free guided tours of the garden, run by volunteers, are given Saturday from 1 to 3pm. The meeting point is outside Tokyo Station's Marunouchi Central Exit. For more information, see the website http://freewalkingtour.org.

1–1 Chiyoda, Chiyoda-ku. ℂ 03/3213-1111. Free admission (you'll be given a token upon entering; turn it in at any gate when you leave). Tues–Thurs and Sat–Sun 9am–5pm (to 4:30pm Mar to mid-Apr and Sept–Oct; to 4pm Nov–Feb). You must enter 30 min. before closing. Closed Dec 23 and Dec 28–Jan 3; open other national holidays. Station: Otemachi, Takebashi, or Nijubashi-mae.

Hama Rikyu Garden Overrated Considered by some to be the best garden in Tokyo (but marred, in my opinion, by skyscrapers in Shiodome that detract from its charm), this urban oasis has origins stretching back 300 years, when it served as a retreat for a former feudal lord and as duck-hunting and falconry grounds for the Tokugawa shoguns. In 1871, possession of the garden passed to the Imperial family, who used it to entertain such visiting dignitaries as Gen. Ulysses S. Grant. Come here to see how the upper classes enjoyed themselves during the Edo Period. The garden contains an inner tidal pool, spanned by three bridges draped with wisteria (views from the south end of the garden are the most picturesque). There are also other ponds; a refuge for ducks, herons, and migratory birds; a promenade along the bay lined with pine trees; a 300-year-old pine; moon-viewing pavilions; and teahouses (powdered green tea and a sweet will cost you ¥500). Plan on at least an hour's stroll to see everything, but the best reason for coming here is to board a ferry from the garden's pier bound for Asakusa, with departures every hour (or more often) between 10:35am and 4:15pm; the fare is ¥720 one-way.

1–1 Hamarikyuteien, Chuo-ku. © **03/3541-0200.** Admission ¥300 adults, ¥150 seniors, free for children 12 and under. Daily 9am–5pm. Station: Shiodome (exit 5, 5 min.) or Tsukiji-shijo (7 min.).

Rikugien Garden ★★ (Finds) Though not as centrally located or as easy to reach as Tokyo's other famous gardens, this one is a must for fans of traditional Japanese gardens and is probably my favorite. It was created in 1702 by a trusted confidante of the shogun, who began as a page and rose to the highest rank as a feudal lord. During the Meiji Era, the founder of Mitsubishi took it over for his second residence and later donated it to the city. What I like most about the garden is that it's dominated by a pond in its center, complete with islands and islets, viewing hills, and strolling paths around its perimeter, providing enchanting views. The garden is especially famous for its changing maple leaves in autumn. Because it takes some effort to reach, you'll probably want to enjoy at least an hour here.

6–16–3 Hon-Komagome, Bunkyo-ku. © **03/3941-2222.** Admission ¥300 adults, ¥150 seniors, free for children 12 and under. Daily 9am–5pm. Station: Komagome (8 min.) or Sengoku (10 min.).

Shinjuku Gyoen ★★ (Kids) Formerly the private estate of a feudal lord and then of the Imperial family, this is considered one of the most important parks of the Meiji Era. It's wonderful for strolling because of the variety of its planted gardens; styles range from French and English to Japanese traditional. This place amazes me every time I come here. The park's 58 hectares (143 acres) make it one of the city's largest, and each bend in the pathway brings something completely different: Ponds and sculpted bushes give way to a promenade lined with sycamores that opens onto a rose garden. Cherry blossoms, azaleas, chrysanthemums, and other flowers provide splashes of color from spring through autumn. The Japanese garden, buried in the center, is exquisite; if you have time only for a quick look at traditional landscaping, you won't be disappointed here. There are also wide grassy expanses, popular for picnics and playing, and a greenhouse filled with tropical plants (closed for renovation until 2011). You could easily spend a half-day of leisure here, but for a quick fix of rejuvenation, 1½ hours will do.

11 Naitocho, Shinjuku-ku. © **03/3350-0151.** Admission ¥200 adults, ¥50 children. Tues–Sun 9am–4:30pm. Station: Shinjuku Gyoen-mae (2 min.) or Sendagaya (5 min.).

Ueno Park (Kids) Ueno Park—on the northeast edge of the Yamanote Line—is one of the largest parks in Tokyo and one of the most popular places in the city for Japanese families on a day's outing. It's a cultural mecca, with a number of attractions, including the prestigious Tokyo National Museum; the National Museum of Western Art; the National Museum of Nature and Science; the delightful Shitamachi Museum, with its displays of old Tokyo; Ueno Zoo; and Shinobazu Pond (a bird sanctuary). The busiest time of the year at Ueno Park is April, during the cherry-blossom season.

Other well-known landmarks in Ueno Park are **Toshogu Shrine,** erected in 1651 and dedicated to Tokugawa Ieyasu, founder of the Tokugawa shogunate; and **Kiyomizu Kannon-do Temple,** completed in 1631 as a much smaller copy of the famous Kiyomizu Kannon-do Temple in Kyoto (see "Shrines & Temples," below). Ueno Park is also a popular refuge for Tokyo's homeless.

For more information on Ueno Park, see the walking tour of Ueno in chapter 8.

Taito-ku. Free admission to the park; separate admissions to each of its attractions. Daily 24 hr. Station: Ueno (1 min.). Tokyo Shitamachi Bus: Ueno Koen Yamashita/Ueno Station.

4 SHRINES & TEMPLES

In addition to the temples and shrines listed here, don't forget **Sensoji Temple** and **Meiji Jingu Shrine** (see "The Top Attractions," earlier).

Kiyomizu Kannon-do Temple   Established in 1631 and moved to its present site overlooking Shinobazu Pond in 1698, this small but important structure is a copy of the famous Kiyomizu Temple in Kyoto (but on a much less grand scale). It was once part of the Kan'eiji Temple precincts that covered Ueno Hill during the Edo Period. Remarkably, the temple survived both the 1868 battle between Imperial and shogunate forces and bombings during World War II. Today, it's one of Tokyo's oldest temples. It enshrines Kosodate Kannon, protectress of childbearing and child-raising; women hoping to become pregnant come here to ask for the goddess's mercy, and those whose wishes have been fulfilled return to pray for their child's good health and protection. Many leave behind dolls as symbols of their children. Once a year, on September 25, a requiem service is held for all the dolls at the temple, after which they are cremated.

Ueno Park, Taito-ku. ☏ 03/3821-4749. Free admission. Daily 7am–5pm. Station: Ueno (3 min.). Tokyo Shitamachi Bus: Ueno Koen Yamashita/Ueno Station.

Toshogu Shrine ★   Come here to pay respects to the man who made Edo (present-day Tokyo) the seat of his government and thus elevated the small village to the most important city in the country. Erected in 1651, it's dedicated to Tokugawa Ieyasu, founder of the Tokugawa shogunate. Like Toshogu Shrine in Nikko, it was built by Ieyasu's grandson, Iemitsu, and boasts some of the same richly carved, ornate design favored by the Tokugawas, especially the Chinese-style gate. Remarkably, it survived the civil war of 1868, the Great Kanto Earthquake of 1923, and even World War II. The pathway to the shrine is lined with massive stone lanterns, as well as 50 copper lanterns donated by daimyo from all over Japan. The shrine, closed, unfortunately, for renovation until 2014, contains some exquisite art, including murals by a famous Edo artist, Kano Tan-yu, and clothing and samurai armor worn by Ieyasu. At the counter to the left you can buy good-luck charms that will supposedly bring you fortune, happiness, and other earthly desires. On a more somber note, a flame on shrine grounds, lit from flames burning in both Hiroshima and Nagasaki, appeals for world peace.

Ueno Park, Taito-ku. ☏ 03/3822-3455. Free admission. Daily 9am–sunset (about 6pm in summer, 4:30pm in winter). Station: Ueno (4 min.). Tokyo Shitamachi Bus: Ueno Koen Yamashita/Ueno Station.

Yasukuni Shrine ★   Built in 1869 to commemorate Japanese war dead, Yasukuni Shrine is constructed in classic Shinto style, with a huge steel *torii* gate at its entrance. During times of war, soldiers were told that if they died fighting for their country, their spirits would find glory here; even today, it's believed that the spirits of some 2.4 million Japanese war dead are at home here, where they are worshipped as deities. During any day of the week, you're likely to encounter older Japanese paying their respects to friends and families who perished in World War II. But every August 15, the shrine is thrust into the national spotlight when World War II memorials are held. Visits by prime ministers have caused national uproars and outrage among Japan's Asian neighbors, who think it improper for a prime minister to visit—and thereby condone—a shrine so closely tied to Japan's nationalistic and militaristic past.

If you can, come on a Sunday, when a flea market for antiques and curios is held at the entrance to the shrine from about 6am to 3pm. On the shrine's grounds is a war memorial museum outlining Japan's military history, the **Yushukan** ★★. It chronicles the rise and fall of the samurai, the colonization of Asia by Western powers by the late 1800s, the Sino-Japanese War, the Russo-Japanese War, and World Wars I and II, though explanations in English are rather vague and Japan's military aggression in Asia is glossed over. Still, a fascinating 90 minutes can be spent here gazing on samurai armor, swords, uniforms, tanks, guns, a Mitsubishi Zero fighter plane, and artillery, as well as such thought-provoking displays as a human torpedo (a tiny submarine guided by one occupant and loaded with explosives) and a suicide attack plane. But the most chilling displays are the seemingly endless photographs of war dead, some of them very young teenagers. In stark contrast to the somberness of the museum, temporary exhibits of beautiful ikebana (Japanese flower arrangements) and bonsai are often held on the shrine grounds in rows of glass cases. Yasukuni Shrine is also famous for its cherry blossoms.

3-1-1 Kudan-kita, Chiyoda-ku. ✆ 03/3261-8326. www.yasukuni.or.jp. Free admission to shrine; Yushukan ¥800 adults, ¥500 students, ¥300 junior-high and high-school students, ¥100 children. Shrine daily 24 hr.; Yushukan daily 9am–5pm. Station: Kudanshita (3 min.) or Ichigaya or Iidabashi (7 min.). On Yasukuni Dori.

5 MORE MUSEUMS

ART MUSEUMS

Bridgestone Museum of Art (Bridgestone Bijutsukan) ★   This is one of Tokyo's best private art museums, with a small but impressive collection of French Impressionist art, as well as Japanese paintings in the Western style dating from the Meiji Period onward. Because there are only 10 small rooms of displays, it makes a quick and worthwhile 1-hour detour if you're in the vicinity. The permanent collection, comprising 500 works shown on a rotating basis, includes works by Monet, Manet, Degas, Sisley, Cézanne, Pissarro, Renoir, Corot, Gauguin, van Gogh, Matisse, Picasso, Modigliani, and Rousseau, as well as Japanese painters Chu Asai, Aoki Shigeru, Kishida Ryusei, and Saeki Yuzo. An audio guide for ¥500 provides historical and biographical background to major works. Special exhibitions, which draw large crowds, are mounted four times a year.

Bridgestone Building, 1–10–1 Kyobashi, Chuo-ku. ✆ 03/3563-0241. www.bridgestone-museum.gr.jp. Admission ¥800 adults, ¥600 seniors, ¥500 students, free for children 14 and under (except during special exhibits). Special exhibits cost more. Tues–Sat 10am–8pm; Sun and holidays 10am–6pm. Closed during exhibit changes. Station: Tokyo (Yaesu Central exit, 5 min.), Kyobashi (Meidi-ya exit, 5 min.), or Nihombashi (Takashimaya exit, 5 min.). On Chuo Dori (with an entrance around the corner on Yaesu Dori), a short walk directly east of Tokyo Station.

(Tips) Museum Savings Pass

Since 2003, a combination ticket called a **Grutt Pass** has been made available every year by the Tokyo Metropolitan Government; it allows free or reduced admission to more than 60 museums, zoos, aquariums, and other attractions throughout the Tokyo area. Costing ¥2,000 and valid for 2 months, it covers all the museum biggies and is available at all participating venues and the city's Tokyo Tourist Information Center. Though the validity of the current pass expires March 31, 2010, it's a good bet that the pass will be extended for another year into 2011. Note that most museums in Tokyo are closed Mondays and for New Year's—generally the last day or so in December and the first 1 to 3 days of January. If Monday happens to be a national holiday, most museums will remain open but will close Tuesday instead. Some of the privately owned museums, however, may be closed on national holidays or the day following every national holiday, as well as for exhibition changes. Call beforehand to avoid disappointment. Remember, too, that you must enter museums at least 30 minutes before closing time. For a listing of current special exhibitions, including those being held in galleries of major department stores, consult *Metropolis,* published weekly and available online at www.metropolis.co.jp.

Hara Museum of Contemporary Art (Hara Bijutsukan)   Japan's oldest museum devoted to contemporary international and Japanese art is housed in a 1930s tiled, Bauhaus-style Art Deco home that once belonged to the current director's grandfather; the building alone, designed by Jin Watanabe, is worth the trip. The museum stages three or four exhibitions annually; some are on the cutting edge of international art, but at least one features works from its own collection, which focuses on paintings and sculptures mainly from the 1950s and 1960s by Japanese and foreign artists and includes works by Andy Warhol, Roy Lichtenstein, Claes Oldenburg, Jackson Pollock, Karel Appel, Robert Rauschenberg, and Frank Stella. Be sure to check out the downstairs toilet by Morimura Yasumasa. After your tour, relax at the lovely greenhouselike cafe with outdoor seating. Plan on spending at least an hour at this museum.

4-7-25 Kita-Shinagawa, Shinagawa-ku. © 03/3445-0651. www.haramuseum.or.jp. Admission ¥1,000 adults, ¥700 high-school and college students, ¥500 children. Tues, Thurs–Sun, and holidays 11am–5pm; Wed 11am–8pm. Closed during exhibition changes. Station: Shinagawa (Takanawa exit, 15 min.).

Mori Art Museum (Mori Bijutsukan) ★★   This is Tokyo's highest museum, on the 53rd floor of the Roppongi Hills Mori Tower. Opened in 2003, it features state-of-the-art galleries with 6m-tall (20-ft.) ceilings, controlled natural lighting, and great views of Tokyo. Innovative exhibitions of emerging and established artists from around the world are shown four times a year, with past shows centering on contemporary Asian, African, and Japanese art. Although the installations alone, ranging from paintings and fashion to architecture and design, are worth a visit, an extra incentive is the attached Tokyo City View observatory, usually included in the museum admission and providing eye-popping views over Tokyo. Plan on at least 90 minutes up here.

Roppongi Hills Mori Tower, 6–10–1 Roppongi, Minato-ku. © 03/5777-8600. www.mori.art.museum. Admission varies according to the exhibit but averages ¥1,500 adults, ¥1,000 high-school and college students, and ¥500 children. Wed–Mon 10am–10pm; Tues 10am–5pm. Station: Roppongi (Roppongi Hills exit, 1 min.).

MOT or Museum of Contemporary Art, Tokyo (Tokyo-to Gendai Bijutsu-kan) ★ The MOT is inconveniently located but well worth the trek if you're a fan of the avant-garde (you'll pass the Fukagawa Edo Museum, described below, on the way, so you may wish to visit both). This modern structure of glass and steel, with a long corridor entrance that reminds me of railroad trestles, houses both permanent and temporary exhibits of Japanese and international postwar art in rooms whose sizes lend themselves to large installations. Although temporary exhibits, which occupy most of the museum space, have ranged from Southeast Asian art to a retrospective of Jasper Johns, the smaller permanent collection presents a chronological study of 40 years of contemporary art, beginning with anti-artistic trends and pop art in the 1960s and continuing with minimalism and cutting-edge contemporary works, with about 100 works displayed on a rotating basis. Included may be works by Andy Warhol, Gerhard Richter, Roy Lichtenstein, David Hockney, Frank Stella, Sandro Chia, Mark Rothko, and Julian Schnabel. Depending on the number of exhibits you visit, you'll spend anywhere from 1 to 2 hours here. It might be useful to know that there are two pleasant places to dine here, a restaurant and a cafe.

4-1-1 Miyoshi, Koto-ku. ℂ **03/5245-4111.** www.mot-art-museum.jp. Admission to permanent collection ¥500 adults, ¥400 college students, ¥250 high-school students and seniors, free for children; special exhibits cost more. Tues–Sun 10am–6pm. Station: Kiyosumi-Shirakawa (exit A3, 15 min.). On Fukagawa Shiroyokan-dori St., just off Mitsume Dori.

The National Art Center, Tokyo ★ Japan's newest national museum doesn't have a collection of its own. Rather, its purpose is to exhibit works organized by Japanese artists' associations, its own curators, and joint efforts by mass media companies and other art institutions. The range of changing exhibitions, therefore, can be staggering, with past exhibitions showing masterworks from the Rijksmuseum Amsterdam; fashion and architecture organized by the Museum of Contemporary Art, Los Angeles; works by Monet and Lalique; and a retrospective on Japanese government-sponsored art exhibitions held the past 100 years. Even the building itself—with an undulating, seductive facade of glass—attracts crowds with its Paul Bocuse restaurant, museum shop, and changing exhibitions by national artists' associations. This museum, the nearby Mori Art Museum, and Suntory Museum of Art, all within walking distance of one another, have been dubbed Art Triangle Roppongi.

7-22-2 Roppongi, Minato-ku. ℂ **03/5777-8600.** www.nact.jp. Admission ¥500–¥1,500 for most exhibitions. Wed–Mon 10am–6pm (to 8pm Fri). Station: Nogizaka (exit 6, 1 min.) or Roppongi (exit 4A or 7, 5 min.)

The National Museum of Modern Art, Tokyo (Tokyo Kokuritsu Kindai Bijutsukan) ★★ This museum houses the largest collection of modern Japanese art under one roof, including both Japanese- and Western-style paintings, prints, watercolors, drawings, and sculpture, all dating from the Meiji Period through the 20th century. Exhibits change four times a year, but names to look for include Kishida Ryusei, Munakata Shiko, Kuroda Seiki, and Yokoyama Taikan. A few works by Western artists, such as Picasso, Klee, and Kandinsky, are also on display as examples of Western artistic styles of the same period. Expect to spend about 1 hour here.

Your admission here allows entry also to the nearby **Crafts Gallery** (ℂ **03/3211-7781**), housed in a handsome Gothic-style brick building constructed in 1910 as headquarters of the Imperial Guard and now used to exhibit contemporary crafts, including pottery, ceramics, kimono, metalwork, glassware, lacquerware, bambooware, and more.

Sightseeing in Tokyo Without Spending a Yen

While it could be argued that simply walking around Tokyo is a free cultural experience, the city abounds in other free attractions and activities as well. Here are some of my favorite free things in Tokyo:

- The Tokyo Metropolitan Government's 45th-floor observatories in Shinjuku, offering surreal views of the city's never-ending sprawl (and on clear days in winter, also of Mt. Fuji)
- Meiji Shrine, Tokyo's most venerable Shinto shrine, surrounded by a dense, peaceful forest
- Harajuku, a lively neighborhood just outside Meiji Shrine, which is packed with teenyboppers in all styles of dress and boutiques that cater to the young (on Sun, kids in *cosplay*—costume play—gather near Harajuku Station)
- Asakusa's Sensoji Temple, Tokyo's oldest and most popular temple, is surrounded by shops selling a wide array of traditional goods, as well as a lot of interesting kitsch
- Tsukiji Fish Market, one of the largest in the world
- East Garden, located next to the Imperial Palace and once the main grounds of Edo Castle (my favorite part is the Japanese-style Ninomaru); free guided tours are offered on Saturdays

Exhibitions change approximately four times a year to reflect the seasons, with most displays concentrating on a specific theme such as bambooware or the works of a single artist. Unfortunately, the exhibition space is very limited; you can tour the place in 30 minutes or less.

3–1 Kitanomaru Koen Park, Chiyoda-ku. © **03/3214-2561.** www.momat.go.jp. Admission ¥420 adults, ¥130 college students, free for children; special exhibits cost more. Tues–Sun 10am–5pm (to 8pm Fri). Station: Takebashi (5 min.).

The National Museum of Western Art (Kokuritsu Seiyo Bijutsukan) ★

Japan's only national museum dedicated to Western art is housed in a main building designed by Le Corbusier and in two more recent additions. It presents a chronological study of sculpture and art from the end of the Middle Ages through the 20th century, beginning with works by Old Masters, including Lucas Cranach the Elder, Rubens, El Greco, Murillo, and Tiepolo. French painters and Impressionists of the 19th and 20th centuries are well represented, including Delacroix, Monet (with a whole room devoted to his work), Manet, Renoir, Pissarro, Sisley, Courbet, Cézanne, and Gauguin. The museum's 20th-century collection includes works by Picasso, Max Ernst, Miró, Dubuffet, and Pollock. The museum is also famous for its 50-odd sculptures by Rodin, one of the largest collections in the world, encompassing most of his major works including *The Kiss, The Thinker, Balzac,* and *The Gates of Hell.* Plan on spending at least an hour here, though frequent—and ambitious—special exhibitions may entice you to linger longer.

- Beer Museum Yebisu (alas, there are no free samples, but at ¥200 a glass, this is certainly the cheapest place to imbibe)
- Tokyo Anime Center, located in Akihabara (which abounds in shops selling anime, manga, and electronics)
- Tokyo Metropolitan Children's Hall, a great public facility for families, with indoor gyms, a rooftop playground, a crafts corner, and monthly events and programs
- Showrooms, including the Sony Building that lets you try out all their newest products; Megaweb, a huge technology playground featuring more than 100 Toyota models and a museum of old cars; and the Panasonic Center, which showcases its products, lets you play games, and even has a fully designed house of the future (reservations are required to see the house)
- Free tours of Shinjuku (offered by the Tokyo Metropolitan Government), as well as Asakusa and Ueno (led by volunteer guides)
- Galleries in department stores, with changing exhibits on everything from ikebana and art to ceramics and crafts
- Festivals, ranging from biggies such as the Sanja Matsuri in Asakusa to events such as Gishi-sai at Sengakuji Temple, which commemorates 47 masterless samurai who avenged their master's death

Ueno Park, Taito-ku. ✆ **03/3828-5131.** www.nmwa.go.jp. Admission ¥420 adults, ¥130 college students, free for children 17 and under and seniors; special exhibits require separate admission fee. Free admission to permanent collection 2nd and 4th Sat of the month. Tues–Sun 9:30am–5pm (to 8pm Fri). Station: Ueno (4 min.). Tokyo Shitamachi Bus: Ueno Koen Yamashita/Ueno Station.

Suntory Museum of Art (Suntory Bijutsukan)   Founded in 1961 and moving to Tokyo Midtown in 2007, this private museum boasts a collection of 3,000 Japanese antique arts and crafts, including lacquerware, ceramics, paintings, glassware, Noh costumes, kimono, scrolls, teaware, and other items, which it displays in themed exhibitions, along with visiting collections. Although modern in design, the museum incorporates such traditional Japanese materials as wood and paper in darkened rooms to create a soothing, inviting atmosphere.

Tokyo Midtown, 9-7-4 Akasaka, Minato-ku. ✆ **03/3479-8600.** www.suntory.com/culture-sports/sma. Admission varies, averaging ¥1,200 adults, ¥900 high-school and college students, free for children. Sun–Mon and holidays 10:30am–6pm; Wed–Sat 10am–8pm. Station: Roppongi (2 min.) or Nogizaka (4 min.).

Ukiyo-e Ota Memorial Museum of Art (Ota Kinen Bijutsukan) ★ (Finds)   This great museum features the private ukiyo-e (woodblock print) collection of the late Ota Seizo, who, early in life, recognized the importance of ukiyo-e as an art form and dedicated himself to its preservation. Although the collection contains 12,000 prints, only 80 to 100 are displayed at any given time, in thematic exhibitions that change monthly and include English-language descriptions. The museum itself is small but delightful. You can tour it in about 30 minutes, and be sure to take a peek in the basement shop with its *furoshiki* (traditional wrapping cloth), handkerchiefs, and other items.

1-10-10 Jingumae, Shibuya-ku. © **03/3403-0880.** www.ukiyoe-ota-muse.jp. Admission ¥700–¥1,000 adults, ¥500–¥700 high-school and college students, ¥200–¥400 junior-high students, free–¥200 children; price depends on the exhibit. Tues–Sun 10:30am–5:30pm (enter by 5pm). Closed from the 27th to end of each month. Station: Harajuku (2 min.) or Meiji-Jingumae (1 min.). Near the Omotesando Dori and Meiji Dori intersection, behind La Forêt.

SPECIALTY MUSEUMS & SHOWROOMS

Beer Museum Yebisu   If you find yourself in Yebisu Garden Place (perhaps to see the Museum of Photography), you may wish to take a 30-minute spin through this showcase of Sapporo breweries. Named after Yebisu Beer, which made its debut in 1890 and to which both Ebisu Station and the surrounding neighborhood owe their names, it presents a high-tech explanation (in Japanese only) of an age-old process. I especially like the gallery of old beer advertisements (featuring almost always women), but it's not always on display. Alas, there are no free samples; visitors must purchase tickets from vending machines at the tasting lounge, but prices are much lower than elsewhere (¥200 for a glass or ¥500 for a sampler of four brews), making the beer here the best reason for a visit.

Yebisu Garden Place, 4–20–1 Ebisu, Shibuya-ku. © **03/5423-7255.** Free admission. Tues–Sun 10am–6pm (enter by 5pm). Station: Ebisu (8 min.). Behind Mitsukoshi department store (take the B1 exit from the store).

Drum Museum (Taikokan) (Kids)   This fourth-floor museum, which you can tour in about 20 minutes, features a collection of more than 600 instruments, displayed on a rotating basis and including traditional Japanese drums as well as a variety of drums from all over the world. With the exception of some of the rare, older pieces (distinguished by a red marking), many of the 200 or so drums always on display can be touched and played, making this a good spot for children. There are also videos of drumming from Japan and around the world. On the ground floor is a shop specializing in Japanese percussion instruments and items used in Japanese festivals, including decorative Japanese drums, lion heads for the lion dance, Japanese flutes, and masks.

Miyamoto Japanese Percussion and Festival Store, 2–1–1 Nishi-Asakusa, Taito-ku. © **03/3842-5622.** Admission ¥300 adults, ¥150 children. Wed–Sun 10am–5pm. Closed holidays. Station: Tawaramachi (2 min.) or Asakusa (5 min.). Tokyo Shitamachi Bus: Ueno Koen Yamashita/Ueno Station. On Kokusai Dori, north of Kaminarimon Dori.

Edo-Tokyo Open Air Architectural Museum (Edo-Tokyo Tatemono-en) ★ (Finds)   Although located on the far western outskirts of Tokyo, this branch of the Edo-Tokyo Museum is a must for architecture buffs. Spread on 7 hectares (17 acres) in the middle of an expansive park, it showcases some two dozen buildings from the late Edo Period to the 1940s, arranged along streets in a village setting. Included are 200-year-old thatch-roofed farmhouses, traditional Japanese- and Western-style residences, a teahouse, soy-sauce shop, bathhouse, photography studio, stationery store, Japanese umbrella shop, police box, and more, filled with related objects and furniture. You'll need at least 2 hours to see everything, plus another 2 hours to get here and back.

3–7–1 Sakura-cho, Koganei-shi. © **042/388-3300.** Admission ¥400 adults, ¥200 children and seniors. Tues–Sun 9:30am–5:30pm (to 4:30pm Oct–Mar). From Shinjuku Station, take the rapid Chuo Line about 30 min. to Musashi-Koganei Station. Take the north exit and board bus no. 2 or 3 (departures every 7 min.) for a 5-min. ride to Koganei Koen Nishi Guchi stop, from which it's a 5-min. walk; or board bus no. 4 or 33 (departures twice an hour) to Edo-Tokyo Tatemono-en-mae stop, from which it's a 3-min. walk.

Many restaurants, hotels, and other establishments in Japan do not have signs giving their names in Roman (English-language) letters. As an aid to the reader, chapter 14 lists the Japanese symbols for all such places described in this guide. Each set of characters representing an establishment name has a number, which corresponds to the number that appears inside the box preceding the establishment's name in the text. Thus, to find the Japanese symbols for, say, **The Former Kusuo Yasuda Residence,** refer to no. 52 on p. 325.

(52) **The Former Kusuo Yasuda Residence** ★ (Finds) Traditional Japanese wooden homes are becoming rare in Tokyo, and even rarer are homes open to the public. That alone makes this residence worth a visit, but its history and unique architectural details are what make it special. Built in 1919 for a prosperous businessman who liked to entertain but who afterwards decided the house was too elegant in which to raise his five children, the house was then acquired by Zenshiro Yasuda and his wife, Mineko, who had lost their home in the 1923 Great Kanto Earthquake. The Yasuda family continued to occupy the house for the next 75 years, and—this is what I find most amazing—they had so much respect for the architectural integrity of the structure that they changed almost nothing. Although it looks rather small and modest from the street, the 598-sq.-m (6,550-sq.-ft.) home is much more than first meets the eye, extending long behind the front facade into a garden and with a grand second floor. The main *Genkan* (foyer), reserved for important guests and the head of the household, is designed after the formal entrance of a samurai residence, while an informal entrance to the right was used by the immediate family, relatives, and friends. In addition to a Japanese-style drawing room with a hearth for formal tea ceremonies, there's also a Western-style drawing room with furniture original to the house, including a piano and Victorola. The bathroom contains a rare floor-level sink in the dressing area, presumably for women kneeling to wash long hair fashionable during the time, but my favorite room is probably the kitchen, state-of-the-art when it was built, with skylights and a central island with a sink, gas stove, ice box, and cellar for storage. In any case, because the house is staffed by volunteers (the house belongs to the non-profit Japan National Trust), open hours are currently limited. You'll probably spend at least a half-hour here.

5–20–18 Sendagi, Bunkyo-ku. (C) **03/3822-2699.** Admission ¥500 adults, ¥200 junior high through college students, free for children 11 and under. Wed and Sat 10:30am–4pm. Closed mid-Aug. Station: Sendagi (Exit 1, 7 min.). Turn left out of the station, take an immediate left again, and then turn right at the stoplight. It will be on the left.

Fukagawa Edo Museum (Fukagawa Edo Shiryokan) ★ (Kids) This is the Tokyo of your dreams, the way it appears in all those samurai flicks on Japanese TV: a reproduction of a 19th-century neighborhood in Fukagawa, a prosperous community on the east bank of the Sumida River during the Edo Period. This delightful museum is located off Kiyosumi Dori on a pleasant tree-lined, shop-filled street called Fukagawa Shiryokan Dori. The museum's hangarlike interior contains 11 full-scale replicas of traditional houses, vegetable and rice shops, a fish store, two inns, a fire watchtower, and tenement homes, all arranged to resemble an actual neighborhood. There are lots of small touches and flourishes to make the community seem real and believable—a cat sleeping on a roof, a snail crawling up a fence, a dog relieving itself on a pole, birdsong, and a vendor shouting his wares. The village even changes with the seasons (with trees sprouting cherry blossoms in spring and threatened by thunderstorms in summer) and, every 45 minutes or so, undergoes a day's cycle from morning (roosters crow, lights brighten) to night (the sun sets, the retractable roof closes to make everything dark). Of Tokyo's museums, this one is probably the best for children; plan on spending about an hour here. Don't confuse this museum with the much larger Edo-Tokyo Museum, which traces the history of Tokyo. *Note:* Closed for renovations until August 2010.

1–3–28 Shirakawa, Koto-ku. ℂ **03/3630-8625.** Call for updated information on admission and hours. Station: Kiyosumi-Shirakawa (3 min.).

Ghibli Museum (Overrated)   Only fans of Japanese animation (anime) may find the obstacles of visiting this unique museum worth the effort—a required advance purchase of tickets (either through JTB offices in Japan or abroad, or through Lawson convenience stores in Japan), admission at a specific date and time, and the museum's location on the outskirts of Tokyo (a 20-min. train ride followed by a 5-min. bus ride). It's the brainstorm of Japan's most famous animation director, Hayao Miyazaki, who is to Japan what Walt Disney is to the U.S., and whose film *Spirited Away* won the Oscar for best animated film in 2002. As expected, the museum is a whimsical flight of imagination, with displays related to Miyazaki's films and a reproduction of his studio, complete with a play area for children, a rooftop garden, and a theater showing 10-minute excerpts of his work. Disappointingly, displays are in Japanese only, so you'll probably spend just an hour here. A consolation: On the same train line to Mitaka is the free **Suginami Animation Museum,** 3–29–5 Kamiogi (ℂ **03/3396-1510;** www.sam.or.jp/flier.htm; station: Ogikubo), with English-language explanations on the history of Japanese animation and a theater showing past and current films; open Tuesday to Sunday from 10am to 6pm.

Mitaka Inokashira Park, 1–1–83 Shimorenjaku, Mitaka City. ℂ **0442/40-2233.** www.ghibli-museum.jp. Admission ¥1,000 adults, ¥700 children 13–18, ¥400 children 7–12, ¥100 children 4–6, free for children 3 and under. Wed–Mon 10am–6pm. Closed periodically for maintenance. From Shinjuku Station, take the JR Chuo Line 20 min. to Mitaka Station; then a 15-min. walk or, from the station's south exit, a 5-min. ride via museum shuttle bus departing every 10 min. (round-trip fare: ¥300).

Jiyugakuen Myonichikan   Fans of Frank Lloyd Wright will want to make a pilgrimage here. Designed by the renowned American architect in 1921 while he was in Tokyo working on the Imperial Hotel, the former girls' school has some notable characteristics, including low-pitched roofs and geometric-patterned windows that resemble Wright's "Prairie House" designs. It's worth taking a break with tea or coffee and a sweet in the dining hall, where you can admire Wright's original light fixtures. A small room devoted to Wright displays photographs of the Imperial Hotel and his other works in Japan. Plan on about 30 minutes here.

2–31–3 Nishi-Ikebukuro, Toshima-ku. ℂ **03/3971-7535.** www.jiyu.jp/tatemono/index-e.html. Admission ¥400, ¥600 with drink and a sweet. Tues–Sun 10am–4pm. Station: Ikebukuo (west exit, 5 min.). Behind the Hotel Metropolitan.

John Lennon Museum ★   Opened on October 9, 2000, the day John Lennon would have turned 60, this museum chronicles the former Beatles musician from his childhood through his early years in Liverpool, the various stages of the Beatles' fame, his relationship with Yoko Ono and their commitment to the peace movement, the breakup of the Beatles, his 5 years as a house husband caring for their son, Sean, and family trips to Japan. It's worth noting that Japanese-only captions mention Lennon's son Julian from his first marriage or the fact that Yoko had a daughter from one of her two previous marriages. Otherwise, the museum does an excellent job with displays of Lennon's hand-written lyrics, trademark wire-rim glasses, leather jacket, motorcycle, U.K. passport, guitars, white Steinway, and other memorabilia, with concert videos and personal footage throughout. Few Lennon fans will probably escape dry-eyed, especially in the Final Room, adorned only with the powerful lyrics of his songs. The Museum Lounge, with listening stations and books, is open only to visitors. This was my teenage son's favorite Tokyo museum. You can easily spend 90 minutes here.

Saitama Super Arena, 2–27 Kamiochiai, Yono-city, Saitama. ✆ 048/601-0009. www.taisei.co.jp/museum. Admission ¥1,500 adults, ¥1,000 high-school and college students, ¥500 children. Wed–Mon 11am–6pm. From Shinagawa or Tokyo Station, take the JR Keihin–Tohoku Line 30–40 min. to Saitama Shin-toshin Station, from which it's a 3-min. walk from the west exit. Or, from Shinjuku, take the JR Saikyo Line to Kita-yono, from which it's a 7-min. walk.

Kite Museum (Tako-no-Hakubutsukan)   This private collection consists of more than 3,000 kites, mainly Japanese, all jam-packed in a few small rooms you can tour in about 30 minutes. They range from miniature kites the size of postage stamps to kites dating from the Taisho Period, some ornately decorated with Kabuki stars, samurai, and animals. There are even hand-painted kites by ukiyo-e master Hiroshige.

Taimeiken Building, 5th floor, 1–12–10 Nihombashi, Chuo-ku. ✆ 03/3275-2704. Admission ¥200 adults, ¥100 children. Mon–Sat 11am–5pm. Closed holidays. Station: Nihombashi (3 min.). Off Eitai Dori, btw. Chuo Dori and Showa Dori and behind Coredo shopping center.

Megaweb (Kids)   This huge technology playground and amusement spot on Odaiba is a Toyota showroom in disguise. For the kids there are several virtual thrill rides, including racing simulators, a motion theater with seats that move to the action, and driverless electric commuter cars (some rides have passenger height restrictions). The History Garage displays models from around the world, mostly from the 1950s through the 1970s. But the complex's main raison d'être is its Toyota City Showcase, with 140-odd Toyota models (many of which you can climb in), including hybrids and racing cars. The Universal Design Showcase is fascinating for its cars designed for people with disabilities (and including Japan's aging population), complete with ramps, seats that swing out for easy access, and car seats that double as wheelchairs, as well as for its display of wheelchairs of the future and everyday products (such as easy-to-use scissors) geared toward people with disabilities. Car buffs and families can probably kill an hour or two here, but serious Toyota fans may want to skip this in favor of the adult-oriented Toyota Auto Salon Amlux, described below. Beside Megaweb is a 113m-tall (371-ft.) Ferris wheel that takes 16 minutes to make a complete turn and costs ¥900 to ride, as well as Leisureland, a huge game arcade. ***Note:*** Megaweb may close in 2012; check the website or contact Tokyo's tourist offices for an update.

Palette Town, 1 Aomi, Koto-ku, Odaiba. ✆ 03/3599-0808. www.megaweb.gr.jp. Free admission, but some activities cost extra. Daily 11am–9pm for most attractions (7pm for the Universal section). Station: Aomi, on the Yurikamome Line from Shimbashi (1 min.); or Tokyo Teleport, on the Rinkai Line (3 min.).

Miraikan—National Museum of Emerging Science and Innovation (Nippon Kagaku Miraikan) ★★ (Kids)   Opened in 2001 on Odaiba, this fascinating educational museum provides hands-on exploration of the latest developments in cutting-edge science and technology, including interactions with robots, virtual-reality rides, and displays that suggest future applications such as noninvasive medical procedures and an environmentally friendly home. Everything from nanotechnology and genomes to space exploration is explained in detail; English-language touch-screens, and a volunteer staff eager to assist in demonstrations and answer questions catapult this to one of the most user-friendly technology museums I've seen (avoid, however, weekends and school holidays, when it's packed with families). A great place to get your brain cells up and running whether you're 8 years old or 80, this museum deserves at least 3 hours.

2–41 Aomi, Koto-ku, Odaiba. ☎ **03/3570-9151**. www.miraikan.jst.go.jp. Admission ¥600 adults, ¥200 children. Wed–Mon 10am–5pm. Station: Telecom Center, on the Rinkai Line; or Fune-no-Kagakukan, on the Yurikamome Line (5 min. from either).

Museum of Maritime Science (Fune-no-Kagakukan) (Kids) The building housing the Museum of Maritime Science is shaped like a ship, complete with an observation tower atop its bridge. Appropriately enough, it's located on Odaiba, reclaimed land in Tokyo Bay, and offers a good view of Tokyo's container port nearby. The museum, which you can tour in about 3 hours, contains an excellent collection of model boats, including wooden ships used during the Edo Period; warships (such as the 1898 battleship *Shikishima*); submarines; ferries; supertankers (such as the *Nisseki Maru,* in use from 1971 to 1985 and the world's largest oil tanker at the time); and container ships. Technical explanations, unfortunately, are mostly in Japanese only, so it's totally worth spending the extra ¥500 for an audio guide. Children love the radio-controlled boats they can direct in a rooftop pond. Moored nearby is the *Soya,* constructed in 1938 as a cargo icebreaker; it served as Japan's first Antarctic observation ship and provides views of living quarters, the galley, and machine rooms. Those with a lot of time on their hands can also visit the *Yotei Maru,* which once ferried the waters between Aomori and Hokkaido before the opening of an underwater tunnel made its job obsolete. With the National Museum of Emerging Science and Innovation nearby, and a public swimming pool (July–Aug) next door, this area of Odaiba is a good destination for families.

3–1 Higashi-Yashio, Shinagawa-ku, Odaiba. ☎ **03/5500-1111**. www.funenokagakukan.or.jp. Admission to Museum (including *Soya* and *Yotei Maru*) ¥700 adults, ¥400 children. Tues–Sun 10am–5pm. Station: Fune-no-Kagakukan, on the Yurikamome Line from Shimbashi (1 min.).

National Museum of Nature and Science (Kokuritsu Kagaku Hakubutsukan) ★ (Kids) Japan's largest science museum covers everything from the evolution of life to Japanese inventions and technology, in expansive, imaginative displays, with plenty of exhibits geared toward children. A highlight is an entire arena of 100-some taxidermic animals from around the world, including a polar bear, camel, gorilla, tiger, bear, and other creatures (some are animals that died at Ueno Zoo). Other highlights include a dinosaur display; a hands-on discovery room for children exploring sound, light, magnetism, and other scientific phenomena; re-created wood and marine habitats; a Japanese mummy from the Edo Period curled up in a burial jar; Hachiko (stuffed, on the second floor of the main building; there's a famous statue of the dog at Shibuya Station); and an extensive exhibition that allows visitors to stroll through some 4 billion years of evolutionary history. You'll want to spend about 2 hours here, more if you have children in tow or if you opt for the audio guide (¥200 extra), recommended since English-language explanations are limited.

Ueno Park, Taito-ku. ☎ **03/5777-8600**. www.kahaku.go.jp. Admission ¥600 adults, free for children. Tues–Sun 9am–5pm (to 8pm Fri). Station: Ueno (5 min.). Tokyo Shitamachi Bus: Ueno Koen Yamashita/Ueno Station.

Open-Air Folk House Museum (Nihon Minka-en) ★★ (Finds) Whereas the Edo-Tokyo Tatemono-en (see above) is an open-air museum of traditional and modern Tokyo homes and buildings mostly dating from the late 1800s to the 1940s, this architectural museum concentrates on rural Japan from centuries past. Located in the neighboring city of Kawasaki, 30 minutes by express train from Shinjuku, it features around 20 traditional houses and other historic buildings, in a lovely setting along wooded hillsides. Most buildings are heavy-beamed thatched houses (the oldest are 300 years old), but there are also warehouses, a samurai's residential gate, a water wheel, and a Kabuki stage from a small fishing village, all originally from other parts of Honshu and reconstructed here. An English-language pamphlet and numerous signs explain each of the buildings, open to the public, so you can wander in and inspect the various rooms, gaining insight into rural Japanese life in centuries past. Plan on spending a half-day here, including round-trip transportation.

7-1-1 Masugata, Tama-ku, Kawasaki. ✆ **044/922-2181.** Admission ¥500 adults, ¥300 high-school and college students and seniors, free for children. Tues–Sun 9:30am–5pm (to 4:30pm Nov–Feb). From Shinjuku Station, take the express Odakyu Line 30 min. to Mukogaoka Yuen Station, from which it's a 15-min. walk.

Panasonic Center ★★ (Finds) Of the many company showrooms around town, this one, near Odaiba, is one of the best. Not only does it display Panasonic's newest products, from HD camcorders to the world's largest plasma TV, but it also addresses environmental issues (from recycling to energy conservation) and how products are evolving to assist Japan's elderly and people with disabilities. You can play the latest Nintendo games, learn about self-cleaning air-conditioners, and see for yourself why tilted drums in washing machines are easier to access. Although there's plenty to see for free, visitors with kids or time on their hands might also want to take in RiSuPia, a hands-on science and mathematics museum where you can play air hockey hitting only prime numbers; learn about probability with the roll of a dice; "paint" a picture using only red, green, and blue; and arrange pillows to complete an abstract puzzle. But coolest of all is the Eco & Ud House, a house of the future designed for four people (parents, child, and grandmother) and incorporating all the latest smart and energy-efficient products, from top shelves in the kitchen that can be pulled out and lowered, to a plasma TV that doubles as a home system, monitoring everything from the house's energy consumption to the child as she walks to school. One-hour free tours of the house (make reservations 1 month in advance) allow you to see or test the function of everything—you can even lie down in the sleep-inducing bedroom if you wish.

2-5-18 Ariake, Koto-ku. ✆ **03/3599-2600.** Free admission to Panasonic Center; RiSuPia ¥500 adults, ¥300 high-school students, free for children. Tues–Sun 10am–6pm. Station: Kokusai-tenjijo, on the Rinkai Line; or Ariake, on the Yurikamome Line (3 min. from either).

Shitamachi Museum (Shitamachi Fuzoku Shiryokan) *Shitamachi* means "downtown" and refers to the area of Tokyo in which commoners used to live, mainly around Ueno and Asakusa. Today there's very little left of old downtown Tokyo, and with that in mind, the Shitamachi Museum seeks to preserve for future generations a way of life that was virtually wiped out by the great earthquake of 1923 and World War II. Shops are set up as they may have looked back then, including a merchant's shop and a candy shop, as well as one of the shitamachi tenements common at the turn of the 20th century. These tenements—long, narrow buildings with one roof over a series of dwelling units separated by thin wooden walls—were the homes of the poorer people. The tenements' narrow back alleyways served as communal living rooms. The museum also displays some personal effects of these residents, including utensils, toys, costumes, and tools, most of which you can pick up and examine more closely. Individuals, many living in shitamachi, donated all the museum's holdings. This museum is small and is recommended only if you don't have time to see the better Edo-Tokyo Museum (see earlier).

WHAT TO SEE & DO IN TOKYO

You can see it in about 20 minutes on your own, but I recommend taking advantage of free guided tours lead by volunteers, who can explain the function of various things you might otherwise miss, such as the fly catcher.

Ueno Park, Taito-ku. ✆ **03/3823-7451**. Admission ¥300 adults, ¥100 children. Tues–Sun 9:30am–4:30pm. Station: Ueno (3 min.). Tokyo Shitamachi Bus: Ueno Koen Yamashita/Ueno Station.

Sony Building   A popular place to kill 30 minutes or so of free time in the Ginza, the Sony Building, open since 1966, offers four floors of showrooms, including the latest in Sony video and digital cameras, portable TVs and HDTVs, DVD and MP3 players, digital photo frames, laptops, and computers, as well as a small Hi-Vision theater. There are also a few PlayStations, but true gamers may want to test their skill at **Sony Computer Entertainment, Inc.,** on Aoyama Dori at 2–9–21 Minami Aoyama (✆ **03/6438-8000**; station: Aoyama 1-chome), open free to the public Monday to Friday 11:15am to 7pm.

5-3-1 Ginza, Chuo-ku. ✆ **03/3573-2371**. Free admission. Daily 11am–7pm. Station: Ginza (B9 exit, 1 min.). At the intersection of Harumi Dori and Sotobori Dori.

Tokyo Metropolitan Museum of Photography (Tokyo-to Shashin Bijutsu-kan) ★   This museum has an impressive 22,000 works in its photographic inventory, ranging from the historical to the contemporary, with about 70% by Japanese photographers. Exhibitions from Japan and abroad, many on the cutting edge of contemporary photography, are shown in one gallery, while another features a rotating exhibit of the museum's holdings (occasionally the permanent collection is usurped by a special exhibition). I can easily spend an hour here, lost in another world.

Yebisu Garden Place, 1-13-3 Mita, Meguro-ku. ✆ **03/3280-0099**. www.syabi.com. Admission to permanent collection ¥500–¥700 adults, ¥400–¥700 students, ¥250–¥600 children and seniors; more for special exhibits. Sat–Sun and Tues–Wed 10am–6pm; Thurs–Fri 10am–8pm. Station: Ebisu (8 min.).

Toyota Auto Salon Amlux Tokyo   I'm not a big car fan, but even I have fun at Amlux. Japan's largest automobile showroom when it opened 20-some years ago, this sophisticated facility holds its own with four floors of exhibition space containing more than 70 vehicles (be sure to stop by the information desk on the first floor for an English-language pamphlet). Everything from sports and racing cars to family, hybrid, handicap-accessible, and luxury cars is on view, all open so that potential buyers can climb inside and play with the dials. There are also race-car simulators, a trumpet-playing robot (weekends only), a play area for toddlers, the Universal Design Corner (with cool gadgets that make life easier for persons with disabilities and the elderly), and exhibits relating to Toyota's plans for the future (such as specialty seats to prevent whiplash). As opposed to Megaweb on Odaiba (see above), which is mainly for entertainment, this is for serious automobile fans.

3-3-5 Higashi Ikebukuro, Toshima-ku. ✆ **03/5391-5900**. www.amlux.jp. Free admission. Tues–Sun 11am–7pm. Station: Higashi Ikebukuro (2 min.) or Ikebukuro (5 min.).

6 SPECTACULAR CITY VIEWS

In addition to the recommendations below, another lofty perch is **Tokyo City View,** an observatory on the 52nd floor of Roppongi Hills' Mori Tower, 6–10–1 Roppongi (✆ **03/6406-6652**; www.roppongihills.com/tcv). Admission here is usually included in the price of the Mori Art Museum (see earlier). Otherwise, it costs a hefty ¥1,500 for adults, ¥1,000 for high-school and university students, and ¥500 for children, so you might as well take in the museum. For an additional ¥300, you can head to the rooftop Sky Deck, the highest open-air observation deck in Japan, where you have unobstructed views over the metropolis. Tokyo City View is open Sunday to Thursday from 10am to 11pm and Friday and Saturday from 10am to 1am. The Sky Deck is open daily from 10am to 8pm (closed during inclement weather).

Tokyo Metropolitan Government Office (TMG) ★★★ (Kids) Tokyo's city hall—designed by one of Japan's best-known architects, Kenzo Tange—is an impressive addition to the skyscrapers of west Shinjuku. The complex comprises three buildings— TMG no. 1, TMG no. 2, and the Metropolitan Assembly Building—and together they contain everything from Tokyo's Disaster Prevention Center to the governor's office. Most important for visitors is TMG no. 1, the tall building to the north that offers the best free view of Tokyo. This 48-story, 240m (787-ft.) structure, the tallest building in Shinjuku, boasts two observatories located on the 45th floors of both its north and south towers, with access from the first floor. Both observatories offer the same spectacular views—on clear winter days, you can even see Mount Fuji—as well as a small souvenir shop and coffee shop (the North Tower also has a Hakuhinkan Toy Park, with fun souvenirs, but a large restaurant annoyingly takes up the entire east side of the observatory). In expensive Tokyo, this is one of the city's best bargains, and kids love it. On the first floor is a Tokyo Tourist Information Center, open daily 10am to 6:30pm.

2–8–1 Nishi-Shinjuku. ✆ **03/5321-1111.** Free admission. Daily 9:30am–10:30pm. Closed Dec 29–Jan 3. Station: Tochomae (1 min.), Shinjuku (10 min.), or Nishi-Shinjuku (5 min.).

Tokyo Tower ★ (Overrated) Japan's most famous observation tower was built in 1958 and was modeled after the slightly smaller Eiffel Tower in Paris. Lit up at night, this 330m (1,083-ft.) tower, a relay station for TV and radio stations, is a familiar and beloved landmark in the city's landscape; but with the construction of skyscrapers over the past few decades (including the TMG, above, with its free observatory), it has lost some of its appeal as an observation platform and seems more like a relic from the 1950s. With its tacky souvenir shops and assorted small-time attractions, this place is about as kitsch as kitsch can be.

The tower has two observatories: the main one at 149m (489 ft.) and the top observatory at 248m (814 ft.). The best time of year for viewing is said to be during Golden Week at the beginning of May. With many Tokyoites gone from the city and most factories and businesses closed down, the air at this time is thought to be the cleanest and clearest. There are several offbeat tourist attractions in the tower's base building, including a wax museum (where you can see the Beatles, a wax rendition of Leonardo's *Last Supper*, Hollywood stars, and a medieval torture chamber), a small aquarium, a museum of holography, a Guinness World Records Museum, and a trick art gallery, all with separate admission fees and appealing mainly to children.

4–2 Shiba Koen, Minato-ku. ✆ **03/3433-5111.** www.tokyotower.co.jp. Admission to both observatories ¥1,420 adults, ¥860 children. Daily 9am–10pm. Station: Onarimon or Kamiyacho (6 min.).

7 ESPECIALLY FOR KIDS

Attractions listed earlier that are good for children include the Edo-Tokyo Museum (p. 173), Drum Museum (p. 192), Fukagawa Edo Museum (closed for renovation until August 2010; p. 193), Ghibli Museum (p. 194), Megaweb (p. 195), National Museum of Emerging Science and Innovation (p. 195), Museum of Maritime Science (p. 196), National Museum of Nature and Science (p. 196), Panasonic Center (p. 197), Tokyo Tower (p. 199), and the observatory of the Tokyo Metropolitan Government Office (p. 199). Ueno and Shinjuku parks (p. 200) are good for getting rid of all that excess energy.

Hanayashiki   Opened in 1853 while the shogun still reigned, this small and rather corny amusement park is Japan's oldest. It offers a small roller coaster, a kiddie Ferris wheel, a carousel, a haunted house, a 3-D theater, samurai and ninja shows, and other diversions that appeal to younger children. Note, however, that after paying admission, you must still buy tickets for each ride; tickets are ¥100 each, and most rides require three to four tickets.

2-28-1 Asakusa (northwest of Sensoji Temple), Taito-ku. 🕐 03/3842-8780. www.hanayashiki.net. Admission ¥900 adults, ¥400 children 5–12 and seniors, free for children 4 and under. Daily 10am–6pm (to 5pm in winter). Station: Asakusa (5 min.). Tokyo Shitamachi Bus: Ueno Koen Yamashita/Ueno Station.

Joypolis Sega   Bored teenagers in tow, grumbling at yet another temple or shrine? Bring them to life at Tokyo's most sophisticated virtual amusement arcade, outfitted with the latest in video games and high-tech virtual-reality attractions, courtesy of Sega. Video games include bobsledding, snowboarding, and car races, in which participants maneuver curves utilizing virtual-reality equipment, as well as numerous aeronautical battle games. There's also a 3-D sightseeing tour with seats that move with the action on the screen, several virtual reality rides (sky diving, anyone?), a virtual aquarium, and much, much more. Most harmless are the Print Club machines, which will print your face on stickers with the background (Mt. Fuji, perhaps?) of your choice. If you think your kids will want to try everything, buy them a passport for ¥3,500 for those 15 and older or ¥3,100 for those under 15 (children younger than 7 get in free but are charged for attractions—note that some activities have height restrictions).

There's a smaller Sega on Dogenzaka slope in Shibuya at 2-6-16 Dogenzaka (🕐 03/5458-2201; station: Shibuya, 2 min.), open daily 10am to midnight and offering arcade and virtual-reality games, but note that because this is in a nightlife area, children under 16 aren't allowed after 6pm, and children under 18 aren't allowed after 8pm.

Tokyo Decks, 3rd floor, Odaiba. 🕐 03/5500-1801. http://sega.jp/joypolis/Tokyo/home_e.shtml. Admission ¥500 adults, ¥300 children; individual attractions an additional ¥300–¥600 each. Daily 10am–11pm. Station: Odaiba Kaihin Koen (2 min.).

National Children's Castle (Kodomo-no-Shiro) ★   Conceived by the Ministry of Health and Welfare to commemorate the International Year of the Child in 1979, the Children's Castle holds various activity rooms for children of all ages (though most are geared to elementary-age kids and younger). The third floor, designed for spontaneous and unstructured play, features a large climbing gym, building blocks, a playhouse, dolls, books, and a preteen corner with billiards, foosball, and other age-appropriate games; there's also an art room staffed with instructors to help children with projects suitable for their ages. On the fourth floor is a music room with instruments the kids are invited to play, as well as a video room with private cubicles where visitors can make selections from a library of English-language and Japanese videos, including Disney films. On the roof is an outdoor playground complete with a wading pool (summer only; ¥200 extra admission) and tricycles, while in the basement is the family pool open to the public weekends only (¥300 for adults, ¥200 for children). Various programs are offered throughout the week, including puppet shows, fairy tales, live music performances, and origami presentations.

5–53–1 Jingumae, Shibuya-ku. © **03/3797-5666.** Admission ¥500 adults, ¥400 children 3–17, free for children 2 and under. Tues–Fri 12:30–5:30pm; Sat–Sun and holidays (including school holidays) 10am–5:30pm. Station: Omotesando (exit B2, 8 min.) or Shibuya (10 min.). On Aoyama Dori btw. Omotesando and Shibuya stations.

Sunshine International Aquarium   On the 10th floor of the World Import Mart Building, this Sunshine City complex is the unlikely home of some 60,000 fish and animals, including dolphins, sea otters, penguins, ocean sunfish (flat as a pancake but up to 4m/13 ft. in circumference and 2 tons in weight), and more. There are also seal performances. Because the aquarium is small (you can see it in about an hour), it's perfect for small children.

World Import Mart Building, 10th floor, Sunshine City, 3–1–3 Higashi Ikebukuro. © **03/3989-3466.** Admission ¥1,800 adults, ¥900 children 4–15, free for children 3 and under. Mon–Fri 10am–6pm; Sat–Sun and holidays 10am–6:30pm. Station: Higashi Ikebukuro (3 min.) or Ikebukuro (7 min.).

Tokyo Disneyland & Tokyo DisneySea ★★★   Virtually a carbon copy of Disneyland back home, this one also boasts the Jungle Cruise, Pirates of the Caribbean, the Haunted Mansion, and Space Mountain. Other hot attractions include Toontown, a wacky theme park where Mickey and other Disney characters work and play; MicroAdventure, which features 3-D glasses and special effects; and Star Tours, a thrill adventure created by Disney and George Lucas.

Opened in 2001 adjacent to Disneyland, **DisneySea,** a theme park based on ocean legends and myths, offers seven distinct "ports of call," including the futuristic Port Discovery marina, with its StormRider, which flies straight into the eye of a storm; the Lost River Delta, with its Indiana Jones Adventure; Mermaid Lagoon, based on the film *The Little Mermaid;* the Arabian Coast, with its Sindbad's Seven Voyages boat ride; and the American Waterfront, with its Tower of Terror. Because DisneySea is unique to Tokyo, I personally think this is the one to see; its installations are a class act.

1–1 Maihama, Urayasu-shi, Chiba. © **047/310-0733.** www.tokyodisneyresort.co.jp. 1-day passport to either Disneyland or DisneySea, including entrance to and use of all attractions, ¥5,800 adults, ¥5,100 seniors, ¥5,000 children 12–17, ¥3,900 children 4–11, free for children 3 and under. Daily 8 or 9am to 10pm, with slightly shorter hours in winter. Station: Maihama, on the JR Keiyo Line from Tokyo Station (1 min.).

Tokyo Dome City   Located in the center of town, next to the Tokyo Dome stadium, this amusement park features a high-tech Ferris wheel called the Big O (hollow in the middle, with no spokes and no hub); the heart-stopping Thunder Dolphin roller coaster, which passes through the Big O at speeds reaching up to 130kmph (81 mph); the Tower Hacker, which drops straight down from a height of 80 m (262 ft.); and a water ride, simulation theater, game arcade, bowling alley, and other amusements packed into cramped quarters.

1–3–61 Koraku, Bunkyo-ku. © **03/5800-9999.** www.tokyo-dome.co.jp. Free admission; individual rides cost ¥400–¥1,000 each. 1-day passport ¥4,000 adults, ¥3,000 children (reduced passports after 5pm). Mon–Fri 10am–9pm; Sat–Sun and holidays 9:30am–9pm. Station: Korakuen (1 min.), Kasuga (2 min.), or Suidobashi (7 min.).

Tokyo Metropolitan Children's Hall (Tokyo-To Jido Kaikan) (Finds)   This is Tokyo's largest public facility for children—and it's absolutely free. There are toddler areas, indoor gyms, computers, a crafts corner, musical instruments, and a rooftop

WHAT TO SEE & DO IN TOKYO

7

ESPECIALLY FOR KIDS

playground (open weekends and holidays), as well as a minitheater with frequent showings of free films and monthly events and programs (in Japanese only). Although the hall is not as extensive or sophisticated as the National Children's Castle, the price is right and it's good for a rainy day. *Note:* Sadly, this facility is slated to close in March 2012 (though a skate park is slated to open nearby).

1-18-24 Shibuya, Shibuya-ku. ✆ **03/3409-6361.** Free admission. Daily 9am–5pm (to 6pm July–Aug). Closed one Mon a month. Station: Shibuya (7 min.) or Hanzomon (exit 11, 3 min.). Off Meiji Dori, on the side street beside Tower Records & Books.

Tokyo Sea Life Park (Kasai Rinkai Suizokuen) ★ ⟨Finds⟩   Located on the shore of Tokyo Bay in Kasai Rinkai Park, this public facility is Tokyo's largest—yet cheapest—aquarium, with tanks displaying marine life of Tokyo Bay and beyond, including the Pacific, Indian, and Atlantic oceans. Hammerhead sharks, bluefin tuna, the giant ocean sunfish, penguins, puffins, a touch tide pool, and a 3-D movie are some of the highlights. The park also contains a beach, a small Japanese garden, a bird sanctuary, and what is claimed to be Japan's largest Ferris wheel (fare: ¥700), making it a good family outing.

Kasai Rinkai Park, 6-2-3 Rinkai-cho, Edogawa-ku. ✆ **03/3869-5152.** www.tokyo-zoo.net/english. Admission ¥700 adults, ¥350 seniors, ¥250 children 12–14, free for children 11 and under. Thurs–Tues 9:30am–5pm (enter by 4pm). Mon–Fri, take the JR Keiyo Line rapid service from Tokyo Station to Shin-Kiba, change to the local Keiyo Line, and get off at the next station, Kasairinkai Koen, from which it's a 5-min. walk. Sat–Sun and holidays, there's rapid service directly to Kasairinkai Koen.

Ueno Zoo   Founded in 1882, Japan's oldest zoo is small by today's standards but remains one of the most well-known zoos in Japan. A vivarium houses amphibians, fish, and reptiles, including snakes and crocodiles. Also of note is the five-storied pagoda dating from the Edo era, along with a teahouse built 350 years ago to receive the shogun when visiting nearby Toshogu Shrine. Shinobazu Pond, on the west end of the zoo, serves as a sanctuary for wild cormorants and other birds. Personally, I can't help but feel sorry for some of the animals in their small spaces, but children will enjoy the Japanese macaques, polar and Hokkaido brown bears, California sea lions, penguins, gorillas, giraffes, zebras, elephants, hippos, deer, and tigers. Expect to spend a minimum of 2 hours here.

Ueno Park, Taito-ku. ✆ **03/3828-5171.** www.tokyo-zoo.net/english. Admission ¥600 adults, ¥300 seniors, ¥200 children 12–14, free for children 11 and under. Tues–Sun 9:30am–5pm (enter by 4pm). Closed some holidays. Station: Ueno (4 min.). Tokyo Shitamachi Bus: Ueno Koen Yamashita/Ueno Station.

8 SPECTATOR SPORTS

For information on current sporting events taking place in Tokyo, ranging from kickboxing and pro wrestling to sumo, baseball, soccer, table tennis, and golf, contact the **Tourist Information Center,** or pick up a copy of the free weekly *Metropolis* magazine.

BASEBALL   Introduced into Japan from the United States in 1873, baseball is as popular among Japanese as it is among Americans. Even the annual high-school playoffs keep everyone glued to their television sets. As with other imports, the Japanese have added their modifications, including cheerleaders. Several American players have proven very popular with local fans; but according to the rules, no more than four foreigners may play on any one team. In recent years, there's been a reverse exodus of top Japanese players defecting to American teams.

There are two professional leagues, the Central and the Pacific, which play from April to October and meet in the Japan Series. In Tokyo, the home teams are the **Yomiuri Giants,** who play at the Tokyo Dome (℡ **03/5800-9999;** station: Korakuen or Suidobashi), and the **Yakult Swallows,** who play at Jingu Stadium (℡ **03/3404-8999;** station: Gaienmae). Other teams playing in the vicinity of Tokyo are the **Chiba Lotte Marines,** who play at Chiba Marine Stadium in Chiba (℡ **043/296-8900**), and the **Yokohama BayStars,** who play in downtown Yokohama Stadium (℡ **045/661-1251**). Advance tickets go on sale Friday, 2 weeks prior to the game, and can be purchased at one of many **Ticket Pia** locations around town (such as the Sony building in Ginza or the Isetan department store annex in Shinjuku; ask your hotel for the one nearest you), except for the Giants, where tickets can be purchased only at Tokyo Dome. Prices for the Tokyo Dome and Jingu Stadium range from ¥1,800 for an unreserved seat in the outfield to ¥6,000 for seats behind home plate. The Giants are so popular, however, that tickets are hard to come by.

SUMO ★★★   The Japanese form of wrestling, known as sumo, began perhaps as long as 1,500 years ago and is still the nation's most popular sport, with wrestlers—often taller than 6 feet and weighing well over 300 pounds—revered as national heroes. A sumo match takes place on a sandy-floored ring less than 4.5m (15 ft.) in diameter; the object is for a wrestler to either eject his opponent from the ring or cause him to touch the ground with any part of his body other than his feet. This is accomplished by shoving, slapping, tripping, throwing, even carrying the opponent. Altogether, there are 48 holds and throws, and sumo fans know them all. Most bouts are very short, lasting only 30 seconds or so. The highest-ranking players are called *yokozuna,* or grand champions; in 1993, a Hawaiian named Akebono was promoted to the highest rank, the first non-Japanese ever to be so honored. Nowadays, there are many high-ranking foreigners.

Sumo matches are held in Tokyo at the **Kokugikan,** 1–3–28 Yokoami, Sumida-ku (℡ **03/3622-1100;** www.sumo.or.jp; station: Ryogoku, then a 1-min. walk; Tokyo Shitamachi Bus: Ryogoku Station). Matches are held in January, May, and September for 15 consecutive days, beginning at around 9:30am and lasting until 6pm; the top wrestlers compete after 3:30pm. The best seats are ringside box seats, but they're snapped up by companies or the friends and families of sumo wrestlers. Usually available are balcony seats, which can be purchased at Ticket Pia locations around town and JTB travel agencies. You can also purchase tickets directly at the Kokugikan ticket office beginning at 9am every morning of the tournament. Prices range from about ¥2,100 for an unreserved seat (sold only on the day of the event at the stadium, with about 400 seats available) to ¥8,200 for a good reserved seat.

If you can't make it to a match, watching on TV is almost as good. Tournaments in Tokyo, as well as those that take place annually in Osaka, Nagoya, and Fukuoka, are broadcast on the NHK channel from 4 to 6pm daily during matches.

Tokyo Strolls

Because Tokyo is a jigsaw puzzle of distinct neighborhoods, it makes sense to explore the city section by section. Below are walking tours of four of Tokyo's most fascinating, diverse, and easily explored neighborhoods. For information on sightseeing and attractions outside these neighborhoods or for additional information on attractions described below, see chapter 7.

WALKING TOUR 1   A S A K U S A

START:	**Hama Rikyu Garden (Shiodome Station) or Asakusa Station (exit 1 or 3)**
FINISH:	**Kappabashi Dori (station: Tawaramachi)**
TIME:	**Allow approximately 5 hours, including the boat ride**
BEST TIMES:	**Tuesday through Friday, when the crowds aren't as big, or Sunday, when you can join a free tour, but:**
WORST TIMES:	**Sunday, when the shops on Kappabashi Dori are closed**

If anything remains of old Tokyo, Asakusa is it. This is where you find narrow streets lined with small residential homes, women in kimono, Tokyo's oldest and most popular temple, and quaint shops selling boxwood combs, fans, sweet pastries, and other products of yore. With its temple market, old-fashioned amusement park, and traditional shops and restaurants, Asakusa preserves the charm of old downtown Edo better than anyplace else in Tokyo. For many older Japanese, a visit to Asakusa is like stepping back to their childhood; for tourists, it provides a glimpse of Tokyo's past.

Pleasure-seekers have flocked to Asakusa for centuries. Originating as a temple town back in the 7th century, it grew in popularity during the Tokugawa regime, as merchants grew wealthy and whole new forms of popular entertainment arose to cater to them. Theaters for Kabuki and Bunraku flourished in Asakusa, as did restaurants and shops. By 1840, Asakusa had become Edo's main entertainment district. In stark contrast to the solemnity surrounding places of worship in the West, Asakusa's temple market had a carnival atmosphere reminiscent of medieval Europe, complete with street performers and exotic animals. It retains some of that festive atmosphere today.

The most dramatic way to arrive in Asakusa is by boat from Hama Rikyu Garden (see stop no. 1, below), just as people used to arrive in the old days. If you want to forgo the boat ride, take the subway directly to Asakusa Station and start your tour from stop no. 2. Otherwise, head to:

❶ Hama Rikyu Garden

Located at the south end of Tokyo (station: Shiodome, exit 5, and then a 5-min. walk), this garden was laid out during the Edo Period in a style popular at the time, in which surrounding scenery was incorporated into its composition. Today, skyscrapers are the only surrounding scenery, but it does contain an inner tidal pool, bridges draped with wisteria, moon-viewing pavilions, and teahouses. (See "Parks & Gardens," in chapter 7, for more details.)

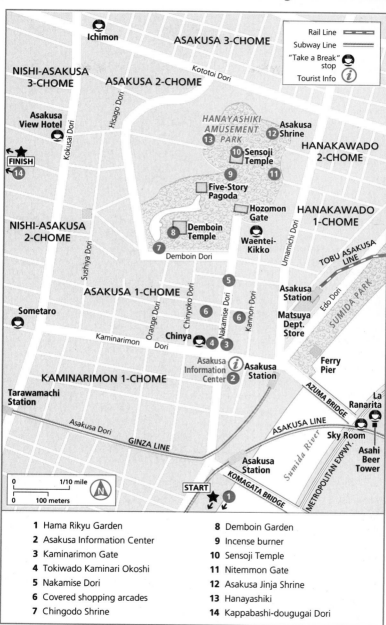

Ichimon

ASAKUSA 3-CHOME

Rail Line
Subway Line
"Take a Break" stop
Tourist Info ℹ

NISHI-ASAKUSA 3-CHOME

ASAKUSA 2-CHOME

Kototoi Dori

Hisago Dori

Asakusa View Hotel

Kokusai Dori

HANAYASHIKI AMUSEMENT PARK
13

Asakusa Shrine **12**

HANAKAWADO 2-CHOME

FINISH

14

10 Sensoji Temple

9

11

Five-Story Pagoda

NISHI-ASAKUSA 2-CHOME

Sushya Dori

8 Demboin Temple

7

Demboin Dori

Hozomon Gate

Waentei-Kikko

HANAKAWADO 1-CHOME

Umamichi Dori

TOBU ASAKUSA LINE

5

ASAKUSA 1-CHOME

Chiryoko Dori

Orange Dori

Nakamise Dori

Kannon Dori

6

6

Asakusa Station

Matsuya Dept. Store

Edo Dori

SUMIDA PARK

Sometaro

Kaminarimon Dori

Chinya **4** **3**

Asakusa Information Center ℹ **2**

Asakusa Station

Ferry Pier

La Ranarita

KAMINARIMON 1-CHOME

Tarawamachi Station

Asakusa Dori

GINZA LINE

AZUMA BRIDGE

ASAKUSA LINE

Sky Room

Asahi Beer Tower

Asakusa Station

Sumida River

METROPOLITAN EXPWY.

0   1/10 mile
0   100 meters

N

START **1**

KOMAGATA BRIDGE

TOKYO STROLLS

8

ASAKUSA

1 Hama Rikyu Garden
2 Asakusa Information Center
3 Kaminarimon Gate
4 Tokiwado Kaminari Okoshi
5 Nakamise Dori
6 Covered shopping arcades
7 Chingodo Shrine
8 Demboin Garden
9 Incense burner
10 Sensoji Temple
11 Nitemmon Gate
12 Asakusa Jinja Shrine
13 Hanayashiki
14 Kappabashi-dougugai Dori

Boats depart the garden to make their way along the Sumida River every 30 to 60 minutes between 10:35am and 4:15pm, with the fare to Asakusa costing ¥720. Although much of what you see along the working river today is only concrete embankments, I like the trip because it affords a different perspective of Tokyo—barges making their way down the river, high-rise apartment buildings with laundry fluttering from balconies, warehouses, and superhighways. The boat passes under approximately a dozen bridges during the 40-minute trip, each one completely different. During cherry-blossom season, thousands of cherry trees lining the bank make the ride particularly memorable.

Upon your arrival in Asakusa, walk away from the boat pier a couple of blocks inland, where you'll soon see the colorful Kaminarimon Gate on your right. Across the street on your left is the:

② Asakusa Information Center

Located at 2–18–9 Kaminarimon (✆ 03/ 6280-6710), the center is open daily from 9:30am to 8pm but is staffed by English-speaking volunteers only from 10am to 5pm. Stop here to pick up a map of the area, use the restroom, and ask for directions to restaurants and sights. On Sundays, volunteers give free 1-hour guided tours of Asakusa at 11am and 2pm (arrive 10 min. earlier). Note the huge Seiko clock on the center's facade—every hour on the hour, from 10am to 7pm, mechanical dolls reenact scenes from Asakusa's most famous festivals.

Across the street is the:

③ Kaminarimon Gate

The gate is unmistakable, with its bright red colors and 100-kilogram (220-lb.) lantern hanging in the middle. The statues inside the gate are of the god of wind to the right and the god of thunder to the left, ready to protect the deity enshrined in the temple. The god of thunder is particularly fearsome—he has an insatiable appetite for navels.

To the left of the gate, on the corner, is:

④ Tokiwado Kaminari Okoshi

This open-fronted confectionery has been selling rice-based sweets (*okashi*) for 250 years and is popular with visiting Japanese buying gifts for the folks back home. It's open daily 9am to 9pm.

Once past Kaminarimon Gate, you'll find yourself immediately on a pedestrian lane called:

⑤ Nakamise Dori

This leads straight to the temple. Nakamise means "inside shops," and historical records show that vendors have sold wares here since the late 17th century. Today Nakamise Dori is lined on both sides with tiny stall after tiny stall, many owned by the same family for generations. If you're expecting austere religious artifacts, however, you're in for a surprise: Sweets, shoes, barking toy dogs, Japanese crackers (called *sembei*), bags, umbrellas, Japanese dolls, T-shirts, fans, masks, and traditional Japanese accessories are all sold. How about a brightly colored straight hairpin—and a black hairpiece to go with it? Or a temporary tattoo in the shape of a dragon? This is a great place to shop for souvenirs, gifts, and items you have no earthly need for—a little bit of unabashed consumerism on the way to spiritual purification.

TAKE A BREAK
If you're hungry for lunch, there are a number of possibilities in the neighborhood. ⑰ **Chinya** (p. 138), 1–3–4 Asakusa, just west of Kaminarimon Gate on Kaminarimon Dori, has been serving sukiyaki and *shabu-shabu* since 1880. Northeast of Kaminarimon Gate is ⑳ **Waentei-Kikko** (p. 140), 2–2–13 Asakusa, offering *obento* lunch boxes and *shamisen* performances. For Western food, head to the other side of the Sumida River, where on the 22nd floor of the Asahi Beer Tower is **La Ranarita Azumabashi** (p. 139), 1–23–1 Azumabashi, a moderately priced Italian restaurant with great views of Asakusa; and the utilitarian **Sky Room** (p. 168) with inexpensive beer, wine, and other drinks.

The Floating World of Yoshiwara

During the Edo Period (1603–1867), prostitution in Japan was not only allowed, it was—along with everything else in feudal Japan—regulated and strictly controlled by the Tokugawa shogunate. Licensed quarters arose in various parts of Edo (now Tokyo), but none was as famous or as long-standing as **Yoshiwara,** the "floating world of pleasure." Opened in 1657 in the midst of rice fields, far outside the city gates upriver from Asakusa, Yoshiwara rose to such prominence that, at its height, as many as 3,000 prostitutes, referred to as "courtesans," worked their trade here. The services they rendered depended on how much their customers were willing to spend. Some men, so they say, stayed for days. Stories abound of how more than a few lost their entire fortunes.

The top-ranked courtesan, known as Tayu, was distinguished by her gorgeous costume, which often weighed as much as 40 pounds and included a huge *obi* (sash) knotted in front. Many of the courtesans, however, had been sold into prostitution as young girls. To prevent their escape, a moat surrounded Yoshiwara, which could be entered or exited only through a guarded gate. The courtesans were allowed out of the compound once a year, during an autumn festival. Such virtual imprisonment was abolished only in 1900. Yoshiwara itself was closed down in 1957, when prostitution became illegal.

Before reaching the end of Nakamise Dori, there are a couple interesting side streets worth exploring. Just 2 blocks north of Kaminarimon Gate are:

6 Two covered shopping arcades

Stretching both to the right and left of Nakamise Dori, these pedestrian-only covered lanes are typical of what you'll see everywhere in Japan—regular streets that became instant shopping centers by covering them with roofs and banning vehicular traffic. This is where the locals shop, with stores selling clothing, household goods, souvenirs, and more.

Farther along Nakamise Dori, to the left, is Demboin Dori (you'll pass some interesting shops selling antiques here). In just a minute's walk, you'll see a small red gate on your right, leading to:

7 Chingodo Shrine

Dedicated to Chingodo, the so-called raccoon dog and guardian against fires and burglars, it affords a view of part of a garden through a fence. This garden is:

8 Demboin Garden

This peaceful oasis in the midst of bustling Asakusa was designed in the 17th century by Enshu Kobori, a tea-ceremony master and famous landscape gardener who also designed a garden for the shogun's castle. Alas, it used to be open to the public, but no longer, so you'll have to content yourself with a glimpse of it here.

Return to Nakamise Dori and resume your walk north to the second gate, which opens onto a square filled with pigeons and a large:

9 Incense burner

This is where worshippers "wash" themselves to ward off or help cure illness. If, for example, you have a sore throat, be sure to rub some of the smoke over your throat for good measure.

The building dominating the square is:

⑩ Sensoji Temple

Sensoji is Tokyo's oldest temple. Founded in the 7th century and therefore already well established long before Tokugawa settled in Edo, Sensoji Temple is dedicated to Kannon, the Buddhist goddess of mercy, and is therefore popularly called the Asakusa Kannon Temple. According to legend, the temple was founded after two fishermen pulled a golden statue of Kannon from the sea. The sacred statue is still housed in the temple, carefully preserved inside three boxes. Even though it's never on display, an estimated 20 million people flock to the temple annually to pay their respects.

Within the temple is a counter where you can buy your fortune by putting a 100-yen coin into a wooden box and shaking it until a long bamboo stick emerges from a small hole. The stick will have a Japanese number on it, which corresponds to one of the numbers on a set of drawers. Take the fortune, written in both English and Japanese, from the drawer that has your number. But don't expect the translation to clear things up; my fortune contained such cryptic messages as "Getting a beautiful lady at your home, you want to try all people know about this," and "Stop to start a trip." If you find that your fortune raises more questions than it answers or if you simply don't like what it has to say, you can conveniently negate it by tying it to one of the wires provided for this purpose just outside the main hall.

To the right (east) of the temple is the rather small:

⑪ Nitemmon Gate

Built in 1618, this is the only structure on temple grounds remaining from the Edo Period; all other buildings, including Sensoji Temple and the pagoda, were destroyed in a 1945 air raid.

On the northeast corner of the grounds is a small orange shrine, the:

⑫ Asakusa Jinja Shrine

This shrine was built in 1649 by Iemitsu Tokugawa, the third Tokugawa shogun, to commemorate the two fishermen who found the statue of Kannon, and their village chief. Its architectural style, called Gongen-zukuri, is the same as Toshogu Shrine's in Nikko. West of Sensoji Temple is a gardenlike area of lesser shrines, memorials, flowering bushes, and a stream of carp. (*Tip:* The most picturesque photos of Sensoji Temple can be taken from here.)

Farther west still is:

⑬ Hanayashiki

This is a small and corny amusement park that first opened in 1853 and still draws in the little ones. (See "Especially for Kids," in chapter 7 for details.)

Most of the area west of Sensoji Temple (to the left when facing the front of the temple) is a small but interesting part of Asakusa popular among Tokyo's older working class. This is where several of Asakusa's old-fashioned pleasure houses remain, including bars, restaurants, strip shows, traditional Japanese vaudeville, and so-called "love hotels," which rent rooms by the hour.

If you keep walking west, past the Asakusa View Hotel, within 10 minutes you'll reach:

⑭ Kappabashi-dougugai Dori

Generally referred to as Kappabashi Dori, Tokyo's wholesale district for restaurant items has shops selling pottery, chairs, tableware, cookware, lacquerware, rice cookers, *noren,* and everything else needed to run a restaurant. You can even buy those models of plastic food you've seen in restaurant displays. Ice cream, pizza, sushi, mugs foaming with beer—they're all here, looking like the real thing. (Stores close about 5pm and are closed Sun.)

> ☕ **WINDING DOWN**
> The **Asakusa View Hotel,** on Kokusai Dori, between Sensoji Temple and Kappabashi Dori, has several restaurants and bars, including the clubby **Ice House,** the hotel's main bar, open daily from 5:30pm. Another good place to end a day of sightseeing is **Ichimon** (p. 258), 3–12–6 Asakusa, near the inter-

> section of Kokusai and Kototoi avenues. Decorated like a farmhouse, it specializes in sake. For inexpensive dining in a convivial, rustic setting, head to ㉓ **Sometaro** (p. 141), 2–2–2 Nishi-Asakusa, just off Kokusai Dori, where you cook your own *okonomiyaki,* or fried noodles, at your table.

WALKING TOUR 2 · HARAJUKU & AOYAMA

START:	Meiji Jingu Shrine (station: Harajuku)
FINISH:	Omotesando Station
TIME:	Allow approximately 4 hours, including stops along the way
BEST TIMES:	The first Sunday of every month, when there's an antiques flea market at Togo Shrine, and every Sunday when teenagers dressed in *cosplay* (costume play) and other costumes hang out near Meiji Jingu Shrine
WORST TIMES:	Monday (when the Ota Memorial Museum of Art is closed), Thursday (when the Oriental Bazaar is closed), and from the 27th to the end of every month (when the Ota Memorial Museum of Art is closed for exhibit changes)

Harajuku is one of my favorite neighborhoods in Tokyo, though I'm too old to really fit in. In fact, anyone over 25 is apt to feel ancient; this is Tokyo's most popular hangout for Japanese teenagers. The young come to see and be seen: Japanese punks, girls decked out in fashions of the moment, and young couples looking their best. I like Harajuku for its vibrancy, sidewalk cafes, street hawkers, and trendy clothing boutiques. It's also the home of Tokyo's most important Shinto shrine, as well as a woodblock-print museum and an excellent souvenir shop of traditional Japanese items.

Nearby is **Aoyama,** a yuppified version of Harajuku, where the upwardly mobile shop and dine. Connecting Harajuku and Aoyama is **Omotesando Dori,** a wide, tree-lined boulevard that forms the heart of this area and is popular for people-watching.

From Harajuku Station, take the south exit (the one closer to Shibuya) and turn right over the bridge, where you will immediately see the huge cypress *torii* **marking the entrance to:**

❶ Meiji Jingu Shrine

Dedicated to Emperor and Empress Meiji, Meiji Jingu Shrine opened in 1920 and remains the most venerable shrine in Tokyo. (See "The Top Attractions," in chapter 7, for more details.) The shrine is surrounded by a dense forest of 365 different species totaling 120,000 trees, donated by people from all over Japan. If it's June, stop off at the Iris Garden, located halfway

on the 10-minute tree-shaded path to the shrine.

> ☕ **TAKE A BREAK**
> If the hike to Meiji Shrine has made you thirsty, stop off at the rustic **Café Mori no Terrace** outdoor pavilion, just inside the entryway to the shrine grounds. Open daily 9am to sunset, it offers coffee, beer, pastries, and ice cream. For something more substantial, wait until you get to Takeshita Dori (described below), where you'll find a **Wolfgang Puck Express** (p. 153), 1–17–1 Jingumae, good for burgers and pizza.

After visiting the shrine, retrace your steps back to Harajuku Station. If it's Sunday, you'll see groups of teenage Japanese—many of them bizarrely dressed—gathered on the bridge over the train tracks and at the nearby entrance to Yoyogi Park. They're all that's left of the masses of teenagers that used to congregate on nearby Yoyogi Dori back when it was closed to vehicular traffic on Sundays. Sadly, authorities decided to open Yoyogi and Omotesando Dori streets to traffic, thereby putting an end to Tokyo's most happening Sunday scene.

At Harajuku Station, continue walking north beside the station to its north exit. Across the street from Harajuku Station's north exit is:

➋ Takeshita Dori

This narrow pedestrian-only street is lined with stores that cater to teenagers. It's usually jam-packed—especially on Sunday afternoons—with young people hunting for bargains on inexpensive clothes, music, sunglasses, jewelry, watches, cosmetics, photos of the latest idols, and more. One shop worth pointing out is **Harajuku Daiso** (✆ **03/5775-9641;** daily 10am–9pm), on the left, one of many bargain variety stores to hit Japan after the recession. It offers four floors of kitchenware, tableware, cosmetics, office supplies, and more, with most items priced at ¥100.

After inching your way along this narrow lane with its flow of humanity, you will eventually find yourself on a busy thoroughfare, Meiji Dori. If it's the first Sunday of the month, turn left (north) onto Meiji Dori, where in a couple of minutes, on your left, you'll see the entrance to:

➌ Togo Shrine

Dedicated to Admiral Heihachiro Togo, who was in charge of the fleet that defeated the Russian navy in 1905 in the Russo-Japanese War, the shrine is now most popular for its flea market held the first Sunday of every month to 2pm. Everything from old chests, dolls, porcelain, and kimono are for sale, spread out on a tree-shaded sidewalk that meanders around the shrine.

Head back south on Meiji Dori where, to your right, just before the big intersection, is:

➍ La Forêt

This building, housing trendy shoe and clothing boutiques, is the ultimate in Tokyo teen cool. The less expensive boutiques tend to be on the lower floors, more exclusive boutiques higher up. (See chapter 9 for details on the shops and department stores listed here.)

Across the street on Meiji Dori is the YM Square building, where on the third and fourth floors is:

➎ Hanjiro

This shop (✆ **03/3796-7303**) is packed to the rafters with secondhand American clothing and its own original designs. Young Japanese love this store, and even my teenage son found things he just had to buy. Somebody is making a fortune here.

Behind La Forêt is one of my favorite museums, the:

➏ Ukiyo-e Ota Memorial Museum of Art

Located at 1–10–10 Jingumae, this museum features the private *ukiyo-e* (woodblock prints) collection of the late Ota Seizo. Exhibitions of the museum's 12,000 prints change monthly and are always worth checking out. (See "More Museums," in chapter 7, for details.)

Across Omotesando Dori is:

➐ Chicago

Specializing in used American clothing, Chicago also stocks used and new kimono, obi, and *yukata* in a far back corner of its basement.

Near La Forêt is Harajuku's major intersection, Meiji Dori and Omotesando Dori. Here, at the intersection at 6–30–1 Jingumae, is one of Harajuku's more unusual shops, appropriately called:

➑ Condomania

Condoms are for sale here in a wide range of sizes, colors, and styles, from glow-in-the-dark to scented. It's open daily 11am to 11pm.

Heading east on Omotesando Dori (away from Harajuku Station), you'll soon see, to your right:

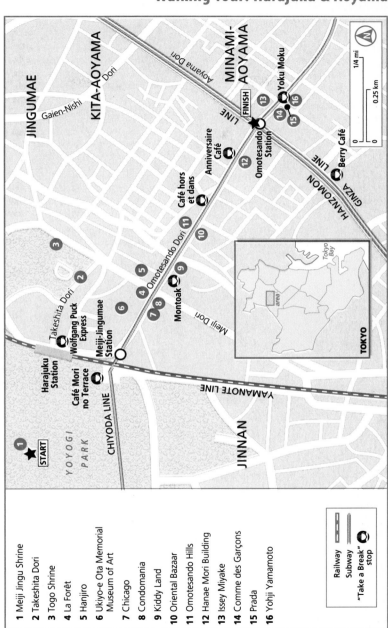

JINGUMAE

KITA-AOYAMA

Gaien-Nishi Dori

Aoyama Dori

MINAMI-AOYAMA

HANZOMON LINE

GINZA LINE

Yoku Moku

Berry Café

FINISH

Omotesando Station

Anniversaire Café

Café hors et dans

Omotesando Dori

Takeshita Dori

Wolfgang Puck Express

Montoak

Meiji Dori

Meiji-Jingumae Station

Harajuku Station

Café Mori no Terrace

CHIYODA LINE

YOYOGI PARK

START

YAMANOTE LINE

JINNAN

TOKYO

Tokyo Bay

area

1/4 mi
0.25 km

1 Meiji Jingu Shrine
2 Takeshita Dori
3 Togo Shrine
4 La Forêt
5 Hanjiro
6 Ukiyo-e Ota Memorial Museum of Art
7 Chicago
8 Condomania
9 Kiddy Land
10 Oriental Bazaar
11 Omotesando Hills
12 Hanae Mori Building
13 Issey Miyake
14 Comme des Garçons
15 Prada
16 Yohji Yamamoto

Railway
Subway
"Take a Break" stop

TOKYO STROLLS

8

HARAJUKU & AOYAMA

9 Kiddy Land

This shop at 6–1–9 Jingumae sells gag gifts and a great deal more than just toys, including enough to amuse undiscerning adults. You could spend an hour browsing here, but the store is so crowded with teenagers that you may end up rushing for the door.

As you continue east on Omotesando Dori (where sidewalk vendors selling jewelry and ethnic accessories set up shop on weekends), to your right will soon be Cat Street, a popular strolling side street lined with more shops selling everything from grungy T-shirts to the latest designs by up-and-coming design talents. On Omotesando Dori, to the right, is also Harajuku's most famous store:

10 Oriental Bazaar

Located at 5–9–13 Jingumae, this is Tokyo's best one-stop shopping spot for Japanese souvenirs. Four floors offer antiques, old and new kimono, Japanese paper products, fans, jewelry, woodblock prints, screens, chinaware, and much more at reasonable prices. I always stock up on gifts here for the folks back home.

On the other side of Omotesando Dori is:

11 Omotesando Hills

This posh commercial and residential shopping center, designed by Tadao Ando, houses upscale clothing and accessory shops, as well as restaurants. Unique is 53 **Hasegawa Sake Shop** (☎ 03/5785-0833), on the third floor, with selected offerings from sake brewers across Japan. There's a stand-up bar, where you can sample sake for ¥400 a cup.

Back on Omotesando Dori and continuing east, you'll pass shops dedicated to the wares of Gucci, Fendi, Armani, Louis Vuitton, and Tod's, but none have been here as long as the:

12 Hanae Mori Building

Near the end of Omotesando Dori, to the right, it was designed in 1978 by Japanese architect Kenzo Tange (who also designed the TMG City Hall in Shinjuku). It houses the entire collection of Hanae Mori, from casual wear to evening wear.

TAKE A BREAK
Harajuku and Aoyama have more sidewalk cafes than any other part of Tokyo. Most conspicuous is the fancy **Anniversaire Café**, 3–5–30 Kita-Aoyama (☎ 03/5411-5988), across from the Hanae Mori Building (see no. 12, above). **Café hors et dans**, 4–11–6 Jingumae (☎ 03/5775-5433), just east of Omotesando Hills on Omotesando Dori, has a second-floor outdoor terrace. **Montoak**, a glass building next to Kiddy Land (see no. 9, above) at 6–1–9 Jingumae (☎ 03/5468-5928), is a hip (so hip it doesn't even bother to hang out a shop sign) multilevel bar/coffee shop with comfy chairs and a second-floor balcony.

At the end of Omotesando Dori, where it connects with Aoyama Dori, is Omotesando Station. You can board the subway here or, for more shopping, cross Aoyama Dori and continue heading east, where you'll pass a number of designer shops. First, on the left at 3–18–11 Minami-Aoyama, is:

13 Issey Miyake

The clothes here are known for their richness in texture and fabrics.

To the right, at 5–2–1 Minami-Aoyama, is:

14 Comme des Garçons

Rei Kawakubo's designs for both men and women are showcased here.

Farther down the street, on the right at 5–2–6 Minami-Aoyama, is:

15 Prada

By far the most interesting design on the block, the building looks like a giant bug eye (to me, at least), its dome structure comprising hundreds of glass bubbles.

Just past Prada, on the right at 5–3–6 Minami-Aoyama, is:

16 Yohji Yamamoto

As with all Yamamoto shops, this store has an interesting avant-garde interior.

Return to Aoyama Dori, where you'll find the Omotesando subway station.

> **WINDING DOWN** Between Comme des Garçons and Yohji Yamamoto is **Yoku Moku,** easy to find at 5–3–3 Minami-Aoyama (ℂ **03/5485-3330**), with its bright blue exterior and terrace. Open daily from 10am to 6:30pm, it's famous for its pastries and desserts. For more sinful pleasures, head to **Berry Café,** 5–10–19 Minami-Aoyama (ℂ **03/5774-7130**), on the left side of Aoyama Dori in the direction of Shibuya. Its berry-topped cakes have to be seen to be believed; even its plastic-food displays look good enough to eat. It's open Monday to Saturday 11am to 9pm and Sunday 11am to 8pm.

WALKING TOUR 3 | UENO

START:	South end of Ueno Park (station: Ueno)
FINISH:	Ameya Yokocho flea market, along the tracks of the Yamanote Line (station: Ueno or Okachimachi)
TIME:	Allow approximately 2 hours, not including stops along the way
BEST TIMES:	Weekdays, when museums and shops aren't as crowded
WORST TIMES:	Monday, when the museums and zoo are closed

Located on the northeast end of the Yamanote Line loop, Ueno is one of the most popular places in Tokyo for Japanese families on a day's outing. Unlike sophisticated Ginza, Ueno has always been favored by the working people of Tokyo and visitors from Tokyo's rural north. During the Edo Period, the area around Ueno was where merchants and craftspeople lived, worked, and played. Ueno was also the site of the enormous Kan'eiji Temple compound, which served as the private family temple and burial ground of the Tokugawa shoguns. Today, Ueno's main drawing card is Ueno Park, the largest park in Tokyo. It's famous throughout Japan for its cluster of historic monuments, zoo, and excellent museums, including the prestigious Tokyo National Museum. If you wish, time your visit to coincide with free, 90-minute walking tours of Ueno every Wednesday, Friday, and Sunday at 10:30am and 1:30pm. Tours depart from Ueno Green Salon, located between JR Ueno Station and the National Museum of Western Art (see no. 5 below for its location).

You will probably arrive in Ueno by either subway or the JR Yamanote Line. Regardless, following the signs, make your way via underground passage to the main entrance of Keisei Ueno Station (terminus of the Skyliner train from Narita Airport and home to a Tokyo Tourist Information Center; daily 9:30am–6:30pm). Outside Keisei Ueno Station's main exit, to the left, are two steep flights of stone stairs leading up to an area of trees. This is the south entrance to:

 Ueno Park

Located atop a broad hill, this was once part of the precincts of Kan'eiji Temple, a huge, 120-hectare (297-acre) complex consisting of a main temple and 36 subsidiary temples. Unfortunately, most of the complex was destroyed in 1868, when 2,000 die-hard shogun loyalists gathered on Ueno Hill for a last stand against the advancing forces of the Imperial army. In 1873, Ueno Park opened as one of the nation's first public parks.

Although quite small compared to New York City's Central Park, this is Japan's largest city park and Tokyo's most important museum district, making it a favorite destination for families and school groups in search of culture, relaxation, and fun. With its 1,000 cherry trees, it's one of the most famous spots for cherry-blossom viewing in the country. It's also a popular hangout for Tokyo's homeless population, which has grown markedly since the recession. You'll see their makeshift cities—cardboard, blue tarp, and even clothes drying on lines—in among the trees.

A landmark near the south entrance to the park is a bronze:

❷ Statue of Takamori Saigo

This is the best-known monument in Tokyo, if not all of Japan. Born in 1827 near Kagoshima on Kyushu Island, the samurai Takamori Saigo rose through the ranks as a soldier and statesman. He helped restore the emperor to power after the Tokugawa shogunate's downfall but later became disenchanted with the Meiji regime when rights enjoyed by the samurai class were suddenly rescinded. He led a revolt against the government that failed and ended up taking his own life in ritual suicide. The statue was erected in the 1890s but later became controversial when Gen. Douglas MacArthur, leader of the U.S. occupation forces in Japan after World War II, demanded its removal because of its nationalistic associations. Saved by public outcry, the statue depicts the stout Saigo dressed in a simple cotton kimono with his hand on his sword.

Ironically, behind the statue of Saigo and slightly to the left is a memorial dedicated to those very men Saigo originally opposed. Here lie the:

❸ Tombs of the Shogitai Soldiers

These were the die-hard Tokugawa loyalists who resisted Imperial forces on Ueno Hill in 1868. Tended by descendants of the soldiers, the grounds contain a small painting depicting the fierce battle.

Behind and to the left of the war memorial, on the other side of the pathway, is:

❹ Kiyomizu Kannon-do Temple

Completed in 1631 as a miniature copy of the famous Kiyomizu Temple in Kyoto and one of the few buildings left standing after the battle of 1868, this is one of the oldest temples in Tokyo. The temple

houses the protectress of childbearing and child-raising, thereby attracting women hoping to become pregnant or whose wishes have been fulfilled. To the right of the main altar is a room full of dolls, left by women to symbolize their children in a gesture they hope will further protect them. (See "Shrines & Temples," in chapter 7, for more information.)

TAKE A BREAK Just east of the tombs of the Shogitai soldiers is **Tokori** (p. 142), serving Korean barbecue at reasonable prices. For a simple snack or a drink, **Café Hibiki** (📞 03/3821-9151), across from the Museum of Western Art (see no. 6 below), is a pleasant coffee shop attached to the Tokyo Cultural Hall (Tokyo Bunka Kaikan), with outdoor seating on fake grass. Open daily 11am to 7pm, it offers desserts and premade sandwiches from a glass display case.

Back on the main promenade, between Kiyomizu Kannon-do Temple and the Tombs of the Shogitai Soldiers, head north, passing the Ueno Royal Museum and Japan Art Academy. Turn right on the lane running between the Tokyo Bunka Kaikan and the National Museum of Western Art. Soon, on your left, beyond an information kiosk and small square, is the:

❺ Ueno Green Salon

Free 90-minute walking tours of Ueno depart from here every Wednesday, Friday, and Sunday at 10:30am and 1:30pm. All you need to do is show up.

Just before the Ueno Green Salon, to your left, is the very good:

❻ National Museum of Western Art (Kokuritsu Seiyo Bijutsukan)

Built in 1959, with a main building designed by French architect Le Corbusier, the museum features works by such Western artists as Renoir, Monet, Sisley, Manet, Delacroix, Cézanne, Degas, El Greco, and Goya; but it's probably most famous for its 50-some sculptures by Rodin.

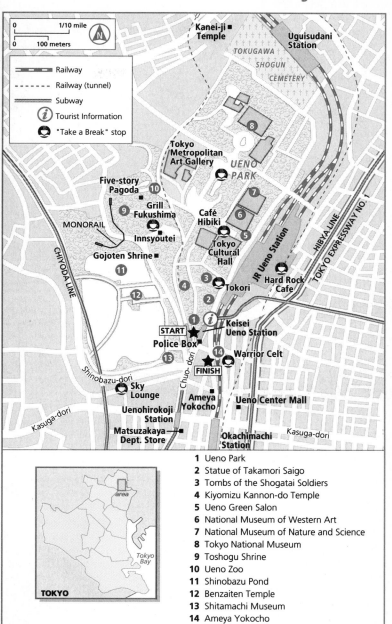

0   1/10 mile
0   100 meters

Railway
Railway (tunnel)
Subway
(i) Tourist Information
"Take a Break" stop

Kanei-ji Temple
Uguisudani Station
TOKUGAWA SHOGUN CEMETERY

Tokyo Metropolitan Art Gallery
UENO PARK

Five-story Pagoda
Grill Fukushima
Café Hibiki
MONORAIL
Innsyoutei
Gojoten Shrine
Tokyo Cultural Hall
JR Ueno Station
Hard Rock Cafe
HIBYA LINE
TOKYO EXPRESSWAY NO. 1

CHIYODA LINE

Tokori

START
Police Box
Keisei Ueno Station
Warrior Celt
FINISH

Shinobazu-dori
Sky Lounge
Ameya Yokocho
Uenohirokoji Station
Matsuzakaya Dept. Store
Ueno Center Mall
Okachimachi Station
Kasuga-dori

TOKYO STROLLS

8

UENO

TOKYO
area
Tokyo Bay
TOKYO

1 Ueno Park
2 Statue of Takamori Saigo
3 Tombs of the Shogatai Soldiers
4 Kiyomizu Kannon-do Temple
5 Ueno Green Salon
6 National Museum of Western Art
7 National Museum of Nature and Science
8 Tokyo National Museum
9 Toshogu Shrine
10 Ueno Zoo
11 Shinobazu Pond
12 Benzaiten Temple
13 Shitamachi Museum
14 Ameya Yokocho

North of the National Museum of Western Art is the:

❼ National Museum of Nature and Science (Kokuritsu Kagaku Hakubutsukan)

This is a great attraction if you're traveling with children (p. 196).

The most important museum in Ueno Park, however, is the one farthest to the north, the:

❽ Tokyo National Museum (Tokyo Kokuritsu Hakubutsukan)

Japan's largest museum and the world's largest repository of Japanese art is the place to see antiques from Japan's past, including lacquerware, pottery, scrolls, screens, ukiyo-e, samurai armor, swords, kimono, Buddhist statues, and much more. If you go to only one museum in Tokyo, this should be it.

Assuming you don't spend the entire day in museums, walk straight south from the National Museum to Ueno Park's main square, marked by an artificial pond with a spouting, dancing fountain. At the end of the square turn right, pass the main entrance to the zoo, and then look for the stone *torii* on the right that marks the entrance to:

❾ Toshogu Shrine

Ueno Park's most famous religious structure—dedicated to Tokugawa Ieyasu, founder of the Tokugawa shogunate—was erected in 1651 by Ieyasu's grandson. Like Nikko's Toshogu Shrine (see chapter 11), it is ornately decorated with brilliant red, blue, green, and gold ornamentation. The pathway leading to the shrine is lined with massive stone lanterns, plus 50 copper lanterns donated by feudal lords from throughout Japan. To the right of the pathway is a five-story pagoda (located on zoo grounds), covered entirely in lacquer and constructed in 1639. The shrine grounds are also famous for their peonies, which bloom both in spring and in winter (fee charged for peony garden).

Unfortunately, the shrine itself is undergoing renovation until 2014, so you won't be able to go inside to see the murals by a famous Edo artist, Kano Tan-yu, and armor worn by Ieyasu. Note, however, the lions decorating the arched, Chinese-style

Karamon Gate—legend has it that when night falls, they sneak down to Shinobazu Pond for a drink. On a lighter note, you'll see signs asking you to refrain from making a bonfire, in case you are contemplating a cookout on these sacred grounds.

TAKE A BREAK
Located just past Toshogu Shrine, **Grill Fukushima** (p. 142) opened in 1876 as one of Japan's first restaurants serving Western food. It remains Ueno Park's most upscale place, serving pricey but quite good classic French cuisine. Next door is the equally old traditional-looking ㉔ **Innsyoutei** (p. 142), serving Japanese set meals.

If you want to skip the zoo, beside Innsyoutei are a row of orange *torii* (made, horrendously enough, out of plastic) and a road leading downhill to Shinobazu Pond (see no. 11, below), passing Gojoten Shrine along the way. Otherwise, retrace your steps to:

❿ Ueno Zoo

Opened in 1882, this is Japan's oldest zoo. Although it seems small by today's standards (with miserably cramped quarters for some of its animals), it draws crowds for its Japanese macaques, polar bears, California sea lions, penguins, gorillas, giraffes, zebras, elephants, deer, and tigers. The zoo's most famous resident, however, a giant panda donated by the Chinese government named Ling Ling, died in 2008. Be sure to see the five-story pagoda mentioned earlier in the walk.

End your tour of the zoo by taking the monorail to:

⓫ Shinobazu Pond

This marshy pond was constructed in the 17th century; teahouses once lined its banks. Now part of the pond has literally gone to the birds: It's a bird sanctuary, especially for cormorants. The pond is filled with lotus plants, a lovely sight when they bloom in August.

There are small boats for rent, and on an island in the middle of the pond, connected to the bank with walkways, is the:

⑫ Benzaiten Temple

This temple is dedicated to the goddess of fortune.

At the southeastern edge of Shinobazu Pond is the:

⑬ Shitamachi Museum (Shitamachi Fuzoku Shiryokan)

Shitamachi means "downtown" and refers to the area of Tokyo where commoners used to live, mainly around Ueno and Asakusa. Displays here include a shitamachi tenement house, as well as everyday objects used in work and play, all donated by people living in the area.

From the Shitamachi Museum, head south on Chuo Dori and turn left on Kasuga Dori, passing Matsuzakaya department store and Ueno Center Mall. Here, at Okachimachi Station, is:

⑭ Ameya Yokocho

This narrow shopping street is located under and along the west side of the elevated tracks of the Yamanote Line between Ueno and Okachimachi stations. Originally a wholesale market for candy and snacks, and after World War II a black market in U.S. Army goods, Ameya Yokocho (also referred to as Ameyacho or Ameyoko) today consists of hundreds of stalls and shops selling at a discount everything from vegetables and cosmetics to handbags and clothes. Early evening is the most crowded time as workers rush through on their way home. Some shops close on Wednesday, but most are open from about 10am to 7pm.

> **WINDING DOWN**
> For drinks with a view and piano music, head to the south end of Shinobazu Pond where, on the 10th floor of the Hotel Park Side, 2–11–18 Ueno, the **Sky Lounge** (✆ **03/3836-5711**) is open daily 5 to 11:30pm (cover charge: ¥500). Attracting a younger crowd is **Warrior Celt** (p. 258), 6–9–2 Ueno, a friendly bar with a nightly happy hour and free live music; it's just a stone's throw from Ameya Yokocho. Also, **Hard Rock Cafe Ueno** (p. 143) is in JR Ueno Station.

WALKING TOUR 4   YANAKA

START:	Tennoji Temple (station: Nippori)
FINISH:	Nezu Temple (station: Nezu)
TIME:	Allow approximately 4 hours, including stops along the way
BEST TIMES:	There is no "best" time, as such, for this walk, but head out early in the day
WORST TIMES:	Monday, when some shops and the Daimyo Clock Museum are closed

Yanaka has been famous for its large concentration of temples since the Edo Period, when most temples and shrines were removed from the inner city and relocated to the outskirts in an attempt to curb the frequent fires that ravaged the crowded shogunate capital. Not only did the religious structures' thatched roofs ignite like tinder, but the land they formerly occupied would also subsequently be cleared and left empty, to act as fire breaks in the otherwise densely populated city. Furthermore, temples on the edge of town could double as forts to protect Edo from invasion. The only invasions Yanaka suffered, however, were friendly ones, as townspeople flocked here to enjoy its peacefulness, wooded hills, paddies, clear streams, and majestic temple compounds. It wasn't long before the wealthy began building country estates here as well, followed by artists and writers who favored Yanaka's picturesque setting and cool breezes.

One of Tokyo's few old quarters to have survived both the 1923 Kanto earthquake and firebombs of World War II, Yanaka is still largely residential, with narrow lanes, small houses, and a few unique museums and traditional shops tucked here and there among the gently sloping hills. Because there are no major attractions or department stores here, the atmosphere of this stroll is markedly different from the bustling liveliness of the previous walking tours—there are few crowds and there's very little traffic. Rather, a trip to Yanaka is like a visit to a small town, where the pace of life is slow and the people have time for one another. If Tokyo is starting to wear on your nerves, come here to refresh yourself. This walk always makes me happy!

The easiest way to get to Yanaka is on the Yamanote Line. Disembark at Nippori Station, take the south exit (the end closest to Ueno Station), and turn left for the west exit. Look for the flight of steps beside a map of the area. After climbing these stairs, you'll soon reach, on the left:

❶ Tennoji Temple

Founded more than 500 years ago, this used to be a grand and impressive complex, 10 times its present size and popular among townspeople as one of Edo's three temples authorized to hold lotteries. The lotteries, however, drew such huge, rowdy crowds that they were banned in the mid-19th century by the Tokugawa shogunate. Then, in 1868, most of the complex was destroyed in the battle between Tokugawa loyalists and Imperial forces on nearby Ueno Hill. Today, Tennoji is quiet and peaceful, with neatly swept grounds and the soothing sounds of chirping birds and chanting monks. The first thing you see upon entering the compound is a seated bronze Buddha, which dates from 1690 and is one of the temple's dearest treasures. Nearby is a standing bronze Jizo, guardian of children's spirits. It was erected by a grieving father more than 60 years ago, following the death of his son in a playground accident; a relief at the base depicts boys playing in school uniform. There's also a small stone statue of Kannon, goddess of mercy.

Walk straight out of the temple compound's main entrance and continue walking on the paved road straight through:

❷ Yanaka Cemetery

Once the burial grounds of Kanei-ji and Tennoji temples and opened to the public in 1874, this is one of Tokyo's largest cemeteries. Among its more than 7,000 tombstones are graves belonging to famous public figures, artists, and writers, some of whom lived in the area. Among the most famous writers buried here are Soseki Natsume (1867–1916) and Ogai Mori (1862–1922), both novelists of the Meiji Era and longtime Yanaka residents. Natsume, whose portrait is featured on the 1,000-yen note, became famous after writing *I Am a Cat,* a humorous look at the follies of human society as seen through the eyes of a cat. Ogai, who at 19 was the youngest graduate ever from the medical school at Tokyo University and who later became surgeon general, was a foremost figure of modern Japanese literature. His works tried to bridge the gap between the traditional and the modern, as Japan moved away from its feudal agrarian past.

Today the cemetery is quite peaceful and empty, but it wasn't always so. During the Edo Period, teahouses along its edge served more than tea, with monks among their frequent customers. One of the teahouse beauties, Osen Kasamori, achieved fame when ukiyo-e master Harunobu immortalized her in several of his works. Most poor girls were looking for patrons, not necessarily one-night stands.

After a minute's walk, to your left, you'll see two sights very strange for a cemetery—a police box and a children's playground. Here, between the two and surrounded by a low fence and hedge, is the:

❸ Foundation of Tennoji Temple's Five-Story Pagoda

First built in 1644 but burned down in 1772, this was reconstructed as the tallest pagoda in Edo. It met its final demise in 1957, when it was burned down by two lovers who then committed suicide.

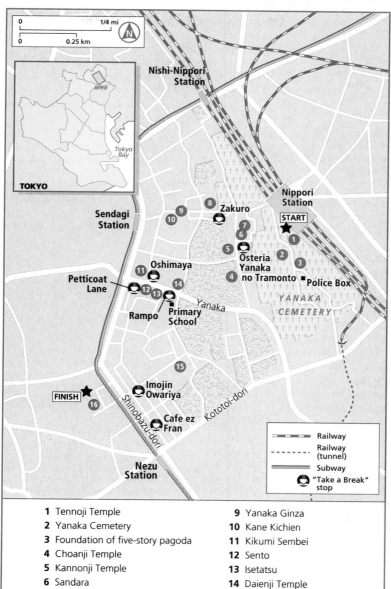

TOKYO STROLLS

8

YANAKA

0 — 1/4 mi
0 — 0.25 km

N

TOKYO

Tokyo Bay

area

Nishi-Nippori Station

Sendagi Station

Nippori Station

START

Zakuro

Osteria Yanaka no Tramonto

Police Box

YANAKA CEMETERY

Oshimaya

Petticoat Lane

Rampo

Primary School

Yanaka

Imojin Owariya

FINISH

Cafe ez Fran

Shinobazu-dori

Kototoi-dori

Nezu Station

Railway
Railway (tunnel)
Subway
"Take a Break" stop

1 Tennoji Temple
2 Yanaka Cemetery
3 Foundation of five-story pagoda
4 Choanji Temple
5 Kannonji Temple
6 Sandara
7 Asakura Choso Museum
8 Midori-ya

9 Yanaka Ginza
10 Kane Kichien
11 Kikumi Sembei
12 Sento
13 Isetatsu
14 Daienji Temple
15 Daimyo Clock Museum
16 Nezu Shrine

Tips **A Note on Japanese Symbols**

Many hotels, restaurants, attractions, and shops in Japan do not have signs giving their names in Roman (English-language) letters. Chapter 14 lists the Japanese symbols for all such places described in this guide. Each set of characters representing an establishment name has a corresponding number in chapter 14, which appears inside the oval preceding the establishment's name in the text. Thus, to find the Japanese symbol for, say, **Sandara,** refer to no. 54 on p. 325.

Take a right at the police box and continue through the cemetery to a residential street, following it 1 block until it ends at a T-intersection. Ahead is a plaque dedicated to Kano Hogai (1828–88), a Japanese painter of the early Meiji Period who incorporated Western techniques into his work and who, along with Okakura Tenshin, is credited for "modernizing" Japanese art. Behind the plaque is:

❹ Choanji Temple

Established in 1669, it was dedicated to the god of longevity, one of Japan's seven lucky gods. During the Edo Period, a pilgrimage to all seven temples, each housing one of the seven gods of fortune, was thought to bring good luck. Now that such pilgrimages have lost their appeal, Choanji seems rather forgotten. In addition to Kano's tomb, located near the center of the temple's graveyard, the temple is notable for its three stone *stupas* dating from the 1200s, erected for the repose of departed souls. They are straight ahead on the main path, by the statues and under the groomed cedars.

Turn left out of Choanji. At the next immediate left down a side street you'll see an old temple wall dating from the Edo Period. It's the only one in the area to have survived fires, earthquakes, and wars. Back on the main road, farther along on the left, is:

❺ Kannonji Temple

A small stone pagoda to the right of its front entrance is dedicated to the 47 *ronin (akoroshi)*, masterless samurai who avenged their master's death and then committed ritual suicide in 1702 (see the box in chapter 3, "The Masterless Samurai"). Their story captured the public's imagination and has become a popular Kabuki play.

Two of the ronin were brothers of a head priest here, and several meetings plotting their revenge allegedly took place on this spot.

TAKE A BREAK
Just a stone's throw farther north, on the right, is **Osteria Yanaka no Tramonto,** 7-17-11 Yanaka (✆ **03/6383-1621**), a simple Italian restaurant offering pasta lunches for ¥1,200 from noon to 2:30pm (closed Wed). Farther along, to the left at the top of the steps to Yanaka Ginza (no. 9 below), is **Zakuro,** 3-14-13 Nishi-Nippori (✆ **03/5685-5313**), one of Tokyo's more eccentric restaurants serving Turkish, Pakistani, and Persian cuisine and open daily 11am to 11pm. After removing your shoes at the door (and donning proffered Mideastern garb if you wish), you'll be led to floor cushions in a big room that resembles a tent, with boards on the floor serving as tables. Set lunches include an all-you-can eat meal for ¥1,000 (last order 3pm). Evenings feature belly dancing and an all-you-can-eat feast for ¥2,000.

Just past Yanaka no Tramonto, also on the right at 7-18-6 Yanaka, is:

❻ ㊴ Sandara

This small crafts shop sells pottery, baskets, and other crafts. It's open Tuesday through Sunday from 10:30am to 6pm. Its name comes from the sacks once used to hold rice.

Past this shop, also on the right, at 7-18-10 Yanaka, is the:

❼ Asakura Choso Museum

With its modern black facade, it looks rather out of place in this traditional neighborhood, but its interior is a delightful mix of modern and traditional architecture. One of Tokyo's most intriguing homes open to the public—but unfortunately closed for renovation until March 2013—it was built in 1936 as the home and studio of Asakura Fumio, a Western-style sculptor known for his realistic statues of statesmen, women, and cats. Noted features include a studio with soaring ceilings, a traditional Japanese house wrapped around an inner courtyard pond famous for its large stones arranged to reflect the Five Confucian Virtues, and a rooftop garden. For now, however, the only thing visible from the street is one of his statues.

Continue past the museum and turn left at the next street (if you take a right here instead, you will end up back at Nippori Station). Keep to the right and walk down the steps. Just past the arched entryway marking the neighborhood's pedestrian-only shopping lane, to your right at 3–13–3 Nishi-Nippori, is:

❽ (55) Midori-ya

This exquisite basket shop (✆ **03/3828-7522**) with several samples on display outside its front door is the store and workshop of Suigetsu Buseki, who coaxes flexible strands of bamboo into beautifully crafted baskets, some of them signed. The shop is known for its use of smoked bamboo, taken from the undersides of thatched farmhouses; the bamboo exhibits a beautiful gloss and subtle color gradation from years of exposure to indoor fire pits. Because such antique pieces of bamboo are increasingly hard to come by, some of the baskets are rightfully expensive but are still less expensive than those at major department stores. You can linger here; the Buseki family is happy to discuss their love for their trade with Japanese-speakers. The Imperial family and visiting dignitaries, including a former U.S. ambassador to Japan, have been among their customers. The shop is open Tuesday to Sunday 11am to 6pm.

Continue your walk through what is one of my favorite streets on this walk:

❾ Yanaka Ginza

This is an ambitious name for an otherwise old-fashioned shopping lane. It's pleasant because it's free from cars and, unlike many shopping streets nowadays, isn't a covered arcade. One Japanese friend told me that it reminds her of neighborhood shopping streets from her childhood. Lining the lane are shops selling both modern and traditional toys, crafts, clothing, sweets, household goods, tofu, rice, fish, and vegetables. One of my favorites is the tea shop:

❿ (56) Kane Kichien

Located about halfway down Yanaka Ginza on the left at 3–11–10 Yanaka (✆ **03/3823-0015**), it sells varieties of tea at the counter toward the back. With all the reported benefits of green tea, you probably know someone who might appreciate a small gift from this store. It's open Monday to Saturday from 10am to 7:30pm.

At the end of the shopping street, turn left and walk for about 5 minutes, passing the Annex Katsutaro Ryokan on the way, until you come to a stoplight and a slightly larger road.

> **TAKE A BREAK**
> Immediately to the left of the stoplight, on the corner, is a noodle shop called (57) **Oshimaya,** 3–2–5 Yanaka (✆ **03/3821-5052**). It's located on the second floor of a modern building but has traditional bamboo screens at the window and an indoor pond with fish. It offers two different kinds of noodles—*soba* and *udon*—served in a variety of ways, including tempura *soba* and curry *soba*. Open every day except Thursday from 11am to 8pm (closed 3–5pm Mon–Fri).

If all you want is a drink, straight ahead at the stoplight is **Petticoat Lane**, 2–35–7 Sendagi (© **03/3821-8859**), a tiny coffee shop open daily 11am to midnight. A minute's walk farther on the right-hand side past Isetatsu (see below) is ⑤⑧ **Rampo**, 2–9–14 Yanaka (© **03/ 3828-9494**), a cozy coffee shop packed with knickknacks, kitsch, and folk art. It offers soft drinks, coffee, and beer; jazz plays softly in the background. Open every day except Monday from 10am to 8pm. Look for the wooden COFFEE SNACK sign above its door.

If you take a right at the stoplight mentioned above, to your right you will soon see:

⑪ ⑤⑨ **Kikumi Sembei**

You can't miss it—look for the beautiful, 130-year-old wooden building, with its traditional open-fronted shop selling Japanese crackers. It's definitely worth a photo. You may even want to buy some of its square-shaped sembei. It's open Tuesday to Sunday from 10am to 7pm (3–37–16 Sendagi; © **03/3821-1215**).

Just beyond the cracker shop is Sendagi Station. Unless you're ready to call it quits, however, turn around and head back in the opposite direction, passing the stoplight and the noodle shop listed above. Almost immediately on your right will be a:

⑫ **Sento**

The *sento*, or public bathhouse, is easily recognizable by its shoe lockers in the entryway and by the chimney rising in the back. Although on the decline, public bathhouses still serve as important gathering places, especially for those without private tubs.

Farther along, on your right on a corner, is:

⑬ ⑥⓪ **Isetatsu**

Isetatsu, 2–18–9 Yanaka (© **03/3823- 1453**), sells items made from Japanese paper, including paper fans, papier-mâché objects, and boxes. Founded in the mid-1800s and run by the Hirose family for four generations, it specializes in *chiyogami*, handmade decorative paper printed

with wood blocks. Some of the designs are the family's own creations; others are taken from family crests used by samurai and members of the court and worn on kimono and armor. The shop is open daily from 10am to 6pm.

As you continue in the same direction (east), on the next block on the left side you'll find:

⑭ **Daienji**

Located at 3–1–2 Yanaka, opposite the grade school and recessed back from the street, this temple is famous for its chrysanthemum fair and honors ukiyo-e master Harunobu, one of Edo's most famous artists; and Osen Kasamori, who worked at one of the many teahouses near Tennoji in the 1760s and achieved fame when Harunobu singled her out as a model for many of his portraits. A copy of Harunobo's portrait of Osen hangs in the small guardhouse to the right at the entrance to the temple grounds, where an English-speaking older man is usually on hand to give brief explanations of Daienji, which has the distinction of housing a Buddhist temple and a Shinto shrine under one roof. The larger stone marker is a monument to Harunobu; the smaller one to the left is Osen's.

Cross the street at the crosswalk, turn left to continue walking in the same direction you've been going, and take the first right (beside the traditional-looking elementary school with an old-fashioned clock). Turn left at the end of the street, and after a couple minutes, to your right, at 2–1–27 Yanaka, will be the:

⑮ **Daimyo Clock Museum (Daimyo Tokei Hakubutsukan)**

Tucked inside an overgrown garden, this one-room display of clocks and watches from the Edo Period (1603–1867) features about 50 examples taken from the museum's extensive collection (displays change annually). On display are huge free-standing clocks, sundials, alarm clocks, pocket watches, and small watches that were attached to *obi* (the sash worn with a kimono). The first clock was brought to

Japan by a missionary in the 16th century, and in typical Japanese fashion was quickly modified to suit local needs. Rather than measuring 24 hours a day, Edo clocks were based on the length of time between sunrise and sunset, so that time varied greatly with the seasons. Clocks had to be set once or twice a day and were so expensive that only *daimyo*, or feudal lords, could afford them. Most daimyo had both a clockmaker and clock setter under their employ, as castles generally contained several huge clocks on their grounds. Apparently, time was of the essence in Japan even back then. Explanations in the museum are in Japanese only, but ask to see an English-language pamphlet. Admission is ¥100. It's open Tuesday to Sunday 10am to 4pm (closed Dec 25–Jan 15 and July–Sept; ℂ 03/3821-6913).

Take a right out of the museum to return to the street you were on, turn left and then left again (note the weirdly shaped pine tree at the corner). Walk down one of the many slopes for which Yanaka is famous and which still has some traditional wooden homes (including a beautiful one on your right). On the left-hand side of the slope, at the end of the street just before the stoplight, is Imojin Owariya, a Japanese sweet shop (see "Winding Down," below). Cross the busy street, Shinobazu-Dori, at the stoplight and continue straight (you'll pass another sento to your left). The road will begin to slope upward, and then, to your right, will be:

⑯ Nezu Shrine

This is one of Tokyo's best-kept secrets. With its brightly colored orange *torii*,

venerable cedars, and manicured azalea bushes, it's a welcome contrast to the austerity of the Buddhist temples that dominate Yanaka. It was built in 1706 by the fifth Tokugawa shogun and features a front courtyard gate of red lacquer with joists in gilt, green, blue, orange, and black. The shrine is most well known, however, for its thousands of manicured azalea bushes. When they bloom in April, this place is heaven—but be prepared for crowds.

To reach Nezu Station, return to Shinobazu-Dori and turn right.

 WINDING DOWN
On the slope upward from Shinobazu-Dori, in the direction of the clock museum, is ⑥⑴ **Imojin Owariya**, 2-30-4 Nezu (ℂ **03/3821-5530**), a plain, tiny Japanese version of a small-town ice-cream parlor. You can get homemade ice cream here, as well as shaved ice with flavorings of sweet-bean paste, lemon, strawberry, or melon. It's open Tuesday through Sunday from 11am to 7pm. On Shinobazu-Dori, between Nezu Shrine and Nezu Station, there's **Cafe ez Fran**, 2-27-1 Nezu (ℂ **03/3828-5511**). Open Tuesday to Sunday 11:30am to 11pm (1am Fri and Sat), it's a coffee shop until 6pm, after which it becomes a bar specializing in beers from around the world.

Shopping

I have never seen people shop as much as the Japanese do. Judging from the crowds that surge through Tokyo's department stores every day, I'm convinced it's the country's number-one pastime. Women, men, couples, and even whole families go on shopping expeditions in their free time, making Sunday the most crowded shopping day of the week—though with today's economic climate, many of them may be just window-shopping.

1 THE SHOPPING SCENE

BEST BUYS Tokyo is the country's showcase for everything from the latest in camera, computer, or music equipment to original woodblock prints and designer fashions. Traditional Japanese crafts and souvenirs that make good buys include toys (both traditional and the latest in technical wizardry), kites, Japanese dolls, carp banners, swords, lacquerware, bamboo baskets, *ikebana* (flower arranging) accessories, ceramics, pottery, iron teakettles, chopsticks, fans, masks, knives, scissors, sake, incense, and silk and cotton kimono. And you don't have to spend a fortune: You can pick up handmade Japanese paper *(washi)* products, such as umbrellas, lanterns, boxes, stationery, and other souvenirs, for a fraction of what they would cost in import shops in the United States. In Harajuku, it's possible to buy a fully lined dress of the latest fashion craze for ¥8,000 or less, and I can't even count the number of pairs of fun, casual shoes I've bought in Tokyo for a mere ¥4,000. Used camera equipment can be picked up for a song, reproductions of famous woodblock prints make great inexpensive gifts, and many items—from pearls to electronic video and audio equipment—can be bought tax-free (see "Taxes," below).

Japan is famous for its electronics, but if you're buying new you can probably find these products just as cheaply, or even more cheaply, in the United States. If you think you want to shop for electronic products while you're in Tokyo, it pays to do some comparison shopping before you leave home so that you can spot a deal when you see one. On the other hand, one of the joys of shopping for electronics in Japan is discovering new, advanced models; you might decide you want that new Sony HD camcorder simply because it's the coolest thing you've ever seen, no matter what the price.

GREAT SHOPPING AREAS Another enjoyable aspect of shopping in Tokyo is that specific areas are often devoted to certain goods, sold wholesale but also available to the individual shopper. **Kappabashi-dougugai Dori** (station: Tawaramachi), for example, is where you'll find shops specializing in kitchenware, while **Kanda** (station: Jimbocho) is known for its bookstores. **Akihabara** (station: Akihabara) is packed with stores selling the latest in electronics, as well as anime-related items. **Ginza** (station: Ginza) is the chic address for high-end international designer brands as well as art galleries. **Aoyama** (station: Omotesando) boasts the city's largest concentration of Japanese designer-clothing stores and an ever-increasing number of international names, while nearby **Harajuku** (stations: Harajuku, Meiji-Jingu-mae, or Omotesando) and **Shibuya** (station: Shibuya) are the places to go for youthful, fun, and inexpensive fashions.

> **Tips** **Buyer Beware**
>
> Ivory is popular in Japan, but it's banned for import into the United States. Beware, therefore, when shopping for antiques, hair ornaments, figurines, or other items that may contain ivory. You should also think twice before buying anything made with tortoise shell, crafted primarily from the shell of the endangered hawksbill sea turtle.

SALES   Department stores have sales throughout the year, during which you can pick up bargains on everything from electronic goods and men's suits to golf clubs, toys, kitchenware, food, and lingerie; there are even sales for used wedding kimono. The most popular sales are for **designer clothing,** usually held twice a year, in July and December or January. Here you can pick up fantastic clothing at cut-rate prices—but be prepared for the crowds. Sales are generally held on one of the top floors of the department store in what's usually labeled the "Exhibition Hall" or "Promotion Hall" in the store's English-language brochure. Stop by the department store's information desk, usually located near the main entrance, for the brochure as well as fliers listing current sales promotions.

TAXES   A 5% consumption tax is included in the price of marked goods, but all major department stores in Tokyo will refund the tax to foreign visitors if total purchases amount to more than ¥10,001 on that day. Exemptions include food, beverages, tobacco, pharmaceuticals, cosmetics, film, and batteries. When you've completed your shopping, take the purchased goods and receipts to the tax refund counter in the store. There are forms to fill out (you will need your passport). Upon completion, a record of your purchase is placed on the visa page of your passport, and you are given the tax refund on the spot. When you leave Japan, make sure you have your purchases with you (pack them in your carry-on); you may be asked by Customs to show them.

SHIPPING IT HOME   Many first-class hotels in Tokyo provide a packing and shipping service. In addition, most large department stores, tourist shops, such as the Oriental Bazaar, and antiques shops, will ship your purchases overseas, including antique furniture.

If you wish to ship packages yourself, the easiest method is to go to a post office and purchase an easy-to-assemble cardboard box, available in several sizes (along with the necessary tape). Keep in mind that packages mailed abroad cannot weigh more than 20kg (about 44 lb.), and that only the larger international post offices accept packages to be mailed overseas (ask your hotel concierge for the closest one). Remember, too, that mailing packages from Japan is expensive (for details, see chapter 12, "Fast Facts").

2 SHOPPING A TO Z

ANIME & MANGA

Although **Akihabara** has long boasted Japan's largest concentration of electronics shops, in recent years it has also gained a reputation as *the* place to shop for manga (Japanese comic books and graphic novels) and items related to anime (Japanese animation) and cosplay (costume play). Anime fans should make a point of stopping by the free **Tokyo**

> **Tips** **A Note on Japanese Symbols**
>
> Many hotels, restaurants, attractions, and shops in Japan do not have signs giving their names in Roman (English-language) letters. Chapter 14 lists the Japanese symbols for all such places described in this guide. Each set of characters representing an establishment name has a number in the appendix, which corresponds to the number that appears inside the oval preceding the establishment's name in the text. Thus, to find the Japanese symbol for, say, **Don Quijote,** refer to no. 62 on p. 326.

Anime Center, just north of the JR Akihabara Station on the fourth floor of UDX (✆ **03/5298-1188;** www.animecenter.jp; Tues–Sun 11am–7pm), with an information desk, a merchandise shop, and a 3-D theater (admission charged for theater only).

One of the best anime/manga chain stores in Japan is **Mandarake,** with a shop in Akihabara, about 4 minutes from JR Akihabara Station at 3–11–2 Soto-Kanda (✆ **03/3252-7007;** www.mandarake.co.jp). Open daily from noon to 8pm, the sleek black building offers eight floors of both new and second-hand goods, including pop and vintage figurines, video games, manga, and posters. Serious shoppers, however, will want to make a pilgrimage to **Nakano Broadway** mall at 5–52–15 Nakano (✆ **03/3388-7004**), a 5-minute walk from the north exit of Nakano Station, where you'll find Mandarake's head store and a slew of other shops dedicated to both new and retro pop goods from Japan and overseas, including software, games, manga, figures, and anime and cosplay fare, all open daily from noon to 8pm. A smaller branch is in Shibuya at 31–2 Udagawacho (✆ **03/3477-0777**), open daily from noon to 8pm.

Otherwise, back in Akihabara, ⟨67⟩ **Kotobukiya,** conveniently located across from JR Akihabara Station, in the Radio Kaikan Building, at 1–15–16 Soto-Kanda (✆ **03/5298-6300**), sells stuffed anime characters, movie props, and figurines (some of them definitely X-rated) from 10am to 8pm daily. It's also worth popping into ⟨62⟩ **Don Quijote,** on Chuo Dori, at 4–3–3 Soto-Kanda (✆ **03/5298-5411;** www.donki.com), which has to be seen to appreciate its jumble of everyday goods too numerous to mention, including maid costumes and even a maid cafe (I don't even want to get into why these are so popular) on the fifth floor. It's open daily from 10am to 5am.

ANTIQUES & CURIOS

In recent years, it has become a buyer-beware market in Japan, mostly due to fake antiques produced in China infiltrating the Japanese market. You shouldn't have any problems with the reputable dealers listed here, but if you're buying an expensive piece, be sure to ask whether there are any papers of authenticity.

In addition to the listings here, other places to look for antiques include the **Oriental Bazaar** and Tokyo's **outdoor flea markets** (see later in this chapter).

Antique Mall Ginza Japanese, European, and some American antiques, collectibles, and odds and ends crowd three floors of Tokyo's largest antiques mall, where you could spend hours browsing among furniture, jewelry, watches, porcelain, pottery, dolls, netsuke, scrolls, glassware, kimono, folk art, and much more. Open Thursday to Tuesday 11am to 7pm. 1–13–1 Ginza, Chuo-ku. ✆ **03/3535-2115.** www.antiques-jp.com. Station: Ginza-Itchome or Kyobashi (3 min.). Btw Chuo Dori and Showa Dori.

Fuji-Torii   Open since 1948, this small, one-room shop in Harajuku specializes in traditional Japanese works of art and antiques, mainly screens, scrolls, woodblock prints (including reproductions), and ceramics. Open Wednesday to Monday from 11am to 6pm; closed the third Monday of the month. 6–1–10 Jingumae, Shibuya-ku. ✆ **03/3400-2777.** www.fuji-torii.com. Station: Meiji-jingumae (2 min.) or Harajuku or Omotesando (5 min.). On Omotesando Dori, next to Kiddy Land.

Ginza Antiques   While not nearly as extensive as the Antique Mall Ginza (see above), the half-dozen or so stalls here on the second floor of the Ginza 5 Building (located under an expressway) offer a variety of high-end antiques, including porcelain, furniture, dolls, kimono, and other treasures from Japan and Europe, interspersed with stalls selling crafts and jewelry. Open daily 10am to 7pm. 5–1 Ginza, Chuo-ku. ✆ **03/5568-2650.** Station: Ginza (exit C1, 1 min.) or JR Yurakucho (2 min.). On Harumi Dori, across from the Hankyu and Seibu department stores.

Kurofune Antiques (Finds   Located in a large house in Roppongi, Kurofune is owned by American John Adair, who, for more than 25 years, has specialized in Japanese antique furniture in its original condition. The largest collection here is of mid- to top-quality pieces, but browsing is a delight even if you can't afford to buy; stock in addition to furniture includes hibachi, fabrics, prints, maps, lanterns, screens, folk art, and the country's largest collection of Japanese baskets. Open Monday to Saturday 10am to 6pm. Closed early April through Golden Week. 47–7–4 Roppongi, Minato-ku. ✆ **03/3479-1552.** www.kurofuneantiques.com. Station: Roppongi (5 min.). From Roppongi Crossing, walk away from Tokyo Tower on Gaien-Higashi Dori, take the diagonal street (Ryudocho-Bijitsukan-dori) to the left (across from Tokyo Midtown), and then take a right at 7-Eleven.

Okura Oriental Art   Established in 1975, this small shop offers Japanese antiques and folk art, including *tansu* (storage chests), hibachi, Imari porcelain, and bamboo ware. Open Tuesday to Saturday 10am to 6pm. 3–3–14 Azabudai, Minato-ku. ✆ **03/3585-5309.** www.okura-art.com. Station: Roppongi, Roppongi 1–chome or Azabu Juban (7–8 min.). Just off Iikura Katamachi Crossing, about halfway btw. Roppongi Crossing and Tokyo Tower.

ARCADES & SHOPPING MALLS

ARCADES IN HOTELS   Shopping arcades are found in several of Tokyo's first-class hotels. Although they don't offer the excitement and challenge of rubbing elbows with the natives, they do offer convenience, English-speaking clerks, and consistently top-quality merchandise. The **Imperial Hotel Arcade** (station: Hibiya) is one of the best, with shops selling pearls, woodblock prints, porcelain, antiques, and expensive name-brand clothing such as Hanae Mori. The **Okura** and **New Otani** hotels also have extensive shopping arcades.

UNDERGROUND ARCADES   Underground shopping arcades are found around several of Tokyo's train and subway stations; the biggest are at **Tokyo Station** (the Yaesu side) and **Shinjuku Station** (the east side). They often have great sales and bargains on clothing, accessories, and electronics. My only complaint is that once you're in an arcade, it seems as if you'll never find your way out again.

SHOPPING MALLS   **Sunshine City** (✆ **03/3989-3331;** station: Higashi Ikebukuro or Ikebukuro) is one of Tokyo's oldest shopping malls, with more than 200 shops and restaurants spread through several adjoining buildings. Its popularity, however, is now challenged by newer and grander shopping centers, including chic **Omotesando Hills** (www.omotesandohills.com; station: Harajuku, Omotesando, or Meiji-Jingumae), with a varied mix of boutiques and restaurants; **Roppongi Hills** (📞 **03/6406-6000;** www.roppongihills.com/en; station: Roppongi), an urban renewal project with approximately 130 shops spread throughout several buildings and along tree-lined streets; and **Tokyo Midtown** (www.tokyo-midtown.com/en; station: Roppongi), with its mix of tony shops, restaurants, and offices.

Caretta Shiodome (www.caretta.jp/english; station: Shiodome), a 47-story monolith just southwest of the Ginza (and across from Hama Rikyu Garden), contains 58 shops and 33 restaurants. While there, stop by the Ad Museum Tokyo, Japan's first museum of advertising, with changing exhibits; admission is free (closed Sun–Mon).

Just across the harbor, on the man-made island of Odaiba (station: Aomi, Tokyo Teleport, or Odaiba Kaihin Koen), is **Palette Town,** an amusement/shopping center that contains the sophisticated, upscale Italian-themed **Venus Fort** (📞 **03/3599-0700**), an indoor mall that evokes scenes from Italy with its store-fronted lanes, painted sky, fountains, plazas, and expensive Italian name-brand boutiques. Nearby, **DECKS Tokyo Beach** (📞 **03/3599-6500**) targets Japanese youths with its Joypolis games arcade and international goods, including imports from the United States, Europe, China, and Hong Kong. I especially like its Daiba 1–chome Syoutengai section (on the fourth floor of Tokyo Deck's "Seaside Mall" section), a remake of mid-1900s Japan, with crafts, kitsch, food, and an old-fashioned games arcade, and Daiba Little Hong Kong department, with its Chinese accessories, souvenirs, and restaurants (on the sixth and seventh floors of the "Island Mall" section of Tokyo Decks). DECKS is connected to **Aqua City** (📞 **03/3599-4700;** www.aquacity.jp), with many more clothing boutiques plus a Toys "R" Us, both a Daiso and Three Minutes Happiness discount shop, and Ramen Kokugi-kan, a ramen theme park with six restaurants from various parts of Japan offering their own takes on the popular noodle dish.

One of Tokyo's biggest malls is **LaLaport Tokyo Bay** (📞 **0120-355-2312** or 03/5446-5143; http://tokyobay.lalaport.net/lala_eng; station: Minami Funabashi) on the eastern outskirts of the city, with a staggering 500-plus shops and restaurants and unbelievable crowds on weekends. It's sensory overload for me, but true mall fanatics might find the experience invigorating. **Urban Dock LaLaport Toyosu** (📞 **03/6910-1234;** http://toyosu.lalaport.jp) is smaller (190 shops and restaurants) but is more accessible (station: Toyosu) and even has a woodblock-print museum, flower garden, and Kidzania, a career-oriented theme park where kids can play in various job environments, from a bank to police station.

ART GALLERIES

The Ginza has the highest concentration of art galleries in Tokyo, with more than 200 shops dealing in everything from old woodblock prints to silk-screens, lithographs, and contemporary paintings. In addition, Japanese department stores almost always contain art galleries, with changing exhibitions ranging from works by European masters to contemporary Japanese pottery. Check the free giveaway *Metropolis* for exhibition listings.

Design Festa Gallery (Finds) Whereas the other galleries below feature traditional and contemporary woodblock prints and works by mostly well-known artists, this alternative and eclectic gallery offers 29 rental rooms to creative types working in any media, whether it's performance art, film, installations, sculpture, jewelry, clothing, or paintings. It's fun to walk through and see what's on offer; even the facade, a riot of colors, is a work of art. Definitely worth a visit if you're in Harajuku. The gallery also gets my kudos for

its Design Festa art events held twice a year at Tokyo Big Sight, featuring more than
8,000 artists from around the world (see "When to Go" in chapter 3). Open daily 11am to 8pm. Closed during Design Festa art event weekends. 3-20-18 Jingumae, Shibuya-ku. ℂ **03/3479-1442.** www.designfesta.com. Station: Harajuku (8 min.) or Meiji-Jingumae (4 min.). From Harajuku Station, take the north exit, walk down Takeshita Dori, cross Meiji Dori and continue walking straight. It will be on a side street to the left.

Nishimura Gallery This gallery, with an unlikely location on the third floor of an office building, represents an even mix of established Japanese and foreign (mainly British) painters and sculptors, including David Hockney, Peter Blake, Paul Davis, Richard Hamilton, Kobayashi Takanobu, Machida Kumi, and Funakoshi Katsura. Open Tuesday to Saturday 10:30am to 6:30pm. 2-10-8 Nihombashi, Chuo-ku. ℂ **03/5203-2800.** www. nishimura-gallery.com. Station: Nihombashi (4 min.). Just off Showa Dori, on a side street north of Takashimaya department store.

Sakai Kokodo Gallery This gallery claims to be the oldest woodblock print shop in Japan. It was first opened back in 1870 in the Kanda area of Tokyo by the present owner's great-grandfather; altogether four generations of the Sakai family have tended the store. It's a great place for original prints, as well as reproductions of such great masters as Hiroshige. (If you're really a woodblock print fan, you'll want to visit the Sakai family's excellent **Japan Ukiyo-e Museum,** in the small town of Matsumoto in the Japan Alps.) Open daily 11am to 6pm. 1-2-14 Yurakucho, Chiyoda-ku (across from the Imperial Hotel's Tower). ℂ **03/3591-4678.** www.ukiyo-e.co.jp/index-e.html. Station: Hibiya (1 min.).

Shiseido Gallery Founded in 1919 by the Shiseido cosmetics company's first president, this is the Ginza's oldest gallery but it occupies very updated quarters in a basement room with super-high ceilings (5m/16 ft.). It features contemporary art by young, promising talent, both Japanese and foreign. Open Tuesday to Saturday 11am to 7pm; Sunday and holidays 11am to 6pm. Tokyo Ginza Shiseido Building, B1, 8-8-3 Ginza, Chuo-ku. ℂ **03/3572-3901.** www.shiseido.co.jp/e/gallery/html. Station: Ginza (3 min.). On Chuo Dori, south of Ginza 4-chome Crossing.

S. Watanabe This 100-year-old shop deals mostly in contemporary woodblock prints with traditional themes, as well as reproduction and antique *ukiyo-e.* Open Monday to Saturday 9:30am to 8pm; holidays 9:30am to 5pm. 8-6-19 Ginza, Chuo-ku. ℂ **03/3571-4684.** Station: Shimbashi (2 min.). On Namiki Dori.

Yoseido Gallery Established in 1953, this shop deals in modern woodblock prints, etchings, silk-screens, copper plates, and lithographs, including lithographs by one of my favorite Japanese artists, Shinoda Toko. Open Monday to Saturday 11am to 7pm. Closed holidays. 5-5-15 Ginza, Chuo-ku. ℂ **03/3571-1312.** www.yoseido.com. Station: Ginza (1 min.). On Namiki Dori near Harumi Dori.

BOOKS

Yasukuni Dori, in Jimbocho, Kanda (station: Jimbocho), is lined with bookstores selling both new and used books, with several dealing in English-language books. Keep in mind, however, that English-language books are usually more expensive in Japan than back home. Still, no bibliophile should pass this street up, especially if your interest is in books related to Japan.

Kinokuniya This is one of Tokyo's best-known bookstores, with one of the city's largest selections of books and magazines in English—including books on Japan, dictionaries and textbooks for students of Japanese, and novels—on its sixth floor. Open daily 10am to 8pm; closed some Wednesdays. Takashimaya Annex, Takashimaya Times Sq. complex. © 03/5361-3301. Station: Shinjuku (south exit, 2 min.).

Kitazawa   On the second floor of Book House, Kitazawa, open since 1902, offers second-hand foreign books, including rare editions, antiquarian books (reservations needed to peruse the antique editions), and a big section on Japan. If you're looking for an out-of-print book, this is your best bet. Open Monday, Tuesday, Thursday, and Friday 11am to 6:30pm, and Saturday, Sunday and holidays from noon to 5:30pm. 2–5 Jimbo-cho, Kanda, Chiyoda-ku. © 03/3263-0011. Station: Jimbocho (1A exit and turn right, 1 min.). On Yasukuni Dori.

Maruzen   This is Japan's oldest bookstore, founded in 1869 but now ensconced in the modern Oazo Building across from Tokyo Station's Marunouchi exit. Its English-language section, on the fourth floor, is huge and well laid out, with everything from dictionaries to travel guides to special-interest books on Japan. It also carries books on science, politics, and history, as well as magazines and paperbacks. If you're searching for a specific title, you'll probably want to come here first. Open daily 9am to 9pm. 1–6–4 Marunouchi. © 03/5288-8881. Station: Tokyo (1 min.). Take the Marunouchi exit from Tokyo Station and turn right (north); it's across the street.

Ohya Shobo   Established in 1882, this delightfully cramped shop in Kanda doesn't have any English-language books, but it does claim to have the world's largest stock of 18th- and 19th-century Japanese illustrated books, woodblock prints, and maps, including maps from the Edo Period. Open Monday to Saturday 10am to 6pm; closed some holidays. 1–1 Jimbocho, Kanda, Chiyoda-ku. © 03/3291-0062. Station: Jimbocho (A7 exit, 3 min.). Turn right (east) onto Yasukuni Dori; it will be on your right, one of the last bookstores.

Tower Records and Books   My friends in Tokyo don't shop anywhere else for their books and magazines, as prices are usually lower here than elsewhere. The seventh floor is devoted to imported publications, with a good selection of English-language books, more than 3,000 different kinds of magazines, and—available via computer printout for a fee—more than 300 newspapers from around the world. Open daily 10am to 11pm. 1–22–14 Jinnan. © 03/3496-3661. Station: Shibuya (Hachiko exit, 5 min.).

DEPARTMENT STORES

Japanese department stores are institutions in themselves. Usually enormous, well-designed, and chock-full of merchandise, they have about everything you can imagine, including museums and art galleries, pet stores, rooftop playgrounds or greenhouses, travel agencies, restaurants, grocery markets, and flower shops. You could easily spend a whole day in a department store—eating, attending cultural exhibitions, planning your

---

Tips   **Department Store Hours**

Japanese department stores are generally open from 10 or 10:30am to 8 or 9pm. They used to close 1 day a week, but now they rarely close, or they close irregularly, though always on the same day of the week (say, on Tues) in no apparent pattern (one month they may be closed the second Tues of the month, but the next month the first or not at all). In any case, you can always find stores that are open, even on Sundays and holidays (major shopping days in Japan).

next vacation, exchanging money, purchasing tickets to local concerts and other events, and, well, shopping.

One of the most wonderful aspects of the Japanese department store is the courteous service. If you arrive at a store as its doors open at 10 or 10:30am, you'll witness a daily rite: Lined up at the entrance are staff who bow in welcome. Some Japanese shoppers arrive just before opening time so as not to miss this favorite ritual. Sales clerks are everywhere, ready to help you. In some stores, you don't even have to go to the cash register once you've made your choice; just hand over the product, along with your money, to the sales clerk, who will return with your change, your purchase neatly wrapped, and an *"Arigatoo gozaimashita"* ("Thank you very much"). Many department stores will also ship your purchases home for you, send them to your hotel, or hold them until you're ready to leave the store. A day spent in a Japanese department store could spoil you for the rest of your life.

Many department stores include boutiques by such famous Japanese and international fashion designers as Issey Miyake, Rei Kawakubo (creator of Comme des Garçons), Hanae Mori, Takeo Kikuchi, Vivienne Westwood, and Paul Smith, as well as a department devoted to the kimono. Near the kimono department may also be the section devoted to traditional crafts, including pottery and lacquerware. Many famous restaurants maintain branches in department stores, but not to be missed is the basement (nicknamed a *depachika,* which is a combination *depa*—from department store—and *chika,* meaning basement), where you'll find one or two levels devoted to foodstuffs: fresh fish, produce, green tea, sake, prepared snacks and dinners, and delectable pastries. There are often free samples of food; if you're hungry, walking through the food department could do nicely for a snack.

To find out what's where, stop by the store's information booth located on the ground floor near the front entrance and ask for the floor-by-floor English-language pamphlet. Be sure, too, to ask about sales on the promotional floor—you never know what bargains you may chance upon.

In Ginza, Yurakucho & Nihombashi

Matsuya Ginza   This is one of my favorite department stores in Tokyo; if I were buying a wedding gift, Matsuya is one of the first places I'd look. It has a good selection of Japanese folk crafts items, kitchenware, kimono, and beautifully designed contemporary household goods, in addition to the usual designer clothes and accessories ("Queen" sizes are on the sixth floor). I always make a point of stopping by the seventh floor's Design Collection, which displays items from around the world selected by the Japan Design Committee as examples of fine design, from the Alessi teapot to Braun razors. Two basement floors are devoted to food. Open daily 10am to 8pm. There's a branch in Asakusa at 1–41–1 Hanakawado (✆ 03/3842-1111; daily 10am–7:30pm). 3–6–1 Ginza, Chuo-ku. ✆ 03/3567-1211. Station: Ginza (2 min.). On Chuo Dori, just a long block north of Ginza 4–chome Crossing.

Matsuzakaya Ginza Tokyo   Established almost 400 years ago, this was the first department store in Japan that did not require customers to take off their shoes at the entrance. It appeals mainly to Tokyo's older generation with its mostly men's and women's clothing, but it does have a pet shop, children's play area, and a Shinto shrine on its roof (along with a beer garden in summer) and the trendy Muji (see "Fashions," later) in its second basement. Its spiffy basement food floor has a small dining corner with tables where you can order sushi, tempura, eel, and other fare. Hours are 10:30am to 7:30pm daily, though some floors, like the basement food floor, stay open until 8pm. 6–10–1 Ginza, Chuo-ku. ℂ **03/3572-1111.** Station: Ginza (2 min.). 1 block from Ginza. 4–chome Crossing on Chuo Dori in the direction of Shimbashi.

Mitsukoshi   This Nihombashi department store is one of Japan's oldest and grandest, founded in 1673 by the Mitsui family as a kimono store. In 1683, it became the first store in the world to deal only in cash sales; it was also one of the first stores in Japan to display goods on shelves rather than have merchants fetch bolts of cloth for each customer, as was the custom of the time. In 2008, Mitsukoshi and Isetan (another big name in department stores; see "In Shinjuku," below) merged their operations, creating the biggest department store company in Japan and overtaking the number one position from rival Takashimaya, below; current Isetan and Mitsukoshi department stores have retained their respective names (though a new outlet opening in 2011 in Osaka will be the first to bear the joint Isetan-Mitsukoshi name).

Today, housed in a building dating from 1914, Mitsukoshi remains one of Tokyo's loveliest department stores, with a beautiful and stately Renaissance-style facade and an entrance guarded by two bronze lions, replicas of the lions in Trafalgar Square. The store carries many international name-brand boutiques, from Chanel to Christian Dior. On its roof is a garden and gardening section, often with a display of bonsai. Its kimono, by the way, are still hot items. Open daily 10am to 8pm. Another branch, located right on Ginza 4–chome Crossing (ℂ **03/3562-1111;** daily 10am–8pm), is popular with young shoppers. 1–4–1 Nihombashi Muromachi, Chuo-ku. ℂ **03/3241-3311.** Station: Mitsukoshimae (1 min.).

Takashimaya   This department store has always provided stiff competition for Mitsukoshi, with a history just as long. It was founded as a kimono shop in Kyoto during the Edo Period and opened in Tokyo in 1933. Today it's one of the city's most attractive department stores, with a Renaissance-style building and gloved elevator operators whisking customers to eight floors of shopping and dining. Naturally, it features boutiques by such famous designers as Chanel, Louis Vuitton, Gucci, Issey Miyake, and more. Its sale of used kimono (look for advertisements in the *Japan Times*) draws huge crowds, even more than the usual 35,000 daily customers. Open daily 10am to 8pm. 2–4–1 Nihombashi (on Chuo Dori), Chuo-ku. ℂ **03/3211-4111.** Station: Nihombashi (1 min.).

Wako   This is one of Ginza's smallest department stores but also one of its classiest, housed in one of the few area buildings that survived World War II. It was erected in 1932 by the Hattori family, founders of the Seiko watch company, and is famous for its distinctive clock tower, graceful curved facade, and innovative window displays. The store's ground floor carries a wide selection of Seiko watches and handbags, while the upper floors carry imported and domestic fashions and luxury items with prices to match. It caters to older, well-to-do customers; you won't find hordes of young Japanese girls shopping here. Open Monday to Saturday 10:30am to 6pm; closed holidays. 4–5–11 Ginza (at Ginza 4–chome Crossing), Chuo-ku. ℂ **03/3562-2111.** Station: Ginza (1 min.).

Yurakucho Hankyu   Connected to Yurakucho Seibu (below), this store carries mostly clothing and accessories, including shoes in its basement; clothing ranges from casual wear to business suits and designer wear. Open Monday and Tuesday 11am to 8:30pm; Wednesday to Friday 11am to 9pm; Saturday and Sunday 11am to 8pm. 2–5–1 Yurakucho, Chiyoda-ku. ℂ **03/3575-2233.** Station: Yurakucho (1 min.) or Hibiya and Ginza (2 min.). In Yurakucho, just east of the elevated JR Yamanote Line tracks and btw. the Hibiya and Ginza subway stations.

Yurakucho Marui   Marui (which uses the symbols O1O1 as store identification, a take on the circle, which is *maru* in Japanese), gained its toehold in the competitive store business by offering easy-to-obtain credit cards to young shoppers buying clothes or setting up households for the first time. This upscale venue, debuting in 2007 beside JR Yurakucho Station, marks the chain's coming-of-age, with cool fashions and accessories aimed at upwardly mobile commuters. Open daily 11am to 8:30pm. 2-7-1 Yurakucho, Chiyoda-ku. 🕻 **03/3212-0101.** Station: Yurakucho (1 min.).

Yurakucho Seibu   This Seibu branch, connected to Yurakucho Hankyu via covered square, contains clothing and accessories mostly for women, with a few floors devoted to men's fashions. All the biggies in Japanese designer names—Issey Miyake, Yohji Yamamoto, Comme des Garçons—are located on the seventh floor, along with others such as Vivienne Westood. Open Monday to Wednesday 11:30am to 8:30pm; Thursday and Friday 11:30am to 9pm; Saturday 11an to 9pm; Sunday and holidays 11am to 8:30pm. 2-5-1 Yurakucho, Chiyoda-ku. 🕻 **03/3286-0111.** Station: Yurakucho (1 min.) or Hibiya and Ginza (2 min.). In Yurakucho near the elevated tracks of the JR Yamanote Line, btw. the Hibiya and Ginza stations.

In Ikebukuro

Seibu   Once the nation's largest department store—and still one of the biggest—Seibu has 47 entrances, thousands of sales clerks, dozens of restaurants, 12 floors, 31 elevators, and more than 100,000 shoppers a day. Two basement floors are devoted to foodstuffs— you can buy everything from taco shells to octopus to seaweed. Dishes are set out so that you can sample the food as you move along, and hawkers yelling out their wares give the place a marketlike atmosphere. Fast-food counters sell salads, grilled eel, chicken, sushi, and other ready-to-eat dishes. The rest of the floors offer clothing, furniture, art galleries, jewelry, household goods, kitchenware, and a million other things. Loft, Seibu's department for household goods and interior design, and Wave, Seibu's CD department, occupy the top four floors of the main building. Many of the best Japanese and Western designers have boutiques here; it also carries large, tall, and petite sizes on the fourth floor. Open Monday to Saturday from 10am to 9pm, Sunday and holidays from 10am to 8pm. 1-28-1 Minami Ikebukuro, Toshima-ku. 🕻 **03/3981-0111.** Station: Ikebukuro (underneath the store).

Tobu/Metropolitan Plaza   Once overshadowed by nearby Seibu, this flagship of the Tobu chain expanded and reopened in 1993 as Japan's largest department store (it has since been overtaken by other stores, including Takashimaya Shinjuku, below). It consists of a main building, a connecting central building, and Metropolitan Plaza. It offers everything from luxury goods and the latest international fashions to hardware, software, toys, daily necessities, and traditional Japanese products (good for souvenirs). On the seventh floor are outlets for Uniqlo and Three Minutes Happiness (see "Fashions" and "Housewares & Interior Design," respectively, later in this chapter). Its basement food floor is massive—food accounts for nearly 20% of Tobu's total sales. Here, too, is the home of the **Japan Traditional Craft Center,** a must for anyone shopping for traditional and contemporary handmade Japanese crafts. Open Monday to Saturday from 11am to 9pm; Sunday and holidays from 11am to 8:30pm. 1-1-25 Nishi-Ikebukuro, Toshima-ku. 🕻 **03/3981-2211.** Station: Ikebukuro (west exit, 1 min.).

In Shinjuku

Isetan   With a history stretching 120 years and attracting more than 30 million customers a year, Isetan is a favorite among foreigners living in Tokyo. Now part of the

Isetan-Mitsukoshi conglomerate, it has a good line of conservative work clothes, as well as contemporary and fashionable styles, including designer goods by Issey Miyake, Yohji Yamamoto, Hanae Mori, Comme des Garçons, Marc Jacobs, and Salvatore Ferragamo, as well as large dress sizes (on the second floor). It has a great kimono section along with all the traditional accessories (obi, shoes, purses). Its basement food hall is legendary, with its dessert and massive chocolate sections an especially illuminating commentary on Japan's obsession with food. An annex offers eight floors of men's clothing and accessories. Open daily 10am to 8pm. 3-14-1 Shinjuku, Shinjuku-ku. ℂ 03/3352-1111. Station: Shinjuku Sanchome (1 min.) or Shinjuku (east exit, 6 min.). On Shinjuku Dori, east of Shinjuku Station.

Takashimaya Shinjuku   Since its opening in 1996, Takashimaya has been the number-one draw in Shinjuku and is packed on weekends. Much larger than Takashimaya's Nihombashi flagship, this huge complex boasts 10 floors of clothing and restaurants (lower floors target the affluent elderly, while upper floors appeal to younger shoppers and families; petite and "queen-size" clothing are on the sixth floor). There's also Tokyu Hands with everything imaginable for the home hobbyist, and Kinokuniya bookstore with English-language books on the sixth floor. Open daily 10am to 8pm. 5-24-2 Sendagaya, Shinjuku-ku. ℂ 03/5361-1111. Station: Shinjuku (1 min.). Across the street from Shinjuku Station's south exit.

In Shibuya

Shibuya is a shopping mecca for the fashionable young, with so many stores that there's a bona fide store war going on. Tokyu and Seibu are the two big names, but in addition to these two, see the "Fashions" section, below.

Seibu   Shibuya's largest department store consists of two buildings connected by pedestrian skywalks, with lots of designer boutiques such as Issey Miyake, Comme des Garçons, Tsumori Chisato, Stella McCartney, Vivienne Westwood, and Vivienne Tam. Nearby are Loft, with household goods, and Movida, a fashion department store with fun young fashions for waifs. See the listing for the main store in Ikebukuro, above. Open Sunday to Wednesday 10am to 8pm, Thursday to Saturday 10am to 9pm. 21-1 Udagawacho. ℂ 03/3462-0111. Station: Shibuya (Hachiko exit, 3 min.).

Tokyu Honten (Main Store)   With its conservative styles in clothing and housewares, the Tokyu chain's flagship store appeals mainly to a 40s-and-older age group. You'll find women's fashions (including departments for larger sizes), men's fashions, children's clothing and toys, arts and crafts, and restaurants. It adjoins the ultramodern Bunkamura complex, the largest cultural center in Tokyo, with cinemas, theater and concert halls, a museum, a bookstore, and cafes. Open daily 11am to 7pm. 2-24-1 Dogenzaka. ℂ 03/3477-3111. Station: Shibuya (Hachiko exit, 7 min.).

ELECTRONICS

The largest concentration of electronics and electrical-appliance shops in Japan is in an area of Tokyo called **Akihabara**, also known simply as Akiba and centered on Chuo Dori (station: Akihabara). Although you can find good deals on video and audio equipment elsewhere (especially just west of Shinjuku Station, where Yodobashi dominates with several stores devoted to electronics), Akihabara is a must-see simply for its sheer volume. With hundreds of multilevel stores, shops, and stalls, Akihabara accounts for one-tenth of the nation's electronics and electrical-appliance sales. An estimated 50,000 shoppers come here on a weekday, 100,000 per day on a weekend. Even if you don't buy anything,

(Fun Facts) The Magical World of Vending Machines

One of the things that usually surprises visitors to Japan is the number of vending machines in the country, estimated to be more than 5.5 million—one for every 20 people. They're virtually everywhere—in train stations, in front of shops, on the back streets of residential neighborhoods. They'll take bills and give back change. Some will even talk to you.

And what can you buy in these vending machines? First, there are the obvious items—drinks and snacks, including hot or cold coffee in a can, but they come in such a bewildering number of choices that it's difficult to make a selection. If you're on your way to someone's house, you might be able to pick up a bouquet of flowers from a machine. Your camera is out of batteries? You may be able to find those, too, along with CDs, film, disposable cameras, sandwiches, and even eggs. Vending machines outside post offices sell stamps and postcards, while those in business hotels sell razors, Cup Noodles, beer, and even underwear.

In the not-too-distant past, things were also sold from sidewalk vending machines that would have met with instant protest in other countries around the world. Cigarettes and beer were available on almost every corner, where even children could buy them if they wanted to; nowadays, however, shoppers must first insert a computer-readable card certifying they're at least 20 years old. I remember a vending machine in my Tokyo neighborhood: By day, it was blank, with no sign as to what was inside; at night, however, the thing would light up, and on display were pornographic comics. Nowadays, pornographic vending machines are very rare, not for moral reasons, but because of the Internet.

Still, if it's available in Japan, it's probably in a vending machine somewhere.

it's great fun walking around. If you do intend to buy, make sure you know what the item would cost back home. Or you may be able to pick up something that's unavailable back home. Most of the stores and stalls are open-fronted, and many are painted neon green and pink. Salespeople yell out their wares, trying to get customers to look at their cellular phones, computers, video equipment, digital cameras, MP3 players, TVs, calculators, watches, and rice cookers. This is the best place to see the latest models of everything electronic; it's an educational experience in itself.

If you are buying, be sure to bargain and don't buy at the first place you hit. One woman I know who was looking for a portable music device bought it at the third shop she went to for ¥4,000 less than what was quoted to her at the first shop. Make sure, too, that whatever you purchase is made for export—that is, with English-language instructions, an international warranty, and the proper electrical connectors. All the larger stores have duty-free floors, where products are made for export, and most shops are open daily from about 10am to 8pm or later.

The largest store is **Yodobashi Akiba,** just east of JR Akihabara Station at 1–1 Hanaoka-cho (© **03/5209-1010;** daily 9:30am–10pm), which offers a staggering amount of electronic-related goods such as cameras, computers, TVs, and rice cookers, but it also offers a slew of other leisure-related items such as games and bicycles (some people fear this monolith will put independent Akiba shop owners out of business). Other reputable stores, with English-speaking staff and models for export, include **Laox,** 15–3 Soto-Kanda (✆ **03/3255-5301**), and **AKKY International,** 1–12–5 Soto-Kanda (✆ **03/5207-5027**), both on Chuo Dori (the latter store also carries Japanese souvenirs in its basement). If you're serious about buying, check these stores first.

In recent years, Akihabara has also earned a reputation as a center for Japanese **pop culture,** including anime, manga (Japanese comics), and cosplay (costume play); see "Anime & Manga," earlier.

For more information on Akihabara, go to www.akihabara-tour.com, where at press time, free 2-hour tours of Akihabara were offered two Saturdays a month at 1pm.

In addition to stores in Akihabara and Shinjuku, there's **LABI Shibuya,** 2–29–20 Dogenzaka (✆ **03/5456-6300;** station: Shibuya), offering seven floors of electronics, including digital cameras, camcorders, cellphones, TVs, computers, software, games and appliances. It's open daily 10am to 10pm.

Cameras

You can purchase cameras at many duty-free shops, including those in Akihabara, but if you're serious about photographic equipment, make a trip to a shop dealing specifically in cameras. If a new camera is too formidable an expense, consider buying a used camera. New models come out so frequently in Japan that older models can be snapped up for next to nothing.

Bic Camera   This huge, eight-floor store near the Ginza offers not only single-lens reflex, large and medium format, and digital cameras, but also computers, DVD and MP3 players, camcorders, watches, toys, and much more. Note, however, that it caters primarily to Japanese; English-speaking sales clerks are scarce, and export models are limited. Ask for the English-language brochure and, if you're buying sensitive equipment, make sure it will work outside Japan and comes with English-language instructions. Open daily 10am to 10pm. There's a branch in Shibuya at 1–24–12 Shibuya (✆ **03/5466-1111;** daily 10am–8pm; station: Shibuya, 2 min.). 1–11–1 Yurakucho, Chiyoda-ku. ✆ **03/5221-1112.** Station: Yurakucho (1 min.).

㊳ Lemon   Its name doesn't inspire confidence, but this company specializes in used and new cameras and lenses from around the world. On the eighth floor are both new and used Japanese and foreign cameras, including digital cameras and large-format models. Leica, Hasselblad, Rolleiflex, Canon, Pentax, and Nikon are just some of the brands available, along with watches and eyeglasses. A camera buff's paradise. Open Monday to Saturday 11am to 8pm, Sunday 11am to 5pm. 4–2–2 Ginza, Chuo-ku. ✆ **03/3567-3131.** Station: Ginza (1 min.). In a green glazed-brick building also housing the Ginza Methodist Church.

Yodobashi Camera   Shinjuku is the photographic equipment center for Tokyo, and this store, 1 block west of the station, is the biggest in the area. It ranks as one of the largest discount camera shops in the world (though the new Yodobashi in Akihabara, above, now surpasses it), with around 30,000 items in stock, and it reputedly sells approximately 500 to 600 cameras daily. Prices are marked, but you can bargain here. In addition to cameras, it sells watches, calculators, computers, and other electronic equipment, though if you're interested specifically in watches, clocks, audio/video equipment, games, and other wares, nearby branches specialize in all of these (ask at the main shop for a map of shops in the area). Open daily 9:30am to 10pm. 1–11–1 Nishi-Shinjuku, Shinjuku-ku. ✆ **03/3346-1010.** Station: Shinjuku (west exit, 3 min.).

The **department stores** and **shopping malls** listed earlier are all good places to check out the latest trends. For inexpensive, basic clothing (think Japanese version of Gap), look for one of the 40-some **Uniqlo** shops in Tokyo selling T-shirts, jeans, socks, shirts, and other clothing for the whole family. A convenient location is 5–7–7 Ginza, on Chuo Dori (𝒞 **03/5569-6781;** station: Ginza). Another popular chain, selling minimalist yet hip cotton clothing in basic colors, is **Muji,** with its flagship located next to the Tourist Information Center at 3–8–3 Marunouchi (𝒞 **03/5208-8241;** station: Yurakucho).

Second-hand clothing, which made its first appearance in Japan after the economic meltdown, is now "in," with several shops catering to young Tokyoites in Harajuku, offering mostly American but also Japanese used clothing. My favorite is **Hanjiro,** on the third and fourth floors of YM Square (and across Meiji Dori from La Forêt, below), at 4–31–10 Jingumae (𝒞 **03/3796-7303**). It carries used clothing in addition to its own original brand. **Kinji** (𝒞 **03/6406-0505**), in the basement of the same building, specializes in used clothing, as does **Chicago,** with two locations in Harajuku, at 26–26 Jingumae (𝒞 **03/5414-5107**), with men's, women's, and children's second-hand clothing, and at 6–31–21 Jingumae (𝒞 **03/3409-5017**), which also sells used kimono at the far corner of the basement.

Otherwise, **Harajuku** and **Shibuya** are the places to go for hundreds of small shops selling inexpensive designer knockoffs, as well as fashion department stores—multistoried buildings filled with concessions of various designers and labels. The stores below are two of the best known and largest.

La Forêt   This is not only the largest store in Harajuku but also one of the most fashionable, appealing mostly to teenage and 20-something shoppers. Young and upcoming Japanese designers are here as well as established names, in boutiques spread on several floors. There's so much to see—from pink frilly dresses to Goth—you can easily kill a few hours here. Open daily 11am to 8pm. 1–11–6 Jingumae, Shibuya-ku. 𝒞 **03/3475-0411.** Station: Meiji-Jingumae (1 min.) or Harajuku (3 min.). On Meiji Dori, just off Harajuku's main intersection of Omotesando Dori and Meiji Dori.

Parco   A division of Seibu, Parco is actually two buildings clustered together and called Parco Part 1 and Part 3 (Part 2 recently closed). Parco Part 1 is the place to go for designer boutiques for men and women, with clothes by Japanese designers, such as Yohji Yamamoto and Tsumori Chisato, and such foreign designers as Anna Sui and Vivienne Westwood. Part 3 is devoted to casual, young fashions. Parco has two sales a year that you shouldn't miss if you're in town—one in January and one in July. Open daily 10am to 9pm. 15–1 Udagawacho, Shibuya-ku. 𝒞 **03/3464-5111.** Station: Shibuya (Hachiko exit, 4 min.)

Designer Boutiques

Ginza is home to international designer names, including Prada, Cartier, Chanel, Christian Dior, and Louis Vuitton. For top Japanese designers, the block between Omotesando Crossing and the Nezu Museum (currently undergoing renovation) in **Aoyama** (station: Omotesando, 2 min.) is the Rodeo Drive of Japan. Even if you can't buy here (steep prices for most pocketbooks), a stroll is de rigueur for clothes hounds and those interested in design. Most shops are open daily from 11am to 8pm. **Issey Miyake** (𝒞 **03/3423-1408**), on the left side as you walk from Aoyama Dori, offers two floors of cool, spacious displays of Miyake's interestingly structured designs for men and women. (His very popular Pleats Please line is around the corner on Aoyama Dori, 3–13–21 Minami Aoyama; 𝒞 **03/5772-7750.**) Across the street is **Comme des Garçons**

(© **03/3406-3951**), Rei Kawakubo's showcase for her daring—and constantly evolving—men's and women's designs. The goddess of Japanese fashion and one of the few females in the business when she started, Kawakubo has remained on the cutting edge of design for more than 3 decades. One of Japan's newer designers, **Tsumori Chisato,** has a shop on the left side of the street (© **03/3423-5170**). Also worth seeking out is **Yohji Yamamoto** on the right (© **03/3409-6006**), where Yamamoto's unique, classically wearable clothes are sparingly hung, flaunting the avant-garde interior space.

Of the many non-Japanese designers to have invaded this trendy neighborhood in recent years, none stands out as much as **Prada** (© **03/6418-0400**), a bubble of convex/concave windows on the right side of the street. On a back street behind Prada are up-and-coming design houses, including **A Bathing Ape** (© **03/3407-2145**), where DJ/fashion designer Nigo sells limited editions of his hip T-shirts and shoes. Down the street, **Y-3** (© **03/5464-1930**), a collaboration between Yohji Yamamoto and Adidas, is a must for those who wish to look fashionable while working out.

On the other side of Aoyama Dori, on Omotesando Dori in the direction of Harajuku, is **Hanae Mori** (© **03/3400-3301**), the grande dame of Japanese design, with everything from separates and men's golf wear to haute couture and wedding gowns on display on three floors of a building designed by Japanese architect Kenzo Tange.

FLEA MARKETS

Flea markets are good places to shop for antiques as well as for delightful junk. You can pick up secondhand kimono at very reasonable prices, as well as kitchenware, vases, cast-iron teapots, small chests, woodblock prints, dolls, household items, and odds and ends. (Don't expect to find any good buys in furniture.) The markets usually begin as early as dawn or 6am and last until 3 or 4pm or so, but go early if you want to pick up bargains. Bargaining is expected. Note that since most markets are outdoors, they tend to be canceled if it rains.

Togo Shrine, 1–5–3 Jingumae, on Meiji Dori in Harajuku (near Meiji-Jingumae and Harajuku stations), has a small antiques market on the first Sunday of every month from 6am to 2pm. It's great for used kimono and curios and is one of my favorites. For more information, see the walking tour of Harajuku and Aoyama in chapter 8.

Nogi Shrine, a 1-minute walk from Nogizaka Station at 8–11–27 Akasaka, has an antiques flea market from dawn to about 2pm the second Sunday of each month except November. It has a lovely setting; the shrine commemorates General Nogi and his wife, both of whom committed suicide on September 13, 1912, to follow the Meiji emperor into the afterlife. Their simple home and stable are on shrine grounds.

Hanazono Shrine, 5–17–3 Shinjuku, near the Yasukuni Dori/Meiji Dori intersection east of Shinjuku Station (Shinjuku Sanchome Station, 5 min.), has a flea market every Sunday from dawn to about 2pm (except in May and Nov, due to festivals).

Yasukuni Shrine, a 3-minute walk from Kudanshita Station, at 3–1–1 Kudanshita, holds a flea market every Sunday from 6am to about 3pm on the long walkway to this very famous shrine (see chapter 7 for information on the shrine and its military museum).

The **Oedo Antique Fair,** held at 3–5–1 Marunouchi, in the courtyard of the Tokyo International Forum, beside Yurakucho Station, claims to be the largest outdoor antiques market in Japan (it has also taken away vendors from Tokyo's other flea markets). Held the first and third Sunday of the month from 9am to 5pm, it features Western antiques (at highly inflated prices), as well as Japanese glassware, furniture, ceramics, furniture, kimono, woodblock prints, and odds and ends. If you hit only one flea market, this should be it.

Finally, the closest thing Tokyo has to a permanent flea market is **Ameya Yokocho** (also referred to as Ameyoko, Ameyokocho or Ameyacho), a narrow street near Ueno Park that runs along and underneath the elevated tracks of the JR Yamanote Line between Ueno and Okachimachi stations. There are about 400 stalls here selling discounted items ranging from vegetables and cosmetics to handbags, tennis shoes, watches, and casual clothes. The scene retains something of the *shitamachi* spirit of old Tokyo. Although housewives have been coming here for years, young Japanese recently discovered the market as a good bargain spot for fashions, accessories, and cosmetics. Some shops close on Wednesdays, but hours are usually daily from 10am to 7pm; early evening is the most crowded time. Don't even think of coming here on a holiday—it's a standstill pedestrian traffic jam.

HOUSEWARES & INTERIOR DESIGN

The **department stores** listed earlier sell home furnishings, including bedding, kitchenware, lighting, and decor.

Daiso   The largest chain of 100-Yen shops in Japan (comparable to dollar stores in the U.S.), with more than 2,500 locations in Japan and abroad, this is also one of the better discount stores, offering mostly its own brand goods, purchased directly from manufacturers (many of which are in China). Items, priced mostly at ¥100 or multiples thereof, include kitchenware, tableware, cosmetics, office supplies, and other household goods and daily necessities, making it a good place to shop for cheap souvenirs such as chopsticks and *ikebana* (flower arranging) accessories. In addition to the four-story shop listed here, there's a branch in Aqua City, Odaiba (✆ 03/3599-7061). Open daily 10am to 9pm. 1-19-24 Jingumae, Shibuya-ku. ✆ 03/5775-9641. www.daiso-sangyo.co.jp/English. Station: Harajuku (north exit, 3 min.) or Meiji-Jingumae (4 min.). On Takeshita Dori, about midway down.

㉒ **Don Quijote**   Teenagers don't seem to mind the jumble of everyday goods offered here, but I find it so packed along its narrow aisles that it makes me feel claustrophobic. It offers household goods and gadgets, sporting goods, electronics, party items, food, and much, much more, including cosplay fare such as maid costumes (a perennial favorite). It's hard to come up with anything Don Quijote *doesn't* sell, but strangely, I never find anything I'm compelled to buy. It's open daily from 10am to 5am. You'll find branches of Don Quijote in Shinjuku, on Yasukuni Dori at 1-16-5 Kabuki-cho (✆ 03/5291-9211), and in Roppongi, on the left side of Gaien-Higashi Dori if walking from Roppongi Crossing toward Tokyo Tower, at 3-14-10 Roppongi (✆ 03/5786-0811), both open a mind-boggling 24 hours. 4-3-3 Soto-Kanda, Chiyoka-ku. ✆ 03/5298-5411. Station: Akihabara (3 min.). On Chuo Dori.

Loft   Loft is Seibu's store for the young homeowner and hobbyist, with tableware, cookware, glassware, bathroom accessories, bed linens, office supplies, stationery, games, and more. Don't miss the sixth-floor variety goods department, filled with an amazing amount of Japanese and American kitsch, party goods (including some weird costumes), and cellphone straps and charms. If you've yearned for a bank in the shape of a toilet, this is the place for you. There's a branch in Ikebukuro's Seibu (discussed earlier). Open daily 10am to 9pm. 21-1 Udagawacho, Shibuya-ku. ✆ 03/3462-3807. Station: Shibuya (Hachiko exit, 4 min.). Behind Seibu B.

Muji   This domestic chain is worth checking out for its plain yet well-designed products, many of them made from recycled materials at affordable prices. Futon, bed linens, kitchen appliances, tableware, storage units, furniture (think rattan and unbleached woods), clothing, cosmetics, and other practical goods are offered at more than 280 locations in Japan, but this is its head store. Open daily 10am to 9pm. 3–8–3 Marunouchi, Chiyoda-ku. ✆ **03/5208-8241**. Station: Yurakucho (2 min.). Across from the Kotsu Kaikan Building (location of the Tourist Information Center).

Three Minutes Happiness   Bargain yen shops are all over Japan, but this is one of my favorites. It carries tableware, household goods, office supplies, cosmetics, sunglasses, clothing (including *tabi* socks, with separation for the big toe and used for thonged footwear), and many other simple items, mostly in bright and happy colors like lime green and sky blue. Let's just hope most of the products give more than 3 minutes of happiness. You'll find branches of this shop in Ikebukuro's Tobu/Metropolitan Plaza and Aqua City on Odaiba (see earlier). Open daily 11am to 9pm. 3–5 Udagawacho, Shibuya-ku. ✆ **03/5459-1851**. Station: Shibuya (Hachiko exit, 5 min.). On the left side of Koen Dori.

Tokyu Hands   Billing itself the "Creative Life Store," Tokyu Hands, part of the Tokyu chain, is a huge department store for the serious homeowner and hobbyist, with everything from travel accessories, *noren* (doorway curtains), chopsticks, and kitchen knives, to equipment and materials for do-it-yourselfers, including paper for shoji. If there's a practical Japanese product you've decided you can't live without (lunchbox? bathroom slippers? hanging laundry rack?), this is a good place to look. You'll also find Tokyu Hands at 1–28–10 Higashi Ikebukuro beside the Sunshine City Building (✆ **03/3980-6111**) and in the Takashimaya Shinjuku complex (✆ **03/5361-3111**). Open daily 10am to 8:30pm. 12–18 Udagawacho, Shibuya-ku. ✆ **03/5489-5111**. Station: Shibuya (Hachiko exit, 6 min.). Near the two Parco buildings.

JAPANESE CRAFTS & TRADITIONAL PRODUCTS

If you want to shop for traditional Japanese folk crafts in the right atmosphere, nothing beats **Nakamise Dori** (station: Akasaka), a pedestrian lane leading to Sensoji Temple in Asakusa. It's lined with stall after stall selling souvenirs galore, from wooden *geta* shoes (traditional wooden sandals) and hairpins worn by geisha to T-shirts, fans, umbrellas, toy swords, and dolls. Most stalls are open from 10am to 6pm; some close 1 day a week. The side streets surrounding Nakamise Dori, including Demboin Dori and a covered pedestrian lane stretching from both sides of Nakamise Dori, are also good bets.

Another good place to search for traditional crafts is **department stores,** which usually have sections devoted to ceramics, pottery, bambooware, flower-arranging accessories, kimono, and fabrics.

Ando   Opened in 1880, this two-story shop probably has Tokyo's largest selection of Japanese cloisonné, including jewelry, vases, and plates, with both traditional and strikingly modern designs. Open Monday to Friday 10am to 6:30pm; Saturday, Sunday and holidays 10:30am to 6:30pm. 5–6–2 Ginza, Chuo-ku. ✆ **03/3572-2261**. Station: Ginza (exit A1, 1 min.). On Harumi Dori, btw. Chuo Dori and Sotobori Dori.

㊿ **Bengara**   Noren are the doorway curtains hanging in front of Japanese restaurants, public bathhouses, and shops, signaling that the establishment is open. Bengara sells more than 400 different models of both traditional and modern noren of various sizes and colors, including those bearing kanji (Chinese characters) or scenes from famous woodblock prints. You can look through catalogs or have a noren custom-made with your own name. Open daily 10am to 6pm; closed the third Thursday of every month.

Blue & White   American Amy Katoh has been the driving force behind this small but unique 27-year-old shop specializing in Japanese modern and traditional crafts, including textiles, *yukata,* porcelain, candles, picture frames, notebooks, fans, and more, mostly in colors of indigo-dyed blue and white. Of note is the creative clothing made especially for this shop, and the crafts designed by artists with disabilities. Open Monday to Saturday 10am to 6pm, Sunday and holidays 11am to 6pm. 2–9–2 Azabu Juban, Minato-ku. ℭ **03/3451-0537.** Station: Azabu-Juban (exit 4, 3 min.) or Roppongi (exit 3, 12 min.).

(65) **Fujiya**   *Tenugui* are cotton hand towels used since the Edo Period for everything from drying off after bathing to headgear. In this small shop they're elevated to works of art, designed by a father-and-son team and featuring more than 200 traditional motifs, including Kabuki actors, festivals, masks, flowers, animals, and much more. Inexpensive gifts, they can be fashioned into scarves, framed as pictures, or used in countless other ways. Open Friday to Wednesday 10am to 6pm. 2–2–15 Asakusa, Taito-ku. ℭ **03/3841-2283.** Station: Asakusa (4 min.). East of Nakamise Dori, beside Hyakusuke (see below).

Hashi Ginza Natsuno   This shop is tiny, but so are the products it sells—chopsticks and chopstick holders, in all designs and colors. There are even chopsticks for children. The quality is high, so you can bet prices are high, too. Open Monday to Saturday 10am to 8pm, Sunday and holidays 10am to 7pm. 5–4–2 178 Jingumae, Shibuya-ku. ℭ **03/3403-6033.** Station: Omotesando (3 min.). Off Omotesando Dori; opposite the Hanae Mori Building, take the small side street (the one btw. McDonald's and Ito Hospital with a harajuku arch across it); it's down this street on the right. Look for the huge chopsticks outside.

(66) **Hyakusuke**   For traditional Japanese cosmetics *(kesho hin),* come to Hyakusuke, a 200-year-old, family-owned shop. During the Edo Period, it did a brisk trade in teeth blackener (white teeth were considered ugly), but today it offers rather mundane products, as well as such traditional treatments as *kombu to funori* (a seaweed hair treatment), *tsubaki* (camellia) oil for healthy hair, and—perhaps most interesting—*uguisu no hun,* nightingale droppings that are said to leave your skin soft and smooth. Simply mix it with a little soap to wash your face. A purchase of ¥1,000 will give you about a month of daily use. Makeup used by geisha and Kabuki actors is also sold here, attracting customers in these traditional professions, but I'm partial to face paper, used on humid days to blot away perspiration and grime. Open Wednesday to Monday from 11am to 5pm. 2–2–14 Asakusa, Taito-ku. ℭ **03/3841-7058.** Station: Asakusa (3 min.). Just east of Nakamise Dori; walking toward Sensoji Temple, turn right after the last shop on Nakamise, pass the two Buddha statues, and turn right again at Benten-do Temple; the shop is on your right, across from the playground.

Japan Sword   Coming here is like visiting a museum. Established more than 100 years ago, this is the best-known sword shop in Tokyo, with a knowledgeable staff and an outstanding collection of fine swords, daggers, sword guards, fittings, and other sword accessories, as well as antique samurai armor. The place also sells copies and souvenir items of traditional swords at prices much lower than those of the very expensive historic swords. Note that antique and modern swords require permission to export, which takes about 2 weeks (the company can ship purchases to you), but you can take replicas with you—just be sure to pack them in checked bags. Open Monday to Friday 9:30am to 6pm, Saturday 9:30am to 5pm. Closed holidays. 3–8–1 Toranomon, Minato-ku. ℭ **03/3434-4321.** www.japansword.co.jp. Station: Toranomon (exit 2, 5 min.) or Kamiyacho (exit 3, 5 min.).

Japan Traditional Craft Center (Zenkoku Dentoteki Kogeihin Senta) **Finds**
Established to distribute information on Japanese crafts and promote the country's artisans, this two-story center is a great introduction to both traditional and contemporary
Japanese design, with English-language explanations. It sells various top-quality crafts
from all over Japan on a rotating basis, so there are always new items on hand. Crafts for
sale usually include lacquerware, ceramics, textiles, paper products, bamboo items, calligraphy brushes, ink stones, fans, metalwork, knives, furniture, and sometimes even
stone lanterns or Buddhist family altars. Prices are high, but rightfully so. Unfortunately,
its location in out-of-the-way Ikebukuro makes a trip here feasible only if you have the
time; otherwise, you're probably better off shopping in the crafts section of a department
store. Open daily from 11am to 7pm. 1st floor of Metropolitan Plaza Building, 1–11–1 Nishi-
Ikebukuro. ✆ 03/5954-6066. Station: Ikebukuro (1 min.).

Kanesoh   Knives and scissors (including gardening scissors) have been sold from this
tiny shop since the 1870s, now in its fifth generation of knife makers. Open daily 11am
to 7pm. 1–18–12 Asakusa. ✆ 03/3844-1379. Station: Asakusa (2 min.). 1 block west of Nakamise
Dori; take the 1st left after passing under Kaminarimon Gate with its huge paper lantern.

67 **Kotobukiya**   This crowded shop specializes in vases and accessories for flower
arranging, of mostly contemporary designs. It also features objects used in tea ceremonies, including cast-iron teapots. Open Monday to Saturday 9:30am to 7pm; Sunday and
holidays 10am to 6:30pm. Closed the first and third Tuesday of each month. 3–18–17
Minami-Aoyama, Minato-ku. ✆ 03/3408-4187. Station: Omotesando (1 min.). On Aoyama Dori,
opposite Omotesando Dori.

Kurodaya   If you're visiting Asakusa, you might want to stop in at this shop. First
opened back in 1856, it sells traditional Japanese paper and paper products, including
kites, papier-mâché masks, boxes, and more. Open Tuesday to Sunday 11am to 7pm.
1–2–5 Asakusa, Taito-ku. ✆ 03/3844-7511. Station: Asakusa (1 min.). Next to Kaminarimon Gate,
to the east.

68 **Kuroeya**   This shop, with an improbable location on the second floor of an office
building near Nihombashi Bridge (the starting point of all main highways leading out of
Edo to the provinces during the feudal era), has been dealing in fine-quality lacquerware
since 1689, including items used in the tea ceremony and items used in everyday life such
as bowls, chopsticks, trays, stacked boxes, coasters, and plates. In recent years it has also
added wine coolers, walking sticks, handbags, jewelry, and other contemporary items to
its inventory. Open Monday to Friday 9am to 5pm. 1–2–6 Nihombashi, Chuo-ku.
✆ 03/3272-0948. Station: Nihombashi (exit B11, 1 min.) or Mitsukoshi-mae (exit B5, 3 min.). Near
Nihombashi Bridge, behind Kinko's (look for the lacquerware display case outside the front
door).

Kyoto-Kan   Dispensing tourist information about Kyoto, Kyoto-Kan also has a small
shop with traditional arts and crafts, including bamboo baskets, fans, Japanese sweets,
sake, pottery, paper products and other items. It also offers a 15-minute tea ceremony
experience Monday to Thursday from 12:30 to 4:30pm (reservations are necessary for
groups of more than five persons) for ¥500 per person, including traditional Japanese tea,
a seasonal sweet, and even the opportunity of trying your own hand at making tea. Open
daily 10:30am to 7:30pm. Closed last Wednesday of the month. 2–1–1 Yaesu, Chuo-ku.
✆ 03/5204-2265. Station: Tokyo (Yaesu Central Exit, 1 min.). Across from Tokyo Station.

(69) **Kyugetsu**   Asakusabashi is Tokyo's wholesale district for retailers of dolls, with several stores lining Edo Dori. This is one of the area's biggest stores, founded in 1830. It sells both modern and traditional dolls; its Japanese dolls range from elegant creatures with porcelain faces, delicate coiffures, and silk kimono, to wooden dolls called *kokeshi.* Hours are Monday to Friday 9:15am to 6pm, Saturday and Sunday 9:15am to 6pm. Closed several days following Children's Day and in mid-August. 1–20–4 Yanagibashi, Taito-ku. ☎ **03/5687-5176.** Station: Asakusabashi (1 min.). In front of the station.

Kyukyodo   Founded in 1633 in Kyoto, this Tokyo branch of the famous incense shop also sells stationery, cards, sheets of Japanese paper, calligraphy brushes, and paper products such as boxes and trays. Open Monday to Saturday 10am to 7:30pm, Sunday and holidays 11am to 7pm. 5–7–4 Ginza, Chuo-ku. ☎ **03/3571-4429.** Station: Ginza. Near Ginza 4–chome Crossing, on the right side of Chuo St. in the direction of Shimbashi.

Oriental Bazaar   If you have time for only one souvenir shop in Tokyo, this should be it. This is the city's best-known and largest souvenir/crafts store, selling products at reasonable prices and offering four floors of souvenir and gift items, including cotton yukata, kimono (new and used), woodblock prints, paper products, fans, chopsticks, Imari chinaware, sake sets, Japanese dolls, pearls, books on Japan, and a large selection of antique furniture. This store will also ship things home for you. Open Friday to Wednesday 10am to 7pm. 5–9–13 Jingumae, Shibuya-ku. ☎ **03/3400-3933.** Station: Meiji-Jingumae (3 min.), Harajuku (4 min.), or Omotesando (5 min.). On Omotesando Dori in Harajuku; look for an Asian-looking facade of orange and green.

(70) **Sukeroku** (**Finds**)   This tiny, truly unique shop sells handmade figures of traditional Japanese characters, from mythological figures to priests, farmers, entertainers, and animals. Included are people of the many castes of the Edo Period, ranging from peasants to feudal lords. Most figures are in the ¥3,000-to-¥5,000 price range, though some are much higher than that. Open daily 10am to 6pm. Nakamise Dori, Asakusa. ☎ **03/3844-0577.** Station: Asakusa (3 min.). It's the next-to-last shop on the right as you walk from Kaminarimon Gate toward Sensoji Temple.

Tsutaya   Tsutaya has everything you might need for *ikebana* (flower arranging) or the Japanese tea ceremony, including vases of unusual shapes and sizes, scissors, and tea whisks. Open daily 10am to 6:30pm. Closed the first, fourth, and fifth Sunday and last Saturday of each month. 5–10–5 Minami-Aoyama, Minato-ku. ☎ **03/3400-3815.** Station: Omotesando (2 min.). On Kotto Dori, near the Kua' Aina hamburger joint.

(71) **Yamamoto Soroban Ten**   When I first came to Japan more than 25 years ago, I often saw older Japanese using an abacus in a shop or restaurant. No longer. Although this shop has been in business for over 65 years and is now in its third generation of owners, I wonder how long it will survive in the world of computers and calculators (only two Japanese towns still produce the abacus, and Japanese children no longer learn how to use them in school). The founder's granddaughter speaks English and will explain how an abacus works. Open Friday to Wednesday 10am to 5pm (holidays 11am–6pm). Closed the third Wednesday of every month. 2–35–12 Asakusa, Taito-ku. ☎ **03/3841-7503.** Station: Asakusa (5 min.). 1 block east of Sensoji Temple's main building, on Umamichi Dori (also spelled Umamiti); look for the giant abacus outside the front door.

Yonoya   This unique shop sells its own handmade boxwood combs, crafted by a seventh-generation comb maker. Its history stretches back 300 years, to a time when women's hairstyles were elaborate and complicated, as many woodblock prints testify.

Today such handcrafted combs are a dying art. The combs here range in price from about ¥2,500 to more than ¥25,000; hair ornaments are also sold. Open Thursday to Tuesday from 10:30am to 6:30pm. 1–37–10 Asakusa, Taito-ku. ✆ 03/3844-1755. Station: Asakusa (3 min.). On Demboin Dori (also spelled Dempoin Dori), just off Nakamise Dori.

72 **Yoshitoku** Yoshitoku has had a shop at this location since 1711, making it Tokyo's oldest wholesale doll and traditional crafts store. It carries a variety of Japanese dolls on its first floor, most traditionally dressed as samurai, geisha, Kabuki actors, sumo wrestlers, and other Japanese personalities. There are also fine—and expensive—dolls representing the Imperial court, dressed in silk kimono that follow the originals down to the minutest detail. Obviously, these dolls are meant not for children's play but for display by collectors. Upstairs are more mundane modern dolls, including stuffed animals. Open daily 9:30am to 5:30pm. Closed Sunday and holidays May 5 to November. 1–9–14 Asakusabashi, Taito-ku. ✆ 03/3863-4419. Station: Asakusabashi (1 min.).

KIMONO

The **Oriental Bazaar** (see "Japanese Crafts & Traditional Products," above) sells new and used kimono, including elaborate wedding kimono. Department stores also sell kimono, notably **Takashimaya** and **Mitsukoshi** in Nihombashi and **Isetan** in Shinjuku. They also have yearly sales of used, rental wedding kimono. Flea markets are another good option for used kimono and yukata, particularly the antiques market at **Togo Shrine** (discussed earlier). There's also a secondhand **kimono stand in Harajuku** open for business every Saturday, Sunday, and holiday from 11am to 5pm on the corner of Meiji Dori and Omotesando Dori. Prices start at ¥500, making them affordable even as gifts for friends.

Chicago This basement shop specializes in used American clothing, but also stocks hundreds of affordable used kimono (including wedding kimono), cotton yukata (for sleeping), and obi (the sash worn around a kimono), all located in its Kimono Corner in the very back left corner of the shop. Open daily 11am to 8pm. 6–31–21 Jingumae, Shibuya-ku. ✆ 03/3409-5017. Station: Meiji-Jingumae (1 min.) or Harajuku (2 min.). On Omotesando Dori, btw. Meiji Dori and Harajuku Station.

Gallery Kawano Antique kimono, obi, and high-quality fabrics are for sale at this small shop, including those that are hand-painted and beautifully embroidered. Open daily 11am to 6pm. 4–4–9 Jingumae, Shibuya-ku. ✆ 03/3470-3305. Station: Omotesandoumae (4 min.). Off Omotesando Dori; opposite the Hanae Mori Building. Take the side street (btw. McDonald's and Ito Hospital, with a harajuku arch over it), turn left at Royal Host restaurant, and then right; it will be on your right.

Hayashi Kimono Established in 1913, Hayashi sells all kinds of kimono, including wedding kimono, cotton yukata, and *tanzen* (the heavy winter overcoat that goes over the yukata), as well as used and antique kimono. If you're buying a gift for someone back home, this is a good place to start. Open Monday to Saturday 10am to 7pm, Sunday 10am to 6pm. In the International Arcade (underneath the JR Yamanote Line's elevated tracks), 2–1–1 Yurakucho, Chiyoda-ku. ✆ 03/3501-4012. Station: Yurakucho (2 min.). Near the Imperial Hotel.

73 **Tatsumi** This small shop in Asakusa sells antique and used kimono and obi at reasonable prices. Open daily 10:30am to 7pm. 1–39–11 Asakusa, Taito-ku. ✆ 03/3843-7606. Station: Asakusa (4 min). On the corner of Demboin Dori and Orange St.

In addition to the department stores and housewares and interior-design shops listed earlier, the best place to shop for items related to cooking and serving is **Kappabashi-dougugai Dori** (station: Tawaramachi), popularly known as Kappabashi and Japan's largest wholesale area for cookware. Approximately 150 specialty stores here sell cookware and everything else restaurants need, including sukiyaki pots, woks, lunchboxes, pots and pans, aprons, knives, china, lacquerware, rice cookers, plastic food (the kind you see in restaurant display cases), noren (Japanese curtains) and disposable wooden chopsticks in bulk. Although the stores are wholesalers selling mainly to restaurants, you're welcome to browse and purchase as well. Stores are closed on Sunday but otherwise open from about 10am to 5pm.

MUSIC

HMV HMV offers five floors of music, from Japanese pop, soul, reggae, rock, and New Age, to jazz, classical, and opera, with listening stages so that you can hear before you buy. Open daily 10am to 11pm. 24–1 Udagawacho, Shibuya-ku. © **03/5458-3411.** Station: Shibuya (Hachiko exit, 3 min.). On the street btw. the two Seibu stores.

Tower Records and Books From classical to new releases to Japanese pop and J-Indie to games to CD-ROMs, it's all here, on six floors. On the seventh floor are imported books and magazines. Open daily 10am to 11pm. Closed some Mondays. 1–22–14 Jinnan, Shibuya-ku. © **03/3496-3661.** Station: Shibuya (Hachiko exit, 5 min.).

PEARLS

Mikimoto, on Chuo Dori not far from Ginza 4–chome Crossing, past Wako department store (© **03/3535-4611**), is Japan's most famous pearl shop. It was founded by Mikimoto Koichi, who in 1905 produced the world's first good cultured pearl. Open Thursday to Tuesday 11am to 7pm. Otherwise, there's a Mikimoto branch (© **03/3591-5001**) in the Imperial Hotel Arcade of the Imperial Hotel (station: Hibiya), where you'll also find **Asahi Shoten** (© **03/3503-2528**), with a good selection in the modest-to-moderate price range; and **Uyeda Jeweller** (© **03/3503-2587**), with a wide selection of pearls in many different price ranges.

TOYS

Hakuhinkan Toy Park This is one of Tokyo's largest and best toy stores, with four floors. In addition to the usual dolls, puzzles, stuffed animals, games, and other items, there's a games arcade on the fourth floor. Open daily 11am to 8pm. 8–8–11 Ginza, Chuo-ku. © **03/3571-8008.** Station: Shimbashi or Ginza (4 min.). On Chuo Dori, near the overhead expressway.

Kiddy Land Toys, games, puzzles, dolls, action figures, and much more are packed into this immensely popular shop, usually so crowded with teenagers that it's impossible to get in the front door. It also has a large selection of gag gifts, including temporary tattoos and who knows what else. Open Monday to Friday 10:30am to 9pm; Saturday, Sunday, and holidays 10am to 9pm. Closed the third Tuesday of some months. 6–1–9 Jingumae. © **03/3409-3431.** www.kiddyland.co.jp. Station: Meiji-Jingumae (2 min.) or Harajuku or Omotesando (5 min.). On Omotesando Dori in Harajuku, near Oriental Bazaar.

Tokyo After Dark

By day, Tokyo is arguably one of the least attractive cities in the world. Come dusk, however, the drabness fades and the city blossoms into a profusion of giant neon lights and paper lanterns, and its streets fill with millions of overworked Japanese out to have a good time. If you ask me, Tokyo at night is one of the craziest cities in the world, a city that never seems to sleep. Entertainment districts are as crowded at 3am as they are at 10pm, and many places stay open until the subways start running after 5am. Whether it's jazz, reggae, gay bars, sex shows, dance clubs, mania, or madness you're searching for, Tokyo has them all.

GETTING TO KNOW THE SCENE
Tokyo has no one center of nighttime activity. There are many nightspots spread throughout the city, each with its own atmosphere, price range, and clientele. Most famous are probably **Ginza, Kabuki-cho** in Shinjuku, and **Roppongi.** Before visiting any of the locales listed in this chapter, be sure to walk around the neighborhoods and absorb the atmosphere. The streets will be crowded, the neon lights will be overwhelming, and you never know what you might discover on your own.

Although there are many bars, discos, and clubs packed with young Japanese of both sexes, nightlife in Japan for the older generations is still pretty much a man's domain, just as it has been for centuries. At the high end of this domain are the **geisha bars,** where highly trained women entertain by playing traditional Japanese instruments, singing, and holding witty conversations—and nothing more risqué than that. Such places are located mainly

in Kyoto and, generally speaking, are both outrageously expensive and closed to outsiders. As a foreigner, you'll have little opportunity to visit a geisha bar unless you're invited by a business associate.

All Japanese cities, however, have so-called **hostess bars;** in Tokyo, these are concentrated in Ginza, Roppongi, Shinjuku, and Akasaka. Hostess bars in various forms have been a part of Japanese society for centuries. A woman will sit at your table, talk to you, pour your drinks, listen to your problems, and boost your ego. You buy her drinks as well, which is one reason the tab can be so high. Most of you will probably find the visit to one not worth the price, as the hostesses usually speak Japanese only, but such places provide Japanese males with sympathetic ears and the chance to escape the worlds of both work and family. Men usually have a favorite hostess bar, often a small place with just enough room for regular customers. The more exclusive hostess bars welcome only those with an introduction.

The most popular nightlife spots are **drinking establishments,** where most office workers, students, and expatriates go for an evening out. These places include Western-style bars, most commonly found in Roppongi, as well as Japanese-style watering holes, called *nomi-ya. Yakitori-ya,* bars that serve yakitori and other snacks, are included in this group. Dancing and live-music venues are also hugely popular with young Tokyoites. At the low end of the spectrum are topless bars, erotic dance clubs (including those that employ Western dancers), sex shows, and massage parlors, with the largest concentration of such places in Shinjuku's Kabuki-cho district.

Impressions

Then I saw for the first time the true beauty of Tokyo, and of all Japanese cities. They are only beautiful at night, when they become fairylands of gorgeous neon: towers and sheets and globes and rivers of neon, in stunning profusion, a wild razzle-dazzle of colors and shapes and movements, fierce and delicate, restrained and violent against the final afterglow of sunset.

—James Kirkup, *These Horned Islands* (1962)

In addition to the establishments listed in this chapter, be sure to check the restaurants listed in the inexpensive category in chapter 6, for a relatively cheap night out on the town. Many places serve as both eateries and watering holes, especially yakitori-ya.

EXTRA CHARGES & TAXES One more thing you should be aware of is the "table charge" imposed on customers by some bars (especially *nomiya*) and many cocktail lounges. Included in the table charge is usually a small appetizer—maybe nuts, chips, or a vegetable; for this reason, some locales call it an *otsumami,* or snack charge. At any rate, the charge is usually between ¥300 and ¥500 per person. Some establishments levy a table charge only after a certain time in the evening; others may add it only if you don't order food from the menu. If you're not sure and it matters to you, be sure to ask before you order anything. Remember, too, that there's a 5% consumption tax, though most menus already include it in their prices. Some higher-end establishments, especially nightclubs, hostess bars, and dance clubs, will add a service charge ranging anywhere from 10% to 20%.

FINDING OUT WHAT'S ON Keep an eye out for *Metropolis* (http://metropolis. co.jp), a free weekly that carries a nightlife section covering concerts, theaters, and events and is available at bars, restaurants, and other venues around town. The *Japan Times* and *Daily Yomiuri* also have entertainment sections.

GETTING TICKETS If you're staying in a higher-end hotel, the concierge or guest-relations manager can usually get tickets for you. Otherwise, you can head to the theater or hall itself. An easier way is to go through one of many ticket services available such as **Ticket PIA,** which has outlets on the first floor of the Sony Building in the Ginza, the Isetan department store annex in Shinjuku, and many other locations in Tokyo; ask your hotel concierge for the one nearest you.

TOKYO AFTER DARK

10

THE PERFORMING ARTS

1 THE PERFORMING ARTS

In addition to the listings below, Tokyo has occasional shows of more avant-garde or lesser-known performing arts, including highly stylized Butoh dance performances by companies such as Sankai Juku, and percussion demonstrations by Kodo drummers and other Japanese drum groups. The publications listed above have complete listings.

TRADITIONAL PERFORMING ARTS

KABUKI Probably Japan's best-known traditional theater art, Kabuki is also one of the country's most popular forms of entertainment. Visit a performance and it's easy to see why—Kabuki is fun! The plays are dramatic, the costumes are gorgeous, the stage settings can be fantastic, and the themes are universal—love, revenge, and the conflict between duty and personal feelings. One probable reason for Kabuki's popularity is that it originated centuries ago as a form of entertainment for the common people in feudal Japan, particularly the merchant class. One of Kabuki's interesting aspects is that all roles—even those depicting women—are portrayed by men.

There are more than 300 Kabuki plays, all written before the 20th century. For a Westerner, one of the more arresting things about a Kabuki performance is the audience. Because this has always been entertainment for the masses, the spectators can get quite lively, adding yells of approval, guffaws, and laughter. Also contributing to the festive atmosphere are the obento lunches and drinks available during intermission.

One of Japan's most prestigious theaters for Kabuki is **Kabuki-za,** 4–12–15 Ginza, which unfortunately closed for demolition in April 2010, with an expected resurrection in a new building in 2013. Although I lament the destruction of the handsome older structure, which boasted a Momoyama-style facade influenced by 16th-century castle architecture, the new theater will undoubtedly incorporate the usual Kabuki stage fittings, including a platform that can be raised above and lowered below the stage for dramatic appearances and disappearances of actors, a revolving stage, and a runway stage extending into the audience.

In any case, until the Kabuki-za's reopening, kabuki performances will be held at the nearby **Shinbashi Enbujo Theater,** 6–18–2 Ginza (© **03/3541-2600,** or 03/5565-6000 for advance reservations; www.shochiku.co.jp/play/kabukiza/theater; station: Higashi-Ginza), as well as other venues in town. Shochiku, a major film and production company that also serves as Tokyo's chief Kabuki production company, stages about eight or nine Kabuki productions a year. Each production begins its run between the first and third of each month and runs about 25 days (there are no shows in Aug). Usually, two different programs are shown; matinees run from about 11 or 11:30am to 4pm, and evening performances run from about 4:30 or 5pm to about 9pm. It's considered perfectly okay to come for only part of a performance. Of course, you won't be able to understand what's being said, but that doesn't matter; the productions themselves are great entertainment. For an outline of the plot, you should rent **English-language earphones** for ¥650, plus a ¥1,000 refundable deposit—these provide a running commentary on the story, music, actors, stage properties, and other aspects of Kabuki. Renting earphones will add immensely to your enjoyment of the play.

Tickets generally range from ¥2,500 to ¥17,000, depending on the program and seat location. Advance tickets can be purchased at the theater box office from 10am to 6pm. You may also make advance reservations by phone (same-day bookings are not accepted). Otherwise, tickets for each day's performance are placed on sale 1 hour before the start of each performance.

Another venue for Kabuki is the **National Theatre of Japan (Kokuritsu Gekijo),** 4–1 Hayabusacho, Chiyoda-ku (© **03/3230-3000;** www.ntj.jac.go.jp; station: Hanzomon, 6 min.). Kabuki is scheduled throughout the year except during February, May, August, and September, when Bunraku (see below) is staged. Matinees usually begin at 11:30am or noon, and afternoon performances at 4:30pm. Most tickets range from about ¥1,500 to ¥8,500, with earphones available for ¥700 plus a ¥1,000 deposit. Tickets can be purchased at the box office (daily 10am to 6pm), by phone, or online.

NOH   Whereas Kabuki developed as a form of entertainment for the masses, Noh was a much more traditional and aristocratic form of theater. During the Edo Period (1603–1867), Noh became the favorite performance art of military rulers; indeed, many feudal lords not only maintained their own Noh stage and troupe but also performed Noh themselves.

In contrast to Kabuki's extroverted liveliness, Noh is very calculated and restrained. The oldest form of theater in Japan, it has changed very little in the past 600 years. Altogether there are about 250 Noh plays, almost all of them created before 1600 and often concerned with supernatural beings, Shinto gods, beautiful women, warriors, mentally confused and tormented people, or tragic-heroic epics. The language is so archaic that today the Japanese cannot understand it at all, which explains in part why Noh does not have the popularity that Kabuki does. Central to Noh are elaborate costumes, masks, and musicians who chant and play the drums and flute.

Because the action is slow, sitting through an entire performance can be tedious unless you are particularly interested in Noh dance and music. In addition, most Noh plays do not have English-language translations. You may want to drop in for just a short while. Definitely worth seeing, however, are the short comic reliefs, called *kyogen,* that make fun of life in the 1600s and are performed between Noh dramas.

Noh is performed at a number of locations in Tokyo, but most famous is the **National Noh Theater (Kokuritsu Nohgakudo),** 4–18–1 Sendagaya, Shibuya-ku (© **03/3423-1331,** or 03/3230-3000 for reservations; www.ntj.jac.go.jp; station: Sendagaya, 5 min.). Opened in 1983, it is dedicated to presenting classical Noh and kyogen, with about three to five performances monthly. Tickets range from about ¥2,600 to ¥4,800 but are often sold out in advance. However, about 30 tickets are held back to be sold on the day of the performance. In addition, privately sponsored Noh performances are also held here, for which the admission varies. Check the *Japan Times* or *Daily Yomiuri* for performance dates and times, or go to www.theatrenohgaku.org/index_e.php for information on Noh performances being staged throughout Japan.

BUNRAKU   Bunraku is traditional Japanese puppet theater, but contrary to what you might expect, the dramas are for adults, with themes centering on love, revenge, sacrifice, and suicide. Popular in Japan since the 17th century, Bunraku is fascinating to watch because the puppeteers, dressed in black, are right on stage with their puppets. They're wonderfully skilled at making the puppets seem like living beings. It usually takes three puppeteers to work one puppet, which is about three-quarters human size. A narrator recites the story and speaks all the parts, accompanied by the *shamisen,* a traditional three-stringed Japanese instrument.

Although the main Bunraku theater in Japan is in Osaka, the **National Theatre of Japan** (see above for information) stages about four Bunraku plays a year (in Feb, May, Aug, and Sept). There are usually two to three performances daily, beginning at 11am, with tickets costing ¥1,500 to ¥6,500. Earphones with English-language explanations are available for ¥550, plus a ¥1,000 deposit.

CONTEMPORARY PERFORMING ARTS

WESTERN CLASSICAL MUSIC   Among the best-known orchestras in Tokyo are the Tokyo Philharmonic Orchestra (© **03/5353-9521;** www.tpo.or.jp), the largest orchestra in Japan and with the longest history; Japan Philharmonic Orchestra

(☎ 03/5378-5911; www.japanphil.or.jp); Tokyo Symphony Orchestra (☎ 044/520-1511; www.tokyosymphony.com); and NHK Symphony Orchestra (☎ 03/3465-1780; www.nhkso.or.jp). They play in various theaters throughout Tokyo, with the majority of performances in Suntory Hall in Akasaka, Bunkamura Orchard Hall in Shibuya, NHK Hall in Shibuya, Tokyo Opera City in Shinjuku, or the Tokyo Geijutsu Gekijo in Ikebukuro. Because the schedule varies, it's best to contact the orchestra directly or check the *Japan Times* or *Daily Yomiuri* to find out whether there's a current performance. Tickets generally start at ¥3,000 or ¥4,000.

TAKARAZUKA KAGEKIDAN This world-famous, all-female troupe stages elaborate musical revues with dancing, singing, and gorgeous costumes. Performances range from Japanese versions of Broadway hits to original Japanese works based on local legends. The first Takarazuka troupe, formed in 1912 at a resort near Osaka, gained instant notoriety because all its performers were women, in contrast to the all-male Kabuki. When I went to see this troupe perform, I was surprised to find that the audience also consisted almost exclusively of women; indeed, the troupe has an almost cultlike following.

Performances, with story synopses available in English, are generally held in March, April, July, August, November, December, and sometimes in June, at **Tokyo Takarazuka Gekijo,** 1–1–3 Yurakucho (☎ 03/5251-2001; www.kageki.hankyu.co.jp/english; station: Hibiya, 1 min.). Tickets, available at the box office or through **Ticket Pia** (with many locations around town), usually range about ¥3,500 to ¥11,000.

SHOW NIGHTCLUBS ★ For unique, casual entertainment, nothing beats an evening at an entertainment nightclub, featuring fast-paced dancing in intimate venues. Although the emcee may speak Japanese only, no translation is necessary for the stage productions, which may center on easy-to-understand themes or include humorous antics. One of the oldest show nightclubs is **Kingyo,** 3–14–17 Roppongi (☎ 03/3478-3000; www.kingyo.co.jp; station: Roppongi, 4 min.), which stages one of the most high-energy, visually charged acts I've ever seen—nonstop action of ascending and receding stages and stairs, fast-paced choreography, elaborate costumes, and loud music. There are a few female dancers, but most of the dancers are males assuming female parts, just like in Kabuki. In fact, many of the performances center on traditional Japanese themes with traditional dress and kimono, but the shows take place in a technically sophisticated setting. There are also satires: One past performance included a piece on Microsoft vs. Apple; another featured aliens from outer space—great fun. It's located in the Roppongi nightlife district near the Roppongi Cemetery. (From Roppongi Crossing, walk toward Tokyo Tower on Gaien-Higashi Dori and take the second left; it's on the right.) Cover is ¥3,500 for shows at 7:30 and 10pm, with additional shows Friday and Saturday at 1:15am (closed Sun and Mon; reservations recommended). You are also required to purchase one drink and one food item, and there's a 20% tax and service charge. Or you can opt for admission packages that include a set meal and drinks beginning at ¥6,000.

I also like **Show Dining Konparuza,** 8–7–5 Ginza (☎ 03/6215-8593; station: Ginza or Shimbashi, 5 min.), also with moving stages and with lively choreography by Makato-san, who also performs. Productions change twice a year, but there's always a traditional number with dancers dressed in kimono, along with performances that act out popular songs or movies. Doors open daily at 6pm, with the first show at 7:30pm. Cover charge is ¥3,000, plus a minimum of one drink and one food purchase. Alternatively, there's an all-you-can-drink set that includes three dishes and the cover charge for ¥5,800.

2 THE CLUB & MUSIC SCENE

THE MAJOR ENTERTAINMENT DISTRICTS

GINZA A chic and expensive shopping area by day, Ginza transforms itself into a dazzling entertainment district of restaurants, bars, and first-grade hostess bars at night. It's the most sophisticated of Tokyo's nightlife districts and also one of the most expensive. Some of the Japanese businessmen you see carousing in Ginza are paying by expense account; prices can be ridiculously high.

Because I'm not wealthy, I prefer Shinjuku, Shibuya, and Roppongi. However, because Ginza does have some fabulous restaurants and several hotels, I've included reasonably priced recommendations for a drink in the area if you happen to find yourself here after dinner. The cheapest way to absorb the atmosphere in Ginza is to wander through it, particularly around Namiki Dori, Suzuran Dori, and their side streets. The "Nightlife & Where to Stay & Dine in Ginza & Hibiya" map on p. 92 will help you locate the Ginza clubs and bars mentioned in this chapter.

SHINJUKU Northeast of Shinjuku Station is an area called **Kabuki-cho,** which undoubtedly has the craziest nightlife in all of Tokyo, with block after block of strip joints, massage parlors, pornography shops, host and hostess clubs, peep shows, love hotels, bars, restaurants, and, as the night wears on, drunk revelers. A world of its own, it's sleazy, chaotic, crowded, vibrant, and fairly safe. Despite its name, Shinjuku's primary night hot spot has nothing to do with Kabuki, though at one time there was a plan to bring culture to the area by introducing a Kabuki theater. The plan never materialized, but the name stuck. Although Kabuki-cho was traditionally the domain of salarymen out on the town, nowadays young Japanese, including college-age men and women, have claimed parts of it as their own; the result is a growing number of inexpensive drinking and live-music venues well worth a visit. The "Nightlife & Where to Stay & Dine in Shinjuku" map on p. 94 will help you locate the area's clubs and bars mentioned in this chapter.

To the east of Kabuki-cho, just west of Hanazono Shrine, is a smaller district called **Goruden Gai,** which is "Golden Guy" mispronounced. Originally a black market and prostitution district after World War II, today it's a warren of five tiny alleyways leading past even tinier bars, each consisting of just a counter and a few chairs. Many of these closet-size bars are closed to outsiders, catering to regular customers, though a growing number of them welcome strangers as well. Although many thought Goruden Gai would succumb to land-hungry developers in the 1980s, the economic recession brought a stay of execution. In fact, in recent years Goruden Gai has experienced a revival, with more than 100 tiny drinking dens lining the tiny streets and attracting artists, musicians, filmmakers, writers, and students. Still, it occupies such expensive land that I fear for this tiny enclave, one of Tokyo's most fascinating.

Even farther east is **Shinjuku 2–chome** (called Ni–chome; pronounced "knee-cho-may"), officially recognized as the gay-bar district of Tokyo. Its lively street scene of mostly gays and some straights of all ages (but mostly young) make this one of Tokyo's most vibrant nightlife districts. It's here that I was once taken to a host bar featuring young hosts in crotchless pants. The clientele included both gay men and groups of young, giggling office girls. That place has since closed down, but Shinjuku is riddled with other spots bordering on the absurd.

The best thing to do in Shinjuku is simply wander. In the glow of neon light, you'll pass everything from smoke-filled restaurants to touts trying to get you to step inside so they can part you from your money. If you're looking for strip joints, topless or bottomless coffee shops, peep shows, porn, or prostitutes, I leave you to your own devices, but you certainly won't have any problems finding them. Be careful, however, of hidden charges, such as exorbitant drink prices, or you may end up spending more than you bargained for.

A word of **warning** for women traveling alone: Forgo the experience of strolling around Kabuki-cho. The streets are crowded and therefore relatively safe, but you may not feel comfortable with so many inebriated men stumbling around. If there are two of you, however, go for it. I took my mother to Kabuki-cho for a spin around the neon, and we escaped relatively unscathed. You're also fine walking alone to any of my recommended restaurants.

ROPPONGI To Tokyo's younger crowd, Roppongi is the city's most fashionable place to hang out. It's also a favorite with the foreign community, including models, business types, English teachers, and tourists staying in Roppongi's posh hotels. Roppongi has more than its fair share of live-music houses, restaurants, discos, expatriate bars, and pubs. Some Tokyoites complain that Roppongi is too crowded, too crass, and too commercialized (and has too many foreigners). However, for the casual visitor, Roppongi offers an excellent opportunity to see what's new and hot in the capital city and is easy to navigate because nightlife activity is so concentrated. There is one huge **caveat,** however: Roppongi's concentration of foreigners has also attracted the unscrupulous, with reports of spiked drinks causing patrons to pass out, only to awaken hours later to find their credit cards missing or fraudulently charged for huge amounts. In other words, never leave your drinks unattended, and you're best off following the buddy system.

The center of Roppongi is **Roppongi Crossing** (the intersection of Roppongi Dori and Gaien-Higashi Dori), at the corner of which sits the Almond Coffee Shop (under renovation until Dec 2010). The shop has mediocre coffee and desserts at inflated prices, but the sidewalk in front is the number-one meeting spot in Roppongi.

If you need directions, there's a conveniently located *koban* (police box) catty-corner from the Almond Coffee Shop and next to a bank. It has a big outdoor map of the Roppongi area showing the address system, and someone is always there to help. The "Nightlife & Where to Stay & Dine in Roppongi" map on p. 159 will help you locate the Roppongi clubs and bars mentioned in this chapter.

If the buzz of Roppongi is too much, a quieter, saner alternative is neighboring **Nishi Azabu,** which has restaurants and bars catering to Japanese and foreigners alike. The center of Nishi Azabu is the next big crossroads, Nishi-Azabu Crossing (the intersection of Roppongi Dori and Gaien-Nishi Dori). Nishi Azabu is about a 10-minute walk from Roppongi Station, past Roppongi Hills in the direction of Shibuya. **Roppongi Hills** is a massive urban development with many restaurants and some bars of its own, while the newest kid on the block, **Tokyo Midtown,** has brought gentrification—and an influx of affluent customers—to Roppongi's nightlife.

OTHER HOT SPOTS Not quite as sophisticated as Ginza or nearly as popular as Roppongi, **Akasaka** nonetheless has its share of hostess bars, both Western and Japanese-style pubs, restaurants, and inexpensive holes-in-the-wall. Popular with executive tycoons and ordinary office workers, as well as foreigners staying in one of Akasaka's many hotels, this district stretches from the Akasaka-mitsuke subway station along three narrow streets, called Hitotsugi, Misuji, and Tamachi, all the way to the Akasaka Station. There are also many Korean restaurants in Akasaka, earning it the nickname "Little Korea." For orientation purposes, stop by the koban (police box) at the huge intersection of Aoyama Dori and Sotobori Dori at Akasaka-mitsuke Station. The "Nightlife & Where to Stay & Dine in Akasaka" map on p. 103 will help you locate the Akasaka spots mentioned in this chapter.

One of the most popular districts for young Japanese by day, **Harajuku** doesn't have much of a nightlife district because of city zoning laws. A few places scattered through the area, however, are good alternatives if you don't like the crowds or the commercialism of Tokyo's more famous nightlife districts. There are also a fair number of sidewalk cafes open late into the night.

Shibuya's **Shibuya Center Gai,** a pedestrian lane just a minute's walk from the Hachiko exit of Shibuya Station (look for the pedestrian lane with the steel arch), is popular with young Japanese for its whirl of inexpensive restaurants, open-fronted shops, bars, fast-food joints, and pachinko parlors. **Ebisu** also has a few very popular expatriate bars.

LIVE MUSIC

The live-music scene exploded in the 1990s and now spreads throughout Tokyo. In addition to the dedicated venues below, several bars offer live music many nights of the week, including Warrior Celt, What the Dickens!, Dubliners' Irish Pub in Shibuya, Vagabond, and Bar Bourbon Street (see "The Bar Scene," below).

Bauhaus   Since 1981, this small club has had the same great house band that plays mostly 1970s and 1980s British and American hard rock, including the music of Led Zeppelin, Queen, Jimi Hendrix, The Who, Aerosmith, The Eagles, Van Halen, Santana, Red Hot Chili Peppers, and others, with music beginning around 8pm. The band puts on quite a show—a bit raunchy at times but very polished. Open Monday to Saturday 7pm to 1am. Closed holidays. Reine Roppongi, 2nd floor, 5–3–4 Roppongi. ✆ 03/3403-0092. Cover ¥2,835. Station: Roppongi (3 min.). From Roppongi Crossing, walk toward Tokyo Tower on Gaien-Higashi Dori and turn right at McDonald's. It's ahead to the right of the parking lot.

Birdland   Open since the 1970s and moving from Roppongi to Akasaka in 2007, this music club used to feature primarily jazz but in the past few years has morphed into the city's number-one spot for Hawaiian music, offered 2 to 3 nights a week in addition to jazz. Yes, you read that right, and if you don't mind the cafeterialike atmosphere, hefty cover charge, and older, appreciative crowd, you might find this place camp enough to qualify as interesting, if not unique. Check Birdland's website for the music schedule. Open Monday to Saturday 6pm to 11pm (music begins at 7pm). Akasaka KT Building, 5th floor, 3–16–7 Akasaka. ✆ 03/3583-3546. www.birdland-tokyo.jp. Cover ¥3,600, plus ¥900 drink minimum and 10% service charge. Station: Akasaka (2 min.) or Akasaka-mitsuke (5 min). On Hitosuji Dori, across from a shrine.

Blue Note   Tokyo's most expensive, elegant jazz venue is cousin to the famous Blue Note in New York. The musicians are top-notch; Sarah Vaughan, Tony Bennett, Chick Corea, David Sanborn, Roberta Flack, the Milt Jackson Quartet, and Tower of Power have all performed here. However, the 300-seat establishment follows the frustrating Japanese practice of selling tickets good for only one set. There are usually two sets nightly, generally at 7 and 9:30pm Monday to Saturday and 6:30 and 9pm Sunday and holidays. 6–3–16 Minami Aoyama. ✆ 03/5485-0088. www.bluenote.co.jp. Cover ¥7,350–¥8,400 for most performances, more for top names. Station: Omotesando (8 min.). Off Kotto Dori.

Body & Soul Since 1974, this low-ceilinged, tiny but cozy basement club with only a few tables and a long bar gives everyone a good view of its mostly jazz performances by Japanese and foreign musicians. Hours are Monday to Saturday 7pm to midnight, with performances at 8:30 and 10:20pm. 6-13-9 Minami Aoyama. ℂ 03/5466-3348. www.bodyand soul.co.jp. Cover ¥3,500–¥4,000 for most sets; ¥5,000 and up for 2 sets. Station: Omotesando (7 min.). On the other side of Roppongi Dori across from Eneos gas station, down a side street and to the left.

Cavern Club If you know your Beatles history, you'll know Cavern is the name of the Liverpool club where the Fab Four got their start. The Tokyo club features Beatles memorabilia and house bands performing Beatles music exclusively—and very convincingly at that. Extremely popular with Japanese and foreigners alike, it's packed on weekends—expect long lines, or call to reserve a table. Hours are Monday to Saturday 6pm to 2:30am (music begins at 7:30pm), Sunday and holidays 6pm to midnight. 5-3-2 Roppongi. ℂ 03/3405-5207. Cover ¥1,890 for men, ¥1,575 for women, plus a 1-drink minimum and 10% service charge. Station: Roppongi (4 min.). Take the side street going downhill on the left side of Almond Coffee Shop, and then take the 1st left; the club will be on the right.

Cotton Club This cool venue is the best proof yet that Marunouchi, which already boasts new skyscrapers, hotels, and designer shops, is on its way to becoming an urban destination. Taking its name from Harlem's legendary establishment and attracting well-heeled business types, this sophisticated supper club, ensconced on the second floor of an office building, offers a wide range of musical entertainment, from traditional and fusion jazz to salsa and modern Hawaiian music, performed by trios, quartets, bands, solo guitarists, and vocalists. Past performers include Rickie Lee Jones, Rita Coolidge, and the Duke Ellington Orchestra. There are usually two seatings, at 7 and 9:30pm (5 and 8pm Sun and holidays). 2-7-3 Marunouchi. ℂ 03/3215-1555. www.cottonclubjapan.co. jp. Cover ¥5,000–¥8,400 for most performances. Station: Tokyo (Marunouchi south exit, 2 min.). Behind (south of) the Central Post Office.

Crocodile Popular with a young Japanese crowd, the eclectic Crocodile describes itself as a casual rock-'n'-roll club, with live bands ranging from rock and blues to jazz-fusion, reggae, soul, experimental, and even country and Hawaiian. It's a good place to check out new Japanese bands; on the fourth Friday of the month, the Tokyo Comedy Store (www.tokyocomedy.com) provides more than 2 hours of live stand-up and improv comedy in English. The club has an interesting interior and a good, laid-back atmosphere. Open daily 6pm to 2am; performances start around 8pm. 6-18-8 Jingumae. ℂ 03/3499-5205. www.crocodile-live.jp. Cover ¥2,000–¥3,000, occasionally more for big acts. Station: Meiji-Jingumae or Shibuya (10 min.). On Meiji Dori halfway btw. Harajuku and Shibuya.

JZ Brat This hotel club promotes both domestic and international jazz performers, including many vocalists, in a breezy setting reminiscent of the '60s. Open Monday to Saturday 5:30 to 11pm. Sometimes closed for private events (call first). Music starts at 7:30pm. Cerulean Tower Tokyu Hotel, 26-1 Sakurgaoka-cho. ℂ 03/5728-0168. www.jzbrat.com. Cover ¥4,200–¥5,250 for most bands. Station: Shibuya (5 min.).

Kento's Kento's was one of the first places to open when the wave of 1950s nostalgia hit Japan in the 1980s; it has even been credited with creating the craze. This is the place to come if you feel like bopping the night away to tunes of the 1950s and 1960s played by live bands. Although there's hardly room to dance, that doesn't stop the largely over-30

Japanese audience from twisting in the aisles as the night wears on. Hours are Monday to Saturday from 6pm to 2:30am, Sunday and holidays from 6pm to midnight. (Also at 8–2–1 Ginza, on the 9th floor, ✆ **03/3572-9161;** and in east Shinjuku at 3–18–4 Shinjuku, on the 6th floor, ✆ **03/3355-6477.**) Daini Reine Building, 5-3-1 Roppongi. ✆ **03/3401-5755.** www.kentos-tokyo.jp. Cover ¥1,890 for men, ¥1,575 for women, plus 10% service charge and 1-drink minimum. Station: Roppongi (4 min.). Take the side street going downhill on the left side of Almond Coffee Shop, and then take the 1st left; the club is on the right.

Liquidroom   This is the most happening place in Ebisu (if not all of Tokyo) for live events, with concerts, well-known DJs, and stage events most nights of the week. Lots of groups kick off their world tours here, in a huge, cavernous room where the energy is so pervasive that the floor vibrates. On the second floor is Time Out Café & Diner, open Monday to Friday noon to midnight or later, Saturday 1pm to 5am, and Sunday from 3 to 10pm. Liquidroom usually opens around 6pm, with live events from about 7 to 10pm or later. 3–16–6 Higashi. ✆ **03/5464-0800.** www.liquidroom.net. Cover ¥3,000–¥6,000, depending on the event. Station: Ebisu (3 min.). Take the west exit, cross Komazawa Dori and turn right, and then turn left at Meiji Dori; it will be almost immediately on your left.

New York Bar   This is one of Tokyo's most sophisticated venues, boasting Manhattan-style jazz and breathtaking views of glittering west Shinjuku. Unfortunately, it's also one of the city's smallest. Consider coming for dinner in the adjacent **New York Grill** (p. 143); it costs a small fortune, but you'll save the cost of the cover. Hours are daily from 5pm, with live music 8pm to midnight (from 7pm on Sun). Park Hyatt Hotel, 52nd floor, 3–7–1–2 Nishi-Shinjuku. ✆ **03/5322-1234.** http://tokyo.park.hyatt.com. Cover ¥2,000. Station: Shinjuku (13 min.), Hatsudai on the Keio Line (7 min.), or Tochomae (8 min.).

The Ruby Room   I've seen living rooms larger than this second-floor venue, home to local acts, open-mic Tuesdays (with a 1-drink minimum), house and techno DJs, and other events. The crowd depends on the music, but because there's no room to move, people dance where they are. The band is close, close, close—any closer and you'd be in the drummer's lap. Open Monday, Tuesday, Friday and Saturday from 7pm or later, depending on the event (some concerts get underway at midnight), until 5am. 2–25–17 Dogenzaka, Shibuya-ku. ✆ **03/3780-3022.** www.rubyroomtokyo.com. Cover ¥1,500–¥2,000 Fri-Sat only, including 1 drink. Station: Shibuya (Hachiko exit, 4 min.). Walk on Dogenzaka to the Prime Building and Royal Host and take the 1st right; keep to the left at the Y intersection.

Shinjuku Pit Inn   This is one of Tokyo's most famous and longest-running jazz, fusion, and blues clubs, featuring both Japanese and foreign musicians. There are two programs daily—from 2:30 to 5pm and from 7:30 or 8pm—making it a great place to stop for a bit of music in the middle of the day. 2–12–4 Shinjuku. ✆ **03/3354-2024.** www.pit-inn.com. Cover, including 1 drink, ¥1,300 for the 2:30pm show (¥2,500 Sat–Sun and holidays), ¥3,000 for the evening shows. Station: Shinjuku Sanchome (3 min.). Northeast of the Shinjuku Dori/Meiji Dori intersection.

STB 139   Popular with well-heeled Japanese, this classy venue in a modern brick building offers a wide range of musical entertainment, from jazz and classical to fusion, Latin, nostalgia, R&B, and Japanese pop, performed mostly by Japanese talent. Open daily from 6 to 11pm, with most shows starting at 7:30 or 8pm. Most people dine here as well: The menu features seafood, pasta, and lighter fare. 6–7–11 Roppongi. ✆ **03/5474-0139.**

http://stb139.co.jp. ¥4,500–¥7,350 for most shows. Station: Roppongi (3 min.). From Roppongi Crossing, take the road downhill from the left side of Almond Coffee Shop; it will be on the right.

DANCE CLUBS & DISCOS

Discos lost popularity after their 1980s heyday, but with the rise of almost cult-figure DJs, dance clubs have witnessed a resurgence in recent years, with Roppongi still boasting more dance clubs than elsewhere in the city. Sometimes the set cover charge includes drinks, which makes for an inexpensive way to spend an evening. Keep in mind, however, that prices are usually higher on weekends and are sometimes higher for men than for women. Although clubs are required by law to close at midnight, many of them ignore the rule and stay open until dawn. You must be at least 20 years old (the legal drinking age in Japan) to enter most clubs.

In addition to the recommendations here, many bars bring in DJs and become mostly dance clubs later in the evening, especially on weekends, including New Sazae, Gaspanic, Enjoy House, Quest, Tokyo Sports Café/Lime, and Arty Farty. See "The Bar Scene" and "Gay & Lesbian Bars," later.

El Café Latino   All the smooth Latin moves make their way to the tiny dance floor of this happening club. It's fun to watch, even if you don't know how to perform salsa, rumba, merengue, or dance to reggaeton (Latin reggae), but if you want to get in the groove, show up for one of the free 30-minute classes at 7pm on Tuesday, Thursday, and Friday. Open Tuesday to Thursday and Sunday 6pm to midnight, Friday and Saturday 6pm to 5am. 3-15-24 Roppongi. ✆ **03/3402-8989.** www.elcafelatino.com. Cover (Fri–Sat only) ¥1,500, including 1 drink. Station: Roppongi (4 min.). From Roppongi Crossing, walk down Gaien-Higashi Dori in the direction of Tokyo Tower, turning left after passing McDonald's on your right, and then turning right at Gaspanic.

Sam & Dave   This Osaka import is party central in Akasaka, with its disco ball, palm trees, black interior, video screens, and events that range from swing night on Wednesdays to DJs on Fridays and Saturdays. Open daily 7pm to 5am. 4-3-6 Akasaka. ✆ **03/3585-0325.** www.samanddave.org. Cover ¥1,000–¥2,000, depending on the event. Station: Akasaka (3 min.) or Akasaka-mitsuke (4 min.). On Hitotsugi Dori.

Tokyo Loose   Young Tokyoites who work in Shinjuku come here after-hours to hang out and to dance to trance, hip-hop, techno, soul, R&B, and house music spun by local DJs. Things don't get hopping until after midnight, and even when the sun comes up it's night at this small basement club that attracts a good mix of Japanese and foreigners, most in their 20s. Happy hour is until 11pm Monday to Thursday, when drinks cost ¥500. Open daily at 8pm, closing when the crowd thins out (about 10am on weekends). 2-37-3 Kabuki-cho. ✆ **03/3207-5677.** www.tokyoloose.com. Cover (Fri–Sat only) ¥1,000, including 1 drink for men, 2 drinks for women. Station: Shinjuku (east exit, 10 min.). North of Koma Stadium, on Hanamichi Dori.

Velours   Every guest is a star, or at least, that's how every clubber is supposed to feel at this posh venue for adults, complete with imported French furniture and a 19th-century Baccarat chandelier. It all might ring a bit pretentious for some, but after the DJ gets things rolling and the drinks kick in, celebrity wannabes might find they're having fun just being who they are. Popular with foreigners and Japanese alike. Open Wednesday to Saturday from 9pm to 5am. 6-4-6 Minami Aoyama. ✆ **03/5778-4777.** Cover ¥2,500 for men, ¥2,000 for women, including 1 drink. Station: Omotesando Roppongi (8 min.). Off Kotto Dori, near Blue Note (see above).

GINZA

See the map on p. 92 for the bars listed in this section.

Ginza Sapporo Lion Yebisu and Sapporo beer are the draw at this large beer hall with its mock Gothic ceiling and faux, kitschy German decor. A large display of plastic foods and an English-language menu help you choose from snacks ranging from yakitori to sausage and spaghetti. The place is popular with older Japanese. Hours are Monday to Saturday from 11:30am to 11pm, Sunday and holidays from 11:30am to 10:30pm. 7–9–20 Ginza. ✆ **03/3571-2590.** Station: Ginza (3 min.). On Chuo Dori not far from the Matsuza-kaya department store.

(74) **Lupin** (Finds) You couldn't find a more subdued place than this tiny basement bar. First opened back in 1928 and little changed over the decades, it features a long wooden bar and booths. Even the staff looks like they've been here since it opened. Because no music is ever played here, it's a great place for conversation. Very civilized. There's a table charge of ¥700 per person, which includes a snack. Heartland beer is on tap. Hours are Tuesday to Saturday from 5 to 11:30pm. 5–5–11 Ginza. ✆ **03/3571-0750.** Station: Ginza (2 min.). In a tiny alley btw. Namiki and Ginza W. 5th St. (look for a nearby torigin sign).

Old Imperial This is the Imperial Hotel's tribute to its original architect, Frank Lloyd Wright, and is the only place in the hotel that contains Wright originals—the Art Deco terra-cotta wall behind the bar, the mural, and the small desk at the entrance. Its clubby atmosphere, low lighting, and comfortable chairs and tables (copies of Wright originals) make it perfect for a quiet drink. Try the Mount Fuji, the bar's own 1924 creation: dry gin, lemon juice, pineapple juice, egg white, and maraschino cherry. Hours are daily 11:30am to midnight. Imperial Hotel, 1–1–1 Uchisaiwai-cho. ✆ **03/3539-8088.** Station: Hibiya (1 min.).

300 Bar You don't want to come here when you're drop-dead tired, because there are no seats in this standing bar. Rather, with all drinks and appetizers priced at ¥315, this is a good place for a quick drink or a place to meet up with friends in the Ginza. It's self-service and, upon entry, you're required to purchase two tickets totaling ¥630, which can be redeemed for two drinks or food items from the 100-plus menu listing everything from cocktails to such snacks as tofu gratin and fried rice balls. There are two locations in the Ginza, the one below and at 8–3–12 Ginza (✆ **03/3571-8300**). Both are open Monday to Saturday 5pm to 2am, Sunday and holidays 5 to 11pm. 5–9–11 Ginza. ✆ **03/3572-6300.** www.300bar.com. Station: Ginza (2 min.). On a side street southeast of the Ginza 4–chome Crossing.

ASAKUSA

See the map on p. 109 for the bars listed in this section.

Daimasu This sake bar offers more than 100 different kinds of sake and shochu by the glass, allowing you to try a variety of different kinds, including seasonal and regional varieties. To start, purchase a ticket booklet for ¥1,000; small glasses start at ¥210. Or, purchase your own alcohol at the shop's adjoining liquor store and drink it at the sake bar for a ¥500 corkage fee. Open daily noon to midnight. 1–2–8 Asakusa. ✆ **03/5806-3811.** Station: Asakusa (3 min.).Just off Nakamise Dori, to the right if walking from Kaminarimon Gate toward Sensoji Temple.

Ichimon   Ichimon takes its name from *mon,* which was the lowest piece of currency used by common people during the Edo Period. *Ichimon* means "one mon." This quirky place, specializing in sake, has a unique system whereby each customer purchases mon, issued here in wooden tokens at the rate of ¥100 for each mon; the tokens are then used to pay for your sake, meal, and ¥700 snack charge. Plan on exchanging about ¥5,000 into mon; mon you don't use can be exchanged for the real thing when you leave. There's no English-language menu, but the usual pub fare is available, including *shumai* (steamed dumplings), duck meatballs, nabe, noodles, and other fare. This is a cozy place, decorated like an old farmhouse with wooden beams, shoji screens, and antiques. Open Monday to Friday 6 to 11pm, and Saturday, Sunday, and holidays 5 to 10pm. 3-12-6 Asakusa. ℂ **03/3875-6800.** Station: Tawaramachi (10 min.) or Asakusa (15 min.). Just northeast of the Kokusai Dori/Kototoi Dori intersection; from the intersection, walk 1 block north on Kokusai Dori and turn right; it's almost immediately on your right, with a big sake barrel above its door.

Sky Room (**Value**   This is a great—albeit simple—place for an inexpensive drink after an active day in historic Asakusa. The Asahi Beer Tower, which sits next to the distinctive building with the golden hops perched on top, belongs to the Asahi Beer company; it's thought to represent a mug of foaming beer. The plain, cafeteria-style bar, perched at the top of the building in the foam next to **La Ranarita Azumabashi** (p. 139), offers great views as well as different kinds of Asahi beer, wine, coffee, tea, and sodas, all priced at ¥600 or less, and a very limited snack menu. With seating for only 26 at a window-side counter, it can be crowded on weekends. Open daily 10am to 9:30pm. Asahi Beer Tower, 22nd floor, 1-23-1 Azumabashi. ℂ **03/5608-5277.** Station: Asakusa (exit 5, 4 min.). On the opposite side of the Sumida River from Sensoji Temple.

UENO

See the map on p. 117 for the bars listed in this section.

Hard Rock Cafe   Located in JR Ueno Station, this chain cafe has the usual rock-'n'-roll memorabilia, American food, extensive drink menu, and loud music. Open daily 7am for breakfast to 11pm. 7-1-1 Ueno. ℂ **03/5826-5821.** Station: JR Ueno (1 min.).

Warrior Celt   This third-floor British pub is somewhat of a novelty in Ueno, especially for its nightly happy hour until 7pm (when beer and spirits are priced at just ¥600) and for its free live music Tuesday, Friday, and Saturday nights. With its international, friendly mix, it's a good place to while away some hours if you find yourself in Ueno after the museums close. Open Sunday to Tuesday 5pm to midnight, Wednesday to Saturday 5pm to 5am. 6-9-22 Ueno. ℂ **03/3836-8588.** Station: Ueno (Hirokoji exit, 5 min.). One block east of the Yamanote elevated train tracks, just a stone's throw from the Ameya Yokocho market. From Ueno Station, take the street to the right of OICity department store; Warrior Celt is on the right, beside the Hotel Chic love hotel.

SHINJUKU

See the map on p. 94 for the bars listed in this section.

Albatross (**Finds**   This tiny bar is one of the 100 or so miniature establishments nestled in Goruden Gai. Located up a narrow flight of stairs and decorated in blood red, it attracts a mostly young crowd—though there's room for only a handful of patrons squeezed along the counter, with additional tiered seating up above. There's a ¥300 snack charge per person. Open daily 8pm to 5am. 1-1-7 Kabuki-cho. ℂ **03/3203-3699.** Station: Shinjuku Sanchome (7 min.). In Goruden Gai, on 5th St. (Gobangai).

> ## ⓘ Tips A Note on Establishments with Japanese Signs
>
> Many hotels, restaurants, attractions, and other establishments in Japan do not have signs giving their names in Roman (English-language) letters. Those that don't are indicated in this guide by an oval with a number that corresponds to a number in chapter 14 that shows the Japanese equivalent. Thus, to find the Japanese symbol for, say, **Volga,** refer to no. 75 on p. 326.

Christon Cafe   This has to be one of the weirdest theme bars I've seen in Tokyo. Decorated like a church with its stained-glass windows, vaulted ceiling, organ music, crosses, and statue of Jesus, it's packed to the rafters despite the ¥300 cover charge. What to order? A Bloody Mary, of course. Hours are Sunday to Thursday 5 to 11:30pm, Friday and Saturday 5pm to 4am. Oriental Wave Building, 8th floor, 5-17-13 Shinjuku. ☎ 03/5287-2426. Station: Shinjuku Sanchome (5 min.). In east Shinjuku, on Yasukuni Dori, just west of Hanazono Shrine.

Dubliners' Irish Pub   Attracting expats and locals alike—mostly in their 30s and 40s—is this chain Irish bar, especially for its weekday happy hour from noon to 7pm (you have to wonder, don't these people work?). A menu lists such perennial favorites as Irish stew, fish and chips, and minced lamb shepherd's pie. Open Monday to Saturday noon to 1am, Sunday noon to 11pm. 3-28-9 Shinjuku. ☎ 03/3352-6606. Station: Shinjuku (east exit, 3 min.). In east Shinjuku, behind Mitsukoshi department store to the southwest, above Sapporo Lion.

New Sazae   After other bars in this predominantly gay district close, those revelers who refuse to call it quits migrate around the corner to this dive. The diverse crowd is a bit rowdy, but if you get this far, you're probably right where you belong. A ¥1,000 cover includes the first drink; drinks thereafter cost ¥700. Hours are Sunday to Thursday 9pm to 5am, Friday and Saturday 9pm to 7am. Ishikawa Building, 2nd floor, 2-18-5 Shinjuku. ☎ 03/3354-1745. Station: Shinjuku Sanchome (4 min.). Southeast of the Yasukuni Dori and Gyoen Dori intersection, behind Bygs, in Shinjuku Ni-chome.

Vagabond   Although most of the night action in Shinjuku is east of the station, the west side also has an area of inexpensive restaurants and bars. This second-floor nightspot has been in operation for more than 30 years and is now managed by the original owner's son, Matsuoka Takahiko. It features a jazz pianist nightly, beginning at 7pm. Although there's no music charge per se, after 7pm there is an obligatory snack charge of ¥500 for the bowl of chips automatically brought to your table. Small and cozy, this place is popular with foreigners who live near Shinjuku Station and with Japanese who want to rub elbows with them; its Guinness brings in customers from the United Kingdom. Hours are Monday to Saturday 5 to 11:30pm, Sunday 5 to 11pm. 1-4-20 Nishi Shinjuku. ☎ 03/3348-9109. Station: Shinjuku (west exit, 2 min.). In west Shinjuku, in the 2nd alley behind (north of) Odakyu Halc.

⑦⑤ **Volga**   Volga, a *yakitori-ya* housed in an ivy-covered two-story brick building, features an open grill facing the street and a smoky and packed drinking hall typical of older establishments that once dotted the country. Its unrefined atmosphere has changed little since it opened here in the 1950s. Rooms are tiny and simply decorated with wooden tables and benches, and the clientele is middle-age. Very Japanese. Get here soon after it opens to be assured a seat. Hours are Monday to Saturday from 5 to 10:30pm. Closed holidays. 1–4–18 Nishi Shinjuku. ✆ **03/3342-4996**. Station: Shinjuku (west exit, 2 min.). In west Shinjuku, on the corner down the street from Vagabond (see above).

SHIBUYA

See the map on p. 155 for the bars listed in this section. In addition to the listings below, you might try **Hobgoblin Shibuya,** on Dogenzaka slope, at 1–3–11 Dogenzaka (✆ **03/6415-4243**), open Monday to Friday from 5pm and weekends from noon. See "Akasaka," below, for a review of this imported chain.

Dubliners' Irish Pub   This bar has several things going for it: It is open all day, is easy to find, has a covered balcony from which to observe the bustle of Shibuya, and offers (usually) free live Irish music every Wednesday from 8pm. It even offers weekday happy hour, from noon to 7pm. Hours are Monday to Saturday noon to 1am, Sunday and holidays noon to 11pm. 2–29–8 Dogenzaka. ✆ **03/5459-1736**. Station: Shibuya (2 min.). Take the Hachiko exit and walk up Dozenzaka; it will be on the right side, on the 2nd floor.

Gaspanic Shibuya   Gaspanic has a well-earned reputation for hard-core partying, but patrons who prefer this Shibuya location over the original Roppongi bar (see below) say it's because the clientele (mostly Japanese and foreigners in their 20s) here tends to be mostly locals and because DJs play what customers want to hear, ranging from the Beatles to rap. Happy hour—when drinks are ¥500—is until 9:30pm daily but all day and night on Thursday. Open daily 6pm to 5am. (Also at 2–10–7 Dogenzaka in Shibuya, same hours; ✆ **03/3780-1731**.) 21-7 Udagawa-cho. ✆ **03/3462-9099**. Station: Shibuya (Hachiko exit, 1 min.). Just past the entrance to Center Gai (Shibuya's nightlife street), on the right side.

EBISU

Enjoy House (Finds)   With its 1960s-style decor, efficient yet relaxed and funky staff, friendly atmosphere, and tiny dance floor, the inimitable Enjoy House is a great place to—well, enjoy yourself. Open Tuesday to Friday from 7pm to 2am, Saturday and Sunday from 3pm to 4am. 2–9–9 Ebisu Nishi. ✆ **03/5489-1591**. Station: Ebisu (west exit, 3 min.). Take the road opposite Komazawa Dori from the koban (police box; next to Softbank) and continue past Peacock grocery store to the juncture where 5 streets converge; it's on the other side of the intersection, on a diagonal street to the left.

What the Dickens!   One of Tokyo's most popular expat bars, What the Dickens! packs 'em in with live bands nightly from 8:30 to 11:30pm (everything from rock and pop to reggae, jazz, blues, Dixieland, and folk), no cover, British beer on tap, and hearty servings of pub grub. Come early for happy hour, available every day except Sunday and holidays from 5 to 7pm. Hours are Tuesday to Thursday 5pm to 2am, Friday and Saturday 5pm to 2am, and Sunday 3pm to midnight. 1–13–3 Ebisu Nishi, 4th floor of the Roob Building. ✆ **03/3780-2099**. www.whatthedickens.jp. Station: Ebisu (west exit, 3 min.). Take the side street running btw. Wendy's and KFC; it's at the end of the 2nd block on the left, on the corner.

ROPPONGI

See the map on p. 159 for the bars listed in this section. Directions are from Roppongi Crossing, Roppongi's main intersection of Roppongi Dori and Gaien-Higashi Dori.

In addition to the listings here, try **Hobgoblin Roppongi,** on Gaien-Higashi Dori in the direction of Tokyo Tower at 3–16–33 Roppongi (🕐 **03/3568-1280**), open daily from Monday to Friday from 5pm and weekends from noon (see "Akasaka," below, for a review).

A971   This Roppongi newcomer attracts a well-heeled crowd due to its location in Midtown, but that doesn't mean it doesn't get down and—well, if not exactly dirty, at least hopping by the wee hours of the morning. The first floor serves as a casual cafe and bar, with sidewalk seating and four computers guests can peruse for free, while the second floor serves as a combination cafe and lounge. The menu offers contemporary cuisine— think local vegetables and the likes of oven-baked fish covered with miso—at surprisingly reasonable prices given its location. Hours are Monday to Saturday 10am to 4am (second floor 11am–2am), Sunday and holidays 10am to midnight (second floor 11am–midnight). Midtown East, 9–7–2 Akasaka. 🕐 **03/5413-3210.** www.a971.com. Station: Roppongi (2 min.). At the entrance to Midtown.

Agave   Tequila fans take note: This is Japan's largest tequila bar, with approximately 500 brands on offer. Margaritas, appetizers (nachos and the like), and cigars are also available. Yes, cigar smoking is allowed in this basement establishment, but an airy domed ceiling, Mexican decor and music, and a friendly staff—not to mention tequila (I like it with chili-pepper salt on the rim)—may make it sufferable for nonsmokers. Hours are Monday to Thursday from 6:30pm to 2am, Friday and Saturday from 6:30pm to 3:30am. 7–15–10 Roppongi. 🕐 **03/3497-0229.** Station: Roppongi (2 min.). Just off Roppongi Dori, on the right side, heading from Roppongi Crossing toward Roppongi Hills and Shibuya (take the second right).

Bar Bourbon Street   The Big Easy is the inspiration for this small, cozy bar with a living-room atmosphere and free live music nightly from 9pm to midnight, mostly blues but sometimes traditional jazz and Dixieland. It offers a large selection of wines by the glass and, of course, bourbons, along with Cajun and New Orleans favorites such as blackened fish and jambalaya. The bar's owner is the organizer of an annual Roppongi *Mardi Gras* party. It's open Tuesday to Saturday 6pm to 2am. 7–8–16 Roppongi. 🕐 **03/5786-2887.** www.bourbonstreet-tokyo.com. Station: Roppongi (5 min.). From Roppongi Crossing, walk away from Tokyo Tower on Gaien-Higashi Dori, turning left at the diagonal street Ryudo-cho Bijitsukan-dori (across from Tokyo Midtown); it will be on your right on a side street after the Times car park.

Bar Del Sole   I like this place for its outdoor terrace and open facade, a rarity in Roppongi. In addition to the usual drinks, it has a snack menu that includes lots of desserts, even ice cream. It opens daily at 11am, closing at midnight Monday to Thursday, 2am Friday and Saturday, and 11pm Sunday and holidays. 6–8–14 Roppongi. 🕐 **03/3401-3521.** Station: Roppongi (4 min.). From Roppongi Crossing, take the road downhill from the left side of Almond Coffee Shop; it will be on the right.

Fiesta International Karaoke Bar   This karaoke bar offers 15,000 English-language songs, including oldies, soul, pop, rock, and heavy metal, along with professional sound equipment and a sound engineer who can make your voice sound better than it really is. Admission is ¥3,500, which includes three drinks and all the songs you care to sing, except on Tuesdays when women pay only ¥2,500. Open Monday 7am to midnight, Tuesday to Saturday 7pm to 5am. 7–9–3 Roppongi. 🕐 **03/5410-3008.** www.fiesta-roppongi.com. Station: Roppongi (3 min.). From Roppongi Crossing, walk away from Tokyo

Tower on Gaien-Higashi Dori, turning left at the diagonal street Ryudocho Bijitsukan-dori (across from Tokyo Midtown); it will be on your left.

Gaspanic Bar   This has long been *the* bar for foreign and Japanese 20-somethings. The music is loud, and after midnight the place gets so crowded that you may see female patrons dancing on the countertops. Thursdays are especially packed—all drinks are only ¥500. Drinks are also just ¥500 daily during happy hour to 9:30pm. In the basement is Club 99, open Thursday to Saturday for dancing. Nearby, Gaspanic Club, on Gaien-Higashi Dori, across from the Roi Building at 3–10–5 Roppongi (✆ **03/3402-7054**), is open daily 6pm to 5am for dancing. All offer the same Thursday and happy-hour drink specials. Large bouncers at all the doors serve as clues that these places can get rough. Hours are daily 6pm to 5am. 3–15–24 Roppongi. ✆ **03/3405-0633**. Station: Roppongi (4 min.). From Roppongi Crossing, walk toward Tokyo Tower on Gaien-Higashi Dori, and turn left at Family Mart.

Geronimo Shot Bar   People either seem to love or hate this place. It's tiny, dominated by a bar in the middle that's surrounded by people who come to drink, dance, and socialize. If the gong sounds, it means someone has bought a shot for everyone there, and this happens more than you might think. Happy hour is until 9pm. Open Monday to Friday 6pm to 5am, Saturday and Sunday 7pm to 5am. 7–14–10 Roppongi. ✆ **03/3478-7449**. www.geronimoshotbar.com. Station: Roppongi (1 min.). On Roppongi Crossing, across from Almond Coffee Shop.

Hard Rock Cafe   If you like your music loud, the Hard Rock Cafe is the place for you. The outside is easily recognizable by King Kong scaling a wall; the inside looks like a modern yuppie version of the local hamburger joint, except, of course, there's the added attraction of all that rock-'n'-roll paraphernalia. Happy hour is Monday to Friday 4 to 7pm. Hours are Sunday to Thursday from 11:30am to 2am, Friday and Saturday from 11:30am to 4am. 5–4–20 Roppongi. ✆ **03/3408-7018**. www.hardrockjapan.com. Station: Roppongi (3 min.). From Roppongi Crossing, walk toward Tokyo Tower on Gaien-Higashi Dori and turn right at McDonald's.

Heartland   This is the New Age reincarnation of a former popular dive, occupying a corner of Roppongi Hills and attracting crowds of mostly expats, from bankers and investors to artistic types. Artwork not only fills the walls but also is projected onto a curved wall behind the bar that acts as a screen. Seating is limited, forcing people to mill around as though it were a private cocktail reception every night of the week, and a DJ on weekends keeps things hopping. What to order? Try the bar's own Heartland microbrew (produced by Kirin). Hours are daily 5pm to 4am. 6–10–1 Roppongi. ✆ **03/5772-7600**. www.heartland.jp. Station: Roppongi (3 min.). From Roppongi Crossing, walk on Roppongi Dori to the end of Roppongi Hills; it will be on the left.

Legends Sports Bar & Grill   Five screens broadcast all the biggest sporting events, including sumo, rugby, soccer, and U.S. sports. Happy hour is limited to 5 to 7pm Monday to Friday, so let's hope your team wins. Otherwise, take solace in the substantial food menu of burgers, sandwiches, and other fare. It's open Sunday to Friday 5pm to 2am, Saturday 2pm to 3am or later. 3–16–33 Roppongi. ✆ **03/3589-3304**. www.legendsports.jp. Station: Roppongi (6 min.). From Roppongi Crossing, walk on Gaien-Higashi Dori toward Tokyo Tower; it will be on your left.

Mogambo   Sister bar to Geronimo Shot Bar (see above), this jungle-themed bar (with the motto, "because it's a jungle out there") is similarly small, with a bar at its center and a convivial atmosphere, especially when someone rings the bell and free shots are poured for all. Many of its customers are regulars, and due to its intimate size, striking up conversation seems effortless. Happy hour is until 9pm daily. It's open Monday to Friday 6pm to 6am, Saturday 7pm to 6am. 6-1-7 Roppongi. ℂ **03/3403-4833**. www.mogambo.net. Station: Roppongi (3 min.). From Roppongi Crossing, take the road downhill from the left side of Almond Coffee Shop and take the first right; it will be on the right.

Paddy Foley's   Easy to find, this lively Irish pub is popular with both Japanese and foreigners. Happy hour is until 7pm (to 6pm weekends), several screens show live sports events (mainly soccer and rugby), and there's occasional live music. It's open Monday to Thursday 6pm to 2am, Friday 5pm to 4am, Saturday 1pm to 4am, and Sunday 3pm to 2am. Roi Building basement, 5-5-1 Roppongi. ℂ **03/3423-2250**. www.paddyfoleystokyo.com. Station: Roppongi (3 min.). On Gaien-Higashi Dori, on the right as you walk from Roppongi Crossing toward Tokyo Tower.

Quest   This sophisticated bar with blood-red walls and illuminated tables attracts a young, international (predominately Aussie) crowd with its Australian beers; daily happy hour (till 10pm); live sports coverage; nightly DJ playing a mix of rock, house, trance, hip-hop, and R&B; and meat pies. It's known mostly, however, for its late hours and doesn't start jumping until after midnight. Every Friday and Saturday there's an after-hours party starting at 4am, when guys have to pay ¥1,000, including one drink) to get in, but gals—I wonder why?—can get in free. Hours are Sunday to Thursday 7pm to 7am, Friday and Saturday 7pm to 10am. 5-3-1 Roppongi. ℂ **03/5414-2225**. www.barquestroppongi.com. Station: Roppongi (4 min.). Take the side street going downhill on the left side of Almond Coffee Shop, and then take the 1st left; it will be on the right.

Seventh Heaven Gentlemen's Club   One of several exotic dance clubs in Tokyo, this one features international dancers (Japanese, Brazilian, European) and is popular with foreign business travelers and Japanese entertaining their clients. Admission is ¥5,500 from 7 to 9pm, including all you can drink and eat, and is ¥7,000 thereafter, including two drinks, but discounts are offered on its website. Women are admitted free on Saturdays. Hours are Monday to Saturday from 7pm to 3am or later. 7-14-1 Roppongi. ℂ **03/3401-3644**. www.seventh-heaven.com. Station: Roppongi (3 min.). From Roppongi Crossing, it's on the left side of Gaien-Higashi Dori as you walk away from Tokyo Tower.

Tokyo Sports Café/Lime   This is a sports bar with attitude, boasting 10 plasma screens showing all major sporting events live, including American football, baseball, NBA basketball, boxing, soccer, rugby, and even cricket, as well as a free billiards table. Yet it also brings in the women with free champagne every Thursday and free shots for models on Friday. Happy hour for everyone is until 9pm (except during major games), and international DJs turn up the heat on Thursday through Saturday nights beginning at 1am. It's open Monday to Saturday 6pm to 5am. 7-13-8 Roppongi. ℂ **03/5411-8939**. Station: Roppongi (1 min.). From Roppongi Crossing, walk toward Shibuya and take the 1st right; it's ahead at the end of the street.

AKASAKA

See the map on p. 103 for the bars listed in this section.

Garden Lounge   If you prefer the view of a Japanese landscape garden to that of neon lights, get to this place before sunset, where you can look out over a 400-year-old garden complete with waterfall, pond, bridges, and manicured bushes. Cocktails begin at a pricey ¥1,400. Hours are daily 7am to 10pm. Hotel New Otani, 4–1 Kioi-cho. ☎ **03/5226-0246.** Station: Nagata-cho or Akasaka-mitsuke (3 min.).

Hobgoblin Akasaka   This U.K. chain import is a welcome addition to Akasaka's night scene and is very popular with expats. It offers eight brews on tap (one of the largest selections in town), satellite TVs broadcasting major sporting events, darts, hearty portions of typical pub fare, and happy hour from 5 to 7pm (Mon–Fri only). Open Monday to Friday 11am to 1am, Saturday and holidays 5pm to 1am. Tamondo Building, basement, 2–13–19 Akasaka. ☎ **03/6229-2636.** Station: Akasaka (exit 2, 2 min.). From the station, turn right onto Akasaka Dori and right at Misuji Dori.

The Mermaid   This cozy British pub in the heart of Akasaka's nightlife district opens to the street, with outdoor picnic tables for overflow. It offers the usual British ales and pub grub, including ale-battered fish and chips, bangers and mash, and burgers, as well as lunch specials and free Wi-Fi for those lugging laptops. Happy hour is Monday to Friday 3 to 7pm and Saturday and Sunday 5 to 7pm. Open Sunday to Thursday 11:30am to midnight, Friday 11:30am to 4am, and Saturday 5:30pm to midnight. 3–10–9 Akasaka. ☎ **03/3584-2006.** Station: Akasaka-mitsuke (2 min.) or Akasaka (4 min.). On Tamachi Dori.

Top of Akasaka   I like to start my evenings in Akasaka with a quiet drink at this fancy and romantic cocktail lounge. With the city of Tokyo as a dramatic backdrop, I can watch the day fade into darkness as millions of lights and neon signs twinkle in the distance. Cocktails average ¥1,730, and there's a cover charge of ¥900 for the piano music after 8pm. *Note:* No children allowed. Hours are Monday to Saturday 5pm to 1am, Sunday and holidays 5 to 11pm. Akasaka Prince Hotel, 40th floor, 1–2 Kioi-cho. ☎ **03/3234-1111.** Station: Nagata-cho or Akasaka-mitsuke (2 min.).

SHINAGAWA

See the map on p. 105 for the bars listed in this section.

Top of Shinagawa   Occupying the whole top floor of the Prince Hotel Shinagawa's Main Tower, the Top of Shinagawa boasts one of the best views of any hotel bar in Tokyo. It offers unparalleled panoramas of Tokyo Bay, Odaiba, the Rainbow Bridge, Mount Fuji, and the Tokyo cityscape. The bar is divided into sections; only the East Lounge (facing the bay) is open during the day, offering a weekday buffet of hot entrees, salad, and dessert for ¥2,500 from 11:30am to 3:30pm—it's very popular with Japanese women (nary a man in sight!). An open restaurant called Prince Court at the center offers fixed-price dinners from ¥6,000. You can also come simply for a drink, but note that the North Bar, facing central Tokyo and open from 5pm to 2am, has a ¥500 table charge. Open daily 11:30am to 2am. Shinagawa Prince Hotel, 4–10–30 Takanawa. ☎ **03/3440-1111.** Station: Shinagawa (2 min.).

4 GAY & LESBIAN BARS

Shinjuku Ni-chome (pronounced "knee-cho-may"), southeast of the Yasukuni Dori and Gyoen Dori intersection (behind the koban [police box] and Bygs Building), is Tokyo's gay and lesbian quarter, with numerous establishments catering to a variety of age groups and preferences, and a lively street scene. Listed below are good places to start (see the maps in chapter 5 for locations); you'll find a lot more in the immediate area by exploring on your own.

Advocates   Attracting both gays and straights, this small bar opens onto the street with a few sidewalk tables and overflowing crowds, making this a good vantage point for watching the street action and for networking. Hours are Monday to Saturday 6pm to 5am, Sunday 6pm to 1am. 2–18–1 Shinjuku. (*C*) **03/3358-3988.** Station: Shinjuku Sanchome (4 min.). On the street behind Bygs, to the right.

Arty Farty   One of Ni–chome's larger gay bars, this is also one of the best places to dance, due to a good sound system and music that ranges from house to hip hop. Although it used to be strictly males only, it recently moved to a new location (across from the legendary Pit Inn jazz house) and threw open its doors to all. A fun climax to a pub crawl in Shinjuku. It's open Sunday to Thursday 7pm to 3am, Friday and Saturday 7pm to 5am. 2–11–7 Shinjuku. (*C*) **03/5362-9720.** Station: Shinjuku Sanchome (3 min.). Northeast of the Shinjuku Dori/Meiji Dori intersection.

Kinsmen   This long-standing second-floor gay bar welcomes customers of all persuasions. It's a pleasant oasis, small and civilized, with occasional live music. Hours are Sunday and Tuesday to Thursday 7pm to 1am, Friday to Saturday 7pm to 3am. 2–18–5 Shinjuku. (*C*) **03/3354-4949.** Station: Shinjuku Sanchome (4 min.).

Kinswomyn   This casual, tiny, but welcoming women-only bar attracts a regular clientele of mainly Japanese but also foreign lesbians. Weekends can get quite crowded, especially when some of the younger patrons start dancing, making weekdays preferable for those seeking a more relaxed, quiet setting. Hours are Wednesday to Monday 8pm to 4am. 2–15–10 Shinjuku. (*C*) **03/3354-8720.** Station: Shinjuku Sanchome (4 min.). On a street behind Kinsmen.

5 MOVIE THEATERS

Going to the movies is an expensive pastime in Tokyo, with admission averaging about ¥1,800 for adults, ¥1,500 for senior-high and college students, and ¥1,000 for children and seniors over 60. Look for weekday specials; some theaters, for example, offer women discounts on Wednesday or late-show discounts. If you want to see one of Hollywood's latest releases (which usually take a few months to reach Japan), you may have to contend with long lines and huge crowds. Movies are shown in the original language, with Japanese subtitles.

Although there are movie theaters spread throughout the metropolis, none is as sophisticated and upscale as **Toho Cinemas,** located in the Roppongi Hills development at 6–10–2 Roppongi (*C*) **03/5775-6090**). It offers seven screens at the usual moviegoing price, plus a Premier Zone with its own bar, Japanese garden, and viewing room with armchair seating and side tables (admission here is a hefty ¥3,000, including one drink). Like many other cinemas, it offers discounted tickets for ¥1,000 on the first day of each month and for ladies on Wednesday (except in the Premier Zone). Unlike other theaters, however, it shows movies Sunday to Wednesday from 10am to midnight, and Thursday, Friday, and Saturday from 10am to 5am (note that city law bans children under 18 inside movie theaters past 11pm).

If you're interested in seeing Japanese classics, your best bet is the **National Film Center,** 3-7-6 Kyobashi, Chuo-ku (✆ **03/5777-8600;** www.momat.go.jp/english/nfc/ index.html; station: Kyobashi). Movies, shown Tuesday through Friday at 3 and 7pm and Saturday and Sunday and holidays at 1 and 4pm, include both Japanese and foreign films (some with English subtitles). Because programs change often, call or check the website to see what's playing and to check show times. A ticket here is ¥500 for adults, ¥300 for students and seniors, and ¥100 for children.

Side Trips from Tokyo

If your stay in Tokyo is 3 days or more, consider an excursion in the vicinity. **Kamakura** and **Nikko,** ranked as two of the most important historical sites in Japan, each represent a completely different but equally exciting period of Japanese history. **Yokohama,** with its thriving port, waterfront development, museums, and great garden, also makes an interesting day trip. **Fuji-Hakone-Izu National Park** serves as a huge recreational playground for the residents of Tokyo. For overnight stays, I heartily recommend **Hakone,** both for its atmosphere and its Japanese-style inns *(ryokan),* where you'll be able to experience a bit of old Japan. **Izu Peninsula** also boasts ryokan and hot-spring resorts, in both seaside and mountain settings. (For more information on ryokan, see "Japanese-style Accommodations," in chapter 5.) Active travelers may want to hike to the top of **Mount Fuji** in summer, while shoppers may head for the pottery village of **Mashiko,** which can be toured on its own or in combination with an overnight trip to Nikko. Because these are popular tourist destinations, try to avoid traveling on weekends and holidays.

Before departing Tokyo, stop by the **Tourist Information Center (TIC)** for pamphlets about Kamakura, Nikko, Hakone, and the Mount Fuji area, some of which provide maps, train schedules, and other useful information (see "Visitor Information," in chapter 12, for the TIC location).

Although all the recommended excursions above can be toured easily on your own, several tour companies offer guided trips for those who wish to leave the particulars of travel to someone else. JTB's **Sunrise Tours** (© **03/5796-5454;** www. jtb-sunrisetours.jp) offers the most extensive choices, with trips to Hakone, Nikko, Kamakura, and beyond, including Kyoto, ski resorts, and annual festivals.

1 KAMAKURA ★★★

51km (32 miles) S of Tokyo

If you take only one day trip outside Tokyo, it should be to Kamakura, especially if you're unable to include the ancient capitals of Kyoto and Nara in your travels. (If you are going to Kyoto and Nara, I would probably choose Nikko, below.) Kamakura is a delightful hamlet with no fewer than 65 Buddhist temples and 19 Shinto shrines spread throughout the town and surrounding wooded hills. Most of these were built centuries ago, when a warrior named Minamoto Yoritomo seized political power and established his shogunate government in Kamakura back in 1192. Wanting to set up his seat of government as far away as possible from what he considered to be the corrupt Imperial court in Kyoto, Yoritomo selected Kamakura because it was easy to defend. The village is enclosed on three sides by wooded hills and on the fourth by the sea—a setting that lends a dramatic background to its many temples and shrines.

Although Kamakura remained the military and political center of the nation for a century and a half, the Minamoto clan was in power for only a short time. After Yoritomo's death, both of his sons were assassinated, one after the other, after taking up military rule. Power then passed to the family of Yoritomo's widow, the Hojo family, who ruled until 1333, when the emperor in Kyoto sent troops to crush the shogunate government. Unable to stop the invaders, 800 soldiers retired to the Hojo family temple at Toshoji, where they disemboweled themselves in ritualistic suicide known as *seppuku*.

Today Kamakura is a thriving seaside resort (its pop. is 173,500), with old wooden homes, temples, shrines, and wooded hills—a pleasant 1-day trip from Tokyo. (There's also a beach in Kamakura called Yuigahama Beach, but I find it unappealing; it's often strewn with litter and unbelievably crowded in summer. Skip it.)

ESSENTIALS

GETTING THERE   Take the **JR Yokosuka Line** bound for Zushi, Kurihama, or Yokosuka; it departs every 10 to 15 minutes from the Yokohama, Shinagawa, Shimbashi, and Tokyo JR stations. The trip takes almost 1 hour from Tokyo Station and costs ¥890 one-way to Kamakura Station. From Shinjuku, take the JR Shonan-Shinjuku Line 1 hour to Kamakura for the same price.

VISITOR INFORMATION   In Kamakura, there's a **tourist information window** (© 0467/22-3350; www.city.kamakura.kanagawa.jp) inside Kamakura Station near the east exit. You can pick up a map here and get directions to the village's most important sights and restaurants. It's open daily 9am to 5:30pm April to September, 9am to 5pm October to March.

ORIENTATION & GETTING AROUND   Kamakura's major sights are clustered in two areas: **Kamakura Station,** the town's downtown with the tourist office, souvenir shops spread along Komachi Dori and Wakamiya Oji, restaurants, and Tsurugaoka Hachimangu Shrine; and **Hase,** with the Great Buddha and Hase Kannon Temple. You can travel between Kamakura Station and Hase Station via the **Enoden Line,** a wonderful small train, or you can walk the distance in about 20 minutes. Destinations are also easily reached by buses departing from Kamakura Station.

SEEING THE SIGHTS

Keep in mind that most temples and shrines open at about 8 or 9am and close between 4 and 5pm.

AROUND KAMAKURA STATION   About a 12-minute walk from Kamakura Station, **Tsurugaoka Hachimangu Shrine** ★★★ (© 0467/22-0315) is the spiritual heart of

---

(Tips) Free Sightseeing Guides

University students of Kanagawa Prefecture volunteer their time to guide foreign visitors in Kamakura as a way to practice their English. You'll find them most weekends outside the east exit of Kamakura Station from about 10am to noon, available for tours on a first-come, first-served basis. To make sure you have a guide, or to reserve for another day of the week, contact Nishimoto Hiroaki at © 080/1526-1000, or send an e-mail to hiroakiarea7177@yahoo.co.jp at least 2 weeks in advance, stating your name, country, number of people in your group, time and date of your request, and phone number of your hotel in Japan. Although the service is free, you should pay for the student's transportation and meal, if applicable.

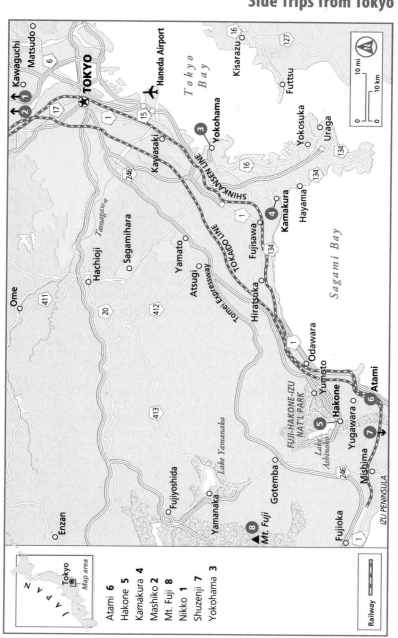

Atami **6**
Hakone **5**
Kamakura **4**
Mashiko **2**
Mt. Fuji **8**
Nikko **1**
Shuzenji **7**
Yokohama **3**

Railway

Fun Facts **Murder & Betrayal at Tsurugaoka Hachimangu Shrine**

As you ascend the 62 steps to the vermilion-painted shrine, note the **gingko tree** to the left that's thought to be about 1,000 years old. This is supposedly the site where Yoritomo's second son was ambushed and murdered back in 1219; his head was never found. Such stories of murder and betrayal were common in feudal Japan. Fearful that his charismatic brother had designs on the shogunate, Yoritomo banished him and ordered him killed. Rather than face capture, the brother committed seppuku. When the brother's mistress gave birth to a boy, the baby was promptly killed. Today, the lotus ponds, arched bridge, pigeons, and bright vermilion sheen of the shrine give little clue to such violent history.

Kamakura and one of its most popular attractions. It was built by Yoritomo and dedicated to Hachiman, the Shinto god of war who served as the clan deity of the Minamoto family. The pathway to the shrine is along Wakamiya Oji, a cherry tree–lined pedestrian lane that was also constructed by Yoritomo back in the 1190s so that his oldest son's first visit to the family shrine could be accomplished in style with an elaborate procession. The lane stretches from the shrine all the way to Yuigahama Beach, with three massive *torii* (traditional entry gate of a shrine) set at intervals along the route to signal the approach to the shrine. On both sides of the pathway are souvenir and antiques shops selling lacquerware, pottery, and folk art. (I suggest you walk to Kamakura Station via Komachi Dori, a fun pedestrian shopping lane that parallels Wakamiya Oji to the west, and return via Wakamiya Oji.)

At the top of the stairs, which afford a panoramic view toward the sea, is the vermilion-colored shrine with its small shrine museum, not worth the ¥100 admission. However, you can get your fortune in English for ¥100 by shaking out a bamboo stick with a number on it and giving it to the attendant. You can also buy a charm to assure good luck in health, driving a car, business, or other ventures. Shrine grounds are always open, free to the public.

Although it's a bit out of the way, it might pay to visit **Zeniarai-Benten Shrine** (© **0467/25-1081**), about a 20-minute walk west of Kamakura Station. This shrine is dedicated to the goddess of good fortune. On the Asian zodiac's Day of the Snake, worshippers believe that if you take your money and wash it in spring water in a small cave on the shrine grounds, it will double or triple itself later on. This being modern Japan, don't be surprised if you see a bit of ingenuity; my Japanese landlady told me that when she visited the shrine she didn't have much cash on her, so she washed something that she thought would be equally as good—her credit card. Fittingly, admission is free. Open daily 8am to 5pm.

AROUND HASE STATION   To get to these attractions, you can go by bus, which departs from in front of Kamakura Station (take any bus from platform no. 1 or 6 to the Daibutsuen-mae stop). Or, for a more romantic adventure, you can go by the **JR Enoden Line,** a tiny train that putt-putts its way seemingly through backyards on its way from Kamakura Station to Hase and beyond. Since it's mostly only one track, trains have to take turns going in either direction. I suggest that you take the bus from Kamakura Station directly to the Great Buddha, walk to Hase Shrine, and then take the Enoden train back to Kamakura Station.

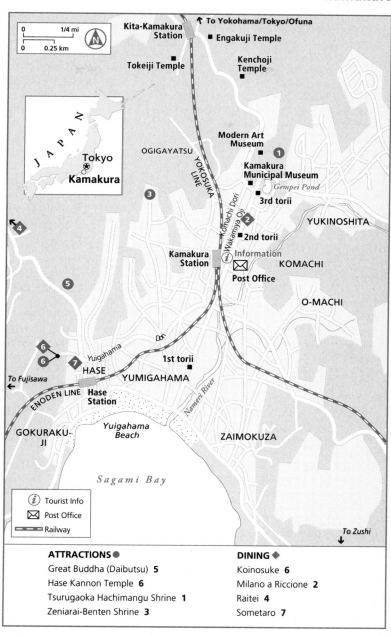

0   1/4 mi
0   0.25 km

N

To Yokohama/Tokyo/Ofuna

Kita-Kamakura
Station

■ Engakuji Temple

Kenchoji
Temple
■

■ Tokeiji Temple

J A P A N

Tokyo

Kamakura

OGIGAYATSU

YOKOSUKA LINE

Modern Art
Museum
■

Kamakura
Municipal Museum
■
Gempei Pond

3rd torii
■

1

3

Komachi Dori

Wakamiya Oji

YUKINOSHITA

2nd torii
■

2

4

Kamakura
Station

i Information

KOMACHI

✉
Post Office

O-MACHI

5

DST

Namen River

6

Yuigahama

1st torii
■

6
7
HASE

YUMIGAHAMA

To Fujisawa ←

ENODEN LINE

Hase
Station

GOKURAKU-
JI

*Yuigahama
Beach*

ZAIMOKUZA

Sagami Bay

i Tourist Info
✉ Post Office
▬ Railway

To Zushi
↓

ATTRACTIONS ●
Great Buddha (Daibutsu) **5**
Hase Kannon Temple **6**
Tsurugaoka Hachimangu Shrine **1**
Zeniarai-Benten Shrine **3**

DINING ◆
Koinosuke **6**
Milano a Riccione **2**
Raitei **4**
Sometaro **7**

Probably Kamakura's most famous attraction is the **Great Buddha** ★★★ (✆ **0467/22-0703**), called the Daibutsu in Japanese and located at **Kotokuin Temple.** Eleven meters (36 ft.) high and weighing 93 tons, it's the second-largest bronze image in Japan. The largest Buddha is in Nara, but in my opinion, the Kamakura Daibutsu is much more impressive. For one thing, the Kamakura Buddha sits outside against a dramatic backdrop of wooded hills. Cast in 1252, the Kamakura Buddha was indeed once housed in a temple like the Nara Buddha, but a huge tidal wave destroyed the wooden structure—and the statue has sat under sun, snow, and stars ever since. I also prefer the face of the Kamakura Buddha; I find it more inspiring and divine, as though with its half-closed eyes and calm, serene face, it's above the worries of the world. It seems to represent the plane above human suffering, the point at which birth and death, joy and sadness, merge and become one. Open daily from 7am to 6pm (to 5:30pm Oct–Mar). Admission is ¥200 for adults and ¥150 for children; I always keep the entry ticket for a bookmark, a nice souvenir. If you want, you can pay an extra ¥20 to go inside the statue—it's hollow—but there's usually a line and I find it claustrophobic.

About a 10-minute walk from the Daibutsu is **Hase Kannon Temple (Hasedera)** ★★★ (✆ **0467/22-6300;** www.hasedera.jp), located on a hill with a sweeping view of the sea. This is the home of an 11-headed gilt statue of Kannon, the goddess of mercy, housed in the Kannon-do (Kannon Hall). More than 9m (30 ft.) high and the tallest wooden image in Japan, it was made in the 8th century from a single piece of camphor wood. The legend surrounding this Kannon is quite remarkable. Supposedly, two wooden images were made from the wood of a huge camphor tree. One of the images was kept in Hase, not far from Nara, while the second was given a short ceremony and then tossed into the sea to find a home of its own. The image drifted 483km (300 miles) eastward and washed up on shore but was thrown back in again because all who touched it became ill or incurred bad luck. Finally, the image reached Kamakura, where it gave the people no trouble. This was interpreted as a sign that the image was content with its surroundings, and Hase Kannon Temple was erected at its present site. Note how each face has a different expression, representing the Kannon's compassion for various kinds of human suffering. Also in the Kannon-do is a museum with religious treasures from the Kamakura, Heian, Muromachi, and Edo periods.

Another golden statue housed here is of **Amida,** a Buddha who promised rebirth in the Pure Land to the West to all who chanted his name. It was created by order of Yoritomo Minamoto upon his 42nd birthday, considered an unlucky year for men. You'll find it housed in the Amida-do (Amida Hall) beside the Kannon-do to the right. Also of interest is the **Kyozo,** with rotating book racks containing sutras (if you give the book racks a spin, it's considered just as auspicious as reading the sutras; but alas, you can do so only on the 18th of each month). **Benten-kutsu Cave** contains many stone images, including one of Benzaiten (seated, with a lute and a money box in front). A sea goddess and patroness of music, art, and good fortune, she is the only female of Japan's Seven Lucky Gods. **Prospect Road** is a 10-minute hiking path featuring flowers in bloom and panoramic views.

As you climb the steps to the Kannon-do, you'll encounter statues of a different sort. All around you will be likenesses of **Jizo,** the guardian deity of children. Although parents originally came to Hase Temple to set up statues to represent their children in hopes the deity would protect and watch over them, through the years the purpose of the Jizo statues changed. Now they represent miscarried, stillborn, or aborted infants. More than 50,000 Jizo statues have been offered here since the war, but the hundreds or so you see now will remain only a year before being burned or buried to make way for others. Some of the statues, which can be purchased on the temple grounds, are fitted with hand-knitted caps, bibs, and sweaters. The effect is quite chilling.

Hase Temple is open daily 8am to 5pm (to 4:30pm Oct–Feb); admission is ¥300 for adults, ¥100 for children.

WHERE TO DINE

In addition to the suggestions below, a simple restaurant called Kaikoan at **Hase Kannon Temple** (described above), serves noodles, desserts, and drinks. After deciding what you want, purchase tickets from a vending machine. It offers a great view, making it a good place for a snack on a fine day; it's open daily from 10am to 4pm.

⑦⑥ **Koinosuke** VARIED JAPANESE   Its location across the square from Kamakura Station and all-day open hours make this a convenient place for a meal, though it lacks atmosphere and therefore is not nearly as memorable as my other recommendations. Still, you can't go wrong ordering one of its many sets, including those with tempura, sashimi, sukiyaki, or steak. The menu is in Japanese only, but there are photos of some of the options.

1–4–1 Komachi, Kamakura. ℂ **0467/25-3740.** Set meals ¥1,900–¥6,930. AE, DC, MC, V. Daily 11am–8:30pm. Station: Kamakura (1 min.). Across the square from the station's east exit, in a modern, gray building.

Milano a Riccione ITALIAN   This is the Japanese branch of a Milan restaurant known for its handmade pasta, seafood, and good selection of wines. Although located in a basement, it opens onto a subterranean courtyard, making it brighter and more cheerful than you would expect. There's an English-language seasonal menu, but the best bargain is the daily set lunch for ¥1,575, which includes an appetizer; a choice of pasta or pizza; and coffee, espresso, or tea. It's the quickest meal you can order, but if you're in a hurry, you should dine elsewhere, as care and time are devoted to the preparation of such meals as sautéed Nagoya cochin chicken with gorgonzola or simmered whole fish. At dinner time, a table charge of ¥315 is levied per person and set meals are available only for two or more diners.

2–12–30 Komachi, Kamakura. ℂ **0467/24-5491.** Reservations required for lunch. Pizza and pasta ¥1,260–¥1,785; main dishes ¥1,785–¥2,572; set dinners ¥4,200–¥4,935; set lunches ¥1,575–¥2,730. AE, DC, MC, V. Thurs-Tues 11:30am–3pm and 5:30–9:30pm (last order). Station: Kamakura (6 min.). On the left side of Wakamiya Oji when walking from Kamakura Station to Tsurugaoka Hachimangu Shrine.

Ⓣ**ips** **A Note on Japanese Symbols**

Many hotels, restaurants, attractions, and other establishments in Japan do not have signs giving their names in Roman (English-language) letters. Chapter 14 lists the Japanese symbols for all such places described in this guide. Each set of characters representing an establishment name has a corresponding number in chapter 14, which appears inside the oval preceding the establishment's name in the text. Thus, to find the Japanese symbol for, say, **Raitei,** refer to no. 77 on p. 326.

⑦ **Raitei** ★★★ Ⓕⁱⁿᵈˢ NOODLES/OBENTO   Though it's a bit inconveniently located, this is the absolute winner for a meal in Kamakura. Visiting Raitei is as much fun as visiting the city's temples and shrines. The restaurant is situated in the hills on the edge of Kamakura, surrounded by verdant countryside, and the wonder is that it serves inexpensive *soba* (Japanese noodles) and *obento* lunchboxes, as well as priestly *kaiseki* feasts. Take the stone steps on the right to the back entry, where you'll be given an English-language menu with such offerings as noodles with chicken, various obento, and kaiseki. The pottery used here comes from the restaurant's own kiln, and you'll sit on rough-hewn wood stools or on tatami. If you make a reservation in advance for kaiseki, you'll dine upstairs in your own private room in a refined traditional setting with great views. The house, once owned by a wealthy landowner, was moved to this site in 1929.

When you've finished your meal, be sure to walk the path looping through the garden past a bamboo grove, Buddhist stone images, and a miniature shrine. The stroll takes about 20 minutes, unless you stop for a beer at the refreshment house, which has outdoor seating and a view of the countryside.

Takasago, Kamakura. Ⓒ **0467/32-5656.** Reservations required for kaiseki. Noodles ¥900–¥1,522; obento lunchboxes ¥3,675; soba set meals ¥2,625; kaiseki feasts from ¥6,300. Entry fee ¥500, which counts toward the price of your meal. AE, DC. Daily 11am–sundown (about 7pm in summer). Bus: no. 4 from platform no. 6 at Kamakura Station or Daibutsuen-mae to Takasago stop (or a 15-min. taxi ride).

⑦⑧ **Sometaro** Ⓥᵃˡᵘᵉ OKONOMIYAKI   Located near the approach to Hase Temple, this small, second-floor restaurant offers do-it-yourself *okonomiyaki* (a kind of Japanese pancake; English-language cooking instructions are available) stuffed with cabbage, bean sprouts, and a choice of a main ingredient such as beef, pork, or shrimp. It also serves *yakisoba* (fried noodles) and *teppanyaki* (grilled steak, seafood or vegetables), all from an English-language menu. The waitress is a bit gruff, but if you can ignore that, you'll enjoy the conviviality of dining here.

3-12-11 Hase, Kamakura. Ⓒ **0467/22-8694.** Reservations recommended for lunch. Main dishes ¥900. No credit cards. Thurs–Tues 11:30am–9pm (last order). Station: Hase (2 min.). On the slope leading to the entrance of Hase Temple, at the beginning on the left side.

2 NIKKO ★★★

150km (93 miles) N of Tokyo

After the publication of James Clavell's novel *Shogun,* many people became familiar with Tokugawa Ieyasu, the powerful real-life shogun of the 1600s on whom Clavell's fictional shogun was based. Quashing all rebellions and unifying Japan under his leadership, Tokugawa established such a military stronghold that his heirs continued to rule Japan for the next 250 years without serious challenge.

Millions of Japanese through the centuries have paid homage to Tokugawa, heading north to Nikko, where **Toshogu Shrine** was constructed in his honor in the 17th century, and where his remains were laid to rest in a mausoleum. Nikko means "sunlight"— an apt description of the way the sun's rays play upon this sumptuous shrine of wood and gold leaf. In fact, nothing else in Japan matches Toshogu Shrine for its opulence. Nearby is another mausoleum containing Tokugawa's grandson, as well as a temple, a shrine, and a garden. Surrounding the sacred grounds, known collectively as **Nikko Sannai** and designated a World Heritage Site by UNESCO in 1999, are thousands of majestic cedar

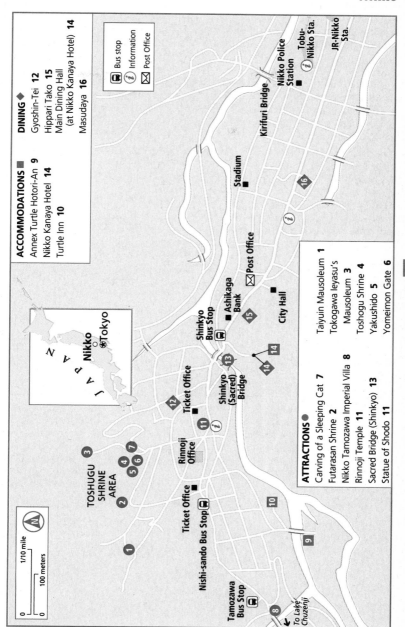

ACCOMMODATIONS ■
Annex Turtle Hotori-An **9**
Nikko Kanaya Hotel **14**
Turtle Inn **10**

DINING ◆
Gyoshin-Tei **12**
Hippari Tako **15**
Main Dining Hall
(at Nikko Kanaya Hotel) **14**
Masudaya **16**

🚌 Bus stop
ⓘ Information
✉ Post Office

ATTRACTIONS ●
Carving of a Sleeping Cat **7**
Futarasan Shrine **2**
Nikko Tamozawa Imperial Villa **8**
Rinnoji Temple **11**
Sacred Bridge (Shinkyo) **13**
Statue of Shodo **11**
Taiyuin Mausoleum **1**
Tokogawa Ieyasu's
  Mausoleum **3**
Toshogu Shrine **4**
Yakushido **5**
Yomeimon Gate **6**

trees in the 200,000-acre **Nikko National Park.** Another worthwhile sight is **Nikko Tamozawa Imperial Villa,** built in 1899.

I've included a few recommendations for an overnight stay. Otherwise, you can see Nikko in a very full day. Plan on 4 to 5 hours for round-trip transportation, 2½ hours for Toshogu Shrine and vicinity, and 1 hour for the Imperial villa.

ESSENTIALS

GETTING THERE   The easiest, fastest, and most luxurious way to get to Nikko is on the privately owned Tobu Line's Limited Express, called the **Spacia,** which departs every hour or more frequently from Tobu's Asakusa Station. The cost is ¥2,620 one-way for the 1-hour-and-50-minute trip on weekdays, and ¥2,720 on weekends and holidays (most trains require a transfer at Shimo-Imaichi Station). All seats are reserved, which means you are guaranteed a seat; if you're traveling on a holiday or a summer weekend, you may wish to purchase and reserve your ticket in advance. Another plus is that there's usually an English-speaking hostess on board who passes out pamphlets on the area and can answer sightseeing questions about Nikko.

To save money, consider purchasing Tobu's World Heritage Pass, which provides round-trip train travel between Asakusa and Nikko via Limited Express, unlimited bus travel in Nikko, and admission to Toshogu Shrine (excluding Ieyasu's mausoleum), Rinnoji Temple, and Futarasan Shrine. Cost of the pass, valid for 2 days and available only to foreign visitors, is ¥3,600 for adults, ¥3,200 for senior high students, ¥3,000 for junior high students, and ¥1,700 for children. You can purchase the pass online at www.tobu.co.jp/foreign or at the Tobu Sightseeing Service Center at Asakusa Station (© 03/3841-2871), open daily 7:45am to 5pm.

Otherwise, you can reach Nikko on Tobu's slower **rapid train** from Asakusa, which costs ¥1,320 one-way and takes 2 hours and 10 minutes, with trains departing every hour or more frequently. There is no reserved seating, which means you might have to stand if trains are crowded.

You can also travel to Nikko via JR train. There are four trains a day from Shinjuku, most requiring a change of trains in Shimo-Imaichi station for onward travel to Nikko. Trips take about 2 hours. If you're visiting **Mashiko** (see later in this chapter), you can save yourself the hassle of buying train tickets from different rail companies (Tobu and JR) by taking the JR Utsunomiya Line (also called Tohoku Honsen Line) from Shinjuku, Shibuya, or Ueno to JR Utsunomiya Station for the bus to Mashiko, and then continuing onward from JR Utsunomiya Station to Nikko (the Tobu Line does not travel btw. Utsunomiya and Nikko). Faster but more expensive is the Shinkansen bullet train from Tokyo to Utsunomiya (there are departures every 20–40 min. and the trip takes about 55 min.), where you change for the train to Nikko (45 min.).

VISITOR INFORMATION   Before leaving Tokyo, pick up the Nikko leaflet from the Tourist Information Center (TIC). It gives the train schedule for both the Tobu Line, which departs from Tobu's Asakusa Station, and JR trains that depart from Shinjuku Station. The TIC also has color brochures with maps of the Nikko area.

Nikko's Tobu and JR stations are located almost side by side in the village's downtown area. **Nikko Tobu Station tourist information counter** (© **0288/53-4511;** www.nikko-jp.org; daily 8:30am–5pm), located inside Tobu Station, has staff who can give you a map, answer basic questions, and point you in the right direction. You can also make hotel and ryokan reservations here for ¥100. The **Nikko Information Center** (© **0288/54-2496;** daily 9am–5pm), located on the left side of the main road leading from the train station to Toshogu Shrine (next to Eneos gas station), has English-speaking staff and lots of information in English about Nikko, including information on public hot springs.

GETTING AROUND   Toshogu Shrine and its mausoleum are on the edge of town, but you can walk from either the JR or Tobu train stations to the shrine in about half an hour. Head straight out the main exit, pass the bus stands, and then turn right. English-language signs point the way throughout town. Keep walking on this main road (you'll pass the Nikko Information Center about halfway down on the left side, as well as souvenir shops) until you come to a T-intersection with a vermilion-colored bridge spanning a river (about a 15-min. walk from the train stations). The stone steps opposite lead up the hill into the woods and to Toshogu Shrine. You can also travel from Tobu Station by bus, getting off at either the Shinkyo (a 7-min. ride) or Nishi Sando (a 10-min. ride) bus stop.

SEEING THE SIGHTS

ON THE WAY TO THE SHRINE   The first indication that you're nearing the shrine is the vermilion-painted **Sacred Bridge (Shinkyo)** arching over the rushing Daiyagawa River. It was built in 1636, and for more than 3 centuries only shoguns and their emissaries were allowed to cross it. Today, you can cross it by paying ¥300, or you can take the modern vehicular bridge for free.

Across the road from the Sacred Bridge, steps lead uphill into a forest of cedar where, after a 5-minute walk, you'll see a statue of **Shodo,** a priest who founded Nikko 1,200 years ago at a time when mountains were revered as gods. In the centuries that followed, Nikko became one of Japan's greatest mountain Buddhist retreats, with 500 subtemples spread through the area. Behind Shodo is the first major temple, Rinnoji Temple, where you can buy a **combination ticket** for ¥1,300 for adults, ¥450 for children; it allows entry to Rinnoji Temple and its garden, Toshogu Shrine, neighboring Futarasan Shrine, and the other Tokugawa mausoleum, Taiyuin. Once at Toshogu Shrine, you'll have to pay an extra ¥520 to see Ieyasu's tomb. Combination tickets sold at the entry to Toshogu Shrine already include Ieyasu's tomb. It doesn't really matter where you buy your combination ticket, since you can always pay the extra fee to see sights not covered. A note for bus riders: If you take the bus to the Nishi Sando bus stop, the first place you'll come to is the Taiyuin Mausoleum, where you can also purchase a combination ticket.

Toshogu Shrine and the other sights in Nikko Sannai are open daily April to October from 8am to 5pm (to 4pm the rest of the year); you must enter at least 30 minutes before closing time.

RINNOJI TEMPLE   Rinnoji Temple (℗ **0288/54-0531**) was founded by the priest Shodo in the 8th century, long before the Toshogu clan came onto the scene. Here you can visit **Sanbutsudo Hall,** a large building that enshrines three 8.4m-high (28-ft.) gold-plated wooden images of Buddha, considered the "gods of Nikko"; today people pray here for world peace. Perhaps the best thing to see at Rinnoji Temple is **Shoyo-en Garden** (opposite Sanbutsudo Hall). Completed in 1815 and typical of Japanese landscaped gardens of the Edo Period, this small strolling garden provides a different vista with each turn of the path, making it seem much larger than it is. Your ticket also gains entrance to a small treasure house, where relics are displayed on a rotating basis.

TOSHOGU SHRINE ★★★   The most important and famous structure in Nikko is Toshogu Shrine (℗ **0288/54-0560**), built by Tokugawa's grandson (and third Tokugawa shogun), Tokugawa Iemitsu, as an act of devotion. It seems that no expense was too great in creating the monument: Some 15,000 artists and craftspeople were brought to Nikko from all over Japan, and after 2 years' work, they erected a group of buildings more elaborate and gorgeous than any other Japanese temple or shrine. Rich in colors and carvings, Toshogu Shrine is gilded with 2.4 million sheets of gold leaf (they could cover an area of almost 2.4 ha/6 acres). The mausoleum was completed in 1636, almost 20 years after Ieyasu's death, and was most certainly meant to impress anyone who saw it as a demonstration of the Tokugawa shogunate's wealth and power. The shrine is set in a grove of magnificent ancient **Japanese cedars** planted over a 20-year period during the 1600s by a feudal lord named Matsudaira Masasuna. Some 13,000 of the original trees still stand, adding a sense of dignity to the mausoleum and shrine.

You enter Toshogu Shrine via a flight of stairs that passes under a huge stone torii gateway, one of the largest in Japan. On your left is a five-story, 35m-high (115-ft.) **pagoda.** Although normally pagodas are found only at temples, this pagoda is just one example of how Buddhism and Shintoism are combined at Toshogu Shrine. After climbing a second flight of stairs, turn left and you'll see the **Sacred Stable,** which houses a sacred white horse. Horses have long been dedicated to Shinto gods and are kept at shrines. Shrines also kept monkeys as well, since they were thought to protect horses from disease; look for the three monkeys carved above the stable door, fixed in the poses of "see no evil, hear no evil, speak no evil"—they're considered guardians of the sacred horse. Across from the stable is **Kami-Jinko,** famous for its carving by Kano Tanyu, who painted the images of the two elephants after reading about them but without seeing what they actually looked like.

The central showpiece of Nikko is **Yomeimon Gate,** popularly known as the Twilight Gate, implying that it could take you all day (until twilight) to see everything carved on it. Painted in red, blue, and green, and gilded and lacquered, this gate is carved with about 400 flowers, dragons, birds, and other animals. It's almost too much to take in at once and is very un-Japanese in its opulence, having more in common with Chinese architecture than with the usual austerity of most Japanese shrines.

You can visit the shrine's main sanctuary, **Hai-den,** comprising three halls: One was reserved for the Imperial family, one for the shogun, and one (the central hall) for conducting ceremonies. You can buy good-luck charms here that will guard against such misfortunes as traffic accidents, or that will ensure good health, success in business, easy childbirth, or other achievements in daily life. To the right of the main hall is the entrance to **Tokugawa Ieyasu's mausoleum.** If it's not already included in your combination ticket, admission is ¥520 extra. After the ticket counter, look for the carving of a sleeping cat above the door, dating from the Edo Period and famous today as a symbol of Nikko (you'll find many reproductions in area souvenir shops). Beyond that are 200 stone steps leading past cedars to Tokugawa's tomb. After the riotous colors of the shrine, the tomb seems surprisingly simple.

On the way out you'll pass **Yakushido,** famous for its dragon painting on the ceiling. A monk gives a brief explanation (in Japanese only) and demonstrates how two sticks struck together produce an echo that supposedly resonates like a bell. Twelve statues here represent the Chinese zodiac calendar.

FUTARASAN SHRINE Directly to the west of Toshogu Shrine is Futarasan Shrine (© **0288/54-0535**), the oldest building in the district (from 1617), which has a pleasant garden and is dedicated to the gods of mountains surrounding Nikko. You'll find miniature shrines dedicated to the god of fortune, god of happiness, god of trees, god of water, and god of good marriages. On the shrine's grounds is the so-called **ghost lantern,**

enclosed in a small vermilion-colored wooden structure. According to legend, it used to come alive at night and sweep around Nikko in the form of a ghost. It apparently scared one guard so much that he struck it with his sword 70 times; the marks are still visible on the lamp's rim. Entrance to the miniature shrines and ghost lantern is ¥200 extra.

TAIYUIN MAUSOLEUM ★   Past Futarasan Shrine is **Taiyuin Mausoleum** (**© 0288/53-1567**), the final resting place of Iemitsu, the third Tokugawa shogun (look for his statue). Completed in 1653, it's not nearly as large as Toshogu Shrine, but it's ornate and serenely elegant nevertheless. To show respect for the first shogun, Taiyuin's buildings face Toshogu Shrine. Tourists usually bypass this shrine, making it a pleasant last stop on your tour of Nikko Sannai.

NIKKO TAMOZAWA IMPERIAL VILLA (TAMOZAWA GOYOUTEI KINEN KOEN) ★★
If you haven't seen the Imperial villas of Kyoto (which require advance planning), this villa, at 8–27 Honcho (**© 0288/53-6767**), is a great alternative. Although it's not as old, having been built in 1899 for Prince Yoshihito (who later became the Taisho emperor) and recently painstakingly restored so that it looks brand new, it has the distinction of being the largest wooden Imperial villa of its era, with 106 rooms, 37 of which are open to the public. In addition, the central core of the villa is actually much older, constructed in 1632 by a feudal lord and brought to Nikko from Edo (present-day Tokyo). Altogether, three emperors and three princes used the villa between 1899 and 1947. A self-guided tour of the villa provides insight into traditional Japanese architectural methods—from its 11 layers of paper-plastered walls to its nail-less wood framing—as well as the lifestyle of Japan's aristocracy. Be sure to wander the small, outdoor garden. Admission is ¥500 for adults, half-price for children. Open Wednesday to Monday 9am to 4:30pm. It's about a 20-minute walk from Toshogu Shrine, or take the bus to the Tamozawa stop.

WHERE TO STAY

If it's peak season (Golden Week, Aug, or Oct) or a weekend, it's best to reserve a room in advance, which you can do by calling a lodging either directly or through a travel agency in Tokyo. Off-peak, you can make a reservation upon arrival at Nikko Tobu Station, either at the **tourist information counter** or at the **accommodations-reservation window** (**© 0288/54-0864;** Mon–Fri 9am–5pm, Sat–Sun and holidays 8:25am–5:55pm), both of which are familiar with the area accommodations and will make all arrangements for you. Note that the charge for booking a room at either of these facilities is ¥100 per person.

Moderate

Nikko Kanaya Hotel ★★ (Finds   Founded in 1873, this distinguished-looking place on a hill above the Sacred Bridge is the most famous hotel in Nikko, combining the rustic heartiness of a European country lodge with elements of old Japan. The present complex, built in spurts over the past 137 years, has a rambling, delightfully old-fashioned atmosphere that fuses Western architecture with Japanese craftsmanship. Through the decades it has played host to a number of VIPs, from Charles Lindbergh to Indira Gandhi to Shirley MacLaine; Frank Lloyd Wright left a sketch for the bar fireplace, which was later built to his design. Even if you don't stay here, you might want to drop by for lunch (see review below). Pathways lead to the Daiyagawa River and several short hiking trails. All rooms are Western-style twins, with the differences in price based on room size, view (river view is best), and facilities. Some 10 rooms have been updated, but

I prefer the older, simpler rooms because they have more character; some have antiques and claw-foot tubs. The best (and priciest) room in the house is the corner room in the 72-year-old wing where the emperor once stayed.

1300 Kami-Hatsuishi, Nikko City, Tochigi 321-1401. (C) **0288/54-0001**. Fax 0288/53-2487. www.kanaya-hotel.co.jp. 70 units. ¥15,015–¥46,200 single; ¥17,325–¥51,970 double. ¥3,465–¥4,620 extra on Fri, Sat, and eve before national holidays; ¥5,775 extra in peak season. AE, DC, MC, V. Bus: From Nikko Tobu Station to the Shinkyo stop, a 5-min. ride. On foot: 20 min. from Nikko Tobu Station (on foot: 20 min.). **Amenities:** 3 restaurants, including the Main Dining Hall; bar; small outdoor heated pool (summer only); outdoor skating rink (in winter). *In room:* A/C, TV, minibar.

Inexpensive

Annex Turtle Hotori-An ★★ **Kids** Owned by the super-friendly family that runs Turtle Inn (see below), this is one of my favorite places to stay in Nikko. One dip in the hot-spring bath overlooking the Daiyagawa River (which you can lock for privacy) will tell you why; at night, you're lulled to sleep by the sound of the rushing waters. A simple but spotless modern structure (all nonsmoking), it's located in a nice rural setting on a quiet street with a few other houses; an adjoining park and playground provide plenty of space for kids to play. All its rooms except one are Japanese style. A plentiful Western-style breakfast costs ¥1,050 in the pleasant living area/dining room. For dinner, you can go to the nearby Turtle Inn (not available Sun, Tues, or Thurs; reservations should be made the day before), or buy a pizza from the freezer and microwave it yourself. There's also a communal refrigerator where you can store food.

8–28 Takumi-cho, Nikko City, Tochigi 321-1433. (C) **0288/53-3663**. Fax 0288/53-3883. www.turtle-nikko.com. 11 units. ¥6,500 single; ¥12,400 double. ¥300 extra per person in peak season. Hot-spring tax ¥150 extra. Special rates for children. Winter discount available. AE, MC, V. Bus: From Nikko Station to the Sogo Kaikan-mae stop, a 7-min. ride; then a 9-min. walk. **Amenities:** Hot-spring baths; computer w/free Internet access at Turtle Inn. *In room:* A/C, TV.

Turtle Inn ★ This excellent, nonsmoking pension, a Japanese Inn Group member, is located within walking distance of Toshogu Shrine in a newer two-story house on a quiet side street beside the Daiyagawa River. The friendly owner, Mr. Fukuda, speaks English and is very helpful in planning a sightseeing itinerary. Rooms are bright and cheerful in both Japanese and Western styles; the five tatami rooms are without a private bathroom. Excellent Japanese dinners (served on local Mashiko pottery) are available for ¥2,100, as are Western breakfasts for ¥1,050. Be sure to order dinner the day before, and note that it's not available on Sunday, Tuesday, or Thursday.

2–16 Takumi-cho, Nikko City, Tochigi 321-1433. (C) **0288/53-3168**. Fax 0288/53-3883. www.turtle-nikko.com. 10 units (3 with bathroom). ¥4,800 single without bathroom, ¥5,600 single with bathroom; ¥9,000 double without bathroom, ¥10,600 double with bathroom. ¥300 extra per person in peak season. Hot-spring tax ¥150 extra. Special rates for children. Winter discounts available. AE, MC, V. Bus: From Nikko Station to the Sogo Kaikan-mae stop, a 7-min. ride; then a 5-min. walk. **Amenities:** Hot-spring baths; computer w/free Internet access. *In room:* A/C, TV, no phone.

WHERE TO DINE

Expensive

Main Dining Hall at Nikko Kanaya Hotel ★★ **Finds** CONTINENTAL Even if you don't spend the night here, the Kanaya Hotel's quaint dining hall with its wood-carved pillars is one of the best places in town for lunch. Because it's beside the Sacred Bridge, only a 10-minute walk from Toshogu Shrine, you can easily combine it with your sightseeing tour. I suggest Nikko's specialty: locally caught rainbow trout available cooked three different ways. I always order mine cooked Kanaya style—covered with soy sauce, sugar, and sake; grilled; and served whole. The best bargain is the set lunch for ¥3,500, available until 3pm, which comes with soup, salad, a main dish such as trout, bread or rice, and dessert. Steak, lobster, salmon, chicken, and other Western fare are also listed on the English-language menu.

Nikko Kanaya Hotel, 1300 Kami-Hatsuishi, Nikko City. ℂ **0288/54-0001.** Reservations recommended during peak season. Main dishes ¥2,900–¥9,240; set lunches from ¥3,500; set dinners ¥9,800. AE, DC, MC, V. Daily 11:30am–3pm and 6–8pm. A 20-min. walk from Nikko Tobu Station.

Moderate

Gyoshin-Tei ★★ VEGETARIAN/KAISEKI   This lovely Japanese restaurant, with a simple tatami room and a view of pines, moss, and bonsai, serves two kinds of set meals—kaiseki and Buddhist vegetarian cuisine—both of which change monthly and include the local specialty, *yuba* (see Masudaya, below). It's one of several restaurants in a parklike setting all under the same management and with the same open hours. Meijino-Yakata (closed Wed), occupying a stone house built 110 years ago as the private retreat of an American businessman, serves Western food such as grilled rainbow trout, veal cutlet, and steak, with set meals ranging from ¥3,990 to ¥8,400. Fujimoto (closed Thurs), in a small stone cottage, serves French food created with Japanese ingredients and eaten with chopsticks. All restaurants offer a set lunch for ¥3,150. The drawback: This place is harder to find than my other recommendations, but it's only a 4-minute walk northeast of Rinnoji Temple.

2339–1 Sannai, Nikko City. ℂ **0288/53-3751.** Reservations recommended. Vegetarian/kaiseki meals ¥3,990–¥5,775; set lunches ¥3,150. AE, DC, MC, V. Fri–Wed 11am–7pm (from 11:30am in winter). A 25-min. walk from Nikko Tobu Station; or bus from Nikko Station to Shinkyo (then a 7-min. walk).

Masudaya ★ YUBA   Only two fixed-price meals are served at this Japanese-style, 80-year-old restaurant, both featuring *yuba,* a high-protein food made from soybeans and produced only in Kyoto and Nikko. Until 100 years ago, it could be eaten only by priests and members of the Imperial family. Now you can enjoy it, too, along with such sides as rice, sashimi, soup, fried fish, and vegetables. Dining is either in a common dining hall (reserve 2 days in advance) or, for the more expensive meals, in private tatami rooms upstairs (reserve 1 week in advance).

439 Ichiyamachi, Nikko City. ℂ **0288/54-2151.** Reservations required. Yuba kaiseki meals ¥3,990 and ¥5,450. No credit cards. Fri–Wed 10:30am–4pm (closes earlier if it runs out of set meals; open Thurs if a holiday). A 5-min. walk from Nikko Tobu Station. On the left side of the main street leading from Tobu Station to Toshogu Shrine, just before the fire station.

Inexpensive

⑦⑨ **Hippari Tako** NOODLES   This tiny, three-table establishment is under the caring supervision of motherly Miki-san, who serves a limited selection of noodle dishes, including ramen and stir-fried noodles with vegetables, as well as *onigiri* (rice balls), vegetarian tempura, and *yakitori* (skewered barbecued chicken). There's an English-language menu, and the walls, covered with business cards and messages left by appreciative guests from around the world, are testimony to both the tasty meals and Miki-san's warm hospitality. A computer allows guests access to the Internet 30 minutes for free.

1011 Kami-Hatsuishi, Nikko City. ℂ **0288/53-2933.** Main dishes ¥650–¥850. No credit cards. Daily 11am–7pm (last order). A 15-min. walk from Nikko Tobu Station. On the left side of the main street leading from Toshogu Shrine, 1 min. before the Nikko Kanaya Hotel and the Sacred Bridge.

SIDE TRIPS FROM TOKYO

3 MASHIKO

100km (62 miles) N of Tokyo

Mashiko is a small village known throughout Japan for its *Mashiko-yaki,* distinctive, heavy, country-style pottery. A visit to Mashiko can be combined with an overnight trip to Nikko (see earlier); both are not far from the town of Utsunomiya, north of Tokyo. Because the major attraction in Mashiko is its pottery shops and kilns, there's little in the way of restaurants and accommodations, so I suggest that you come here just for the day, and return to Tokyo or travel on to Nikko before nightfall. Plan on spending about 3 hours in Mashiko, plus several hours for transportation.

Mashiko's history as a pottery town began in 1853, when a potter discovered ideal conditions in the nearby mountain clay and red pine wood for firing. It wasn't until 1930, however, that Mashiko gained national fame, when the late Hamada Shoji, designated a "Living National Treasure," built a kiln here and introduced Mashiko-ware throughout Japan. Other potters have since taken up his technique, producing ceramics for everyday use, including plates, cups, vases, and tableware. There are about 50 pottery shops in Mashiko (along with about 300 kilns) where you can browse and watch craftspeople at work. Pottery fairs, held twice a year in late April/early May and late October/early November, attract visitors from throughout Japan.

ESSENTIALS
Getting There
You must first take a train from Tokyo to Utsunomiya; transfer there for a bus to Mashiko.

BY TRAIN   The fastest but most expensive way to reach Utsunomiya is aboard the **Tohoku Shinkansen,** which departs from Tokyo Station and Ueno every 20 to 40 minutes and arrives in Utsunomiya approximately 55 minutes later; the one-way fare is ¥4,290 for an unreserved seat. Otherwise, take the **JR Utsunomiya** (also called the Tohoku Honsen) rapid train from Shinjuku, Shibuya, or Ueno Station, which departs approximately every hour and takes 90-some minutes to reach Utsunomiya JR station (¥1,890 one-way). If you're stopping off in Mashiko on your way to Nikko, note that only JR trains (not the Tobu Line) travel between Utsunomiya and Nikko (see "Nikko," earlier).

BY BUS   Upon reaching Utsunomiya JR station, take the west exit to the bus terminal just outside the station. Buses operated by the Toya Bus company (✆ **028/662-1080**) depart from platform no. 14 approximately every hour, taking about 1 hour to reach Mashiko and costing ¥1,100 one-way. Alight at the **Sankokanmae bus stop.**

VISITOR INFORMATION   There's a **tourist information counter** at JR Utsunomiya station (✆ **028/636-2177**), open daily 8:30am to 8pm, where you can obtain information on buses heading to Mashiko. In Mashiko, the **tourist information office** is inconveniently located at the tiny Mashiko train station, open daily 8:30am to 5:30pm (✆ **0285/70-1120**).

WHAT TO SEE & DO
Once you alight from the bus at the Sankokanmae stop, turn left at the stoplight just ahead for the **Mashiko Reference Collection Museum,** also called (80) **Mashiko Sankokan** (✆ **0285/72-5300**), a compound of several thatch-roofed farmhouses and

exhibition halls that served as Hamada Shoji's workshop and home from 1925 until his death in 1978 at the age of 83. Galleries here showcase about 30 of his works, as well as his private collection of Eastern and Western glass, ceramics, fabrics, furniture, and paintings, including pieces by Bernard Leach and Kanjiro Kawai. You can also see his "climbing kiln," built along the slope of a hill. Plan on at least a half-hour here. Admission is ¥800 for adults, half-price for children. It's open Tuesday through Sunday 9:30am to 4:30pm; closed New Year's and February.

A 7-minute walk from Mashiko Sankokan (reached by backtracking to the bus stop and then turning left at the first stoplight) is **Ceramic Art Messe Mashiko,** or **Togei Messe Mashiko** (© 0285/72-7555), a visitor's complex devoted to pottery, woodblock prints, and changing art exhibits. Works by Hamada, as well as pieces by Mashiko potters and pottery from around Japan, are on display, along with a former thatched home that once belonged to Hamada. Admission is ¥600 for adults, half-price for children. The complex is open Tuesday to Sunday 9:30am to 5pm (to 4pm in winter).

SHOPPING

The main reason people come to Mashiko is to shop. Alongside the Togei Messe complex is one of the largest shops, **Mashiko Pottery Center,** or ⑧⑴ **Mashikoyaki Kyohan Center** (© 0285/72-4444; daily 9am–5:30pm). On the other side of the Kyohan Center is the **main street** of Mashiko, where you'll find dozens of shops offering a vast selection of pottery created by the town's potters. Wander in and out—you're sure to find something you like.

4 YOKOHAMA

29km (18 miles) S of Tokyo

Few attractions in Yokohama warrant a visit if you're just in Japan for a short time. If you're in Tokyo for an extended period, however, Yokohama is a pleasant destination for an easy day trip. Be sure to make time for wonderful Sankeien Garden; although a mere 100 years old, it ranks on my long list as one of the top gardens in Japan.

A rather new city in Japan's history books, Yokohama was nothing more than a tiny fishing village when Commodore Perry arrived in the mid-1800s and demanded that Japan open its doors to the world. The village was selected by the shogun as one of several ports to be opened for international trade, transforming it from a backwater to Japan's most important gateway. Yokohama subsequently grew by leaps and bounds and was a pioneer when it came to Western goods and services, boasting Japan's first bakery (1860), photo studio (1862), beer brewery (1869), cinema (1870), daily newspaper (1870), public restroom (1871), and ice cream (1879).

Now Japan's second-largest city with a population of almost 3.6 million, Yokohama remains the nation's largest international port and supports a large international community, with many foreigners residing in the section called the Bluff. Yokohama has an especially large Chinese population and Japan's largest Chinatown, whose restaurants serve as a mecca for hungry Tokyoites. Befitting a city known for its firsts, Yokohama constructed Japan's first and largest urban development project more than a decade ago—**Minato Mirai 21,** with a conference center, museums, hotels, shopping centers, and restaurants. Hard to imagine that a mere 150 years ago, Yokohama was a village of 100 houses.

GETTING THERE   Because many Yokohama residents work in Tokyo, it's as easy to get to Yokohama as it is to get around Tokyo. Although Yokohama Station is the city's main train station, I suggest taking a train from Tokyo that will take you farther to Sakuragicho, Minato Mirai, or Motomachi Chukagai station, since most attractions are clustered here. (However, if you're headed first to Sankeien Garden, you'll want to disembark at Yokohama Station and transfer to bus no. 8 at the east exit.) Best is the **Minato Mirai Line** (of the Tokyu-Toyoko private company), which departs from Shibuya and reaches Minato Mirai in about 30 minutes on the limited express. A one-way fare costs ¥440; an all-day Minato Mirai Line pass, including transportation from Shibuya and back, is worth the cost of ¥840. Alternatively, the **JR Keihin-Tohoku Line** travels through Ueno, Tokyo, Yurakucho, Shimbashi, and Shinagawa stations before continuing on to Sakuragicho, with the journey from Tokyo Station taking approximately 40 minutes and costing ¥540 one-way.

VISITOR INFORMATION   There are several Tourist Information Centers in Yokohama, but probably the most convenient and easiest to find is **Sakuragicho Station Tourist Information Center** (𝒸 045/211-0111; daily 9am–7pm), located in a kiosk outside JR Sakuragicho Station in the direction of Minato Mirai and its Landmark Tower. The main office, the **Yokohama Convention & Visitors Bureau,** is located in the Sangyo Boeki Center (nicknamed Sambo Center), 2 Yamashita-cho, Naka-ku (𝒸 045/641-4759; www. welcome.city.yokohama.jp/tourism; Mon–Fri 9am–5pm), close to the Silk Center and Yamashita Park. Both have excellent city maps and brochures.

Next door to the Convention & Visitors Bureau, in the Silk Center, is the **Kanagawa Prefectural Tourist Office** (𝒸 045/681-0007; www.kanagawa-kankou.or.jp; Tues–Sun 10am–6pm), with information on Hakone and Kamakura, both in Kanagawa Prefecture.

GETTING AROUND   If you start your day in Yokohama at either Sakuragicho or Minato Mirai Station, you can visit the museums and attractions there and then walk onward to Yamashita Park via a waterfront promenade (about a 30-min. walk, with a stop, perhaps, at the Red Brick Warehouse shopping mall on the way). If you prefer not to walk, there's a red retro-looking tourist bus called the **Akai Kutsu,** which makes the rounds of central Yokohama, including Sakuragicho Station, Minato Mirai, Yamashita Park, and Chinatown throughout the year, with departures every 20 to 30 minutes and costing ¥100 per ride (pick up a map and timetable at the Sakuragicho Station tourist office). To reach Sankeien Garden, take bus no. 8, which departs from Yokohama Station's east exit and passes Minato Mirai, Chinatown, and Yamashita Park on its way to the garden. If you end the day with a meal at Chinatown, you can catch the Minato Mirai Line back to Shibuya at nearby Motomachi Chukagai Station.

SEEING THE SIGHTS

MINATO MIRAI   There's no mistaking **Minato Mirai 21** (www.minatomirai21.com) when you see it—it looks like a vision of the future with its dramatic monolithic buildings. It boasts a huge state-of-the-art convention facility, three first-class hotels, Japan's tallest building, office buildings, two great museums, and an amusement park. It's all a bit too sterile for my taste, but its museums make a visit here worthwhile.

If you arrive at Sakuragicho Station, take the moving walkway that connects the station to the Landmark Tower in Minato Mirai in 5 minutes. Otherwise, the Minato Mirai Line will deposit you directly in the middle of the massive urban development.

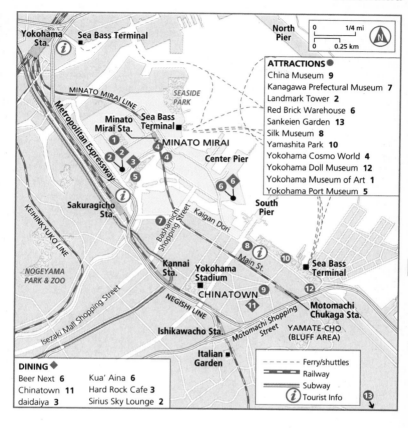

ATTRACTIONS ●
China Museum **9**
Kanagawa Prefectural Museum **7**
Landmark Tower **2**
Red Brick Warehouse **6**
Sankeien Garden **13**
Silk Museum **8**
Yamashita Park **10**
Yokohama Cosmo World **4**
Yokohama Doll Museum **12**
Yokohama Museum of Art **1**
Yokohama Port Museum **5**

DINING ◆
Beer Next **6**   Kua' Aina **6**
Chinatown **11**   Hard Rock Cafe **3**
daidaiya **3**   Sirius Sky Lounge **2**

- - - - - Ferry/shuttles
━━━━━ Railway
━━━━━ Subway
ⓘ Tourist Info

    There are several shopping malls in Minato Mirai, including Queen's Square, Yokohama World Porter's, Landmark Plaza, Jack Mall, and the restored Red Brick Warehouse, but the area's most conspicuous building is **Landmark Tower,** Japan's tallest building and also with Japan's highest observatory in a building. The fastest elevator in the world will whisk you up 270m (886 ft.) in about 40 seconds to the 69th floor, where there's an observation room called **Sky Garden** (✆ **045/222-5030;** daily 10am–9pm, to 10pm Sat). From here you can see the harbor with its container port and Yokohama Bay Bridge, as well as almost the entire city and even, on clear days in winter, Mount Fuji. However, its admission fees—¥1,000 for adults, ¥800 for seniors and high-school students, ¥500 for elementary and junior-high students, and ¥200 for children—make it too expensive in my book. Better is Landmark Tower's 70th-floor **Sirius Sky Lounge;** although there's a cover charge, its atmosphere is more relaxing (see below).
    Maritime buffs should spend an hour checking out the **Yokohama Port Museum (Yokohama Minato Hakubutsukan),** 2–1–1 Minato Mirai (✆ **045/221-0280;**

www.nippon-maru.or.jp), which concentrates on Yokohama's history as a port, beginning with the arrival of Perry's "Black Ships." Other displays chart the evolution of ships from Japan and around the world from the 19th century to the present, with lots of models of everything from passenger ships to oil tankers and a full-scale simulator that lets you bring a cruise ship into Yokohama's port. Kids like the three telescopes connected to cameras placed around Yokohama and the captain's bridge with a steering wheel; sailing fans enjoy touring the 96m (315-ft.), four-masted *Nippon-Maru* moored nearby, built in 1930 as a sail-training ship for students of the merchant marines. Admission is ¥600 for adults and ¥300 for children. The museum is open Tuesday to Sunday 10am to 5pm.

The most important thing to see in Minato Mirai is the **Yokohama Museum of Art** ★, 3–4–1 Minato Mirai (© 045/221-0300), which emphasizes 20th-century art by Western and Japanese artists in its ambitious goal to collect and display works reflecting the mutual influence of Europe and Japan on modern art since the opening of Yokohama's port in 1859. The light and airy building, designed by Kenzo Tange and Urtec, Inc., features exhibits from its permanent collection—which includes works by Cézanne, Picasso, Matisse, Leger, Max Ernst, Dalí, and Japanese artists—that change three times a year (you can tour its four rooms in about 30 min.), as well as special exhibitions on loan from other museums. Open Friday through Wednesday from 10am to 6pm. Admission is ¥500 for adults, ¥300 for high-school and college students, and ¥100 for children. Special exhibitions cost more.

It would be hard to miss **Yokohama Cosmo World** (© 045/641-6591), an amusement park spread along both sides of a canal: It boasts one of the largest Ferris wheels in the world. Other diversions include a roller coaster that looks like it dives right into a pond (but vanishes instead into a tunnel), a haunted house, a simulation theater with seats that move with the action, kiddie rides, a games arcade, and much more. Admission is free but rides cost ¥300 to ¥700 apiece. The park is open 11am to 8pm in winter and 11am to 10pm in summer; closed most Thursdays (except in summer).

IN & AROUND YAMASHITA PARK You can walk to Yamashita Park from Minato Mirai's Cosmo World in less than 30 minutes along a waterfront promenade. Along the way you'll pass the **Red Brick Warehouse (Aka Renga),** located in the Shinko-cho district of Minato Mirai (© 045/227-2002). This restored waterfront warehouse is home to dozens of shops selling crafts, furniture, housewares, clothing, and jewelry, as well as restaurants, with most shops open daily 11am to 8pm. If you don't want to walk, take the Minato Mirai Line to either Nihon Odori or Motomachi Chukagai Station, from which Yamashita Park is about a 5-minute walk.

Laid out after the huge 1923 earthquake that destroyed much of Tokyo and Yokohama, Yamashita Park is Japan's first seaside park, a pleasant place for a stroll along the waterfront where you have a view of the city's mighty harbor and Bay Bridge. Across the gingko-lined street from Yamashita Park are two worthwhile special-interest museums. At the west end (closest to Minato Mirai) is the Silk Center, where you'll find both the prefectural tourist office and the excellent **Silk Museum** ★★, 1 Yamashita-cho, Naka-ku (© 045/641-0841; www.silkmuseum.or.jp; station: Nihon Odori). For many years after Japan opened its doors, silk was its major export, and most of it was shipped to the rest of the world from Yokohama, the nation's largest raw-silk market. In tribute to the role silk has played in Yokohama's history, this museum has displays showing the metamorphosis of the silkworm and the process by which silk is obtained from cocoons, all well documented in English; from April to October, you can even observe live cocoons and silkworms at work (compared to the beauty they produce, silkworms are amazingly ugly).

The museum also displays various kinds of silk fabrics, as well as gorgeous kimono and reproduction Japanese costumes from the Nara, Heian, and Edo periods. Don't miss this museum, which takes about 30 minutes to see; surprisingly, it's never crowded. Open Tuesday through Sunday from 9am to 4:30pm; admission is ¥500 for adults, ¥300 for seniors, ¥200 for students, and ¥100 for children.

At the opposite end of Yamashita Park is the **Yokohama Doll Museum,** 18 Yamashita-cho (© 045/671-9361; www.museum.or.jp/yokohama-doll-museum; station: Motomachi Chukagai), which boasts a collection of approximately 13,000 dolls from 140 countries, with about 1,300 dolls on display. A trip through the museum begins with a collection of old Western dolls introduced to Japan when Yokohama opened as an international harbor, as well as Japanese dolls sent to the West. Exhibits that follow show dolls from around the world dressed in their native costume, popular international figures of the past few decades (from Hello Kitty to R2-D2 of *Star Wars* fame), antique dolls (including those produced by such famous doll makers as Lenci and Jumeau), and Japanese dolls, from *hina* (elaborate dolls representing the empress and emperor, used for the March Hina Festival) to *kokeshi* (simple wooden dolls). It's open 10am to 6:30pm; closed the third Monday of every month (except July, Aug, and Dec). Admission is ¥500 for adults and ¥150 for children. Plan on spending about 30 minutes here.

Not far from Yamashita Park is **Chukagai,** Japan's largest Chinatown, with hundreds of souvenir shops and restaurants; see "Where to Dine," below.

SANKEIEN GARDEN ★★★ In my opinion, **Sankeien Garden** (© 045/621-0634; www.sankeien.or.jp) is the best reason to visit Yokohama. Although not old itself, this lovely park contains more than a dozen historic buildings that were brought here from other parts of Japan, including Kyoto and Nara, all situated around streams and ponds and surrounded by Japanese-style landscape gardens. The park, divided into an Inner Garden and Outer Garden, was laid out in 1906 by Tomitaro Hara, a local millionaire who made his fortune exporting silk. As you wander along the gently winding pathways, you'll see a villa built in 1649 by the Tokugawa shogunate clan, tea arbors, a 500-year-old three-story pagoda, and a farmhouse built in 1750 without the use of nails. The gardens are well known for their blossoms of plums, cherries, wisteria, azaleas, irises, and water lilies, but no matter what the season, the views here are beautiful.

Plan on at least 2 hours to see both gardens. Sankeien is open daily from 9am to 5pm (you must enter the Inner Garden by 4pm, the Outer Garden by 4:30pm). Admission is ¥500 for adults, ¥300 for seniors, and ¥200 for children. The easiest way to reach Sankeien Garden is by bus no. 8, which departs from platform no. 2 at Yokohama Station's east exit (near Sogo department store) and winds its way past Sakuragicho Station, past Chinatown (via Hon-cho Dori), and through Kannai before it reaches the Honmoku-Sankeien-mae bus stop 30 minutes later (the bus stop is announced in English).

GREAT FOR KIDS If you have children, you may wish to get on their good side by taking them to **Yokohama Hakkeijima Sea Paradise,** Hakkeijima (© 045/788-8888; www.seaparadise.co.jp), a combination seaside amusement park and aquarium. Among the dozen thrill rides are a roller coaster that juts over the sea, a fiberglass boat that shoots the currents, a tower ride that lets you "fall" 105m (344 ft.) at bloodcurdling speed, and a carousel. The aquarium features such popular animals as sea otters, Atlantic puffins, polar bears, penguins, and belugas; an underwater tunnel moves visitors past stingrays, moray eels, and exotic tropical fish. There are also marine mammal shows featuring dolphins, belugas, and seals. Admission to the aquarium and its shows costs ¥2,700 for adults, ¥2,200 for seniors, ¥1,600 for children 6 to 15, and ¥800 for children 4 to 5.

Individual thrill rides range from ¥300 to ¥1,000. Otherwise, a combination "free" pass good for everything costs ¥4,900 for adults and ¥3,500 or ¥2,000 for children, depending on their age.

The aquarium is open mid-March through August, from about 9am to 8 or 9pm, depending on the season, with shorter winter hours. It takes approximately 1 hour to reach Hakkeijima Sea Paradise from Yokohama Station. Take the JR Negishi Line from Yokohama Station to Shin-sugita, and then transfer to the Seaside Line to Hakkeijima Station. Or, take the Keihin Kyuko Line from Shinagawa or Yokohama Station to Kanazawa Hakkei Station to catch the Seaside Line.

WHERE TO DINE

CHUKAGAI (CHINATOWN)   Located in Yamashita-cho, a couple blocks inland from Yamashita Park and next to Motomachi Chukagai Station of the Minato Mirai Line, Chinatown has more than 500 restaurants and shops lining two main streets and dozens of offshoots. Tokyoites have long been coming to Yokohama just to dine; many of the restaurants have been owned by the same families for generations. Most serve Cantonese food and have plastic-food displays, English-language menus, or pictures of their dishes, so your best bet is to wander around and let your budget be your guide. Most dishes run ¥850 to ¥3,000, and set lunches go for ¥900 to ¥1,200. Larger restaurants accept credit cards; those that do display them on the front door. Most Chinatown restaurants are open from 11 or 11:30am to 9:30pm or later; some close Tuesday or Wednesday, but there are always other restaurants open.

While here, you might want to take a spin through the **China Museum (Yokohama Daisekai),** 97 Yamashita-cho (© 045/681-5588), an eight-story building with an interior that replicates Shanghai of the 1920s and '30s (Shanghai and Yokohama are sister cities), with re-created street scenes, artisans producing traditional crafts, souvenir shops, and a food court with stalls offering dishes from around China, most priced less than ¥800. It's open Sunday to Thursday 10am to 9pm, and Friday and Saturday 10am to 10pm.

MINATO MIRAI   For sophisticated surroundings or just a romantic evening cocktail, take the elevator up to the 70th floor of Landmark Tower, where you'll find the Yokohama Royal Park Hotel Nikko's **Sirius Sky Lounge** ★ (© 045/221-1111), with stunning seaside views. It serves a buffet lunch for ¥3,500 daily from 11:30am to 2:30pm, which often centers on a changing, ethnic cuisine but also offers items such as salmon, lamb, and pizza. After lunch, it's teatime until 5pm. From 5pm to 1am daily, Sirius is a cocktail lounge (no one under 20 years old allowed) and levies a cover charge: ¥1,050 per person from 5 to 7pm and again from 11pm to 1am; ¥2,100 for live music from 7 to 11pm. It offers a small, a la carte dinner menu, as well as set dinners for ¥6,300 and ¥9,450.

Nearby, a good place for a drink or a hamburger is the local branch of the **Hard Rock Cafe,** located on the first floor of Queen's Square Yokohama Tower A (© 045/682-5626; daily 11am–11pm). Nearby, on the fourth and fifth floors of the Queen's Square Yokohama, is a branch of **daidaiya** (© 045/228-5035; daily 11am–3pm and 5–10:30pm). See p. 163 and p. 168, respectively, for reviews of these restaurants.

The 1911 renovated Red Brick Warehouse (see above) also has fast-food outlets, including a **Kua' Aina** burger shop (© 045/227-5300; p. 151), but for something more substantial, head to the third floor for **Beer Next** (© 045/226-1961; daily 11am–10pm [last order]), which strives admirably to create an international cuisine that goes down well with beer. Pizza, pasta, rotisserie roast chicken, and seared tuna with garlic oil and soy sauce are just some of the dishes offered; prices range from ¥1,470 to ¥2,310.

5 HAKONE ★★★

97km (60 miles) SW of Tokyo

Part of **Fuji-Hakone-Izu National Park,** Hakone is one of the closest and most popular weekend destinations for residents of Tokyo. Beautiful Hakone has about everything a vacationer could wish for—hot-spring resorts, mountains, lakes, breathtaking views of Mount Fuji, and interesting historical sites. You can tour Hakone as a day trip if you leave early in the morning and limit your sightseeing to a few key attractions, but adding an overnight stay—complete with a soak in a hot-spring tub—is much more rewarding. If you can, travel on a weekday, when modes of transportation are less crowded and some hotels offer cheaper weekday rates.

ESSENTIALS

GETTING THERE & GETTING AROUND   Getting to and around Hakone is half the fun! An easy loop tour you can follow through Hakone includes various forms of unique transportation: Starting out by train from Tokyo, you switch to a small three-car tram that zigzags up the mountain, then change to a cable car, and then to a smaller ropeway, and end your trip with a boat ride across Lake Ashi, stopping to see major attractions along the way. From Lake Ashi (that is, from the villages of Togendai, Hakone-machi, or Moto-Hakone), you can then board a bus bound for Odawara Station (a 1-hr. ride), where you board the train back to Tokyo. These same buses also pass by all the recommendations listed below, which is useful if you wish to complete most of your sightseeing the first day before going to your hotel for the evening. A bus runs directly between Togendai and Shinjuku in about 2 hours (fare: ¥1,960).

Odakyu operates the most convenient network of trains, buses, trams, cable cars, and boats to and around Hakone. The most economical and by far easiest way to see Hakone is with Odakyu's **Hakone Free Pass** which, despite its name, isn't free but does give you a round-trip ticket on the express train from Shinjuku Station to Odawara or Hakone Yumoto and includes all modes of transportation in Hakone listed above and described below. The pass lets you avoid the hassle of buying individual tickets and gives nominal discounts on most Hakone attractions. A 2-day pass costs ¥5,000 and a 3-day pass is ¥5,500. Children pay ¥1,500 and ¥1,750, respectively.

The trip from Shinjuku to Odawara via Odakyu Express takes 90 minutes, with departures two to four times an hour. In Odawara, you then transfer to another train for a 15-minute trip to Hakone Yumoto; trains depart four times an hour. If time is of the essence or if you want to ensure a seat during peak season, reserve a seat on the faster and more luxurious **Odakyu Romance Car,** which travels from Shinjuku all the way to Hakone Yumoto in 1½ hours and costs an extra ¥870 one-way with a Hakone Pass (you can still make a stopover in Odawara to see the castle, if you wish).

All these passes can be purchased at any station of the Odakyu Railway. In Tokyo, the best place to purchase Hakone Free Pass tickets is Shinjuku Station, at the **Odakyu Sightseeing Service Center,** located on the ground floor near the west exit of Odakyu Shinjuku Station (© **03/5321-7887;** www.odakyu.jp/english; daily 8am–6pm), where you can obtain English-language sightseeing information in addition to purchasing tickets. If you wish, you can also buy 1- or 2-day do-it-yourself package tours that include round-trip transportation to Hakone, meals, sightseeing, and hotel stays.

VISITOR INFORMATION   Before leaving Tokyo, pick up the "Hakone and Kamakura" leaflet available from the Tourist Information Center; it provides transportation information for throughout the Hakone area. A color brochure called "Hakone National Park" includes sightseeing information and contains a map of the Hakone area. See "Visitor Information," in chapter 3 for TIC locations. The Odakyu Sightseeing Service Center, above, also has a wealth of information, including the useful *Timetable of Traffic in Hakone,* a booklet which lists the schedules for all forms of transportation in Hakone.

In Odawara, the **Odawara Tourist Information Center** (✆ 0465/33-1521; daily 9am–5pm) is inside Odawara Station. In Hakone Yumoto, the **Yumoto Tourist Office** (✆ 0460/85-8911; daily 9:30am–6pm Apr–Nov, to 5:30pm Dec–Mar) is across the street from Hakone Yumoto Station.

LUGGAGE   If you plan to return to Tokyo, I suggest you leave your luggage in storage at your Tokyo hotel or at Shinjuku Station and travel to Hakone with only an overnight bag. If you're traveling onward to, say, Kyoto, you can leave your bags at a check-in counter at Hakone Yumoto Station, open daily 8am to 10pm (a large bag costs ¥500 a day). Or if you deliver your bags to the **Hakone Carry Service** (✆ 0460/86-4140) at Hakone Yumoto Station between 8:30am and noon, it will transport your bags to your Hakone accommodations by 3pm. The next day, it can also pick up your bags at your hotel at 10am and deliver them to Yumoto Station by 1pm, where they will keep them until 7pm. The service costs ¥700 to ¥1,000 per bag, depending on the size and weight, and is available daily year-round.

WHAT TO SEE & DO

If you decide to spend only 1 day in Hakone, you should leave Tokyo very early in the morning and plan on visiting just a few key attractions—I recommend the **Hakone Open-Air Museum, Owakudani Nature Trail,** and, if time permits, **Hakone Check Point** and/or **Narukawa Art Museum.** Keep in mind that most forms of transportation (like the ropeway), as well as museums, close at 5pm.

If you're spending the night—and I strongly urge that you do—you can arrange your itinerary in a more leisurely fashion and devote more time to Hakone's attractions. You may wish to travel only as far as your hotel the first day, stopping at sights along the way and in the vicinity. The next day you could continue with the rest of the circuit through Hakone. Or you can opt to complete most of your sightseeing the first day, and then backtrack to your accommodations or reach it by bus from Togendai, Hakone-machi, or Moto-Hakone.

ODAKYU TRAIN TO HAKONE

Regardless of whether you travel via the Odakyu Romance Car or the ordinary Odakyu Express, your train will stop at Odawara Station, considered the gateway to Hakone. If you've never seen a Japanese castle and won't have another opportunity to see one, consider visiting **Odawara Castle,** Odawara Joshi-koen (✆ 0465/23-1373). A 10-minute walk from Odawara Station (take the east exit out of the station and turn right), this three-tiered, four-story castle dates from the 1500s, was dismantled in 1870 by the Meiji government because of its associations with the shogun regime, and was rebuilt in 1960. Its keep contains a small historical museum relating to the castle, including models of castles, palanquins used to transport people up and down mountains during the Edo

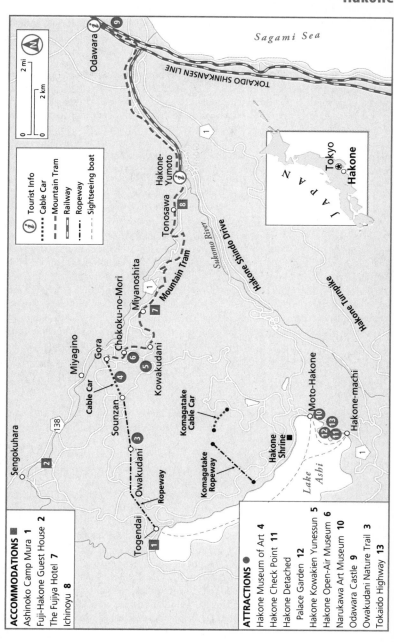

ACCOMMODATIONS ■

Ashinoko Camp Mura **1**
Fuji-Hakone Guest House **2**
The Fujiya Hotel **7**
Ichinoyu **8**

ATTRACTIONS ●

Hakone Museum of Art **4**
Hakone Check Point **11**
Hakone Detached
Palace Garden **12**
Hakone Kowakien Yunessun **5**
Hakone Open-Air Museum **6**
Narukawa Art Museum **10**
Odawara Castle **9**
Owakudani Nature Trail **3**
Tokaido Highway **13**

Legend:
(i) Tourist Info
..... Cable Car
--- Mountain Tram
═══ Railway
-·-· Ropeway
----- Sightseeing boat

Sagami Sea

TOKAIDO SHINKANSEN LINE

Odawara

JAPAN
Tokyo
Hakone

Hakone-Yumoto

Tonosawa

Sukomo River

Hakone Shindo Drive

Miyanoshita

Chokoku-no-Mori

Mountain Tram

Miyagino

Gora

Sengokuhara

Cable Car

Sounzan

Owakudani

Kowakudani

Ropeway

Togendai

Komagatake
Cable Car

Komagatake
Ropeway

Hakone Turnpike

Hakone
Shrine

Moto-Hakone

Hakone-machi

*Lake
Ashi*

138

1

2 mi
2 km

Period, mirrors, Noh masks, lacquerware, and samurai armor and weapons. The tower affords a panoramic view of the surrounding park (which contains a free, small zoo). You can see it all in less than 30 minutes. Admission is ¥400 for adults and ¥150 for children. It's open daily from 9am to 5pm.

SCENIC RAILWAY TO GORA

At Hakone Yumoto Station, the end stop on the Odakyu train, transfer to the **Hakone Tozan Railway,** in operation since 1919. This delightful, mountain-climbing, three-car electric tram winds its way through forests and over streams and ravines as it travels upward to Gora, making several switchbacks along the way. The entire trip from Hakone Yumoto Station to Gora takes only 40 minutes, but the ride through the mountains is beautiful, and this is my favorite part of the whole journey. The railway, which runs every 10 to 15 minutes, makes about a half-dozen stops before reaching Gora, including **Tono-sawa** and **Miyanoshita,** two hot-spring spa resorts with a number of old ryokan and hotels. Some of the ryokan date back several centuries, to the days when they were on the main thoroughfare to Edo, called the old Tokaido Highway. Miyanoshita is the best place for lunch. See "Where to Dine," and "Where to Stay," below.

For relaxing hot-spring bathing en route, pay a visit to the thoroughly modern, sophisticated public bath called **Hakone Kowakien Yunessun** ★★ (✆ **0460/82-4126;** www. yunessun.com/english). To reach it, disembark from the Hakone Tozan Railway at Kowakudani and then take a 15-minute taxi or bus ride (bus stop: Kowaki-en). This self-described "Hot Springs Amusement Park & Spa Resort" offers a variety of both indoor and outdoor family baths, which means you wear your bathing suit. In addition to indoor Turkish, Roman, and salt baths, there's also a children's play area with slides and a large outdoor area with a variety of small baths, including those mixed with healthy minerals and—I am not making this up—coffee, green tea, sake, and wine. For those who desire more traditional bathing, there's the Mori No Yu, with both indoor and outdoor baths separated for men and women (you don't wear your suit here). Most people who come stay 2 to 3 hours. Admission is ¥3,500 to Yunessun, ¥1,800 to Mori No Yu, or ¥4,000 to both; if you have a Hakone Free Pass, you'll pay ¥2,800, ¥1,400, or ¥3,200, respectively. Children pay half-fare. Upon admission, you'll be given a towel, robe, and wristband to pay for drinks and extras (rental suits are available), so you can leave all valuables in your assigned locker. Yunessun is open daily 9am to 7pm March to October, 9am to 6pm in November to February; Mori No Yu is open 9am to 9pm year-round.

The most important stop on the Hakone Tozan Railway is the next-to-the-last stop, Chokoku-no-Mori, where you'll find the famous **Hakone Open-Air Museum (Chokoku-no-Mori Bijutsukan)** ★★★ (✆ **0460/82-1161;** www.hakone-oam.or.jp), a minute's walk from the station. With the possible exception of views of Mount Fuji, this museum is, in my opinion, Hakone's number-one attraction. Using nature as a dramatic backdrop, it showcases sculpture primarily of the 20th century in a spectacular setting of glens, formal gardens, ponds, and meadows. There are 400 sculptures on display, both outdoors and in several buildings, with works by Carl Milles, Manzu Giacomo, Jean Dubuffet, Willem de Kooning, Barbara Hepworth, and Joan Miró, as well as more than 25 pieces by Henry Moore, shown on a rotating basis. The Picasso Pavilion contains works by Picasso from pastels to ceramics (it's one of the world's largest collections) and photographs of the artist's last 17 years of life taken by David Douglas Duncan. The Picture Gallery is devoted to changing exhibitions. Several installations geared toward children allow them to climb and play. I could spend all day here; barring that, count on staying at least 2 hours. Be sure to stop off at the "foot onsen" near the Picture Gallery, where you can immerse your tired feet in soothing, hot-spring water. The museum is open daily 9am to 5pm; admission is ¥1,600 adults, ¥1,100 university and high-school students and seniors, and ¥800 children. Your Hakone Free Pass gives you a ¥200 discount.

BY CABLE CAR TO SOUNZAN

Cable cars leave Gora every 20 minutes or so and arrive 9 minutes later at the end station of Sounzan, making several stops along the way as they travel steeply uphill. One of the stops is Koen-Kami, from which it's only a minute's walk to the **Hakone Museum of Art** (✆ **0460/82-2623**). This five-room museum displays Japanese pottery and ceramics from the Jomon Period (around 4000–2000 B.C.) to the Edo Period, including terra-cotta *haniwa* burial figures, huge 16th-century Bizen jars, and Imari ware. What makes this place particularly rewarding are the bamboo grove and small but lovely moss garden, shaded by Japanese maples, with a teahouse where you can sample Japanese tea for ¥630. It is most beautiful in autumn. Open Friday through Wednesday from 9:30am to 4:30pm (to 4pm Dec–Mar); admission is ¥900 for adults, ¥700 for seniors, ¥400 for university and high-school students, and free for children. The Hakone Free Pass gives you a ¥200 discount. Plan on spending about a half-hour here, more if you opt for tea.

BY ROPEWAY TO TOGENDAI

From Sounzan, you board a ropeway with gondolas for a long, 30-minute haul over a mountain to Togendai on the other side, which lies beside Lake Ashi, known as Lake Ashinoko in Japanese. Note that the ropeway stops running at around 5:15pm in summer and 4pm in winter.

Before reaching Togendai, however, get off at Owakudani, the ropeway's highest point, to hike the 30-minute **Owakudani Nature Trail** ★. *Owakudani* means "Great Boiling Valley," and you'll soon understand how it got its name when you see (and smell) the sulfurous steam escaping from fissures in the rock, testimony to the volcanic activity still present here. Most Japanese commemorate their trip by buying boiled eggs, cooked here in the boiling waters, available at the small hut midway along the trail.

ACROSS LAKE ASHI BY BOAT

From Togendai you can take a pleasure boat across Lake Ashi, also referred to as "Lake Hakone" in some English-language brochures. Believe it or not, a couple of the boats plying the waters are replicas of a man-of-war pirate ship. It takes about half an hour to cross the lake to Hakone-machi (also called simply Hakone; *machi* means "city") and Moto-Hakone, two resort towns right next to each other on the southern edge of the lake. This end of the lake affords the best view of Mount Fuji, one often depicted in tourist publications. Boats are in operation year-round (though they run less frequently in winter and not at all in stormy weather); the last boat departs around 5pm from the end of March to the end of November. Otherwise, buses connect Togendai with Moto-Hakone, Odawara, and Shinjuku.

After the boat ride, if you're heading back to Tokyo, buses depart for Odawara near the boat piers in both Hakone-machi and Moto-Hakone. Otherwise, for more sightseeing, get off the boat in Hakone-machi, turn left, and walk about 5 minutes on the town's main road, following the signs and turning left to **Hakone Check Point (Hakone Seki-sho)** ★ (✆ **0460/83-6635**), on a road lined with souvenir shops. This is a reconstructed guardhouse originally built in 1619 to serve as a checkpoint along the famous Tokaido

Highway, which connected Edo (present-day Tokyo) with Kyoto. In feudal days, local lords, called *daimyo,* were required to spend alternate years in Edo; their wives were kept in Edo as virtual hostages to discourage the lords from planning rebellions while in their homelands. This was one of several points along the highway that guarded against the transport of guns, spies, and female travelers trying to flee Edo. Passes were necessary for travel, and although it was possible to sneak around it, male violators who were caught were promptly executed, while women suffered the indignity of having their heads shaven and then being given away to anyone who wanted them. Inside the reconstructed guardhouse, which was rebuilt on the site of the original checkpoint using traditional carpenter tools and architectural techniques of the Edo Period, you'll see life-size models reenacting scenes inside a checkpoint. A small museum has displays relating to the Edo Period, including items used for travel, samurai armor, and gruesome articles of torture. Open daily from 9am to 5pm (until 4:30pm Dec–Feb); admission is ¥500 for adults and ¥250 for children. Your Hakone Free Pass gives you a ¥100 discount. It shouldn't take more than 20 minutes to see everything.

Just beyond the Hakone Check Point, at the big parking lot with the traditional gate, is the **Hakone Detached Palace Garden (Onshi-Hakone-Koen),** which lies on a small promontory on Lake Ashi and has spectacular views of the lake and, in clear weather, Mount Fuji. Originally part of an Imperial summer villa built in 1886, the garden is open to the public 24 hours and admission is free. It's a great place for wandering. On its grounds is the **Lakeside Observation Building** (daily 9am–4:30pm), with displays relating to Hakone Palace, destroyed by earthquakes.

If you take the northernmost exit from the garden, crossing a bridge, you'll see the neighboring resort town, **Moto-Hakone** down the road. Across the highway and lined with ancient and mighty cedars is part of the old **Tokaido Highway** itself. During the Edo Period, more than 400 cedars were planted along this important road, which today stretches 2½km (1½ miles) along the curve of Lake Ashi and makes for a pleasant stroll (unfortunately, a modern road has been built right beside the original one). Moto-Hakone is a 5-minute walk from the Detached Palace Garden.

In Moto-Hakone, **Narukawa Art Museum** ★★ (**© 0460/83-6828;** www.narukawa-museum.co.jp) is worthwhile and located just after you enter town, up the hill to the right when you reach the orange torii gate. It specializes in modern works of the *Nihonga* style of painting, developed during the Heian Period (794–1185) and sparser than Western paintings (which tend to fill in backgrounds and every inch of canvas). Large paintings and screens by contemporary Nihonga artists are on display, including works by Yamamoto Kyujin, Maki Susumu, Kayama Matazo, Hirayama Ikuo, and Hori Fumiko. Changing exhibitions feature younger up-and-coming artists, as well as glassware. I wouldn't miss it; views of Lake Ashi and Mount Fuji are a bonus. Open daily 9am to 5pm; admission is ¥1,200 for adults, ¥900 for high-school and university students, and ¥600 for children.

WHEN YOU'RE DONE SIGHTSEEING FOR THE DAY

Buses depart for Hakone Yumoto and Odawara from both Hakone-machi and Moto-Hakone two to four times an hour. Be sure to check the time of the last departure; generally it's around 8pm, but this can change with the season and the day of the week. (The bus also passes two of the accommodations recommended below, The Fujiya Hotel and Ichinoyu, as well as Yunessun hot-spring baths; another bus will take you to Fuji-Hakone Guest House.) Otherwise, the trip from Moto-Hakone takes approximately 30

WHERE TO STAY

Japan's ryokan sprang into existence to accommodate the stately processions of daimyo and shogun as they traversed the roads between Edo and the rest of Japan. Many of these ryokan were built along the Tokaido Highway, and some of the oldest are found in Hakone. Most accommodations cost more during peak travel times like Golden Week, school holidays, New Year's, weekends, and national holidays.

Expensive

The Fujiya Hotel ★★★ (Finds The Fujiya, which was established in 1878, is quite simply the grandest, most majestic old hotel in Hakone; indeed, it might be the loveliest historic hotel in Japan. I love this hotel for its comfortably old-fashioned atmosphere, including such Asian touches as a Japanese-style roof and long wooden corridors with photographs of famous guests, from Einstein to Eisenhower. A landscaped garden out back, with a waterfall, pond, greenhouse, outdoor pool, and stunning views over the valley, is great for strolls and meditation. There's also a small hotel museum and an indoor thermal pool and hot-spring public baths (hot-spring water is also piped in to each guest's bathroom). Even if you don't stay here, come for a meal or tea.

There are five separate buildings, all different and added on at various times in the hotel's long history, but management has been meticulous in retaining its historic traditions. Rooms are old-fashioned and spacious with high ceilings and antique furnishings. The most expensive rooms are the largest, but my favorites are those in the Flower Palace, which has an architectural style that reminds me of a Japanese temple and seems unchanged since its 1936 construction. Be sure to ask the front desk for the hotel's map of the surrounding village and leaflets describing how to reach sightseeing spots in Hakone from the hotel.

Note: A limited number of the least expensive rooms in the main building (dating from 1891) are available for foreigners at a special discounted rate, in dollars, based on the hotel's age. However, the special rate is not available on Saturday, the night before national holidays, during Golden Week, the month of August, or New Year's. And if these discounted rooms are sold out, you'll pay the regular rate.

359 Miyanoshita, Hakone-machi, Kanagawa-ken 250-0404. © **0460/82-2211.** Fax 0460/82-2210. www.fujiyahotel.jp. 146 units. Special rates for foreigners (excluding tax and service charge): $131 single or double in 2010, $132 in 2011. Regular rates: ¥20,040–¥44,190 single or double; ¥5,670–¥13,860 extra on Sat, night before holiday, and peak travel times. AE, DC, MC, V. Station: Miyanoshita (Hakone Tozan Railway; 5 min.). Bus: From Odawara or Moto-Hakone to Miyanoshita Onsen stop (1 min.). **Amenities:** 3 restaurants (see "Where to Dine," below); bar; golf course; hot-spring baths; Jacuzzi; indoor/outdoor pools; room service; sauna; Wi-Fi in lobby; hotel museum. *In room:* A/C, TV, hair dryer, minibar.

(82) **Ichinoyu ★★** Located near Tonosawa Station (on the Hakone Tozan Line) next to a roaring river, this delightful, rambling wooden building stands on a tree-shaded winding road that follows the track of the old Tokaido Highway. Opened more than 380 years ago, Ichinoyu is now in its 15th generation of owners. It claims to be the oldest ryokan in the area and was once honored by the visit of a shogun during the Edo Period. Old artwork, wall hangings, and paintings decorate the place. The ryokan has only tatami rooms, the oldest dating from the Meiji Period, more than 100 years ago. My favorites are the Take, Kotobuki, and Matsue rooms, old-fashioned and consisting mainly of

SIDE TRIPS FROM TOKYO

11

HAKONE

seasoned and weathered wood; they face the river and have private outdoor baths, also with views of the river. (Rooms with private *rotenburo,* or outdoor hot-spring baths, cost ¥3,000 extra.) Both the communal tubs and the tubs in the rooms are supplied with hot water from a natural spring. The price you pay depends on your room, the meals you select (served communally in a dining room), and the time of year you visit; rooms for single travelers are not available.

90 Tonosawa, Hakone-machi, Kanagawa-ken 250-0315. ☏ 0460/85-5331. Fax 0460/85-5335. http://english.ichinoyu.co.jp/honkan/index.html. 24 units (12 with bathroom). ¥8,400–¥15,225 per person including 2 meals. Higher rates on Sat, night before holiday, and peak travel times. AE, DC, MC, V. Station: Tonosawa (Hakone Tozan Railway; 6 min.). Bus: From Odawara or Moto-Hakone to Tonosawa bus stop (2 min.). **Amenities:** Hot-spring baths. *In room:* A/C, TV, fridge.

Inexpensive

Ashinoko Camp Mura (Kids) Because you're in a national park, you might be inclined to enjoy nature by roughing it in a cabin beside Lake Ashi, just a 10-minute walk from the ropeway to Sounzan and the boat to Hakone-machi. Operated by Kanagawa Prefecture and also with tent camping, it offers row and detached (more expensive and closer to the lake) cabins that sleep up to six persons, each with two bedrooms, a bathroom, a living room with cooking facilities and tableware, and a deck with picnic table. However, there is no supermarket in nearby Togendai, so you'll either want to bring your own food or dine at the camp's restaurant, which offers both Japanese and Western selections (reservations required for lunch and dinner). There's a hiking trail around the lake. A great place for kids. Open year-round.

164 Hakone-machi, Moto-Hakone, Kanagawa 250-0522. ☏ 0460/84-8279. Fax 0460/84-6489. 36 units. Peak season ¥26,250 row cabin, ¥31,500 detached cabin; off season ¥15,750 row cabin, ¥21,000 detached cabin. No credit cards. Bus: Togendai, from Odawara (1 hr.) or Shinjuku (2 hr.), and then a 10-min. walk. **Amenities:** Restaurant; rental bikes; barbecue grills. *In room:* Kitchenette.

Fuji-Hakone Guest House It's a bit isolated, but this Japanese Inn Group member offers inexpensive, spotlessly clean lodging in tatami rooms, all nonsmoking. A 20-some-year-old house, situated in tranquil surroundings set back from a tree-shaded road, is run by a man who speaks very good English and is happy to provide sightseeing information, including a map of the area with local restaurants. Some of the rooms face the Hakone mountain range. Pluses are the communal lounge area with fridge, microwave, computer (¥100 for 30 min.), TV and even a piano, and the outdoor hot-spring bath (for which there's an extra ¥500 charge).

912 Sengokuhara, Hakone, Kanagawa 250-0631. ☏ 0460/84-6577. Fax 0460/84-6578. http://hakone.syuriken.jp/hakone. 14 units (none with bathroom). ¥5,250–¥6,300 single; ¥10,500–¥12,600 double; ¥15,750–¥16,800 triple. Plus ¥150 hot-spring tax per person. Peak season and Sat–Sun ¥1,000–¥2,000 extra. Minimum 2-night stay preferred. Western breakfast ¥840 extra. AE, DC, MC, V. Bus: Hakone Tozan (included in the Hakone Free Pass) from Togendai (15 min.) or from Odawara Station (50 min.) to the Senkyoro-mae stop (announced in English), and then a 1-min. walk. **Amenities:** Hot-spring bath; free Wi-Fi in lobby. *In room:* A/C, TV.

WHERE TO DINE

For casual dining, the Hakone Open-Air Museum has a pleasant restaurant, **Bella Foresta,** overlooking the park's fantastic scenery and offering a buffet lunch daily from 11am to 3:30pm for ¥1,980. Also sporting a view is the even less formal restaurant **Owakudani Sky,** on the third floor of the Owakudani Ropeway Station, serving curry rice, noodles, and other fare for less than ¥1,200.

Main Dining Room ★★ CONTINENTAL   Hakone's grandest, oldest hotel, conveniently located near a stop on the three-car Hakone Tozan Railway, is a memorable place for a good Western meal. The main dining hall, dating from 1930, is very bright and cheerful, with a high and intricately detailed ceiling, large windows with Japanese screens, a wooden floor, and white tablecloths. The views of the Hakone hills are impressive, and the service by the bow-tied waitstaff is attentive. For lunch you can have such dishes as crab curry, beef stew, fried prawn, rainbow trout, and sirloin steak. The excellent dinners, with seatings at 6 and 8pm, feature elaborate set courses or a la carte dishes ranging from scallops and grilled lamb to chicken, rainbow trout, and steak. Afterward, be sure to tour the landscaped garden.

In the Fujiya Hotel, 359 Miyanoshita, Hakone-machi. *©* **0460/82-2211.** Reservations required for dinner. Main dishes ¥2,200–¥7,500; set dinners ¥11,500–¥23,100); set lunches ¥5,000–¥12,000. AE, DC, MC, V. Daily noon–2pm (to 2:30pm Sat–Sun and holidays) and 6–8:30pm. Station: Miyanoshita on the Hakone Tozan Railway (5 min.).

---

6 MOUNT FUJI

100km (62 miles) SW of Tokyo

Mount Fuji, affectionately called "Fuji-san," has been revered since ancient times. Throughout the centuries Japanese poets have written about it, painters have painted it, pilgrims have flocked to it, and more than a few people have died on it. Without a doubt, this mountain has been photographed more than anything else in Japan.

Mount Fuji is stunningly impressive. At 3,766m (12,355 ft.), it's the tallest mountain in Japan, towering far above anything else around it—a cone of almost perfectly symmetrical proportions. It is majestic, grand, and awe-inspiring. To the Japanese it symbolizes the very spirit of their country. Though it's visible on clear days (mostly in winter) from as far away as 161km (100 miles), Fuji-san, unfortunately, is almost always cloaked in clouds. If you catch a glimpse of this mighty mountain, consider yourself extremely lucky. One of the best spots for views of Mount Fuji is **Hakone** (see earlier).

ESSENTIALS

There are four ascents to the summit of Mount Fuji (and four descents), each divided into 10 stations of unequal length, with most climbs starting at the Go-go-me, or the Fifth Station, about 1,400m to 2,400m (4,593–7,874 ft.) above sea level. From Tokyo, the **Kawaguchiko-Yoshidaguchi Trail** is the most popular and most easily accessible, as well as the least steep. The "official" climbing season is very short, only from July 1 to August 31. Climbers are discouraged from climbing outside the season, due to low temperatures, super-strong winds, and no emergency services. To beat the crowds—and I do mean crowds—try to schedule your climb on a weekday during the first 2 weeks of July, before the start of Japan's school vacation (around July 20).

GETTING THERE   The easiest way to reach the Kawaguchiko Fifth Station is by **bus** from Shinjuku Station. In July and August there are six buses daily that travel directly from Shinjuku Station to Kawaguchiko Trail's 5th Station, costing ¥2,600 one-way and taking almost 2½ hours. Otherwise, there are also buses that go to Kawaguchiko Station in 1 hour and 45 minutes and cost ¥1,700 one-way; from Kawaguchiko Station there are buses onward to the Fifth Station, with this trip taking approximately 45 minutes and costing another ¥1,500 one-way or ¥2,000 round-trip. Buses, which depart a 2-minute walk from the west side of Shinjuku Station in front of the Yasuda Seimi no. 2 Building, require reservations, which you can make at the **Keio Highway Bus Reservation Center (Keio Kosoku Bus Yoyaku Center; ℂ 03/5376-2222)** or a travel agency such as JTB. Less frequent **Fujikyu Buses (ℂ 0555/72-5111)** depart from Tokyo Station's Yaesu south exit for Kawaguchiko Station for ¥1,700, but the trip takes an hour longer.

VISITOR INFORMATION   More information and train and bus schedules can be obtained from the **Tourist Information Center,** including a leaflet called "Mount Fuji and Fuji Five Lakes." See "Visitor Information," in chapter 3. Another good source is Fujiyoshida City's official website, www.city.fujiyoshida.yamanashi.jp, which carries information on the Kawaguchiko-Yoshidaguchi Trail, bus schedules from Tokyo, mountain huts, and other information. Finally, there's a tourist information office at Kawaguchiko Station (**ℂ 0555/72-6700**), open daily 9am to 5pm during climbing season.

CLIMBING MOUNT FUJI

Mount Fuji is part of a larger national park called **Fuji-Hakone-Izu National Park.** Of the handful of trails leading to the top, most popular for Tokyoites is the **Kawaguchiko-Yoshidaguchi Trail,** which is divided into 10 different stages; the Fifth Station, located about 2,475m (8,120 ft.) up and served by bus, is the usual starting point. From here it takes about 6 hours to reach the summit and 3 hours for the descent.

PREPARING FOR YOUR CLIMB   Because of snow and inclement weather from fall through late spring, the best time to make an ascent is during the "official" climbing season from July through August. Keep in mind that this is not a solitary pursuit. Rather, more than 400,000 people climb Fuji-san every year, mostly in July and August and mostly on weekends—so if you plan on climbing Mount Fuji on a Saturday or a Sunday in summer, go to the end of the line, please.

You don't need climbing experience to ascend Mount Fuji (you'll see everyone from grandmothers to children making the pilgrimage), but you do need stamina and a good pair of walking shoes. The climb is possible in tennis shoes, but if the rocks are wet, they can get awfully slippery. You should also bring a light plastic raincoat (which you can buy at souvenir shops at the Fifth Station), since it often rains on the mountain, a sun hat, sunglasses, sunscreen, water, snacks, a sweater for the evening, gloves, socks, tissues (for pay toilets, which may not have toilet paper), and a flashlight (or headlamp) if you plan on hiking at night. Keep in mind, too, that it gets very chilly on Mount Fuji at night. Even in August, the average temperature on the summit is 41°F (5°C). Finally, there are places to eat and rest on the way to the top, but prices are high, so carry as many snacks and liquids with you as you can.

Don't be disappointed when your bus deposits you at **Kawaguchiko Fifth Station,** where you'll be bombarded with souvenir shops, restaurants, and busloads of tourists; most of these tourists aren't climbing to the top. As soon as you get past them and the blaring loudspeakers, you'll find yourself on a steep rocky path, surrounded only by scrub brush and the hikers on the path below and above you. After a couple of hours, you'll probably find yourself above the roiling clouds, which stretch in all directions. It will be as if you are on an island, barren and rocky, in the middle of an ocean.

STRATEGIES FOR CLIMBING TO THE TOP   The usual procedure for climbing Mount Fuji is to take a morning bus, start climbing in early afternoon, spend the night near the summit, get up early in the morning to climb the rest of the way to the top, and then watch the sun rise (about 4:30am) from atop Mount Fuji. (You can, of course, also

The first documented case of someone scaling Mount Fuji is from the early 8th century. During the Edo Period, pilgrimages to the top were considered a purifying ritual, with strict rules governing dress and route. Women, thought to defile sacred places, were prohibited from climbing mountains until 1871.

wake up in time to see the sun rise and then continue climbing.) At the summit is a 1-hour hiking trail that circles the crater. Hikers then begin the descent, reaching the Fifth Station before noon.

There are about 16 **mountain huts** along the Kawaguchiko Trail above the Fifth Station, but they're very primitive, providing only a futon and toilet facilities. Some have the capacity to house 500 hikers. The cost is ¥5,250 per person without meals, ¥7,350 with two meals. Some huts charge ¥1,000 extra for Friday or Saturday night. When I stayed in one of these huts, dinner consisted of dried fish, rice, miso soup, and pickled vegetables; breakfast was exactly the same. Still, unless you want to carry your own food, I'd opt for the meals. Note that most huts are open only in July and August; book as early as you can to ensure a place. I recommend **Seikanso** at the Sixth Station (© **0555/24-6090;** www.seikanso.jp), with flush toilets and open from July to mid-October; **Toyokan Hut** at the Seventh Station (© **0555/22-1040**), or **Taishikan Hut** at the Eighth Station (© **0555/22-1947**). Call the **Japanese Inn Union of Mount Fuji** at © **0555/22-1944** for more information.

In the past few decades, there's been a trend in which climbers arrive at the Fifth Station late in the evening and then climb to the top during the night with the aid of flashlights. After watching the sunrise, they then make their descent. That way, they don't have to spend the night in one of the huts. My days of walking up a mountain through the night, however, are far behind me, but this is certainly an option if your time is limited.

Climbing Mount Fuji is definitely a unique experience, but there's a saying in Japan: "Everyone should climb Mount Fuji once; only a fool would climb it twice."

7 IZU PENINSULA

Atami: 107km (66 miles) SW of Tokyo; Shuzenji: 140km (87 miles) SW of Tokyo

Whenever Tokyoites want to spend a night or two at a hot-spring spa on the seashore, they head for Izu Peninsula. Jutting into the Pacific Ocean southwest of Tokyo, Izu boasts some fine beaches and a dramatic coastline marked in spots by high cliffs and tumbling surf. It also has a verdant, mountainous interior with quaint hot-spring resorts. However, even though the scenery is at times breathtaking and Izu offers a relaxing respite from bustling Tokyo, there's little of historical interest to lure a short-term visitor to Japan; make sure you've seen both Kamakura and Nikko before you consider coming here.

Keep in mind also that Izu's resorts are terribly crowded during the summer vacation period from mid-July to the end of August. If you do travel during the peak summer season, make accommodations reservations at least several months in advance. Otherwise, there are hotel, ryokan, and *minshuku* reservation offices in all of Izu's resort towns that will arrange accommodations for you. Be aware, however, that if a place has a room still open at the last minute in August, there's probably a reason for it—poor location, poor service, or unimaginative decor.

Before you leave Tokyo, be sure to pick up the leaflet "The Izu Peninsula" at the Tourist Information Center.

ATAMI

Atami means "hot sea." According to legend, once upon a time, local fishermen, concerned about a geyser spewing forth into the sea and killing lots of fish and marine life, asked a Buddhist monk to intervene on their behalf and to pray for a solution to the problem. The prayers paid off when the geyser moved itself to the beach; not only was the marine life spared, but Atami was also blessed with hot-spring water the townspeople could henceforth bathe in. It's rumored that Tokugawa Ieyasu (1543-1616), Japan's most famous shogun, was so enamored by the quality of Atami's hot-spring waters that he ordered barrels of it delivered to his castle in Edo (present-day Tokyo).

Today, Atami—with a population of 40,000—is a conglomeration of hotels, ryokan, restaurants, pachinko parlors, souvenir shops, and a sizable red-light district, spread along narrow, winding streets that hug steep mountain slopes around Atami Bay. Although I find the setting picturesque, the city itself isn't very interesting—in fact, its economy is severely depressed, and because it has none of the fancy shops and nightlife to attract a younger generation, mostly older Japanese vacation here, giving the town an old-fashioned, unpretentious atmosphere. In any case, this is the most easily accessible hot-spring seaside resort from Tokyo, and it has a wide beach flanked by a half-mile boardwalk, a wonderful art museum, and several other attractions that make it popular even on just a day trip.

Essentials

GETTING THERE From Tokyo Station, it's 40 to 50 minutes by **Shinkansen bullet train;** be sure to check the schedule beforehand, as the Hikari bullet train stops at Atami only three times a day (though the slower Kodama bullet trains run more frequently). The fare is ¥3,570 for an unreserved seat. You can also take the **JR Odoriko** or **Super View Odoriko,** which travels from Tokyo Station to Atami in 1 hour and 15 or 20 minutes, with the fare ranging from ¥3,190 to ¥4,270, depending on the train. Slower is the local **JR Tokaido Line** for ¥1,890, which takes about 1 hour and 40 minutes.

VISITOR INFORMATION The **Atami Tourist Information Office** (adjacent to a coffee shop) is to the left as you exit the train station (© **0557/81-5297;** daily 9am–5:30pm; to 5pm Oct–Mar). No English is spoken, but English-language literature and a map are available, including the very useful "Atami Walking Guide." You'll also find information on Atami online at www.atamispa.com.

GETTING AROUND Buses serve major sightseeing attractions in Atami. If you're spending the day here, you might wish to purchase a 1-day ticket for the **YuYu Bus,** which has two routes, both making circuitous trips through town and departing Atami Station every 35 minutes. You can leave and reboard as often as you wish, or you can stay on for a tour of the city. The cost is ¥800 for adults and ¥400 for children.

Seeing the Sights

Atami's must-see is the **MOA Art Museum** ★, 26–2 Momoyama-cho (© **0557/84-2511;** www.moaart.or.jp), housed in a modern building atop a hill with sweeping views of Atami and the bay. It's a 5-minute bus ride from Atami Station on the YuYu Bus; or take a bus from platform 4 to the last stop (fare: ¥160). The museum's entrance is dramatic—a long escalator ride through a tunnel—but the museum itself concentrates on traditional Asian art, including woodblock prints by Hokusai, Hiroshige, and their contemporaries; Chinese ceramics; Japanese bronze religious art; and lacquerware. Although some 200 items from the 3,500-piece private collection are changed monthly, keep an eye out for a few things always on display: the Golden Tea Room (a remake of Toyotomi Hideyoshi's tea room), a Noh theater, and a tea-storage jar with a wisteria design by Edo artist Nonomura Ninsei, a National Treasure. Another National Treasure, displayed only 1 month a year (Feb), is a gold-leaf screen of red and white plum blossoms by Ogata Korin, whose residence next door is also part of the museum. It takes about an hour to tour the museum, open Friday through Wednesday from 9:30am to 4:30pm; admission is ¥1,600 for adults, ¥1,200 for seniors, ¥800 for university and high-school students, free for children.

I also love 83 **Kiunkaku,** 4–2 Showa-cho (© **0557/86-3101;** YuYu bus: Kiunkaku stop), built in 1919 as the private villa of a shipping magnate, converted to a ryokan in 1947, and now open to the public. It's an eclectic mix of Japanese and Western architectural styles, with stained-glass windows, fireplaces, parquet floors, gaily painted European furniture, and tatami rooms, wrapped around a lovely inner garden. It was once a favorite haunt of famous Japanese writers (including Mishima Yukio); who wouldn't feel inspired here? Allow 30 minutes to tour the facilities, open Thursday to Tuesday from 9am to 5pm. Admission is ¥500 for adults, ¥300 for university and high-school students, and free for children.

Finally, if you're here on a Saturday or Sunday, try to catch the 11am dancing performance of the **Atami Geisha,** at Geigi Kenban (across from City Hall), 17–13 Chuo-cho (© **0557/81-3575;** YuYu bus: Shiyakusho-mae). Although reservations are not required for the 30-minute show, I advise making one anyway to assure getting a seat, as these performances are very popular with the older generation. Stick around after the show; most of the geisha come out to greet the audience, and you can ask to have your picture taken standing next to a performer. Admission, including tea and a Japanese sweet, is ¥1,300.

Where to Stay

84 **Taikanso** ★★   Located on a pine-shaded mountain slope above the city, this beautiful ryokan was built in 1938 as the private villa of a steelworks owner and was named after his friend Yokoyama Taikan, a famous Japanese painter. Ten years later it was converted to a Japanese inn; since then, it's been expanded into several buildings connected by covered pathways and meandering streams, adhering to a Kyoto style of architecture popular in the 16th century. Various styles of rooms are available, with the most expensive (including the room where Taikan stayed) offering the best views, the most space, and the best meals (Western-style breakfasts available on request). Rooms are tatami, but beds can be installed upon request. The ultimate in luxury is the oldest unit, a three-room suite with a sitting alcove and cypress tub, where Queen Beatrix of the Netherlands stayed with her husband and three sons. Although all the rooms boast hot-spring water for the tubs, there are three public baths with open-air bathing, saunas, and Jacuzzis, as well as three private baths with outdoor baths and views over Atami (extra fee for these: ¥2,100). Be sure to wander the corridors and garden with its 300-year-old pines, stopping off at the footbaths on the third floor of the annex, where you can soak your feet, order drinks, and look out over the town.

7-1 Hayashigaoka-cho, Atami City, Shizuoka 413-0031. © **0557/81-8137.** Fax 0557/83-5308. www. atami-taikanso.com. 44 units. ¥29,550–¥70,000 per person. Rates include 2 meals. ¥3,150–¥5,000 extra per person Sat–Sun, holidays, and peak season. AE, DC, MC, V. Take a taxi from Atami Station, a 4-min. ride. **Amenities:** 2 restaurants; coffee shop; nightclub; indoor/outdoor hot-spring baths; sauna. *In room:* A/C, TV, minibar, hair dryer, Internet.

Where to Dine

(85) **Home Run Sushi** (Value) SUSHI For excellent sushi, head to this simple, 30-year-old one-room restaurant near the waterfront, with both counter and table seating. There's no English-language menu, but there are plastic-food displays of various sushi sets. I have no idea why this place is called Home Run—one of Japan's many mysteries.

5-1 Nagisacho, Atami City. © **0557/82-7300.** Sushi set meals ¥1,050–¥2,000. AE, DC, MC, V. Daily 11:45am–3pm and 5–10pm. A 10-min. walk from Atami Station, at the end of Ginza Dori St., on a corner to the left.

SHUZENJI

Whereas Atami, above, is popular for its seaside setting, Shuzenji Onsen is Izu Peninsula's most famous mountain spa. Nestled in a valley and straddling both sides of a river, it has a history stretching more 1,200 years, when one of Japan's most revered figures in Japanese Buddhism, Kobo Daishi, discovered a hot spring here and founded Shuzenji Temple. Today, Shuzenji, home to some 16,000 residents, is a small mountain village easily navigated on foot. Most people come for a night or two, staying in a ryokan, soaking in restorative hot-spring baths, strolling along the town's narrow streets to a few historic sights, and feasting on meals featuring local cuisine. Along with Shuzenji Temple, there are several historic sites tied to the Minamoto clan, who established a shogunate government in Kamakura in the 12th century (see "Kamakura," earlier in this chapter).

Essentials

GETTING THERE The rail gateway to Shuzenji is Mishima, a minor stop on the Shinkansen bullet train. The Hikari bullet train stops at Mishima about six times a day, though the slower Kodama bullet train stops more frequently; be sure to check the schedule beforehand. In any case, it takes 45 to 60 minutes by bullet train from Tokyo Station to Mishima, where you can then transfer to the **Izu-Hakone Railway**'s Sunzu Line for the 30-minute ride onward to Shuzenji. The fare for the entire journey is ¥4,390 for a reserved seat. Alternatively, you can save money by taking the slower **JR Tokaido Line** from Tokyo to Mishima, and then board the Izu-Hakone Railway bound for Shuzenji; the fare for this is ¥2,710 and takes about 3 hours. If you're coming from Atami, take the JR Tokaido Line 12 minutes to Mishima for ¥320, and then transfer to the Izu-Hakone Railway for another ¥500.

You can also reach Shuzenji by Odakyu's **Tokai Bus** (© 0570/01-1255) from Tokyo's Shinjuku Station. Travel time is 2 hours and 45 minutes, and the fare is ¥2,500 one-way or ¥4,500 round-trip. There are two departures daily (at the time of going to press, at 9:15am and 6:35pm), and reservations are required.

VISITOR INFORMATION The **Shuzenji Tourist Information Office** (© 0558/72-2501) is located inside Shuzenji Station, to the right after exiting the ticket gate. There's no English-speaking staff, but you can pick up a pamphlet with a map. It's open daily 9am to 5pm.

GETTING AROUND Shuzenji Spa (Shuzenji Onsen), with its ryokan, hot-spring baths, Shuzenji Temple, and other sights, is a 30-minute walk from Shuzenji Station, so you'll probably want to take the local bus. Buses depart Shuzenji Station approximately every 10 or 15 minutes from stop no. 1 bound for "Shuzenji Onsen," the last stop. The fare is ¥210. Once you're ensconced in your ryokan, you can walk everywhere. English-language signs direct you to major attractions.

Seeing the Sights

Shuzenji Onsen spreads along the Katsura River. In the center of the spa town, in the river bed, is **Tokko-no-yu,** the oldest hot spring in Izu. According to legend, in 807 Kobo Daishi saw a young boy washing his ill father in the cold water of Katsura River. Taking pity, Kobo Daishi struck a rock in the riverbed with an iron club *(tokko),* causing the rock to split open and release a hot spring that cured the sick father. Today, a pavilion along the river marks the historic spot.

After discovering Tokko-no-yu, Kobo Daishi founded **Shuzenji Temple,** just steps away from Katsura River on a small hill. Because of its associations with the great Buddhist leader, the temple flourished and a village sprang up around it. During the Kamakura Period (1185–1333), Shuzenji Temple became a stage for two tragic events resulting from the Minamoto clan's bitter family feud. First, Minamoto Yoritomo, who established the Kamakura shogunate but feared that his younger brother Noriyori had ambitions to take over, had Noriyori imprisoned here in 1193. Noriyori, who had proved his bravery by acting as commander in chief in the defeat of the rival Heike clan, subsequently killed himself. Later, Yoritomo's son, Yoriie, the second Kamakura shogun, was assassinated in Shuzenji while enjoying his bath at nearby Hakoyu spa, reportedly through poison added to his bathwater. The present temple building dates from 1883, when it was rebuilt following a mysterious fire. The Shuzenji Treasure House contains items relating to the temple, including the tokko said to have belonged to Kobo Daishi and Yoriie's death mask. You'll also find a statue of Dainichi Nyorai, given to the temple by Hojo Masako, wife of Yoritomo, in honor of her son Yoriie. Admission to the treasure house, open daily 8:30am to 4pm, is ¥300; temple grounds are open daily 6am to 5pm.

Across the river from Shuzenji Temple is **Hakoyu,** now a modern hot-spring public bath housed in an eye-catching tower. You can bathe in its tub made of *hinoki* cypress for ¥350. It's open daily from noon to 9pm.

Nearby is the **Bamboo Forest Path,** a pedestrian walkway through a bamboo grove, as well as **Shigetsuden,** the oldest wooden structure in Izu. Yoriie's mother, Masako, ordered construction of Shigetsuden to house several thousand rolls of Buddhist scriptures, donated to console the soul of her son Yoriie. It is thought that most of the scriptures were sent later to Edo (present-day Tokyo) by order of the Tokugawa shogunate, though one roll is displayed at Shuzenji Temple's Treasure House. Beside Shigetsuden is **Minamoto Yoriie's Grave,** marked by a stone pillar erected in 1703 by Shuzenji Temple's head priest to mark the 500th anniversary of Yoriie's death. The eldest son of Yoritomo, Yoriie was only 18 when he became the second shogun and was placed under house arrest in Shuzenji after only 5 years of reign. He was 23 when murdered in his bath by assassins from Kamakura. Three stones behind the pillar mark the graves of Yoriie, his concubine, and their son.

A walking trail leads across the river to **Minamoto Noriyori's Grave.** Other hiking trails lead through the surrounding mountain scenery, including the 5-km (3-mile) Okunoin Walking Trail leading to Okunoin, where Kobo Daishi is said to have practiced meditation as a youth.

Walking directions are from Shuzenji Onsen bus terminal.

Very Expensive

(86) Yagyu-no-Sho ★★★   This elegant sanctuary, surrounded by a wall and beautiful garden complete with streams, pond, mossy ground, and bamboo groves, sits on the edge of Shuzenji and feels like it's deep in the countryside. It was built some 40 years ago, a replica of the original Yagyu-no Sato in Nara, and offers 16 rooms, each one with a different atmosphere and unique architectural details, from ceiling designs to door pulls. They range from standard rooms, located in the main building accessible by elevator and decorated with antiques, to villas with their own private garden and open-air bath. The inn's most popular room is Tsukikage, with its own balcony over a pond and open-air bath. Kyoto-style kaiseki meals, with local specialties and mountain vegetables, are served in your room, and the owner's wife speaks English. If you're looking for a pampered mountain retreat, this place fits the bill.

1116–6 Shuzenji Onsen, Izu-shi, Shizuoka 410-2416. © **0558/72-4126.** Fax 0558/72-5212. www.yagyu-no-sho.com. 16 units. ¥40,050–¥68,400 per person. Rates include 2 meals. ¥2,100 extra per person Sat and nights before holidays. AE, MC, V. From the bus terminal, turn right and follow the main road; it will be on your right (7 min.). **Amenities:** Indoor/outdoor hot-spring baths. *In room:* A/C, TV, hair dryer, minibar.

Moderate

(87) **Arai Ryokan ★★**   Open since 1872, this is one of Shuzenji's most acclaimed inns. It has welcomed many Japanese celebrities over the decades, from writers and artists to Kabuki actors. It's located right in the center of the village, beside the river and just a stone's throw from Shuzenji Temple and the Bamboo Forest Path. Its 15 structures, all registered as national cultural assets and situated around a river-fed pond, include a delightful main building where you're served a welcome tea on an old-fashioned wooden veranda, a wooden covered bridge leading to rooms, and a 90-year-old public bath built in the style of Horyuji Temple in Nara—without the use of nails. Rooms are spread through several buildings constructed during different times in the inn's long history, including standard rooms with and without private bathroom and more elaborate rooms that face the pond and Katsura River. Seasonal meals are served in your room. This inn is highly recommended for its nostalgic atmosphere.

970 Shuzenji Onsen, Izu-shi, Shizuoka 410-2416. © **0558/72-2007.** Fax 0558/72-5119. www.arairyokan. net. 30 units (15 with bathroom; 12 with toilet only; 3 without bathroom). ¥21,000–¥38,000 per person. Rates exclude tax and service charge. Rates include 2 meals. AE, MC, V. From the bus terminal, turn right and follow the main road; it will be on your left, past Shuzenji Temple (3 min.). **Amenities:** Indoor/outdoor hot-spring baths; indoor hot-spring pool (summer only); free Internet in lobby. *In room:* A/C, TV, hair dryer, minibar.

Inexpensive

(88) **Goyokan**   This family-run inn, in a warehouse-style building of black tiles topped with white mortar, opened about 20 years ago. Sandwiched between Shuzenzji's main road and the Katsura River, near the bus terminal, it offers simple but clean tatami rooms, some with views of the river. Note that no dinner is served and no single accommodations are available.

765–2 Shuzenji Onsen, Izu-shi, Shizuoka 410-2416. © **0558/72-2066.** Fax 0558/72-8212. www.goyokan. co.jp. 11 units (none with bathroom). ¥6,450 per person without breakfast; ¥7,500 per person with breakfast. Rates include tax. No credit cards. Across the street from the bus terminal, to the left (1 min.). **Amenities:** Indoor hot-spring baths. *In room:* A/C, TV, fridge, no phone.

Where to Dine

(89) Nanaban (Value) NOODLES   Nanaban is famous in Shuzenji for its buckwheat noodles, but you may have to work a bit to release your meal's special aroma and flavors. Most popular is the Zendera Soba, which you prepare by grinding your own sesame seeds and then grating fresh wasabi root, all of which is added to your soba along with soy sauce (you can take any extra wasabi root home with you). Other soba and *udon* dishes are also available, including those with mountain vegetables and tempura. There's no English-language menu, but there's a plastic food display outside and the menu has pictures. After taking your shoes off at the entrance, you'll be seated at a low table with leg wells, surrounded by antiques and gleaming wood.

761-1-3 Shuzenji Onsen, Izu-shi. (C) **0558/72-0007.** Set meals ¥1,260–¥1,890. No credit cards. Fri–Wed 10–4pm. Across the street from the bus terminal, to the left (1 min.); look for the statue of the raccoon dog and the bamboo fountain.

Fast Facts

1 FAST FACTS: TOKYO

If you can't find answers to your questions here, call the **Tourist Information Center** (© **03/3201-3331**), open daily from 9am to 5pm; the city-run **Tokyo Tourist Information Center** (© **03/5321-3077**), open daily from 9:30am to 6:30pm, or the **TIC TOKYO** (© **03/5220-7055**), open daily 10am to 7pm. Another good source for information is the **Foreign Residents' Advisory Center** (© **03/5320-7744**), which can answer a wide range of topics from problems concerning daily life in Japan and emergency numbers to Japanese customs; it's open Monday to Friday from 9:30am to noon and 1 to 5pm. Finally, if you're staying in a first-class hotel, another valuable resource is the concierge or guest-relations desk; the staff there can tell you how to reach your destination, answer general questions, and even make restaurant reservations for you.

AREA CODES The area codes for Tokyo are © **3,** if calling from abroad, and © **03,** if calling from within Japan.

BABYSITTERS Most major hotels can arrange babysitting services, but expect to pay a minimum of ¥5,000 for 2 hours. Some hotels have day-care centers for young children, though they are no less expensive. See individual hotel listings or "Family-Friendly Hotels" in chapter 5.

BUSINESS HOURS **Government offices and private companies** are generally open Monday through Friday 9am to 5pm. **Banks** are open Monday through Friday 9am to 3pm (but usually will not exchange money until 10:30 or 11am,

after that day's currency exchange rates come in). Neighborhood **post offices** are open Monday through Friday 9am to 5pm; some major post offices (located in each ward) stay open until 7pm.

Department stores are open from about 10am to 8 or 9pm. Most are open daily but may close irregularly. **Smaller stores** are generally open from about 10am to 8pm, closed 1 day a week. Convenience stores such as 7-Eleven and Family Mart are open 24 hours.

Keep in mind that **museums, gardens,** and **attractions** stop selling admission tickets at least 30 minutes before the actual closing time. Similarly, **restaurants** take their last orders at least 30 minutes before the posted closing time (even earlier for *kaiseki* restaurants). Most museums are closed on Monday; if Monday is a national holiday, however, museums will usually remain open and close on the following day, Tuesday, instead.

DRINKING LAWS The legal drinking age is 20. Beer, wine, and spirits are readily available in grocery stores, some convenience stores, and liquor stores. Many bars, especially in nightlife districts such as Shinjuku and Roppongi, are open until dawn. If you intend to drive in Japan, you are not allowed even one drink.

DRUGSTORES There is no 24-hour drugstore *(kusuri-ya)* in Tokyo, but ubiquitous 24-hour convenience stores, such as 7-Eleven, Lawson, and Family Mart, carry such things as aspirin. If you're looking for specific pharmaceuticals or familiar health-care products, a good bet is the **American Pharmacy,** in the basement of the Marunouchi Building, 2–4–1 Marunouchi, Chiyoda-ku (© **03/5220-7716;** Mon–Fri 9am–9pm, Sat 10am–9pm, and Sun and holidays 10am–8pm). It carries imported cosmetics, vitamins, and other items and has many of the same over-the-counter drugs you can find at home (many of them imported from the U.S.) and can fill American prescriptions—but note that you *must first visit a doctor in Japan* before foreign prescriptions can be filled, so it's best to bring an ample supply of any prescription medication with you.

EARTHQUAKES Kobe's tragic 1995 earthquake brought world-wide attention to the fact that Japan is earthquake-prone. Approximately 200 earthquakes can be felt in Tokyo each year, but there are many more that are too small to detect. However, in the event of an earthquake you can feel, there are a few precautions you should take. If you're indoors, take cover under a doorway, against a wall, or under a table, and do not go outdoors. If you're outdoors, stay away from trees, power lines, and the sides of buildings; if you're surrounded by tall buildings, seek cover in a doorway. If you're near a beach or the bay, evacuate to higher ground to avoid danger in case of a tsunami. Never use elevators during a quake. You should be sure to note emergency exits wherever you stay. All hotels supply flashlights, usually found attached to your bedside table. In case of major emergencies, there are emergency shelters throughout the city.

ELECTRICITY The electricity throughout Japan is 100 volts AC, but there are two different cycles in use: In Tokyo and in regions northeast of the capital, it's 50 cycles, while in Nagoya, Kyoto, Osaka, and all points to the southwest, it's 60 cycles. In any case, it's close enough to the American system that I've never encountered any problems plugging my American

electronics, including laptops and camera rechargers. Leading hotels in Tokyo often have two outlets, one for 110 volts and one for 220 volts (with the appropriate plugs used in the U.S. and Europe), so you can use most American or European appliances (electric razors, travel irons, laptops, and so forth) during your stay. Otherwise, plugs are the same as in the U.S., two flat parallel pins.

EMBASSIES & CONSULATES The visa or passport sections of most embassies are open only at certain times during the day, so it's best to call in advance.

U.S. Embassy: 1–10–5 Akasaka, Minato-ku, near Toranomon subway station (© **03/3224-5000;** http://japan. usembassy.gov; consular section Mon–Fri 8:30am–noon and Mon–Tues and Thurs–Fri 2–4pm; phone inquiries Mon–Fri 8:30am–1pm and 2–5:30pm).

Canadian Embassy: 7–3–38 Akasaka, Minato-ku, near Aoyama-Itchome Station (© **03/5412-6200;** www.international. gc.ca/missions/japan-japon/menu-eng. asp; consular section Mon–Fri 9:30–11:30am; embassy Mon–Fri 9am–12:30pm and 1:30–5:30pm).

British Embassy: 1 Ichibancho, Chiyoda-ku, near Hanzomon Station (© **03/5211-1100;** http://ukinjapan.fco. gov.uk/en; Mon–Fri 9am–12:30pm and 2–5:30pm; consulate inquiries Mon–Fri 9:15am–2:15pm).

Embassy of Ireland: Ireland House, 2–10–7 Kojimachi, Chiyoda-ku, near Hanzomon Station, exit 3 (© **03/3263-0695;** www.irishembassy.jp; Mon–Fri 10am–12:30pm and 2–4pm).

Australian Embassy: 2–1–14 Mita, Minato-ku, near Azabu-Juban Station, exit 2 (© **03/5232-4111;** www.australia. or.jp; consular section Mon–Fri 9am–5:30pm; embassy Mon–Fri 9am–12:30pm and 1:30–5pm).

New Zealand Embassy: 20–40 Kamiyama-cho, Shibuya-ku, a 15-minute walk from Shibuya Station (📞 03/3467-2271; www.nzembassy.com/japan; Mon–Fri 9am–5:30pm; call for consular hours).

EMERGENCIES The national emergency numbers are 📞 **110** for **police** and 📞 **119** for **ambulance** and **fire** (ambulances are free in Japan unless you request a specific hospital). You do not need to insert any money into public telephones to call these numbers. However, if you use a green public telephone, it's necessary to push a red button before dialing. If you call from a gray public telephone or one that accepts only prepaid cards, you won't see a red button; it that case simply lift the receiver and dial.

HOLIDAYS See "When to Go," in chapter 3.

HOSPITALS Large hospitals in Japan are open only a limited number of hours (designated hospitals remain open for emergencies, however, and an ambulance will automatically take you there). Otherwise, you can make appointments at these hospital clinics to see a doctor: **The International Catholic Hospital (Seibo Byoin),** 2–5–1 Naka-Ochiai, Shinjuku-ku, near Mejiro Station on the Yamanote Line (📞 03/3951-1111; http://catholic toshima.web9.jp/english/seibohospital. html; clinic hours Mon–Sat 8–11am; closed third Sat each month; walk-ins accepted); **St. Luke's International Hospital (Seiroka Byoin),** 9–1 Akashi-cho, Chuo-ku, near Tsukiji Station on the Hibiya Line (📞 03/3541-5151; www. luke.or.jp; Mon–Fri 8:30–11am; appointment necessary for some treatments); and **Japan Red Cross Medical Center (Nihon Sekijujisha Iryo Center),** 4–1–22 Hiroo, Shibuya-ku (📞 03/3400-1311; www.ned. jrc.or.jp; Mon–Fri 8:30–11am; walk-ins only), whose closest subway stations are Roppongi, Hiroo, and Shibuya—from there, you should take a taxi.

Otherwise, many first-class hotels offer medical facilities or an in-house doctor.

Both your embassy and the **AMDA International Medical Information Center** (📞 03/5285-8088; www.amdainternational.com; Mon–Fri 9am–5pm) can refer you to medical professionals who speak English.

The following clinics have some English-speaking staff and are popular with foreigners living in Tokyo: **Tokyo Midtown Medical Center,** an affiliate of Johns Hopkins and located on the sixth floor of Midtown Tower, 9–7–1 Akasaka, Minato-ku, near Roppongi Station (📞 03/5413-7911; www.tokyomidtown-mc.jp; Mon–Fri 10:30am–1pm; accepts walk-ins, appointment, and emergencies); **The International Clinic,** 1–5–9 Azabudai, Minato-ku, within walking distance of Roppongi or Azabu-Juban stations (📞 03/3582-2646; Mon–Fri 9am–noon and 2–5pm, Sat 9am–noon; walk-ins only); and **Tokyo Medical & Surgical Clinic,** 3–4–30 Shiba-koen, Minato-ku, near Kamiyacho, Onarimon, or Shiba-koen stations and across from Tokyo Tower (📞 03/3436-3028; www.tmsc.jp; Mon–Fri 9–11:30am and 2–4:30pm, Sat 9am–noon; appointment only).

At the Tokyo Medical & Surgical Clinic, above, is the **Tokyo Clinic Dental Office** (📞 03/3431-4225; Mon–Thurs 9am–6pm and Sat 9am–5pm). Just a 3-minute walk away is the **United Dental Office,** 2–3–8 Azabudai, Minato-ku (📞 03/5570-4334; http://uniteddental office.com; Mon–Tues and Thurs–Sat 9am–1pm and 2–6pm). Tokyo Midtown Medical Center (see above) also has a **Dental Clinic;** call 📞 03/5413-7912 for an appointment.

INTERNET ACCESS See "Staying Connected," in chapter 3.

LANGUAGE English is widely understood in major hotels, restaurants, and shops, but it's hit-or-miss elsewhere. See "Dealing with the Language Barrier," in chapter 2, and a list of common phrases in Japanese in chapter 13.

LAUNDROMATS All upper- and most midrange hotels offer laundry and dry-cleaning services (but it's expensive, with a laundered shirt costing about ¥400). Note that for same-day service, it's usually necessary to hand over your laundry by 10am. Many hotels do not offer laundry service on Sundays or holidays. Several Japanese-style accommodations in the budget category have coin-operated washers. Otherwise, coin laundries (as they're known in Japan) can be found in residential areas; ask your hotel for the nearest one. Many hotel guest rooms have a pull-out laundry line over the tub for hand washables.

LEGAL AID Contact your embassy if you find yourself in legal trouble. The **Legal Counseling Center,** 1–4 Yotsuya, Shinjuku (© **03/5367-5280;** www.horitsu-sodan.jp; station: Yotsuya), is operated by three bar associations and provides legal counseling with English interpreters Monday to Friday 1 to 4pm.

LOST & FOUND If you've forgotten something on a subway, in a taxi, or on a park bench, don't assume it's gone forever—if you're willing to trace it, you'll probably get it back. If you can remember where you last saw it, the first thing to do is telephone the establishment or return to where you left it; there's a good chance it will still be sitting there. If you've lost something on the street, go to the nearest police box *(koban);* items found in the neighborhood will stay there for 3 days or longer.

If you've lost something in a taxi, have someone who speaks Japanese contact the **Tokyo Taxi Center,** 7–3–3 Minamisuma, Koto-ku (© **03/3648-0300**). For JR trains, go to the nearest station master's office (usually near the exit) or call the **JR East Infoline** (© **050/2016-1603**). For items lost in the **subway,** go to the nearest subway station; after 1 day, lost items are kept at Ueno Station's Lost and Found Center (© **03/3834-5577**) for 3 to 4 days.

Eventually, every unclaimed item in Tokyo ends up at the Central Lost and Found Office of the **Metropolitan Police Board,** 1–9–11 Koraku, Bunkyo-ku (© **03/3814-4151;** Mon–Fri 8:30am–5:15pm; station: Iidabashi).

Be sure to notify all your credit card companies the minute you discover your wallet has been lost or stolen, and file a report at the nearest police precinct. Your credit card company or insurer may require a police report number or record of the loss. Most credit card companies have an emergency toll-free number to call if your card is lost or stolen; they may be able to wire you a cash advance immediately or deliver an emergency credit card in a day or two. **Visa**'s emergency number in Japan is © **00531/11-1555. American Express** cardholders can call © **03/3220-6220,** and for traveler's checks it's © **0120/779-656. MasterCard** holders should call © **00531/11-3886** in Japan, and **Diner's Club** holders should call © **0120-074-024** in Japan.

LUGGAGE & LOCKERS At Narita International Airport, delivery service counters will send luggage to your hotel the next day (or from your hotel to the airport) for about ¥1,690 to ¥2,000 per bag. Coin-operated lockers are located at all major JR stations, such as Tokyo, Shinjuku, and Ueno, as well as at most subway stations. Lockers cost ¥300 to ¥600 per day, depending on the size.

MAIL If your hotel cannot mail letters for you, ask the concierge for the location of the nearest post office, recognizable by the red logo of a capital T with a horizontal line over it. Mailboxes are bright orange-red; the left slot is for domestic mail while the slot on the right is for mail to foreign countries. It costs ¥110 to airmail letters weighing up to 25 grams and ¥70 to mail postcards to North America and Europe. Domestic mail costs ¥80 for letters weighing up to 25 grams, and ¥50 for postcards. Post offices throughout Japan are also convenient for their ATMs, which accept international bank cards operating on the PLUS and Cirrus systems, as well as MasterCard and Visa.

Although all post offices are open Monday through Friday from 9am to 5pm, major post offices in each ward remain open to 7pm. The **Shibuya Central Post Office,** 1–12–13 Shibuya (© **03/5469-9907;** station: Shibuya), has longer business hours than most: Monday through Friday 9am to 9pm; and Saturday, Sunday, and holidays 9am to 7pm. An after-hours counter remains open throughout the night for mail and packages, making it the only 24-hour post office in town. *Note:* The Central Post Office, built in 1931 near Tokyo Station, is closed for major renovation until approximately 2012.

As for mailing packages, your hotel may have a shipping service. Otherwise, you can mail packages abroad only at larger post offices. Conveniently, they sell cardboard boxes in several sizes with the necessary tape. Packages mailed abroad cannot weigh more than 20kg (about 44 lb.). A package weighing 10kg (about 22 lb.) will cost ¥6,750 to North America via surface mail and will take about a month to arrive. Express packages, which take 3 days to North America and can weigh up to 30kg (66 lb.), cost ¥12,550 for 10kg (22 lb.).

For English-language postal information, call © **0570-046111** Monday through Friday between 8am and 10pm, weekends and holidays between 9am and 10pm, or check the website **www.post. japanpost.jp**.

NEWSPAPERS & MAGAZINES Three English-language newspapers are published daily in Japan: the *Japan Times* and the *Daily Yomiuri* (the former with a weekly supplement from *The Observer* and the latter with a weekly supplement from *The Washington Post*), as well as the *International Herald Tribune/Asahi Shimbun.* Hotels and major bookstores carry the international editions of such newsmagazines as *Time* and *Newsweek.* You can also read the *Japan Times* online at www. japantimes.co.jp and the *Daily Yomiuri* at www.yomiuri.co.jp/dy.

PASSPORTS For information on obtaining passports, please contact the following agencies:

For Residents of Australia Contact the **Australian Passport Information Service** at © **131-232,** or visit the government website at www.passports.gov.au.

For Residents of Canada Contact the central **Passport Office,** Department of Foreign Affairs and International Trade, Ottawa, ON K1A 0G3 (© **800/567-6868;** www.ppt.gc.ca).

For Residents of Ireland Contact the **Passport Office,** Setanta Centre, Molesworth Street, Dublin 2 (© **01/671-1633;** www.irlgov.ie/iveagh).

For Residents of New Zealand Contact the **Passports Office** at © **0800/225-050** in New Zealand, or 04/474-8100; or log on to www.passports.govt.nz.

For Residents of the United Kingdom Visit your nearest passport office, major post office, or travel agency, or contact the **United Kingdom Passport Service** at © **0870/521-0410,** or search its website at www.ukpa.gov.uk.

For Residents of the United States To find your regional passport office, either check the U.S. Department of State website or call the **National Passport Information Center** toll-free number (© **877/487-2778**) for automated information.

POLICE The national emergency telephone number is © **110.** For nonemergency criminal matters or concerns, the **Metropolitan Police Department** maintains an English-language telephone counseling service for foreigners at © **03/3501-0110** Monday through Friday from 8:30am to 5:15pm.

SMOKING The legal age for purchasing tobacco products and smoking in Japan is 20. Smoking is banned in public areas, including train and subway stations and office buildings. In most wards (city districts), nonsmoking ordinances ban smoking on sidewalks but allow it in marked "Smokers Corner" areas, usually near train stations. Many restaurants have nonsmoking sections, though bars do not.

TAXES A 5% consumption tax is imposed on goods and services in Japan, including hotel rates and restaurant meals. Although hotels and restaurants are required to include the tax in their published rates, you might come across one that has yet to comply (especially on English-language menus which may not be updated regularly). In Tokyo, hotels also levy a separate accommodations tax of ¥100 per person per night on rooms costing ¥10,000 to ¥14,999; rates ¥15,000 and up are taxed at ¥200 per night per person. Some hotels include the local tax in their published rack rates; others do not.

In addition to these taxes, a 10% to 15% **service charge** will be added to your bill in lieu of tipping at most of the fancier restaurants and at moderately priced and upper-end hotels. Thus, the 15% to 20% in tax and service charge that will be added to your bill in the more expensive locales can really add up. Most *ryokan,* or Japanese-style inns, include a service charge but not a consumption tax in their rates. If you're not sure, ask. Business hotels, *minshuku* (private-home lodging), youth hostels, and inexpensive restaurants do not impose a service charge.

As for **shopping,** a 5% consumption tax is also levied on most goods. (Some of the smaller vendors are not required to levy tax.) Travelers from abroad, however, are eligible for an exemption on goods taken out of the country, although only the larger department stores and specialty shops seem equipped to deal with the procedures. In any case, most department stores grant a refund on the consumption tax only when the total amount of purchases for the day exceeds ¥10,000. You can obtain a refund immediately by having a sales clerk fill out a list of your purchases and then presenting the list to the tax-exemption counter of the department store; *you will need to show your passport.* Note that no refunds for consumption tax are given for food, drinks, tobacco, cosmetics, film, or batteries.

TELEPHONES For information on how to make calls or where to rent mobile phones in Japan, see "Staying Connected" in chapter 3. For directory assistance in Tokyo, dial ℭ **104.**

TELEVISION Almost nothing is broadcast in English; even foreign films are dubbed in Japanese. Most upper-range hotels, however, offer **bilingual televisions** (meaning you can switch the language from Japanese to English, but only if the program or movie was originally in English), though very few (and fairly dated) English movies and sitcoms are broadcast each week. The plus of bilingual TV is that you can listen to the nightly national news broadcast by NHK at 7 and 9pm. Otherwise, major hotels in Tokyo have cable TV with English-language programs, including CNN broadcasts (sometimes in Japanese only) and BBC World as well as in-house pay movies. But even if you don't understand Japanese, I suggest that you watch TV at least once; maybe you'll catch a samurai series or a sumo match. Commercials are also worth watching. ***Note:*** Japan switches from analog to digital broadcasting in July 2011. Many hotels have already replaced their old TV sets with new equipment, but some of the cheapest accommodations may upgrade only a few rooms at a time because of the extra expense.

A word on those **pay video programs** offered by hotels and many resort *ryokan:* Upper-range hotels usually have a few choices in English, and these are charged automatically to your bill. Most business hotels usually offer only one kind of pay movie—generally "adult entertainment" programs. If you're traveling with children, you'll want to be extremely careful about selecting your TV programs. Many adult video pay channels appear with a simple push of the channel-selector button, and they can be difficult to get rid of. In budget accommodations, you may come across televisions with coin boxes attached to their sides or, more common nowadays, vending machines in the hallway offering prepaid cards. These are also for special adult entertainment videos. Now you know.

TIME Japan is 9 hours ahead of Greenwich Mean Time, 14 hours ahead of New York, 15 hours ahead of Chicago, and 17 hours ahead of Los Angeles. Because Japan does not go on daylight saving time, subtract 1 hour from the above times if you're calling the United States in the summer.

Because Japan is on the other side of the International Date Line, you lose a day when traveling from the United States to Asia (if you depart the U.S. on Tues, you'll arrive on Wed). Returning to North America, however, you gain a day, which means that you arrive on the same day you leave. (In fact, it can happen that you arrive in the U.S. at a time earlier than when you departed from Japan.)

TIPPING One of the delights of being in Japan is that there is no tipping—not even to waitresses, taxi drivers, or bellhops. If you try to tip them, they'll probably be confused or embarrassed. Instead, you'll have a 10% to 15% service charge added to your bill at higher-priced accommodations and restaurants. That being said, you might want to tip, say, your room attendant at a high-class ryokan if you've made special requests or meals are served in your room; in that case, place crisp, clean bills (¥3,000 to ¥5,000) in a white envelope on the table of your room at the beginning of your stay; but it's perfectly fine, too, if you choose not to tip.

TOILETS If you're in need of a restroom in Tokyo, your best bets are train and subway stations, big hotels, department stores, and fast-food chains such as McDonald's. Use of restrooms is free in Japan, and though most public facilities supply toilet paper, it's a good idea to carry a packet of tissues.

In parks and some restaurants, especially in rural areas, don't be surprised if you go into some restrooms and find men's urinals and private stalls in the same room. Women are supposed to walk right past the urinals without noticing them.

Many toilets in Japan, especially those at train stations, are **Japanese-style toilets:** They're holes in the ground over which you squat facing the end that has a raised hood. Men stand and aim for the hole. Although Japanese lavatories may seem uncomfortable at first, they're actually much more sanitary because no part of your body touches anything.

Otherwise, Western-style toilets in Japan are usually very high-tech. Called **washlets,** these combination toilet/bidets have heated toilet seats, buttons and knobs directing sprays of water of various intensities to various body parts, and even lids that raise when you open the stall. But alas, instructions are usually in Japanese only. The voice of experience: Don't stand up until you've figured out how to turn the darn spray off.

VISAS Most foreign tourists, including Americans, Canadians, Australians, New Zealanders, and citizens of the United Kingdom and Ireland, do not need visas to visit Japan. Nationals of countries that do not have reciprocal visa exemption arrangements with Japan must obtain a visa. A Temporary Visitor's Visa allows tourists to stay in Japan for up to 90 days. Applicants must apply in person to a Japanese Embassy or a consulate with a valid passport, two passport photos taken within the past 6 months, two official visa application forms, and documents certifying the purpose of the visit.

VISITOR INFORMATION The **Japan National Tourism Organization (JNTO)** publishes a wealth of free, colorful brochures and maps covering Tokyo and other cities. These include a tourist map of Tokyo, brochures of popular destinations near Tokyo, and "The Tourist's Language Handbook," a phrase booklet to help foreign visitors communicate with the Japanese.

Japan Online: You can reach JNTO via the Internet at **www.jnto.go.jp** (and at www.japantravelinfo.com for North American travelers; at www.seejapan.co.uk for British travelers; and at www.jnto.org.au for Australian travelers), where you can read up on what's new, view maps, get the latest weather report, find links to online hotel reservation companies and tour companies, and browse through information ranging from hints on budget travel to regional events. JNTO also showcases local tourism attractions, Japanese cuisine, and other topics on YouTube at www.youtube.com/VisitJapan.

The **Tokyo Metropolitan Government** maintains a website, at **www.tourism.metro.tokyo.jp**, as does the **Tokyo Convention & Visitors Bureau**, at **www.tcvb.or.jp**. A different perspective is provided by bloggers living in Tokyo at **http://tokyo.metblogs.com**.

The **JNTO Overseas:** If you'd like information on Japan before leaving home, contact one of the following JNTO offices.

In the **United States:** 11 West 42nd Street, 19th Floor, New York, NY 10036 (☏ 212/715-1205; visitjapan@jntonyc.org); and Little Tokyo Plaza, 340 E. Second St., Ste. 302, Los Angeles, CA 90012 (☏ 213/623-1952; info@jnto-lax.org).

In **Canada:** 481 University Ave., Ste. 306, Toronto, ON M5G 2E9, Canada (☏ 416/366-7140; info@jntoyyz.com).

In the **United Kingdom:** Fifth Floor, 12 Nicholas Lane, London EC4N 7BN, England (☏ 020/7398-5678; info@jnto.co.uk).

In **Australia:** Level 7, 36–38 Clarence St., Sydney NSW 2000, Australia (no phone service; travelinfo@jnto.org.au).

In **Tokyo:** JNTO maintains three tourist offices, known as **Tourist Information Centers (TICs),** in Tokyo and in its airport to handle inquiries from foreigners and the general public about Tokyo and the rest of Japan and to provide free maps and sightseeing materials. You can even make reservations here for inexpensive accommodations throughout Japan at no extra charge.

If you arrive by plane at **Narita International Airport,** you'll find TICs in the arrivals lobbies of Terminal 1 (☏ 0476/30-3383) and Terminal 2 (☏ 0476/34-5877), both open daily from 8am to 8pm. Otherwise, the main TIC is in the heart of Tokyo at 2–10–1 Yurakucho (☏ 03/3201-3331; station: Yurakucho), within walking distance of the Ginza. It's located on the 10th floor of a rather obscure office building next to Yurakucho Station called the **Kotsu Kaikan Building** (look for the building's circular top). Assuming you're able to find them, the TIC staff is courteous and efficient; I cannot recommend them highly enough. In addition to city maps (such as the "Tourist Map of Tokyo") and sightseeing materials, the office has more information on the rest of Japan than any other tourist office, including pamphlets and brochures on major cities and attractions such as Nikko and Kamakura. Hours are daily 9am to 5pm.

There's also the new **TIC TOKYO,** facing the Nihombashi exit of Tokyo Station, at 1–8–1 Marunouchi (☏ 03/5220-7055; www.tictokyo.jp). Open daily 10am to 7pm, it dispenses information on traveling throughout Japan, and books accommodations, tours, and even air tickets.

Another great source of information is the **Tokyo Tourist Information Center,** operated by the Tokyo Metropolitan Government and located on the first floor of the Tokyo Metropolitan Government (TMG) Building no. 1, 2–8–1 Nishi-Shinjuku (𝒞 **03/5321-3077**; www.tourism.metro.tokyo.jp; station: Tochomae or Shinjuku). You'll probably want to come here anyway for the great views from TMG's free observation floor. The center dispenses pamphlets, its own city map (which is a great complement to the one issued by JNTO), and handy one-page detailed maps of various city districts, from Ueno to Roppongi. It's open daily 9:30am to 6:30pm. Other city-run information counters are located at Keisei Ueno Station (𝒞 **03/3836-3471**), open daily 9:30am to 6:30pm, and at Haneda Airport (𝒞 **03/5757-9345**), open daily 9am to 10pm.

Tourist Publications: Be sure to pick up *Event Calendar* at the TIC, a monthly leaflet listing festivals, antiques and crafts fairs, and other events throughout the metropolitan area. Of the many free giveaways available at the TICs, restaurants, bars, bookstores, hotels, and other establishments visitors and expats are likely to frequent, the best is the weekly *Metropolis* (http://metropolis.co.jp), with features on Tokyo, club listings, and restaurant and movie reviews. Look also for the free *Japanzine* (www.seekjapan.jp/japanzine) and *att.Japan* (www.att-japan.net). Weekly entertainment sections on theater, films, and special events are published in the English-language newspapers, appearing on Friday in the *Japan Times* and on Thursday in the *Daily Yomiuri.*

WATER The water is safe to drink anywhere in Japan, although some people claim it's too highly chlorinated. Bottled water is readily available.

2 AIRLINE WEBSITES

MAJOR AIRLINES

Aeromexico
www.aeromexico.com

Air Canada
www.aircanada.com

Air France
www.airfrance.com

Air India
www.airindia.com

Air New Zealand
www.airnewzealand.com

Air Tahiti Nui
www.airtahitinui-usa.com

Asiana Airlines
http://us.flyasiana.com

Alitalia
www.alitalia.com

All Nippon Airways
www.ana.co.jp

American Airlines
www.aa.com

British Airways
www.british-airways.com

Cathay Pacific
www.cathaypacific.com

China Airlines
www.china-airlines.com

Continental Airlines
www.continental.com

Delta Air Lines
www.delta.com

EgyptAir
www.egyptair.com

Hawaiian Airlines
www.hawaiianair.com

Japan Airlines
www.jal.com

Jetstar Airways
www.jetstar.com

KLM Royal Dutch Airlines
www.klm.com

Korean Air
www.koreanair.com

Lufthansa
www.lufthansa.com

Northwest Airlines
www.nwa.com

Qantas Airways
www.qantas.com

Philippine Airlines
www.philippineairlines.com

Singapore Airlines
www.singaporeair.com

Swiss Air
www.swiss.com

Thai Airways International
www.thaiair.com

Turkish Airlines
www.thy.com

United Airlines
www.united.com

US Airways
www.usairways.com

Virgin Atlantic Airways
www.virgin-atlantic.com

A Glossary of Useful Japanese Terms

Needless to say, it takes years to become fluent in Japanese, particularly in written Japanese, with its thousands of *kanji*, or Chinese characters, and its many *hiragana* and *katakana* characters. If you know even a few words of Japanese, however, they will not only be useful but will delight Japanese people you meet in the course of your trip.

PRONUNCIATION

In pronouncing the following vocabulary, remember that there's very little stress on individual syllables (pronunciation of Japanese is often compared to Italian). Here's an approximation of some of the sounds of Japanese:

a	*as in* father
aa	*held slightly longer than* a
e	*as in* pen
i	*as in* pick
ii	*held slightly longer than* i
o	*as in* oh
oo	*held slightly longer than* o
u	*as in* boo
uu	*held slightly longer than* u
g	*as in gift at the beginning of words; like* ng *in* sing *in the middle or at the end of words*

Vowel sounds are almost always short unless they are pronounced doubled, in which case you hold the vowel a bit longer. *Okashi,* for example, means "a sweet," whereas *okashii* means "strange." As you can see, even slight mispronunciation of a word can result in confusion or hilarity. (Incidentally, jokes in Japanese are nearly always plays on words.) Similarly, double consonants are given more emphasis than only one consonant by itself.

USEFUL WORDS & PHRASES
Basic Terms

Yes	**Hai**
No	**Iie**
Good morning	**Ohayo gozaimasu**
Good afternoon	**Konnichiwa**
Good evening	**Konbanwa**
Good night	**Oyasuminasai**

Hello   **Haro** (or **Konnichiwa**)
How are you?   **Ogenki desu ka?**
How do you do?   **Hajimemashite?**
Goodbye   **Sayonara** (or **Bye-Bye**)
Excuse me/Pardon me/I'm sorry   **Sumimasen**
Please (when offering something)   **Doozo**
Please (when requesting something)   **Kudasai**
Thank you   **Domo arigato**
You're welcome   **Doo-itashimashite**

Basic Questions & Expressions

I'm American   **Amerikajin desu**
I'm Canadian   **Canadajin desu**
I'm English   **Igirisujin desu**
Sorry, I don't speak Japanese   **Sumimasen, Nihongo wa hanasemasen**
Do you understand English?   **Eigo wa wakarimasu ka?**
Do you understand?   **Wakarimasu ka?**
I understand   **Wakarimasu**
I don't understand   **Wakarimasen**
Can I ask you a question?   **Otazune shitaino desuga?**
Just a minute, please   **Chotto matte kudasai**
How much is it?   **Ikura desu ka?**
It's expensive   **Takai desu**
It's cheap   **Yasui desu**
Where is it?   **Doko desu ka?**
When is it?   **Itsu desu ka?**
What is it?   **Kore-wa, nan-desu-ka?**
I like it   **Suki desu** (pronounced "ski")
Where is the toilet?   **Toire wa, doko desu ka?**
My name is . . .   [Your name] **to mooshimasu**
What is your name?   **O-namae wa, nan desu ka?**
What time do you open/close?   **Nanji ni akimasuka? Nanjini shimarimasuka?**
Credit card   **Kurejitto kaado**
Too expensive   **Takasugimasu**
This one   **Kore**
That one   **Are**

Travel Expressions & Directionals

Where is . . . ?   **Doko desu ka . . . ?**
Where is the train station?   **Eki wa, doko desu ka?**
Train station   **Eki**
Airport   **Kuukoo**

Subway **Chika-tetsu**

Bus **Basu**

Taxi **Takushii**

Airplane **Hikooki**

Train **Densha**

Bullet train **Shinkansen**

Limited express train (long distance) **Tokkyu**

Ordinary express train (doesn't stop at every station) **Kyukoo**

Rapid train **Kaisoku densha**

Local train (one that stops at every station) **Kakueki teisha** (or **futsu**)

I would like a reserved seat, please. **Shiteiseki o kudasai.**

I would like a seat in the nonsmoking car, please. **Kinensha no shiteiski o kudasai.**

Where should I transfer? **Norikae wa doko desu ka?**

Unreserved seat **Jiyuseki**

Platform **Platto-hoomu**

Ticket **Kippu**

Destination **Ikisaki**

One-way ticket **Katamichi-kippu** (or **katamichiken**)

Round-trip ticket **Oofuku-kippu** (or **oofukuken**)

I would like to buy a ticket. **Kippu ichimai o kaitai no desu kedo.**

I would like to buy two tickets. **Kippu nimai o kaitai no desu kedo.**

Exit **Deguchi**

Entrance **Iriguchi**

North **Kita**

South **Minami**

East **Higashi**

West **Nishi**

Left **Hidari**

Right **Migi**

Straight ahead **Massugu**

Is it far? **Tooi desu ka?**

Is it near? **Chikai desu ka?**

I'm lost. **Maigoni narimashita.**

Can I walk there? **Aruite ikemasu ka?**

Street **Dori** (or **michi**)

Tourist Information Office **Kanko annaijo** (or **kanko kyookai**)

Where is the tourist office? **Kanko annaijo wa, doko desu ka?**

May I have a map, please? **Chizu o kudasai?**

Police **Keisatsu**

Police box **Koban**

Post office **Yuubin-kyoku**

I'd like to buy a stamp. **Kitte o kaitai no desu kedo.**

Bank **Ginkoo**
Hospital **Byooin**
Drugstore **Yakkyoku**
Convenience store **Konbiniensu stoaa**
Embassy **Taishikan**
Department store **Depaato**
Downtown area **Hanka-gai**
Passport **Pasupooto**
I want to go to . . . **. . . e ikitai desu.**
I want to go to the station. **Eki e ikitai desu.**
What time does . . . leave? **. . . nanjini shuppatsu desu ka?**
Train **Densha**
Subway **Chikatetsu**
Bus **Basu**
Ferry **Ferii**

Lodging Terms

Hotel **Hoteru**
Japanese-style inn **Ryokan**
Japanese-style lodging in a family home **Minshuku**
Youth hostel **Yuusu hosuteru**
Cotton kimono **Yukata**
Room **Heya**
Do you have a room available? **Heya ga arimasu ka?**
Does that include meals? **Shokuji wa tsuite imasu ka?**
Tax **Zei**
Service charge **Saabisu**
Key **Kagi**
Balcony **Beranda**
Hot-spring spa **Onsen**
Outdoor hot-spring bath **Rotenburo**
Bath **Ofuro**
Public bath **Sentoo**
Where is the nearest public bath? **Ichiban chikai sentoo wa, doko desu ka?**
I would like a room with one bed/two beds. **Singuru** (single bed), **Daberu** (double-size bed), **Tsuin** (twin beds) **no heya o onegaishimasu.**
Does it have a private bathroom? **Heya ni wa ofuro** (tub) **toire** (toilet) **ga tsuitemasuka?**
I'd like a private bathroom. **Basu toile tsuki no heya o onegaishimasu.**
Does the window open? **Kono mado wa akimasuka?**

Dining Terms & Phrases

Restaurant **Resutoran** (serves Western-style food)
Dining hall **Shokudoo** (usually serves Japanese food)

Coffee shop	**Kissaten**
Japanese pub	**Izakaya** or **Nomiya**
Western food	**Yooshoku**
Japanese food	**Washoku**
Breakfast	**Chooshoku**
Lunch	**Ohiru/lanchi**
Dinner	**Yuushoku**
I'd like to make a reservation.	**Yoyaku oneigai shimasu.**
I'd like to pay the bill.	**Okanjyoo o oneigai shimasu.**
Menu	**Menyu**
Japanese green tea	**Ocha**
Black (Indian) tea	**Koocha**
Coffee	**Koohi**
Water	**Mizu**
Lunch or daily special, set menu	**Teishoku** (Japanese food)
Lunch or daily special, set menu	**Coosu,** or **seto** (usually Western food)
What do you recommend to eat?	**Nani ga osusume desu ka?**
This is delicious.	**Oishii desu.**
Thank you for the meal.	**Gochisoo-sama deshita.**
I would like a fork, please.	**Fooku o kudasai.**
I would like a spoon, please.	**Supuun o kudasai.**
I would like a knife, please.	**Naifu o kudasai.**

May I have some more, please? (if you're asking for liquid, such as more coffee, or food) **Moo sukoshi kudasai?**

May I have some more, please? (if you're asking for another bottle—say, of soda or sake) **Moo ippon kudasai?**

May I have some more, please? (if asking for another cup—say, of coffee or tea) **Moo ippai kudasai?**

I would like sake, please.	**Osake o kudasai.**
I would like a cup of coffee, please.	**Koohi o ippai kudasai.**
I would like the set meal, please.	**Seto o kudasai** or **Teishoku o kudasai.**
Soda	**Tansan**
Salt	**Shio**
Pepper	**Koshoo**
Baked	**Yaku**
Fried	**Ageru/furai**
Not fried	**Agemonode nai**
Broiled	**Yaku**
Steamed	**Musu**
Grilled	**Yaki**
Well done	**Yoku yaku**
Raw	**Nama**
Rare	**Reaa**

I'm a vegetarian. **Bejitarian desu.**

I can't eat meat/pork. **Oniku/butaniku ga taberemasen.**

I'm allergic to . . . **. . . no alelugii desu.**

Nuts **Nattsu/kinomi**

Milk **Gyuunyuu/miruku**

Shellfish **Kai**

Food

Anago Conger eel

Ayu A small river fish, or sweet fish; a delicacy of western Japan

Chu-hai Shochu Shochu (see below) mixed with soda water and flavored with syrup and lemon

Dengaku Lightly grilled tofu (see below) coated with a bean paste

Dojo Small, eel-like river fish, or loach

Fugu Pufferfish (also known as blowfish or globefish)

"Genghis Khan" or **Jingisu khan** Mutton and vegetables grilled at your table

Gohan Rice

Gyoza Chinese fried pork dumplings

Kaiseki Formal Japanese meal consisting of many courses and served originally during the tea ceremony

Kamameshi Rice casserole topped with seafood, meat, or vegetables

Kushiage (also **kushikatsu** or **kushiyaki**) Deep-fried skewers of chicken, beef, seafood, and vegetables

Maguro Tuna

Makizushi Sushi (see below), vegetables, and rice rolled inside dried seaweed

Miso Soybean paste, used as a seasoning in soups and sauces

Miso-shiru Miso soup

Mochi Japanese rice cake

Nabe A one-pot stew, usually cooked at the table

Nattoo Fermented soybeans

Nikujaga Stew of beef, potato, and carrot, flavored with sake (see below) and soy sauce; popular in winter

Oden Fish cakes, hard-boiled eggs, and vegetables, simmered in a light broth

Okonomiyaki Thick pancake filled with meat, fish, shredded cabbage, and vegetables or noodles, often cooked by diners at their table

Ramen Thick, yellow Chinese noodles, served in a hot soup

Sake (also **Nihon-shu**) Rice wine

Sansai Mountain vegetables, including bracken and flowering fern

Sashimi Raw seafood

Shabu-shabu Thinly sliced beef quickly dipped in boiling water and then dipped in a sauce

Shochu Japanese whiskey, made from rice, wheat, or potatoes

Shojin-ryori Japanese vegetarian food, served at Buddhist temples

Shooyu Soy sauce

Shuumai   Steamed Chinese pork dumplings

Soba   Buckwheat noodles

Soomen   Fine white wheat vermicelli, eaten cold in summer

Sukiyaki   Japanese fondue of thinly sliced beef cooked in a sweetened soy sauce with vegetables

Sushi (also **nigiri-zushi**)   Raw seafood placed on top of vinegared rice

Tempura   Deep-fried food coated in a batter of egg, water, and wheat flour

Teppanyaki   Japanese-style steak, seafood, and vegetables cooked by a chef on a smooth, hot, tableside grill

Tofu   Soft bean curd

Tonkatsu   Deep-fried pork cutlets

Tonkotsu   Pork that has been boiled for several hours in miso, shochu, and brown sugar

Udon   Thick white wheat noodles

Unagi   Grilled eel

Wasabi   Japanese horseradish, served with sushi

Yakisoba   Chinese fried noodles, served with sautéed vegetables

Yakitori   Charcoal-grilled chicken, vegetables, and other specialties, served on bamboo skewers

Yudofu   Tofu simmered in a pot at your table

Matters of Time

Now	**Ima**	Morning	**Asa**
Later	**Ato de**	Night	**Yoru**
Today	**Kyoo**	Afternoon	**Gogo**
Tomorrow	**Ashita**	Holiday	**Yasumi** (or **kyujitsu**)
Day after tomorrow	**Asatte**	Weekdays	**Heijitsu**
Yesterday	**Kinoo**	1 hour	**Ichijikan**
Which day?	**Nan-nichi desu ka?**	2 hours	**Nijikan**
What time is it?	**Nan-ji desu ka?**	8 hours	**Hachijikan**
Daytime	**Hiruma**		

Days of the Week

Sunday	**Nichiyoobi**	Thursday	**Mokuyoobi**
Monday	**Getsuyoobi**	Friday	**Kinyoobi**
Tuesday	**Kayoobi**	Saturday	**Doyoobi**
Wednesday	**Suiyoobi**		

Months of the Year

January	**Ichi-gatsu**	July	**Shichi-gatsu**
February	**Ni-gatsu**	August	**Hachi-gatsu**
March	**San-gatsu**	September	**Ku-gatsu**
April	**Shi-gatsu**	October	**Juu-gatsu**
May	**Go-gatsu**	November	**Juuichi-gatsu**
June	**Roku-gatsu**	December	**Juuni-gatsu**

Numbers

1	**Ichi**	20	**Nijuu**
2	**Ni**	30	**Sanjuu**
3	**San**	40	**Shijuu** (or **yonjuu**)
4	**Shi**	50	**Gojuu**
5	**Go**	60	**Rokujuu**
6	**Roku**	70	**Nanajuu**
7	**Shichi** (or **nana**)	80	**Hachijuu**
8	**Hachi**	90	**Kyuuju**
9	**Kyuu**	100	**Hyaku**
10	**Juu**	1,000	**Sen**
11	**Juuichi**	10,000	**Ichiman**
12	**Juuni**		

Other General Nouns

Fusuma   Sliding paper doors

Gaijin   Foreigner

Geta   Wooden sandals

Haori   Short kimono-like jackets (sometimes worn over a kimono), traditionally worn by men

Irori   Open-hearth fireplace

Izakaya (or **Nomiya**)   A Japanese-style bar or pub, with beer, sake, and Japanese food, generally open only from 5 or 6pm

Jinja   Shinto shrine

Kotatsu   Heating element placed under a low table (which is covered with a blanket) for keeping your legs warm

Nihonjin   Japanese person

Noren   Short curtains hung outside shops and restaurants to signify they are open

Rotenburo   Outdoor hot-spring bath

Shoji   White paper sliding windows

Tatami   Rice mats

Tera (or **dera**)   Temple

Tokonoma   Small, recessed alcove in a Japanese room used to display a flower arrangement, scroll, or art object

Torii   Entrance gate of a Shinto shrine, consisting usually of two poles topped with one or two crossbeams

Washlet   Bidet toilet

Yukata   Cotton kimono worn for sleeping

Zabuton   Floor cushions

14

A Japanese-Character Index

INDEX

See also Accommodations and Restaurant indexes, below.

ACCOMMODATIONS